Lecture Notes in Computer Science   7143

Commenced Publication in 1973
Founding and Former Series Editors:
Gerhard Goos, Juris Hartmanis, and Jan van Leeuwen

Malay K. Kundu   Sushmita Mitra
Debasis Mazumdar   Sankar K. Pal (Eds.)

Perception and Machine Intelligence

First Indo-Japan Conference, PerMIn 2012
Kolkata, India, January 12-13, 2012
Proceedings

 Springer

Volume Editors

Malay K. Kundu
Sushmita Mitra
Indian Statistical Institute (ISI)
Machine Intelligence Unit
Kolkata, India
E-mail: {malay,sushmita}@isical.ac.in

Debasis Mazumdar
Centre for Development of Advanced Computing (C-DAC)
Kolkata, India
E-mail: debasis.mazumdar@cdac.in

Sankar K. Pal
Indian Statistical Institute (ISI)
Kolkata, India
E-mail: sankar@isical.ac.in

ISSN 0302-9743   e-ISSN 1611-3349
ISBN 978-3-642-27386-5   ISBN 978-3-642-27387-2 (eBook)
DOI 10.1007/978-3-642-27387-2
Springer Heidelberg Dordrecht London New York

Library of Congress Control Number: 2011944041

CR Subject Classification (1998): I.4, I.5, H.5, I.2, H.3-4, F.1

LNCS Sublibrary: SL 6 – Image Processing, Computer Vision, Pattern Recognition, and Graphics

Typesetting: Camera-ready by author, data conversion by Scientific Publishing Services, Chennai, India

Printed on acid-free paper

Springer is part of Springer Science+Business Media (www.springer.com)

Message from the General Chair

Machine intelligence (MI) is a core concept for integrating various advanced technologies with the basic task of pattern recognition and learning. The objective is to give machines the ability to learn, adapt, reason, make decisions, and display behaviors not explicitly programmed into their original capabilities. Intelligent autonomous systems (IAS) is the physical embodiment of machine intelligence. Characteristics to be achieved in the system include: tractability, robustness, flexibility and close resemblance with human-like decision making, among others.

Perception engineering is an integral part of machine intelligence. The concept of perception-based engineering is essentially to integrate the different aspects of the human sensory responses into system and product design.

The First Indo-Japan Conference on Perception and Machine Intelligence (PerMIn 2012) primarily focused on different theoretical, generic and applied research issues of MI and perception engineering. Articles included in the proceedings provide original contributions in MI or perception, using classic as well as modern computing paradigms. Various real-life application areas considered include – speech recognition, image processing, biometrics, cognitive systems, e-nose and e-tongue, behavioral modeling, document processing, remote sensing, data security and bioinformatics. All these, coupled with several keynote and plenary talks by eminent scientists, made this interdisciplinary event an ideal platform to both theoretical and applied researchers as well as practitioners for collaborative research.

I take this opportunity to thank C-DAC, Kolkata, for holding the conference. I hope they will organize similar conferences regularly in successive years. It may be mentioned here that my scientific association with C-DAC, Kolkata, started in the early 1990s when it was called ER&DCI and located in a small unit at Taratala, and the Machine Intelligence Unit (MIU) was just formed at the Indian Statistical Institute, Kolkata. Thanks are due to its two former Executive Directors G.K. Deb and Amiya Baran Saha for their vision, and Rajat Moona, Director General, C-DAC and A.K. Nath, Executive Director, C-DAC, Kolkata, for their continuous support and inspiration. Special thanks to Shri Debasis Mazumder and Soma Mitra for their initiative and co-ordination, and the members of the Organizing, Program and other Committees for their sincere effort in making it a reality. Thanks are also due to all the financial sponsors for their support towards this endeavor, and Springer for publishing the PerMIn 2012 proceedings in their prestigious LNCS series.

November 2011   Sankar K. Pal

Preface

It is our great pleasure to welcome you to the proceedings of the First Indo-Japan Conference on Perception and Machine Intelligence (PerMin 2012), held in Kolkata, India, during January 12–13, 2012. PerMin 2012 was jointly organized by C-DAC, Kolkata, India, in collaboration with the National Institute of Information and Communication Technology, Japan, along with technical support from the Machine Intelligence Unit (MIU), Indian Statistical Institute, Kolkata.

This conference is the first of its kind to be held in Kolkata, the nerve center of the economy and culture of eastern India. The primary motivation behind the conference was to present the state of the art in scientific results, bridging the gap between academia and industry for the purpose of catalyzing collaborative research and development in perception engineering and machine intelligence.

PerMIn 2012 addressed both theories and applications of the different facets of engineering and machine intelligence considering them individually as well as in integration. We hope the conference met the expectations of academicians, researchers, professionals and engineers. We are thankful to the members of the International Program Committee for extending their support in various forms to make a strong technical program. The conference received around 100 submissions from countries across the globe. Each submitted paper was reviewed by at least two referees, and we ultimately selected only 45% of the submitted papers.

We express our gratitude to Jeremy Wolfe, O. Yamaguchi, S. Mukhopadhaya and N.R. Pal, for accepting our invitation to be the keynote and plenary session speakers. We further take the opportunity to express our gratefulness to Rajat Moona, Director General C-DAC and A.K. Nath, Executive Director, C-DAC, Kolkata, for their continuous inspiration behind the scenes.

We would like to express our sincere thanks to the members of the Organizing Committee for their whole-hearted support. Special mention must be made of the Organizing Chair S. Mitra, Finance Chair Nabarun Bhattacharya, and the joint conveners of the Organizing Committee C. Saha and Sri. A. Das. I. Dutta of the Machine Intelligence Unit of ISI Kolkata did a great job and we express our sincere thanks to him.

We gratefully acknowledge the financial support provided by different organizations as listed here. Without their support it would have been impossible to hold this conference. Last but surely not least, we thank Alfred Hofmann, Springer, Heidelberg, for extending his cooperation in publishing the PerMI 2012 proceedings. Finally, we would like to thank all the contributors for their enthusiastic response.

November 2011

Malay K. Kundu
Sushmita Mitra
Debasis Mazumdar
Sankar K. Pal

Organization

PerMIn 2012 was organized by the Centre for Development of Advanced Computing (C-DAC), Kolkata, and in collaboration with the National Institute of Information and Communication Technology (NICT), Japan, and in technical collaboration with the Indian Statistical Institute (ISI), Kolkata.

PerMIn 2012 Conference Committee

General Chair

Sankar K. Pal	ISI, Kolkata, India

Program Chairs

M.K. Kundu	ISI, Kolkata, India
S. Mitra	ISI, Kolkata, India
S. Mitra	C-DAC, Kolkata, India

Program Co-chairs

D. Mazumdar	C-DAC, Kolkata, India
K. Ghosh	ISI, Kolkata, India

Organizing Chair

S. Mitra	C-DAC, Kolkata, India

Patrons

Srikumar Banerjee	Department of Atomic Energy, Government of India
Rajat Moona	Director General, C-DAC, India

Advisory Committee

Rama Chellappa	University of Maryland, USA
Andrzej Skowron	Warsaw University, Poland
Andrey Legin	St. Petersburg State University, Russia
Hiroya Fujisaki	University of Tokyo, Japan
B. Yegnanarayana	IIT, Hyderabad, India
Kazumasa Enami	NICT, Japan
Kashiko Kodate	Japan Women's University, Japan
Dwijesh Dutta Mazumdar	Indian Statistical Institute, Kolkata, India
Navin Vasishta	Department of Science and Technology, India
A.K. Nath	C-DAC, Kolkata, India

Program Committee

Tinku Acharya	Videonetics Technology Private Limited, India
Stefano Baldassi	University of Florence, Italy
Rajib Bandyopadhyay	Jadavpur University, India
Roberto Baragona Sapienza	University of Rome, Italy
Tapan Kumar Basu	Indian Institute of Technology, Kharagpur, India
Bhargab B. Bhattacharya	Indian Statistical Institute, India
Kanad Kishore Biswas	Indian Institute of Technology, Delhi, India
Sambhunath Biswas	Indian Statistical Institute, India
Basabi Chakraborty	Iwate Prefectural University, Japan
Bhabotosh Chanda	Indian Statistical Institute, India
Bidyut Baran Chaudhuri	Indian Statistical Institute, India
Subhasish Choudhuri	Indian Institute of Technology, Bombay, India
Santanu Choudhury	Indian Institute of Technology, Delhi, India
Sukhendu Das	Indian Institute of Technology, Madras, India
Rajat K. De	Indian Statistical Institute, India
Ashish Ghosh	Indian Statistical Institute, India
Phalguni Gupta	Indian Institute of Technology, Kanpur, India
Masahide Kaneko	University of Electro-Communications, Japan
Dmitry Kirsanov	St. Petersburg State University, Russia
Akihisa Kodate	Tsuda College, Japan
Amit Konar	Jadavpur University, India
Shyamal Kumar Dasmandal	Indian Institute of Technology, Kharagpur, India
Pradipta Maji	Indian Statistical Institute, India
Pabitra Mitra	Indian Institute of Technology, Kharagpur, India
Suman Mitra	Dhirubhai Ambani Institute of Information and Communication Technology, India
Dipti Prasad Mukherjee	Indian Statistical Institute, India
Jayanta Mukherjee	Bhaba Atomic Research Centre, India
C.A. Murthy	Indian Statistical Institute, India
B.L. Narayana	Yahoo, India
Hitoshi Ohnishi	The Open University of Japan
K.R. Ramakrishnan	Indian Institute of Science, Bangalore, India
Sudeep Sarkar	University of South Florida, USA
Eriko Watanabe	University of Electro-Communications, Japan
Tatsuya Yamazaki	National Institution of Information and Communications Technology, Japan
Koichi Yoshida	Alpha M.O.S., Japan

Additional Reviewers

Bandyopadhyay, Asok
Banerjee, Meenakshi
Basu, Joyanta
Basu, T.K.
Bhattacharya, Nabarun
Bhattacharyya, Nabarun
Biswas, Sujoy
Chanda, Kunal
Choudhury, Lopamudra
Chowdhury, Manish
Das, Nabanita
Das, Sitansu Kumar
Das, Sudeb
Dhara, Bibhas Chandra
Kapinaiah, Viswanath
Kar, Guruprasad

Khan, Soma
Konar, Amit
Kotwal, Ketan
Maity, Santi P.
Meher, Saroj K.
Mukherjee, Bhaswati
Mukherjee, Snehasis
Ohnishi, Hitoshi
Parua, Suparna
Prasanna, Srm
Saha, Baidyanath
Saha, Chandrani
Sen, Debashis
Singh, Y. Kirani
Sinha, Sitabhra
Sur, Arijit

Organizing Committee

Soma Mitra	C-DAC, Kolkata
Nabarun Bhattacharyya	C-DAC, Kolkata
Debasis Mazumdar	C-DAC, Kolkata
Rajib Bandyopadhyay	Jadavpur University
Asim Sarkar	C-DAC, Kolkata
Sunil Kumar Banerjee	C-DAC, Kolkata
Jayanta Kumar Roy	C-DAC, Kolkata
Sandipan Sourav Kar	C-DAC, Kolkata
Chandrani Saha	C-DAC, Kolkata
Gargi Bag	C-DAC, Kolkata
Apurba Das	C-DAC, Kolkata
Sonali Dhali	C-DAC, Kolkata
Santanu Ranjan Dutta	C-DAC, Kolkata
Somnath Chakroborty	C-DAC, Kolkata
Kunal Chanda	C-DAC, Kolkata
Suparna Parua	C-DAC, Kolkata
Munmun Chakroborty	C-DAC, Kolkata
Washef Ahmed	C-DAC, Kolkata
Arup Saha	C-DAC, Kolkata
Milton S. Bepari	C-DAC, Kolkata
Anal H. Warsi	C-DAC, Kolkata
Joyanta Basu	C-DAC, Kolkata
Soma Khan	C-DAC, Kolkata
Tulika Basu	C-DAC, Kolkata

Rajib Roy	C-DAC, Kolkata
Amitava Akuli	C-DAC, Kolkata
Arun Jana	C-DAC, Kolkata
Devdulal Ghosh	C-DAC, Kolkata
Abhra Pal	C-DAC, Kolkata
Subrata Sarkar	C-DAC, Kolkata
Vamsi Shri Krishnan	C-DAC, Kolkata
Aryya Sen	C-DAC, Kolkata

Sponsoring Organizations

- Department of Science Technology (DST), Government of India
- Department of Information Technology (DIT), Government of India
- Council of Scientific Industrial Research (CSIR), Government of India
- Board of Research in Nuclear Sciences (BRNS), Department of Atomic Energy (DAE), Government of India
- Centre for Development of Advanced Computing (C-DAC), Kolkata
- e-AgriEn Program, C-DAC, Kolkata

Table of Contents

Keynote Paper

Plenary Papers

Contributory Papers

Perception

Human Computer Interaction

E-Nose and E-Tongue

Machine-Intelligence and Application

Image and Video Processing

Speech and Signal Processing

The Rules of Guidance in Visual Search

Jeremy M. Wolfe

Visual Attention Lab, Brigham and Women's Hospital & Harvard Medical School
wolfe@search.bwh.harvard.edu

Abstract. It is impossible to identify all objects in the visual world at the same time. Accordingly, we must direct attention to specific objects in order to fully recognize them. The deployment of attention is far from random. Attention is guided toward likely targets by a limited set of stimulus attributes such as color and size ("classic guidance"). Attention is also guided by a number of scene-based properties. Thus, if we were looking for sheep, we would expect them on surfaces that could support sheep, not in mid-air. We use information about the 3D layout of a space to determine which objects could plausibly be sheep-sized in that space. This paper briefly reviews the diverse set of guiding properties and the rules that govern their use.

1   Classic Feature Guidance

Imagine that you are looking out over some rolling pasture, dotted with shrubs, rocks, trees, and sheep. Perhaps there a few farm buildings and an assortment of other animals. You are looking for one, particular sheep. She is identifiable by some distinctive mark, though it is not easy. Let us suppose that she is in your current field of view. How do you locate her? Even though she is visible, you will need to search. We are incapable of recognizing all of the objects in the visual world at the same time. The computational demands for a visual system that could process the world in parallel are simply too great [1, 2].To cope with this fundamental limitation, we have attentional mechanisms that select one or a small number of objects for recognition at any one moment [3]. If the objects of attention need to be fixated, then the rate of processing is about 3-4 per second, the rate of saccade production [4]. However, if not limited by eye movements, search can proceed at a rate of 20-40 items per second [5] and this appears to be the case whether or not the eyes are free to move [6]. There is a debate about whether this reflects an ability to examine several objects in parallel on each fixation or whether it reflects the ability to covertly deploy attention to one item after another at 20-40 items per second. We hold an intermediate position but the answer is not central to the topic of this chapter [7].

What is central to this chapter is the question of what is selected. While you would need to search for the specific sheep, you would not search at random. Your attention will be guided to some objects rather than other objects. This is the core idea of Guided Search [8-10]. In this chapter, we will briefly review the rules of guidance by basic features that have emerged over the last 25 years of research ("classic guidance") and

M.K. Kundu et al. (Eds.): PerMIn 2012, LNCS 7143, pp. 1–10, 2012.

we will describe several forms of scene-based guidance that become important when we search real scenes and not just arrays of elements on blank backgrounds.

1.1   The Basic Visual Search Paradigm

In classic visual search experiments, the observer is asked to look for a target among a variable number of distractors. The total number of items presented is the set size and the behavioral measures of interest are the response times (RTs) and the accuracy. In Figure 1, the target is the sheep (a very schematic sheep) with a "T" marking among

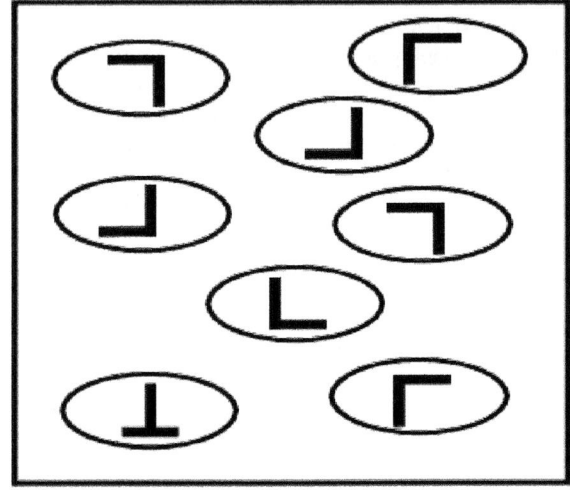

Fig. 1. Find the T

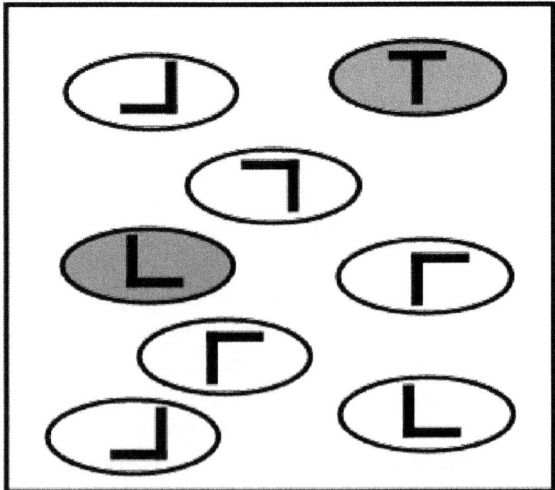

Fig. 2. The T, if present, is in a dark oval

distractors with L markings. If the Ts and Ls were large enough to make fixation unneccessary, RTs for this task would increase linearly with set size and the slope of the RT x Set Size function would be about 25 msec/item for target present trials and slightly more than twice that for target absent trials [11]. However, if you were informed that the T, if present, was on a dark sheep, as in Figure 2, you could use the color/luminance information to guide attention to the two dark items. This reduces the effective set size by a factor of 4 and will reduce the resulting RT x Set Size slopes by a comparable amount [12]. This second search is *guided*.

1.2   Features and Dimensions

There is a limited set of attributes that will guide attention in this manner. The exact number is open to debate but somewhere between 1 and 2 dozen attributes would be a reasonable estimate. Lists of candidate attributes are reviewed elsewhere [13]. They include uncontested properties like color, size, motion, and orientation as well as less firmly established properties like shininess and numerosity. In models, like Triesman's original Feature Integration Theory [5], these attributes are represented in spatially organized maps that might correspond to separable modules in the nervous system [14]. It turns out to be important to distinguish between the representation of a "feature" like red as opposed to a dimension like "color". For example, consider a very simple search for a "singleton" target defined by a single attribute like a color or an orientation. If the defining attribute can change on each trial, observers behave differently if the difference between successive targets is a change within a dimension (e.g. a red target followed by a green one) or between dimensions (e.g. red followed by vertical) [15].

1.3   Bottom-Up Guidance and Salience Maps

In Figure 2, your attention would be attracted to the dark items, simply because they differ from the other items in the vicinity. This is "bottom-up guidance", a term more or less synonymous with what is usually meant by "salience". Both terms refer to the stimulus-driven aspect of guidance. Computational theories have proposed "salience maps" in which the level of activation at a location corresponds to the magnitude of the difference between the features at that location and the features at neighboring locations [16][17]. Psychophysical data supports the idea of a map that combines representations of multiple dimensions into a single, dimensionless map [18] and various physiological loci have been proposed to house this representation [19][20, 21]. Salience map models do quite well in predicting where observers will look in scenes when they have no specific task other than to look at the scene [22].

1.4   Top-Down Guidance

Bottom-up guidance and local salience will not fully account for your search for the hypothetical sheep. There is no guarantee that the target sheep will be particularly salient. However, once you have a specific target in mind, it is possible to modulate the salience map based on that goal. Thus, in Figure 3, various items might be salient for various reasons.

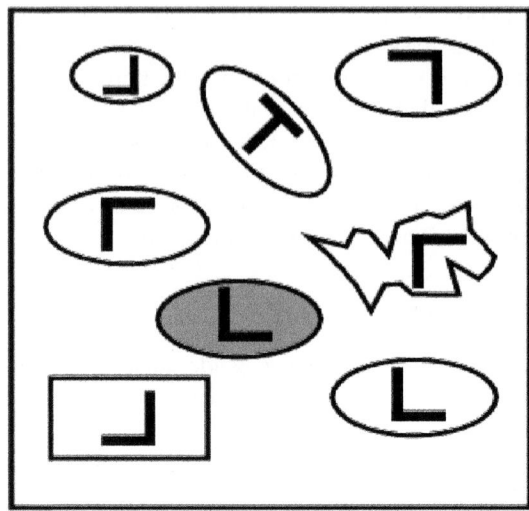

Fig. 3. Top-down guidance makes it possible to guide attention to a small item or a jagged item or to other features as needed

If you are told, however, that the T is likely to be in a tilted item, you will be able to guide attention on the basis of orientation. If you were told that the target was a jagged item, you could guide attention to items based on their shape (though we are not really clear on the precise nature of the shape features in search). Instead of a simple bottom-up salience map, models like Guided Search have a "priority map" [23] that combines inputs from all features/dimensions in a weighted manner where the weights can be influenced by the top-down needs of the observer. Thus, if the target is likely to be small, higher weights would be assigned to the "size" dimension and the "small" feature within that dimension.

1.5   Objects of Attention

Classic salience maps, even with top-down components, are computed from raw feature information. They guide attention to redness, leftward motion, etc. Humans, on the other hand, pretty clearly direct attention to objects [24]. Attention is directed to the red *object*, not merely to red. Indeed, if attention is directed to part of an object it tends to spread to 'fill' the entire object [25]. As a consequence, salience maps that include an object representation, are able to model human eye movements better than purely spatial maps [26].

1.6   The Rules of Classic Feature Guidance

Guidance is highly rule-governed. In the interest of space, we will simply state some of the rules. Further discussion and illustrations can be found in the citations:

a) Search for an item becomes harder as the similarity between target and distractors increases [27].

b) Search for a target becomes harder at the heterogeneity of the distractors increases [27].

c) Guidance is based on relatively coarse-coding of features. Thus, while a difference of 3 degrees between the orientations of two lines would be easy to discriminate once the lines were attended, the same 3 degree difference will not support efficient guided search. That would likely require a difference of greater than 10 degrees [28].

d) Guidance is based on categorical coding of features. Thus, it is easier to find the only categorically "steep" orientation in a display than it is to find a target that is not categorically unique, even if the steep and not steep targets are otherwise equivalently different from their distracters [29].

e) Guidance can be based on its own specialized coding of features. For example, in guidance by color, search for a desaturated red (pink) among saturated (red) and unsaturated (white) distractors is much faster than search for other desaturated targets (pale green, pale blue) even after perceptual differences are carefully controlled [30].

1.7   Conjunctions and Guidance by Multiple Features

In Figure 4, the T, if present, is in a white, jagged item. A quick search will reveal that the white jagged item does not contain a T. The search is quick because you can guide attention to the intersection of white and jagged items, guiding attention to two attributes at the same time [8]. Indeed, it is possible to guide attention to multiple attributes [31] though others argue that the guidance takes place, one feature after the other, in rapid succession [32].

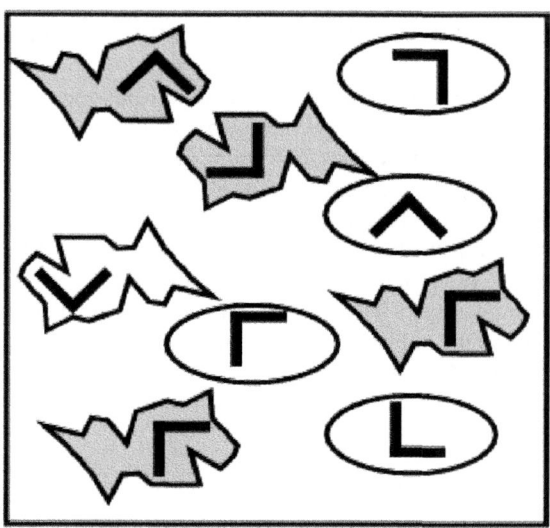

Fig. 4. Conjuction search: The target, T, if present, will be in a jagged, white object

Guidance by multiple features also comes with rules. While it is possible to guide to a color and a shape, it is not possible to guide efficiently to a target defined by two colors. In Figure 5, the target is the pink-green item (light-dark if you are reading this in black & white). It is not hard to find with only 8 items in the display but it does requires a random search [33]. It is much easier to find the pink object with the green part on the right of Figure 5 because it is possible to guide to the color of the whole and the color of the part at the same time [34].

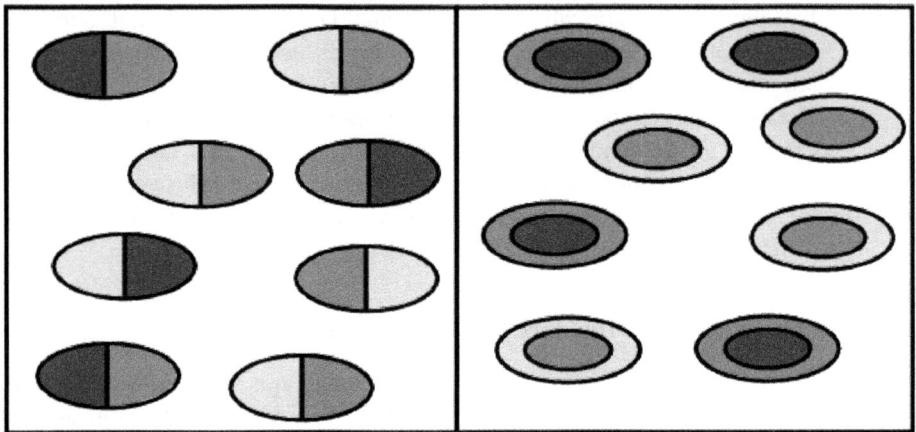

Fig. 5. On the left, search for the item that is pink-green item (light-dark in the black & white version). On the right, search for the pink item with a green part. Within dimension conjuctions are hard to find unless one attribute defines the whole object while another defines a part.

2   Beyond Classic Guidance: Searching in Scenes

The ability to guide to multiple features at the same time does not explain our ability to search in the real world. If classic guidance, by itself, were adequate, then it should be possible to search efficiently for one object (e.g. a sheep) in a display of other objects. One would simply guide to a set of sheep features. However, searches for arbitrary objects in random arrays are inefficient [35]. Searches for objects in scenes are much more efficient [36] though it is hard to quantify this efficiency because it is nearly impossible to count the set size in a real scene (Try it in Figure 6). The efficiency of search in scenes is based on forms of guidance that depend on the presence of scene structure. In this final section, we will briefly describe these forms of guidance using Figure 6 as an example.

2.1   Size X Depth Guidance

Look for people in Figure 6. Your ability to do this efficiently is based, in part, on your ability to compute the "gist" of the scene in a fraction of a second [37] without the need to divide the scene into identified objects, first. Part of that rapid gist calculation is an assessment of the 3D layout of the scene [37]. We can also calculate

Fig. 6. Look for people. The efficiency of this search relies on scene-based guidance.

the size of defined regions in the scene without necessarily knowing what they are. Given the 2D sizes of proto-objects [38] in the image and an estimate of the 3D layout of the scene, there are only a few items in this scene that could be plausible humans. This size x depth information guides you toward the human on the sidewalk. It may cause you to miss the same image of a human, cut out and placed in the doorway on the left. That 'human' object is not human-sized in this scene.

2.2 Semantic and Syntactic Guidance

You were willing to look for humans in Figure 6 because it is a scene where humans would plausibly appear. Moreover, you probably did not spend much time looking for people on the roof. People might stand there, but it is unlikely. We can call this sort of guidance, based on an understanding of the meaning of scene, "semantic" guidance [39]. Like size depth guidance, it may be based on information about the 'gist' of a scene, extracted very rapidly, without the need to identify individual objects [40].

Your search for humans was also guided by the implied physics of the scene. While people could be on the roof, it would be very unlikely for them to float in empty space [41]. We can call this guidance, based on the rules that govern the physical placement of objects, "syntactic guidance".

2.3   Memory and Episodic Guidance

Finally, if you remember that there is an unusually small human in the doorway on the left, you can use that memory to guide the deployment of attention back to the doorway. The role of memory in search is a complex topic [42]. For present purposes, we can say that, of course, your memory for previously encountered objects guides search for those objects. However, that guidance is comparatively slow and in many cases in the lab and, perhaps, many in the real world, the other forms of guidance discussed here, both classic and scene-based, will get your attention to the object before the relevant information can be extracted from episodic memory.

3   Conclusion

If we return to the search for that one, special sheep from the start of this article, it should be clear than many forms of guidance would contribute to your ability to find the sheep. Only a subset of objects will be the correct sheep size in the 3D world of this scene. Sheep come in only a few colors and shapes. They tend to be roughly horizontal. They stand on roughly horizontal surfaces. The search may still be hard. Guidance can only do so much if, for instance, there are hundreds of sheep in the scene. Nevertheless, in spite of our processing limitations, guided search makes it possible to find what we are looking for in a world full of distractors.

References

1. Tsotsos, J.: A Computational Perspective on Visual Attention. MIT Press, Cambridge (2011)
2. Tsotsos, J.K.: Analyzing vision at the complexity level. Brain and Behavioral Sciences 13, 423–469 (1990)
3. Treisman, A.: Feature binding, attention and object perception. Philos. Trans. R Soc. Lond. B Biol. Sci. 353, 1295–1306 (1998)
4. Findlay, J.M.: Visual attention: the active vision perspective. Perception ECVP abstract, S1 (2000)
5. Treisman, A., Gelade, G.: A feature-integration theory of attention. Cognitive Psychology 12, 97–136 (1980)
6. Zelinsky, G.J., Sheinberg, D.L.: Eye movements during parallel / serial visual search. J. Experimental Psychology: Human Perception and Performance 23, 244–262 (1997)
7. Wolfe, J.M.: Moving towards solutions to some enduring controversies in visual search. Trends Cogn. Sci. 7, 70–76 (2003)
8. Wolfe, J.M., Cave, K.R., Franzel, S.L.: Guided Search: An alternative to the Feature Integration model for visual search. J. Exp. Psychol. - Human Perception and Perf. 15, 419–433 (1989)
9. Wolfe, J.M.: Guided Search 2.0: A revised model of visual search. Psychonomic Bulletin and Review 1, 202–238 (1994)
10. Wolfe, J.M.: Guided Search 4.0: Current Progress with a model of visual search. In: Gray, W. (ed.) Integrated Models of Cognitive Systems, Oxford, New York, pp. 99–119 (2007)

11. Wolfe, J.M., Palmer, E.M., Horowitz, T.S.: Reaction time distributions constrain models of visual search. Vision Res. 50, 1304–1311 (2010)
12. Egeth, H.E., Virzi, R.A., Garbart, H.: Searching for conjunctively defined targets. J. Exp. Psychol: Human Perception and Performance 10, 32–39 (1984)
13. Wolfe, J.M., Horowitz, T.S.: What attributes guide the deployment of visual attention and how do they do it? Nature Reviews Neuroscience 5, 495–501 (2004)
14. Zeki, S.: Localization and globalization in conscious vision. Annu. Rev. Neurosci. 24, 57–86 (2001)
15. Found, A., Muller, H.J.: Searching for unknown feature targets on more than one dimension: Investigating a 'dimension weighting' account. Perception and Psychophysics 58, 88–101 (1996)
16. Koch, C., Ullman, S.: Shifts in selective visual attention: Towards the underlying neural circuitry. Human Neurobiology 4, 219–227 (1985)
17. Itti, L., Koch, C., Niebur, E.: A model of saliency-based visual attention for rapid scene analysis. IEEE Trans. Pattern Anal.Mach. Intell. 20, 1254–1259 (1998)
18. Zehetleitner, M., Krummenacher, J., Geyer, T., Hegenloh, M., Müller, H.: Dimension intertrial and cueing effects in localization: support for pre-attentively weighted one-route models of saliency. Attention, Perception, & Psychophysics 73, 349–363 (2011)
19. Bisley, J.W., Goldberg, M.E.: Attention, Intention, and Priority in the Parietal Lobe. Annual Review of Neuroscience 33, 1–21 (2010)
20. Zhaoping, L., May, K.A.: Psychophysical tests of the hypothesis of a bottom-up saliency map in primary visual cortex. PLoS Comput. Biol. 3, e62 (2007)
21. Thompson, K.G., Bichot, N.P.: A visual salience map in the primate frontal eye field. Prog. Brain Res. 147, 249–262 (2004)
22. Parkhurst, D., Law, K., Niebur, E.: Modeling the role of salience in the allocation of overt visual attention. Vision Res. 42, 107–123 (2002)
23. Serences, J.T., Yantis, S.: Selective visual attention and perceptual coherence. Trends Cogn. Sci. 10, 38–45 (2006)
24. Goldsmith, M.: What's in a location? Comparing object-based and space-based models of feature integration in visual search. J. Experimental Psychology: General 127, 189–219 (1998)
25. Egly, R., Driver, J., Rafal, R.D.: Shifting attention between objects and loctions: Evidence from normal and parietal lesion subjects. J. Experimental Psychology: General 123, 161–177 (1994)
26. Einhauser, W., Spain, M., Perona, P.: Objects predict fixations better than early saliency. Journal of Vision 8, 1–26 (2008)
27. Duncan, J., Humphreys, G.W.: Visual search and stimulus similarity. Psychological Review 96, 433–458 (1989)
28. Foster, D.H., Ward, P.A.: Asymmetries in oriented-line detection indicate two orthogonal filters in early vision. Proc. R. Soc. Lond. B 243, 75–81 (1991)
29. Wolfe, J.M., Friedman-Hill, S.R., Stewart, M.I., O'Connell, K.M.: The role of categorization in visual search for orientation. J. Exp. Psychol: Human Perception and Performance 18, 34–49 (1992)
30. Lindsey, D.T., Brown, A.M., Reijnen, E., Rich, A.N., Kuzmova, Y.I., Wolfe, J.M.: Color channels, not color appearance or color categories, guide visual search for desaturated color targets. Psychol. Sci. 21, 1208–1214 (2010)
31. Wolfe, J.M.: Bound to guide: A surprising, preattentive role for conjunctions in visual search. Journal of Vision 10, 1289 (2010)

32. Huang, L.: What is the unit of visual attention? Object for selection, but Boolean map for access. Journal of Experimental Psychology: General 139, 162–179 (2010)
33. Wolfe, J.M., Yu, K.P., Stewart, M.I., Shorter, A.D., Friedman-Hill, S.R., Cave, K.R.: Limitations on the parallel guidance of visual search: Color X color and orientation X orientation conjunctions. J. Exp. Psychol: Human Perception and Performance 16, 879–892 (1990)
34. Wolfe, J.M., Friedman-Hill, S.R., Bilsky, A.B.: Parallel processing of part/whole information in visual search tasks. Perception and Psychophysics 55, 537–550 (1994)
35. Vickery, T.J., King, L.-W., Jiang, Y.: Setting up the target template in visual search. J. of Vision 5, 81–92 (2005)
36. Wolfe, J.M., Alvarez, G.A., Rosenholtz, R.E., Kuzmova, Y.I.: Visual search for arbitrary objects in real scenes. Atten Percept Psychophys 73, 1650–1671 (2011)
37. Oliva, A.: Gist of the scene. In: Itti, L., Rees, G., Tsotsos, J. (eds.) Neurobiology of Attention, pp. 251–257. Academic Press / Elsevier, San Diego, CA (2005)
38. Rensink, R.A.: Seeing, sensing, and scrutinizing. Vision Res. 40, 1469–1487 (2000)
39. Torralba, A., Oliva, A., Castelhano, M.S., Henderson, J.M.: Contextual guidance of eye movements and attention in real-world scenes: The role of global features on object search. Psychological Review 113, 766–786 (2006)
40. Greene, M.R., Oliva, A.: The briefest of glances: the time course of natural scene understanding. Psychol. Sci. 20, 464–472 (2009)
41. Vo, M.L.H., Henderson, J.M.: Does gravity matter? Effects of semantic and syntactic inconsistencies on the allocation of attention during scene perception. Journal of Vision 9, 1–15 (2009)
42. Vo, M.L.-H., Wolfe, J.M.: Does repeated search in scenes need memory? Looking AT versus looking FOR objects in scenes. J. Exp. Psychol: Human Perception and Performance (in press, 2011)

Smart Sensing System for Human Emotion and Behaviour Recognition

N.K. Suryadevara, T. Quazi, and Subhas C. Mukhopadhyay

School of Engineering and Advanced Technology
Massey University, New Zealand
S.C.Mukhopadhyay@massey.ac.nz

Abstract. In this study, we reported a smart sensing system for detecting Human Emotion and Behaviour Recognition. The inhabitant emotions are sensed based on information from the physiological sensors as happiness, sadness, stressed and neutral. Also, we defined two new wellness functions to determine the regularity of house-hold activities and foresee changes in the domestic activity behaviour. Developed intelligent program was tested at different elderly houses living alone and the results are encouraging. The developed system is less cost, reliable and robust in realizing functional condition of the inhabitant both emotionally and physically.

Keywords: Wireless Sensor Networks, Human Emotion, Activities of Daily Living, Wellness, Smart Home.

1 Introduction

1.1 Human Emotion

Human Emotions play a vital role in people's everyday life. It's a mental state that does not arise through free will, and is often accompanied by physiological changes. Therefore it is very important to monitor these changes as this will help in early detection of various emotional problems related to stress, anxiety, panic attacks etc. Once these problems have been detected, they can be treated at any early stage before it becomes too serious.

In the past different approaches have taken place to detect and evaluate human emotions. EEG analyses the nervous system to provide information about emotions. Image Processing recognizes emotions by changes in facial expression. The tone of speech is another way of emotion detection. Text is also used to monitor changes in human emotion. In this project, physiological signals e.g. heart rate, skin temperature and skin conductance, are used to recognize human emotions.

In an average adult, the heart goes through a full cardiac cycle seventy times a minute .This means that a healthy heart rate at rest is sixty to eighty beats per minute (BPM). Any irregularities in human heart rate can be due various factors. The most common heart pounding at rest can be due stress, panic attacks, anxiety or other heart

M.K. Kundu et al. (Eds.): PerMIn 2012, LNCS 7143, pp. 11–22, 2012.

problems. Therefore it is important to monitor the heart rate continuously which would help in finding a relationship between heart rate and changes in physical environment.

Continuous monitoring of body temperature is very important. Generally a human skin temperature is between 32-35°C. However, there are many causes of variation from these values. The most common reasons for changes in skin temperature at room temperature include fever, stress, anxiety, panic attacks, dehydration, etc. Therefore it is important to monitor the skin temperature as it is influenced by changes in emotion i.e. stress and anxiety. These changes in temperature will help in finding out the correlation between temperature and changes in human emotion.

Human skin has electrical properties that change relatively quickly and are closely related to psychological and physiological processes [1]. Changes in electro-dermal activity (EDA) and skin conductance are related to changes in eccrine sweating gland which are, in turn, related to activity in the sympathetic branch of the autonomic nervous system (ANS). Therefore, skin conductance has become an important tool to help find human emotions in the form of Galvanic Skin Response (GSR).

1.2   Current Research Works on Home Monitoring for Recognizing Activities of Daily Living

A variety of systems for monitoring and functional assessment for elder care have been proposed and developed in recent times. Monitoring activities of the person based on camera based sensors or CCD cameras are reported [2, 3] in which the images of the person are taken and analyzed. In real practice applications such as surveillance and security make full use of camera based system but for home monitoring activities it lacks a huge acceptability among the elderly.

Other than camera, infrared based Small Motion Detectors (SMDs), passing sensors, operation detectors and IR motion sensors have been incorporated in house for monitoring the human activity behaviour and the interpretation of human activity is limited to only to a few human activities. There are number of projects available on wearable health devices [4, 5] integrated with sensors to provide continuous monitoring of person's health related issues and activity monitoring. Also, systems using RFID communication technology in elderly center were introduced [6] .Although these devices are for specific purposes, they have severe concerns related to security, privacy and legal aspects [7].

Systems like remote human monitoring using wireless sensor networks [8] were introduced. Also, monitoring and modeling of inhabitant activities of daily living were incorporated [9]. Adding to the hardware setup mentioned earlier diversity of machine learning methods has been proposed for human activity recognition in smart environments e.g. Hidden Markov models and fuzzy logic [10]. However, in real circumstances, using supervised machine learning methods is not practical, as it requires complex processing of data such as labeling of data at run-time. More over, offline analysis has been studied for predicting activity recognition and abnormal situation [11]. Offline analysis mechanisms may not be apt in applying for real time data processing system processing of inhabitant activity behaviour analysis.

There is a huge demand for an electronic system with intelligent mechanism, less cost, flexible, robust and accurate for monitoring basic Activities of Daily Living (ADLs) behaviour of inhabitant living alone so that care can be taken at right time by informing to the care taker.

Activity recognition and predicting abnormal bahaviour are two important functions to be done in timely manner rather than offline. Hence, real-time processing of data is a must for recognizing behaviour pattern of the inhabitant and predicting abnormal situations. An initial decline or change in regular daily activities can suggest changes to the health and functional abilities of the elderly person.

2   System Description

The Smart Sensing System for Human Emotion and Behaviour Recognition consists of two parts, can be used together or separately. In one system a wearable device has been developed to monitor physiological parameters (such as body temperature, heart rate, body conductance etc.) of a human subject. The system consists of an electronic device which is worn on the wrist and finger, by the person. Using several sensors to measure different vital signs, the person is wirelessly monitored within his own home in a smart home.

Based on the measured physiological parameters, the emotion of the person such as happiness, sadness, stressed situation etc are determined. Depending on the situation the system can set off an alarm, allowing help to be provided to the person, if necessary.

In the second system, the design intricacies and implementation details of a wireless sensors network based safe home monitoring system targeted for the elder people to provide a safe, sound and secured living environment in the society has been targeted in this research. The system is designed to support people who wish to live alone but, because of old age, ill health or disability, there is some risk in this, which worries their family or friends. The system works on the principle of using wireless sensor units to monitor the appliance throughout a house and detect when certain desired electrical as well as non-electrical appliances such as bed, toilet, water-use etc. are used for their living. A central controller unit queries the sensor units and logs the data into a PC at a pre-defined rate. Communication between the Sensor Units and the controller is using radio-frequency wireless media. Based on the Sequence of the sensor events the behaviour and the wellness of the elderly is determined.

The wellness of the elderly dictates whether the person is safe and sound at home. Since no vision sensors (camera or infra-red) are used, the system is non-invasive, respects privacy and has found wide acceptance among the elderly.

2.1   Human Emotion Recognition System

The human emotion recognition module consists of physiological sensors, signal conditioning circuit, a C8051 Silabs microcontroller, communication medium (Zigbee unit) and a computer for displaying and storing the results.

The Human Emotion detection system consists of a box which has a microcontroller, a Zigbee module (router) and signal condition circuits residing inside while the IR LED, phototransistor, temperature sensor and GSR electrodes on the surface which would be in direct contact with the hand as seen below in fig 1.

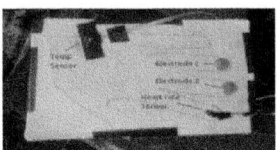

Fig. 1. Subject's hand on the system and System setup with all sensors for data collection

Heart Rate Sensor Unit

The heart rate sensor used in this project is based on the concept of near infrared spectroscopy (NIRS). The reason for using this approach is that near infra-red sensors are inexpensive, non-invasive, compact, reliable and good for continuous monitoring.

The custom made heart rate sensor consists of an infra-red LED (OP180) with a wavelength of 940nm by Optek Technology and an infra-red phototransistor (SDP8406) by Honeywell. A low power quad operational amplifier (LM324) is used for the amplification of the signals. The heart rate sensor requires 3.3V to operate which is provided by the microcontroller. The output of from the sensor is a digital signal which is input into the digital port of the microcontroller.

The digital signal from the microcontroller is used to measure beats per minute (BPM). The appropriate code is written in Silabs IDE which is provided with the Silabs C8051 microcontroller.

The program sends software ticks every 10μsec intervals. The frequency/minute is stored in K. The BPM_tick_value stores the number of ticks between falling edges. The BPM is calculated by dividing the frequency by the tick value.

Skin Temperature Sensor Unit

Skin temperature is measured using DS600 analog-output temperature sensor by Maxim - Dallas semiconductor. The DS600 requires 2.7-5.5V to operate which is provided by the microcontroller. It provides an accuracy of ±0.5°C over a range of -20 to 100°C.The output from the sensor is an analogue voltage which is proportional to temperature in °C and is given by the formula.

$$T\ (°C) = (Vout - VOS) / (\Delta V/\Delta T), \text{ where } VOS = DC \text{ offset, } 509mV$$

$$\Delta V/\Delta T = \text{Typical output gain, } +6.45 \text{ mV/ }°C \tag{1}$$

Galvanic Skin Response (GSR) Sensor Unit

The galvanic skin response consists of 2 electrodes. One electrode is connected to 3.3V provided by the microcontroller. The second electrode is connected to a 68K resistor and 100nF capacitor. The output from this circuit is a voltage which enters the analogue input of microcontroller and displayed on the screen.

2.2   Behaviour Recognition System

For recognizing activities of daily life Zigbee modules of star structure are configured to capture the sensor data based on the usage of house hold appliances and store data in the computer system for further data processing. Collected sensor data is of low level information containing only status of the sensor as active or inactive and identity of the sensor.

Electrical appliance monitoring sensor units are connected to appliances like Microwave Oven, Water Kettle, Toaster, Room Heater, Television and Dishwasher as they are regularly used by the inhabitant. Force sensor units are attached to Bed, Couch, Toilet and Dining chair to monitor their usage. Fabricated contact sensors are fixed to the Fridge and Grooming cabinet to detect the open and close door operations for recognizing the usage of these appliances.

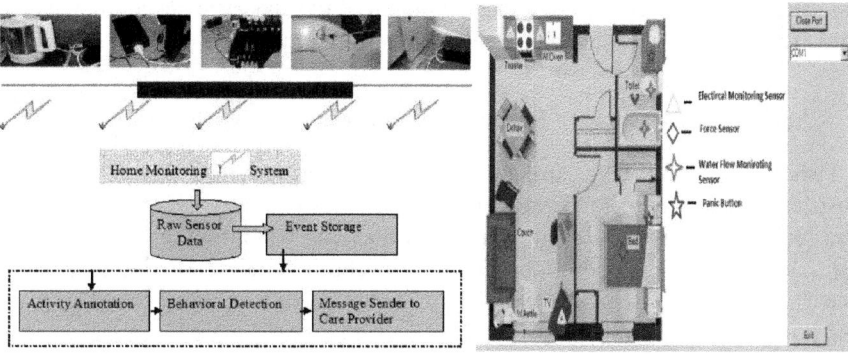

Fig. 2. Architecture of the developed system with few sensors, functional description of activity recognition and front end of data collection

A)   Architecture of the sensor network

As shown in fig 2, intelligent home monitoring system based on ZigBee wireless sensors has been designed and developed to assist and monitor the elderly people. Fig: 1 depicts the structural design of the developed system. Wireless Sensor Network is designed and developed by following IEEE standard 802.15.4 of ZigBee. Communication is established and managed by the functional set of the modem configuration with appropriate values for Network, security, serial and I/O interfacing.

B)   Data Collection Unit

The user interface of our developed system provides connection to the sensor network for capture of data in real-time processing, the corresponding sensor icon will be highlighted to display if the connected house-hold appliance is active. At any point, of execution elderly activity can be known by viewing to the front end of the system. Captured raw sensor data are collected, and stored in the processing unit in the form of event based activity (i.e.) when status (active or inactive) of the sensor is changed.

3   Recognition Procedures

3.1   Human Emotion Recognition Process

From the system description presented in section 2.1, classification of different emotions is performed on different data set of classes aiming at distinctive emotions. K means clustering were performed on the data collected from the features for distinguishing the emotions. This technique is a form of unsupervised learning that helps to find the intrinsic constitution in the data. Using clustering, it is possible to find the related points without actually knowing the labels. Hence those attributes may be found that contribute to the points being similar to others as well as those which make is dissimilar from others [12].

As K means clustering is applicable to fairly large data sets and use other heuristics to find good initial centres, we can cluster different people skin temperature, heart rate and GSR values to classify them into appropriate emotions like Happy, Sad, Neutral and Stress. The centroid converges to a local optimum of the cluster to specify the number of centres. The results of this method are shown in results section.

3.2   Activities of Daily Life Recognition Process

Fig 3 shows the multi-level structure of recognizing activities of daily living. The lowest level of the multi-level structure of Activities of Daily Life mapping consists of the sensor systems used to generate sensor events when they are activated in the home. The next level is chore identification. A chore is defined as the association of sub-activity related to sensor event. This is to be monitored when the elderly uses a house-hold device for some purpose.

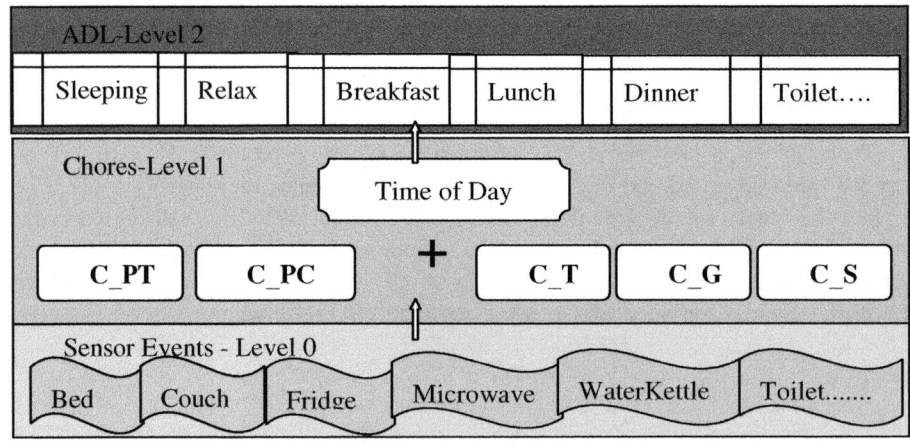

Fig. 3. ADLs are recognized from a Multi-level structure of sensor events

Fragment of chore are identified by the parts of sensor events that correspond to a particular chore. However, sensor event may not properly map to corresponding chores. In order to have proper chore identification, we followed a mathematical model of Laplace smoothing. The basic idea is to find the maximum-probable parts of text related to sensor event and estimate probabilities of sensor event stream text to identify chores. This technique does not need any training data to estimate the maximum likelihood of the chore. Also, time granularity is added so that the behaviour detection system will be aware of what time of day an ADL is getting executed. Implementation details are described in following section.

3.2.1 Activity Labeling

Activity labeling for the activities of daily living of the inhabitant during real-time monitoring of appliances use is directly done with the help of 'sensor events'. Activities like Sleeping, Dining, Toileting and Self Grooming were recognized based on the **Sensor-ID status and Time of the Day**. Activities like preparing Breakfast/Lunch/Dinner, Watching Television and Preparing Tea are recognized with the help of a probabilistic learning method of Naïve Bayes model along with add-one Laplace smoothing technique.

Sub-activity (Chore) identification process is as follows: We denote different sub-activities with unique letters as Preparing Tea (Chore_PT) = A, Preparing Coffee (Chore_PC) = B, Preparing Toast (C_TS) = C. If Water Kettle sensor is active then we get the stream of letters A, B, indicating it may be used for preparing tea or preparing coffee.

Similarly, if Fridge sensor unit is active then A, B, C letters and Teabag container sensor unit is active then the letter 'A'. If the inhabitant uses house-hold appliances Water Kettle, Fridge, and Teabag container in any sequence then the letter stream generated are: A,A,B,C,A or A,B,C,A,B,A or A,A,B,A,B,C etc., here, our task is to identify maximum probable sub-activity (chore) from the sensor stream event letters.

The best chore (sub-activity) for the stream of letters generated by the sensor events is given by the maximum likelihood estimate as the conditional probability which is the relative frequency of letter (t) in stream of letters belonging to chore (c). To eliminate zeroes for the probability of unseen event we use add-one, Laplace smoothing. Eq (2) describes the probability of term (set of letters) belonging to a particular class of sub-activity.

$$P(t \mid c) = \frac{N_{ct} + 1}{\sum\limits_{t' \in V} (N_{ct'} + 1)} = \frac{N_{ct} + 1}{\sum\limits_{t' \in V} N_{ct'} + K'} \tag{2}$$

Where t is a term containing set of letters, c is class of sub-activity (chore). N_{ct} is the number of times a particular letter occurs in class 'c'. V is the set of letters. $K' = |V|$ is the number of unique letters.

From the fig 4 the maximum likelihood stream of "(A, B, A, B, C, A)" letters belong to chore preparing tea (C_PT).Similarly, other chores are identified. Once the individual chores are identified they are mapped to next level along with the time of day to recognize appropriate ADL. Fig 5 shows the part of the annotated activities during the run time of the system.

Sensor Events (Any Order)	Stream of Letters "t"	Belonging to Class "c"	P(t | c)
Water Kettle, Fridge, Tea_Bag	A,B,A,B,C,A	P(A,B,A,B,C,A | Prep_Tea(A))	0.0109739
		P(A,B,A,B,C,A | Prep_Coffee(B))	0.0133333
		P(A,B,A,B,C,A | Prep_Toast (C))	0.0020576
Fridge, Toaster	A,B,C,C	P(A,B,C,C | Prep_Tea(A))	0.0185185
		P(A,B,C,C | Prep_Coffee(B))	0.0185185
		P(A,B,C,C | Prep_Toast (C))	0.0277777
Coffee_Bag, Fridge, Water Kettle	B,A,B,C,A,B	P(B,A,B,C,A,B | Prep_Tea(A))	0.0019753
		P(B,A,B,C,A,B | Prep_Coffee(B))	0.0046296
		P(B,A,B,C,A,B | Prep_Toast (C))	0.0020576

Fig. 4. Likelihood of the sensor event stream of letters belonging to a particular sub-activity class

Sensor-ID/ Status	Connected to Appliance	Type of Sensor	Time of Usage	Annotated Activity	Run Time Data
18(Active)	Bed	Pressure Sensor	09:00pm to 06:00am	Sleeping(SL)	2011-6-9 21:02:10 18 ON SL begin 2011-6-10 05:50:10 18 OFF SL end
11/12/13 (active)	Microwave Oven/ Water Kettle/ Toaster	Electrical sensor	6:00am to 10:00am	Breakfast(BF)	2011-6-5 06:16:42 11 ON BF begin 2011-6-5 06:21:35 11 OFF BF end
14(Active)	TV	Electrical sensor	14->19 or 19->14	Watching TV(WTV)	2011-6-6 17:20:35 14 ON TV begin 2011-6-6 17:20:45 19 ON WTV begin 2011-6-6 18:05:39 19 OFF WTV end 2011-6-6 18:06:05 14 OFF TV end
25(Active)	Fridge	Contact	25->12 or 12->25	Preparing Tea(PT)	2011-6-9 10:15:20 25 ON FR begin 2011-6-9 10:15:50 12 ON PT begin 2011-6-9 10:15:45 25 OFF FR end 2011-6-9 10:16:50 12 OFF PT end

Fig. 5. Activity labeling during runtime of the system

3.3 Wellness Determination of Inhabitant

We introduced two wellness functions to determine the wellness of the inhabitant person under the monitoring environment. The first function is to determine the non-usage or inactive duration of the appliances. The second function is to determine the over-usage of household appliances. The two functions are β_1 and β_2, used to determine the wellness of inhabitant based on the usage of house hold appliances.

Wellness function β_1: **The wellness function, designated as 'β_1' is defined as**

$$\beta_1 = \left(1 - \frac{t}{T}\right) \quad (3)$$

Where β_1 =Wellness function of the inhabitant based on Inactive measurement of appliances, t = Time of Inactive duration of all appliances (i.e.) duration time no appliances are used, T= Maximum inactive duration during which no Appliances are used. If β_1 is equal to 1.0 indicates the inhabitant is under healthy situation. If β_1 is less than 1.0 and goes below 0.5 the situation indicates some abnormal situation.

Wellness function β2: **The wellness function, designated as 'β$_2$' is defined as**

$$\beta 2 = 1 + \left(1 - \frac{Ta}{Tn} \right) \tag{4}$$

Where β_2 = Wellness function of the inhabitant based on excess usage measurement of appliance, T_a=Actual usage duration of any appliance, T_n =Maximum usage during of use time of appliance.

Under normal condition, $T_a < T_n$ (i.e.) No Abnormality.

Only if $T_a > T_n$ then β2 is calculated using the eq. (4). The value of β_2 close to 1 to 0.8 may be considered as normal situation. If β_2 goes less than 0.5 indicates excess usage of the appliance and may lead to an abnormal condition.

4   Results

Wireless Sensor Network(WSN) consisting of six electrical sensors, four force sensors, two contact switch sensor units and a integrated unit of physiological sensor unit are installed in the home to monitor inhabitant behaviour and human emotion detection. Along with the wireless sensor network a laptop installed with the developed intelligent software connected with Zigbee module acting as coordinator is associated with WSN to collect and monitor the inhabitant behaviour. Program for Data Acquisition, Activity recognition, wellness determination and emotional detection functions are programmed for monitoring the inhabitant activities and physiological conditions using Microsoft Visual Studio.

The fabricated sensor modules along with Zigbee components are configured to have effective communication with Zigbee coordinator for recording sensor values in the system for processing of data. Fig 7, 9 shows the accuracy of data received with respect to other standard devices. Received sensor data is recorded in different files of the software system and simultaneously do file processing for determining wellness function values.

The signal from the sensors were input in the program which was then stored as a text file. These data points were then used for feature extraction of four basic emotions i.e. happy, sad, stressed and neutral. We used data mining Weka [13, 14] software tool for K-means clustering for feature extraction purpose. We used six data sets for recognizing happy, sad, stress and neutral emotions. A part of this data set was used for training purpose. Once the training was complete the next step was to test the data without the training data. Fig 6 shows the clustering of collected data for recognizing four emotions has Happy, Sad, Stress and Neutral.

The results obtained were encouraging to go for large data sets to have more recognition values for emotions based on skin temperature, heart rate and GSR values.

"β1 and β2" functions can tell us, how well the inhabitant activity is being performed. Active duration of every sensor is recorded during one week of trial run and is given in tables: accordingly, maximum duration of each appliance is derived. Then during the testing phase β2 are calculated using the eq 4, is shown in tables 1.

The value of β2 close to 1 to 0.8 may be considered as normal situation. If β2 goes less than 0.8 indicates excess usage of the appliance and if less than 0.5 may lead abnormal condition. Similarly, β1 are calculated according to the eq 3. are determined to be a regular activity. The calculations of β1 and β2 are done simultaneously when the sensor activity status is plotted on the respective files. Wellness functions were helpful in deducing no appliance and excess used by the inhabitant at their houses.

It can be observed from the tables: that there are instances (values denoted in bold) of excess usage of the appliances by the inhabitants during one week of the testing phase, (i.e.) Subject 1 has one instance of over usage of appliance couch Also, they are verified with the ground truth of the respective subjects. It can be inferred from the results that the results of wellness functions are able to determine how well (regular) the inhabitant is performing their daily activities in using their household appliances and encouraging to be applied in real-time monitoring for predicting the irregular behaviour of the inhabitant. Fig 8 shows the percentage use of home appliances during one week of training period at a subject house. MO = Microwave Oven, TR= Toaster, WK= Water Kettle, AD= Audio device, HT=Heater, TV=Television, DC=Dining Chair, BD=Bed, CO=Couch, TO= Toilet and NA denotes: No Appliance used.

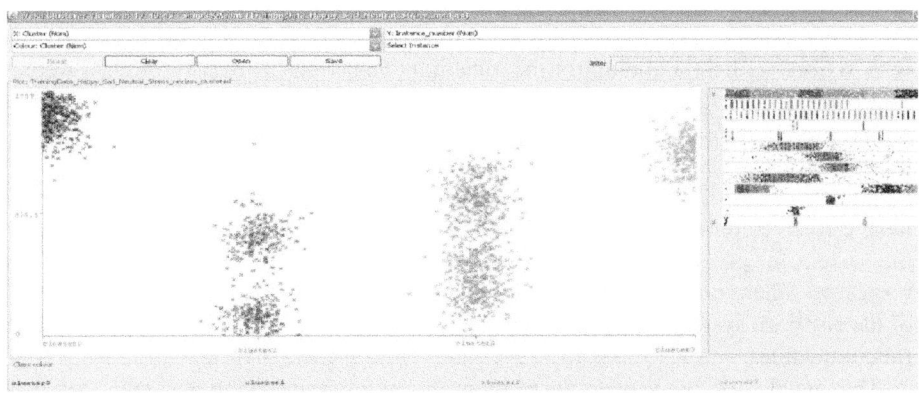

Fig. 6. Clustering of the physiological parameters data

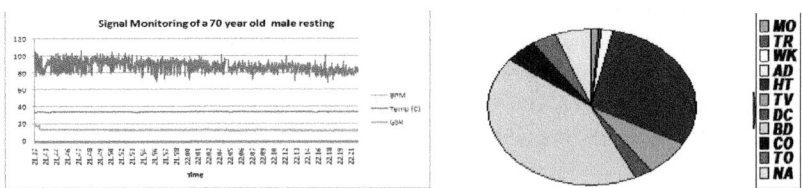

Fig. 7. Data monitoring for a 70 year old male   **Fig. 8.** Percentage use of different appliances at a subject house

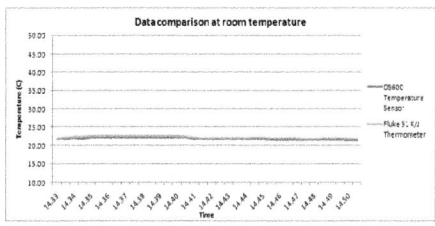 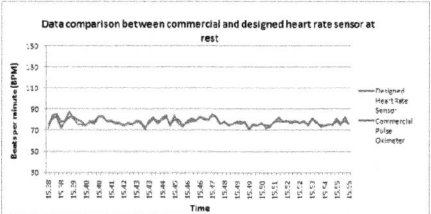

Fig. 9. Data comparison of the DS600 temperature sensor and a Fluke 51K/J thermometer at room temperature and Data comparison of the designed heart rate sensor and a commercial pulse oximeter

Table 1. Subject1 maximum active duration of the appliances during one week trial run and during one week testing phase

Date/Appliance	Maximum Active Duration(hh:mm:ss)				
	Bed	Toilet	Chair	TV	Couch
05/06/2011(Sun)	9:35:40	0:12:20	0:17:45	1:10:50	0:57:45
06/06/2011(Mon)	7:50:10	0:10:35	0:15:35	0:45:20	1:45:50
07/06/2011(Tue)	9:20:10	0:14:45	0:25:28	2:15:10	2:30:10
08/06/2011(Wed)	8:45:50	0:13:55	0:10:20	1:45:50	0:55:20
09/06/2011(Thu)	8:35:25	0:12:20	0:19:45	1:55:30	2:20:10
10/06/2011(Fri)	8:50:25	0:15:45	0:20:35	1:30:20	1:30:45
11/06/2011(Sat)	9:25:15	0:10:55	0:28:30	1:40:10	2:10:35
Maximum	9:35:40	0:15:45	0:28:30	2:15:10	2:20:10

Date/Appliance	Maximum Active Duration(hh:mm:ss)			
	Bed, β_1	Toilet, β_1	Chair, β_1	Couch, β_1
12/06/2011(Sun)	9:25:20, 1.01795	0:11:10, 1.291005	0:18:55, 1.336257	1:27:45, 1.3736
13/06/2011(Mon)	7:20:45, 1.23436	0:12:15, 1.222222	0:16:25, 1.423977	3:15:50, 0.602854
14/06/2011(Tue)	8:50:37, 1.078257	0:10:45, 1.31746	0:20:18, 1.287719	2:45:20, 0.82045
15/06/2011(Wed)	9:15:15, 1.035466	0:12:55, 1.179894	0:34:30, 0.789474	1:15:20, 1.46253
16/06/2011(Thu)	9:35:35, 1.000145	0:15:20, 1.026455	0:13:15, 1.535088	2:50:40, 0.78204
17/06/2011(Fri)	8:30:55, 1.11247	0:13:45, 1.126984	0:25:25, 1.145324	1:45:50, 1.24456
18/06/2011(Sat)	10:25:15, 0.913868	0:12:15, 1.222222	0:18:40, 1.384675	1:55:35, 1.175386

5   Conclusion

The human emotion feature extractions haven't been fully realized into real time analysis. At present the emotions are been determined based on the offline clustering process. As far as the sensor units are concerned the developed system has shown accurate and reliable readings. The system is capable of wirelessly communicating with the computer and storing data into computer for processing. The system once fully designed and constructed will be capable of extracting various types of emotions from the provided signals. The in-house sensing system is a wireless sensor network, in which each node can detect the presence of inhabitant when using the appliances. Real-time activity behaviour recognition of the inhabitant and determination of wellness function of the inhabitant using the activity of appliances was encouraging as the system was stable in executing the tasks for a couple of weeks.

The developed software for the system is augmented with wellness functions to provide intelligence in determining the habitual behaviour of the inhabitant. This can be extended for predicting the abnormal behaviour of the inhabitant in a smart home environment. Also, the system can be executed for required number of months to derive the optimal maximum utilization of the appliances used by the inhabitant then test for the efficiency of the wellness functions to predict the abnormal behaviour of the inhabitant in using the daily household appliances. Extensive analyses have to be conducted in predicting the abnormal situation of the inhabitant for the developed system.

References

1. Figner, B., Murphy, R.O.: Using skin conductance in judgment and decision making research. In: Schulte-Mecklenbeck, M., Kuehberger, A., Ranyard, R. (eds.) A Handbook of Process Tracing Methods for Decision Research. Psychology Press, New York
2. Zhongna, Z., Wenqing, D., Eggert, J., Giger, J.T., Keller, J., Rantz, M., He, Z.: A real-time system for in-home activity monitoring of elders. In: Proceedings of the Annual International Conference of IEEE Engineering in Medicine and Biology Society, EMBC 2009, September 3-6, pp. 6115–6118 (2009)
3. George, P., George, X., George, P.: Monitoring and Modeling Simple Everyday Activities of the Elderly at Home. In: Proceedings of the 7th IEEE Consumer Communications and Networking Conference, CCNC 2010, vol. 007(01), pp. 1–5 (January 2010)
4. Jian, K.W., Liang, D., Wendong, X.: Real-time Physical Activity classification and tracking using wearable sensors. In: Proceedings of the 6th International Conference on Information, Communications & Signal Processing, pp. 1–6 (December 2007)
5. Yu-Jin, H., Ig-Jae, K., Sang, C.A., Hyoung-Gon, K.: Activity Recognition using Wearable Sensors for Elder Care. In: Proceedings of the 2nd International Conference on Future Generation Communication and Networking, FGCN 2008, December 13-15, vol. 2, pp. 302–305 (2008)
6. Hung, K.P., Tao, G., Wenwei, X., Palmes, P.P., Jian, Z., Long Ng, W., Chee, W.T., Nguyen, H.C.: Context-aware middleware for pervasive elderly homecare. IEEE Journal on Selected Areas in Communications 27(4), 510–524 (2009)
7. Moshaddique, A.A., Kyung-sup, K.: Social Issues in Wireless Sensor Networks with Healthcare Perspective. The International Arab Journal of Information Technology 8(1), 34–39 (2011)
8. Seon-Woo, L., Yong-Joong, K., Gi-Sup, L., Byung-Ok, C., Nam-Ha, L.: A Remote Behavioral Monitoring System for Elders Living Alone. In: Proceedings of the International Conference on Control, Automation and Systems, ICCAS 2007, pp. 2725–2730 (2007)
9. Lymberopoulos, D., Bamis, A., Eixeira, T., Savvides, A.: BehaviorScope: Real-Time Remote Human Monitoring Using Sensor Networks. In: Proceedings of the International Conference on Information Processing in Sensor Networks, IPSN 2008, pp. 533–534 (April 2008)
10. Medjahed, H., Istrate, D., Boudy, J., Dorizzi, B.: Human activities of daily living recognition using fuzzy logic for elderly home monitoring. In: Proceedings of the IEEE International Conference on Fuzzy Systems, pp. 2001–2006 (2009)
11. Nazerfard, E., Rashidi, P., Cook, D.J.: Discovering Temporal Features and Relations of Activity Patterns. In: IEEE International Conference on Data Mining Workshops (ICDMW), pp. 1069–1075 (2010)
12. Murugappan, M., Rizon, M., Nagarajan, R., Yaacob, S., Zunaidi, I., Hazry, D.: EEG Feature Extraction for Classifying Emotions using FCM and FKM. International Journal of Computers and Communications 1(2), 21–25 (2007)
13. Witten, H.I., Frank, E.: Data Mining: Practical machine Learning tools and techniques. Morgan Kaufmann Pub. (2005)
14. Hall, M., Frank, E., Holmes, G., Pfahringer, B., Reutemann, P., Witten, I.H.: The WEKA Data Mining Software: An Update. SIGKDD Explorations 11(1) (2009)

Fuzzy Rule-Based Approaches
to Dimensionality Reduction

Nikhil Ranjan Pal

Indian Statistical Institute, 203 B.T. Road, Calcutta, India
`nikhil@isical.ac.in`, `nrpal59@gmail.com`

Abstract. In this talk we deal with the problem of dimensionality reduction in a fuzzy rule-based framework. We consider dimensionality reduction through feature extraction as well as through feature selection. For the former approach, we use Sammon's stress function as a criterion for structure-preserving dimensionality reduction. For feature selection we propose an integrated framework, which embeds the feature selection task into the classifier design task. This method uses a novel concept of feature modulating gate and it can exploit the subtle nonlinear interaction between the tool (here a fuzzy rule based system), the features and the task at hand. This method is then extended to Takagi-Sugeno (TS) model for function approximation/prediction problem. The effectiveness of these methods is demonstrated using several data sets.

Keywords: Dimensionality reduction, Fuzzy Rule Based Systems, Sammon's Stress, Supervised method, Unsupervised method.

1   Introduction

Success of any decision making system, designed based on data, usually depends on the features used to design the system and use of more features is not necessarily good. This is true irrespective of whether the system is a pattern classification system or a function approximation type system. Hence a lot of effort is given to reduce the dimensionality of the data before they are used to design the system. Dimensionality reduction can be realized through either feature extraction or feature selection. Given a data set $X = \{\mathbf{x}_1, \mathbf{x}_2, \cdots, \mathbf{x}_n\}; \mathbf{x}_i \in R^p$, dimensionality reduction can be viewed as a mapping from the p dimensional input space to a q dimensional output space ($q < p$), $M : R^p \rightarrow R^q$, such that M is obtained by optimizing some criterion. Note that, the task of feature selection can also be expressed through M. If the task at hand is of classification, then typically the classification error is used as the criterion, while when the task is of function approximation (or prediction), the prediction error is the common criterion of choice. Such dimensionality reduction methods are known as supervised methods as each data point is associated with a target output. Dimensionality reduction can also be done when we do not know the task for which the reduced data will be used. In other words, dimensionality reduction can also be done when the given data points are not associated with any target values as

M.K. Kundu et al. (Eds.): PerMIn 2012, LNCS 7143, pp. 23–27, 2012.

in case of classification. Dimensionality reduction methods for such data sets are called unsupervised methods. For an unsupervised method one needs to use a task independent criterion for feature extraction/selection. In this talk we shall consider both unsupervised and supervised methods.

2   Fuzzy Rule Based Approaches

The problem of dimensionality reduction can be solved using many computational approaches such as neural networks, fuzzy logic, and evolutionary computing [2007, 1997, 2006, 2004]. Here we shall restrict ourselves to only fuzzy rule based approaches [2002]. The main advantage of a fuzzy rule based system lies in its interpretability. Moreover, it is less likely to make poor generalization. Here, first we shall discuss how fuzzy rule based systems can be used for dimensionality reduction through feature extraction when the data points are not associated with any target values.

2.1   Dimensionality Reduction via Feature Extraction

A good criterion for dimensionality reduction would be to preserve the "structure" of the original data into the lower dimensional data. This can be achieved if we can preserve the neighborhood relation in the projected data. The neighborhood relation can be preserved to a great extent if we can preserve the inter-point distances. This is what we do here. Specifically, we use Sammon's stress function [1969] as our criterion to reduce dimensionality through extraction. The sammon's stress function is defined as

$$SE = \frac{1}{\sum_{i<j} d_{ij}^*} \sum_{i<j} \frac{(d_{ij}^* - d_{ij})^2}{d_{ij}^*}. \tag{1}$$

In (1) $d_{ij}^* = d(\mathbf{x}_i, \mathbf{x}_j), \mathbf{x}_i, \mathbf{x}_j \in X$ and $d_{ij} = d(\mathbf{y}_i, \mathbf{y}_j), \mathbf{y}_i, \mathbf{y}_j \in Y$, where $d(\mathbf{x}_i, \mathbf{x}_j)$ be the Euclidian distance between $\mathbf{x}_i$ and $\mathbf{x}_j$, and $\mathbf{y}_i$ is the q-dimensional projection of $\mathbf{x}_i$. Sammon's algorithm finds Y minimizing the error function SE using the gradient descent algorithm. Note that, Sammon's algorithm does not have prediction ability.

Now we deal with the unsupervised feature extraction problem using a supervised framework and equip Sammon's method with prediction ability. First, we generate a lower dimensional representation Y of X minimizing SE. In this way we get a data set (X, Y) such that $\mathbf{x}_i \in X \subset R^p$ is associated with a $\mathbf{y}_i \in Y \subset R^q$. The data set (X, Y) is then used to find a fuzzy rule base RB with a view to realizing $RB(\mathbf{x}_i) = \mathbf{y}_i$. The rules could be of Mamdani-Assilian (MA) [1975] type or Takagi-Sugeno (TS) [1985] type. The MA and TS rules are of the forms:

MA rule : If $\mathbf{x}$ is CLOSE to $\mathbf{v}_i^x$ then $\mathbf{y}$ is CLOSE to $\mathbf{v}_i^y$;
TS rule : If $\mathbf{x}$ is CLOSE to $\mathbf{v}_i^x$ then $\mathbf{y} = u_i(\mathbf{x})$.

Here $\mathbf{v}_i^x \in R^p$ and $\mathbf{v}_i^y \in R^q$. Typically $\mathbf{v}_i^x$ and $\mathbf{v}_i^y$ are obtained as cluster centers by clustering the augmented data set X^*, where

$$X^* = \left\{ \mathbf{x}_i^* = \begin{pmatrix} \mathbf{x}_i \in \mathcal{R}^p \\ \mathbf{y}_i \in \mathcal{R}^q \end{pmatrix} \in \mathcal{R}^{p+q},\ i = 1, \cdots, n \right\} \text{ and}$$

$$V^* = \left\{ \mathbf{v}_i^* = \begin{pmatrix} \mathbf{v}_i^x \in \mathcal{R}^p \\ \mathbf{v}_i^y \in \mathcal{R}^q \end{pmatrix} \in \mathcal{R}^{p+q},\ i = 1, \cdots, c \right\} \text{ is the set of cluster centers.}$$

Here $\mathbf{v}_i^x = (v_{i,1}^x, \cdots, v_{i,p}^x)^T$. Usually the antecedent part, if $\mathbf{x}$ is CLOSE to $\mathbf{v}_i^x$, is written as a conjunction of p atomic clauses: If x_1 is CLOSE to v_{i1}^x and x_2 is CLOSE to v_{i2}^x and $\cdots$ and x_p is CLOSE to v_{ip}^x. The function $u_i(.)$ for the TS case primarily models the behavior of the input-output relation in the neighborhood of $\mathbf{v}_i^y$; here we shall consider a linear function of the inputs. For the MA model, the rule base is initialized using the clustering output and then refined by gradient descent to minimize the square-error between the rule base output and the actual output. Like the MA model, the rule antecedents for the TS model are also initialized based on the clustering results and then the consequents are obtained by the least-square-error estimate. The rule antecedents are then refined using gradient descent. Further details about extraction of the initial rules, their refinement, estimation of the consequent parameters etc. can be found in Pal et al. [2002]. We note here that unlike sammon's method, the fuzzy rule based system has predictability.

Although features extracted by such methods are quite useful, often they are difficult to interpret because of nonlinear integration of many features. The identity of the original features is lost in the generated/extracted features. So, next we shall present a framework for dimensionality reduction through feature selection again using fuzzy rule based systems.

2.2   Dimensionality Reduction via Feature Selection

This is an integrated approach [2008] where feature selection is embedded into the main task of system identification. The system could be a classifier or a function approximation type system. A function approximation type system uses either the MA type rules or the TS type rules, which we have already described. A classifier system, on the other hand, uses rules of a slightly different form: $Rule_i$: If x_1 is CLOSE to v_{i1}^x and x_2 is CLOSE to $v_{i2}^x \cdots$ and x_p is CLOSE to v_{ip}^x then class is c_i. For a given test object, the class that is associated with the rule yielding the maximum firing strength, is taken as the class of the test object.

At the beginning of learning, our method assumes that all features are poor / derogatory features and the system picks up the required feature during learning. The main philosophy behind the scheme is as follows: A bad feature should not have any impact on the fringing strength of a rule irrespective of its linguistic value that is involved in the rule. Note that the firing strength of a fuzzy rule is computed using a T-norm and $T(1, x) = x \forall x \in [0, 1]$. We associate a feature modulator $M(\lambda)$ (we call it a feature modulating gate) with a tunable parameter λ. Typically the feature modulator is a monotonic differentiable function with range [0,1]. One possible choice for the modulator is : $M(\lambda) = \frac{1}{1+exp(-\lambda)}$ and the modulated membership value is computed as $\mu' = \mu^{M(\lambda)}$; λ is a scalar variable. We call λ the modulator parameter, which modulates the membership value, μ. We emphasize that irrespective of the number of linguistic values defined on a linguistic variable, there is *exactly one* modulator for each feature or linguistic variable.

The modulator is initialized in such a manner that at the beginning of training all modulated membership values are *almost* 1 and then the modulator is learnt using the gradient descent algorithm to minimize the classification error. If a feature is important (i.e., if it can reduce the system training error), then the corresponding feature modulating gate will be opened faster, while if a feature is derogatory (i.e., it cannot reduce the error), the associated gate will not open. Thus, at the end of the training the modulating gates for useful features will be opened while those for bad features will not. A unique attribute of this approach is that it can exploit subtle nonlinear interactions between features, the problem (that we intend to solve), and the tool (that is used to solve the problem). The adaptation of this method for the MA model is straightforward because the consequents of MA rules do not involve the inputs. Since the consequents of Takagi-Sugeno type systems involve the input features, we make suitable modification to propagate the effect of the modulator (hence of the associated features) into the consequents. Further details about the classifier systems can be found in Pal [2007], while the details for the TS systems can be obtained from Pal and Saha [2008]. Our approach can deal with necessary features, indifferent features, and derogatory features in an appropriate manner. This approach can be adapted to other computational intelligence frameworks such as neural networks without much difficulty.

3   Results

The proposed methods are illustrated using several well known benchmark data sets. For structure-preserving dimensionality reduction we consider a few data sets whose geometric structures are known so that we can assess the quality of the results. On the other hand, for feature selection, we use several data sets from the UCI Machine learning repository. Similarly, to illustrate the effectiveness of the proposed method for the TS models, we also use several well known data sets. The proposed methods are found to do their targeted jobs quite satisfactorily. Many results by each of these methods can be found in Pal et al. [2002], Pal [2007] and in Pal and Saha [2008].

4   Conclusions

In this talk we have presented two fuzzy rule based approaches to dimensionality reduction. The first approach uses Sammon's stress function as a criterion for feature extraction in a lower dimension. Our method equips Sammon's method with prediction ability. In the second approach we have discussed two methods for feature selection keeping in view the classification and function approximation type problems. These two methods use a novel concept of feature modulating gates, which can also be used, with minor adaptation, for feature selection using multilayer perceptron or radial basis function networks.

References

[1999] Pal, N.R.: Soft Computing for Feature Analysis. Fuzzy Sets and Systems 103, 201–221 (1999)

[1969] Sammon Jr., J.W.: A nonlinear mapping for data structure analysis. IEEE Trans. Computers C-18, 401–409 (1969)

[2002] Pal, N.R., Vijay Kumar, E., Mandal, G.: Fuzzy logic approaches to structure preserving dimensionality reduction. IEEE Trans. Fuzzy Systems 10(3), 277–286 (2002)

[2008] Pal, N.R., Saha, S.: Simultaneous structure identification and fuzzy rule generation for Takagi-Sugeno models. IEEE Trans. Syst., Man and Cybern. -B 38(6), 1626–1638 (2008), doi:10.1109/TSMCB.2008.2006367

[1997] De, R., Pal, N.R., Pal, S.K.: Feature analysis: Neural network and fuzzy set theoretic approaches. Pattern Recognition 30(10), 1579–1590 (1997)

[2004] Chakraborty, D., Pal, N.R.: A neuro-fuzzy scheme for simultaneous feature selection and fuzzy rule-based classification. IEEE Trans. Neural Networks 15(1), 110–123 (2004)

[2006] Chakraborty, D., Pal, N.R.: Selecting Useful Groups of Features in a Connectionist Framework. IEEE Transactions on Neural Networks 19(3), 381–396 (2008)

[1975] Mamdani, E.H., Assilian, S.: An experiment in linguistic synthesis with a fuzzy logic controller. Int. J. Mach. Studies 7(1), 1–13 (1975)

[1985] Takagi, T., Sugeno, M.: Fuzzy identification of systems and its application to modeling and control. IEEE Trans. Syst., Man, Cybern. SMC-15(1), 116–132 (1985)

[2007] Pal, N.R.: A fuzzy rule based approach to identify biomarkers for diagnostic classification of cancers. In: IEEE Int. Conf. Fuzzy Systems, Fuzz-IEEE 2007, pp. 1–6 (2007), doi:10.1109/FUZZY.2007.4295533

Face Recognition Technology and Its Real-World Application

Osamu Yamaguchi

Power and Industrial Systems R&D Center
TOSHIBA Corporation Power System Company, Tokyo, Japan
samu1.yamaguchi@toshiba.co.jp

Abstract. Facial image processing is a promising tool for consumer electronics and social infrastructure systems. In recent years, digital processing of a facial image can easily be performed with the spread of digital image apparatus, such as a digital camera and a mobile phone, by improvement of throughput of a computer. The performance of the face detection that is basic of the facial image processing improves drastically, and the computational cost has also decreased. It is the reason why that has expanded the application to various appliances. This paper introduces our group's facial image processing algorithm as an example and trends of various applications using facial image processing in consumer electronics field and social infrastructure systems.

1 Introduction

"Face" plays an important role in human communication. There are three roles. The first role is to express an intention expressed by the face direction and gaze direction. The second is the role of individual personal identifiers, the last is the role showing the emotional internal condition of each people. In order to realize these three roles by digital appliance, there are the technologies of understanding a face and generating the imagery of a face. As technology of understanding a face, face detection, face tracking, individual identification, gender and age classification, and facial expression recognition are studied widely. On the other hand, as technology of generating the imagery of a face, there are beautiful skin correction, red-eye remover, facial expression synthesis, automatic facial caricature, digital make up simulation and so on.

Facial image processing, which is the example of application of advanced pattern recognition technology, is applied in all the scenes of a home and society as man-machine interface. In recent years, digital processing of a facial image can easily be performed with the spread of digital image apparatus, such as a digital camera and a mobile phone, by improvement of throughput of a computer.

This paper introduces our group's facial image processing algorithm as an example and trends of various applications using facial image processing in consumer electronics field and social infrastructure systems.

M.K. Kundu et al. (Eds.): PerMIn 2012, LNCS 7143, pp. 28–34, 2012.

2   Brief History of Face Recognition

Facial image processing research by computer has about 50 years of history. In Japan, the research report about a facial image processing was already presented from Sakai laboratory of Kyoto University at the second half of the 1960s. Prof. Kanade began with his early work on automated face recognition[1].

The big trend started at the beginning of the 90's with Eigenface that had been proposed by Turk and Pentland[2]. The research of face recognition was activated and the researcher of pattern recognition and computer vision field paid attention to it. In the second half of the 90s, the group of Malsburg of USC proposed Elastic Bunch Graph Matching (EBGM) for face recogntion[3]. They started a venture business and made up the technology which was felt that it approached by the practical use of the facial recognition.

Research on face detection technology based on face/non-face classifier was developed by Rowley[4]of MIT and Sung[5]of CMU almost simultaneously. However, these face detection algorithms were too slow. The high-speed face detection algorithm[6] which Viola and Jones developed made the real-time processing in the beginning of the 21st century. It means one big step towards utilization of facial image processing. Moreover, these researches were introduced into machine learning framework for computer vision field.

3   Facial Image Processing Techniques

3.1   Face Detection

As facial image processing technology for understanding a face, the most important and fundamental technology is the face detection function. Face detection identifies and locates human faces in an arbitrary image regardless of their position, scale, pose and illumination. The face detection problem is challenging as it needs to account for all possible appearance variation caused by lighting condition, color of face, illumination change, facial features, occlusions, etc. As previously mentioned, most face detection algorithms are based on Viola-Jones algorithm[6] based method using AdaBoost and Haar-like features. Our face detection[12] adopt joint Haar-like feature, which is based on co-occurrence of multiple Haar-like features, for detecting faces in images. Feature co-occurrence, which captures the structural similarities within the face class, makes it possible to construct an effective classifier. The joint Haar-like feature can be calculated very fast and has robustness against addition of noise and change in illumination.

3.2   Facial Feature Localization

In order to extract the individual feature and individual attribute information correctly, it is necessary to localize the feature point of facial parts correctly. Since this facial parts detection performance influences the performance of subsequent processing greatly, the stability and accuracy are required. Facial parts detection is mainly focused on the eye detection because most of the methods adopt feature based on the positions of both eyes. However, it is necessary to use plural feature points to deal with the variation of face direction, facial expression and individual difference.

The Active Shape Models[7] represents a parametric deformable model where a statistical model of global shape variation from a training set is built. To fit the multiple facial feature for input image, it iteratively modifies model points to fit local neighborhood. Active Appearance Models[8] is also deformable template method of matching statistical models of appearance to images. A set of model parameters control not only shape modes but also textural intensity information from training data.

Our group proposes a method [20] for fast and accurate extraction of feature points such as pupils, nostrils, mouth edges, and so on. This method achieves a high accuracy at a low computing cost by combining shape extraction with pattern matching. In particular, it uses a separability filter to extract feature point candidates for pupils, nostrils, mouth edges, and the like. Next, it uses pattern matching based on the subspace method to select the correct feature points from the candidates.

Moreover, we propose an efficient and generic facial feature localization method based on a weighted vector concentration approach[21]. Our method does not require any specific priors on facial shape but implicitly learns its structural information from training data.

3.3   Face Recognition

In the face recognition process, the individual feature of face to specify the person is generated by using the facial parts position. In general, the facial recognition method is divided into the feature extraction and pattern recognition.

As global appearance descriptors, gray value (image intensity) feature and its variations are generally utilized. In contrast, two of the most successful local appearance descriptors, Gabor wavelets[3] and Local Binary Patterns (LBP)[9] are made available for face representation. Compared to image intensity, Gabor wavelet is less sensitive to illumination changes. LBP is also basically very resistant to lighting changes and is a descriptor that captures small texture details.

Since the global appearance descriptors are sensitive to the face direction and lighting environment condition, our group has proposed methods for correcting them [16][17][23].

Since each feature sets are of high dimension, dimensionality reduction techniques could generally be adopted, Principal Component Analysis (PCA), Nonnegative Matrix Factorization (NMF), Independent Component Analysis (ICA) and Canonical Correlation Analysis (CCA), etc. Recently, kernelized techniques of them are known to be effective nonlinear feature extractors.

Our recognition approach is based on the Subspace Method. The Subspace Method is a classic method of pattern recognition, and has been applied to various tasks. The Mutual Subspace Method[22][13] is an extension of the Subspace Methods, in which canonical angles between two subspaces are used to define similarity between two sets of patterns. The various methods are applied to face recognition[14][15][18] [19]in our group.

4   Applications

Facial image processing technology can roughly be classified into two groups. One is the technology for understanding a face and another is the technology for generating the imagery of a face. The technology of face detection, face tracking, individual identification, gender or age estimation, facial expression recognition, and fatigue measurement or sleepiness is widely studied as technology for understanding a face.

As technology for generating the imagery of a face, research and development of a skin image retouch, red eyes remover, a facial expression synthesis, automatic facial caricature making, and digital makeup etc. are also spreading quickly.

In Japan, research and development of facial image processing are very prosperous, and the importance of facial image processing is recognized widely and leads the world especially in applicable fields:

1. Digital equipment field

   The automatic image compensation function in the auto focus of a digital camera or a video camera, a printer or a photograph development machine is put in practical use for the purpose of the application which leads to the improvement in quality of image of a photograph and video. Moreover, it is applied to the person authentication, video indexing, photograph arrangement in PC and a cellular phone, etc.

2. Entertainment field

   There is also much service for enjoying a photograph of his/her face. The improvement in photograph quality of image of a photo sticker booth, and the fortune-telling service and photograph disguise service by the photograph of face are used focusing on the younger age group. Facial image processing is also introduced into the handheld game console.

3. Security field

   Face recognition technology has become commonplace in the field of security, for example, suspicious person detection in a station, an airport and a commercial facility, immigration control, and the access control to an institution.

4. Social networking service field

   Most personal photos that are shared online are embedded in social networking service such as Facebook. Facebook is now the top photo-sharing site on the Web with billions of photos in total. Demand for recognizing a facial feature from the large number of images is growing rapidly.

5   Challenges for the Future

There are 7 billion people on the planet in 2011. Can face recognition algorithms identify 7 billion people? The number of submitted paper on major conference of facial image processing has not decreased. Face recognition as a familiar study subjects will remain the same as character recognition. The followings are issues for face recognition in the future.

– High accuracy face recognition

  About the performance benchmark of recognition, there are the vender test and grand challenge which are performed by a U.S. standard technical research center (NIST) taking the leadership. Evaluation in a practical environment and large-scale data are essential. The target will significantly change from the frontal face to the profile face, from a quiescent state to free walking situation and from indoor to outdoor.

– Importance of attribute classifier

  Soft biometrics[10] is a key feature for classifying the unknown person. The attribute classifier not only contributes to the improvement of face recognition performance but also to the acquisition of describable visual attributes (gender, race, age, hair color, etc.) This kind of information is valuable for various applications for consumer electronics and social infrastructure systems.

– High performance facial expression and attitude recognition

  In the communication among computers and people, in order to perform detailed and interactive response system more tailored to his/her situation, it is important technology to understand the intention of the person. Focusing on the smile recognition in the facial expression, it has already been commercialized in several applications. Creating a large corpus for facial expression recognition, gaze recognition and behavior recognition, it is necessary to realize a higher precision as well as improved speech recognition performance by a large corpus.

References

1. Kanade, T.: Picture Processing by Computer Complex and Recognition of Human Faces. doctoral dissertation, Kyoto University (1973)

2. Turk, M., Pentland, A.: Eigenfaces for recognition. Journal of Cognitive Neuroscience 3(1), 71–86 (1991)
3. Wiskott, L., Fellous, J., Kruger, N., von der Malsburg, C.: Face Recognition by Elastic Bunch Graph Matching. IEEE Transactions on Patrern Analysis and Machine Intelligence 19(7), 775–779 (1997)
4. Rowley, H.A., Baluja, S., Kanade, T.: Neural network-based face detection. IEEE Transactions on Pattern Analysis and Machine Intelligence 20(1), 23–38 (1998)
5. Sung, K., Poggio, T.: Example-based learning for viewbased human face detection. IEEE Transactions on Pattern Analysis and Machine Intelligence 20, 39–51 (1998)
6. Viola, P., Jones, M.: Robust real-time face detection. International Journal of Computer Vision (IJCV) 57(2), 137–154 (2004) (Originally appeared in CVPR 2001)
7. Cootes, F.T., Taylor, J.C., Cooper, H.D., Graham, J.: Active shape models - their training and application. Computer Vision and Image Understanding 61, 38–59 (1995)
8. Cootes, F.T., Edwards, J.G., Taylor, J.C.: Active appearance models. IEEE Transactions on Patrern Analysis and Machine Intelligence 23(6), 681–685 (2001)
9. Ahonen, T., Hadid, A., Pietikainen, M.: Face description with local binary patterns: Application to face recognition. IEEE Transactions on Patrern Analysis and Machine Intelligence 28(12), 2037–2041 (2006)
10. Jain, A.K., Dass, S.C., Nandakumar, K.: Soft Biometric Traits for Personal Recognition Systems. In: Zhang, D., Jain, A.K. (eds.) ICBA 2004. LNCS, vol. 3072, pp. 731–738. Springer, Heidelberg (2004)
11. Kumar, N., Berg, A.C., Belhumeur, P.N., Nayar, S.K.: Attribute and Simile Classifiers for Face Verification. In: IEEE International Conference on Computer Vision (ICCV), pp. 365–372 (2009)
12. Mita, T., Kaneko, T., Stenger, B., Hori, O.: Discriminative Feature Co-Occurrence Selection for Object Detection. IEEE Transaction on Pattern Analysis Machine Intellgence 30(7), 1257–1269 (2008)
13. Yamaguchi, O., Fukui, K., Maeda, K.: Face recognition using temporal image sequence. In: Proceedings of Third IEEE International Conference on Automatic Face and Gesture Recognition, pp. 318–323 (1998)
14. Fukui, K., Yamaguchi, O.: Face Recognition using multi-viewpoint patterns for robot vision. In: 11th International Symposium of Robotics Research (ISRR 2003), pp. 192–201 (2003)
15. Nishiyama, M., Yamaguchi, O., Fukui, K.: Face Recognition with the Multiple Constrained Mutual Subspace Method. In: Kanade, T., Jain, A., Ratha, N.K. (eds.) AVBPA 2005. LNCS, vol. 3546, pp. 71–80. Springer, Heidelberg (2005)
16. Nishiyama, M., Yamaguchi, O.: Face Recognition Using the Classified Appearance-based Quotient Image. In: Proceedings Seventh IEEE International Conference on Automatic Face and Gesture Recognition (FG 2006), pp. 49–54 (2006)
17. Kozakaya, T., Yamaguchi, O.: Face Recognition by Projection-based 3D Normalization and Shading Subspace Orthogonalization. In: Proceedings Seventh IEEE International Conference on Automatic Face and Gesture Recognition (FG 2006), pp. 163–168 (2006)
18. Fukui, K., Stenger, B., Yamaguchi, O.: A Framework for 3D Object Recognition Using the Kernel Constrained Mutual Subspace Method. In: Narayanan, P.J., Nayar, S.K., Shum, H.-Y. (eds.) ACCV 2006. LNCS, vol. 3852, pp. 315–324. Springer, Heidelberg (2006)
19. Nishiyama, M., Yuasa, M., Shibata, T., Wakasugi, T., Kawahara, T., Yamaguchi, O.: Recognizing Faces of Moving People by Hierarchical Image-Set Matching. In: CVPR Workshop Biometrics 2007, pp. 1–8 (2007)

20. Yuasa, M., Kozakaya, T., Yamaguchi, O.: An Efficient 3D Geometrical Consistency Criterion for Detection of a Set of Facial Feature Points. In: Proceedings of the IAPR Conference on Machine Vision Applications (IAPR MVA 2007), pp. 25–28 (2007)
21. Kozakaya, T., Shibata, T., Yuasa, M., Yamaguchi, O.: Facial feature localization using weighted vector concentration approach. Image Vision Comput. (IVC) 28(5), 772–780 (2010)
22. Maeda, K.: From the Subspace Methods to the Mutual Subspace Method. In: Cipolla, R., Battiato, S., Farinella, G.M. (eds.) Computer Vision. SCI, vol. 285, pp. 135–156. Springer, Heidelberg (2010)
23. Nishiyama, M., Hadid, A., Takeshima, H., Shotton, J., Kozakaya, T., Yamaguchi, O.: Facial Deblur Inference using Subspace Analysis for Recognition of Blurred Faces. IEEE Transactions on Pattern Analysis and Machine Intelligence 33(4), 838–845 (2011)

Contextual Effects in the Visual Cortex Area 1 (V1) and Camouflage Perception

Atanendu Sekhar Mandal

Central Electronics Engineering Research Institute
Pilani – 333031, Rajasthan, India
mailto:atanu@ceeri.ernet.in, atanendusekhar.mandal@gmail.com

Abstract. The cells in the visual cortex area 1 (V1) and area 2 (V2) show context dependent modulation in their responses. Suppressive as well as modulatory effects from stimuli well outside the classical receptive field are observed. This is attributed to the long-range horizontal connections in the visual cortex. In our work we have carried out contextual effect experiments with our corticocortical connections model. Our simulation results confirm the suppressive as well as the modulatory effects. We are proposing that the surround effect phenomenon can be used for camouflage perception.

Keywords: LGN, Receptive Field, CRF, reverse correlation, surround fields, contextual effects.

1   Introduction

Considerable evidence starting with the work of Hubel and Wiesel [1] in sixties shows that areas surrounding the classical receptive field can modulate cell's response. Knierim and Van Essen [2], Gilbert and Wiesel [3] and several other researchers ([4], [5], [6], [7]) have shown that in the primary visual cortex, the response of a cell gets modulated in presence of surrounding textured patterns. It is also observed that cells respond more strongly to a stimulus in which there is a contrast in orientation between the center and the surround than to a stimulus, which lacks such contrast. A general suppression in neuronal responses is observed whenever the surrounding pattern orientation matches with the optimal orientation for which the response of the center is highest. Modulatory effects from stimuli well outside the classical receptive field (CRF) (the 13x13 section in fig. 3) have been demonstrated as early in the visual pathway (fig. 1) as the retina and the lateral geniculate nucleus (LGN) in cats and monkeys. These observations suggest that visual cortical processing as early as in V1 is involved in complex visual perception. Simple visual attributes like orientation, colour, disparity are not merely extracted by a cell through its tiny and discrete RF. Context dependent modulation of a cell response may have its neural substrate in the long range horizontal connections between cells in the same area as well as in feedback connections from higher cortical areas (see Lamme et. al. [5]). The massive feedback projection from V1 to LGN, the function of which is not properly understood, might contribute to suppressive effects.

M.K. Kundu et al. (Eds.): PerMIn 2012, LNCS 7143, pp. 35–41, 2012.

Of the possible mechanisms proposed in literature as possible causes for surround effects, the long range horizontal connections within the striate cortex is of direct interest related to this work as contextual modulation in V1 has been interpreted as neural substrate of many psychophysical phenomena such as figure-ground segregation ([8], [9]), tilt-illusion [3], and perceptual pop-out ([10], [2], [6]).

For measurement of contextual effect, CRF has to be estimated reliably. Otherwise, the measured CRF will be a subset of the actual CRF and the left out region of CRF is likely to be confused with surround stimuli. For studying CRF we have to estimate the CRF for our simulated cortical cells. For estimating the CRF we have used the reverse correlation technique.

In section 2, a developmental model for corticocortical connections has been presented. Determination of receptive field (RF) has been discussed in section 3 and the contextual effect experiments along with simulation results are given in section 4. In section 5, a proposal for camouflage perception is stated. The conclusion and future works are given in section 6 followed by the references.

2   A Developmental Model of Corticocortical Connections

The visual pathway and the corresponding three-layer representation are shown in figure 1(a) and 1(b).

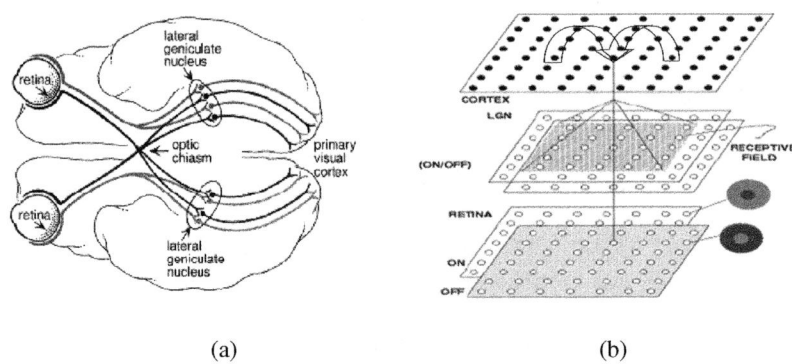

(a)   (b)

Fig. 1. (a) The visual system consisting of the eye, the lateral geniculate nucleus and the visual cortex (Source: [7]); (b) Three layer representation of the visual system. In the retina and in the LGN, ON and OFF cells are shown as two separate layers (Source: [12]).

As shown above, a cortical cell gets connections from a group of cells from the LGN, called its Receptive Field (RF) besides receiving connections from others cells within the cortical area. In the three-layer model, retinal cells receive input from visual space and transmit it to the LGN. There are ON- center and OFF- center retinal cells sending output to ON- and OFF- center LGN cells respectively. Each cortical cell receives input from both ON- and OFF-types of LGN cells. Due to computational complexity we have chosen our cortex to be of the size 50 x 50. The retinal layer is modeled as two 2D 30x30 ganglion cells lying one over the other, the first sheet corresponding to ON-center and the other to OFF-center ganglion cells. ON- and OFF-LGN layers are modeled as two 2D 30x30 sheets lying one over the other. In our model, a cortical cell has an effective receptive field size of 13 x 13. Here 13 x 13 is only a bounding box of the receptive fields. The actual RFs are of varying sizes and shapes.

For the details of the retinal cell's spatial receptive field, temporal response functions and mechanism for generation of spikes, the model in Wörgötter and Koch [11] is used. The parameters are adjusted [12] so that the spikes from LGN cells are 40 spikes/sec [13]. The output layer models layer 4 cortical cells as this layer is the main recipient of afferent connections. The model includes excitatory as well as inhibitory cells.

The short range lateral connections within the cortical area have been modeled [14] as:

$$\dot{w}_{ij} = (\gamma_1 - W^T W)(\gamma_2 - YY^T)w_{ij}f_{dist}(i,j)O_iO_j \qquad (1)$$

In this model, the synaptic weight w_{ij} between cell i and cell j depends on the outputs of the cells O_i and O_j. The output of two different cortical cells will be high if they are excited simultaneously and their orientation preferences match with that of the excitation. Here O_i and O_j are the average number of output spikes from cortical cells i and j respectively. The term (γ_1-W^TW) enforces competition for resources among axonal branches in the ith cortical cell. Competition for a pre-synaptic resource where a pre-synaptic cell has a fixed amount of resource to distribute among its branches constrains the number of axonal branches a cortical cell can maintain. $W=\|w_{ij}\|$ is a matrix of scalars with outgoing weights w_{ij} is as elements. Similarly the term (γ_2-YY^T) enforces competition among other cortical cells for target space on the dendrites of the ith cortical cell. The axons from other cortical cells are competing for neurotrophic factors, growth or survival promoting factors, released by the postsynaptic cells upon which the axons innervate. $Y=\|y_{ij}\|$ is a matrix of scalars with incoming weights to i^{th} cell with y_{ij} is as elements. $f_{dist}(i,j)$ is the distance function. The horizontal connections exhibit not only modular specificity but also axial specificity [8]. With the distance function $f_{dist}(i,j)$ we have tried to model this axial specificity.

To obtain the spike response of the cells we have used a feed-forward three-layer visual pathway model used by Bhaumik and Mathur [12] after incorporating the corticocortical connections model in it. The response of cortical cells at a given time is calculated using the SRM model (Spike response model) [9] after due modifications.

3   Determination of Receptive Field (RF)

Receptive field (RF) of a cortical cell can be obtained by applying the technique of reverse correlation as is used in the experimental studies. The modeled RFs were mapped using the reverse correlation technique [17]. The visual area corresponding to the RF cell, as shown in fig. 3, is divided into a 20x20 grid and small bright and dark rectangular bars (3x1 grid units in size) are shown in random order in the retina of the visual pathway model. The resulting train of action potentials is noted. A correlation delay of zero is chosen (as we have not modeled any delay in the feed-forward path from retina to cortex), and each spike is assigned to the stimulus that preceded it by the correlation delay. Then for each stimulus that evoked a response (spike), one 2-D histogram grid is incremented at the coordinates corresponding to each stimulus location by the number of times it generated a spike. Separate histograms are used for the bright and the dark bars. Final RF is given by the difference of bright and dark histogram. Figure 2 shows the RF of a cortical cell as obtained by reverse correlation.

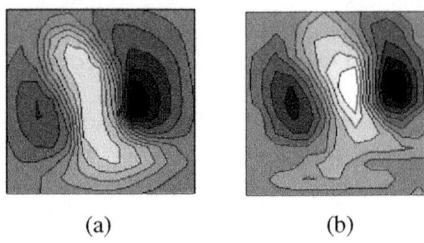

(a)   (b)

Fig. 2. RF of a cortical cell shown (a) as a set of LGN weights, (b) as obtained through reverse correlation

We define RF determined by LGN connection as the CRF for our simulated cortical cells. The CRF of the cells correspond to $4.8° \times 4.8°$ of visual space (79 x 79 grid space in Fig. 3).

4   Contextual Effect Experiments

The setup for contextual effect experiment is shown in Fig. 3. The Cortex is of size 50x50; LGN and the retina are of size 30x30 each. The visual space corresponding to the retina is 164x164. For any cortical cell shown by a hashed circle in Fig. 3, the corresponding receptive field (RF) in the LGN is determined first. It is shown by the black square space (13x13) in the LGN. The visual space corresponding to the RF is shown by the hashed square (79x79). The space just outside this region is the surround field.

For simulating contextual effects, ten sinusoidal grating stimuli with orientations ranging from $0°$ to $180°$ are applied in this hashed zone i.e. the CRF of a cell. Outside the CRF is the surround region. In the surround region we have applied sinusoidal grating stimulus having the same orientation as the preferred orientation of the cortical cell under study or orthogonal orientation to preferred orientation of the cell.

In Fig. 4 we have shown the response of cell (31,13) and cell (40,25). Cell (31,13) shows an iso-orientation felicitation of 5.74% and orthogonal orientation suppression of 8.74%. Cell (40,25) an iso-orientation suppression of 5% and orthogonal orientation suppression of 5.9%. Reported contextual effect [11] ranges from no suppression to 100% suppression and a few cells show facilitatory effect. In our simulated cells the contextual effect is limited by cortex size and both suppression and felicitation in our simulated cells are relatively low, less than 10%. In cat 44% of cells is reported to have lower than 10% suppression and in layer 4 no cell show 100% suppression [18].

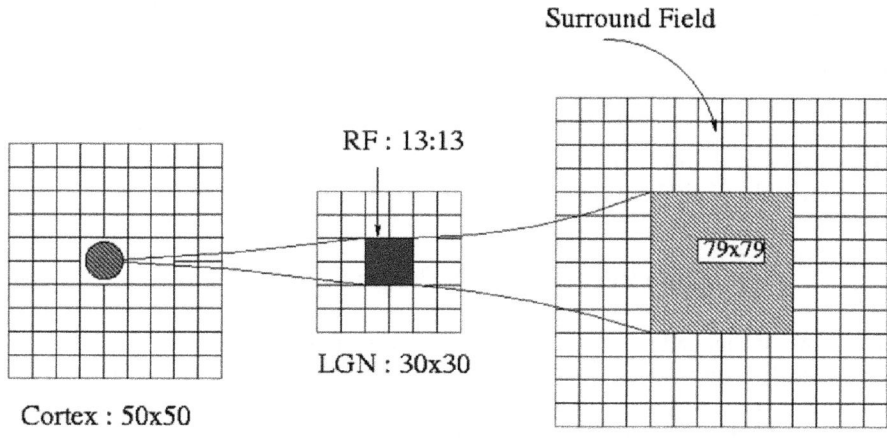

Fig. 3. The setup contextual Effects experiments

In fig. 6(a) we have iso-orientation facilitation and orthogonal orientation suppression. In fig. 6(b) we have both iso-orientation and orthogonal orientation suppression. This short of behaviour is also reported by Gilbert and Wiesel [3]. Iso-orientation suppression (fig. 4(b)) is the most common reported phenomena [2].

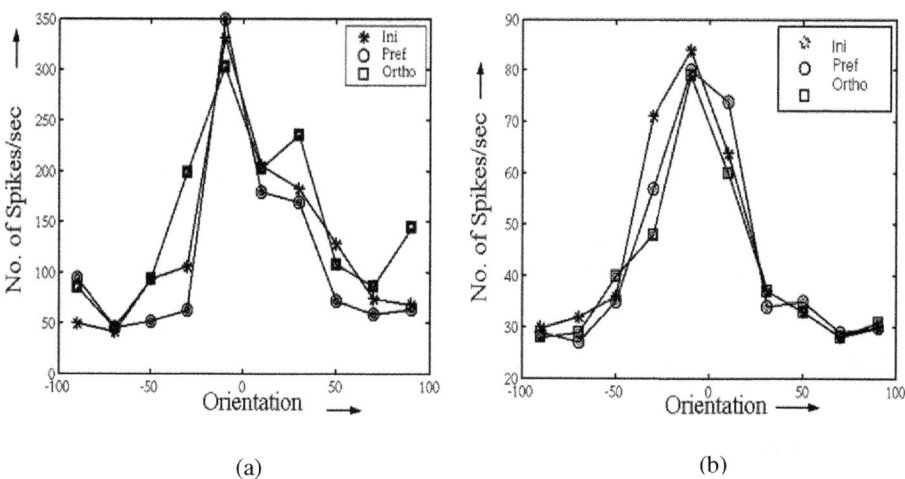

(a)   (b)

Fig. 4. (a) Contextual effect is shown for cell (31,13). (b) Contextual effect in cell (40,25). Response marked with '*' denotes that the cell was simulated with sinusoidal grating input only in the CRF of the cell. Responses marked with open circle denote the surround is simulated with a grating having the same orientation as the preferred orientation of the cell under study. Responses marked with open square represent the surround being simulated by a grating having orthogonal orientation to the preferred orientation of the cell.

In monkeys, decreasing the contrast of the center stimulus from near saturation to the middle of the dynamic range of the cell tends to change cross-orientation facilitation into suppression while leaving iso-orientation suppression unchanged [19]. In cats, iso-orientation suppression at high contrast levels of the center stimulus changes to facilitation, when its contrast is reduced [20]. In a different stimulus paradigm, iso-orientated surround stimuli can also facilitate the response of a neuron.

In the light of all these findings our results are extremely encouraging.

5   Camouflage Perception: A Proposition

The context dependent modulation of the responses of the cortical cells can be exploited for the perception of camouflaged object. From the response of cells, any object having similarity with its surroundings can be identified. When the patterns in the surround field is similar to the pattern in the CRF, the response of the cortical cell will be different with respect to the responses of other cells and a group of such cell responses will make the neural signature which can be perceived and thereby enabling identification of the location of the camouflaged object.

6   Conclusions and Future Works

In this paper, we have studied surround effect in our simulated layer 4 cortical cells. In our experiments in the simulation environments, we have obtained suppressive as well as facilitated responses. Based on these results, it is proposed that the context dependent modulation of the responses of cortical cells can be used for camouflage detection. The model used here is for simple cells. Development of models for complex cells which can be used to interpret visual scenes of complex nature are needed as a combination of both simple and complex cells can be used for handling natural scenes. Further, development of an artificial cortex for the actual neural signature generation and its interpretation in real time for camouflage perception are some of the works that can be done in the future.

Acknowledgement. We would like to acknowledge the contribution of Shri Suthirtha Sanyal, a project associate in the lab. He developed the code for reverse correlation technique. Also we would like to thank Shri Sanjeev Kumar, project assistant, for his help in the manuscript preparation.

References

1. Hubel, D.H., Wiesel, T.N.: Receptive fields and functional architecture in two non-striate visual areas (18 and 19) of the cat. Journal of Neurophysiology 28, 229–289 (1965)
2. Knierim, J.J., Van Essen, D.C.: Neuronal Responses to Static Texture Patterns in Area V1 of the Alert Macaque Monkey. J. Physiology 67, 961–980 (1992)
3. Gilbert, C.D., Wiesel, T.N.: The Influence of Contextual Stimuli on the Orientation Selectivity of Cells in Primary Visual Cortex of the Cat. Vision Res. 30(11), 1689–1701 (1990)

4. Li, W., Their, P., Wehrhahn, C.: Contextual influence on orientation discrimination of humans and responses of neurons in V1 of alert Monkeys. J. Neurophysiol. 83, 941–954 (2000)
5. Lamme, V.A., Super, H., Spekreuse, H.: Feedforward, horizontal and feedback processing in the visual cortex. Curr. Opin. Neurobiol. 8, 529–535 (1998)
6. Nothdurft, H.C., Gallant, G.L., Van Essen, D.C.: Response modulation by texture surround in primate area V1: correlates of "popout" under anesthesia. Vis. Neurosci. 16, 15–34 (1999)
7. Sengpiel, F., Sen, A., Blakemore, C.: Characteristics of surround inhibition in cat area 17. Exp. Brain Res. 116, 216–228 (1997)
8. Lamme, V.A.: The neurophysiology of figure ground segregation in primary visual cortex. J. Neurosci. 15, 1605–1615 (1995)
9. Zipser, K., Lamme, V.A., Schiller, P.H.: Contextual modulation in primary visual cortex. J. Neurosci. 16, 7376–7389 (1996)
10. Kastner, S., Nothdurft, H.C., Pigarev, I.N.: Neuronal correlates of pop-out in cat striate cortex. Vision Res. 37, 371–376 (1997)
11. Wörgotter, F., Koch, C.: A detailed model of the primary visual pathway in the cat: Comparison of afferent excitatory and intracortical inhibitory connection schemes for orientation selectivity. J. Neuroscience 11, 1959–1979 (1991)
12. Bhaumik, B., Mathur, M.: A cooperation and competition based simple cell receptive field model and study of feed-forward linear and nonlinear contributions to orientation selectivity. J. Comp. Neurosci. 14, 211–217 (2003)
13. Cheng, H., Chino, Y., Smith, E., Hamamoto, J., Yoshida, K.: Transfer characteristics of lateral geniculate nucleus X neurons in the cat: effects of spatial frequency and contrast. J. Neurophysiology 74, 2548–2557 (1995)
14. Bhaumik, B., Mandal, A.S.: An Integrated Feedforward and Recurrent Model for layer 4 Cortical Cells in the Visual Cortex. In: Proceedings International Symposium: Building the Brain, NBRC, Manesar, December 15-17 (2003)
15. Bosking, W.H., Zhang, Y., Schofield, B., Fitzpatrick, D.: Orientation Selectivity and the Arrangement of Horizontal Connections in Tree Shrew Cortex. J. Neuroscience 17, 2112–2127 (1997)
16. Gerstner, W.: Spiking Neurons. In: Mass, W., Bishop, C.M. (eds.) Pulsed Neural Networks, pp. 3–54. MIT Press, Cambridge (1999)
17. Jones, J.P., Palmer, L.A.: The two-dimensional spatial structure of simple receptive fields in cat striate cortex. Journal of Neurophysiology 58, 1187–1211 (1987a)
18. Walker, A., Ohzawa, I., Freeman, R.D.: Suppression outside the classical cortical receptive field. Visual Neuroscience 17, 369–379 (2000)
19. Levitt, J.B., Lund, J.S.: Contrast dependence of contextual effects in primate visual cortex. Nature 387, 73–76 (1997)
20. Polat, U., Mizobe, K., Pettet, M.W., Kasamatsu, T., Norcia, A.M.: Collinear stimuli regulate visual responses depending on cell's contrast threshold. Nature 391, 580–584 (1998)
21. Nicholls, J.G., Martin, A.R., Wallace, B.G.: From Brain to Neuron, 3rd edn., p. 562. Sinauer Associates Inc. (1992)

Affective Information Processing and Representations

Dana Sugu[1] and Amita Chatterjee[1,2]

[1] School of Cognitive Science, Jadavpur University
[2] Presidency University
danasugu@research.jdvu.ac.in

Abstract. Affective information processing is analysed considering the emotion circuits within the brain substrates of emotionality. Based on Gärdenfors' [8] conceptual spaces model we try to examine an emotion episode from its elicitation to the differentiation into affective processes. An *affective-conceptual spaces model* is developed taking in consideration Panksepp's [20] nested BrainMind hierarchies.

Keywords: Affective-conceptual spaces model - Affective concepts - Affective representation - Primal affects, Emotions - Cognitions - Hierarchical controls.

1   Introduction

Affective information processing can be seen as a transformation of the representational forms of information to construct an internal representation that is useful for emotions from the external representation as stimuli. Our concern is related to how affective information processing is transformed from the stimuli to the organism and how it is expressed in affective states as reflected in its behaviour. The brain is frequently considered an information processing machine. It takes in information from physical changes in the environment, sensory information, integrates it with remembered or genetically coded information and produces behaviour. In any information processing system, questions to be considered are what is being encoded, what is the mechanism used to transmit the information, how reliable is the mechanism, and how the information is utilized or decoded. Tooby and Cosmides [32] assert that the goal of cognitive neuroscience is 'to map the information processing structure of the human mind and to discover how this computational organization is implemented in the physical organization of the brain'.

Affective information processing is relatively independent of cognitive loads imposed as secondary tasks [10], can be processed within a few hundred milliseconds after the presentation of the priming [5], can occur even when participants are unaware of the stimuli processed affectively, and is unaware of the appraisal of the stimuli presented [2]. In this context, we [30] proposed that the arousal of the brain's emotional network initiates the emotion of surprise which is seen to transform the passive habitual perceptual experience into an affective experience by relating the event/stimulus to the observer. Surprise in this context stands for pure arousal (activation). Motivational drives of approach or withdrawal are amplified by the relevance of the stimulus for the organism's well being. According to the relevance

M.K. Kundu et al. (Eds.): PerMIn 2012, LNCS 7143, pp. 42–49, 2012.

and significance the stimulus bears to the organism, the appraisal processes initiate the affective experience. The purpose of our present study is to indicate the brain's mechanism used in transmitting the affective information, and the components and functions involved in such processing. Our study focuses on the implementational level [14], the brain structures and the neurological basis involved in the elicitation, intensity and differentiation of emotion. (*See* [15] for a detailed review regarding the computational and the algorithmic levels.)

2   Brain Arousal and Affective Information Processing

If we consider two sentences 'an avian has stolen my pancake' and 'a bird has stolen my pancake,' the first one contains the word 'avian' that is less likely to occur in an informal conversation. Compared to the second sentence, it is more surprising and carries additional information, according to Shannon's information theory [27]. The amount of information conveyed by a message or an event increases as the amount of uncertainty becomes greater. The entropy of the information theory is a measure of uncertainty and the uncertainty is taken as a measure of the amount of information conveyed by a particular message or event. Basically, the more we know about a thing, the less uncertain it becomes -   hence there is less entropy and the less information about it.

Pfaff [22] considers the arousal of the central nervous system (CNS) the fuelling drive mechanism that potentiates behaviour while specific motives and incentives explain why an animal does one thing rather than another. He proposed a 'generalized arousal' theory of the CNS that throbs beneath all the specific mental functions and emotional dispositions. The arousal of the CNS depends on surprise and unpredictability. Uncertain events provide more information, as disorder maximizes information flow, unlike order which minimizes it. The salient environment changes, stimuli with high inherent information content provoke the firing of the dopamine neurons. The dependence of dopamine neuronal excitability upon unpredictability, salience and surprise fits in perfectly with the application of the information theory to arousal systems. The autonomic nervous system (ANS) attends emotional arousal and reacts to uncertainty, surprise and change. The ANS handles the visceral, vascular and metabolic changes coordinating responses with the state of the CNS. The information theory has been proven useful in the analyses of arousal mechanisms of the CNS [26, 28].

3   Affective Systems of the Brain

Appraisal theories of emotion are prevalent and dominant in the academic research on affective science [1, 7, 11, 12, 16, 17, 24, 25, 29]. The basic idea they share is that the cognitive component is placed at the very onset of the emotional episode, preceding bodily responses. However, a significant number of recent studies emphasize the need for rising above the 'cognitive revolution' and seek to understand emotion circuits within the brain substrates of emotionality. [3, 21, 4]

Marr's [14] third level of information processing deals with the implementation that specifies the physical realization of the processes in the brain. We shall consider Panksepp's [18] seven subcortical neural affective systems of emotional arousal (SEEKING, RAGE, FEAR, PANIC, LUST, CARE and PLAY) of which the SEEKING system motivates the organism to pursue resources needed for survival. Watt [33] considers this system as distinct from the other prototype emotional systems. Lesions to this system cause organisms to lose the ability to organize any coherent emotional state, creating akinetic mutism and a virtual loss of emotion [34].

SEEKING patterns have been observed following novel environments or familiar environments containing novel objects. The mammalian brain contains a foraging / exploration / investigation / curiosity / interest / expectancy / SEEKING system that leads organisms to eagerly pursue the fruits of their environment – from food to knowledge. This system responds unconditionally to the homeostatic imbalances and environmental incentives. The SEEKING system drives and operates many mental complexities that humans experience as persisting feelings of interest, curiosity and sensation seeking, and it gradually helps cement the perception of causal connections in the world. It seems to translate correlations in environmental events into perception of causality and it may be a major source of 'confirmation bias', the tendency to selectively seek evidence for our hypotheses. The SEEKING system appears to control appetitive activation – the search, foraging and investigatory activities – so that the organism might exhibit consummatory behaviours – eating, drinking, copulating, etc. and it is ingrained within the mammalian brain. Positive expectancy and anticipatory states emerge through its interaction with higher brain mechanisms such as the frontal cortex and hippocampus that generate plans by mediating higher-order temporal and spatial information processing. If the outcome of this interaction is unexpected or unanticipated then the 'cognitive or expectancy reset' mechanism takes place, involving the cognitive dissonance. We [30, 31] proposed that the organism would, at that time, experience the emotion of surprise. Thus, the emotion of surprise is initiated by a sudden arousal of the SEEKING system. Panksepp[1] suggested that this could probably be tested in humans by seeing whether surprise is attenuated by dopamine-blocking agents. Moors [15] notes that the elicitation problem can be seen as part of the intensity problem; the presence or absence of an emotion can be considered to be dependent on intensity. In our proposed mechanism of elicitation of emotion, the intensity / activation / arousal initiates the emotion of surprise in an otherwise regular behaviour time. Depending on its intensity it may or may not initiate affective processes.

Panksepp [20] envisions a three-level 'nested' hierarchy – 'two-way paths of causality' – reflecting both bottom-up and top-down functions: (i) a primary level reflecting the inbuilt functions of the brain; (ii) a secondary level describing behavioural changes arising from automatic and largely unconscious mechanisms of learning and memory; and (iii) a tertiary level revealing the emotion–cognition interpenetrance, the ruminative functions that yield bottom-up evolutionary controls and allow top-down regulatory controls (*see* Fig. 1). This level is responsible for language, thought, arts and culture.

---

[1] Personal correspondence, 1 November 2009.

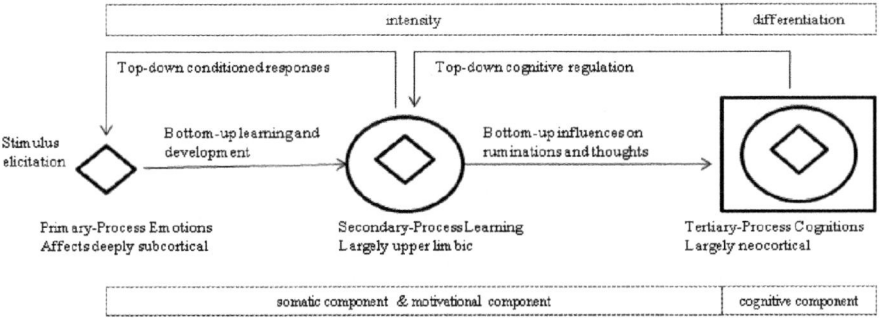

Fig. 1. Schematic conception of nested hierarchies where primary process affects are foundational and re-represented at higher levels of MindBrain processing. Adapted from Panksepp [20].

4   Affective-Conceptual Spaces Model

It is usually accepted that an emotional episode is wider than the emotion itself. According to Moors [15], in an emotional episode there are several components such as cognitive, feeling, motivational, somatic and motor. Such an episode would have to answer several problems, such as emotion elicitation, intensity and differentiation. Among the components involved in an emotional episode we [30, 31] recently proposed the following order: somatic, motivational, cognitive, feeling and motor. In our premises, the emotion of surprise connects the emotional arousal with the cognitive appraisal. Thus, we presume that physiological arousal (intensity/activation) is the basis of qualitative distinctions (valence) among various emotional experiences. In this respect the arousal, responsible for the initiation and the intensity of emotional experiences, would initiate appraisal processes, responsible for the qualitative (valence) differentiation between diverse emotional states. Thus, we proposed that an emotionally charged stimulus/event that interrupts a passive habitual perceptual experience, being produced whenever the sensory representation of the ongoing process is changed, alters habituation into dishabituation, eliciting the experience of surprise, which would be appraised as different affective states, according to the valence, positive or negative, attributed to the stimulus by the individual. By passive habitual perceptual experience we mean an experience when the organism is sufficiently regular in its behaviour, a state that requires minimal 'energy'.

The emotion of surprise is seen to transform the passive habitual perceptual experience into an affective experience by relating the event/stimulus to the perceiver, who can further evaluate its relevance to oneself. The differentiation among different affective states is engendered culturally by social learning. The stimuli elicit positive or negative emotions, expressed by varied vernacular terms such as anger, fear, disgust, happiness or sadness. The individual's attentional resources would try to answer the question, "What is this X to my Y?", where X stands for the target (stimulus) while Y is replaced by the individual's essential requirements, such as safety, purpose, progress, or pleasure, when it is threatened, fulfilled or lost, opposed and offended respectively. In each of these cases, a different affective state follows, as the case of the question, "What is this lion to my safety?" would lead to the experience of fear.

Trying to understand how emotional information and its representation is modeled, we used Gärdenfors' geometrical model of representation based on conceptual spaces. Gärdenfors introduced the *conceptual spaces model* to represent information at the conceptual level which can explain several aspects in cognitive science as well as in biological systems. The model is based on using geometrical structures that hold similarity relations modeled in a neural way. The conceptual space is built up from geometrical representations based on a number of quality dimensions. The epistemological role of the conceptual spaces is to serve as a tool in sorting out various relations between perceptions. The primary function of the quality dimensions is to represent various 'qualities' of the object, such as temperature, weight, brightness, pitch, height, width and depth. Stimuli are judged as being similar or different on the basis of quality dimensions. The dimensions assign properties to stimuli and specify the relations among them. These dimensions are the building blocks of representations at the conceptual level. At the phenomenal or psychological level, quality dimensions of the interpretation concern cognitive structures such as perception, memory, etc. of different organisms, including humans. The goal is to explain natural cognitive processes by psychophysical measurements that determine the structure of how perceptions are represented. An affective-conceptual space could be identified as a collection of one or more quality dimensions that are correlated in various ways, as the fearfulness and the threat dimensions co-vary in the space of fear.

There are quality dimensions that seem to be innate or develop very early in life. From the evolutionary point of view, the sensory dimensions are hardwired; we do not have to learn to hear or see or taste, etc., although learning can help differentiate the content of what we hear, see or taste. Sensory domains are extremely important for basic activities like finding food, avoiding danger, orienting in the environment. Quine [23] notes that innate quality dimensions are needed to make learning possible. Without the prior spacing of quality, habits cannot be acquired and all stimuli would be equally alike and different.

Some quality dimensions of human conceptual spaces are not directly generated from sensory inputs. They are based on shared knowledge, culture of a community, and Freyd [6] argued that culture and the interaction between people generates constrains on conceptual spaces. Furthermore, some quality dimensions are introduced by science. When the discoveries in science bring a change in the quality dimensions a shift of conceptual spaces occurs.

Gärdenfors' model introduced three levels of representations: the subconceptual, the conceptual or intermediate and the symbolic. Bringing this model to affective states, the subconceptual level is adopted when describing the dynamic properties of the physical processes driving the organism. At the conceptual level, the conceptual difference is made between different affective states. The symbolic level deals with the 'naming' of the various affects the organism experiences. At the subconceptual level of description, the organism's emotional processing is explained at a sensory level. According to our proposal, the physiological arousal (intensity/activation) initiates the emotion of surprise. The sensory system perceives an affectively charged stimulus/event that interrupts a passive perceptual experience and arouses the experience of surprise. At the conceptual level, the organism creates or recognizes previous concepts and 'labels' the stimulus depicted at the subconceptual level by the sensory system. The conceptual space is created by the quality dimensions. In affective studies there are three emotion dimensions proposed: arousal/activation, valence and dominance. These emotion dimensions estimate the data received from the subconceptual level. At the symbolic level, we are able to express and communicate the meaning 'labeled' at the conceptual level.

As Gärdenfors points out, the conceptual and the symbolic levels are bidirectional – the conceptual level functions as a semantic domain for the symbols, and the symbolic level generates expectations that control the focus of attention at the conceptual level. In our opinion, the focus of attention would rather be connected with the subconceptual level as it is the level that initiates the bottom-up information processing.The bridge that connects the subconceptual and the conceptual level is the expectation built up by the symbolic level. If the expectation failure leads to the emotion of surprise then the organism perceiving the stimulus at the subconceptual level will search into the conceptual level and try to deal with the novel input.

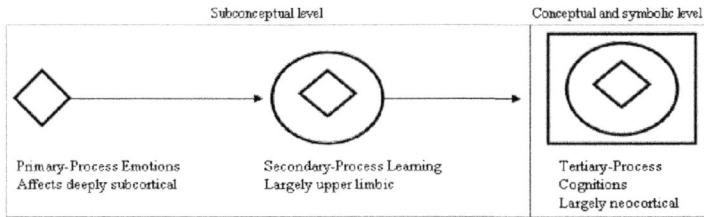

Fig. 2. Graphic representation of an emotion episode: the *affective-conceptual spaces model*

Figure 2 is a graphic representation of an emotional episode. The *affective conceptual spaces model* is proposed as a framework for representing affective information at the conceptual level. The stimulus is analysed at the three levels proposed by Gärdenfors – the subconceptual, the conceptual and the symbolic levels. Panksepp's primary and secondary levels are considered to belong to the subconceptual level. Within the subconceptual level, the somatic component of the emotional episode is represented by the psychological arousal that elicits the emotion of surprise. Emotions act as motivational amplifiers [13] and that calls for the motivational component of the emotional episode. At the conceptual level, the cognitive component attributes 'value' to the stimulus by appraisal processes and the stimulus is labeled with a certain valence, positive or negative, according to the effect it produces on the organism. The organism experiences an affective state which at the symbolic level could be 'named' fear, anger, disgust, sadness or happiness. The intensity of the stimulus is analysed at the subconceptual level. The differentiation of the affective states takes place at the conceptual and symbolic levels. At the subconceptual level the representations are organism centred while at the conceptual and symbolic levels they are stimulus centered.

The affective-conceptual spaces model allows us to explain the mechanism of emotion elicitation and differentiation into different affective states. It also supports the idea that culture and shared knowledge play a distinct role in building up our conceptual spaces. The main advantage offered by the proposed model is that it can serve as an explanatory framework for recent claims of neuroscience research with regard to the fast, non-conscious and automatic perception of stimuli (Panksepp's primary and secondary levels). Unlike other existing models of affective responses (symbolic network models, exemplar models and subsymbolic network models), the affective-conceptual spaces model offers details regarding the elicitation of an automatic emotion episode (at the subconceptual level) and provides an account of how previous experiences and culture outlined the differentiation of the affective experience (at the conceptual and symbolic level).

The proposed affective-conceptual spaces model is mainly concerned with the implementation level. The algorithmic level involves finding out the appropriate procedure in order to enable the 'input' (stimulus) to be differentiated into "outputs" of different affective states. These specific steps (or algorithms) employed to solve the information differentiation of the output could be realized with the help of multi-net systems generally used for developing models for biological processes that combine artificial neural nets (ANN) with algorithms that mimic the natural process of biological evolution, i.e. genetic algorithms (GA). Both models, ANN and GA, find extensive applications in intelligent search, machine learning and optimization problems and imitate "the remarkable ability of the human mind to reason and learn in an environment of uncertainty and imprecision" [35]. We expect that such multi-net systems could benefit from our proposed model that combines entropy, uncertainty and surprise, as they typically stand for essential 'instigators' in human learning processes.

References

1. Arnold, M.B.: Emotion and personality. Columbia University Press, New York (1960)
2. De Houwer, J., Hermans, D.: Do feelings have a mind on their own? In: De Houwer, J., Hermans, D. (eds.) Cognition & Emotion: Reviews of Current Research and Theories. Psychology Press, Hove (2010)
3. Cromwell, H.C., Panksepp, J.: Rethinking the cognitive revolution from a neural perspective: How overuse/misue of term 'cognition' and the neglect of affective controls in behavioral neuroscience could be delaying process in understanding the BraiMind. Neuroscience and Biobehavioral Reviews (2011)
4. Damasio, A.: The self comes to mind. Pantheon, New York (2010)
5. Fockenberg, D., Koole, S.L., Semin, G.R.: Backward affective priming: Even when the prime is late, people still evaluate. Journal of Experimental Social Psychology 42, 799–806 (2006)
6. Freyd, J.: Shareability: the social psychology of epistemology. Cognitive Science 7 (1983)
7. Frijda, N.H.: The emotions. Cambridge University Press, New York (1986)
8. Gärdenfors, P.: Conceptual Spaces: The Geometry of Thought. MIT, Cambridge (2000)
9. Glass, A., Holyoak, K., Santa, J.: Information processing and social cognition. Cognition (1979)
10. Klauer, K.C., Teige-Mocigemba, S.: Controllability and resource dependence in automatic evaluation. Journal of Experimental Social Psychology 43, 648–655 (2007)
11. Lazarus, R.S.: Psychological stress and the coping process. McGraw-Hill, New York (1966)

12. Lazarus, R.S.: Emotion and adaptation. Oxford University Press, New York (1991)
13. Marion, R.: The Boy Who Felt No Pain. Addison-Wesley, Mass (1990)
14. Marr, D.: Vision: A Computational Approach. Freeman & Co., San Francisco (1982)
15. Moors, A.: Theories if emotion causation: A review. In: De Houwer, J., Hermans, D. (eds.) Cognition & Emotion: Reviews of Current Research and Theories. Psychology Press, Hove (2010)
16. Oatley, K., Johnson-Laird, P.N.: Towards a cognitive theory of emotions. Cognition and Emotion 1, 29–50 (1987)
17. Ortony, A., Clore, G.L., Collins, A.: The cognitive structure of emotions. Cambridge University Press, Cambridge (1988)
18. Panksepp, J.: Affective Neuroscience: The Foundations of Human and Animal Emotions. Oxford University Press, New York (1998)
19. Panksepp, J. (ed.): Textbook of biological psychiatry, pp. 75–110. Wiley, Hoboken (2004)
20. Panksepp, J.: What is an emotional feeling? Lessons about affective origins from cross-species neuroscience. Motivation and Emotion, 1–12 (2011a)
21. Panksepp, J.: Cross-species affective neuroscience decoding of the primal affective experiences of humans and related animals. PLoS One (2011b)
22. Pfaff, D.: Brain Arousal and Information Theory: Neural and Genetic Mechanisms. Howard University Press, Cambridge (2006)
23. Quine, W.V.O.: Natural kinds. In: Ontological Relativity and Other Essays, pp. 114–138. Columbia University Press, New York (1969)
24. Roseman, I.J., Antoniou, A.A., José, P.E.: Appraisal determinants of emotions: Constructing a more accurate and comprehensive theory. Cognition and Emotion 10(3), 241–277 (1996)
25. Scherer, K.R.: On the nature and function of emotions: A component process approach. In: Scherer, K.R., Ekman, P. (eds.) Approaches to Emotion, pp. 293–317. Lawrence Erlbaum Associates, Inc., Hillsdale (1984)
26. Schneidman, E., Still, S., Berry II, M.J., Bialek, W.: Network information and connected correlations. Phys. Rev. Lett. 91(23), 87–101 (2003)
27. Shannon, C.E.: A mathematical theory of communication. AT&T Labs Tech., J. 24, 49–65 (1948)
28. Sharpee, T., Rust, N.C., Bialek, W.: Analyzing neural responses to natural signals: maximally informative dimensions. Neural Comput. 16(2), 223–250 (2004)
29. Smith, C.A., Ellsworth, P.C.: Patterns of cognitive appraisal in emotion. Journal of Personality and Social Psychology 48, 813–838 (1985)
30. Sugu, D., Chatterjee, A.: Flashback: Reshuffling emotions. IJHI 3(1), 109–135 (2010)
31. Sugu, D., Chatterjee, A.: Gärdenfors' Conceptual Spaces and Affective Representations. IJHI 4(1), 11–17 (2011)
32. Tooby, J., Cosmides, L.: Toward mapping the evolved functional organization of mind and brain. In: Gazzaniga, M.S. (ed.) The New Cognitive Neuroscience, pp. 1167–1178. MIT Press, Cambridge (2000)
33. Watt, D.F.: Panksepp's common sense view of affective neuroscience is not the commonsense view in large areas of neuroscience. Consciousness and Cognition 14, 81–88 (2005)
34. Watt, D.F., Pincus, D.I.: Neural substrates of consciousness: Implications for clinical psychiatry. In: Panksepp, J. (ed.) Textbook of Biological Psychiatry, pp. 75–110. Wiley, Hoboken (2004)
35. Zadeh, L.A.: The role of fuzzy logic in the management of uncertainty in Expert Systems. Fuzzy Sets and Systems 11, 199–227 (1983)

Face Image Retrieval Based on Probe Sketch Using SIFT Feature Descriptors

Rakesh S.[1], Kailash Atal[2], Ashish Arora[2], Pulak Purkait[3], and Bhabatosh Chanda[3]

[1] Dept. of Computer Science, National Institute of Technology Karnataka, Surathkal
[2] Department of EEE, IIT Guwahati, Guwahati
[3] ECSU, Indian Statistical Institute, 203, B.T. Road, Kolkata
{rakesh.s.mysore,atalkailash,ashish.arora.iitg}@gmail.com,
{chanda,pulak_r}@isical.ac.in

Abstract. This paper presents a feature-based method for matching facial sketch images to face photographs. Earlier approaches calculated descriptors over the whole image and used some transformation and matched them by some classifiers. We present an idea, where descriptors are calculated at selected discrete points (eyes, nose, ears...). This allows us to compare only prominent features. We use SIFT (Scale Invariant Feature Transform) to extract feature descriptors at the annotated points in the sketches and experiment with various methods to retrieve photos. Experimental results demonstrate appreciable matching performances using the presented feature-based methods at a low computational cost.

Keywords: Forensic sketch, image registration, annotated points, SIFT feature descriptors.

1   Introduction

The problem of retrieving facial photos resembling a sketch from gallery of photos has received substantial attention from research community, security agencies, crime investigators etc. An important application of this is to assist law enforcement. During a criminal activity, the photo image of the suspect is generally not available. The criminals are sensitive to not leave behind any trace of their identity in the form of fingerprint or any other biometric. In such situations a recollected description of eyewitnesses is used by forensic artist to draw an estimate sketch of the culprit. The law enforcement agencies need assistance to automatically retrieve photos of potential suspects from the criminal photo database based on available sketch. Since the sketch is not an exact portrayal of the culprit, it becomes difficult to match real-time sketches exactly to their corresponding photos. Additional difficulties are posed due to difference in modalities of sketches and photos. Considering these challenges, criminal investigators are generally interested in the top N retrieved results because of low probability of finding an exact match and relatively higher likelihood of finding a correct match in these retrieved photos. This reduces the burden of investigators to

M.K. Kundu et al. (Eds.): PerMIn 2012, LNCS 7143, pp. 50–57, 2012.

manually search for the exact match of the sketch in the whole database and saves crucial time. It also helps the witness and artist to modify the sketch drawing of the suspect based on retrieved results.

Our proposed solution to the problem is somewhat in between face recognition and image retrieval. In former case only exact match is considered, while in the latter any object of same category provides an acceptable solution. In this paper we study two interesting and related problems: similar visual feature extraction from sketches and photos, and comparing features of the sketch-photo pairs. In order to solve the problem we use SIFT algorithm to extract visual descriptors at key points on facial sketches and photos such as eyes, nose, ears, lips etc on registered image. We extend our approach by performing experiments using obtained feature vectors to correctly retrieve photos of true subject based on probe sketch. Rest of the paper is organized as follows. Section 2 presents the relevant works of recent past. Proposed method and its performance analysis are given in section 3 and 4 respectively. Finally concluding remarks are placed in section 5.

2   Related Work

Most previous research works on sketch to photo matching has concentrated on linear or non-linear approaches like Eigen-transformation (Tang and Wang [11], [9]) and Markov random field (Wang and Tang [10]). These studies share a common approach of synthesizing sketches from photos and then matching these synthesized sketches with probe sketch or synthesizing a photo from probe sketch (Purkait and Chanda [13]) and matching the synthesized photo against the gallery of photo database.

Recent works implement SIFT (Karle, Li and Jain [2], B. Klare and A. Jain[8]) or LBP (Ahonen, Hadid, and Pietikainen [4]) on the whole image which use feature descriptors to create distinct identity of a person. Local descriptors like SIFT [6], LBP [4] and CITE [5] are commonly employed in numerous real time applications such as face photo retrieval. These descriptors diminish the effect of difference in modalities of sketch and photo while still maintaining the distinct identity of a person. Image based feature descriptors have shown success in face recognition in the past years [7].

3   Proposed Method

In this section, we give a detailed explanation of our approach to retrieve photos based on probe sketch. This has distinctly two parts : Training and Test. Training starts with manually annotating key points on the Training set of corresponding sketch-photo pairs. Note that a corresponding pair consists of a sketch and a photo image of same subject. Images are then registered with common shape, called mean shape, using the annotated key points. In case of probe sketch key points are obtained by using active shape model (ASM). This is followed by computation of SIFT descriptors at annotated points. We finally demonstrate the ability to match sketches to photos by directly using Euclidean distance between SIFT feature, Projection Angle method of the SIFT feature and also their combination with the geometric position of the annotated key points. The algorithm may summarily be represented by the following steps:

3.1   Annotating Points

Ordinarily using SIFT on a sketch or a photo of size 500X500 pixels generates descriptors at around 2000 points on the image. Other methods like slicing a photo or sketch in small patches and computing SIFT features in those patches involves computation in very high dimensions. Such methods are often accompanied by use of PCA[1] or LFDA[2]. However points in regions near eyes, lips, nose ears etc. are potential for high distinctness for a person. So we adopted a new approach of calculating SIFT features only at selected points in these regions. During Training we manually marked 41 points on all sketch-photo pairs at identical locations on all images using am_tools [12] however Active Shape Model (ASM) ([3]) can be used to do this automatically for a given probe sketch at the time of testing. ASM is a statistical model of the shape of object in training image which iteratively deform to fit to an object in a new image. It captures the natural variability within a class of shapes. The model is built by learning the patterns of variability of annotated points of a training database.Fig.1 shows 41 key points annotated on sketch-photo pairs.

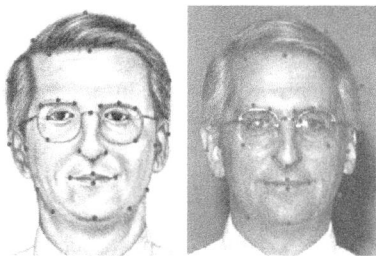

Fig. 1. Annotated Points on corresponding sketch-photo pair from FERET database

3.2   Image Registration

The feature at key point based representation requires each sketch and photo image to be registered onto a common platform. This is done by transforming the image suitably such that the mean and standard deviation of the annotated points of the images database become the same.

Firstly the images are normalized by rotating by the angle between the horizontal axis and the line joining mid-point of the eyes. Now for this rotated image I_i calculate the mean (x_{im}, y_{im}), of all new 41 points. We do the same for all the images in the database, thus fetching a set of means $\{(x_{1m}, y_{1m}), (x_{2m}, y_{2m}), ..., (x_{nm}, y_{nm})\}$ of n images $\{I_1, I_2, ..., I_n\}$. Then we compute the global mean (x_{gm}, y_{gm}) of these n means. To make the images mean centered, we translate each image I_i in x direction by $x_{gm} - x_{im}$ and in y direction by $y_{gm} - y_{im}$ to get (x'_{ki}, y'_{ki}).

The final step of registration is scaling. We scale images in such a way that the standard deviation of Euclidean distance of the annotated points about the global mean (x_{gm}, y_{gm}) is same for all. We first compute the local standard deviation of an all the images and scale them by a ratio of mean standard deviation to local standard deviation using the following transformation.

$$\begin{bmatrix} x''_{ki} \\ y''_{ki} \\ 1 \end{bmatrix} = \begin{bmatrix} scale & 0 & (1-scale).x_{gm} \\ 0 & scale & (1-scale).y_{gm} \\ 0 & 0 & 1 \end{bmatrix} \begin{bmatrix} x'_{ki} \\ y'_{ki} \\ 1 \end{bmatrix}.$$ (1)

After these three steps – rotation, translation and scaling, all the images would be registered to the same platform.

3.3   Feature Extraction

Visual features are computed at 41 key points. The underlying assumption is that the features extracted from eyes, nose or ears are sufficiently distinct for each. Since we have marked the points in a fixed order, it preserves correspondence while comparing features of a photo and sketch. Suppose $\mathbf{P}=(P_1,P_2,...,P_k)^T$ and $\mathbf{S}=(S_1,S_2,...,S_k)^T$ are feature vectors extracted from photo and sketch respectively. Now

$$\mathbf{S'} = \mathbf{AS}.$$ (2)

where k x k matrix A stands for cross modality transformation which takes sketch features to domain of photo features. Thus to retrieve photo from sketch, we need to match $\mathbf{P}$ with $\mathbf{S'}$ and not with $\mathbf{S}$. Now if A can be diagonalized with transform matrix W, i.e., A= $\mathbf{W}^T \mathbf{D} \mathbf{W}$ then equation (2) reduces to $\mathbf{S'} = \mathbf{W}^T \mathbf{DWS}$ or

$$\mathbf{WS'} = \mathbf{DWS}.$$ (3)

Under the assumption that every element of feature vector carry equal amount of information, the diagonal matrix D becomes λI. Then equation (3) may be written as

$$\mathbf{S'} = \lambda \mathbf{S}.$$ (4)

That means in transform domain sketch and photo features are related by a scalar multiplier. SIFT feature, due to its inherent property, satisfies this criterion approximately. This is because SIFT descriptor identifies the scale and dominant orientations at the selected points. The orientation(s), scale and selected locations enables SIFT to construct a canonical view for the point that is invariant to similarity transforms. The reader is referred to [6] for more detailed description on SIFT. Unlike the conventional method we are not using SIFT key point detection, rather the SIFT feature descriptors are computed at predetermined 41 locations. These features are well-suited for sketch-photo matching because they describe the distribution of the direction of edges in the face, which is the information common to both sketches and photos.

SIFT descriptors at j^{th} point in i^{th} photo, $P_i(j)$ is considered as a column vector with 128 elements, where j varies from 1 to 41. $P_i(j)$ is normalized. Similarly $S_k(j)$ represents normalized SIFT descriptors at jth point in k^{th} sketch, i.e., $P_i = (P_i(1),P_i(2), ..., P_i(41))^T$ and $S_k = (S_k(1), S_k(2), ..., S_k(41))^T$.

Suppose $X_{Pk}=(X_P(1), Y_P(1), X_P(2), Y_P(2),...,X_P(41),Y_P(41))$ represents normalized coordinates of key points on photo image. X_{Sk} can be similarly defined for sketch image.

3.4   Recognition and Retrieval Methods

In order to retrieve suitable photos against a probe sketch, S_{probe} , ASM is used to automatically annotate 41 key points on the probe sketch as mentioned   in section 3.1 followed by computation of SIFT descriptors at the annotated key points. And all the descriptors of target photos P_i are computed prior to recognition process. Now suppose dissimilarity between X_{Sprobe} and X_{Pi} is measured as $d(X_{Sprobe}, X_{Pi})$ and similarity   that between photo and sketch SIFT descriptors S_{probe} and P_i as $d(S_{probe}, P_i)$. Hence, overall dissimilarity between photo and sketch may be measured as

$$E_i = \lambda d(X_{Sprobe}, X_{Pi}) + (1 - \lambda)d(S_{probe}, P_i) . \tag{5}$$

where λ is a parameter that determines the importance of coordinates and SIFT features. The dissimilarity measure is defined next.

3.4.1   Projection Angle Based Dissimilarity Measure

In this approach, SIFT descriptor at each of the 41 points is considered as a column vector with 128 elements as mentioned in section 3.1. Based on these values $d(S_{probe}, P_i)$ may be computed as follows:

i. Find the mean vector P_m for photos and S_m for sketches from training images. This step is computed during training period.

ii. Subtract P_m from all the face-photos and S_m from   the probe sketch to get, $P_i' = P_i - P_m$ and $S_{probe}' = S_{probe} - S_m$.

iii. Find the angle $\theta_i(j)$ between $P_i'(j)$ and S_{probe}' (j), by taking dot product.

iv. Find the mean angle, $\theta_{mean,i}$ between S_{probe}' and P_i':

$$\theta_{mean,i} = \frac{\sum_{j=1}^{41} \theta_i(j)}{41} . \tag{6}$$

v. $\theta_{mean,i}$ is the measure of $d(S_{probe}, P_i)$ between S_{probe} and P_i for this case.

3.4.2   Euclidean Distance Based Dissimilarity Measure

It is a simple and most trivial approach used for comparing distance between vectors. In this approach, we compute the mean of Euclidean distance between the corresponding SIFT features of the probe sketch S_{probe} and i^{th} photo P_i after converting it to S_{probe}' and P_i' as mentioned in the methodology for   Projection Angle Method to get $d(S_{probe}, P_i)$. In essence, this method is same as Projection Angle method except in step(iii) where Euclidean distance is computed between two vectors instead of dot product.

Finally the dissimilarity between probe sketch and photo is computed using equation (5) for a suitable value of λ. Hence the best match for a probe sketch is a photo for which the dissimilarity measure E_i is minimum. In case of N photos to be retrieved, lowest N dissimilarity values are considered.

4   Experimental Results and Discussion

In this section, we present the performance of our system using 969 photo-sketch pairs from the FERET database[14, 15]. We have divided our database into 2 parts- 569 for training and 400 for testing. We have repeated the experiment with 5 such random splits and the average performance of the various methods is reported in Table 1 below. The results are shown for two cases – (1) using SIFT only and (2) that value of λ for which best average result is obtained.

Table 1. Comparison of accuracy (precision %) for 400 testing sketch-photo pairs

No of photos retrieved	1	5	10	20	30	40	50
Euclidean Distance Method (SIFT only)	74.7	88.35	92.95	95.1	96.65	97.7	98.2
Euclidean Distance Method	77.25	89.7	93.9	96.1	97.3	98.0	98.45
Projection Angle Method (SIFT only)	79.95	91.45	94.6	97.7	98.55	98.9	99.15
Projection Angle Method	83.85	93.65	96.3	98.3	99.1	99.5	99.7

For the case ($\lambda = 0$), the accuracy of both methods for all the ranks is relatively lower when compared against the case ($\lambda \neq 0$). λ was determined experimentally under the constraint to maximize accuracy. This shows that not SIFT features alone, but their weighted combination with the geometric distance between key points on the registered photos and probe sketch is a better measure of dissimilarity between the two. This is shown in Fig.2.

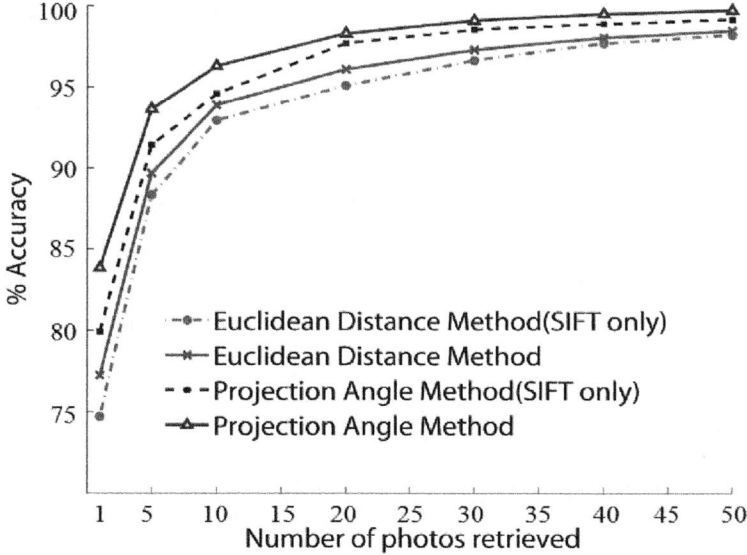

Fig. 2. Comparison of Euclidean Distance Method and Projection Angle Method

Fig. 3. Poor photo-sketch pairs in FERET

The accuracy of 83.85% for a correct match in first retrieval and that of 96.3% in top ten retrievals using Projection Angle Method is appreciable considering the fact that database of comparison of 400 photo-sketch pairs in our case is reasonably high. The fact that the accuracy of a correct match in top 50 retrievals using this method goes close to 99.7% must be of interest for people developing real time applications.

Our choice of 400 sketch-photo pairs is random. We did not perform the test separately for males and females. Nor was there any distinction on the basis of race or origin as tried upon in the earlier work by A.K. Jain et al.[2]. The FERET database also includes some poor sketch for photo of the same subject making our work even more difficult. In some cases, a person in photo has spectacles which is not found in the corresponding sketch. Some of these cases are shown in Fig 3. In the background of these complicacies, we may consider our results highly appreciable.

5   Conclusion

Matching or retrieving photos from sketch is a difficult problem. Forensic sketches pose challenges due to inability of a witness to exactly remember the appearance of a suspect which results in inaccurate sketches. Also sketches drawn with pencil has altogether a different modality in comparison with face photos.

Our work presents an alternative approach to retrieve photos from sketch using SIFT descriptors at annotated key points. Our work indirectly highlights the contribution of the information hidden within the geometrical position of eyes, lips, ears etc. in face recognition. Many opportunities for future research stem from the results shown in this work. The proposed approach matches over 100 sketch –photo pairs in less than a minute with a good accuracy. The major contribution of this paper is fusion of linear and non-linear approaches(annotated points and SIFT feature descriptors) which makes real time matching of sketches with photos possible at low computational cost.

References

1. Ke, Y., Sukthankar, R.: PCA-SIFT: A Distinctive Representation for local images descriptors. In: IEEE Computer Society Conference on Computer Vision and Pattern Recognition (CVPR 2004), vol. 2 (2004)
2. Klare, B.F., Li, Z., Jain, A.K.: Matching Forensic Sketch to Mug Shot photos. IEEE Trans. on Pattern Analysis and Machine Intelligence

3. Cootes, T.F., Taylor, C.J., Cooper, D.H., Graham, J.: Active Shape Models-their training and application. Computer Vision and Machine Understanding 61(1), 38–59 (1995)
4. Ahonen, T., Hadid, A., Pietikainen, M.: Face description with local binary patterns: Application to face recognition. IEEE TPAMI 28(12), 514–518, 2037 (2006)
5. Zhang, W., Wang, X., Tang, X.: Coupled Information-Theoretic Encoding for Face Photo-Sketch Recognition. In: IEEE Computer Society Conference on Computer Vision and Patter Recognition
6. Lowe, D.: Distinctive image features from scale-invariant key points. IJCV 60(2), 91–110 (2004)
7. Mikolajczyk, K., Schmid, C.: A Performance Evaluation of Local Descriptors. IEEE Trans. Pattern Analysis and Machine Intelligence 27(10), 1615–1630 (2005)
8. Klare, B., Jain, A.: Sketch to Photo Matching: A Feature-Based Approach. In: Proc. SPIE Conf. Biometric Technology for Human Identification VII (2010)
9. Tang, X., Wang, X.: Face Sketch Recognition. IEEE Trans. Circuits and Systems for Video Technology 14(1), 50–57 (2004)
10. Wang, X., Tang, X.: Face Photo-Sketch Synthesis and Recognition. IEEE Trans. Pattern Analysis and Machine Intelligence 31(11), 1955–1967 (2009)
11. Tang, X., Wang, X.: Face Sketch Synthesis and Recognition. In: Proc. IEEE Int'l Conf. Computer Vision, pp. 687–694 (2003)
12. The University of Manchester,
    http://personalpages.manchester.ac.uk/staff/
    timothy.f.cootes/tfc_software.html
13. Purkait, P., Chanda, B., Kulkarni, S.: A Novel Technique for Sketch to Photo Synthesis. In: 7th International Conference on Computer Vision, Graphics and Image Processing (ICVGIP 2010), Chennai, pp. 224–231 (December 2010)
14. Jonathon Phillips, P., Wechsler, H., Huang, J., Rauss, P.J.: The FERET database and evaluation procedure for face-recognition algorithms. Image Vision Computer 16(5), 295–306 (1998)
15. The FERET Database, http://www.itl.nist.gov/iad/humanid/feret/

Effect of Perceptual Anchorage Points on Recognition of Bangla Characters

Asok Bandyopadhyay[1], Bhaswati Mukherjee[1], and Bidyut Baran Chaudhuri[2]

[1] Centre for Development of Advanced Computing
Plot-E2/1, Block GP, Sector-v, Salt Lake, Kolkata-700091
[2] Computer Vision & Pattern Recognition Unit,
Indian Statistical Institute, 203, B.T. Road
Kolkata-700108
asok.bandyopadhyay@cdac.in, bbcisical@gmail.com

Abstract. Character recognition (Printed and Handwritten) system has become an extremely useful tool in Human Computer Interaction. Handwriting is a complex perceptual motor task generating linguistic information. Characters reflect shape distinction needed to perceive different phonetic information of words. We have explored 'perceptual processes' of character recognition for developing a cognitive model. Especially, we tried to extract the Perceptual Anchorage Points in the character. An experiment was performed to identify Perceptual anchorage points in a character both for handwritten as well as printed character of different Bangla script fonts including fonts used in Bangladesh. A set of important points and shapes has been found in the experiment. It is noted that deletion of these regions from characters greatly reduces the human cognition of characters.

Keywords: Character Recognition, Human Computer Interaction, Perceptual Anchorage Points, Bangla Handwritten Characters.

1   Introduction

Communication is an indispensable part of civilized society. Orthographic mode of communication is considered as one of the most efficient and reliable means of interaction in daily lives. Human-friendly interfaces are expected to support human handwriting and printed characters as a major input modality. Although apparently simple, it has a highly complex cortical, cerebellar and neuromuscular dynamics [1]. Attneave has shown that important perceptual information is concentrated at the curve and corner points of line-drawing sketches [2]. For characters, we call such important points as 'perceptual anchorage points' as mentioned by Anquetil and Lorette [3]. Such points are of importance for human recognition of characters. If they are absent or get distorted, the perception can be substantially hampered.

For automatic recognition of text too, the recognition accuracy may go down if such points are not properly considered. Conversely, if these features are accounted

M.K. Kundu et al. (Eds.): PerMIn 2012, LNCS 7143, pp. 58–65, 2012.

then the accuracy may increase. Some studies along this line have been done in forensic applications for handwriting authentication and person identification [4]. Also, corners, end-points, crossing points etc. have been used in handwriting OCR. However, in these studies such features are detected on ad-hoc basis, not using human perceptual experiments. The present paper is an attempt to fill this gap on handwriting recognition of Indian text. To the best of our knowledge, such work has not been done for OCR or OHCR applications in Indian Languages in general and Bangla, in particular. In our approach we have given emphasis to find the anchorage points along with their order of significance through human perceptual experiments and attempted to use them to improve the recognition accuracy of Bangla character recognition, which essentially reflects the novelty of our reported work.

Bangla is the second most popular script and language in the Southeast Asia. Almost 250 million people of Eastern India and Bangladesh use this language thereby making it the fifth most popular in the world [5]. Script wise Bangla is quite complex, being alpha-syllabic and conjunct forming in nature. Experiments conducted by Fred Attenueave have revealed that human visual system has specialized neurons to detect the directional curve, corner and end point. So, they play significant role in perception and memorization of line drawing including alphabets. We propose to segment 2D curves at these "perceptual anchorage points", namely discontinuity points, angular points, critical or singular points and multiple points of order k. In our effort, a handwritten character/cluster is characterized by structure- or- shape based representation of a stroke in which a stroke is represented as a string of shape features [6]. For plane curves the main properties are continuity, differentiability and curvature; therefore we define as "catastrophe points" the points where the curve is disrupted, the angular points and the cusps [8] [9].

2   Perceptual Anchorage Points

Perceptual anchorage points specifically refers to the Points of Discontinuity (DP), Angle Points (AP), Cusp Point (CP), Cross Point(CrP) or Multiple points of k order (MP), Loop Point (LP), Bump Point (BP).The concept of Perceptually Anchorage Points was utilized by the Anquetil and Lorette for English character recognition[3]. Points of Discontinuity are 2D piecewise continuous curves corresponding to pen-ups or pen-downs. Each part of a curve delimited by two successive pen-ups is called a component [7]. If pen down point coincides with pen up point for a stroke then it is called Angle Point, where the angle theta (θ) can be of any value $0^\circ< \theta < 180^\circ$ [7]. Cusp points are points of spikes, i.e.where the first derivative does not exist. There is a K angle between two half-tangent T1 and T2.Multiple points are self-intersecting points of the curve. The 'K' number of branches of the curve defines the order of the corresponding multiple point. A Loop point is formed by unification of interior point and end-point. If the pen-down point is traversed again during stroke drawing and if the pen-up point is different from pen down point then it is a loop point. Bump Point is an interior point where the derivative of either x (t) or y (t) with respect to 't' vanishes. Table1 elaborates significant Perceptual Anchorage Points used in Bangla characters.

Table 1. Examples of perceptual anchorage points

Perceptual Anchorage Points	Corresponding Examples
Point of Discontinuity(DP)	
Angle points(AP)	
Cusp Point(CP)	
Multiple points of k order /Cross Point (XP)	
Loop Point(LP)	
Bump Point(BP)	

3   Methodology

Our experimentation started with the objective of finding the importance of anchorage points in recognizing Bangla handwritten characters through some sample handwritten data collected from different persons .A data collection format comprising of characters in the form of incomplete curves has been prepared. The incompleteness of curve refers to the missing link at the points of discontinuity, cusps points, bump points, loop points, angle points, cross-point etc . The incompleteness of a character in specified location was done by taking into account the total number of pixels in a character image and by deleting a specific percentage of pixels around a particular point. Such deviated patterns were developed for handwritten as well as for printed characters with four different fonts namely Likhon, BN Bidisha, Solaiman Lipi (A font from neighboring country, Bangladesh) and BN TT Durga. Solaiman Lipi has been taken to generalize our observation over larger cross section of Bengali speaking people. At a time 3 different characters with different degree of incompleteness were presented to the subjects and thereby asking to write the actual character perceived against each distorted character. Handwritten Data has been collected from a standardized sample comprising of fifty subjects (almost equal in number for each sex) in the age group of 18-40 years. All Subjects were graduates with Bangla as first language up to Higher Secondary level. Printed character samples of four different fonts were also taken in to account.

4   Data Analysis and Result

The data obtained from the subjects has been statistically treated using SPSS Version 17.0(Statistical Package for Social Sciences) for its proper evaluation and generalization. The main parametric statistical tool used was t-test, most commonly applied when the data follows a normal distribution, an assumption taken here [8] [9]. In this case we have taken independent one-sample t-test in which the population mean is equal to a specified value μ_0. The statistical evaluation revealed the possibility of correct recognition for each character under different levels of deviations. Analysis of the data has also revealed the significance level of "anchorage points" mandatory for perception of that particular character accurately [10].

The significance level of anchorage points across the four mentioned fonts was also determined. Fonts do play a role in perceiving the shape of the character. Some fonts inherently are very distinct and clear whereas others are not. As for example Likhon is very prominent font whereas BN TT Durga is not Recognition accuracy thus gets affected by the appearance of the character, especially in absence of the Anchorage Points. The following table (Table 2.) illustrates the same. The character, ক shown below is of font size 18 in case of Likhon but of size 24 for rest all of the cases(so as to maintain the proportionality).Thus for printed character also the significance of Anchorage Points across all four fonts was seen (including True type and Open type).

The distribution pattern of standard scores yielded a near normal distribution; hence parametric statistic like t-test was used to find level of significance of anchorage points. It has been observed that absence of cusps generates maximum perceptual failure, i.e., cusps play the most significant role in anchoring the perception of a particular character. Next to the cusps comes the Bump Points, Loop points, Points of Discontinuity and Cross-points. A Bar Chart representing the above result is given below (Fig.1). It is understood that the lower the recognition rate in absence of a particular perceptual point, the higher is its perceptual significance.

Table 2. Effect of fonts on the recognition accuracy across four different fonts

Fonts	Character	Deviation	Recognition Accuracy
Likhon	ক	কং	0.80
Solaiman Lipi	ক	কং	0.70
BN Bidisha	ক	কং	0.70
BN TT Durga	ক	কং	0.50

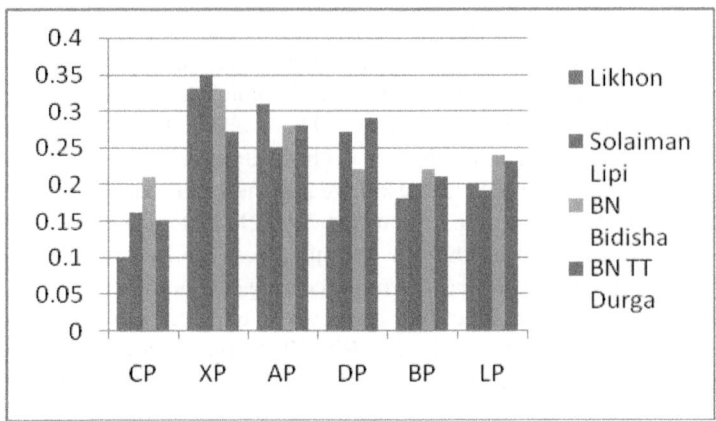

Fig. 1. Hierarchical chart of Anchorage Points of printed characters across different fonts

ANOVA (Analysis of Variance) test was carried out to see whether there is any between the mentioned categories of fonts [11]. SPSS (Statistical Package for Social sciences version 17.0) was used for implementing ANOVA. Table 3 Represents the ANOVA chart for four different fonts.

Table 3. Table representing the ANOVA output among four different fonts

ANOVA						
Source of Variation	SS	df	MS	F	P-value	F critical
Between Groups	0.01	3	0.003 3	0.59	0.622	3.09 8
Within Groups	0.11	20	0.005 5			
Total	0.12	23				

Where,
SS=Sum of Squares.
df= Degrees of Freedom.
 MS=Mean of   Squares.
 F=F ratio
F critical= Critical value of F at a particular confidence.

The results revealed that at 0.05 Confidence level there is no significant difference among the fonts with respect to the order of importance of Anchorage Points. The results implicate that the order of significance of Anchorage Points is independent of different type of fonts.

The hierarchical significance level of anchorage points in handwritten characters is depicted in Fig.2. As obtained in printed characters (across different fonts), the Cusp point has maximum significance in handwritten character recognition as well. Obliteration of Cusp points leads to maximum perceptual failure in comparison to other anchorage points.

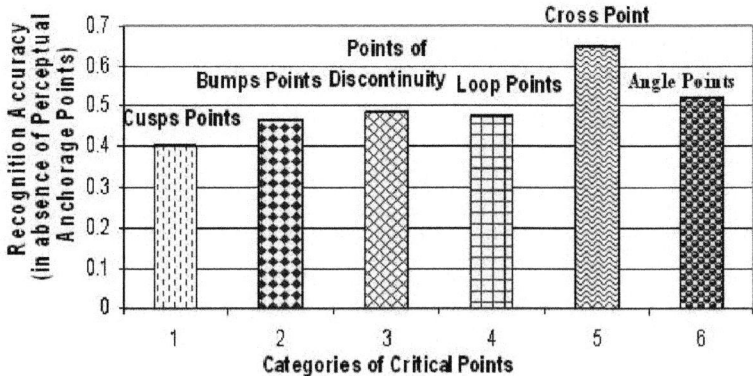

Fig. 2. Hierarchical chart of Anchorage Points in Handwritten Characters

5   Application of the Cognitive Model for Bangla OHCR

List of the perceptual anchorage points for Bangla characters along with their order of significance has been prepared. Using our already developed Online Handwritten character Recognition algorithm for Bangla we find confusion matrix for similar shaped characters and then utilize the level of significance of perceptual anchorage points to differentiate them . The confusion matrix will help us to classify characters by clustering similar shaped characters in a particular group and then the perceptual information will distinguish the characters with in that group, by reducing misrecognition rate to improve the recognition accuracy[12]. We have used two sets of features. Feature set 1 consists of eight directional Line terminals using eight Directional chain coding system. Feature set 2 consists of shape features based on perceptual anchorage points. Matching process is executed in two passes. In pass 1 only Line terminals were used as features and in pass 2 shape features like cusp point, cross point, loop point, angle points and bumps of a stroke are used. For classification we have used DTW (Dynamic Time Warping) classifier. Experimental results show the effect of Anchorage points (shape features used in pass 2) by combining outputs of pass 1 and 2 of the online Bangla recognizer. About 20,873 data samples consisting of Bangla alphanumeric characters, vowel modifiers, Conjunct characters, symbols etc. were collected from 10 native writers.

After necessary filtering of the data, experiment was carried out on 10,300 data samples. To get the effect of anchorage points on recognition accuracy, we have adopted the following Methodology for testing our Bangla online recognizer:

1. 10 sets of data (each set consists of 206 elements) are utilised from each of five native writers (out of ten).
2. 3 sets of them are used as test data input for testing the system recognition performance.
3. Writer dependent testing: Reference Templates of Stroke-base are made of remaining 7 sets of data of the same Writer.

The following table (Table 4) represents the percentage of recognition accuracy under Experimental condition (Without Anchorage points) and Controlled condition (With Anchorage Points).

Table 4. Experimental Results

Overall Recognition Rate (%)		
Writer	With out Anchorage points	With Anchorage Points
1	79.6	93.7
2	79.2	96.4
3	81.5	97.3
4	81.1	96.0
5	78.5	93.2

6   Conclusion

An attempt has been made to locate certain points or shapes within a character, which anchors the perception for that character both in case of handwritten as well as printed character. We have identified some points within each character, which are perceptually relevant. After obtaining the relevant anchorage points within a character we have also tried to get the holistic view of the anchorage points and draw a comparative analogy among different anchorage points in terms of their perceptual significance. The above experiment revealed the highest significance of cusp point in handwritten character as well as in printed character across all considered fonts. The fact that there is no significant difference among the fonts with respect to the order of importance of anchorage points at 0.05 level of confidence also got highlighted. Current observations on significance level of different anchorage points based on the cognitive experiment described above matches with the approach of already developed Online Bangla character recognizer of CDAC, Kolkata which produces very good recognition accuracy. The present experimental study suffers from some limitations. Although we have taken into account the handwritten characters as well as printed characters with font variation across different perceptual anchorage points, we are yet to explore the other perceptual aspects of a character like the bilateral symmetry, perceptual dominance of a particular half like upper or lower, and right or left [10][12].

Acknowledgements. The work has been executed under the project National Programme on Perception Engineering (NPPE), funded by DIT, MCIT, Govt. of India. Authors sincerely acknowledge the support and encouragements given by Col. A.K.Nath ,Executive Director, C-DAC Kolkata.

References

1. Simner Marvin, L., Graham, L.C., Thomassen, A.J.W.M.: Handwriting and drawing research: basic and applied issues. IOS Press (1989)
2. Fred, A.: Applications of Information theory to Psychology. Holt, New York (1959)
3. Anquetil, E., Lorette, G.: Perceptual Model of Handwriting Drawing Application to the Handwriting Segmentation. In: ICDAR 1997 (August 1997)
4. Ploux, S.: Handwriting Recognition. An Example of Perception and Action Coupling. In: Advances in Handwriting & Drawing: A Multidisciplinary Approach, Europia (1994)
5. Chaudhuri, B.B., Pal, U.: A complete printed Bangla OCR system. Journal of Pattern Recognition 31(5), 531–549 (1998)
6. Asok, B.: Online Handwritten Character Recognition System for Bangla. In: Proceedings of International Conference on Information Processing, ICIP, Bangalore (August 2008)
7. Rejean, P., Srihari, S.N.: IEEE On-line and Off-line Handwriting Recognition: A comprehensive survey. IEEE (2000)
8. Schomaker, L.R.B., Thomassen, A.J.W.M., Teulings, H.L.: A computational Model of Cursive Handwriting, Computer Recognition and Human Production of Handwriting, pp. 153–177. World Scientific (1989)
9. Thom, R.: Structural stability and morphogenesis. W.A. Benjamin Inc. (1975)
10. Salomon, A.D.: Visual field factors in the perception of direction. Amer. J. Psychologie 60, 68–88 (1947)
11. Richard, J., Miller, Freund's: Probability and Statistics for Engineers, Department of Statistics. University of Wisconsin, Madison (2005)
12. Napper, L.J.: Method and apparatus for decoding handwritten characters, Balmain, AU (2000)

Scaling Properties of Mach Bands and Perceptual Models

Ashish Bakshi[1] and Kuntal Ghosh[1,2]

[1] Machine Intelligence Unit
[2] Center for Soft Computing Research
Indian Statistical Institute, 203 B.T. Road, Kolkata-108, India
ashishbakshi1@gmail.com, kuntal@isical.ac.in

Abstract. Mach bands are the pronounced light and dark bands visible where a luminance plateau meets a ramp as in a penumbra. A great deal of effort has been devoted to study these in order to understand the underlying neural circuitry. A number of theoretical models, linear and non-linear, have consequently been proposed starting from the seminal studies of Ernst Mach himself. In this work we demonstrate why no linear model of visual perception can explain the Mach band illusion although many such attempts have been made starting from that of Mach to some recent ones. From the same approach, we also systematically demonstrate why the Mach bands are weak or inexistent at step changes of intensity. A new aspect, viz. the scaling properties of the widths of Mach band has been studied to provide a unified approach to solve both these problems in vision.

Keywords: Mach bands, luminance steps, intensity ramps, gradients, vision models.

1 Introduction

Mach bands are the pronounced light and dark bands, visible near points of rapid variation of intensity gradients. As shown in Fig 1 if two intensity plateaus are interpolated by a uniform gradient then a bright band can be seen at the points where the gradient meets the higher plateau and a dark band can be seen where the gradient meets the lower plateau. These illusory bands are now referred to as the Mach bands after the Austrian physicist Ernst Mach who first observed them in 1865 (Ratliff, 1965). The Mach bands are not only present in laboratory or artificial situations. They may easily be observed at the edge of practically all shadows where light or dark lines will surround the penumbra, the reason why the Fomm's striae (Fomm, 1896) in determining the wavelength of X-ray from diffraction experiments turned out to be nothing but results of Mach band illusions and a serious mistake in Physics was corrected (Wind 1899). For the same reason this brightness perception illusion was also found to be the culprit in the well-known discrepancy in determination of earth's radius from its shadow during lunar eclipse and the correct explanation was finally provided by physiological/perceptual optics rather than by physical or geometrical optics. But the Mach bands still remain an excellent subject of study in linking perception with underlying neural mechanisms. In the present work, we have studied the scaling

M.K. Kundu et al. (Eds.): PerMIn 2012, LNCS 7143, pp. 66–74, 2012.
© Springer-Verlag Berlin Heidelberg 2012

properties of the Mach bands and their implication in perceptual modeling and explaining a long standing problem in visual perception.

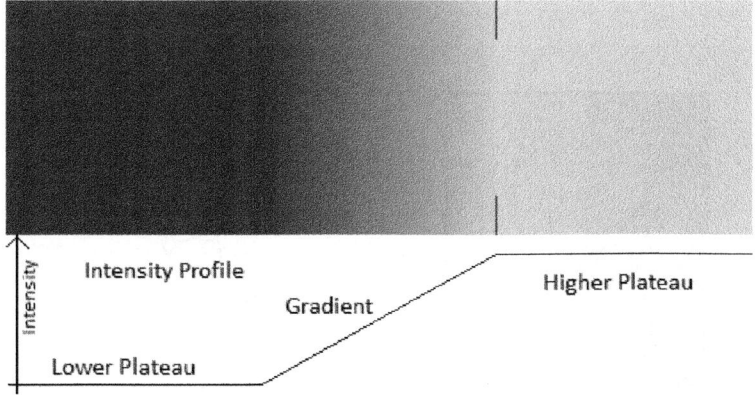

Fig. 1. Vertical bright band and dark bands (the Mach bands) can be seen clearly where the gradient meets the plateaus. Even though the intensity is a monotonically increasing function, intensity peaks and troughs are perceived at the positions of discontinuity of intensity gradient.

2   The Statement of the Problem

The most significant contribution of the study of Mach bands from its outset lies in its establishing an intimate link between perception, its underlying neural mechanisms and computational theories. To explain his own observations, E. Mach himself proposed a mathematical model of visual perception from retinal images (Ratliff, 1965). He stated: *"Let us call the intensity of illumination u on a uniform mat plane where u = f(x, y). Thus, the brightness sensation v of the corresponding retinal point is given by: $v = u - m(d^2u / dx^2 + d^2u / dy^2)$."* This equation also happens to be the first computational model for Mach bands, a linear one. The assumption behind this model in the words of Mach himself was: *"The illumination of a retinal point will, in proportion to the difference between this illumination and the average of the illumination on neighboring points, appear brighter or darker, respectively depending on whether the illumination of it is above or below that average. The weight of the retinal points in this average is to be thought of as rapidly decreasing with distance from the particular point considered* (Ratliff, 1965)."

Mach's model therefore clearly points towards the existence of a center-surround smoothing mechanism in retina and exactly a century passed after these words were uttered, when the probing microelectrodes of the physiologists, Rodieck and Stone (1965) discovered the truth of this scientific prophecy. Their discovery of lateral inhibition in retinal Ganglion cells led to the second model, again a linear one, viz. the Difference of Gaussian (DOG) model that could also provide similar explanation to the occurrence of Mach bands. Here is the DOG model: $DOG(\sigma_1, \sigma_2, x) = A_1 \exp\left(-x^2/2\sigma_1^2\right) - A_2 \exp\left(-x^2/2\sigma_2^2\right)$ where, A_1 and A_2 represent the weights, while σ_1 and σ_2 represent in one dimension, the scales of the classical centre and the antagonistic surround respectively. The model can easily be extended to two dimensions as in case of Mach's model by using 2-D Gaussians.

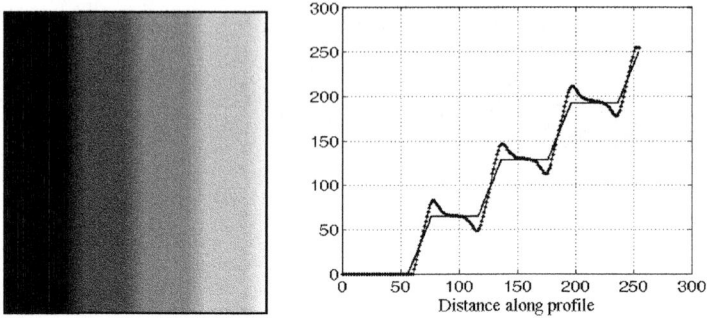

Fig. 2. A 2D trapezoidal waveform (Ratliff and Hartline 1959) used to study the neural responses of limulus eye is demonstrated in staircase form. The linear DOG model reproduces overshoots and undershoots (the thicker dotted line) indicating the bright and dark Mach bands visible at the top and the bottom of each ramp (the thinner solid line) as experimentally reported.

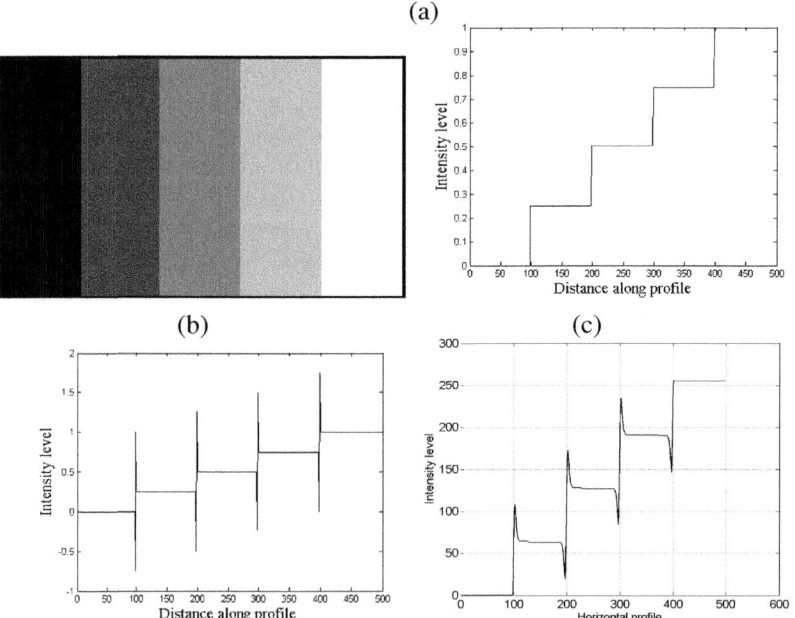

Fig. 3. The Chevreul illusion representing step staircase luminance distribution (a) has been simulated by both Mach's model (b) and the DOG model (c). Both predict the existence of Mach bands at the step edges which contradict the experimental results of Ratliff et al. (1983).

A few years before this discovery, Ratliff and Hartline (1959) studied the neural responses of limulus ommatidia to a luminance ramp of the type known to elicit Mach bands to observe that the responses actually displayed undershoots and overshoots at the inflection points. In Fig. 2 we demonstrate the result of applying the DOG model to a trapezoidal staircase like stimulus like the one used by Ratliff and Hartline (1959). The results confirm the efficacy of this linear model of lateral inhibition.

The third linear model was established by David Marr (1982) who actually combined the concepts of the previous two models (those of Mach and Rodieck-Stone) by proposing a new Laplacian of Gaussian (LOG) model. The LOG will also produce similar results as in Fig. 2.

The problem with these linear models becomes evident when we examine the Chevreul illusion representing step staircase luminance distribution, an illusion that is also sometimes loosely referred to as the Mach band illusion especially in image processing books (e.g. Gonzalez and Woods 2003). The result of applying any of the previously mentioned linear models to this illusion has been shown in Fig. 3. The results predict the strong existence of Mach bands at the step transitions which totally contradicts the visual percept according to the experiments performed by Ratliff et al. (1983) who proved that steps actually inhibit Mach bands. Hence despite the success of the lateral inhibition based theories a shadow of doubt is cast on these linear models towards understanding such perceptual phenomena.

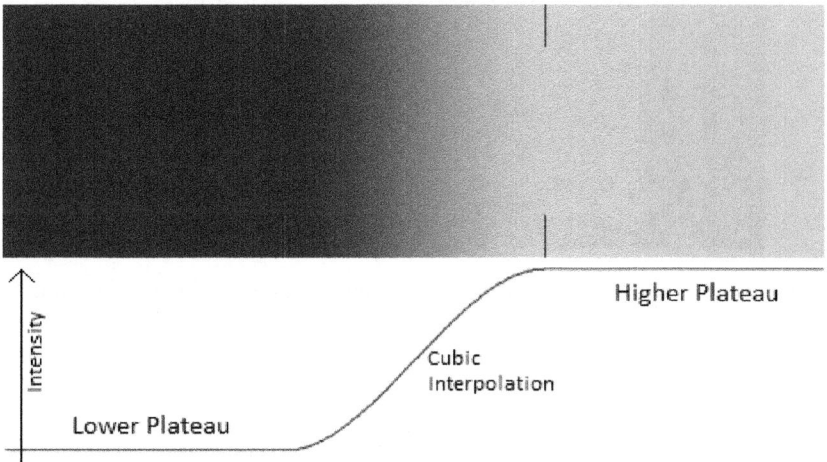

Fig. 4. The higher and lower intensity plateaus have been interpolated by a cubic equation such that there are no discontinuities of slope. No intensity peaks or troughs can now be seen as unambiguously as in Fig 1 above.

3   The Proposed Approach

The Mach bands have already proved to be an excellent paradigm to probe early vision mechanisms like the role of edges in early vision (Marr, 1982), the nature of lateral inhibition (Ratliff, 1965), the importance of phase information (Morrone et al., 1986), multi-channel information processing (Fiorentini et al., 1990), linearity in visual system (Kingdom and Moulden, 1992) and so on, leading to various theories for explaining the Mach bands. Of these the last three approaches mentioned are practically all multi scale models of vision. Some of these provide in their own way explicit though qualitative explanations for the absence of Mach bands at luminance steps (Pessoa, 1996). On the other hand the Grossberg-Todorovic model (1988) which though attempts to provide quantitative explanation depending on filling-in mechanism fail to account for the fact that Mach bands are strong at ramps but weak or inexistent at steps. Some other quantitative models like Ghosh et al.'s (2006) Extraclassical receptive field (ECRF) model or Yu et al.'s (2004) Inverse DOG (IDOG) model however display such weaker responses. But the question of linearity or nonlinearity in modeling, especially in explaining the variable percepts for luminance steps and ramps have not been to our knowledge systematically dealt so far. The ECRF for example is a linear model. The contribution of the present work is to show explicitly why linear models will always be inappropriate in solving Mach bands. Furthermore, by demonstrating the scaling properties of the width of Mach bands it also shows why they practically vanish at luminance steps.

Fig. 5. Every horizontal line in this image has the same brightness profile as any horizontal line below except for an added offset. The offset itself increases as we move from bottom to top, but the gradient remains unchanged. The Mach band width is also perceived as unchanged from bottom to top.

Our approach is first to exhibit that a sharp variation of intensity gradients is essential for the generation of Mach bands. If the intensity plateaus are interpolated by a cubic equation (Fig. 4), without any discontinuities in the slope, then no bands can be seen as unambiguously as before (Fig. 1). Next we show in Fig. 5 that the width of a Mach band is a function of the gradients only and does not depend on the absolute levels of brightness at a particular point. Every horizontal line in the image has the same brightness profile as any horizontal line below except for an added offset. The offset itself increases as we move from bottom to top. The inspection of Fig. 5 clearly reveals that the width of the Mach band is constant throughout from top to bottom. Therefore it can be concluded that the width of the Mach band is a function only of the intensity gradients on the left and right of the band, i.e.

$$width = f(s_l, s_r)$$

where s_l is the gradient on the left and s_r is the gradient on the right of the band. It is likewise easy to show that if the image is inverted left to right then also the width remains unchanged. Therefore

$$f(s_l, s_r) = f(-s_r, -s_l)$$

Based on this approach we are now going to show more decisive results on the scaling properties of the width of Mach bands.

4   Results and Discussion

In Fig 6, the set of pictures shown are horizontally scaled up versions of a single picture as a result of which the horizontal gradients are scaled down. The widths of the clearly visible Mach bands seem to be scaled up proportionally in size. Mathematically this can be written as:

$$f(ks_l, ks_r) = \frac{1}{k} f(s_l, s_r)$$

At smaller scales the bands are thin and sharp while at larger scales the bands are wide and less prominent. Note particularly that at the smallest scale the Mach band is hardly visible since the band itself has been compressed into a very thin line. This is expressed by:

$$\lim_{|s_l| \to \infty} f(s_l, s_r) = 0$$

This explains why Mach bands are weak or inexistent at step changes of intensity.

To further elucidate this scaling property we constructed an image in which the region of gradient increases linearly in size (Fig 7). Here one can clearly see that the band itself diverges outwards as we move from top to bottom. This divergence must be in proportion to the distance from the top since the band flares out like rays of light emanating from the top. If the band did not expand in proportion to the scaling factor then we would have observed a curvature in the width of the Mach band as it flares outwards from the top. In the context of our previous assumption that the width of a Mach band is a function of the neighbourhood gradients, this scaling property implies that

$$f(s_l, 0) \propto \frac{1}{|s_l|}$$

Also if the gradients on both sides are nearly equal then the width is very large. As $s_l \to s_r$, $f(s_l, s_r) \to \infty$, i.e.

$$\lim_{s_l \to s_r} f(s_l, s_r) = \infty$$

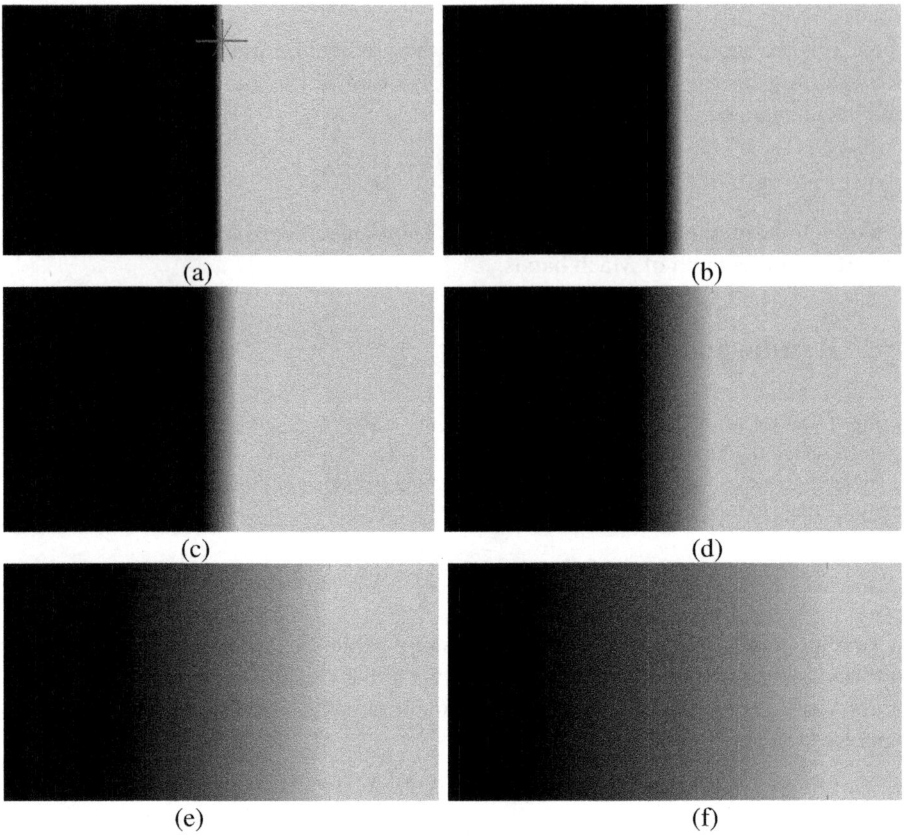

Fig. 6. Figures (a) through (f) are scaled horizontally by the factors 2:5:10:20:60:80 or in other words the horizontal gradients are in reverse order respectively

Fig. 7. The region of intensity gradient increases linearly in size from zero at the top to widest at the bottom. The bright Mach band can be clearly seen as a slanting band radiating from the center at the top towards the south-east direction. The band is clearly thinner at the top and wider at the bottom.

The above two equations can be combined in the single equation

$$width = f(s_l, s_r) \propto \left| s_l^n - s_r^n \right|^{-\frac{1}{n}}$$

Where n is a real number. Such a power law seems to be likely therefore because of the scaling nature of the width of Mach band. Thus we have been able to show that the no linear model can explain the Mach band illusion or in other words any model in visual perception that attempts to explain the Mach bands have to incorporate non-linearities in receptive field unlike the original propositions of Mach (Ratliff 1965), Marr (1982) or Rodieck and Stone (1965). Such non-linearities may be originated from the extra-classical receptive fields also (Ghosh et al. 2006).

5   Conclusion

We have proposed a condition that must be satisfied by any model of the brightness induction illusion concerning Mach bands. We also saw the reason why no Mach bands are visible for a step change in intensity. This suggests the requirement of a model in which the length scales of the filter function is itself derived from the input image. The DOG or any other linear model, because of containing fixed length scales, is unable to produce illusions with very large or very small length scales. An adaptive model whose length scales change depending on the input image is therefore very much in need. But the exact form in which the length scales depend on the input image remains to be discovered. Such models may find potential application in the designing of novel robust visual capturing or display systems and also automatic detection and correction of perceived incoherence in the luminance of video display panels, where accurate perception of intensity level can often be critical.

Acknowledgement. The first author would like to acknowledge the Council of Scientific and Industrial Research (CSIR) for their financial support and also the Indian Statistical Institute (ISI) for providing the infrastructure required for the completion of this work.

References

Fiorentini, A., Baumgartner, G., Magnussen, S., Schiller, P., Thomas, G.: The perception of brightness and darkness: relation to neuronal receptive fields. In: Spillman, L., Werner, J. (eds.) Visual Perceptions: The Neurophysiological Foundations, pp. 129–161. Academic Press (1990)

Fomm, L.: The wavelength of Roentgen-rays. Annalen der Physik 59, 350–353 (1896)

Ghosh, K., Sarkar, S., Bhaumik, K.: A possible explanation of the low-level brightness–contrast illusions in the light of an extended classical receptive field model of retinal ganglion cells. Biol. Cyb. 94, 89–96 (2006)

Gonzalez, R.C., Woods, R.E.: Digital Image Processing, 2nd edn. Pearson Education, Third Indian Reprint (2003)

Grossberg, S., Todorovic, D.: Neural dynamics of 1-D and 2-D brightness perception. Perception and Psychophysics 43, 241–277 (1988)

Kingdom, F.A.A., Moulden, B.: A multi-channel approach to brightness coding. Vis. Res. 32, 1565–1582 (1992)

Marr, D.: Vision: A Computational Investigation into the Human Representation and Processing of Visual Information. W. H. Freeman and Company, New York (1982)

Morrone, M.C., Ross, J., Burr, D.C., Owens, R.: Mach bands are phase dependent. Nature 324, 250–253 (1986)

Pessoa, L.: Mach band attenuation by adjacent stimuli. Perception 25, 425–442 (1996)

Ratliff, F.: Mach bands: quantitative studies on neural networks in the retina. Holden-Day, San Francisco CA (1965)

Ratliff, F., Hartline. H.K.: The responses of limulus optic nerve fibers to patterns of illumination on the receptor mosaic. J. Gen. Physiol. 42, 1241–1255 (1959)

Ratliff, F., Milkman, M., Rennert, N.: Attenuation of Mach bands by adjacent stimuli. Proc. Natl. Ac. Sc. 80, 4554–4558 (1983)

Rodieck, R.W., Stone, J.: Analysis of receptive fields of cat retinal ganglion cells. Journal of Neurophysiol. 28, 833–849 (1965)

Wind, C.H.: Zur demonstration einer von E. Mach entdeckten optischen Tauschung. Physik. Zeit. 1, 112–113 (1899)

Yu, Y., Yamauchi, T., Choe, Y.: Explaining Low-Level Brightness-Contrast Illusions Using Disinhibition. In: Ijspeert, A.J., Murata, M., Wakamiya, N. (eds.) BioADIT 2004. LNCS, vol. 3141, pp. 166–175. Springer, Heidelberg (2004)

Psycho-Visual Evaluation of Contrast Enhancement Algorithms by Adaptive Neuro-Fuzzy Inference System

Apurba Das and Suparna Parua

Centre for Development of Advanced Computing (CDAC), Kolkata, India
{apurba.das,suparna.parua}@cdac.in

Abstract. Image information maximization is an alternative method of contrast enhancement of images. There are plenty of algorithms for contrast enhancement of poor illumination images. In present paper we have proposed a novel method of psycho-visual evaluation of contrast enhancement algorithms. Adaptive Neuro-Fuzzy Inference System (ANFIS) is used here for classification of well known contrast enhancement algorithms. The metric/feature of contrast enhancement is modeled including image statistics both in spatial and frequency domain. The perception inspired model is then used for automatic classification of algorithms depending on the strength of contrast enhancement.

Keywords: Adaptive Neuro-Fuzzy Inference System (ANFIS), Contrast Enhancement, skewness, kurtosis, ANOVA, phycho-visual perception.

1 Introduction

Contrast enhancement [CoEnh] is a basic technique of image processing to be applied in the primary stage of image pre-processing to make the image contents distinguishable. Some methods of tuning the parameters of well known contrast enhancement algorithms are also proposed [1], [2], [3] where they claim to get the desired histogram with guarantee. We can therefore reframe the problem as a problem of image entropy maximization [4] in terms of psycho-visual judgment of human, as the final objective is to extract the image content even from a poorly captured image in terms of significantly high or low intensity. But, undue randomness present in the image increases calculated entropy [4] which may mislead us, but the undue randomness would be discarded by psycho-visual judgment.

The objective of the present work is to define a measure of contrast enhancement. The metric is derived from the input (poor illumination) and output (corrected illumination) image statistics of the enhancement algorithm. Inclusion of ratio of high to low frequency content present in input and output images is also an important feature for the proposed measure. From six chosen algorithms of contrast enhancement from INFace toolbox [5], we have tabulated the input image and six output images to undergo a survey. From the human psycho-visual evaluation by ANOVA (analysis of variance), we have then categorized the contrast enhancement algorithms to three classes, depending on their quality of improvement and formed the

M.K. Kundu et al. (Eds.): PerMIn 2012, LNCS 7143, pp. 75–83, 2012.

training set. Here we have used Adaptive Neuro-Fuzzy Inference System (ANFIS) for classification, as ANFIS has shown significant results in modeling nonlinear functions. In ANFIS, the membership function parameters are extracted from a data set that describes the system behavior. The ANFIS learns features in the dataset and adjusts the system parameters according to a given error criterion [6], [7].

In the next section we have presented the survey for proposed psycho-visual evaluation of contrast enhancement algorithms. The result of the survey is then statistically modeled by ANOVA [8] to form the training matrix. In section three, different texture statistics and frequency domain characteristics to be used as features are described in brief. In section four, an Adaptive Neuro-Fuzzy Inference System (ANFIS) is trained to classify the contrast enhancement algorithms and validated by several test images and different algorithms.

2   ANOVA on Psycho-Visual Judgment

In statistics, analysis of variance (ANOVA) is a collection of statistical models, and their associated procedures, in which the observed variance in a particular variable is partitioned into components attributable to different sources of variation. In its simplest form ANOVA provides a statistical test of whether or not the means of several groups are all equal [8]. The purpose of two-way ANOVA is to find out whether data from several groups have a common mean. Here, a platform for psycho-visual survey is designed. We have taken three groups of people as our subject, depending on their ages. The three groups namely child (5 to 15 years), adult (15 to 45 years) and old (over 45 years) are formed. Each of the subjects is given one original image and six enhanced images. The subjects are then asked to find the best improvement of illumination with respect to the original one. The result of the survey is shown in Fig. 1 and reported in Table 1.

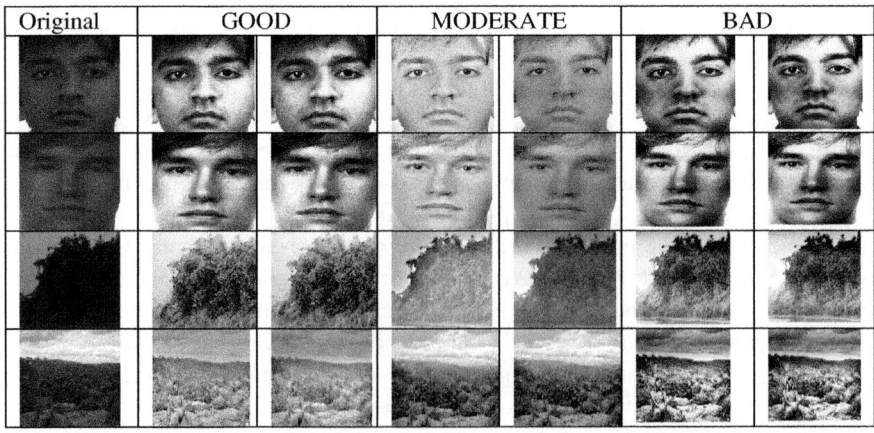

Fig. 1. Survey Result: Training set from Phycho-visual judgment of human

Table 1. Psycho-Visual Survey Report

Age group	Algo. 1	Algo. 2	Algo. 3	Algo. 4	Algo. 5	Algo. 6
Child	26	25	45	18	24	18
Adult	21	40	63	10	24	24
Old	11	21	27	6	34	31

Table 2. 2-way ANOVA Table

```
                    ANOVA Table

Source      SS          df      MS          F       Prob>F

Columns     1896.67     5       379.333     3.93    0.0313
Rows        225.33      2       112.667     1.17    0.3505
Error       966         10      96.6
Total       3088        17
```

The function returns the p-value for the null hypothesis that all samples in matrix presented in Table 1 are drawn from the same population. In Table 2, the p-value for column is 0.03, (i.e., 3 out of 100) which indicates the null hypothesis false for column samples. Similarly, the p-value for rows is 0.35, i.e., 35 out of 100 indicates the null hypothesis true for row samples. The test of ANOVA proves that human judgment is not at all age variant but the quality of contrast enhancement are not same for all the six sample algorithms taken from INFace toolbox [5]. Next, we have labeled the algorithms by the mean performance of ANOVA. We have grouped the performance of algorithms as 'good', 'moderate', and 'bad' in terms of psycho-visual evaluation of human judgment. These labels would then be used to train a supervised classifier designed by ANFIS described in section 4.

3   Feature Selection

Studies on the improvement on texture statistics both in spatial and frequency domain is done in the present section. In literature [9], [10] researchers found satisfactory stable results by defining textures in terms of statistical moments and ratio of high frequency to low frequency content present in a particular image. The feature selection steps are as follows:

1. Calculate mean, variance, skewness, kurtosis and high frequency (HF) to low frequency (LF) content present in the each original image and six improved images.
2. Relative modification of the statistical moments and HF to LF ratios by respective contrast enhancement algorithms are fitted into an entropy based decision tree to know the feature hierarchy [10], [11] which essentially returns the most discriminative features.

3. As expected, the decision tree returns 3 most discriminative features $\Delta\alpha^4$, Δsk, and $\Delta\frac{HF}{LF}$ defined as

$$\Delta\alpha^4 = \left|\frac{kurtosis\ of\ original\ image - kurtosis\ of\ modified\ image}{kurtosis\ of\ original\ image}\right| \quad (1)$$

$$\Delta sk = \left|\frac{skewness\ of\ original\ image - skewness\ of\ modified\ image}{skewness\ of\ original\ image}\right| \quad (2)$$

$$\Delta\frac{HF}{LF} = \left|\frac{\frac{HF}{LF}\ of\ original\ image - \frac{HF}{LF}\ of\ modified\ image}{\frac{HF}{LF}\ of\ original\ image}\right| \quad (3)$$

As we know, as the fourth order statistical moment, kurtosis is the measure of peakness and the third order statistical moment, skewness is the measure of asymmetry of the intensity distribution, they can really be suitable features for classification among CoEnh algorithms. But, these features are not sufficient to form a training set, as we obtain similar kurtosis value for 'good' and 'bad' quality CoEnh algorithms (Fig. 2). Therefore we have also included the third feature $\Delta\frac{HF}{LF}$ for better classification.

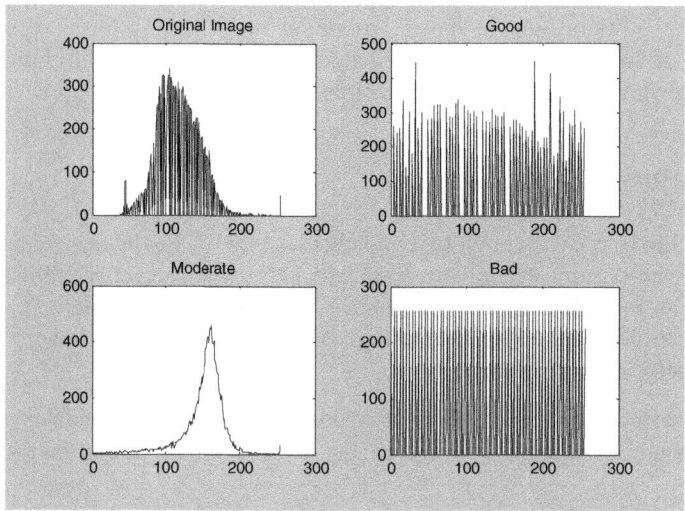

Fig. 2. Histogram improvement by different class of CoEnh Algo.

 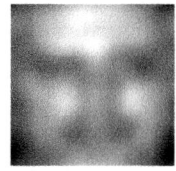 

Fig. 3. Extraction of high and low frequency content from an image

4   ANFIS Based Classifier Design for Contrast Enhancement

Neuro-fuzzy systems harness the power of the two paradigms: Fuzzy logic and artificial neural network (ANN) by utilizing the mathematical properties of ANN in tuning rule-based fuzzy systems that approximate the way humans process information. A specific approach in neuro-fuzzy development is the adaptive neuro-fuzzy inference system (ANFIS), which has shown significant results in modeling nonlinear functions. The ANFIS learns features in the data set and adjusts the system parameters according to a given error criterion [6], [7]. In the present problem also, we have found ANFIS suitable as, the relationship between the three selected features with class levels (output) are grossly non-linear shown in Fig. 4.

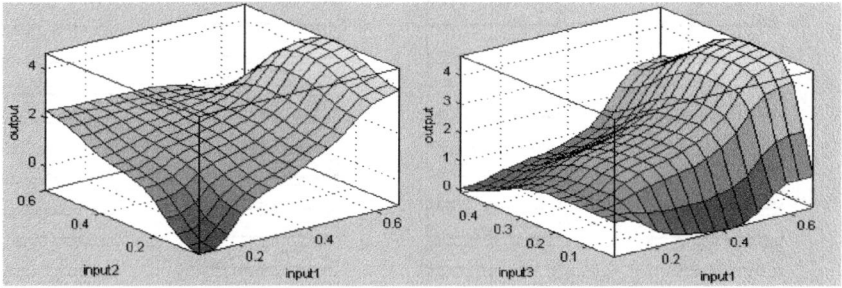

Fig. 4. Decision surface for three chosen features

4.1   Architecture of ANFIS

The ANFIS is a fuzzy Sugeno model put in the framework of adaptive systems to facilitate learning and adaptation [6], [7]. Such framework makes the ANFIS modeling more systematic and less reliant on expert knowledge. To present the ANFIS architecture, 27 fuzzy if-then rules based on a first order Sugeno model are considered:

Rule1. If (in1 is in1mf1) and (in2 is in2mf1) and (in3 is in3mf1) then (output is out1mf1)

Rule2. If (in1 is in1mf1) and (in2 is in2mf1) and (in3 is in3mf2) then (output is out1mf2)

....

Rule27. If (in1 is in1mf3) and (in2 is in2mf3) and (in3 is in3mf3) then (output is out1mf27)

It can be noted that, the number of rule is formed by taking all valid combinations. Therefore, the number of rules for three features (taking 1 membership at a time from three) $= {}^3C_1 \times {}^3C_1 \times {}^3C_1 = 27$, as shown in Fig. 5. Here we have chosen Gaussian membership functions as it exhibits minimum settling time and the error saturation is very close to zero. For training the ANFIS, we have used the hybrid method of learning which applies a combination of the least-squares method and the back-propagation gradient descent method for training FIS membership function parameters to emulate a given training data set.

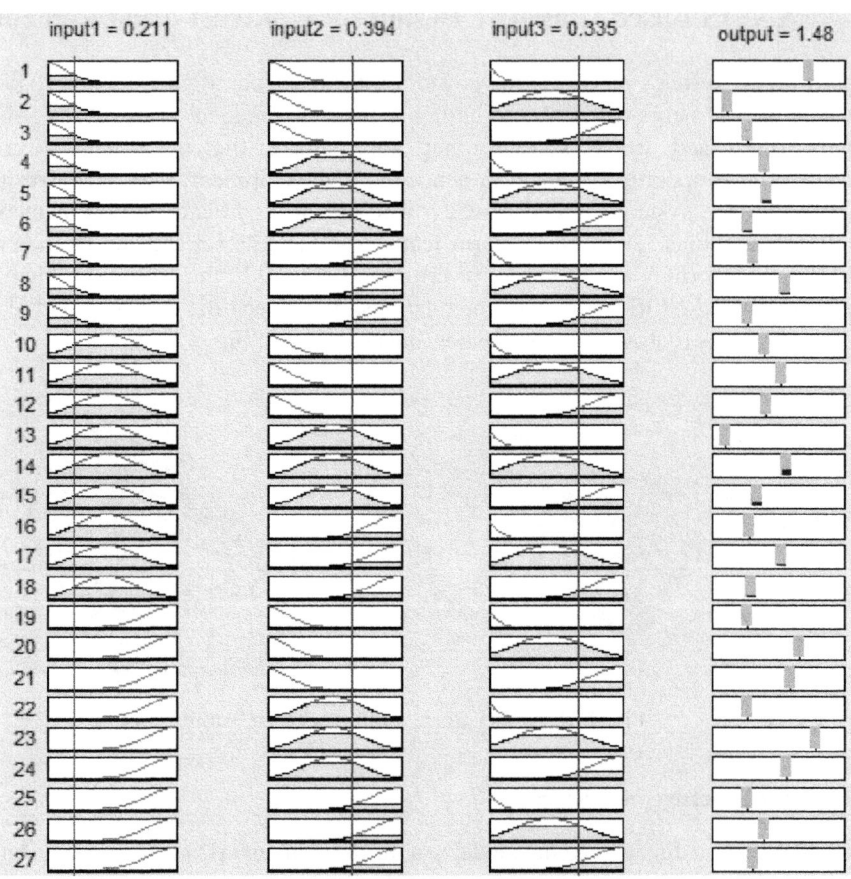

Fig. 5. List of Fuzzy rules for three chosen features

The three membership functions $\mu_{GOOD}(input1), \mu_{MOD}(input1)$, and $\mu_{BAD}(input1)$ are shown in Fig. 6(a). Similarly the membership functions are also formed for other two input features as shown in Fig. 6(b) and 6(c). In the figure, input signifies feature.

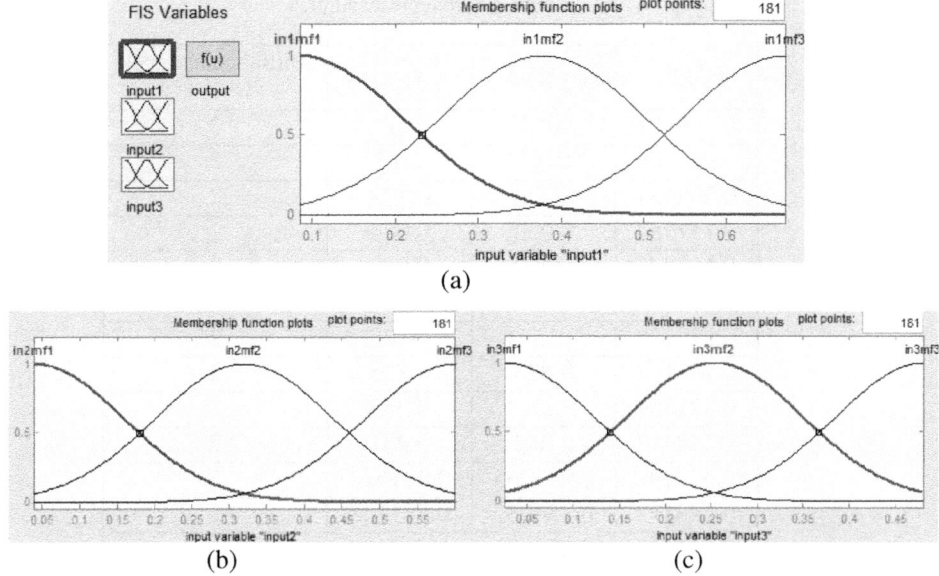

Fig. 6. Membership functions for each feature (a) kurtrosis, (b) skewness, (c) HF/LF

The proposed ANFIS model structure, comprising the 27 aforesaid rules, is presented in the Fig. 7.

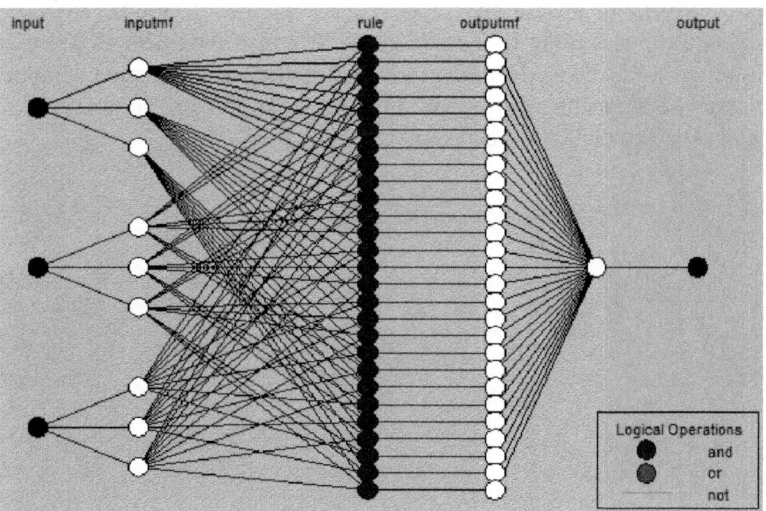

Fig. 7. ANFIS model structure

Now, a large number of images are processed through a number of other well known algorithms. The developed Fuzzy Inference system is tested for 1000 set of images for different CoEnh algorithms. Performance of fifteen random results are presented in Table 3.

Table 3. Fifteen test samples

$\Delta\alpha^4$	Δsk	$\Delta\dfrac{HF}{LF}$	Initial class level
0.169904	0.0729	0.07	2
0.236706	0.0498	0.12	2
0.208434	0.0323	0.109	2
0.157382	0.056	0.084	2
0.163897	0.0615	0.083	2
0.254545	0.4	0.2	2
0.277778	0.4583	0.2	2
0.148148	0.833	0.105	2
0.421569	0.24	0.353	2
0.529412	0.052	0.471	2
0.627291	0.043065	0.421644	2
0.648112	0.254082	0.441128	2
0.662639	0.263071	0.503399	2
0.680634	0.031784	0.501207	2
0.607424	0.315402	0.418779	2

The test matrix is assigned by arbitrary class number 2. After going through the proposed ANFIS, we obtain the proper class number 1(Good), 2(Moderate) and 3(bad). The output is quite in agreement with human judgment as presented in the confusion matrix (Table 4). Here the rate of classification for 'good', 'moderate' and 'bad' classes of algorithms are (283/333)x100 = 84.98%, (234/334)x100 = 70.05% and (290/333)x100 = 87.08%, respectively.

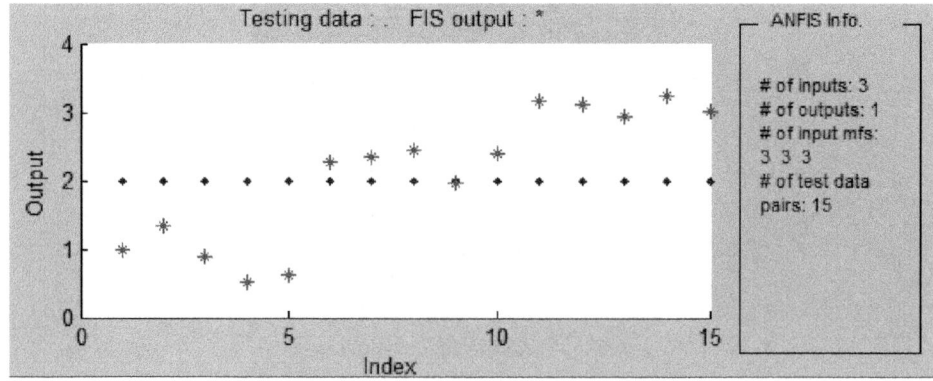

Fig. 8. Performance of FIS for test data

Table 4. Confusion Matrix of ANFIS Vs Psycho-visual evaluation

Actual class levels obtained from psycho-visual evaluation	ANFIS created class levels		
	C1	C2	C3
S1	283	31	19
S2	67	234	33
S3	10	33	290

5   Conclusion

In the present work we have classified the contrast enhancement algorithms based on their quality of improvement of image intensity (contrast). As the training set is formed by human psycho-visual judgment, the method of classification may be considered to be stable and rigid. For any new set of images or any new algorithm of contrast enhancement, we can map the performance onto any of three of our defined clusters. In future, dependency of image type on quality of contrast enhancement can also be studied.

References

1. Sen, D., Pal, S.K.: Automatic Exact Histogram Specification for Contrast Enhancement and Visual System Based Quantitative Evaluation. IEEE Trans. on IP (2010)
2. Sen, D., Pal, S.K.: Novel Automatic Exact Histogram Specification for Contrast Enhancement in Images. IEEE (2010/2011)
3. Coltuc, D., Bolon, P., Chassery, J.M.: Exact Histogram specification. IEEE Trans. Image Processing 15, 1143–1152 (2006)
4. Shanon, C.E.: A mathematical theory of communication. Bell Syst. Tech. J. 27, 379–423 (1948)
5. Struc, V.: The INface toolbox for illumination invariant face recognition, http://www.face-rec.org/source-codes/
6. Jang, J.S.R.: ANFIS: adaptive network based fuzzy inference system. IEEE Trans. Syst., Man Cybern. 23(3), 665–683 (1993)
7. Jang, J.S.R.: Self-learning fuzzy controllers based on temporal back-propagation. IEEE Trans. Neural Networks 3(5), 714–723 (1992)
8. Spiegel, M.R., Schiller, J., Srinivasan, A.: Theory and Problems of Probability and Statistics, 2nd edn. Schaum S Outline Series. Tata McGraw Hill (2004)
9. González, R.C., Woods, R.E.: Digital Image Processing, 2nd edn. Prentice Hall (2002)
10. Parua, S., Das, A., Mazumdar, D., Mitra, S.: Determination of Feature Hierarchy from Gabor and SIFT features for face Recognition. In: EAIT 2011. IEEExplore (2011)
11. Quinlan, J.R.: C4.5 programs for machine learning. Morgan Kaufmann Publishers (1992)

Theory of Mind in Man-Machine Interactions

Fumito Hamada[1] and Edson T. Miyamoto[2]

[1] Mitsui Mining & Smelting, Japan
[2] University of Tsukuba, Institute of Literature and Linguistics,
Tennodai 1-1-1, Tsukuba, Ibaraki, Japan
miyamoto@alum.mit.edu

Abstract. We report questionnaire data investigating people's reactions to the directions provided by a hypothetical QA system, in order to understand how they interpret a given query. The discussion is couched within theory of mind, which provides a metaphor for research to improve man-machine communication by requiring a representation for the user's representation of the world to be introduced.

Keywords: QA systems, Turing test, theory of mind.

1   The Turing Test

The Turing test has generated much debate in philosophy and theoretical AI but it has been less helpful in suggesting ways of improving actual systems. The Loebner prize, a competition implementing a version of the Turing test, has been criticized on various grounds (Shieber, 1994). From the point of view of improving current systems, one concern is that people often base their judgements on superficial cues (e.g., a machine is judged to be human if it lies or makes spelling mistakes, a person with encyclopedic knowledge of Shakespeare is judged to be a machine). But analyses of transcripts from the Loebner prize suggest that pragmatics may help explain why some machine responses are strange as in the following dialogue between a machine *A* and a person *B* (Saygin & Ciceklib, 1999; also Samad, 2008, on pragmatics and machine-machine interactions).

A: *What part of the country are you from?*
B: *I come from Perth, which is in Western Australia.*
A: *Western Australia occupies the entire western third of the country, bordered by the Indian Ocean to the west, South Australia and the Northern Territory to the east, the Timor Sea to the north, and the Southern Ocean to the south.*

A's reply is not appropriate because it violates Grice's *Maxim of Quantity* (Saygin & Ciceklib, 1999; also Hamada, 2011, and references therein). Pragmatics and Grice's maxims in particular provide helpful, intuitive posthoc analyses, but fail to provide a framework to improve machine performance (how much is too much information?). We suggest that work on *theory of mind* (imputing mental states to others based on unobservables and generating a theory to predict their behavior; Premack & Woodruff, 1978) may frame the problem in more helpful

M.K. Kundu et al. (Eds.): PerMIn 2012, LNCS 7143, pp. 84–89, 2012.

ways. For example, in the dialogue, A may build a model of B's model of the world, based among other things on B's utterance. Note that B could have simply answered "I come from Perth" but by adding "which is in Western Australia" B may be signalling modesty, assuming Perth not well-known and most people unaware of its location. If so, a reply stating that A does know where the city is and always wanted to visit a roster of its attractions, would constitute a long but perhaps not too long a reply. Pragmatics could suggest, not unreasonably, that quantity is hence overridden (e.g., by the *Maxim of Relation*). But the point is that the inferences necessary (which are beyond current systems, but see the general discussion) for A's reply to be appropriate (in terms of quantity, relation, and so on) will depend on A keeping a record of B's likely representation of the world, and interpreting it appropriately. Two questionnaires inspired by theory of mind are reported to elaborate on that premise.

2   Questionnaires 1 and 2

In experiments related to theory of mind (Baron-Cohen, Leslie & Frith, 1985; Wimmer & Perner, 1983), children are tested to verify whether they can differentiate between reality (e.g., the marble is in the box) and the beliefs of a character (the doll believes the marble is in the basket) by choosing what the character will do (will the doll look for the marble in the box or in the basket?). In our case, given a user's query (e.g., where is professor Takahashi's office?), a hypothetical QA system can give a literal reply (room 2C103) but it can also add information to fill further potential gaps in the user's knowledge (the professor is not in his office today). Participants rated the dialogues and decided where the user should go (e.g., room 2C103). The intention of the user is unclear (e.g., is it to go to room 2C103 or to meet the professor or...?) and we want to determine what participants' representations of the user's intentions are by investigating how the extra information and its format affect ratings and decisions.

2.1   Method

Participants. A total of 72 participants (36 in Questionnaire 1 and 36 in Questionnaire 2), undergraduates at the University of Tsukuba, volunteered to participate as part of a class activity. (Throughout, *user* will refer to a fictitious person who asks a query to the system; *participants* are the actual people who took part in the experiment by responding to one of the questionnaires.)

Materials. Participants read fictitious exchanges between a human user and a hypothetical QA system that provides information about the University of Tsukuba. Three contexts, each one with three versions (Long, Medium, Short), were created. In one context, the user is in Akihabara in Tokyo (about an hour by train from the main Tsukuba campus) and asks 'Where is the office of professor Taro Takahashi?'. There were three types of responses from the QA system.

Short answer: short, literal reply to the query (e.g., *It is in Tsukuba city, Tenn-odai 1-1-1, room 2C103.*).

Medium answer: the Short answer plus further information (e.g., *Prof. Taka-hashi teaches a class on encryption for on-line business once a month and most attendees are working professionals. * Today is the third Thursday of the month. ** The Tokyo campus office telephone number is 03-1111-9999.*).

Long answer: the Medium answer plus further information (at the points indicated with asterisks), including percentages to make it sound machine-like (e.g., ** There is a 95% probability that the class is held in Tokyo. ** The probability that prof. Takahashi is teaching at the Tokyo campus is 91%. Please, call to confirm.*).

The context uses the fact that the university has two campuses. The professor has his laboratory on the main campus in Tsukuba, but on the day that the dialogue takes place he is likely to be teaching at the Akihabara campus. The user is at Akihabara station where the train leaves for Tsukuba, and participants have to decided whether the user should take the train to Tsukuba. The decision depends on how the query is interpreted: literally (the user needs to go to the lab; e.g., to fix the air-conditioner) or non-literally (e.g., to meet the professor).

After the dialogue, there were three questions. In Question 1, participants rated on a 7-point scale whether the QA system's response was machine-like ('1') or human-like ('7') and, in Question 2, whether the user would be satisfied with it ('1', not at all, to '7', extremely satisfied).

Based on their choice for Question 3 (whether the user should go to Tsukuba), participants were directed to different points in the questionnaire. Those who chose to go to Tsukuba, were told that nobody was in the professor's lab and according to the campus office the professor was at the Akihabara campus. Participants who chose not to go to Tsukuba, were told that the user bumped into a friend and found out that the professor was at the nearby Akihabara campus. In both scenarios, participants answered to two questions (same as Questions 1 and 2) to determine how their perception of the QA system evolved.

Two other contexts following the same design were created asking for directions to get to one of the on-campus cafeterias (which was closing early) and to an auditorium (where a conference was to be held but was moved elsewhere).

Procedure and data analysis. The three versions (Short, Medium, Long) of the three contexts were distributed according to a Latin Square design creating three different lists so that each list contained one version from each context printed on a separate page. Each participant saw one list.

The results of a previous questionnaire indicated that ratings for Question 2 (satisfaction levels) were comparable to ratings for the usefulness of the QA system's reply (see Hamada, 2011, for details), thus the usefulness question was to be eliminated in Questionnaire 1. However, because of a mistake in the files, the question on usefulness was printed in some of the versions. Although the extra question is unlikely to have affected the other questions, a replication was conducted as Questionnaire 2 making sure that all versions of all three contexts had only the questions described in the previous section. Moreover, we had expected that all participants reading the Short answer would choose the literal destination (e.g., Tsukuba), but a few participants chose not to go, thus we added a new question in Questionnaire 2 asking for the reason for the decision.

Analyses of variance were conducted over means for participants (F_1) and for items (F_2). Mean squared errors in the participant analyses were used to calculate *95% confidence intervals for differences between means* (95% CIs), which provide a lower bound for pairwise comparisons (Loftus & Masson, 1994).

2.2   Results

Analyses including questionnaire (1 and 2) as a factor revealed no main effect or interactions with the factors manipulated, therefore the results for the two questionnaires were collapsed and are reported together unless otherwise indicated.

Table 1. Results for the two questionnaires collapsed

Questions:	Initial		Decision	Don't go		Go	
	1	2	3	4	5	6	7
	human	satisfied	go	human	satisfied	human	satisfied
Short	3.06	4.12	76.8%	2.65	2.19	2.64	3.11
Medium	2.42	3.97	68.3%	2.35	2.41	2.39	3.08
Long	2.29	4.29	23.2%	2.60	4.74	2.47	3.76

Table 1 is divided in four parts. The Initial columns (Questions 1 and 2) are the participants' ratings immediately after reading the dialogue. In the column Decision are the responses to Question 3, the percentage of participants who chose to go to the literal destination (i.e., the destination according to the literal interpretation of the query; e.g., Tsukuba). Columns Don't-go (4 and 5) and Go (6 and 7) are the ratings after the decision was made in Question 3. Columns labelled *human* (1, 4 and 6) are how human the system's response was and the columns *satisfied* (2, 5 and 7) are how satisfactory the response was (in all ratings, 7 was the maximum score).

In Question 1 (the initial impression of the system's reply as human-like), the effect of response type (Short, Medium, Long) was reliable $(F_1(2,140)=7.71, P<.001; F_2(2,4)=14.79, P<.05)$ as the Short answer had higher ratings than the the Medium and Long, but the latter two did not differ (95% CI=.14).

Participants' decision (Question 3) was affected by response type $(F_1(2,138)=31.49, P<.001; F_2(2,4)=22.25 P<.01)$ as the Short led to more *go* decisions than the Medium, and the Medium more than the Long (95% CI=.14). Questionnaire 2 included a question asking participants to explain why they decided not to go to the literal destination after reading the Short reply, and all justifications were that this type of reply contained insufficient information.

For the participants who chose *don't-go*, satisfaction (Question 5) was reliably affected by the type of response $(F_2(2,4)= 23.26, P<.01;$ because the number of participants was not equal across conditions only item analyses are reported) as the Long was rated higher than the Short and Medium, but the latter two did not differ (95% CI= 1.72, based on the item analysis). We also compared satisfaction initially (Initial/Question 2) to satisfaction after choosing *don't-go* (Don't-go/Question 5). Satisfaction decreased reliably in the Short and Medium conditions (from 4.12 to 2.19; and from 3.97 to 2.41), while there was a trend for an increase in the Long condition (from 4.29 to 4.74; 95% CI= .95, based on the item analysis).

The remaining differences were not statistically reliable.

In sum, a short reply is felt to be more human-like initially (Question 1) even if satisfaction levels are similar to longer replies (Question 2). But a short reply is also more likely to lead people to go to the literal destination (76.8% in Question 3). Providing more information without justifications can decrease the number of people who go to the literal destination (Medium: 68.3%) but not nearly as much as when justifications are given (Long: 23.2%). After a *don't-go* decision was made, satisfaction lowered in the Short and Medium conditions, but it trended higher in the Long condition. Thus, a longer response with appropriate justification helps people avoid the literal destination. This may seem unsurprising, but note that the user's actual goal was never stated, nevertheless participants' reaction is consistent, the extra information was used with the assumption that the user wanted to meet the professor (and not go to the lab itself) and thus provided a more satisfactory response.

Human-like ratings remained fairly low throughout. In particular, the low rating for the Long condition in Question 1 may come as a surprise (especially since satisfaction in Question 2 was relatively high at 4.29), but recall that the crucial information in the Long condition was always given as a percentage making it sound machine-like. The numbers could be translated into adverbs (e.g., 91% to "highly likely") but this would only add ambiguity. If the system can calculate a probability, then that number should be reported and the user can decide how to interpret it. Some may point to people's uneasiness with such numbers; but weather forecasts in Japan provide precipitation percentages based on which people decide on a daily basis whether to carry an umbrella. This is the kind of situation where mimicking superficial features of human speech is not necessary helpful. That is, sounding human-like does not necessarily translate into more effective interfaces.

3   General Discussion

Current QA systems are usually based on some type of a system database (SDB, for short) to store and organize the knowledge that the system has about the world. Given a query Q, the system searches the SDB for an appropriate answer. Research on theory of mind suggests that it is also necessary to include a user database (UDB) to keep track of the user's mental states, a model of the user's model of the world. The UDB can be built based on the query or queries made by the user, environmental variables (time, place), constraints (e.g., the user knows this is a system about the University of Tsukuba, and is unlikely to ask questions about other universities), and so on. The UDB is virtually the same as the SDB, it has all the entries that the SDB has but many or most of its entries lack the actual information. So, given the query "where is prof. Takahashi's lab?", the UDB contains a form for this professor with a feature *name* whose value is *Takahashi*, but other features (e.g., lab, phone number, schedule) are likely to have no value associated with them. In particular, given the query, the feature lab in the UDB must be null (the user does not know where the lab is), but the crucial point is which other values are missing and need to be provided. Thus, based on the UDB, the system can infer information the user may not possess (e.g., the professor's schedule for today) and the incorrect assumptions the user may be making because of faulty knowledge (the professor is in his office today).

Inferences on such UDBs are not trivial, but theory of mind is never trivial. Children do not succeed in related tasks until fairly late (about 5 or 6 years old; e.g., Baron-Cohen, Leslie & Frith, 1985). The questionnaires reported suggest rudimentary uses for UDBs. Given a query asking about a professor's lab, the system should provide the answer to the literal interpretation, but should also list related potentially relevant information (the professor's schedule, classes, phone number, recent publications, whether his lab air-conditioner has been fixed). Listing everything would be overwhelming to the user. Perhaps just listing an index with the kinds of information available (but not the information itself) and asking whether the user would like to see the detailed content would help ameliorate the clutter. But also crucial is the ordering of the indexed items. For example, if a user asks about the professor's lab, the professor's schedule should take priority over his recent publications. This kind of ordering can be obtained from questionnaire data; but it can also be collected as the system is used. The frequency that users choose to see an item can be fed into a machine learning algorithm to decide item order for future replies. All this can be done without theory of mind, but keeping a record of the likely model the user has of the world should provide a more methodic and constrained approach to the problem.

References

Baron-Cohen, S., Leslie, A., Frith, U.: Does the autistic child have a "theory of mind"? Cognition 21, 37–46 (1985)

Hamada, F.: Jinkotino tyuringu tesutoniokeru kaiwaaiteno siko moderu keisei. Graduation thesis. College of Japanese Language & Culture, University of Tsukuba (2011)

Loftus, G.R., Masson, M.E.J.: Using confidence intervals in within-subject designs. Psychonomic Bulletin & Review 1, 476–490 (1994)

Premack, D., Woodruff, G.: Does the chimpanzee have a theory of mind? The Behavioral and Brain Sciences 4, 515–526 (1978)

Samad, T.: Pragmatics and its implications for multiagent systems. Journal of Mind Theory 0, 193–216 (2008)

Saygin, A.P., Ciceklib, I.: Pragmatics in human-computer conversations. Journal of Pragmatics 34, 227–258 (2002)

Shieber, S.M.: Lessons from a restricted Turing Test. Communications of the Association for Computing Machinery 37, 70–78 (1994)

Wimmer, H., Perner, J.: Beliefs about beliefs: Representation and constraining function of wrong beliefs in young children's understanding of deception. Cognition 13, 103–128 (1983)

Face Recognition System Invariant to Light-Camera Setup

Naman Dauthal, Surya Prakash, and Phalguni Gupta

Department of Computer Science and Engineering,
Indian Institute of Technology Kanpur, 208016, India
{dauthal,psurya,pg}@cse.iitk.ac.in

Abstract. This paper proposes an efficient face recognition system where images are acquired under different camera positions and lighting conditions. Active Appearance model is used to obtain shape and appearance information from faces in the form of feature vectors. Bilinear model then works upon these vectors to obtain style specific basis matrices in the training phase. In the test phase the bilinear model uses elastic net regularization to determine stable content vectors using style specific basis matrix. Euclidean distance between content vectors of two images is used to take decision on matching. The proposed system has been tested on 1255 images of 108 subjects. Experiment results reveal that the system achieves an accuracy of 95% when five top best matches are considered in a closed set identification setup.

Keywords: Active Appearance Model, Elastic Net, Bilinear Model, Ridge Regression, Lasso.

1 Introduction

Face is a well accepted biometric trait. In [6], Jain and Pankanti have justified the increasing popularity of face as a biometric trait for identification and authentication. The biggest challenge is to recognize a known face in a novel state of illumination, viewpoint, expression or age. It is observed that the intra-person variation in availabe images, obtained under different capturing conditions, may be greater than the inter-person variation which leads to incorrect results. Image representations like edge maps, image intensity derivatives have been commonly used to overcome illumination effects. In [1] the insufficiency of these representations to overcome variation due to change in the direction of illumination has been discussed.

Shin et al. [9] have used the bilinear model regularized by ridge regression to design an illumination invariant face recognition system. Lee and Kim [7] have used the same technique for expression invariant face recognition. The bilinear model is a technique that learns the interaction between two important factors -the style and content- of some common observations tasks.

Ridge regression [5] is a shrinkage technique that stabilizes a typical regression model by constraining variance of the computed parameter vector. The lasso [11] is another such shrinkage method that bounds the size of coefficients. It however forces coefficients to shrink to zero thus offering interpretable sparse models. Also lasso is

M.K. Kundu et al. (Eds.): PerMIn 2012, LNCS 7143, pp. 90–97, 2012.

known to perform better when irrelevant features are present. The downside with lasso is that a closed form to the objective function cannot be formulated.

This paper proposes an efficient face recognition system invariant to camera and light setup. It uses bilinear model regularized by a more general shrinkage technique, the elastic net, which offers a compromise between the ridge regression and lasso.

The paper is organized as follows: Section 2 discusses the three preliminary techniques namely the Active Appearance Model, the Bilinear model and the Elastic net used in the proposed system. Section 3 discusses proposed system along with the experimental results. Section 4 provides the concluding remarks.

2   Preliminaries

2.1   Active Appearance Model

Cootes et al. [3] have proposed Active Appearance Model (AAM) as a statistical tool that combines the shape and appearance of an object into a single parameter, builds the object model, learns the correlation between model-displacement and difference image and uses this correlation to fit the model to novel images.

Each face image is landmarked with n points which define the shape vector s of an AAM:

$$\mathbf{s} = (x_1, y_1, x_2, y_2, ..., x_n, y_n) \ . \tag{1}$$

Since an AAM allows linear shape variation, the shape s can be expressed as a mean shape $\mathbf{s}_0$ plus a linear combination of k shape vectors $\{\mathbf{s}_i, i = 1, 2, \cdots, k\}$:

$$\mathbf{s} = \mathbf{s}_0 + \sum_{i=1}^{k} \alpha_i \mathbf{s}_i = \mathbf{s}_0 + \mathbf{P}_s \boldsymbol{\alpha} \ . \tag{2}$$

where α_i are the shape parameters and $\mathbf{s}_i$ are the shape eigenvectors that together form the set $\mathbf{P}_s$ of orthogonal modes of shape variation. The landmark meshes are first normalised using Procrustes analysis to remove the effect of translation, rotation and scaling. Principal Component Analysis (PCA) is then applied to obtain the shape eigenvectors $\mathbf{s}_i$. Only k eigenvectors corresponding to the k largest eigenvalues are considered.

Similarly, the appearance g of an AAM is defined as the sum of mean appearance $\mathbf{g}_0$ and a linear combination of l appearance eigenvectors $\{\mathbf{g}_i, i = 1, 2, \cdots, l\}$:

$$\mathbf{g} = \mathbf{g}_0 + \sum_{i=1}^{l} \tau_i \mathbf{g}_i = \mathbf{g}_0 + \mathbf{P}_g \boldsymbol{\tau} \ . \tag{3}$$

where τ_i are the appearance parameters and $\mathbf{g}_i$ are the appearance eigenvectors that together form the set $\mathbf{P}_g$ of orthogonal modes of appearance variation. The face meshes are first warped onto the mean mesh $\mathbf{s}_0$. Delaunay Triangulation is followed by a piecewise affine warp to shape normalise the training images. PCA is applied to these warped images and the appearance eigenvectors corresponding to l largest eigenvalues taken.

The shape and appearance information from α and τ of each face image is then integrated which is the essence of combined AAMs. To combine the shape and appearance information, a diagonal matrix ψ, showing changes in the appearance with a change in each model parameter, is computed. The shape and appearance parameters for each image are then integrated in a vector $\mathbf{b}$ as:

$$\mathbf{b} = \begin{pmatrix} \psi\alpha \\ \tau \end{pmatrix} = \begin{pmatrix} \psi\mathbf{P}_s^T(\mathbf{s} - \mathbf{s}_0) \\ \mathbf{P}_g^T(\mathbf{g} - \mathbf{g}_0) \end{pmatrix} . \tag{4}$$

These $\mathbf{b}$ vectors for all the faces are arranged into a matrix. PCA is applied on this matrix to get orthogonal feature bases $\mathbf{b}_i$. The vector $\mathbf{b}$ corresponding to a face can be expressed as a linear combination of these bases (or eigenvectors):

$$\mathbf{b} = \mathbf{b}_0 + \sum_{i=1}^{m} y_i \mathbf{b}_i . \tag{5}$$

where $\mathbf{b}_0$ is the mean of all $\mathbf{b}$'s, and $\mathbf{y}$ is the shape-appearance parameter for the face.

2.2   Asymmetric Bilinear Model

Tenenbaum and Freeman [10] have introduced the bilinear model as an "expressive representation" of the interaction between the two factors of some common tasks. Thus a letter and font, a phoneme and speaker accent, a face and its viewing condition are some observations with two factors that have "a mathematical property of separability". The interaction between these factors can be learned during training and then used for classification, extrapolation and translation tasks.

Let the light-camera setup (style) s and content c be represented by vectors $\mathbf{a}^s$ and $\mathbf{b}^c$ having dimensionalities I and J respectively. The symmetric bilinear model can then be expressed as:

$$y_k^{sc} = \sum_{i=1}^{I} \sum_{j=1}^{J} w_{ijk} a_i^s b_j^c . \tag{6}$$

where i, j and k denote the components of style, content and observation vectors, respectively. Each $\mathbf{w}_{ij}$ is a K-dimensional interaction vector representing the interaction between the ith style component and j^{th} content component. K is the length of observation vector $\mathbf{y}$ that we have obtained from AAM.

The Asymmetric model uses style specific basis matrices which are essentially the interaction terms w_{ijk} varied according to style. The style specific terms are computed as:

$$w_{jk}^s = \sum_i w_{ijk}^s a_i^s . \tag{7}$$

These w_{jk} terms, for a particular style s, form a matrix $\mathbf{W}^s$ which is essentially a style-specific linear mapping. This mapping can render a face (feature vector) in style s when the content factor $\mathbf{b}^c$ is found from the following:

$$y_k^{sc} = \sum_j w_{jk}^s b_j^c . \tag{8}$$

$$\mathbf{y}^{sc} = \mathbf{W}^s \mathbf{b}^c . \tag{9}$$

Model Training. Learning the model from a set of observations involves to find the optimal interaction matrix $\mathbf{W}$. The feature vectors of C subjects in S styles are stacked into a single $SK \times C$ matrix $\mathbf{Y}$:

$$\mathbf{Y} = \begin{bmatrix} \mathbf{y}_{11} & \cdots & \mathbf{y}_{1C} \\ \vdots & \ddots & \vdots \\ \mathbf{y}_{S1} & \cdots & \mathbf{y}_{SC} \end{bmatrix} = \mathbf{WB} . \tag{10}$$

where $\mathbf{B}$ is a matrix of content vectors $\{\mathbf{b}^l, l = 1, 2, \cdots, C\}$ and $\mathbf{W}$ is given as:

$$\mathbf{W} = \begin{bmatrix} \mathbf{w}_1^1 & \mathbf{w}_2^1 & \cdots & \mathbf{w}_J^1 \\ \mathbf{w}_1^2 & \mathbf{w}_2^2 & \cdots & \mathbf{w}_J^2 \\ \vdots & & \ddots & \vdots \\ \mathbf{w}_1^S & \mathbf{w}_2^S & \cdots & \mathbf{w}_J^S \end{bmatrix} . \tag{11}$$

The style specific basis $\mathbf{W}^s$ can be found by peforming Singular Value Decomposition (SVD) of $\mathbf{Y}$ that yields three matrices U, S and V so that:

$$\mathbf{Y} = USV^T \tag{12}$$

In lieu of (10), first J columns of US can be taken as $\mathbf{W}$ while the first J rows of V^T can be taken as $\mathbf{B}$.

Testing. The matrix $\mathbf{W}$ can be used to find the content vector of an unknown face provided the associated light-camera setup is known. Given a test face we use a Support Vector Machine (SVM) multicategory classifier to find the style information s and compute $\mathbf{b}$ as:

$$\mathbf{b} = (\mathbf{W}^s)^\dagger \mathbf{y} . \tag{13}$$

The usual setup for linear regression has predictors $\{w_{kj}^s, j = 1, 2, \cdots, p = J\}$ and the observations $\{y_k, k = 1, 2, \cdots, n = K\}$. The regression model solves for $\hat{\mathbf{b}}$ as:

$$\hat{\mathbf{b}} = \underset{\mathbf{b}}{\mathrm{argmin}} \sum_{k=1}^{n} \left(y_k - b_0 - \sum_{j=1}^{p} w_{kj}^s b_j \right)^2 . \tag{14}$$

2.3 Regularizing with Elastic Net

When the data are strongly correlated, the corresponding $\mathbf{b}$ parameters can grow very large in different directions, cancelling each other's effect (so that the objective function is indeed minimized). This results in a highly destablized model as even a small change in an observation $\mathbf{y}$ may produce uncontrollably different $\mathbf{b}$ values. There exist different regularization techniques to trade bias with imprecision. The essence of most, is to include a penalty term in the objective function.

The *elastic-net* penalty, proposed by Zou and Hastie [12] as a compromise between the ridge regression ($\alpha = 0$) and lasso ($\alpha = 1$), is given as:

$$P_\alpha(\mathbf{b}) = \sum_{j=1}^{p} \left[\frac{1}{2}(1 - \alpha)b_j^2 + \alpha|b_j| \right] . \qquad (15)$$

Ridge regression does not produce a parsimonious model i.e. retains all the predictors while lasso ($\alpha = 1$) tends to keep only one variable from a group of variables that exhibit high correlations. The elastic-net overcomes these drawbacks while outperforming the lasso in prediction accuracy. The objective function with elastic net penalty is

$$\min_{(b_0,\mathbf{b})\in\mathbf{R}^{p+1}} \left[\frac{1}{2N} \sum_{k=1}^{N} (y_k - b_0 - (\mathbf{w}_k^s)^T\mathbf{b})^2 + \lambda P_\alpha(\mathbf{b}) \right] . \qquad (16)$$

where λ is the regularization parameter. In [4], the cyclical coordinate descent methods have been used to solve the objective function (16). The coordinates b_j are updated one by one in a cyclic fashion. For each coordinate, the least square coefficient on the partial residual is computed, soft thresholding applied for lasso followed by proportional shrinkage for ridge penalty.

3   Proposed System

This section describes an efficient face recognition system which can handle the issues occurred due to change in camera positions and lighting conditions while acquiring images. It uses the bilinear model regularized by a technique that offers a compromise between ridge and lasso. Initially a training set is considered and style basis matrices W^s are computed. The training set contains face images of subjects in different styles. Active appearance model(AAM) is used to get the feature vector of each face image. These feature vectors y_{ij} for j^{th} subject in i^{th} style contains information about the shape and appearance of face and are stacked into a single matrix $\mathbf{Y}$. Singular Value Decomposition on stacked feature vector matrix $\mathbf{Y}$ is used to compute $\mathbf{W}$. This matrix $\mathbf{W}$ is used to compute the content vectors of gallery images. The feature vectors determined from AAM and the style of image, which is same and known for all images in gallery, are used to find the content vector. This is done by solving a convex optimization problem represented by equation (16). The penalty term in the objective function corresponding to this problem ensures that the computed content vectors have minimal variance hence better stability of the model. To test the proposed system, probe set having test faces in different styles are considered. An SVM classifier is used to determine the style s of all faces in probe set. This style information is used to extract the style specific basis $\mathbf{W^s}$ from $\mathbf{W}$. The feature vector determined from AAM and $\mathbf{W^s}$ is used to compute content vector for all faces in probe set. Finally Euclidean distance between the content vector of a test image in the probe set and that of every image in the gallery set is computed. These distances are used to determine the top 5 best matches in the gallery set against the test face image.

We have used a subset of MUCT face database [8] which consists of 3755 faces with 76 manual landmarks for each face. Each subject is photographed with five webcams,

a, b, c, d and e. Camera a has been positioned in front of the face, b has been fixed 36 cm right from a, c is 40 cm right from a while d and e have been fixed 38 cm above and 40 cm below a respectively. In addition, ten different lighting setups are used and each subject is photographed with two or three lighting setups.

We have selected images of 108 subjects, camera views a, b, d and e and all three lighting sets t, u and v. Thus 15 (3 lighting sets × 4 camera views) different styles have been used for each subject. Further not all images of camera b are included since landmarks corresponding to hidden positions in this view have been marked as $(0, 0)$. We use 1255 images of which 108×3 belong to each of camera views a, d and e while remaining 283 images belong to camera view b. Of 108 subjects, 54 are randomly chosen for training and remaining 54 for gallery and probe sets.

Fig. 1 provides accuracy of the proposed system, with different lengths of content vectors (from 6 to the number of training subjects ie C). The accuracies are computed for four different values of the regularization parameter where the number of training subjects is 50 with $\alpha = 0.5$. This is repeated 8 times using different combinations of training subjects. Fig. 1 suggests that the accuracy increases intially with the content vector length but starts declining after reaching a maximum value. The λ values of 0.015 and 0.025 yield higher accuracy than the bilinear model ($\lambda = 0$). But for $\lambda(= 0.05)$, the accuracy reduces due to too much shrinking.

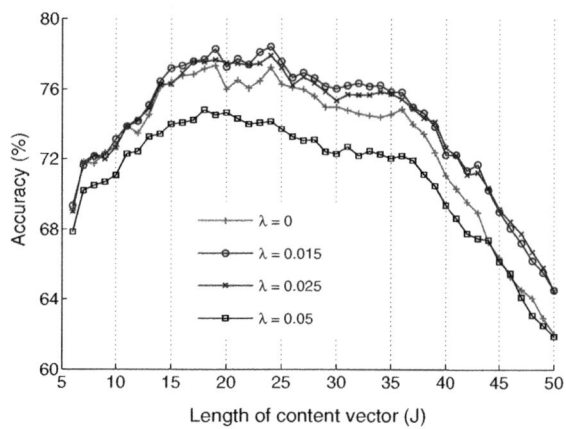

Fig. 1. Accuracy of System with Different Lengths of Content Vector for λ Different Values

Again two experiments with 50 and 70 training subjects have been conducted to test the accuracy of the system for different values of λ and α. The λ values ranging from 0 to 0.1 in steps of 0.005 and α values ranging from 0.1 to 1.0 in steps of 0.05 are used to form different models. The accuracies are computed on test images and plotted in Fig. 2. Fig. 2a shows the accuracy for top best match while the accuracy for the top 5 best mathces is given in Fig. 2b. Accuracy of the system has been found to be 95% when top best 5 matches are considered.

The accuracy remains constant for $\lambda = 0$ ie the bilinear model. It increases with the increase of λ upto a point and then starts declining with further increase in λ values. For small values of λ, the accuracy increases with α while for higher values closer to 0.1, accuracy drastically falls while going from ridge dominance (α closer to 0) to lasso dominance (α closer to 1). This suggests to give greater weight to L2 norm for higher values of λ and to L1 norm for smaller values. To further support our conclusion we try to find the distribution of content vector parameters with α and λ. Fig. 3 plots the 9th, 14th and 19th coefficients of the content vector of a particular person. The content vector shrinks for the second model but stretches again with third.

In all experiments, an SVM multicategory classifier [2] is used to get the style s of probe images. The classifier may fail to classify a fraction of images correctly. The accuracy achieved with SVM classifier is compared with the accuracy achieved with perfect classification (ie. using known style information about probe images) in terms

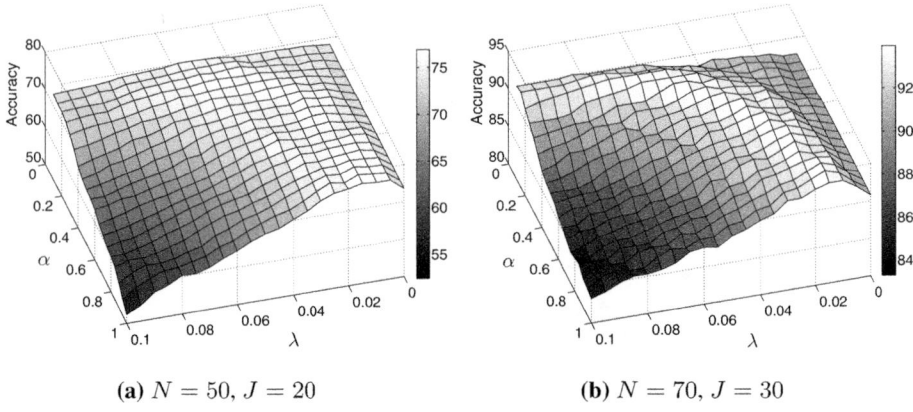

(a) $N = 50, J = 20$ (b) $N = 70, J = 30$

Fig. 2. Accuracy with different models

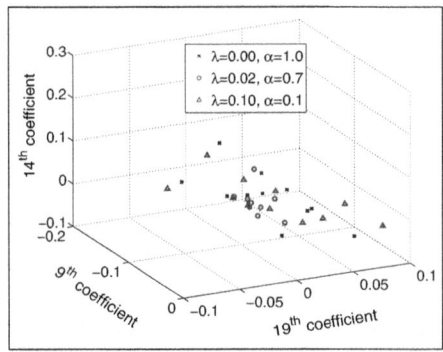

Fig. 3. Distribution of content parameter vector parameters with different models

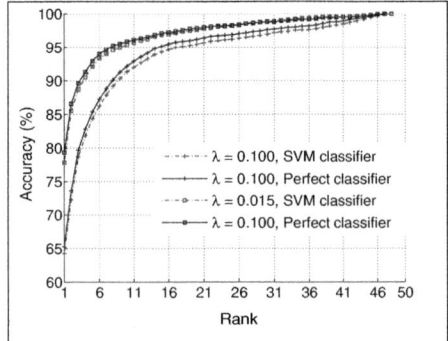

Fig. 4. CMC curves for accuracy with SVM and perfect classification $\alpha = 0.5$

of the cumulative match characteristics (CMC) curves. Fig. 4 suggests that the match accuracy with the real classifier is only slightly lower than the accuracy achievable with perfect classification of the styles of faces in the probe set.

4 Conclusion

This paper has used the bilinear model to design an efficient face recognition system which is invariant to the effect of changes due to camera position and different lighting setups. The accuracy has improved by the using a compromise between ridge regressin and lasso in the bilinear model. Accuracy of the system has been found to be 95% when top best 5 matches are considered.

References

1. Adini, Y., Moses, Y., Ullman, S.: Face recognition: The problem of compensating for changes in illumination direction. IEEE Transactions on Pattern Analysis and Machine Intelligence 19(7), 721–732 (1997)
2. Chang, C.C., Lin, C.J.: LIBSVM: A library for support vector machines. ACM Transactions on Intelligent Systems and Technology 2, 27:1–27:27 (2011), software available at http://www.csie.ntu.edu.tw/~cjlin/libsvm
3. Cootes, T.F., Edwards, G.J., Taylor, C.J.: Active Appearance Models. In: Burkhardt, H., Neumann, B. (eds.) ECCV 1998. LNCS, vol. 1407, pp. 484–498. Springer, Heidelberg (1998)
4. Friedman, J.H., Hastie, T., Tibshirani, R.: Regularization paths for generalized linear models via coordinate descent. Journal of Statistical Software 33(1), 1–22 (2010), http://www.jstatsoft.org/v33/i01
5. Hoerl, A.E., Kennard, R.W.: Ridge regression: Biased estimation for nonorthogonal problems. Technometrics 12(1) (1970)
6. Jain, A.K., Pankanti, S.: Beyond fingerprinting. Scientific American Magazine, 78–81 (2008)
7. Lee, H.-S., Kim, D.: Expression-invariant face recognition by facial expression transformations. Pattern Recognition Letters 29(13), 1797–1805 (2008)
8. Milborrow, S., Morkel, J., Nicolls, F.: The MUCT Landmarked Face Database. Pattern Recognition Association of South Africa (2010), http://www.milbo.org/muct
9. Shin, D., Lee, H.S., Kim, D.: Illumination-robust face recognition using ridge regressive bilinear models. Pattern Recognition Letters 29(1), 49–58 (2008)
10. Tenenbaum, J., Freeman, W.T.: Separating style and content with bilinear models. Neural Computation 12, 1247–1283 (2000)
11. Tibshirani, R.: Regression shrinkage and selection via the lasso. Journal of the Royal Statistical Society, Series B 58(1), 267–288 (1996)
12. Zou, H., Hastie, T.: Regularization and variable selection via the elastic net. Journal of the Royal Statistical Society, Series B 67(2), 301–320 (2005)

Representing Feature Quantization Approach Using Spatial-Temporal Relation for Action Recognition

Sarvesh Vishwakarma and Anupam Agrawal

Indian Institute of Information Technology-Allahabad
Jhalwa, Allahabad 211012, India
{rs51,anupam}@iiita.ac.in

Abstract. In this paper we propose an efficient & intuitive algorithm for the design of feature vector quantization using space-time interest point in video surveillance. The performance of activity recognition is generally depend upon the quantity of significant features but with proper feature quantization one can delivered the same performance with less number of features. The basic characteristics of algorithm are discussed and demonstrated by experiment. It is scalable in nature and work efficiently under varying conditions. In an experiment section, we show that our novel feature quantization approach takes less number of features in compared to standard quantization, while delivering the same performance.

Keywords: Spatio-temporal Feature, Feature Quantization, Action Recognition, Histogram.

1   Introduction

Human Action Recognition in computer vision involves object detection, tracking and recognition of their activities. Among them action recognition has a vital role in many applications. Even great efforts have been done on this, the activity recognition is still an open and challenging problem.

In many vision-related problems, feature extraction and their optimal quantization are the key operation for the human action recognition. Two methods, model-based approach and model-free approach, are generally used by the researcher of in this field. In many circumstance the model-based approaches are not suited because of its complexity. While in the model-free approach, low-level image features are used to represent human movement. An efficient feature quantization algorithm with model based approach is developed to take the advantage of extracted features from the region of interest. It is used by the selection process and classifier to correctly classify the video into its activity class. A recent survey by Turaga et al. [4] focuses on how the high-level recognition is performed by assigning action class-label on image features just extracted from input video stream.

M.K. Kundu et al. (Eds.): PerMIn 2012, LNCS 7143, pp. 98–105, 2012.
© Springer-Verlag Berlin Heidelberg 2012

Several other approaches use the local & global feature that derived from the space-time 3D model. Local features are interest points lie under the rectangular area where the motion of limb is occurring frequently.

The action recognition can be metamorphose into the classification on the basis of spatial-temporal features in the domain of video images. In the present work Benezeth et al. [5] have made an effort to extract the time-line feature. The variation present in all such pack with leveled class of activity used to train the classifier.

The remaining paper is organized as follows. Section 2 gives a brief description of related work on feature correlation statistics. In section 3, our novel feature quantization scheme and the feature map are explained. Finally, experimental results are presented in section 4, followed by the conclusion in section 5.

2   Related Work

Research in video surveillance has made great progresses in recent years, such as background substraction, video indexing, crowd counting, crowd behavior analysis in public places. Zarka et al. [3] used "Star" skeletonization to detect object class and their actions. Liu and Yang et al. [6] exploited the local feature vector.

Blank et al. [9] extract local features (interest point) at every frame and concatenated them temporally to describe the overall motion of human activities. Savarese et al. [2] developed a methodology to get spatio-temporal propinquity information among features. They measured feature co-occurrence patterns in a local 3-D region, making histograms called ST-correlograms. Liu and Shah et al. [8] also considered correlational statistics among features. Likewise, Laptev et al. [1] constracted spatio-temporal histograms by dividing space-time volume into many small sectors.

3   Interest Points, Quantization, and Feature Selection

In this section, an overview of interest point is given. Then, feature quantization is summarized and feature selection is explained.

3.1   Interest Points

Let assume an action video V consists of N image frames. It is represented as $V = [I_1, I_2, I_3, I_4, I_5, \ldots, I_t, \ldots, I_N]$; where $I[x][y][t] \equiv I_t$ and x, y represent position of pixel value on t^{th} image frame. The advantage of converting video into three dimensions array is that algorithm can explore any pixel from any frame.

Interest points are local spatio-temporal features which describe human actions in video. Dollar et al. [10] extract sparse spatio-temporal local interest points from 3D volumes by applying two separate filters in linear and temporal dimension; filters are

$$R = (I * g * h_{ev})^2 + (I * g * h_{od})^2 \qquad (1)$$

where $g(x, y; \sigma)$ is the 2D Gaussian smoothing kernel, applied only along the spatial dimensions, and h_{ev} and h_{od} are quadrature pair of 1D Gabor filters applied temporally. These are defined as $h_{ev}(t; \tau, \omega) = -\cos(2\pi t \omega)e^{-t^2/\tau^2}$ and $h_{od}(t; \tau, \omega) = -\sin(2\pi t \omega)e^{-t^2/\tau^2}$.
    we have used 2D Gabor filter.

$$g(x, y) = s(x, y)w_r(x, y) \qquad (2)$$

where s(x,y) is known as carrier and it is a complex sinusoid.

$$s(x, y) = \exp(j(2\pi(v_o x + u_o y) + O_i)) \qquad (3)$$

where O_i defines the orientation of the filter & 3 orientation are considered: $O_{i=1,2,3} = \{0°, 45°, 90°\}$ and v_o & u_o are the spatial frequencies of the sinusoid controlling the scale of the filter. $w_r(x, y)$ is an envelope and denote a 2D Gaussian-shaped function.

$$w_r(x, y) = \exp\left(-\left(\frac{x^2}{\rho^2} + \frac{y^2}{\rho^2}\right)\right) \qquad (4)$$

ρ defines width of $w_r(x, y)$. Here we can take $\rho = 11$.

3.2   Feature Quantization

Following the preprocessing and normalization, 10 state-of- the-art local and global features are extracted. The extracted local features [7] are: height & width ratio of cloud $\mathcal{C}_s^\tau$; absolute speed $\mathcal{C}_s^{sp}$; density of interest point within the cloud $\mathcal{C}_s^D$; vertical distance between centroid of object and cloud $\mathcal{C}_s^{vd}$; horizontal distance between centroid of object and cloud $\mathcal{C}_s^{hd}$; height ratio $\mathcal{C}_s^{hr}$ & width ratio $\mathcal{C}_s^{wr}$ between object and cloud; amount of overlap between object area & cloud area $\mathcal{C}_s^{O_\tau}$. The global features are: a height & width ratio $\mathcal{O}_t^\tau$; and absolute speed $\mathcal{O}_t^{sp}$. As the values of the features vary in different ranges, each dimension of the feature vector is normalized to a mean of $\mu_o = 0$ and variance of 1. Features are frame dependent so we have to quantize number of features independent of number of frames present in video. As each frame contain $8 \times S + 2$ features. We have taken $S = 6$ so, number of features per frame would be equal to 50. If number of frames in a video are 400 then total number of features would be equal to 20000 which degrades the robustness of algorithm. To reduce dimensionality of feature space a histogram $\mathcal{H}_\mathcal{F}$ of N_b bins is made, with a condition N_b is far less number of frames (see Algorithm 1). In this method, the problem of clustering $8 \times S + 2$ features into $T \times N$ clusters in the kernel feature space is formulated as an optimization problem that involves estimation of a $(T \times N)$-by-$(8 \times S + 2)$ indicator matrix $|\mathcal{X}_\mathcal{T}|$ whose elements are the membership values of each of the $8 \times S + 2$ features to the $T \times N$ clusters.

Algorithm 1. Feature Quantization

Require: $|\mathcal{V}| = \{|V_1|_{N \times 50}, |V_2|_{N \times 50}, |V_3|_{N \times 50} \ldots, |V_T|_{N \times 50}\}$
  $where\, V_{i \in \{1,2,\ldots,T\}} = \{I_1, I_2, \ldots, I_t \ldots, I_N\}, S = 6.$
Ensure: Histogram $\mathcal{H}_{\mathcal{F}}$
  $\mathcal{X}_1 = V_1 \,\&\, j = 2$
  while $j \leq T$ **do**
    $\mathcal{X}_j = \mathcal{X}_{j-1} \| V_j$
    $j \leftarrow j + 1$
  end while
  Matrix $|\mathcal{X}_T|_{(T*N) \times (8S+2)}$
  for $c = 1$ to $8 \times S + 2$ **do**
    for $r = 1$ to $T \times N$ **do**
      Find Quantized Values $\widehat{\mathcal{X}_T} \Leftarrow |\mathcal{X}_T|$
    end for
  end for
  Get $\widehat{\mathcal{V}} \Leftarrow \widehat{\mathcal{X}_T}$
  for $c = 1$ to $8 \times S + 2$ **do**
    for $i = 1$ to T $in\ set$ $\mathcal{V}$ **do**
      Compute Histogram $\mathcal{H}_{\mathcal{F}} \Leftarrow \widehat{\mathcal{V}}$
    end for
  end for

3.3 Feature Selection

For improving the performance of a recognition system, feature selection is performed: features with high significance are selected; features with low significance are excluded from the feature set. In literature, there exists a number of selection strategies, e. g. the Relevant Factor (RF, see [7]). The RF has been applied on the features used in clouds of interest points accumulated over multiple temporal scales in [7] for the first time. Given the feature quantization model described in the previous paragraph, We compute relevant factor for each features. We wish to estimate the value of relevant factor $\mathcal{R}_{f_i}$ vary within the class and across the class. We arrange them in decending order and selected 10% of it for KTH and 40% of it for WEIZMANN dataset. The higher value of $\mathcal{R}_{f_i}$ define the most desire candidate for feature selection.

The KNN (k Nearest Neighbor) classifier is used to classify the input video based on their similarity with training video data set. For a given unlabeled video, we find the k closest labeled videos in the training data set and assign the video to the activity class that appears frequently within the k-subset. For improving the

4 Experiments and Discussion

To verify the correctness and effectiveness of our algorithm, we systematically apply it to several published datasets. The KTH dataset [14] is used to test the action recognition; and the WEIZMANN dataset [15] are used to check robustness.

4.1   Public Dataset

We have tested our system on the KTH dataset and the Weizmann dataset. The KTH dataset is a large-scale dataset that contain 600 video clips of six actions performed four times by 25 people. Each video contain repeated execution of a single action in a resolution of 160×1200 25 frames per second.

The Weizmann dataset consists of 10 action categories with 9 people, resulting in 90 videos. The evaluation was done in a leave-one-out manner: 8 subjects were used for training, and the remaining one for testing. The experiment was repeated for all 9 persons, and the results were averaged.

4.2   Comparison

Two experiments are conducted using standard quantization and our novel feature quantization. The selected features are depicted as feature map. All experiments are evaluated using varying number of features with {100, 500, 1000, 1500, 2000}. The training set is used to estimate the parameters, which are optimized on the validation set. The results are shown in Fig. 1. The best performing parameters are used to perform activity recognition on the dataset (see Table 1)

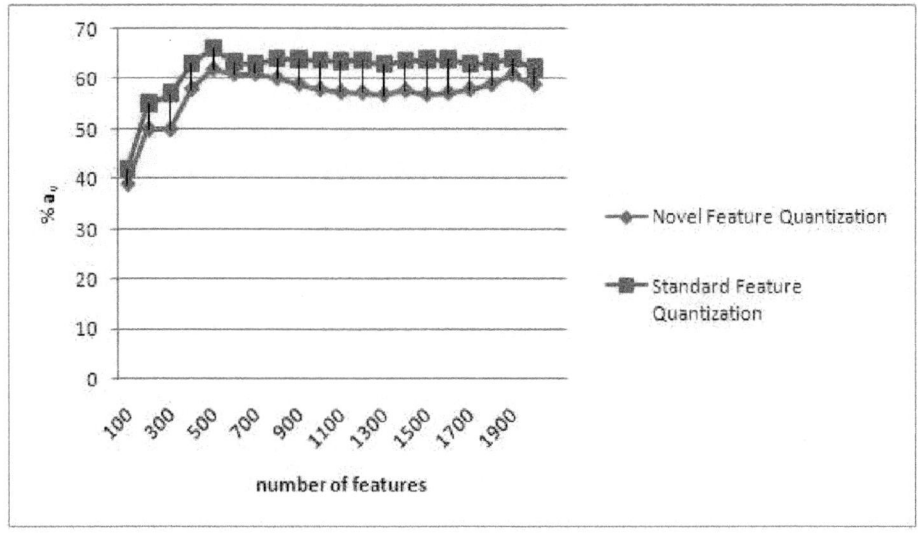

Fig. 1. Performance comparison between standard and novel feature quantization

In the first experiment, feature selection is performed on the features applying standard quantization which uses all 2000 features. Peak performance is reached for $N = 2000$, yields a $a_v = 60.4\%$. For the second experiment however using novel feature quantization as described in section 3 yields a $a_v = 59.7\%$. This improvement is statistically significant and can be achieved for all video frames. When comparing the results of both, for the best performing parameters and

$N = 2000$ on the test data (dataset), a relative drop of -0.7% can be observed. However this change is not significant so, both perform equally. The main advantage with our feature quantization compared to standard quantization is that feature sets containing less number of features delivering the same performance.

Table 1. Comparison with other approaches

APPROACH	KTH	WEIZMANN
Proposed method	93.84%	96.7%
Jia Liu et al. [6]	73.50%	87.50%
Bregonzio et al. [7]	93.17%	96.66%
Dollar et al. [10]	81.17%	85.2%
Liu et al. [8]	94.16%	–
Kovashka et al. [12]	94.53%	–
Yan et al. [13]	90.3%	–
Shabani et al. [11]	–	93.5%

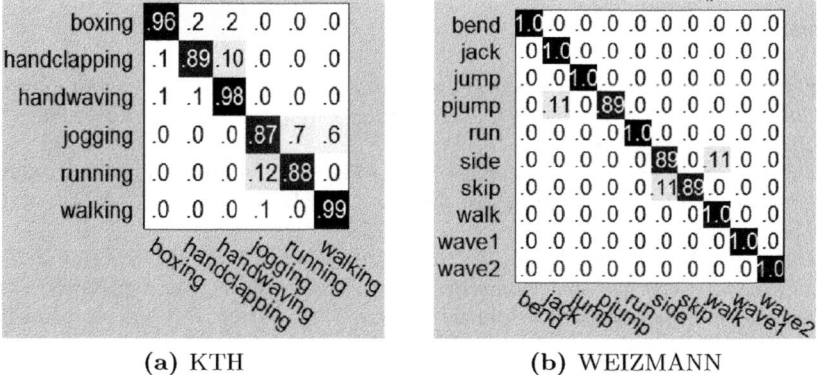

(a) KTH   (b) WEIZMANN

Fig. 2. Confusion Matrices

The accuracy of our method is 93.84% for KTH dataset and for WEIZMANN it is 96.7%, which is better than most of other approaches. The miss classification caused by our approach are summarized in the form of confusion matrices. The results of the experiment on both datasets are displayed in Fig. 2. It can be observed that the running, jogging and walking actions easily mixed up in KTH dataset. In the case of WEIZMANN dataset the pjump, jack, side & walk actions mixed up. Table 1 is provided for comparing the approaches. In Jia Liu experiments [6] nearly 26.5% and 12.5% samples were misclassified in KTH dataset and WEIZMANN dataset respectively. In our experiments the misclassification are 8% (KTH) & 4% (WEIZMANN). It indicates that our method can discriminate a series of similar actions such as jogging and running, which are also single out efficiently, with an accuracy of 87% in KTH dataset. It is however, fractious to make a fair comparison. Their method requires a background substraction procedure, global motion compensation and so on. We observed that our model is universal in the sense that it aims to offer a generic framework for human motion, Compared with other approaches our approach is more robust, easier to compute and simpler to understand.

5   Conclusions

We have proposed a feature vector quantization approach for action recognition framework. The quantization error is not distributed equally among the features when standard feature quantization is applied. Hence, the significant of the features is influenced by both quantization and recognition during feature selection. Our approach is capable of deriving an even distribution of quantization error among the quantized dimensions of the feature vector and each feature equally contribute in quantization process. Our system summarizes typical activities and interactions in the scene, segments the video sequence both temporally and spatially, supports the spatial temporal distribution of interest points for identification of various short or long duration activities.

References

1. Laptev, I., Marszalek, M., Schmid, C., Rozenfeld, B.: Learning realistic human actions from movies. In: IEEE Conference on Computer Vision and Pattern Recognition, pp. 1–8 (2008)
2. Savarese, S., Delpozo, A., Niebles, J., Fei-Fei, L.: Spatial-temporal correlatons for unsupervised action classification. In: Proc. IEEE Workshop on Motion and Video Computing, pp. 1–8 (2008)
3. Zarka, N., Alhalah, Z., Deeb, R.: Real-Time Human Motion Detection and Tracking. In: 3rd International Conference on ICTTA, vol. 08, pp. 1–6 (2008)
4. Turaga, P., Chellappa, R., Subrahmaniam, V.S., Udrea, O.: Machine Recognition of Human Activities: A Survey. IEEE Transactions on Circuits and Systems for Video Technology 18 (11), 1473–1488 (2008)
5. Benezeth, Y., Jodoin, P.M., Emile, B., Laurent, H., Rosenberger, C.: Review and Evaluation of Commonly-Implemented Background Subtraction Algorithms. In: 19th IEEE International Conference on ICPR, pp. 1–4 (2008)
6. Liu, J., Yang, J., Zhang, Y.: Action Recognition by Multiple Features and Hypersphere Multi-class SVM. In: 20th IEEE International Conference on ICPR, pp. 3744–3747 (2010)
7. Bregonzio, M., Gong, S., Xiang, T.: Recognising Action as Clouds of Space-Time Interest Points. In: IEEE International Conference on CVPR, pp. 1948–1955 (2009)
8. Liu, J., Shah, M.: Learning human actions via information maximization. In: IEEE Conference on Computer Vision and Pattern Recognition, pp. 1–8 (2008)
9. Blank, M., Gorelick, L., Shechtman, E., Irani, M., Basri, R.: Actions as Space-Time Shapes. In: 10th IEEE International Conference on ICCV, vol. 02, pp. 1395–1402 (2005)
10. Dollar, P., Rabaud, V., Cottrell, G., Belongie, S.: Behavior Recognition via Sparse Spatio-Temporal Features. In: 2nd Joint IEEE Workshop on Visual Surveillance and Performance Evaluation of Tracking and Surveillance, vol. 02, pp. 65–72 (2005)

11. Shabani, A.H., Zelek, J.S., Clausi, D.A.: Human Action Recognition using Salient Opponent-Based Motion Features. In: 7th Canadian Conference on Computer and Robot Vision, pp. 362–369. IEEE Computer Society (2010)
12. Kovashka, A., Grauman, K.: Learning a Hierarchy of Discriminative Space-Time Neighborhood Features for Human Action Recognition. In: IEEE Conference on Computer Vision and Pattern Recognition, pp. 2046–2053 (2010)
13. Yan, X., Luo, Y.: Making Full Use of Spatial-Temporal Interest Points: An Adaboost Aproach for Action Recognition. In: 17th IEEE International Conference on Image Processing, pp. 4677–4680 (2010)
14. Schuldt, C., Laptev, I., Caputo, B.: Recognizing human actions: a local SVM approach (2004), http://www.nada.kth.se/cvap/actions/
15. Gorelick, L., Blank, M., Shechtman, E., Irani, M., Basri, R.: Actions as Space-Time Shapes (2005),
http://www.wisdom.weizmann.ac.il/vision/SpaceTimeActions.html

Human Computer Interaction with Hand Gestures in Virtual Environment

Siddharth S. Rautaray, Anand Kumar, and Anupam Agrawal

Indian Institute of Information Technology, Allahabad, India
{sr.rgpv,linkinanand,anupam69}@gmail.com

Abstract. With the ever increasing and flourishing phenomena of growth in virtual environments based upon computer systems; demands for new kind of interaction devices have emerged. The present used devices like keyboard, mouse and pen are cumbrousome within these promising applications. The developments of user interfaces influence the changes in the Human-Computer Interaction (HCI). This paper focuses to design an application using computer vision and gesture recognition techniques which develop a relatively economic input device of interacting with virtual games using hand gestures. The architecture of the gesture recognition system comprises of different image processing techniques like camshift, and Lucas Kanade technique for tracking of hands and its gestures. Haar like features locates the position of the hand and recognizes the gesture being made by such located hand image. The modeling of gestures has been done for recognition through matching the feature of defects present in the hand with the assigned gestures. The virtual game is created using Open GL library. The application uses seven gestures for manipulating the virtual game. This main connotation of this hand gesture recognition system is providing a substitute for input devices while making interaction during the virtual games. Hence instead of making effort to develop a new vocabulary of hand gesture we have matched control instruction set of mouse to subset of most discriminating hand gestures, so that we get a robust interface.

Keywords: Human computer interaction, Hand gestures, Virtual environment.

1 Introduction

The user interfaces in vogue are seldom designed with the dexterity performance in desired virtual reality. The key board, mouse etc lack the sensitivity desired in virtual reality application. Eventually the researchers working the area of Human Computer Interaction made a common emphasis to design and develop the user interfaces capable enough fulfill the intended performance criteria desired in the virtual environment. Such interfaces can be developed by exploiting the phenomena of instinctive communication and manipulation accomplishments of humans facilitating the human computer interaction even at the further higher degree.

Most of the users abhor the complexities of the present interaction devices and methods because of the time and attempts needed for understanding the functionalities

M.K. Kundu et al. (Eds.): PerMIn 2012, LNCS 7143, pp. 106–113, 2012.
© Springer-Verlag Berlin Heidelberg 2012

and the chances of failures arising out of the cognitive burden. Besides some interaction steps involving the swiftness in reflex such as double-click, and drop & drag dissuades users particularly elderly or affected by some physical or cognitive disorder [1]. Hence Human computer Interaction (HCI) is persistently in pursuance of being inexpensive, easier in use, versatile and fast which may contribute to the virtual environment to make a world where the interaction feels real.

For achieving submergence within a virtual environment, user shall be capable in interacting efficaciously in the virtual world. The term efficaciously here explicitly indicates the capacity to minimizing the cognitive load and maximizing goal success [2]. For accomplishing it, a successful a 3D user interface should be natural, intuitive, powerful enough and simple to learn which allow the users to carry through the necessitated tasks. The present contact based devices like accelerometers, data glove [3], sensors/actuators and other input devices used to capture the user movement and control the selection, manipulation and movements of objects in virtual scenes [4]. These devices are obstructed by number factors such as awkwardness, unintuitive, rigidity, and prone to distortion from the physical environment.

The present paper describes an application designed for human computer interaction which uses different computer vision techniques for recognizing hand gestures and their interaction with game in virtual environment. The objective of the current application is to use a natural device free interface that recognizes the hand gestures as commands. The paper is further subdivided as follows: state of art is surveyed in section 2. Section 3 provides the architecture design of the vision based gesture recognition system. Section 4 introduces an experimental setup and functioning of the application. Results and analysis of the recognition system has been shown in section 5. Section 6 performs the testing and analysis of the designed system. The effort ends in Conclusion and future work that is in the section 7. References used by the application are summarized in last section.

2   State of Art

To improve the interaction in qualitative terms in virtual environment it is coveted that the means of interaction ought to be as innate as possible. Gestures, especially expressed by hands have become a popular means of human computer interface now days. Human gestures can be defined as a meaningful body movement which involves physical motilities of different parts of body like fingers, hands etc with aim to express purposeful information or communicating with the environment [5]. Gesture input can be categorized into different categories depending on various characteristic [6]. One of the categories is deictic gesture that refers to reaching for something or pointing an object. Accepting or refusing an action for an event is termed as mimetic gestures. It is useful for language representation of gestures. An iconic gesture is way to define an object or its features. Liu and Lovell [7], proposed an interesting technique for real time tracking of hand capturing gestures through a web camera and Intel Pentium based personal computer. The proposed technique is implemented without any use of sophisticated image processing algorithms and hardware. Controlling VLC media player using hand gesture recognition is done in real time environment using vision based techniques [8]. Xu et al. [9] used contact based devices like accelerometer and EMG sensors for controlling virtual games. Conci et al. [1] designs an interactive virtual blackboard by using video processing and gesture recognition engine for giving commands, writing and manipulating objects on a projected visual interface. Lee et al. [10] developed a Virtual Office Environment System (VOES), in which avatar is used navigate and interact with other participants. For controlling the avatar motion in the system a continuous hand gesture system is designed which uses state automata to segment continuous hand gesture and to remove meaningless motion.   Xu et al. [11] presents a hand gesture recognition system for a virtual Rubik's Cube game control that is controlled by EMG and 3D accelerometer to provide a user-friendly interaction between human and computers. In this the signals segments the meaningful gestures from the stream of EMG signal inputs.

There are several studies on the hand movements especially gestures, by modeling the human body and creating a amalgamate body of cognition. This makes it possible to face the problem from a mathematical viewpoint [12]. The major drawbacks of such techniques are they are very complex and highly sophisticated for developing an actionable procedure to make the necessary jigs and tools for any typical application scenarios.

3   Vision Based Gesture Recognition System

The application uses an integrated approach for hand gesture recognition. It recognizes static hand gestures. Figure 1 shows the architecture design of vision based gesture recognition system. Images are captured from camera and passed through following phases/algorithms. The procedure starts by acquisition phase.

The background subtraction is done in the HSV color space for removing the illumination changes where the hand is to be modeled for simplifying the input. As the initialization phase is over, the haar cascade [13] classifier is responsible for locating hand position and classifying gestures (open, close, pointing, etc.). Haar-Like characteristics is features that digitalize images to analyze images in object recognition applications.

In this paper, we use simple rectangular Haar-Like Features as our approach. The simple Haar-like features are called as they are figured likewise with the coefficients within the Haar wavelet transform which is further used in Viola and Jones algorithm [14]. The Haar-like characteristics are also comparatively robust to the noise and lighting changes as the features will figure the gray level deviation between the rectangles (black and the white). The noise and lighting variations also strike the pixel measures on the entire characteristic region, which could be counteracted. The hand is tracked using background subtraction and motion detection. The noise generated in the application is reduced using eroding and dilation. The application uses the Camshift and Lucas Kanade Optical Flow technique for tracking of hand. The following step was implemented to attain a robust hand motion tracking thin the video sequence. This is done by using CAMSHIFT tracking algorithm [15]. This tracking algorithm is modified version of a tracking mean shift algorithm that is a robust non-parametric iterative technique for climbing density gradient to obtain the modality of probability distributions. As the mean shift algorithm is designed for static distribution, CAMSHIFT is developed for dynamic distributions. This unique feature makes the system robust to track dynamic objects in video, where parameters of the object changes dynamically over time. This makes the search window size dynamically adjustable. CAMSHIFT is based on colors, thus it requires the availability of color histogram of the objects within the video sequences. As mentioned earlier, the color model was built in the HSV domain on the basis of the hue component. The spatial mean value is computed by selecting the parameters of the search window. This makes the search window moved towards center of the image in subsequent steps. Once the search window is centered computing is done through the centroid with first-order instant for x,y. The process is continued till it arrived at the point of junction.

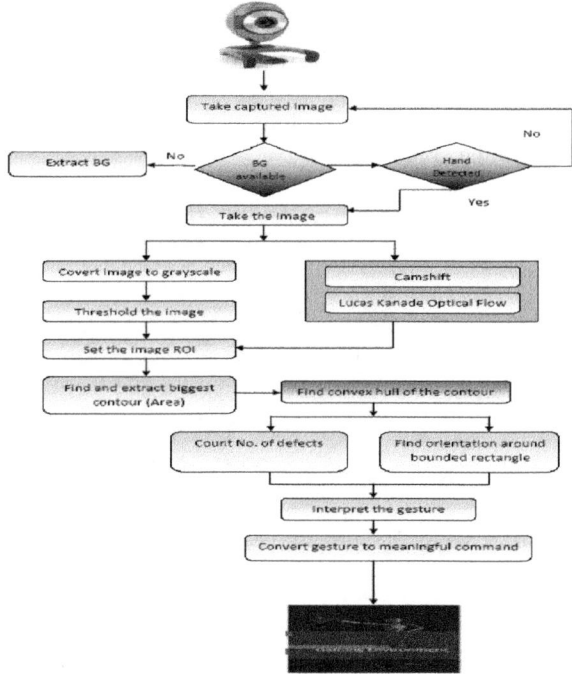

Fig. 1. Virtual game architecture

The tracking technique is made more robust by using Lucas-Kanade optical flow [16]. It provides an accurate local tracking. Though the best solutions to the tracking problem has been obtained by employing the pyramidal execution of Lucas–Kanade classical algorithm [16]. This method makes use of residual pixel displacement vector. It minimizes the error in matching [17]. As the hand is tracked a contour is mapped with the corresponding hand which further extracts corresponding convex hull (area). The recognition has been done through modeling of the hand by mapping to the number of defect formed in it. The system tracks the defects brought forth by the hand gestures and maps to a meaningful command that has been assigned in the application. The application tracks the gestures performed by the hand (defects formed) and maps to the appropriate action assigned in the gesture vocabulary.

4   Experiments

The gesture recognition system used for interactions with virtual game has been developed using OpenCV libraries and implemented in C++.

The application starts with placing the palm in front of capturing device. The webcam then detects the user's hand by creating a rectangle as showed in figure 2.

Fig. 2. Hand Detected

Figure 3 shows the different gestures along with their assigned commands (functions) to control the application.

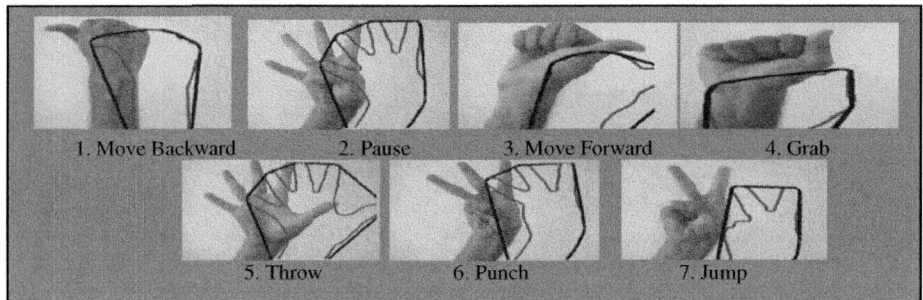

Fig. 3. Designing of gesture vocabulary

5   Results

The virtual game animations (front end) have been designed using OpenGL library. Practical experiments show that our application is implemented well in environments with little noises (i.e., existence of objects whose color is similar to human skin) and with the balanced lightning condition. Execution of the experimental set up of virtual gaming environment resulted in the implementation of different gestures for different commands of the game as is depicted by the figure 4. Where in the figure 4 (a) represents the gesture based command interface of the virtual game with specific depiction of the move backward gesture used for browsing various menu options of the virtual game. Figure 4 (b) represents the virtual game application implemented for the experimental setup of the gesture based user interface. The move forward gesture stands for the command for controlling the movements of birds in the virtual game as depicted in figure 4 (c). The hand gesture used for grabbing of the stick by the virtual human is shown in figure 4 (d). Hand gesture of showing three fingers corresponds to the punching of the bird command in the virtual gaming environment as depicted in figure 4 (e). The hand gesture for throwing the stick towards the bird is shown in figure 4 (f) and jump of the virtual human in figure 4 (g) respectively, and the corresponding hand gestures are five fingers for throwing the stick and two fingers for jump of the virtual human.

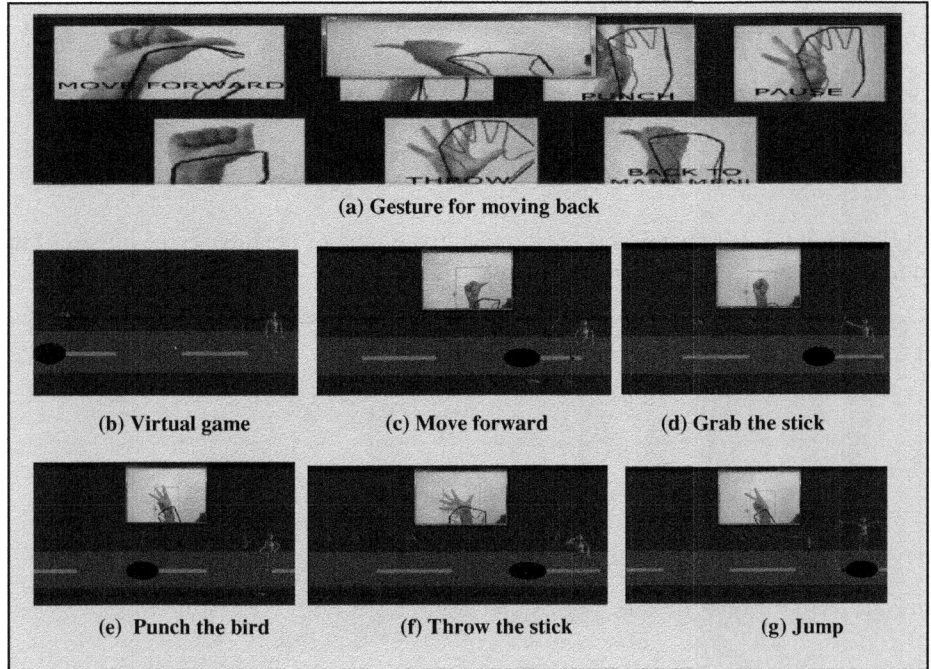

(a) Gesture for moving back

(b) Virtual game   (c) Move forward   (d) Grab the stick

(e) Punch the bird   (f) Throw the stick   (g) Jump

Fig. 4. Results of the interaction of virtual game using hand gestures

6   Testing and Analysis

The performance and viability of the gesture recognition system is carried in the experimental setup where we have interacted with the virtual game. Table 1 exemplifies the number of hits and misses occur during interaction with virtual game by different users through different hand gestures based commands implemented in the gesture based menu.

The performance have been further tested for the application in different environmental condition based on variations in parameters like lighting changes, number of different users etc. Also the application has been implemented for different gestures that could be associated with different possible commands in the virtual game. The result presents a maximum recognition rate of 93 % in the case of jump gesture followed by gesture for move forward with the recognition rate of 90%, lowest recognition rate is for the pause hand gesture that is of 76 %.The punch, move backward and throw gestures are having a recognition rate of 86% and 83% respectively.

Table 1. Hand gesture recognition results

S.No.	Gesture	No. of users played	No. of hits	No. of misses	Recognition rate (%)
1	Move Backward	30	25	5	83.33
2	Pause	30	23	7	76
3	Move Forward	30	27	3	90
4	Grab	30	24	6	80
5	Throw	30	25	5	83
6	Punch	30	26	4	86
7	Jump	30	28	2	93

The below Figure 5 presents the comparative graph of the hits versus misses of the attempts of gesture based commands by the user.

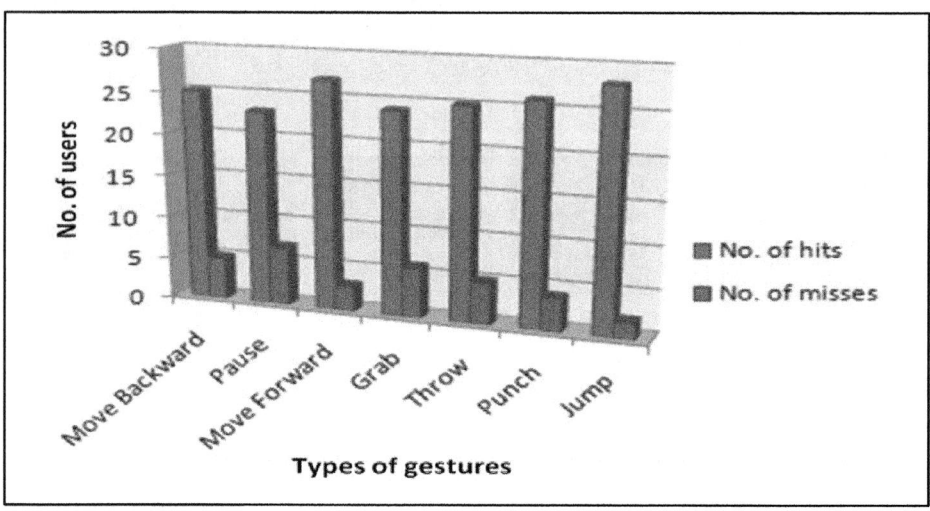

Fig. 5. Comparison of different gestures hits and misses

7   Conclusion and Future Work

The most important advantage of the usage of hand gesture based input modes is that using these techniques the user can interact from a distance without using any computing devices like mouse etc. The application of virtual game controlling through hand gestures proposed and implemented in the present paper provides a suitable efficient and user friendly interface between human and computer for interaction with virtual game using hand gestures. The application also provides a flexibility of defining gestures based on the user interest for specific command which make the application more users friendly and more useful for physically challenged people.

The present application though seems to be feasible and to a greater extent user friendly in comparison to the traditional gaming input modes is somewhat less robust in recognition phase. An attempt to make the input modes less constraints dependent for the users hand gestures has been preferred. But robustness of the application may be increased by applying some more robust algorithms that may help to reduce noise and blur motion in order to have more accurate translation of gestures into commands.

References

1. Conic, N., Cerseato, P., De Natale, F.G.B.: Natural Human- Machine Interface using an Interactive Virtual Blackboard. In: Proceeding of ICIP 2007, pp. 181–184 (2007)
2. O'Hagan, R.G., Zelinsky, A., Rougeaux, S.: Visual gesture interfaces for virtual environments. Interaction with Computers 14, 231–250 (2002)
3. Karlsson, N., Karlsson, B., Wide, P.: A glove equipped with finger flexion sensors as a command generator used in a fuzzy control system. IEEE Trans. on Instrumentation and Measurement, 1330–1334 (1998)
4. van Krevelen, D.W.F., Poelman, R.: A Survey of Augmented Reality Technologies, applications and limitation. The International Journal of Virtual Reality 9(2), 1–20 (2010)
5. Mitra, S., Acharya, T.: Gesture Recognition: A survey. IEEE Transactions on Systems, Man and Cybernetics, Part C: Applications and Reviews 37, 311–324 (2007)
6. Eisenstein, J., Davis, R.: Visual and linguistic information in gesture classification. In: Proceedings of 6th International Conference on Multimodal Interfaces, pp. 113–120. ACM Press (2004)
7. Liu, N., Lovell, B.: Mmx-accelerated Realtime Hand Tracking System. In: Proceedings of IVCNZ 2001 (2001)
8. Rautaray, S.S., Agrawal, A.: A Novel Human Computer Interface Based On Hand Gesture Recognition Using Computer Vision Techniques. In: Proceedings of ACM IITM 2010, pp. 292–296 (2010)
9. Xu, Z., Xiang, C., Wen-hui, W., Ji-hai, Y., Lantz, V., Kong-qiao, W.: Hand Gesture Recognition and Virtual Game Control Based on 3D Accelerometer and EMG Sensors. In: Proceedings of IUI 2009 (2009)
10. Lee, C.S., Ghyme, S.W., Park, C.J., Wohn, K.: The Control of avatar motion using hand gesture. In: Proceeding of Virtual Reality Software and Technology (VRST), pp. 59–65 (1998)
11. Zhang, X., Chen, X., Li, Y., Lantz, V., Wang, K., Yang, J.: A framework for Hand Gesture Recognition Based on Accelerometer and EMG Sensors. IEEE Trans. on Sytems, Man and Cybernetics- Part A: Systems and Humans, 1–13 (2011)
12. Yi, B., Harris Jr., F.C., Wang, L., Yan, Y.: Real-time natural hand gestures. In: Proceedings of IEEE Computing in Science and Engineering, pp. 92–96 (2005)
13. Chen, Q., Georganas, N.D., Petriu, E.M.: Realtime Vision-based Hand Gesture Recognition Using Haar-like Features. In: Proceedings of IEEE Instrument and Measurement Technology Conference, pp. 1–6 (2007)
14. Viola, P., Jones, M.: Rapid object detection using boosted cascade of simple features. In: Proceedings of Computer Vision and Pattern Recognition, pp. 511–518 (2001)
15. Bradski, G.R.: Computer video faces tracking for use in a perceptual user interface. Intel Technology Journal Q2, 1–15 (1998)
16. Yves, B.J.: Pyramidal implementation of the Lucas-Kanade feature tracker. Microsoft Research Labs, Tech. Rep. (1999)
17. Shi, J., Tomasi, C.: Good Features to track. In: Proceedings of IEEE Conference on Computer Vision and Pattern Recognition, pp. 593–600 (1994)

Interval Type-2 Fuzzy Model for Emotion Recognition from Facial Expression

Amit Konar[1], Aruna Chakraborty[2], Anisha Halder[1],
Rajshree Mandal[1], and Ramadoss Janarthanan[3]

[1] ETCE Department, Jadavpur University, Kolkata-32, India
konaramit@yahoo.co.in, {halder.anisha,rajshree.mondal}@gmail.com
[2] Department of Computer Science and Engineering,
St. Thomas College of Engineering and Technology, Kolkata, India
aruna_stcet@rediffmail.com
[3] Department of IT, Jaya Engg. College, Chennai
srmjana_73@yahoo.com

Abstract. The paper proposes a new approach to emotion recognition from facial expression of a subject by constructing an Interval type-2 fuzzy model. An interval type-2 fuzzy face-space is first constructed with the background knowledge of facial features of different subjects for different emotions. The fuzzy face-space thus created comprises primary membership distributions for m facial features, obtained from n subjects, each having l-instances of facial expression for a given emotion. Second, the emotion of an unknown facial expression is determined based on the consensus of the measured facial features with the fuzzy face-space. The classification accuracy of the proposed method is as high as 88.66 %.

Keywords: Emotion Recognition, Feature extraction, Type-2 primary membership, Type-2 secondary membership, Interval Type-2 Fuzzy set.

1 Introduction

There exists extensive works on emotion recognition from facial expression. The study undertaken so far aimed at improving the performance of emotion classification by either selecting suitable features [1], [2], [8] or by identifying the right classifier [3], [4], [5]. However, we are afraid there is hardly any reported work on emotion recognition from facial expression using type-2 fuzzy sets. It is known that type-2 fuzzy sets can eliminate both intra- and inter- personal level uncertainties, which naturally appears in the encoded signals obtained from its fuzzy membership. Usually the fuzzy membership curves are constructed based on individual's personal opinion, which often is bottlenecked because of personal bias or inaccuracy for lack of sufficient knowledge. The problem of uncertainty management in emotion recognition due to intra- and inter- personel variations in features is taken care of in this paper using interval type-2 fuzzy sets (IT2FS).

The paper provides an alternative approach to emotion recognition from an unknown facial expression, when the emotion class of individual facial expression of a large number of experimental subjects is available. IT2FS is used to

M.K. Kundu et al. (Eds.): PerMIn 2012, LNCS 7143, pp. 114–121, 2012.

construct a fuzzy face space based on the measurements of a set of features from a given set of facial expressions carrying different emotions. An unknown facial expression is classified into one of several emotion classes by determining the maximum support of an emotion class to a given set of measurements of a facial expression. The class having the maximum support is declared as the emotion of the unknown facial expression. In spirit, this is similar to how a fuzzy rule based system for pattern classification.

The paper is divided into 5 sections. In section 2, we propose the principle of uncertainty management in fuzzy face-space for emotion recognition. Section 3 provides the experimental details. Performance Analysis based on statistical measurements is given in secion 4. Conclusions are listed in section 5.

2   Uncertainty Management in Fuzzy Face-Space for Emotion Recognition

This section provides a general overview of the proposed scheme for emotion recognition using type-2 fuzzy sets. Here, the emotion recognition problem is considered as uncertainty management in fuzzy space after encoding the measured facial attributes by type-2 fuzzy sets.

Let $F = f_1, f_2, , f_m$ be the set of m facial features. Let $\mu_{\widetilde{A}}(f_i)$ be the primary membership in [0,1] of the feature f_i to be a member of set $\widetilde{A}$, and $\mu(f_i, \mu_{\widetilde{A}}(f_i))$ be the secondary membership of the measured variable f_i in [0,1]. If the measurement of a facial feature, f_i, is performed p times on the same subject experiencing the same emotion, and the measurements are quantized into q intervals of equal size, we can evaluate the frequency of occurrence of the measured variable f_i in q quantized intervals. The interval containing the highest frequency of occurrence then can be identified, and its centre,m_i, approximately represents the mode of the measurement variable f_i. The second moment, σ_i, around m_i is determined, and an exponential bell-shaped (Gaussian) membership function centered on m_i and with a spread σ_i is used to represent the membership function of the random variable f_i. This function represents the membership of f_i to be CLOSE-TO the central value, m_i. It may be noted that a bell-shaped (Gaussian-like) membership curve would have a peak at the centre with a membership value one, indicating that membership at this point is the largest for an obvious reason of having the highest frequency of f_i at the centre.

On repetition of the above experiment for variable f_i on n subjects, each experiencing the same emotion, we obtain n such membership functions, each one for one individual subject. Naturally, the measurement variable f_i now has both intra- and inter-personal level uncertainty. The intra-personal level uncertainty occurs due to pre-assumption of the bell-shape (Gaussian distribution) of the membership function, and the inter-personal level uncertainty occurs due to multiplicity of the membership distribution for n subjects. Thus a new measurement for an unknown person can be encoded using all the n-membership curves, giving n possible membership values, thus giving rise to uncertainty in the fuzzy space. The uncertainty involved in the present problem has been addressed here by IT2FS based approach. We now briefly outline the approach.

2.1   Principles Used in the IT2FS Approach

The primary membership distributions for a given feature f_i corresponding to a particular emotion taken from n-subjects together forms a IT2FS $\widetilde{A}$, whose FOU is bounded by a lower and an upper membership curves $\underline{\mu}_{\widetilde{A}}(f_i))$ and $\underline{\mu}_{\widetilde{A}}(f_i))$ respectively, where

$$\underline{\mu}_{\widetilde{A}}(f_i)) = Min\{\mu_{\widetilde{A}}^1(f_i), \mu_{\widetilde{A}}^2(f_i), ..., \mu_{\widetilde{A}}^n(f_i)\} \tag{1}$$

$$\overline{\mu}_{\widetilde{A}}(f_i)) = Max\{\mu_{\widetilde{A}}^1(f_i), \mu_{\widetilde{A}}^2(f_i), ..., \mu_{\widetilde{A}}^n(f_i)\} \tag{2}$$

are evaluated for all f_i, and $\mu_{\widetilde{A}}^j(f_i), 1 \leq j \leq n$ denotes the primary membership distribution of feature f_i for subject j in IT2FS.

Fig. 1 provides the FOU for a given feature f_i. Now for a given measurement f_i', we obtain an interval $[\underline{\mu}_{\widetilde{A}}(f_i'), \overline{\mu}_{\widetilde{A}}(f_i')]$ representing the entire span of uncertainty of the measurement variable f_i' in the fuzzy space, induced by n primary membership distributions: $\mu_{\widetilde{A}}^j(f_i), 1 \leq j \leq n$. The interval $[\underline{\mu}_{\widetilde{A}}(f_i'), \overline{\mu}_{\widetilde{A}}(f_i')]$, is evaluated by replacing f_i by f_i' in (1) and (2) respectively.

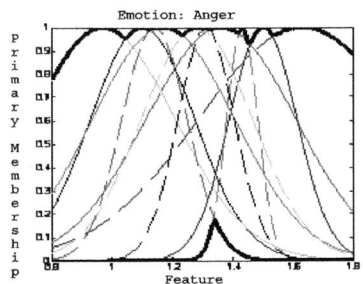

Fig. 1. FOU for feature Mouth-Opening

If there exist m different facial features, then for each feature we would have such an interval, and consequently we obtain m such intervals given by $[\underline{\mu}_{\widetilde{A}}(f_1'), \overline{\mu}_{\widetilde{A}}(f_1')], [\underline{\mu}_{\widetilde{A}}(f_2'), \overline{\mu}_{\widetilde{A}}(f_2')], ..., [\underline{\mu}_{\widetilde{A}}(f_m'), \overline{\mu}_{\widetilde{A}}(f_m')]$.

The proposed IT2FS reasoning system employs a particular format of rules, commonly used in fuzzy classification problems [6]. Consider for instance a fuzzy rule, given by

Rc: if f_1 is $\widetilde{A_1}$ AND f_2 is $\widetilde{A_2}$..... AND f_m is $\widetilde{A_m}$ then emotion class is c.

Here, f_i for i=1 to m are m-measurements (feature value) in the interval type-2 fuzzy sets $\widetilde{A_1}, \widetilde{A_2}, ...\widetilde{A_m}$ respectively, given by

$$\widetilde{A_1} = [\underline{\mu}_{\widetilde{A}}(f_i), \overline{\mu}_{\widetilde{A}}(f_i)], \forall i \tag{3}$$

Since an emotion is characterized by all of these m features, to find the overall support of the m features (m measurements made for the unknown subject) to the emotion class c represented by the n primary memberships, we use the fuzzy meet operation

$$s_c^{min} = Min\{\underline{\mu}_{\tilde{A}}(f_1^/), \underline{\mu}_{\tilde{A}}(f_2^/), ..., \underline{\mu}_{\tilde{A}}(f_m^/)\} \tag{4}$$

$$s_c^{max} = Min\{\overline{\mu}_{\tilde{A}}(f_1^/), \overline{\mu}_{\tilde{A}}(f_2^/), ..., \overline{\mu}_{\tilde{A}}(f_m^/)\} \tag{5}$$

Thus we can say that the unknown subject is experiencing the emotion class c at least to the extent s_c^{min}, and at most to the extent s_c^{max}.

To reduce the non-specificity associated with the interval S_{c-i}, different approaches can be taken. For example, the most conservative approach would be to use lower bound, while the most liberal view would to use the upper bound of the interval as the support for the class c. In absence of any additional information, a balanced approach would be to use center of the interval as the support for the class c by the n primary memberships to the unknown subject. This idea is supported by Mendel [7]. We compute the centre, S_c of the interval S_{c-i},

$$S_c = (s_c^{min} + s_c^{max})/2. \tag{6}$$

Thus S_c is the degree of support that the unknown facial expression is in emotion class c.

Now to predict the emotion of a person from his facial expression, we determine S_c for each emotion class. Presuming that there exist k emotion classes, let us denote them by $S_1, S_2, ..., S_k$ for emotion class 1, 2,..., k, respectively. Since a given facial expression may convey different emotions with different degrees, we resolve the conflict by ranking the S_i for i = 1 to k, and thus determine the emotion class r, for which $S_r \geq S_i$ for all i following the Rule R_c.

To make the algorithm robust, we consider association of fuzzy encoded measurements with emotion class by considering the weakest reliability of the joint occurrence of the fuzzy measurements, and identify the winning emotion class having this measure of reliability superseding the same of other emotion classes.

3   Experimental Details

In this section, we present the experimental details of emotion recognition using the principles introduced in section 2. We here consider 5 emotion classes, (i.e., k=5) including anger, fear, disgust, happiness and relaxation. The experiment is conducted with two sets of subjects: a) the first set of n (=10) subjects is considered for designing the fuzzy face-space and, b) the other set of 30 facial expressions taken from 6 unknown subjects are considered to validate the result of the proposed emotion classification scheme. Five facial features, (i.e., m=5) have been used here to design the type-2 fuzzy face-space.

We now briefly overview the main steps of feature extraction followed by fuzzy face-space construction and emotion recognition of an unknown subject using the pre-constructed face-space.

3.1 Feature Extraction

In order to extract the facial features from emotionally expressive facial images, it is essential to list down the most important features of the face. From earlier research results [5], it is evident that the most important regions for recognizing the emotion of a person are the eyes and lips. This motivated us to select the following features: Left Eye Opening (EO_L), Right Eye Opening (EO_R), Distance between the Lower Eyelid to Eyebrow for Left Eye (LEE_L), Distance between the Lower Eyelid to Eyebrow for Right Eye (LEE_R), and Maximum Mouth opening (MO) including lower and upper lips. Fig. 2 explains the above facial features on a selected facial image.

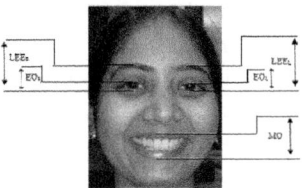

Fig. 2. Facial Features

3.2 Creating the Type-2 Fuzzy Face-Space

The Interval Type-2 fuzzy face-space contains only the primary membership distributions for each facial feature. Since we have 5 facial features and the experiment includes 5 distinct emotions of 10 subjects, we obtain $10 \times 5 \times 5 = 250$ primary membership curves. These 250 membership curves are grouped into 25 heads, each containing 10 membership curves of ten subjects for a specific feature representing a given emotion. One illustration of one such group of 10 membership distributions for the feature EO_L for emotion disgust is given in Fig. 3.

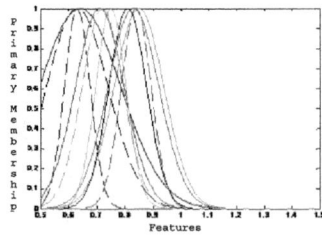

Fig. 3. Membership distributions for emotion disgust and feature EO_L

3.3   Emotion Recognition of an Unknown Subject

The emotion recognition problem addressed here attempts to determine the emotion of an unknown person from her facial expression. To keep the measurements in an emotional expression normalized and free from distance variation from the camera focal plane, we construct a bounding box, covering only the face region, and the reciprocal of the diagonal of the bounding box is used as a scale factor for normalization of the measurements. The normalized features obtained from Fig.4 are enlisted in Table 1. We now briefly explain the experimental results obtained by IT2FS approach.

Fig. 4. Facial Image of an unknown subject

Table 1. Extracted Features of Fig. 4

EO_L	EO_R	MO	LEE_L	LEE_R
0.026	0.026	0.135	0.115	0.115

IT2FS-based Recognition: The IT2FS based recognition scheme considers a fuzzy face space of 5 sets of 10 primary membership distributions as in Fig. 3, where each set refers to one particular feature obtained from 10 sources for an individual emotion. Consequently, for 5 distinct emotions we have 25 such sets of primary membership distributions. Table 2 provides the evaluation of type-2 primary membership values for a feature: EO_L consulting 10 primary distributions obtained from 10 subjects, representative of the facial expression for disgust. The range of these memberships is given in the last column of Table 2. For each feature we obtain 5 Tables like Table 2, each one for a given emotion. Thus for 5 features, we would have altogether 25 such tables. Table 3 provides the results of individual range in primary membership for each feature experimented under different emotional conditions. For example, the entry (0-0.12) corresponding to the row Anger and column EO_L, gives an idea about the extent of the EO_L for the unknown subject matches with known subjects from the emotion class Anger. The results of computing fuzzy meet operation over the range of individual features taken from facial expressions of the subjects under same emotional condition are given in Table 3. The average of the ranges along with its centre value is also given in Table 3. It is observed that the centre has the largest value (=0.3115) for the emotion: happiness.

Table 2. Calculated Type-2 Primary Membership Values for the Feature:EO_L under Emotion: Disgust

Feature	Primary Memberships (μ_{pri})	Range $(min\{\mu_{pri}\}, max\{\mu_{pri}\})$
	0.65	
	0.10	
	0.15	
	0.45	
EO_L(pri)	0.18	0.08-0.65
	0.55	
	0.08	
	0.41	
	0.16	
	0.12	

Table 3. Calculated Feature Ranges and Centre Value for each Emotion

Emotion	Range of Primary Membership for					Features Range S_j^c after fuzzy meet operation (centre)
	EO_L	EO_R	MO	LEE_L	LEE_R	
Anger	0-0.12	0-0.133	0.37-0.864	0.001-0.425	0.003-0.434	0-0.12(0.06)
Disgust	0.08-0.65	0.079-0.67	0-0.474	0.03-0.54	0.03-0.47	0-0.47(0.235)
Fear	0.001-0.0422	0-0.053	0.284-0.826	0.027-0.554	0.031-0.629	0-0.0422(0.0211)
Happiness	0-0.623	0-0.649	0.593-0.926	0.32-0.735	0.284-0.86	0-0.623(0.3115)
Relaxed	0-0.274	0-0.272	0-0.004	0.057-0.528	0.051-0.562	0-0.004(0.002)

4   Performance Analysis

The performance of the proposed emotion classification algorithm is compared with j other algorithms using McNemer's test . Let, $f_A(.)$ and $f_B(.)$ be two classifier outputs obtained by algorithm A and B respectively. In McNemar's test we active a null hypothesis $P_{R,x}[f_A(x) = f(x)] = P_{R,x}[f_B(x) = f(x)]$, where $f(.)$ is actual mapping from $x \in$ traing set R, and P is the probability. Using this hypothesis, we define a statistic, $Z = (|n_{01} - n_{10}| - 1)^2/(n_{01} + n_{10})$, where n_{01} be the number of examples misclassified by A but not by B and n_{10} be the number of examples misclassified by B but not by A. Here we consider, A be our IT2FS algorithm and B is one of the following 3 algorithms: Radial

Basis Function(RBF), Multilayer Perceptron(MLP), and Principal Component Analysis(PCA). Considering the above statistic, we note that the null hypothesis is always rejected, claiming better performance of the classification with others.

5   Conclusion

The paper proposed a simple and time-efficient scheme for emotion recognition from a pre-constructed type-2 fuzzy face-space. Experiments reveal that the classification accuracy of emotion by considering IT2FS is as high as 88.66%. The classical rule based method for emotion classification depends largely on the relational matrix used to represent implication relations. In the present context, the emotion analysis is performed intentionally on the fuzzy encoded measurement space to make the system performance robust.

References

1. Guo, Y., Gao, H.: Emotion Recognition System in Images Based on Fuzzy Neural Network and HMM. In: Proc. 5th IEEE Int. Conf. on Cognitive Informatics (ICCI 2006). IEEE (2006)
2. Zhao, H., Wang, Z., Men, J.: Facial Complex Expression Recognition Based on Fuzzy Kernel Clustering and Support Vector Machines. In: Third International Conference on Natural Computation (ICNC 2007). IEEE (2007)
3. Kharat, G.U., Dudul, S.V.: Neural Network Classifier for Human Emotion Recognition from Facial Expressions Using Discrete Cosine Transform. In: Conference on Emerging Trends in Engineering and Technology. IEEE (2008)
4. Chakraborty, A., Konar, A., Chakraborty, U.K., Chatterjee, A.: Emotion Recognition From Facial Expressions and Its Control Using Fuzzy Logic. IEEE Transactions on Systems, Man and Cybernetics (2009)
5. Kobayashi, H., Hara, F.: The recognition of basic facial expressions by neural network. Trans. Soc. Instrum. Contr. Eng. 29(1), 112–118 (1993)
6. Cordon, O., del Jesus, M.J., Herrera, F.: A proposal on reasoning methods in fuzzy rule-based classification systems. Int. J. of Approximate Reasoning 20 (1999)
7. Mendel, J.M.: On the importance of interval sets in type-2 fuzzy logic systems. In: Proc. Joint 9th IFSA World Congress 20th NAFIPS Int. Conf., Vancouver, BC, Canada, July 25-28, pp. 1647–1652 (2001)
8. Valstar, M., Pantic, M.: Fully Automatic Facial Action Unit Detection and Temporal Analysis. In: Proceedings of the 2006 IEEE Computer Society Conference on Computer Vision and Pattern Recognition Workshop, CVPRW 2006 (2006)

Augmenting Language Tools for Effective Communication

Nandini Bondale and Gaurav Gupta

STCS, Tata Institute of Fundamental Research, Mumbai, India
nandini@tifr.res.in, gauravgupta123@gmail.com

Abstract. Wide spread use of the Internet and tools available on it, help users to communicate well. Good vocabulary is a prerequisite for effective communication, whether written or spoken. Sometimes, while composing text, the user gets stuck for an appropriate word, even though the concept to be communicated is clear in the mind. In this paper, we propose a language tool called 'WordCoin', to suggest the appropriate word options based on the concepts expressed for the intended word. We study the utility of existing dictionaries and networks for such an application. Importantly, we also study how far user's interpretation of a word matches with the meanings quoted in the dictionary. Our study shows, there is a lot of difference between the two. We need to augment the tools to supply the appropriate word based on these observations.

Keywords: Language tool, dictionary, WordCoin, semantic networks.

1   Introduction

Humans use linguistic communication, largely in the form of speech and writing. In the history, writing follows speech. Whether speech or writing, we use symbols to communicate our thoughts, feelings, concepts and abstractions. Language is a rule based communication system composed of meaningful elements and is hierarchically structured. The rules of semantics help us to associate words or phrases with meanings. The rules of syntax help us to arrange the words in proper order.

Communication in the Internet age relies heavily on text. There are useful language tools available for effective written communication. A word whose meaning is unclear can be looked up in the dictionary with ease. Similarly, while composing text, synonyms and related words can be looked up in a thesaurus [1]. Grammar-check can be done on the input text and corrections suggested. Tools like spell-check or thesaurus assume that the basic idea is expressed in a single word by the user. However, there come moments when the user is stuck for the appropriate word while writing, even though the concept or meaning is clear in the mind. At this juncture, we need a tool suggesting the intended word matching the description of the concept given by the user. Need of such tools have been proposed by researchers [2]. We propose a language tool called 'WordCoin', based on our experiment.

M.K. Kundu et al. (Eds.): PerMIn 2012, LNCS 7143, pp. 122–128, 2012.
© Springer-Verlag Berlin Heidelberg 2012

2   What Is 'WordCoin'?

The task of WordCoin is to propose the appropriate words when the user is stuck while composing text. Following examples give some such situations:

1. 'Birds chirp, Dogs bark, Cock - ??'
2. 'Dense air, cannot see clearly, may/may not rain' - ??

At this juncture users need something more than a thesaurus or dictionaries because they don't have a 'search word'. WordCoin is expected to provide the words 'doodle' and 'fog' respectively for above examples. These proposals are based on the concept described by the user which may or may not contain any related word i.e. synonym. We expect WordCoin to be able to work as follows:

Input: puncturing the skin with needles
Output: Tattoo, Acupuncture, Prick

Input: break into many pieces
Output: Shatter, Destroy, Fragment, Disintegrate, Crush

The tool can exist either as a standalone application or an integrated part of a word processor. It could also potentially go through large sections of text and pick out phrases and sentences, to suggest specific words to replace them, making the text shorter, clearer and more precise.

3   Study of Reference Language Tools

In order to design WordCoin, we studied existing language tools assisting users to compose the text and also studied networks, potentially useful for WordCoin.

3.1   Existing Dictionaries

'Onomasiological dictionary' refers to the dictionary which finds word from an idea. Such dictionary is also referred as 'reverse dictionary', although the term is confusing. Sierra [2] lists various types of dictionaries, printed as well as online, falling under this category and compares their output for practical use. He concludes that there is still a gap in the user's need and the solution provided.

The Oxford Reverse Dictionary [3] in the printed form loses the very purpose of such a dictionary. Here, the words are organized by subject. E.g. words related to 'Plants' are categorized into one chapter, words related to 'Travel and Transportation' categorized into another chapter and so on. Searching for the required word in such a form is an inefficient procedure.

'OneLook Reverse Dictionary' [4] is available in electronic form. It works by collecting data from all possible online dictionary applications. In this manner, it searches for the user search terms in the meaning of all possible dictionary words and returns those words which contain the input terms in the meaning. In this effort, the resultant words will be moderately accurate and the probability of finding target words will depend more or less on supplying input terms that match the words in the meaning.

'One word substitution' exercises are a part of the English grammar curriculum and are useful in précis writing. There are several lists available on the Internet mentioning the one word for a phrase or sentence, to help users in this exercise. But they are very limited in scope, although they provide a good starting point.

At this stage, it is interesting to find out whether users think of concepts and words exactly the same way as quoted in the dictionaries. We conducted an experiment to find out what people think when they see a word in isolation. This will be described in section 4.

3.2   Existing Semantic Networks

In this section we highlight some of the semantic networks useful for WordCoin application.

WordNet [5] is an online lexical reference system. It defines 'synsets' of synonymous words representing a single lexical concept and includes word-to-word relations. Its database consists of lexical entries corresponding to unique orthographic forms. Each form is associated with a set of senses. For example, the word 'bass' could mean low-frequency output of a radio or audio system or a type of fish. The numbers in front of some senses are the frequency values obtained from SemCor corpus [6]. This simple listing of lexical entries looks like an ordinary dictionary. However, WordNet contains a set of domain-independent lexical relations which hold among synsets or lemmas, i.e. lexical or semantic pointers, which are useful for WordCoin.

MIT's ConceptNet [7] links the network much more densely i.e. uses a much larger number of relationships, as compared to Wordnet. The training data used for semantic network has been obtained from the Open Mind Commonsense Project [8] and the network is automatically populated using this data. It suggests a model on how one could potentially connect the data for the 'WordCoin' application described in this paper.

ResearchCyc is yet another useful resource for WordCoin, from Open Cyc project [9].

4   Our Experiment

We conducted an experiment to see what concepts people think of, when they see a word in isolation and how much it matches with the dictionary meaning.

A list of 110 uncommonly used yet recognizable words in English was collected, from common sources like newspaper crosswords, magazine texts etc. Uncommonness of words was decided using polysemy count as the criteria, where a lower count indicates infrequent usage. Table 1 lists some sample words used in the experiment.

Table 1. List of sample words

Abandon	Ambiguous	Blackmail	Comment	Conscious
Celebrity	Deed	Disclose	Drench	Fame
Humiliate	Jingle	Laundry	Museum	Nudge
Ritual	Sacred	Scrap	Transition	Vision

The list of words was divided randomly into a set of 5 words each, making a total of 21 sets. These 21 word sets were uploaded on a website. Internet users were invited to type in the meaning of the words, as they interpret it, in the text-box provided next to the word, without referring to any dictionary or consulting other people. No statistical or personal information was collected from the users. Each set of words had an equal probability of getting picked by the system. After the user filled up the responses for a set, we provided an option to randomly select another word set. In this way, we were able to obtain nearly equal number of responses for each word set.

Table 2. A word and its meaning as interpreted by people participating in the experiment

Word	Interpretation by people
Humiliate	angry, to insult someone, to embarrass, to get insulted, to hurt someone's dignity, to lower the dignity, cause to feel shame, to tease a person beyond its limit and which his heart cries out, embarrass the other person, to impose things which the concerned person hates
Mantra	few words of wisdom, brahmins recite it to fool followers, religious rhymes, something that everybody follows or try to do, a trick for shortening the time taken to accomplish a certain feat, a magical spell, a chant or a spell, the procedure of doing something easily, sanskrit shlok, any inspiring enchants or shlokas, formula, repetition of lines
Whirlpool	water being sucked in, a body of water swirling towards a central point, a waterplace or a pool which is constantly whirling or rotating, circular movement of water which sucks things into it, something whirly, water forming a round formation and swallowing what comes in its path at the center, a strong force of water moving in circular motion, a pool of swirling water in the middle of ocean, a big circular kind of thing, storm in ocean, revolving water, water gone crazy and going hey-wire, to go round and round, a swivel formed in water, it is some kind of storm which sets in the sea

Data was also collected in the written format from the people known to us. A list of 30 words was presented to them and they were asked to write the meaning of the word as they interpret it. More than a total of 1000 responses were obtained. Table 2 shows the sample word and the responses received. At this stage we are interested in the qualitatively different responses received and not really the statistics. For easy comparison, Table 3 gives the dictionary meaning of the same words as in Table 2.

Table 3. A word and its meaning as per the Oxford English Dictionary

Word	Dictionary meanings
Humiliate	make (someone) feel ashamed and foolish by injuring their dignity and pride
Mantra	(originally in Hinduism and Buddhism) a word or sound repeated to aid concentration in meditation, a Vedic hymn, a statement or slogan repeated frequently
Whirlpool	a quickly rotating mass of water in a river or sea into which objects may be drawn , typically caused by the meeting of conflicting currents, a turbulent situation from which it is hard to escape, (also whirlpool bath) a heated pool in which hot aerated water is continuously circulated

5   Observations

Following observations, from the experiment as well as the study of our survey, show that more experimentation and preparation is still required to design WordCoin.

5.1   From the Experimental Data

It was interesting to see how people interpreted a single word in a variety of different manner. For the task in hand, we analysed the data to see how far it matches with the dictionary meaning. As evident in Table 2, the experimental data obtained from the hundreds of responses we received, was more than enough to convince us that people's interpretation of words is far dissimilar to concise and precise definitions of the dictionary. People relate words by many other relationships and do not necessarily think in the way a dictionary defines the words to be. Hence it was clear that using an actual dictionary for the WordCoin application was inadequate and would not lead us to an efficient system.

5.2   From the Survey of Reference Tools

Existing semantic networks that were studied connected words with a much higher level of abstraction compared to how real people described and connected actual words. It was proven that none of the existing data networks would provide us the kind of accuracy that would be required in this application.

A dense semantic network had to be developed, which could model, as closely as possible, the relationships that a human mind relates various concepts and words by.

6   Proposed Approach to Build WordCoin

Major requirement of WordCoin is to have the semantic network in a format that can be efficiently and easily incorporated in the application and provides a solid base to both the WSD and Semantic Searching modules of the application.

The responses received from people as part of our experiment were studied to extract a finer list of relationships between words. For example, the following relationships were extracted: 'Jingle is 'soundOf' Bells', 'Red is 'colorOf' Strawberry', where, 'jingle' and 'red' are the words provided in the experiment and 'sound of Bells', and 'color of Strawberry' are the responses obtained. Hence 'sound of', as well as 'color of' is the extracted relationship.

We deduced that relationships themselves will form a hierarchy of their own. It is important to be able to recognize the hierarchical structure and collect together relationships falling under the same category and connect the synsets in the ontology only by the lowest level of relationships obtained. In the above case, both the 'soundOf' and 'colorOf' relationships can be grouped as 'propertyOf', which is already a part of Wordnet. So instead of connecting synsets with relationships like 'propertyOf', we connect them through 'soundOf' and 'colorOf'. We also retain the fact that 'soundOf' and 'colorOf' are sub-properties of 'propertyOf' in a separate relationship hierarchy.

Growing the semantic network by capturing finer and finer relationships between Synsets can only be done manually to begin with. However, openly available data sets like 'The Open Mind Commonsense Project' can be used as the data corpus, instead of seeding the data ourselves. The semantic graph can be modeled as an ontology and an OWL API, like OWL-QL [10], can be used for querying the network. The OWL implementation [11] of WordNet can be chosen as the starting point.

Implementation of a system which is able to deduce related words from a given input would require going through multiple levels of processing. At the first stage, basic preprocessing like running the input through a spell checker is required. The next step will be to figure out parts-of-speech for the input concept using a POS tagger like the Brill Tagger [12]. The POS data obtained via the previous step helps in the morphological parsing (stemming) of individual words in the input, which can be performed using Morphy [13], since it provides POS based stemming. Next, we proceed to disambiguating the word sense for each of the words in the input concept. This could be done using a known semantic distance metric, as in Hirst and St. Onge [14] or Jiang – Conrath [15] or by our own metric generated. The newly formed finer connections using the experimental data such as 'colorOf', 'soundOf', etc. will make calculation of semantic distances more accurate compared to existing semantic networks. We then perform the actual search in the ontology to suggest the appropriate words. As a first degree of approximation, we could propose synsets in the close proximity of the disambiguated synsets. These synsets act as the output of the WordCoin application.

7   Conclusions

We studied how people interpret words in isolation and found that it is dissimilar to the precise and concise meaning given in the dictionary. We found that various resources on the Internet are of no help, when the user is stuck for an appropriate word, as they require a 'search word' for their utility. Existing word networks, which relate words by concepts, provide a good starting point for a more semantically denser network needed for the task of providing the appropriate word for the concept. Our approach to build the WordCoin is mentioned in brief. This tool will not only make communication effective, but it has applications in the areas of language learning, language translation and to build cognitive models.

Acknowledgments. We would like to thank Prof. TV Sreenivas, Indian Institute of Science, Bangalore for his invaluable comments and contributions while preparing the manuscript. We also thank the Internet community and our friends and family members for their contribution in providing the data for our experiment.

References

1. Olsen, M.: ARTFL project: ROGET'S thesaurus (1991)
2. Sierra, G.: The onomasiological dictionary: a gap in lexicography. In: Proceedings of EURALEX (2000)
3. Edmonds, D.: The Oxford Reverse Dictionary. Oxford University Press, Oxford (1999)
4. OneLook Reverse Dictionary, http://onelook.com/reverse-dictionary.shtml
5. Fellbaum, C.: WordNet: An Electronic Lexical Database. The MIT Press (1998)
6. SemCor Corpus, http://www.cse.unt.edu/~rada/downloads.html#semcor
7. MIT ConceptNet, http://csc.media.mit.edu/conceptnet
8. Open Mind Commonsense, http://openmind.media.mit.edu
9. OpenCyc, http://www.cyc.com/opencyc
10. Fikes, R., Hayes, P., Horrocks, I.: OWL-QL - A Language for Deductive Query Answering on the Semantic Web. Journal of Web Semantics (2004)
11. van Assem, M., Gangemi, A., Schreiber, G.: Conversion of WordNet to a standard RDF/OWL representation. In: Proceedings of the Fifth International Conference on Language Resources and Evaluation (2006)
12. Brill, E.: A Simple Rule Based Part Of Speech Tagger. In: Proceedings of the Third Conference on Applied Natural Language Processing, ANLC (1992)
13. WordNet Morphy, http://wordnet.princeton.edu/man/morphy.7WN.html
14. Hirst, G., St-Onge, D.: Lexical chains as representations of context for the detection and correction of malapropisms. In: Fellbaum, C. (ed.) WordNet: An Electronic Lexical Database. The MIT Press, Cambridge (1998)
15. Jiang, J.J., Conrath, D.W.: Semantic Similarity Based on Corpus Statistics and Lexical Taxonomy. In: Proceedings of International Conference Research on Computational Linguistics (ROCLING X), Taiwan (1997)

Design and Evaluation of a Cognition Aware File Browser for Users in Rural India

Debmalya Sinha and Anupam Basu

Department of Computer Science and Engineering,
Indian Institute of Technology, Kharagpur
Kharagpur, India

Abstract. Among GUI Users throughout the world, the File Browsers are important programs for daily computer use. Making the interface "cognition-aware" results in significant reduction in cognitive load specially for the less technology-aware users while learning and using the interface for file browsing tasks. In this paper we propose SahajBrowser, a special type of cognition-aware, Navigational File Browser for digital technology inexperienced, neo-computer literates in rural India. The novel design of its treeview and abilities to open multiple folders at once, provides more assistance for human cognition and for certain file browsing tasks, performs better than the other widely used Spatial and Navigational file browsers. With a KLM-GOMS model analysis, we will compare 4 browsers of different type and conclude that the design of SahajBrowser is the most time efficient of them all.

1 Introduction

User Interfaces (UIs) are the bridge between user and a computer system. It provides the assistance which enables the user to do the work more easily and faster. For using any UI, a human user has to learn the interface and relate each action taken on the UI (like a mouse click) with the actual task done in behind. For these reasons, users' cognition comes first while designing an UI; i.e. how easily the user can learn and use the UI. As a result, UIs are often made as a projection of an existing worldview (eg: the desktop metaphor for office workers) of the user, so that he does not have to learn the interface and can relate to it naturally. Failing to do this results in high cognitive load while trying to learn and adopt the new worldview and map that to the computer interface. For example, a poor farmer in rural India is not familiar with the concept Desktop in real life. Learning and adopting the Desktop based UI for them will be a tough task while most people all over the world are using it without any glitch. A *cognition-aware* UI can take care of reducing the cognitive load of learning and using the interface for these users.

In recent times, many government and private projects are setting up Internet kiosks across villages in India. The target users are low literate rural people, unaware of digital technology. Users have to learn to use the interface of these deployed computers first for a considerable amount of time and then actually

M.K. Kundu et al. (Eds.): PerMIn 2012, LNCS 7143, pp. 129–136, 2012.
© Springer-Verlag Berlin Heidelberg 2012

use it. The challenge is to make a cognition-aware UI which provides necessary cognitive assistance to be intuitive for them to adapt; so that they can learn to work with the system without much cognitive load and in less learning time.

We have been developing such a cognition aware file browser, **SahajBrowser**, as a part of "**Sahaj Linux**"[2], a Linux based Gnome Desktop wrapper exclusively for users in rural India. The folder hierarchy is a tough concept to grasp for the beginners. SahajBrowser has a unique tree-view to show folder contents hierarchically that provides cognitive assistance for the beginners in terms of Schema Acquisition and Short Term Memory management to make the concept more graspable for them. In addition to this, SahajBrowser goes out of the common discreet file browsing tasks like open, copy, paste, delete, etc. and optimizes the use of full file browsing activity like file/folder rearranging, traversing and comparing folders, etc.

In this paper, we will be discussing how SahajBrowser provides assistance for the making the process of cognition of the UI easier for the user. We also discuss how the design is efficient in file browsing activities compared with other browsers. The next section (section 2) describes the design of SahajBrowser and the cognition awareness of it. After that, in section 3 we present a file browsing activity which we model and analyze with KLM-GOMS[7][5] to compare the completion time of the activity in section 4 and show that the SahajBrowser design is more efficient than the existing file browser.

2   A Cognition Aware File Browser - SahajBrowser

2.1   Design Issues of File Browsers

Unlike recent 3D interfaces, the 2D mouse based approaches are cost effective, and is not necessarily mapped with sophisticated mental models. For this reason we will restrain our scope only with mouse based 2D file browsers. File Browsers provide the interface to interact with files (Open Create, Delete, etc), browse them and arrange them by cut-copy-paste operations. The goal of designing the interface of a file browser is to speed up firstly the learning time for the target user and secondly, the task completion time after the user has learned the interface. We have the following design issues for speeding up learning time in a file browser.

1. **Showing the Relationship between Parent and Child Folders:** The concept of a folder containing into another folder and hence creating a hierarchy-of-folders is the first concept to grasp for the new learners. A folder can contain a file or another folder. And on opening such a folder, a file browser shows the contents of the opened folder. A file browser has the task to show the contents of a filesystem in such a manner that the relationship between parent and child folders becomes clear. Traditional spatial File Browsers does not show the parent folder and the contents of it at the same time clearly. As at a point of time, either a parent folder is shown or a child folder is shown, but not both. This incurs much cognitive load for the

new users to relate to the concept of folder hierarchy. Later we discuss that in our proposed browser, we made an unique Treeview design which answers this problem.

Every file browser does the same basic job of opening, deleting, copy pasting files and folders. However, an entire *file browsing activity* like rearranging several files from several folders into other folders, or comparing the contents of the folders by traversing them is constructed of those basic services (open,cut-copy-paste etc.) which a file browser provides. The goal is to propose a design which emphasizes on to make these everyday file folder related activities of a user easy and fast. While creating, opening, and deleting tasks are trivial for any file browser interface, we focus mainly on organizing and viewing files efficiently.

2. **Organizing files:** selecting files from multiple folders at once : In daily life, organizing files into one suitable folder is a frequent job for a user. The most intuitive way is to opening the source folders, selecting the files to be copied, and then paste them into the destination folders. No file browser supports selection from multiple folders at a time, resulting copying files from one folder to another and repeating the process for all the source folders all over.

3. **Showing large amount of child folders tactically:** Though the Treeview browsers can not select from multiple folders, they can , however, open multiple folders. Problem arises when there are a large number of child folders in the folders. While showing the list of the folders in the traditional Treeview, the list gets too large to handle.

2.2   SahajBrowser Design

The proposed design of SahajBrowser solves the issues described in section 2.1. Unlike the conventional File Browsers, it is designed for directly doing the file/folder activity rather than just providing interface for basic open-delete-cut-copy-paste type constructs. For example, the design enables the user to arrange files or folders efficiently using the same cut-copy-paste mechanism, but in a easy, intuitive and much faster way. Below we discuss what design of SahajBrowser enables a user doing such tasks faster.

1. SahajBrowser **allows users to open multiple directories at once**. The conventional tabbed browsers (Example: Nautilus in Linux, Windows Explorer and Xplorer2 in Windows, Finder in Macintosh etc.) can also open multiple directories but do not show them all at once because the design is to hide that part of the viewport by the tabbed panes.

2. In SahajBrowser, **users can select multiple files from multiple folders at the same time**. E.g. in conventional file browsers, if a user selects file X from directory A and then selects another file Y from directory B, her previous selection of file X from A gets ignored and only the selection of the later file Y is retained. In SahajBrowser, we create a selected file list which allows to select both the files, X from folder A and file Y from folder B.

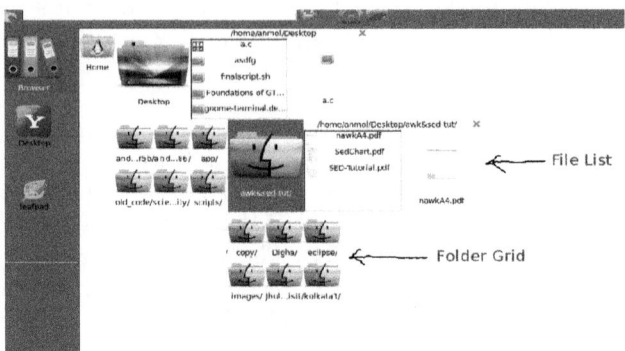

Fig. 1. SahajBrowser design - NEW version

3. SahajBrowser has a compact Treeview design (fig.2.2) which **decreases firstly the mouse pointing time** while traversing directories and secondly, **makes finding the parent-child folder relationship cognitively easier** to the user than the layered approach in conventional browsers.

In the following sections, we will prove that this design performs better than the existing file browsers.

2.3   Cognition Awareness in SahajBrowser Design

We have included two types of cognition awareness, as described in section 1 in SahajBrowser. The design we propose in SahajBrowser firstly helps building the mental model for the abstract concepts like folder hierarchy through **Schema Acquisition**. It also manages the STM of the user to reduce cognitive load while using the UI.

The schema acquisition is a learning technique where the schema is a cognitive construct that organizes the input information according to the way they will be perceived and used by the users. Newer schema adds and forms a connection (though not necessarily always) with earlier schema and thus helps building users' mental model for the specified UI. For example, showing folders and files in a treelike hierarchical construct helps to acquire the notion of parent-child hierarchy of folders in an UNIXlike filesystem.

From the users' viewpoint, this abstract concept of folder hierarchy is difficult to grasp for novice users using non treeview browsers. SahajBrowser provides an unique treeview(fig.2) to show the folders and files in a hierarchical design(see fig.2.2). Seeing a tactically placed child folders under just below its parent folder helps users visualize the hierarchy, thus acquiring a schema for the concept and building the mental model for it. This piece of information generates a schema in users' mind which will be useful for every file browser related tasks and even to acquire more new schema like copy and pasting file/folders etc.

Short term memory management is another very important job for a cognition aware UI. The information user processes in real time resides in the short term memory (STM) of the user. This has a very short data-retaining time. If the STM is not refreshed frequently, previous information in it makes way for new information and itself gets vanished. For example, if there is a need to make user remember a particular thing, it can be showed along with the new information to refresh the short term memory of the user.

As STM is volatile, humans tend to forget what is not refreshed from time to time unless the schema or notion of it is acquired in the Long Term Memory(LTM). In any widely used spatial or navigational browser, users can only open one folder at a time. This way, novice users tend to forget what was in the previous folder before because the information about the new folder contents deletes the previous information in the STM of the user. If there is a way for showing multiple folders simultaneously(fig:2), the STM of the user can be refreshed by seeing the previous information along with the new ones. In SahajBrowser, user can open multiple folders at a time and view the contents(fig:2). This way the STM can be refreshed and the user do not need to *remember* the previous folder's content resulting decreased cognitive load.

After this description of cognitive assistances provided by SahajBrowser, in the next sections, we will describe a file browsing activity and compare the time needed to to complete them by KLM-GOMS modeling.

3   Description of File Rearranging Activity

As described in section 2.2, the design of SahajBrowser targets to reduce interaction time for whole file browsing activity instead of the basic tasks like open, copy etc. Below we describe **File rearranging activity** which exploits the ability of SahajBrowser to show multiple folders and select from them.

In this task, we will copy multiple files from multiple directories into a single destination directory. It is also equal to the task with more than one destination directories and will produce similar results. This task is very useful while arranging files from various folders. In example, users often download or copy various types of files into arbitrary places and the order is generally not maintained while copying/downloading. The user may rearrange their music files into a single organized Music directory cleanly sorted by singers. We model this task for four different browsers using KLM-GOMS model to calculated estimated task completion times in section 4 and compare the results in section 4.3.

There will be two versions of the SahajBrowser to compare for the task, along with Nautilus as a Spatial browser and Windows Explorer as a Navigational (treeview) browser. Here we will show that the treeview browsers like Windows Explorer and SahajBrowser are much more time-efficient than the spatial ones and among the treeview browsers, SahajBrowser performs better.

4   Analysis of File Rearranging Activity

4.1   File Rearranging Task Analysis

As described in section 3, we will model a file rearranging task for the comparison between four file browsers using **KLM-GOMS** model and calculate the interaction time in mSec to compare the results. Users will only use a mouse to give inputs to the system. No keyboard or other inputs like speech has been used for the task. In the next subsections, we describe the task and present the ideas to complete that task for all the four browsers to compare. For the KLM-GOMS analysis, we will assume average level of directories as 4 where level is the number of folders in the path of that folder.

4.2   GOAL Description and Analysis

Our primary Goal is to copy a set of files from different folders of different levels and hierarchies into a single folder. In example, we want to copy file a, b and c from the directory **/home/user1/music** (level 3) and file **w, x, y** and **z** from folder **/home/user2/Downloads/media** (level 4) to the directory **/home/user3/Desktop/Songs** (level 4). Here we copy files from directories of different hierarchy and levels into another directory.

Nautilus: The idea is first to open a source folder (by subgoal open folder), select the set of the files to be copied (by subgoal select), press the copy button and go back to the root of the source folder hierarchy by pressing the up button for (lev) times where *lev* is the source folder level. After that open the destination folder and press the paste button to paste the selected files into the destination folder. Now we have k number of such source folders to copy from. So we repeat the above mentioned procedure for k times to complete the task. The KLM-GOMS analysis of Nautilus gives task completion time: 35400 ms.

Explorer: The idea is to first open the destination folder in the Treeview. Then we open one source folder and select the set of files from it and press the copy button. Next we select the destination folder and press the paste button to paste the selected files. We repeat this process for all the K source folders to complete the task.
    The KLM-GOMS analysis of Explorer gives task completion time: 34000 ms.

SahajBrowser-OLD: The idea is to open all the K source folders all at a time. Unlike other browsers, both the versions of SahajBrowser can open and show multiple folders all at once and the user can select files from multiple folders at a time. It is like selecting file X from folder Y and file A from folder B and keeping both the selections. By this feature, we select all the files to copy from all the open folders and press the copy button. Next, we open the destination folder D and press the paste button to paste all the selected files. The KLM-GOMS analysis gives task completion time: 21600 ms.

SahajBrowser-NEW: The idea is same with the idea of SahajLinux-OLD. The only change in SahajLinux-NEW is, unlike the older version which opens file list of a folder in a separate pane, it integrates the file list with the folder itself. In the old version, after opening a folder, the user had to locate the corresponding file list in the separate pane. That requires a significant extra time and cognitive overhead. The new version of SahajBrowser cuts that time and cognitive load by displaying the file list where the folder is opening.

The KLM-GOMS analysis of gives task completion time: 20000 ms.

4.3   Comparison of File Rearrange Task

While building a new design for a file browser, our hypothesis was to target the whole file browsing activity rather than the single tasks like Open, Create, Delete, cut-copy-paste operations. We described the design first and showed that the design helps users to learn and use the Interface of it. From the graph at fig.2(b) above, Treeview Browsers are more Time-efficient than the rest. The success of the Treeview browsers over the conventional browsers is behind their ability to open multiple folder window at once. This saves the extra overhead of going back up in the directory path hierarchy in the non-treeview browsers. Now the three treeview models we have analyzed, SahajBrowser is better efficient than all. The reason behind this is the ability of SahajBrowser to select multiple files from multiple directories all at once.

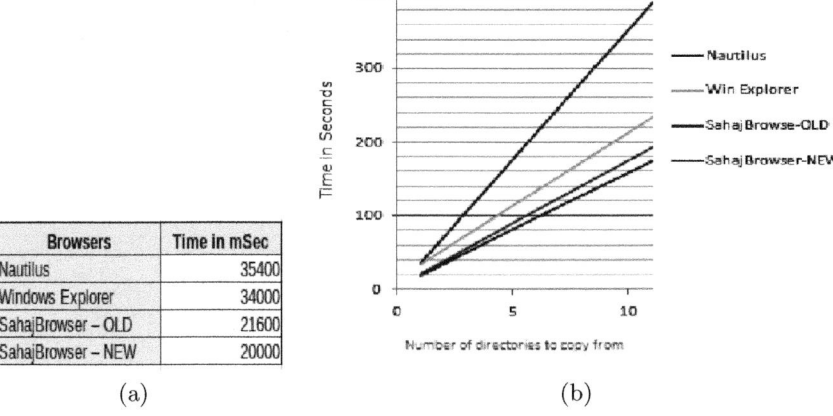

Browsers	Time in mSec
Nautilus	35400
Windows Explorer	34000
SahajBrowser – OLD	21600
SahajBrowser – NEW	20000

(a)   (b)

Fig. 2. Comparison of File Rearrange Task completion time

5   Future Scope

The design of SahajBrowser and the complete SahajLinux is still evolving. While this work lays the foundation of the design that makes it more efficient among the contemporary browsers, we are also working on to make it more intuitive to learn and use for the neo-computer literates. We are doing user interaction surveys as well to know how this design helps users' cognition towards file browsing.

In our next work, we hope to present the cognitive load analysis from user interaction surveys of various other features of the SahajBrowser and SahajLinux itself to prove efficiency for file browsing tasks and show that it is actually easier to learn and use for the neo-computer literates.

Acknowledgements. We thank SNLTR, Kolkata for funding the Sahaj Linux project; Mr. Tirthankar Dasgupta, Mr. Soumyajit Dey, Mr. Sandipan Mandal and Miss Haimabati Dey, IIT Kharagpur, for various helps in process of the research and development of Sahaj Linux and SahajBrowser.

References

1. Shen, S.-T., Woolley, M., Prior, S.: Towards culture-centred design. Interacting with Computers 18(4), 820–852 (2006)
2. Sinha, D., Mandal, S., Basu, A.: Sahaj Linux. In: 2010 IEEE Students' Technology Symposium (TechSym), pp. 318–324 (2010)
3. John, B.E., Kieras, D.E.: The GOMS family of user interface analysis techniques: comparison and contrast. ACM Transactions on Computer-Human Interaction (TOCHI) 3(4) (December 1996)
4. Kieras, D.: Using the Keystroke-Level Model to Estimate Execution Times
5. Card, S., Morn, T.P., Newell, A.: The keystroke-level model for user performance with interactive systems. Communications of the ACM 23, 210–396 (1980)
6. Card, S., Moran, T.P., Newell, A.: The Psychology of Human-Computer Interaction. Lawrence Erlbaum Associates, Hillsdale (1983)
7. John, B., Kieras, D.E.: Using GOMS for user interface design and evaluation: Which technique? ACM Transactions on Computer-Human Interaction 3(4), 287–319 (1996a)

Shiksha: A Novel Architecture for Tele-teaching Using Handwriting as a Perceptually Significant Temporal Media

Amit Singhal, Santanu Chaudhury, and Sumantra Dutta Roy

Electrical Engineering Department, IIT Delhi, New Delhi, India-110016
{amit.singhal,santanuc,sumantra}@ee.iitd.ac.in

Abstract. In this paper we present Shiksha – an integrated architecture which incorporates handwritten illustrations captured and rendered in a temporal fashion synchronized with audio and video data. The architecture of Shiksha permits non-linear growth in the form of multiple hierarchically organized play streams. We have developed an asynchronous multimedia conferencing application in which the users are provided with an authoring and rendering environment to record and view lectures. It also allows the users to ask and reply to doubts in the previously stored lectures making it a fully interactive but asynchronous system.

Keywords: Handwriting, Tele-teaching, Video Conferencing, Web Server.

1   Introduction

Use of integrated audio, video and text is a part of various experiential meeting, lecture capture and collaborative systems like [1], [2], [3], [4], [5], [6]. Beyond audio and video, some systems [3], [1], [7] have also captured the corresponding whiteboard data or slides. Among the handwriting enabled systems, [8] have designed and developed a virtual notepad which takes handwriting inputs from the user and stores it in the form of strokes without applying any recognition. Apoerri [9] has developed tools to annotate audio-video segments using handwritten data which is however stored as images. Schilit et al [10] have used a tablet and pen based system to enable a user to underline, highlight, or scribble comments on online documents. But none of the works has yet experimented with using handwriting as a temporal medium, and capturing and presenting the same in synchronization with the corresponding audio and video. Recognizing handwriting as a data type in itself, rather than limiting it by applying handwriting recognition, opens up a new and natural way of expression.

The major contribution in this paper is integrated document architecture, named as Shiksha, which integrates handwritten notes as a temporal medium synchronized in time with the corresponding audio and video data. It is an improvement over the architecture proposed in [11], specifically for the purpose of tele-teaching. Other unique features of Shiksha are as follows:

M.K. Kundu et al. (Eds.): PerMIn 2012, LNCS 7143, pp. 137–144, 2012.
© Springer-Verlag Berlin Heidelberg 2012

— Support for audio and video, along with handwritten illustrations.
— Integration of multiple play streams into a single logical document entity. This feature allows non-linear growth of the document, i.e. new play streams can be added and existing play streams can be modified.
— Integrated mechanisms to capture, transfer and render the media content in a mutually synchronized way, thus avoiding need to invoke separate applications or the use of attachments.

In the next section, we present the perceptual aspects in design. After that, we present the integrated document architecture for Shiksha. In the later sections, we describe an asynchronous video conferencing application in which we demonstrate the effective and immersive communication made possible by using Shiksha.

2   Perceptual Aspects in Design

Presentation without the presence of a person is not very effective as people tend to lose their interest. Hence, visual component becomes an integral part of the system. But then we also need to keep in mind the high bandwidth requirements for video-based systems. So, the main challenge is to hold the attention of the user, albeit the given bandwidth constraint. There has to be a judicial mixture of handwriting, audio and video. The resultant environment should give the user an experience similar to sitting in an actual classroom. For this purpose, a portion of the available bandwidth would be reserved for the continuous streaming of the audio and handwriting. The remaining bandwidth would be used for video. For small bandwidth, the video cannot be presented as a continuous stream. To solve this problem, there would be a small window (as shown in Fig. 1) which would show the video for small intervals along with the continuous stream of the audio and handwriting. These small intervals would be appropriately chosen on the basis of the lecture content. In between these intervals the video would disappear, thus saving on the bandwidth. The video would reappear at the next relevant instant in the lecture. This would use the given bandwidth in an optimal manner, and also provide an immersive experience to the user.

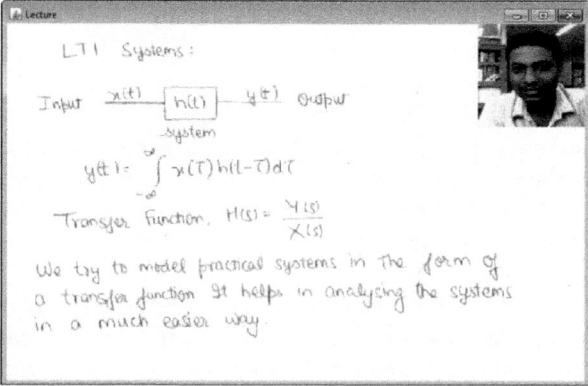

Fig. 1. Small video window on the handwriting panel

3   Document Architecture

Shiksha is a logical document entity which is an integration of multiple hierarchically organized play streams. A play stream can comprise multiple media streams which are rendered in synchronization using playback. In this section, we describe the encoding of the media streams particularly the handwritten data, synchronization of different media streams, viewing and rendering of Shiksha.

We have chosen 'QuickTime' as the video data-encoding format. For audio coding, we have used the 'wav' format. The handwriting stream is stored in the form a text file as a sequence of (x,y) coordinates of pen strokes. The current system design is flexible enough to allow change in the audio, video encoding formats. Change in the audio-video encoding formats does not affect the synchronization relations between the audio, video and the corresponding handwritten data.

Handwriting as a temporal medium is known as ink. It is more natural to draw, write, sketch using a pen rather than using a keyboard and mouse. The novel concept that has been employed in the design of this system is the preservation of temporal characteristics of handwritten data. This further enhances the communication experience, as the temporal characteristics of handwriting are captured and preserved while it is rendered back at the recipient end, giving the user the feel that the other person is writing in front of him. To facilitate use of ink data across devices and different system architectures, it is required to have a standardized representation. With the objective of having a universal standard for representing handwriting or ink, the Multi-modal Interaction working group at W3C has initiated work on one such standard named InkML, i.e. Ink Markup Language [12] which supports a complete and accurate representation of digital ink and allows temporal representation through the use of time-stamps. A typical ink document format is shown below.

```
<ink >
<captureDevice>
<channelDef name="T">
<representation type="integer" units="ms"
relativeTo="trace"/>
</channelDef>
</captureDevice>
<traceFormat id="default">
<regularChannels>
</ channel name="X" type="integer />
</ channel name="Y" type="integer />
</ channel name="T" type="integer />
</regularChannels>
</traceFormat>
<trace id="t001" timeOffset="5"> 10 20 100 11 20
120 13 20 215 19 21 290 </trace>
</ink >
```

It shows 3 channels, X, Y (which denote the x, y coordinates of each pixel of the stroke), and T which denotes the time-stamp when it was drawn. Each stroke of handwritten data is denoted as a trace and identified by a unique trace identifier.

The timeOffset contains the time-stamp when rendering of this trace is to be started. The relativeTo tag defines that the T values are relative to beginning time-stamps of individual traces. The T channel format is specifically defined in the beginning of the document using the channelDef tag. The tag regularChannels denotes that the channels embedded inside it will always have data for each pixel, i.e. all the three data values will always be present for each pixel. In our system design we have kept the different media streams in their respective containers. The advantage of this approach as against the option of having a single container for all the different media streams is that it makes the packaging independent of the audio video formats and avoids hassles of multiplexing the intermittent hand written data with the more continuous audio visual content.

3.1   Synchronization of Media Streams

To enable the temporal capture and synchronization of handwritten data with audio and video, we propose a time-stamp based synchronization mechanism for intra-media and inter-media synchronization of hand-written data. The synchronization between the consecutive data units of a temporal medium is termed as intra-media synchronization whereas that across such temporal media is termed as inter-media synchronization [13]. In our system, Java Media Framework has been used. The three media: Audio, Video, and Handwriting are transmitted over the network as two different streams (Audio-Video combined + Handwriting). We have focused on addressing the issues related to intra-media and inter-media synchronization of handwritten data since this task has not been addressed earlier.   Every time the user starts authoring a document, the authoring environment starts a message clock which counts milliseconds from 0 onwards. When the user writes anything, the pen device generates events. The authoring environment responds to these events by noting down the pixel coordinates and the time-stamps derived from the message clock and stores this information in a text file.

When playing back the document, the renderer reads the stored text file containing the pixel coordinates and the time-stamps when they are to be rendered. The synchronization is done by buffering the received handwriting stream and not directly displaying on the handwriting panel and waiting for the client to receive the next 40ms time-stamped data of merged audio-video stream. Once the wait is over, the buffered handwriting data is displayed on the panel. Synchronizing the handwritten data to the message clock time rather than the time-stamps on audio-video helps make the system audio-video codec independent as well as independent of any effect of transcoding. Further the solution is applicable to different message types viz. audio-video, audio only, video only, etc.

The temporal arrangement of different play streams is achieved through synchronization based on virtual axis which is a subtype of axes based synchronization [13]. It supports the use of several virtual axes to create a virtual coordinate space. If each document path is assumed to be a virtual axis then its immediate child paths are arranged with respect to this axis, i.e. with respect to its parent stream time. This approach has a distinct advantage rather than using a global time axis to manage the document path hierarchy. Whenever a new path is added to the hierarchy, its start time is calculated with respect to the main path.

3.2   Viewing and Editing in Shiksha

Shiksha can have multiple play streams which can be organized in the form of a tree. The play stream which has got no parent is called as the root play stream. A user is presented with a hierarchical view of the different play streams in a Shiksha. The user can select the stream which he would like to watch. He can also use a tracker bar to locate a time point at which he would want to begin watching the selected play stream. The audio and video contents of the message first get downloaded on the local machine of the user, and it gets played from there. In addition, it supports multiple users to access the system at one time. The user can also select the child streams he is interested in watching rather than having to view them all. This provides instant access to the message segment the user is interested in viewing, rather than having to wait until the whole message is downloaded. During playback of a play stream the user is presented with the option of loading and viewing any concurrent child stream(s). The user may continue watching the parent stream or may select a child stream in which case the content of the child stream is played by the rendering engine.

Since Shiksha allows non-linear growth of the document, a new play stream can be linked to any point on an existing play stream. The added stream is considered as a child of the parent stream and it carries information about the ID of the parent stream and the time offset (from the start of the parent stream) for the point at which it is linked to the parent stream.

4   Deploying Shiksha for Asynchronous Video Conferencing System

We have developed an authoring and rendering engine for Shiksha. As an application of such integrated documents, we have developed a client-server based multimedia conferencing system in congruency with the paradigm of asynchronous communication. It basically acts as an ecosystem of offline lecture dissemination. A schematic diagram for the application is shown in Fig. 2.

4.1   Implementation Details

The implementation has been done in java. The various components involved are briefly described below.

GlassFish Server. The application is hosted on a GlassFish server. GlassFish is an open source application server project led by Sun Microsystems for the Java EE platform. It uses a derivative of Apache Tomcat as the servlet container for serving Web content, with an added component called Grizzly for scalability and speed.

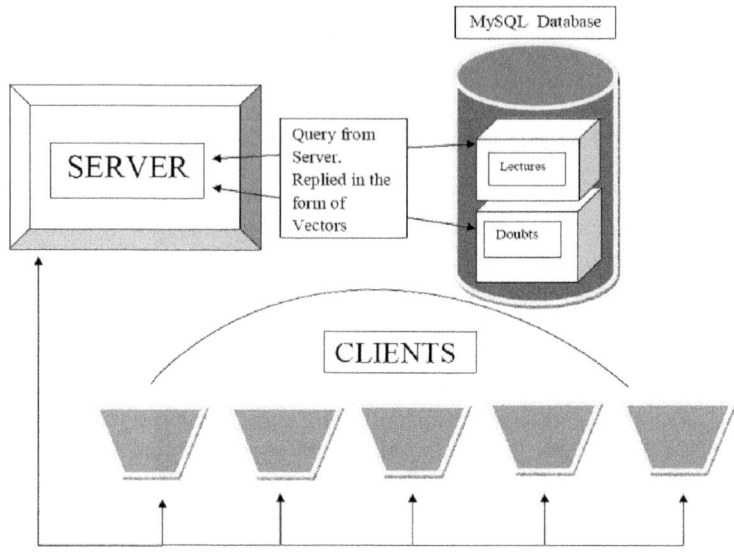

Fig. 2. Schematic Diagram

MySQL Database. The next step is creation of a Database. This is done using MySQL. MySQL is a relational database management system (RDBMS) that runs as a server providing multi-user access to a number of databases. The database has two tables: Lectures and Doubts as shown in Fig. 2. Lecture table stores all the details of the lecture and doubts stores the details of the doubts. These lectures and their corresponding doubts and comments are available for viewing to the clients and further additions can be made to them.

Java Servlets. There are five Java servlets which handle the calls from different clients and are responsible for separate functionalities. The call to these servlets is made in different points on the setup and playback timeline of the client application. Apart from handling the client requests, server provides the option of recording new lectures and adding clarifications in between the lecture in much the same way as the client adds doubt/comment to the lecture. This is achieved through two dedicated Java applications installed on the server.

The application can also be accessed through browser by entering the URL of the web server. The link of opening the required Java application is provided on the web page which when clicked by the user starts the properly guided lecture watching session on his/her terminal. This functionality is achieved by converting the executable JAR application file into a Java Web Start Application and deploying it onto the web server for direct access. The file available on the web page is essentially a JNLP (Java Network Launch Protocol) file. The web server is currently a local server at the multimedia lab in IIT Delhi which can be moved to a larger server space outside the IIT, if situation demands (increase in traffic/hits).

4.2   Functioning

View Lecture. When a client requests to view a lecture, then the server application sends a query to the database, which in turn refers to the lecture table and the available choice of the lectures is presented to the user. Since it is a repository of lectures and there will be more than one lecture, the user can chose which lecture he wants to view. A second choice is presented to the user, as to which doubt threads is he interested in viewing. Now the server accesses all the files – lectures, doubts, and comments related to that particular lecture thread and sends them to the client. All the files are stored in the client's cache, from where they are ready to be played back. Depending upon his choice, the lecture playback starts with the desired doubt threads popping in at their relevant timeline locations.

Raising a Doubt. During the lecture playback, the user might have questions or doubts in his mind. There is a system in place so that a user can conveniently ask his doubt. The user can ask a new doubt at any stage by clicking at the button 'Ask a new doubt', which would pause the playback of the lecture. His camera, microphone and the handwriting panel are activated and the query is sent to the server after the recording. The doubt also gets stored in the form of two different streams (Audio-Video combined + Handwriting). Once a doubt has been asked, there is an option to respond to it in the form of a new button 'Respond to Doubt'. On a future access of the particular lecture thread by any user, this recent doubt also appears in the playback options.

5   Conclusions

The use of Shiksha with its support for audio-visual and handwritten illustrations facilitates an experiential recording of events and near live interaction among the users. There are many schools and colleges in distant parts of India which do not have adequate teaching resources. By using this application, we can reach to those students and help them with their studies. By using a projector at the client end, the lecture experience seems almost as if a teacher is standing in front and delivering it. The option to ask and reply to doubts makes the system interactive also. In addition, the option to shut video also allows us to save bandwidth in real life situations. Since the system is asynchronous, the lecture can be viewed at any convenient time instead of following a fixed schedule.

References

1. Bargeron, D., Grudin, J.: As users grow more savvy: Experiences with an asynchronous distance learning tool. In: 37th Annual Hawaii International Conference on System Sciences, pp. 96–105 (January 2004)
2. Curran, K.: A web-based collaboration teaching environment. IEEE Multimedia 9(3), 72–76 (2002)

3. Brotherton, J.A., Bhalodia, J.R., Abowd, G.D.: Automated Capture, Integration and Visualization of Multiple Media Streams. In: IEEE International Conference on Multimedia Computing and Systems, pp. 54–63 (1998)
4. Jain, R., Kim, P., Li, Z.: Experiential Meeting System. In: ACM SIGMM Workshop on Experiential Telepresence, California, USA, pp. 1–12 (November 2003)
5. Hess, C.K., Lin, D., Nahrstedt, K.: VistaMail: An Integrated Multimedia Mailing System. IEEE Multimedia, 13–20 (October-December 1998)
6. Watt, J.H., Walther, J.B., Nowak, K.L.: Asynchronous Videoconferencing: A Hybrid Communication Prototype. In: International Conference on System Sciences, pp. 13–21 (January 2002)
7. LeeTiernan, S., Grudin, J.: Fostering Engagement in Asynchronous learning through collaborative multimedia annotation. Technical Report Microsoft Research Technical Report MSR-TR-2000-91, 22, Microsoft Research Technical Report MSR-TR-2000-91, 22 (September 2000)
8. Poupyrev, I., Tomokazu, N., Weghorst, S.: Virtual Notepad: Handwriting in Immersive VR. In: IEEE Virtual Reality Annual International Symposium, pp. 126–132 (March 1998)
9. Apoerri, A.: How to make audio/video an easy to use and share as text. In: ASIST 2002, Philadelphia, USA (2002)
10. Schilit, B.N., Golovchimlq, G., Price, M.N.: Beyond paper: Supporting active reading with free form digital ink annotations. In: ACM SIGCHI Conference on Human Factors Computing Systems, Los Angeles, California, United States, pp. 249–256 (1998)
11. Harit, G., Mankar, V., Chaudhary, S.: Patra: A novel document architecture for integrating handwriting with audio-visual information. In: 9th International Conference on Document Analysis and Recognition (ICDAR), pp. 699–703 (September 2007)
12. I. I. M. Language. W3C Working Draft, http://www.w3.org/TR/InkML/
13. Blakowski, G., Steinmetz, R.: A media synchronization survey: Reference model, specification, and case studies. IEEE Journal on Selected Areas Communication 14, 5–35 (1996)

A New Motion Based Fully Automatic Facial Expression Recognition System

Chandrani Saha, Washef Ahmed, and Soma Mitra

Centre for Development of Advanced Computing (CDAC), Kolkata, Plot E-2/1,
Block GP, Sector V, Salt Lake City, Kolkata, 700091, India
{chandrani.saha,washef.ahmed,soma.mitra}@cdac.in

Abstract. In this paper, a new motion based person-independent fully
Automatic Facial Expression Recognition system is introduced. The system uses gradient based optical flow for muscle movement estimation
from video. Decision tree generated rule base is used for recognition purpose. The performance of the system is validated by human psycho-visual
judgment.

Keywords: Basic facial expression recognition system, Gradient based
optical flow, Decision tree.

1 Introduction

Human Computer Interaction (HCI) is a very recent area of thrust which requires
the information processing systems to model the human behavior precisely. A
facial expression is indeed a human behaviour which reflects the a person's internal emotional states. Appearance or dynamical change in muscular arrangement
in the face in response to internal emotional state of the mind are designated
as the emotional facial expressions. Facial expression analysis has been an active research topic for psychologists and behavioral scientists since the work
of Darwin [1]. Research in the area of Automatic Facial Expression Analysis
(AFEA) was brought into focus of pattern recognition community through the
pioneering work of Takeuchi and Nagao [2]. The principal task of AFEA is to
analyze the basic emotional facial expressions proposed by Ekman [3]. Ekman
and his colleagues conducted various experiments on human judgment on still
photographs of posed facial behavior and concluded that six discrete basic emotional expressions can be recognized universally, namely, happiness, surprise,
disgust, fear, anger and sadness. They also proposed that facial expressions are
results of certain Facial Actions and they introduced the Facial Action Coding
System (FACS) [4] designed for human observers to detect subtle changes in
facial appearance. It is a system that linguistically describes all possible visu-
ally detectable facial changes in terms of 44 so-called Action Units (AUs). To
date, Pattern recognition researchers mostly rely on Ekman's theory of expressions and most of the existing expression recognition systems concerned with
recognition of facial actions and six discrete basic emotional facial expressions.

M.K. Kundu et al. (Eds.): PerMIn 2012, LNCS 7143, pp. 145–154, 2012.

Keamey and McKenzie [5] reported on a self-adaptive expert facial expression recognition system that converts facial data into a set of face actions and then this into a set of emotion labels. The system recognizes 36 different face actions but uses hand-measured manually supplied face image data that is difficult to track automatically. Essa and Pentland [6] proposed a method for recognition of facial expressions based on differential patterns of optical flow. They used spatio-temporal templates to recognize 2 face actions and 3 prototypic emotional expressions. However templates are unsuitable for face action recognition since for each individual face action and each combination of various face actions a separate template should be defined. Cohn et al. [7] proposed an optical-flow-based method for discriminating between AUs in the eyebrow, eye and mouth regions. The method can identify 8 individual AUs and 7 AUs combinations.The method requires a manual labeling of some facial landmarks in the first frame of the examined image sequence. Also the method performs only AU identification and does not deal with expression classification. Pantic and Rothkrantz [8] presented a prototype of an Integrated System for Facial Expression Recognition (ISFER) which utilized a framework for hybrid facial feature tracking and an Expert System for face action tracking and multiple emotional classification of facial expressions. But the system deals with still face images, not with image sequences which contains more dynamic information about facial expressions.

In the present paper a new motion based fully automatic person-independent system has been proposed for Automatic Facial Expression Recognition (AFER) from video. The system relies on gradient based optical flow for feature extraction and decision tree for the expression recognition. The input to the system is a video displaying facial expression. The face region is detected from a video sequence using Haar based face detector. Gradient based optical flow is computed locally within the Region of Interest (ROI). The first and second order flow projection statistics is taken as feature attributes. During the training of the system, decision tree is trained to generate a rule base. The trained system recognizes basic expressions based on the rule base. The training and performance evaluation of the system is done on the facial expression video database developed by CDAC, Kolkata [9].

The rest of the paper is organized as follows: Section 2 gives the system overview. Section 3 describes the computation of Region of Interest (ROI). The feature vector computation within ROI is given in section 4. Section 5 describes the rule base generation by training a decision tree. Accuracy of the proposed expression recognition system is given in section 6 . The performance of the proposed system is validated by human psycho-visual judgement in section 7. Section 8 gives the conclusion and future work.

2   System Overview

The schematic diagram of the proposed facial expression recognition system is given in Fig. 1(a).

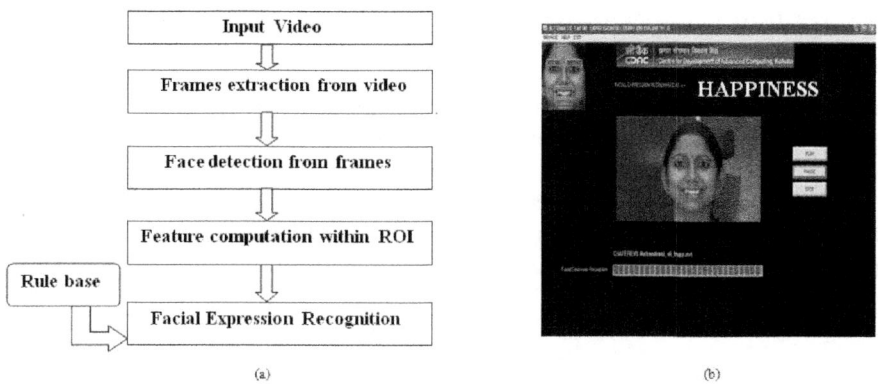

Fig. 1. (a) Schematic diagram and (b) Snapshot of the facial expression recognition system (top left corner shows extracted frame with ROI)

The system takes a video as input and extracts the significant frames at an interval chosen experimentally. The frame carrying good amount of face deformation with respect to the previous one is called as significant frame. The next step is the automatic detection o face regions from the frames by Haar wavelet based face detector [10]. The detected face region is normalized maintaining the aspect ratio. The windows over the Region of Interest (ROI) on the face is extracted using a priori information. In the next step, gradient-based optical flow [11] is computed within the ROI. The mean and standard deviation of the projection of flow vectors on the window axes are calculated, which act as feature vector for recognition. In final step, a trained decision tree generated rule base performs the recognition. The snap shot of the system is given in Fig. 1(b).

3 Extraction of Facial Regions Deformed Maximally during Expression Display - Computation of Region of Interest(ROI)

In the proposed system, feature computation is done locally within certain regions in which maximum change in frame intensity occurs due to movement of a specific muscle group [4] for displaying all six basic expressions. To find these regions, a priori information is gathered based on experiment. From the test expression video sequences, the frame with neutral face and apex of expression are chosen manually and the facial regions are then detected. The gradient based optical flow is then computed globally on the face region comparing the neutral face and the face in the apex of the expression. The next subsection describes briefly the computation of optical flow vectors using gradient based method.

3.1   Computation of Optical Flow Vector Using Gradient Based Method

Optical Flow is the apparent motion of brightness patterns in an image sequence. A gradient based method to compute the components of optical flow (u,v) from a pair of images was proposed by Horn and Schunck in their seminal paper [11]. The algorithm assumes that as points move, their brightness E(x,y) at a point (x,y) does not change significantly within a small time interval. This imposes brightness constraint which generates an ill-posed problem for obtaining two components of optical flow vector. The linear equation obtained from brightness constraint is given by,

$$uE_x + vE_y + E_t = 0 \tag{1}$$

Here, E_x, E_y and E_t are the derivatives of E(x,y) along x, y and time (t) respectively. Horn and Schunck additionally assumed smoothness of the flow vector field, which imposes smoothness constraint on the problem. The equation obtained from smoothness constraint is given by,

$$\nabla^2 u + \nabla^2 v = 0 \tag{2}$$

These two constraint equations are solved iteratively to obtain numerical estimate of optical flow velocity components. The next subsection describes how optical flow vectors detect the maximally deformed facial region during expression display.

3.2   Extraction of Region of Interest (ROI)

As already stated, optical flow vectors are computed globally to quantify the deformation resulting from muscle movements during displaying emotional expressions. Experiment has been conducted with six basic emotional facial expressions for 50 subjects. For each expression, upto 20 percent of the maximum magnitude of the flow vector has been considered to identify maximally deformed face region. Any flow vector less than this threshold is considered as noise and not considered as the representative of the expression related muscle movement. The generated optical flow vector for the six basic expressions is shown in Fig. 2. From the experiment, magnitude of optical flow is found to be high in thirteen (13) major regions which suffer from maximum deformations during display of all six basic expressions. These regions are listed in second coloumn of Table 1. This experimental result acts as a priori information to the proposed system for automatically extracting local windows over the ROI on a face. Fig. 6 shows the local windows placed on a neutral face. These windows are drawn on a face based on anthropometric model of human face used to locate the most important facial feature areas from face images [12]. The proposed recognition system computes feature vectors within these 13 windows. The proposed recognition system computes feature vectors within these 13 windows.

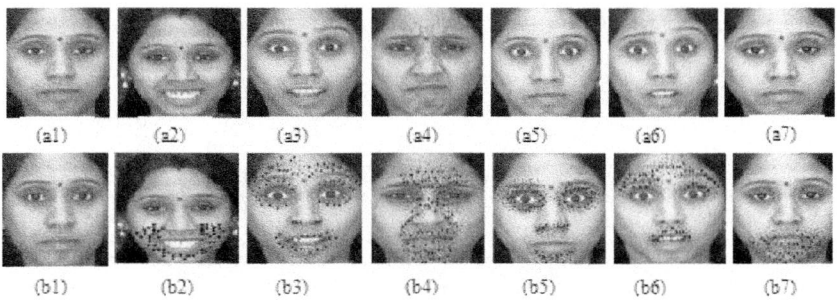

Fig. 2. (a1)Neutral,(a2) Happiness, (a3) Surprise, (a4) Disgust, (a5) Anger, (a6) Fear, (a7) Sadness, (b1)- (b7) Optical flow generated by comparing (a1)-(a7) with (a1)

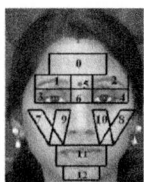

Fig. 3. Regions of Interest (ROI)

4   Computation of Feature Vectors within ROI

In the current work, localized optical flow vector is computed within the 13 windows mentioned in second coloumn of Table 1 as described in the previous section. The direction of orientation of the windows with global horizontal axis is taken as the window symmetry axis. Projection P_{ij} of optical flow vectors $\overrightarrow{U}_{ij}(\overrightarrow{X})$ is taken on the long symmetry axis of ith window for the jth pixel:

$$P_{ij} = \overrightarrow{U}_{ij}(\overrightarrow{X}).\overrightarrow{n_i} \qquad (3)$$

Where $\overrightarrow{U}_{ij}(\overrightarrow{X}) = (u_{ij}(x,y), v_{ij}(x,y))$ is the optical flow vector in j^{th} pixel $\overrightarrow{X} = (x,y)$ of ith window computed from two successive significant frames. $\overrightarrow{n_i}$ is the unit vector along the axis of ith window (i= 0,...,12). In the proposed work, the mean and standard deviation of the flow projections within the 13 windows are taken to compute the feature vectors. So there are 26 dimensional feature vector denoted by $A_0, A_1, ..., A_{25}$ and listed in third coloumn of Table 1.

With these feature vectors, the recognition of the six expressions is performed by the proposed system using a rule base generated by a trained decision tree.

5   Rule Base Generation Using Decision Tree

Decision tree [13] is a popular classification method that results in a flow-chart like tree structure where each node denotes a test on an attribute value and each

Table 1. List of ROI and abbreviation of computed feature vectors

Sl. no.	Regions	Feature vector (Mean,Standard Deviation)
0	Forehead	A_0,A_1
1	Right eye brow	A_2,A_3
2	Left eye brow	A_4,A_5
3	Right eye	A_6,A_7
4	Left eye	A_8,A_9
5	Middle of two inner brows	A_{10},A_{11}
6	Nasion (root of nose)	A_{12},A_{13}
7	Right cheek	A_{14},A_{15}
8	Left cheek	A_{16},A_{17}
9	Right nasalobial region	A_{18},A_{19}
10	Left nasalobial region	A_{20},A_{21}
11	Mouth	A_{22},A_{23}
12	Chin	A_{24},A_{25}

branch represents an outcome of the test. The tree leaves represent the classes. In the current work, the discriminatory power of each attribute is evaluated using Shanon's entropy. In the present work, the decision tree program C5.0 developed by J. Ross Quinlan [14] has been used for the classification of facial expressions. The computed 26 dimensional feature vectors $A_0,A_1,....,A_{25}$ mentioned in the previous section are used as attributes to the decision tree since they capture the discriminatory characteristics of optical flow vectors to classify six basic expressions. The sample space consists of facial expression video database of 50 subjects, divided into training set of 30 subjects and test set of 20 subjects. The database is developed by CDAC, Kolkata under constrained illumination and head pose.

For training the decision tree, 30 subjects are taken from the database displaying video sequence of 6 basic facial expressions. 4 frames (neutral frame and three significant frames) are chosen from each video sequence to compute optical flow. (30X6X3)= 540 training cases are generated with which a decision tree is constructed using C 5.0. The training time of the decision tree is very fast. The generated tree is depicted in Fig 4. The leaf nodes of the tree are the six basic facial expressions: Happiness (H), Surprise (S_u), Anger (A), Fear (F), Disgust (D) and Sadness (S_a). The attribute usage of the decision tree is given in Table 2. The attribute A_{23} (standard deviation of flow projection in mouth) has the maximum entropy and hence the maximum discriminatory feature. This signifies that mouth region carries the maximum information about facial expression. This is obvious because mouth is the maximum deformable facial feature and as a result suffers maximum deformation during expression display.

The rule base generated from the decision tree has been tested on 20 Indian subjects of CDAC, Kolkata facial expression database displaying six basic emotional facial expressions. Like the training set, 4 frames are chosen from each

Fig. 4. Decision tree for facial expression recognition. (a) Main tree, (b)Sub-tree originated from Node 1 of main tree, (c),(d) and (e)- Sub-trees originated from Node 1', 2' and 3' of (b) respectively.

sequence starting from neutral to apex. By generating optical flow vectors from successive significant frames, 360 test cases are generated. The result of test case evaluation is expressed by the confusion matrix given in Table 3.

6   Result

The overall accuracy of automatic recognition of facial expressions performed by the proposed system, tested on CDAC, Kolkata facial expression video database of 50 subjects is given in Table 4. The system recognizes expression in approx. 2 sec from a video of approx. length 10-12 sec in a PC with intel Pentium IV processor, 2 GB RAM and 320 GB hard disk, with Win 7 OS installed.

7   Validation of the Performance of the Proposed System by Human Psycho-visual Judgement

In statistics, Analysis of Variance (ANOVA) [15] is a procedure, in which the observed variance in a particular variable is partitioned into components

Table 2. Attribute usage of decision tree

Attribute	% usage	Attribute	% usage	Attribute	% usage
A_{23}	100%	A_{20}	76%	A_{14}	48%
A_{25}	46%	A_0	46%	A_{21}	42%
A_{24}	30%	A_3	27%	A_9	27%
A_{22}	27%	A_1	27%	A_8	26%
A_5	23%	A_7	23%	A_6	22%
A_{19}	21%	A_{10}	18%	A_{16}	17%
A_{12}	15%	A_{17}	13%	A_{17}	13%
A_4	10%	A_{15}	5%	A_{13}	5%
A_{18}	2%				

Table 3. Evaluation on test data from CDAC, Kolkata facial expression database

	Happiness	Surprise	Anger	Fear	Disgust	Sadness
Happiness	60					
Surprise	12	48				
Anger			51		9	
Fear		22		38		
Disgust			14		46	
Sadness			8	10	14	28

Table 4. Performance accuracy

Expression	Accuracy(%)
Happiness	98.1
Surprise	80.0
Anger	72.0
Fear	58.1
Disgust	92.3
Sadness	51.0

attributable to different sources of variation. ANOVA provides a statistical test to find out whether the means of several groups are all equal or not. In the present work, the recognition efficiency of the proposed system is evaluated by human judgment with the help two-way ANOVA. Human judges from Indian culture with three different age groups - child (10-17 years), young (18-45 years) and old (46-60 years), are asked to manually classify the basic expressions contained in the training set of 30 subjects. 3 frames are chosen from each video sequence to generate 90 images for each expression. The result of the judgment is tabulated in Table 5 (no. of rows (a)=3 and no. of coloumns (b)=6).

The first null hypothesis (H_0^1)scrutinized under the test is framed as, "there exists no significant variation in the mean of the six class centres of the basic expressions".

The ANOVA table (Table 6) shows that, at the 0.05 level of significance, with degree of freedom 2,10, $F_{.95} = 4.1$. Since, $4.1 > 0.00$, there is no significant difference in human recognition of facial expressions across different age groups.

Table 5. Human judgment about CDAC, Kolkata facial expression database

	Happiness	Surprise	Anger	Fear	Disgust	Sadness
Child	117	99	126	108	54	36
Young	108	81	108	117	72	54
Old	108	108	117	99	63	45

Table 6. ANOVA table

Variation	Degree of freedom	Mean Square	F	$F_{.95}$
$V_r=0.00$	a-1=3-1=2	$S_r^2=V_r/(a-1)=0.00$	$F=S_r^2/S_e^2=0.00$ df:2,10	4.1
$V_c=12852$	b-1=6-1=5	$S_c^2=V_c/(b-1)=2570.40$	$F=S_c^2/S_e^2=94.50$ df:5,10	3.33
$V_e=272$	(a-1)(b-1)=10	$S_e^2=V_e/(a-)(b-1)=27.20$		
$V=15572$	ab-1=17			

With 5,10 degrees of freedom, $F_{.95} = 3.33$. Since $3.33 < 94.50$, the ANOVA test also proves that there is a significant difference in recognition of different facial expressions within the dataset. Now, from Table 3 and Table 4 it is observed that the recognition accuracy of the proposed system is different for different expressions. Thus the recognition performance of the proposed facial expression recognition system is validated by the psycho-visual evaluation by human judgment.

8   Conclusion and Future Work

In this paper, a new motion based person independent system has been proposed for fully automatic basic facial expression recognition. The system uses dynamic information about facial expression embedded in video. Gradient based optical flow estimates the facial muscle motion. A decision tree generated rule base is used to recognize the expressions. The training of the decision tree is very fast and the proposed system recognizes basic expressions in acceptable time with acceptable accuracy. Performance of the system is validated by human psycho-visual judgment with the help of ANOVA test. The system recognizes expressions accurately with restricted head movement. The future work is directed to expression recognition in presence of spontaneous head movement and also towards estimation of facial expression intensity.

Acknowledgement. The research is supported by Strategic India-Japan Cooperative Programme (INT/JAP/JST/P-08/2007 dated 25.07.2008) and is jointly conducted by CDAC, Kolkata, India and NICT, Japan. The continuous encouragement of Col. A.K. Nath (retired), Executive Director, CDAC, Kolkata and the collaboration of Dr. Tatsuya Yamazaki, NICT, Japan is greatly acknowledged.

References

1. Darwin, C.: The expression of Emotions in Man and Animals. Univ. Chicago Press (1965)
2. Takeuchi, A., Nagao, K.: Communicative Facial Displace as a New Conversational Modality. In: Proc. A.C.M INTERCHI, pp. 187–193 (1993)
3. Ekman, P., Friesen, W.V., Ellsworth, P.: Emotion in the Human Face. Oxford University Press (1972)
4. Ekman, P., Friesen, W.V.: Facial Action Coding System (FACS): Manual. Consultng Psychologists Press, Pal Alto (1978)
5. Keamey, G.D., McKenzie, S.: Machine Interpretation of Emotion. Cognitive Science 17(4), 589–622 (1993)
6. Essa, I., Pentland, A.: Coding, analysis, interpretation and recognition of facial expression. IEEE Transaction on Pattern Analysis and Machine Intelligence 19(7), 757–763 (1997)
7. Cohn, J.F., Zlochower, A.J., Lien, J.J., Kanade, T.: Feature-Point Tracking by Optical Flow Discriminates Subtle Differences in Facial Expression. In: Proc. 3rd IEEE FG, pp. 396–401 (1998)
8. Pantic, M., Rothkrantz, L.J.M.: An Expert System for Multiple Emotional Classification of Facial Expressions. In: Proc. of IEEE International Conference on Tools with Artificial Intelligence, ICTAI 1999 (1999)
9. chandrani.saha@cdac.in
10. Viola, P., Jones, M.J.: Robust real-time face detection. International Journal of Computer Vision 57(2), 137–154 (2004)
11. Horn, B.K.P., Schunck, B.G.: Determining optical flow. Artificial Intelligence 17, 185–203 (1981)
12. Farkas, L.G.: Anthropometry of the head and face. Raven Press, New York (1994)
13. Gupta, G.K.: Introduction to data mining with case studies. Prentice Hall of India Private Limited (2006)
14. http://www.rulequest.com/index.html
15. Spiegel, M.R., Schiller, J., Srinivasan, A.R.: Theory and Problems of Probability and Statistics, 2nd edn. Schaum's Outline Series. Tata McGrawHill (2004)

Profiling Scotch Malt Whisky Spirits from Different Distilleries Using an Electronic Nose and an Expert Sensory Panel

Koichi Yoshida[1], Emiko Ishikawa[1], Maltesh Joshi[2], Hervé Lechat[2], Fatma Ayouni[2], and Marion Bonnefille[2]

[1] Alpha M.O.S. Japan K.K., JowatakanawaBldg. 8F, 1-5-4 Takanawa, Minato-ku, 108-0074, Tokyo, Japan
[2] Alpha M.O.S. S.A., 20 avenue Didier Daurat, 31400, Toulouse, France

Abstract. Spirits from different Scotch malt whisky distilleries exhibit distinct sensory characteristics. To ensure the future diversity of this spirit category and sustainability of individual distilleries, it is vital that such differences can be maintained. In this research the characteristics of spirits from six distilleries were profiled using an electronic nose (e-nose) and by an expert sensory panel. The instrumental method used a flash GC-based e-nose, the HERACLES. The e-nose produced compositional data that could clearly discriminate between the spirits according to distillery of origin. This discrimination was based on levels of a range of volatile compounds that could potentially influence flavor. The sensory panel provided quantitative data on the levels of sixteen aroma attributes in the spirits. This showed clear differences in flavor among the distilleries. Although the separation obtained using the two approaches was not directly comparable, correlations were observed between peaks in the e-nose chromatograms and certain aroma attributes, indicating that the two techniques are complementary.

Keywords: sensory analysis, sensory profiling, electronic nose, sensory panel.

1   Introduction

Alcoholic drinks are mainly characterized by their specific sensory attributes. To describe, compare or benchmark various brands or products, a detailed descriptive sensory analysis is often needed. It is commonly achieved through human panel testing. More recently analytical instruments such the electronic nose and the electronic tongue have been employed for the analysis of the organoleptic features of several alcoholic beverages [1], such as beers [2], wines [3, 4], or liquors [5, 6].

This study focuses on spirits from different Scotch malt whisky distilleries that exhibit distinct sensory characteristics. To ensure the future diversity of this spirit category and sustainability of individual distilleries, it is vital that such differences can be maintained. Flavor is complex, with differences being due to variations in composition resulting from the processing parameters and raw materials used in their manufacture.

M.K. Kundu et al. (Eds.): PerMIn 2012, LNCS 7143, pp. 155–162, 2012.

This paper has the particularity to characterize malt whisky spirits from six different distilleries using 2 techniques: instrumental analysis thanks to an electronic nose and human assessment through a sensory panel, then to compare the two methods. As a first step, the instrument was used to control and describe slight differences between various products. In a second step, a quantitative sensory evaluation was conducted by an expert panel. The panel results were then correlated with the electronic nose measurement.

2   Material and Method

2.1   Samples

Unmatured malt whisky spirits were collected from six different distilleries (A to F), representing a total of 58 samples. Sample codes and alcohol strengths are shown in Table 1.

Table 1. Whisky samples description

Sample	% of Alcohol	Sample	% of Alcohol	Sample	% of Alcohol
A1	69.7	D1	72	F1, F6	69.2
A2 - A3	68.8	D2	72.6	F2	68.9
A4 - A10	69.8	D3	71.8	F3, F5, F8 - F10	69.3
B1	68.1	D4	72.1	F4	69.1
B2, B4 - B6, B9, B10	68.4	D5	72.3	F7	68.9
B3	63.5	D6	71.9		
B7	67.9	D7	71.7		
B8	68.2	D8	70.7		
C1	70.4	E1, E2	70.8		
C2, C3	70.0	E3, E4	71.0		
C4, C8	69.9	E5, E6, E9	70.6		
C5 - C7	70.5	E7, E8	70.3		
C9, C10	70.1	E10	70.7		

2.2   Equipment

The HERACLES Electronic Nose (Alpha MOS, France) is based on the technology of ultra fast chromatograph and includes two short columns (2m) of different polarities (DB5 apolar and DB1701 slightly polar), coupled to 2 Flame Ionization Detectors (FID). Therefore, the 2 chromatograms obtained simultaneously, allow a sharper identification of chemical compounds.

The Tenax trap located before columns allows pre-concentrating of the injected fraction before rapid thermo desorption in order to improve the sensitivity. With high heating rates (up to 20°C/second), the time of analysis is very short (some seconds) and an analysis can be run every 4 minutes.

2.3   Analytical Conditions

The assays on the whisky spirits were carried out on the chromatography based E-Nose (HERACLES) equipped with a set of columns DB5 / DB1701. The data processing was operated with the AlphaSoft software. Sampling was achieved with an HS100 autosampler. Each sample was injected on HERACLES e-nose in triplicate using the same optimized method (Table 2).

Table 2. HERACLES e-nose parameters for spirits analysis (headspace injection)

Parameter	Value
Quantity of sample	1g in a 10mL vial
Sample incubation	10 min at 100°C
Syringe temperature	110°C
Injected volume	5mL
Sampling time	23s
Trap temperature	40°C
Trap pre-purge time	30 s
Trap desorption temp.	250°C
Trap purge time	60 s
Injection time	2000 ms
Injector temperature	200°C
Column temp. program	40°C (2s) to 220°C (2s) @ 3°C/s
Column pressure program	16 psi
FID temperature	230°C
Acquisition time	50 s

2.4   Sensory Evaluation Analytical Conditions

Sensory evaluation was carried out by an expert panel. Composite samples from each distillery were prepared. These were diluted to 20% abv using water and presented in blind coded glasses to the panel. Panelists were asked to score the spirits according to intensity of 16 aromas listed below, which previous experience have been found to be the key attributes of unmatured malt whisky spirits: Pungent, sulfury, meaty, solventy, fruity/estery, green/grassy, floral, cereal, sweet, soapy, peaty, feinty, oily, sour, stale and clean.

Scoring was carried out using a 0-3 line scale. Analysis of Variance (ANOVA) was carried out to determine which, if any, of the attributes differed among the samples. Data were then summarized by calculating average scores across the panel.

3   Results and Discussion

3.1   Electronic Nose Discrimination

Analysis of the spirits showed globally similar profiles at low retention times (between 0 and 10s) for the main volatile compounds. Consequently, a focus on lower intensity peaks was made. This highlighted the presence of several possibly flavor related, compounds characteristics of each set of samples.

Comparison of the six distilleries showed differences in peak intensity after 10 seconds. A focus on intensity axis (0 to 75 000 au) revealed two types of profiles (Fig.1), with several peaks at specific retention times (15, 34, and 45s on DB5) being present in different proportions based on the origin of the spirit:

▶   A first type of profile (Distilleries D and A) showed lowest volatile composition compared to the second profile (Distilleries B, E, and F).

▶   Distillery C had the highest concentration for medium volatile compounds.

These chemical variations may be due to differences in processing parameters or even raw materials used at the different distilleries.

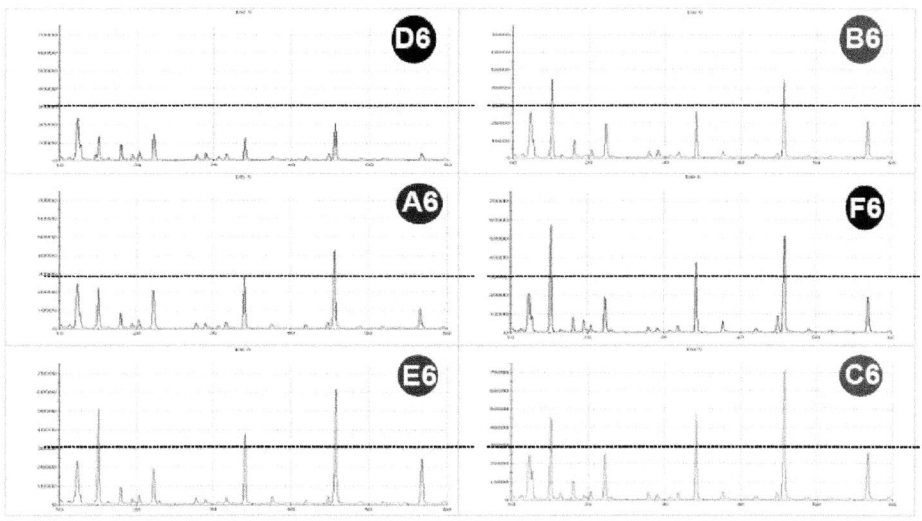

Fig. 1. HERACLES e-nose chromatograms for the 6 types of whisky spirit - Focus on 10 to 60 s on DB5 column

The chromatographic profile could be represented as an odor map using a Principal Component Analysis (PCA) (Fig.2). The various samples are represented according to their relative volatile contents on a 2-axis graph with PC1 giving 56% of the information and PC2 explaining 22% of the relevant information. This PCA plot showed clustering of the samples from each distillery, indicating that the instrument could discriminate spirits according to their origin. Samples dispersion was relatively homogeneous, except for Distillery E which showed two distinct subgroups of samples: E8 to E10, which were close to Distillery F, and samples E1 to E7, which were closer to Distillery B. Samples were numbered in chronological order according to date of production, so this change in composition may be due to a change in the production parameters or raw materials at a particular point in time.

Additionally, two groups could be distinguished:

- ▶ Group 1: Distilleries A & D
- ▶ Group 2: Distilleries B, E & F and Distillery C slightly discriminated on the PC2 axis.

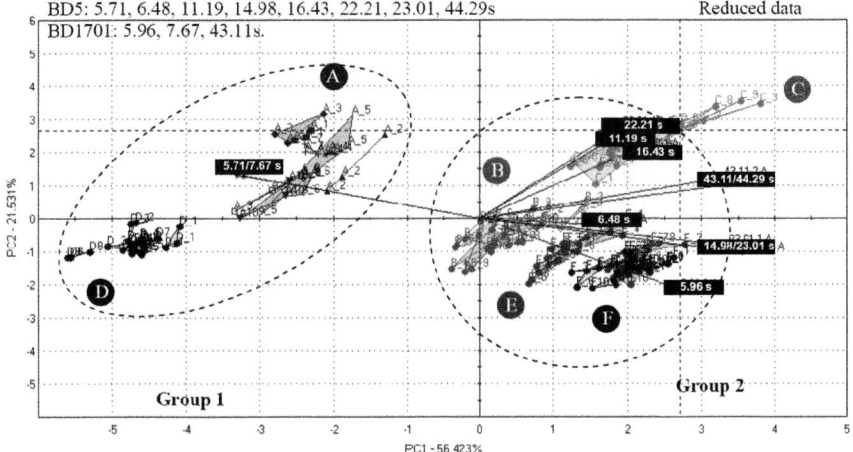

Fig. 2. Odor map (PCA) of whisky spirit samples on HERACLES e-nose

From the chromatograms, it seemed that four molecules characterized each type of spirit. Identification was possible using GC/MS. Sulfides and furans were identified. These are Maillard molecules which are known to have very potent Sulfury or Roast odors. The higher concentration of these molecules in some spirits may mask the other molecules such as esters, ketones and alcohols, which have fruity and green/grassy aromas but are less odorous that Maillard molecules.

3.2   Sensory Analysis Results

The average panel scores, along with the results of the ANOVA (Analysis of Variance) are shown in Table 3.

Table 3. Sensory data for composite spirit samples from each distillery

Samp-Code	Distillery A	Distillery B	Distillery C	Distillery D	Distillery E	Distillery F	ANOVA
Pungent	1.17	1.21	1.37	1.24	1.19	1.34	ns
Sulfury	0.84	0.99	1.73	0.94	1.41	0.97	p<0.0001
Meaty	0.39	0.54	1.36	0.51	1.06	0.65	p<0.0001
Solventy	0.91	0.71	0.53	0.67	0.64	0.77	p=0.0854
Fruity/estery	0.92	0.98	0.31	0.73	0.62	1.01	p<0.0001
Green/grassy	0.86	0.88	0.50	0.90	0.61	0.88	p=0.0026
Floral	0.86	0.71	0.33	0.64	0.58	0.60	p=0.0068
Cereal	0.66	0.88	0.96	0.86	0.78	0.96	ns
Sweet	0.76	0.56	0.34	0.49	0.43	0.45	p=0.0056
Soapy	0.54	0.45	0.47	0.49	0.50	0.54	ns
Peaty	0.42	0.37	0.54	0.61	0.46	0.39	p=0.0553
Feinty	1.08	1.01	1.53	1.23	1.17	1.15	p=0.0336
Oily	0.85	0.60	0.95	0.71	0.87	0.74	ns
Sour	0.73	0.73	0.79	0.73	0.64	0.80	ns
Stale	0.61	0.49	0.77	0.98	0.83	0.62	p=0.0053
Clean	1.55	1.53	0.74	1.13	1.06	1.41	p<0.0001

The average panel scores were further summarized using PCA (Fig. 3). Comparison of this PCA plot with the one obtained for the HERACLES e-nose data showed that the distribution of samples was different. This indicates that the two techniques are complementary.

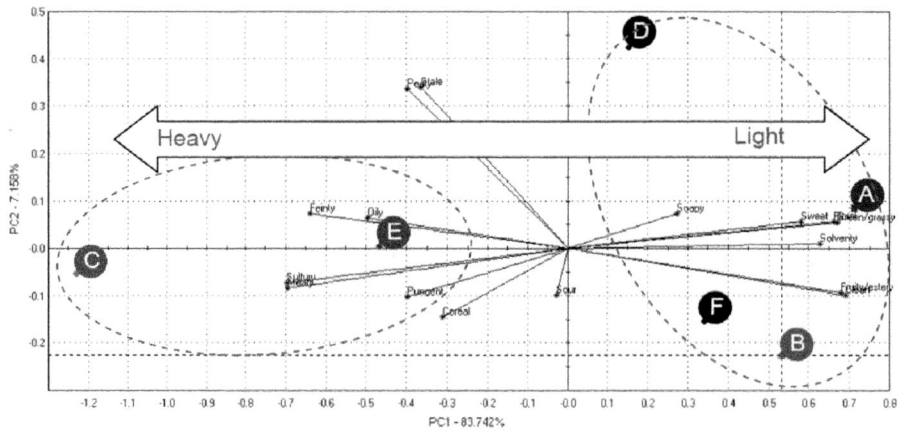

Fig. 3. Principal Components Analysis (PCA) – sensory analysis results

3.3   Correlation Results

Correlation coefficients between the HERACLES and sensory panel data are shown in Table 4. Peak 16.43 showed a good correlation with many sensory attributes: Sulfury, Meaty, and Feinty descriptors (+ve), Fruity, Green, and Floral (- ve).

Table 4. Sensory Correlation coefficient between area of HERACLES peaks and sensory data

Heracles variable	5.71 (1)	6.48 (1)	11.19 (1)	14.98 (1)	16.43 (1)	22.21 (1)	23.01 (1)	44.29 (1)	5.96 (2)	7.67(2)	43.11(2)
Pungent	-0.54	0.46	0.22	0.38	0.64	0.35	0.24	0.45	0.20	-0.48	0.46
Sulfury	-0.42	0.32	0.36	0.43	0.89	0.49	0.54	0.64	0.11	-0.43	0.65
Meaty	-0.49	0.40	0.32	0.50	0.86	0.47	0.59	0.68	0.20	-0.50	0.68
Solventy	0.41	-0.13	-0.04	-0.31	-0.77	-0.10	-0.41	-0.34	-0.17	0.40	-0.35
Fruity/estery	0.06	-0.21	-0.22	-0.04	-0.82	-0.38	-0.19	-0.36	0.25	0.06	-0.37
Green/grassy	0.32	-0.34	-0.40	-0.38	-0.83	-0.55	-0.51	-0.65	-0.04	0.35	-0.66
Floral	0.53	-0.39	-0.19	-0.44	-0.85	-0.33	-0.46	-0.53	-0.20	0.50	-0.54
Cereal	-0.68	0.26	0.04	0.47	0.51	0.04	0.35	0.32	0.44	-0.61	0.33
Sweet	0.63	-0.40	0.06	-0.54	-0.65	-0.06	-0.55	-0.44	-0.43	0.61	-0.43
Soapy	0.19	0.42	-0.18	-0.06	-0.50	0.03	-0.15	-0.06	-0.02	0.17	-0.09
Peaty	0.39	0.00	-0.33	-0.51	0.35	-0.16	-0.39	-0.32	-0.55	0.43	-0.31
Feinty	-0.15	0.35	0.24	0.06	0.84	0.44	0.10	0.37	-0.24	-0.12	0.39
Oily	0.04	0.46	0.34	0.08	0.56	0.61	0.18	0.47	-0.27	0.01	0.48
Sour	-0.24	0.21	0.31	0.05	0.32	0.34	-0.17	0.17	-0.07	-0.16	0.21
Stale	0.31	0.15	-0.55	-0.33	0.14	-0.32	-0.19	-0.30	-0.30	0.31	-0.32
Clean	0.18	-0.30	-0.06	-0.13	-0.78	-0.25	-0.25	-0.34	0.10	0.17	-0.34

The fact that a number of sensory descriptors, rather than a single flavor, correlated with this peak is due to the inter-relationships among sensory attributes, i.e. as heavy (sulfury, meaty, and feinty) aromas increase, lighter (fruity, green, and floral) aromas tend to decrease. GC/MS analysis identified Peak 16.43 as furfuryl ethyl ester. Further sensory work would be required to determine whether or not this compound is directly responsible for the observed differences in aroma among malt whisky spirits.

4   Conclusion

The information given by the HERACLES e-nose, GC/MS and sensory data provides complementary representations of malt whisky spirit heterogeneity. Although the information given by HERACLES e-nose could not replace the sensory panel on all sensory descriptors , some important attributes such as Sulfury, Meaty, Feinty, Fruity, Green, and Floral were highly correlated (positively or negatively) with the HERACLES data.

From GC/MS analysis, it appeared that furfuryl ethyl ether seemed to be one of the most important molecules for explaining the characteristic differences in odor between spirits from different distilleries, though other molecules such as sulfides may also be important.

In this study, the e-nose was shown to be able to discriminate between malt whisky spirits from different distilleries. However, it may also have further application as a quality control tool to detect anomalies in spirit character within an individual distillery.

References

1. Ragazzo-Sanchez, J.A., Chalier, P., Chevalier, D., Calderon-Santoyo, M., Ghommidh, C.: Identification of different alcoholic beverages by electronic nose coupled to GC. Sensors and Actuators B 134, 43–48 (2008)
2. Li, W., Pickard, M.D., Beta, T.: Evaluation of Antioxidant Activity and Electronic Taste and Aroma Properties of Antho-Beers from Purple Wheat Grain. J. Agric. Food Chem. 55, 8958–8966 (2007)
3. Berna, A.Z., Trowell, S., Clifford, D., Cynkar, W., Cozzolino, D.: Geographical origin of Sauvignon Blanc wines predicted by mass spectrometry and metal oxide based electronic nose. Analytica Chimica Acta 648, 146–152 (2009)
4. Wang, Y.W., Wang, J., Zhu, Q.H.: Detecting and Classification of Wine Using an Electronic Tongue. Packaging and Food Machinery (May 2009)
5. Zhang, J., Zhao, L., Ouyang, Y.-F., Gao, H.-Y., Yang, Y.-J., Yin, J.-Y.: Applications of Modern Equipment Analytical Techniques in Sensory Evaluation of Liquor. Food Science (October 2007)
6. Gao, Y.-M., Liu, Y.-F., Li, Y.-X., Li, J.-M., Shi, B.-X., Ni, Y.-Y.: Electronic Nose Fingerprint of Liquor of Main Flavor Types. Liquor Making Science & Technology (2008)

Quality Control and Rancidity Tendency of Nut Mix Using an Electronic Nose

Koichi Yoshida[1], Emiko Ishikawa[1], Maltesh Joshi[2], Hervé Lechat[2],
Fatma Ayouni[2], and Marion Bonnefille[2]

[1] Alpha M.O.S. Japan K.K., JowatakanawaBldg. 8F, 1-5-4 Takanawa,
Minato-ku, 108-0074, Tokyo, Japan
[2] Alpha M.O.S. S.A., 20 Avenue Didier Daurat, 31400, Toulouse, France

Abstract. Nuts are rich in polyunsaturated fats, which are particularly sensitive to lipid oxidation. A Flash GC based electronic nose was used to identify the causes of rancidity in nut mixes and to monitor global sensory quality. Five appetizers of different sensory qualities, all composed of the same nut types, were considered. It was shown that peanuts were the most critical ingredients in the development of rancidity off-flavors. Pecans and cashew nuts also presented a relatively high concentration of off-odors, but their relatively low proportion in the final mix made them less critical towards rancidity. As for Brazil nuts, almonds and hazelnuts, containing lower amounts of volatile compounds, they proved to have a low impact on the overall mix aroma.

Keywords: sensory analysis, electronic nose, off-odors, rancidity control, pattern recognition, sensory profiling, chemical composition.

1 Introduction

The aroma profile and volatile profile of food products can be analyzed by GC/MS. This technique allows identifying the chemical compounds after separation. Another technique consists of using an electronic nose, which performs a global analysis of the volatile profile of products, as the human nose, and can deliver both chemical and sensory information. This instrument has already been used to analyze the volatile profile of various food products such as fruits [1], vegetables [2], cheese [3], fish [4], or oils [5]. For many food products, it is important to reliably assess and monitor sensory features that play an important role in consumers' acceptance.

Nuts are rich in polyunsaturated fats, which are particularly sensitive to lipid oxidation that generates characteristic off-odors. In appetizer mixes, each type of nuts has a different contribution to potential overall rancidity. Therefore, it is important to identify the causes of possible rancidity to monitor the global sensory quality of these appetizers.

After having received a claim from a consumer about an unpleasant off-flavor in their product, a manufacturer needed to explain the origin of the defect. The analysis of the overall aroma profile of 5 mixes containing 6 types of nuts was conducted using HERACLES Flash GC based E-Nose (Alpha MOS, France). The objective was to determine which nuts most contributed to bad quality.

M.K. Kundu et al. (Eds.): PerMIn 2012, LNCS 7143, pp. 163–170, 2012.

2   Material and Method

2.1   Equipment

Over the last decade, "electronic sensing" or "e-sensing" technologies have undergone important developments from a technical and commercial point of view. Among them, electronic noses have been designed to mimic the human sense of olfaction in order to detect and recognize odors and flavors. Basically, an electronic nose consists of a sample delivery system, a detection system and a computing system for pattern recognition.

When headspace injection mode is used, the sample delivery system enables the generation of the headspace (volatile compounds) by heating the sample at a constant temperature under agitation. The system then injects this headspace into the detection system of the electronic nose. The detection system is the "reactive" part of the instrument. Various technologies can be employed to detect volatile compounds: gas sensor arrays, mass spectrometry or gas chromatography.

The computing system works to combine the multiple raw data recorded from the detection part, which represents the input for the multivariate statistical processing. This part of the instrument performs global fingerprint analysis and provides results and representations that can be easily interpreted. Moreover, the electronic nose results can be correlated to those obtained from other techniques (sensory panel, GC, and GC/MS).

In this study, the electronic nose used, the HERACLES, is based on the technology of ultra fast gas chromatography with liquid or headspace injection modes. The HERACLES electronic nose was used to perform headspace analysis of the nut appetizers. This instrument is based on the technology of ultra fast gas chromatography with liquid or headspace injection modes.

In order to increase analysis sensitivity, it includes an embedded Tenax trap located before the columns for pre-concentration of the injected fraction prior to rapid thermo desorption. The instrument features two short columns of different polarities (DB5 apolar and DB1701 slightly polar), coupled to 2 Flame Ionization Detectors (FID). Therefore, two chromatograms are obtained simultaneously.

The electronic nose was operated through its specific AlphaSoft software for instrument monitoring and statistical data processing. The AlphaSoft was used with AroChembase module consisting of a library of chemical compounds with name, formula, CAS number, molecular weight, Kovats retention Index, sensory attributes, and related bibliography. This will allow characterizing the chemical compounds detected on the chromatograms with both chemical and sensory information.

From the early days of these instruments, they have been used to analyze oily food products such as edible oils, to follow up shelf life [6], control the sensory quality [7] or compare sensory profiles [8]. In this study, a HERACLES instrument was employed to perform headspace analysis of the nut appetizers with an aim to compare the odor profile of various nuts and to get information on the behavior towards oxidation and sensory ageing.

2.2   Analytical Conditions

Headspace method was set up to analyze the volatile profiles of the appetizers. This method consists of heating the sample (in this case a solid sample) for a determined time period in order to homogenize the headspace phase i.e. the volatile compounds generated by the sample. Then a fraction of the headspace is collected and injected into the electronic nose for analysis.

For this study, the use of large vials (100mL) was particularly suitable to analyze entire nuts (easier sample preparation with no cutting) and larger quantities of product therefore more representative of the samples. Table 1 describes the analytical parameters applied for the analysis.

Table 1. HERACLES e-nose parameters for nut mix odor analysis (headspace injection)

Parameter	Value
Quantity of sample	30g in a 100mL vial
Sample incubation	20 min at 30°C
Sampling time	24 s
Injection temperature	200°C
Trap temperature	40°C
Trap pre-purge time	5 s
Trap desorption temp.	250°C
Trap purge time	50 s
Injection time	3000 ms
Column temp. program	40°C (2s) to 270°C (2s) @ 5°C/s
Column pressure program	16 psi
FID temperature	280°C
Acquisition time	50 s
Time between 2 injections	4 min

2.3   Samples

Five appetizer samples of different sensory qualities were analyzed with HERACLES electronic nose. The nut mixes were composed of: peanuts (58% in weigh), almonds (22%), cashew nuts (9%), Brazil nuts (6%), pecan nuts (3%), and hazelnuts (2%). The five samples were previously assessed by the company internal sensory panel (Table 2) to determine their overall sensory quality (good, medium, or bad).

Table 2. Samples designation and sensory panel results

Sample	Assessed Quality	Sensory panel evaluation	
		Detected Off-flavors	Nuts with off-flavors
G1	Good	None	-
M2	Medium	Slightly rancid	Peanuts
B3	Bad	Rancid	Peanuts, cashews, pecans
B4	Bad	Rancid	Peanuts, cashews, pecans
B5	Bad	Slightly rancid	Peanuts

Detailed information can be found in literature about chemical and lipidic composition of nuts. This information gives first indications on the tendency of each nut to oxidize. Thus unsaturated fatty acids are known to be more likely to oxidize than saturated fatty acid.

Conversely, the tocopherols are known to protect against lipid oxidation, δ- and γ-tocopherol being more protective against oxidation than α- and β-tocopherol [9]. From the lipidic and chemical composition, it could be suspected that almonds or cashew nuts would develop a lower rancidity than pecan or hazelnuts for example. However, these data on the chemical composition do not give direct and global sensory information on the product. That is why HERACLES E-Nose analysis (Table 1) was conducted to get both an overall sensory profiling and chemical composition information.

3   Results

3.1   Chromatograms

The comparison of chromatograms showed significant differences in volatile compounds profile between the different nut mixes (Fig. 1). Bad products clearly show higher contents in volatile compounds. The characterization of these volatile compounds will help find and explain their origin and the possible causes of defects.

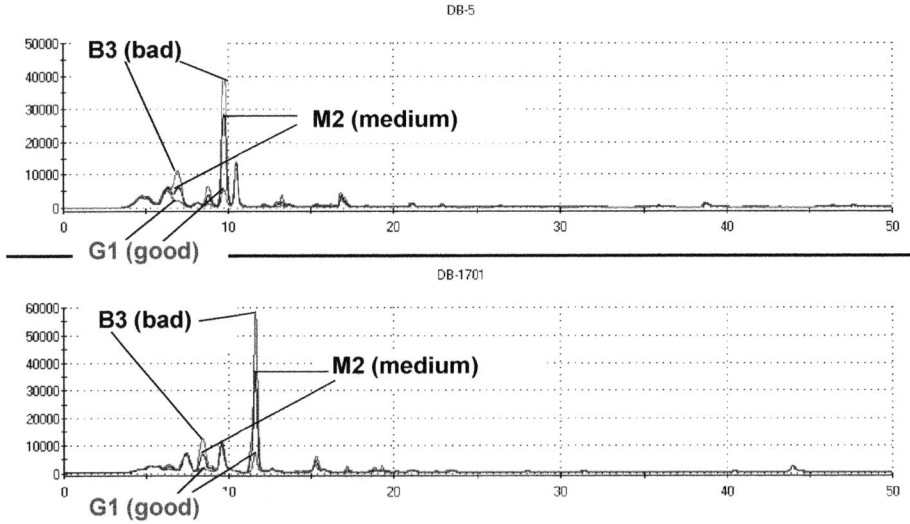

Fig. 1. Superimposed chromatograms of 3 mixes of different qualities, on the 2 HERACLES columns

3.2   Characterization of Volatile Compounds

The nature of the main volatile compounds detected in the headspace of nut mix samples was investigated using their Kovats retention indices (Table 3) and the AroChembase library. The main volatile compounds mostly correspond to secondary oxidation molecules: aldehydes, ketones and alkanes, which confirm that the presence of volatile compounds is strongly related to an oxidation phenomenon.

Table 3. Characterization of nut mix volatile compounds based on their Kovats Index

Retention time		Kovats Index		Possible matching compounds
DB5	DB1701	DB5	DB1701	
4.8	4.7	491	506	Pentane
6.3	7.4	630	722	2-butenal
6.9	8.4	667	765	Furfural
8.7	11.4	749	860	Pentanal/ 1-penten-3-one
9.7	11.7	786	877	2-pentenal
12.9	15.3	883	980	Hexanal
13.3	15.3	892	980	Heptanal
13.3	19.3	892	1085	Octanal

3.3   Odor Map

To globally compare products' aroma, a general odor map based on Principal Component Analysis (PCA) was generated using all chromatograms peaks. In this study, E-Nose analysis confirmed the sensory panel results, since samples were clearly differentiated based on the 3 odor qualities linked to rancidity (Fig. 2).

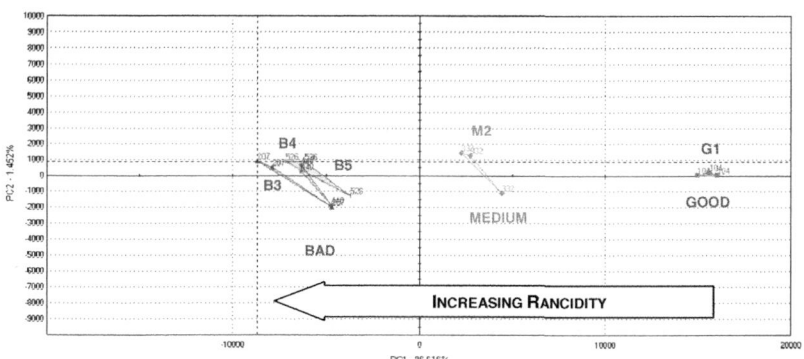

Fig. 2. Principal Component Analysis of Nut Mix Samples

The next step would consist of evaluating each type of nut individually to determine which ones mainly contribute to the global rancidity defect.

3.4   Individual Aroma Analysis of Each Nut Type

In each mix, the nuts were separated by type (peanuts, almonds, cashew nuts, Brazil nuts, pecan nuts, and hazelnuts). Then each type of nuts was analyzed individually with the E-Nose and their aroma profiles compared with the corresponding mix. The analytical conditions were the same as the ones previously applied for the mixes analysis (Table 1).

Fig. 3 represents the odor map of bad B3 mix and its different nut components. The same odor maps built for the 2 other bad samples (B4, B5) and the medium quality sample (M2) showed a similar distribution of the nuts. In bad and medium quality samples, peanuts were the nuts having the volatile profile closest to nut mix aroma.

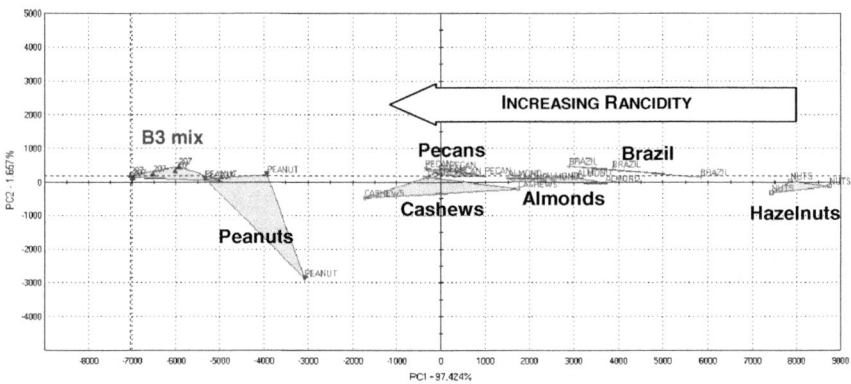

Fig. 3. Odor map of B1 mix and individual nuts based on principal component analysis (PCA) using selected peaks of HERACLES e-nose

To precisely evaluate the volatile compounds content and thus their propensity to oxidize, the Euclidean distance between a blank and each mix, then between the same blank and each type of nuts isolated, was calculated based on HERACLES E-Nose measurement (Fig. 4).

The Euclidean distance is calculated as follows:

$$D\,(X,Y) = \sqrt[2]{\sum_{i=1}^{n}(X_i - Y_i)^2} \tag{1}$$

Where Xi [respectively Yi] is the surface of the ith peak among the n selected peaks of the mix (or nut) [resp. the blank]. In case of several repeated analyses of each sample, Xi [respectively Yi] are defined by:

$$X_i = \frac{\sum_{j=1}^{p}(X_{i,j})}{p} \tag{2}$$

Where p is the number of repetition and $X_{i,j}$ is the surface of the ith peak of the jth mix (or nut) analysis.

$$Y_i = \frac{\sum_{j=1}^{q}(Y_{i,j})}{q} \tag{3}$$

Where q is the number of repetition and $Y_{i,j}$ is the surface of the ith peak of the jth blank analysis. The higher the distance, the higher the volatile compounds content in the mix (or nut).

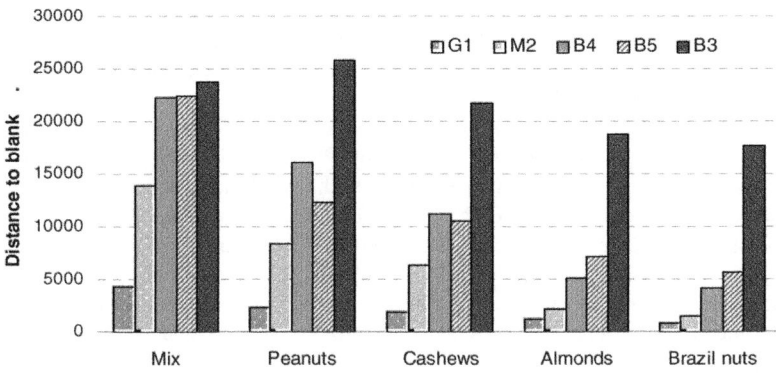

Fig. 4. Odor distance between a blank and each mix or each individual nut type of the mixes (calculated from E-Nose measurement)

The distance for hazelnuts, which was very low, is not presented in the graph. Peanuts and cashew nuts are the most concentrated in volatile compounds, which are linked with lipid oxidation and rancidity. Thus, peanuts are by far the most responsible for the off-odor in bad mixes. Cashew nuts could also have an important impact on final flavor of nut mix. Even in the good mix (G1), the different nuts show the same ranking based on volatile compounds content, but with much lower concentrations. This may indicate that the oxidation rate is the same in the various mixes.

4   Conclusion

The global aroma analysis performed thanks to HERACLES E-Nose showed that peanuts are the most critical ingredients in the development of rancidity off-flavors in nuts mixes. Indeed, among the 6 types of nuts contained in the appetizer, peanuts contain the highest level of volatile compounds. Moreover, as this nut accounts for approximately 60% of the mix mass, the quality of this constituent must be carefully and strictly monitored.

Pecans and cashew nuts also present a relatively high concentration of rancidity off-odors. However, the relatively low proportion of these nuts in the final mix (especially for pecan nuts) makes them less critical towards rancidity. As for Brazil nuts, almonds and hazelnuts, that contain relatively lower amounts of volatile compounds, they have a low impact on the overall mix aroma.

Globally, in order to guarantee the quality of nuts mixes, a quality control of each ingredient should be achieved before blending. This quality control should be conducted in priority on peanuts and cashew nuts, but the analysis of other minority nuts should not be neglected either.

References

1. Lebrun, M., Plotto, A., Goodner, K., Ducamp, M.-N., Baldwin, E.: Discrimination of mango fruit maturity by volatiles using the electronic nose and gas chromatography. Postharvest Biology and Technology 48, 122–131 (2008)
2. Zawirska-Wojtasiak, R., Siwulski, M., Mildner-Szkudlarz, S., Wąsowicz, E.: Studies on the Aroma of Different Species and Strains of Pleurotus Measured by GC/MS, Sensory Analysis and Electronic Nose. Acta Sci. Pol., Technol. Aliment. 8(1), 47–61 (2009)
3. Trihaas, J., Vognsen, L., Nielsen, P.V.: Electronic nose: New tool in modelling the ripening of Danish blue cheese. International Dairy Journal 15, 679–691 (2005)
4. Haugen, J.E., Chanié, E., Westad, F.K., Jonsdottir, R., Bazzo, S., Labrèche, S., Marcq, P., Lundby, F., Olafsdottir, G.: Rapid control of smoked Atlantic Salmon (salmosalar) by electronic nose: correlation with classical methods. Sensors and Actuators B 116, 72–77 (2006)
5. Mildner-Szkudlarz, S., Jelen, H.H.: The potential of different techniques for volatile compounds analysis coupled with PCA for the detection of the adulteration of olive oil with hazelnut oil. Food Chemistry 110, 751–761 (2008)
6. Shiers, V., Adechy, M.: Use of multi-sensor array devices to attempt to predict shelf-lives of edible oils. Seminars in Food Analysis 3, 43–52 (1998)
7. Bazzo, S., Loubet, F., Tang, T., Hewitt-Jones, J.D., Engelen-Cornax, C.E.M., Quadt, J.F.A.: Quality control of edible oil using an electronic nose. Seminars in Food Analysis 3, 15–25 (1998)
8. Gonzalez, Y., Perez, J.L., Moreno, B., Garcia, C.: Classification of vegetable oils by linear discriminate analysis of Electronic Nose. Analytica Chimica Acta 384, 83–94 (1999)
9. Karleskind, A.: Manuel des Corps Gras. Lavoisier Tech. & Doc. (1992)

Estimation of Aroma Determining Compounds of Kangra Valley Tea by Electronic Nose System

Devdulal Ghosh[1,*], Ashu Gulati[2], Robin Joshi[2],
Nabarun Bhattacharyya[1], and Rajib Bandyopadhyay[3]

[1] Centre for Development of Advanced Computing, (C-DAC), Kolkata, Saltlake, Kol-91
{devdulal.ghosh,nabarun.bhattacharya}@cdac.in
[2] Institute of Himalayan Bioresource Technology, Palampur (H.P.) 176061
ashugulati@ihbt.res.in, robinsjoshi@gmail.com
[3] Instrumentation Engineering Department, Jadavpur University (2nd Campus), Kolkata
rb@iee.jusl.ac.in

Abstract. Aroma is a major factor for quality evaluation of finished tea. Professional tea tasters distinguish the aroma of finished tea and decide the valuation of tea. Since tea tasters' being humans their evaluations could be subjective. Instruments like spectrophotometer, high-performance liquid chromatography (HPLC) and gas liquid chromatography(GLC) measure the chemical/volatile compounds polyphenols, catechins and flavour profile of tea[b]. But these instruments are costly, time consuming, take long time to prepare the sample and also needs expert manpower to operate. Besides Electronic Nose (E-Nose) is also used by different tea factories to supplement the work of a tea taster for predicting the tea taster like score of finished tea. E-Nose can give tea taster like score within one and half minute and easy to operate. This paper describes the estimation of tea compounds responsible for tea aroma by E-Nose.

Keywords: Electronic nose, HPLC, GLC, Spectrophotometer, Chemical Compound.

1 Introduction

1.1 About Indian Tea

Tea[c] which is available in the market is in fact 'Made Tea' or processed tea. There are different types of tea say Green tea, Black tea, Instant Tea. There different tea manufacturing like India, Kenya and Sri Lanka In India, there are three distinctly different tea-growing regions. These regions are geographically separated, thereby producing three entirely different teas both in style and in taste/flavor. The three regions are: Darjeeling (North-Eastern India), Assam (far North-East India) and Nilgiri (South India). Apart from the above three distinct tea growing regions tea is also grown in Kerala, Karnataka, Himachal Pradesh, Uttaranchal, Sikkim, Orissa, Bihar,

---

* Corresponding author.

M.K. Kundu et al. (Eds.): PerMIn 2012, LNCS 7143, pp. 171–179, 2012.
© Springer-Verlag Berlin Heidelberg 2012

Arunachal Pradesh, Tripura, Manipur, Nagaland, Mizoram & Meghalaya and in the adjacent plain areas of Dooars and Terai of West Bengal.

Kangra[d,e] district is situated in the North-West Indian state of Himachal Pradesh. The craggy Dhauladhar range towers over the Kangra Valley, where in the foothills lies India's smallest tea region with its own tea town of Palampur in Himachal Pradesh, India. Uniquely, it's the only tea region in India that comprises exclusively China or China-hybrid tea bushes. The China leaf, when processed according to quality norms, yields a distinctive brew that's golden in colour, with a sweet undertone and astringency similar to Darjeeling teas.

1.2   About Electronic Nose

An electronic nose uses an array of non-specific broadly tuned sensors to discriminate odours [a,g]. The odours are analyzed by sensor array data with pattern recognition methods [8]. A customized electronic nose set-up has been developed such that the same can be used in production floor of tea processing units for monitoring of volatile emission pattern during the fermentation process. The electronic nose consists of (a) sensor array, (b) micro-pump with programmable sequence control, (c) PC-based data acquisition and (d) olfaction software as illustrated in Fig. 1.

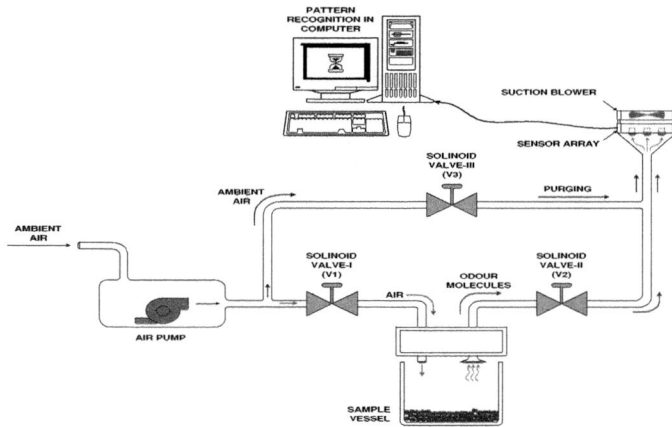

Fig. 1. Customized electronic nose set-up

The experimental sniffing cycle consists of automated sequence of internal operations: (i) headspace generation, (ii) sampling, (iii) purging and (iv) dormancy before the start of the next sniffing cycle. Headspace generation ensures adequate concentration of volatiles released by tea within the sample holder by blowing regulated flow of air on the sample. During sampling, the sensor array is exposed to a constant flow of volatiles through pipelines inside the electronic nose system. During purging operation, sensor heads are cleared with blow of fresh air so that the sensors can go back to their baseline values. The programmable time dormancy cycle is the suspended mode of the electronic nose between two consecutive sniffing cycles.

The specially designed software, called olfaction software, controls the PC-based data acquisition and automated operation of all these cycles. The software has got features like programmable sequence control, dynamic fermentation profile display, data logging, alarm annunciation, data archival, etc. The software has been developed in LabVIEW® of National Instruments. Experimental conditions during the investigation of the different stages of the fermentation process of black tea are as follows:Heating Time= 65 sec, Amount of fermenting tea sample = 50 grams, , Headspace generation time = 30s, Data Collection Time = 50s, , Purging time = 100s, Airflow rate = 5 ml/s.

1.3   About Chemical Analysis Procedure

Gas liquid chromatography (GLC)[f] is a chromatographic technique that can separate a mixture of compounds and is used in biochemistry and analytical chemistry to identify, quantify and purify the individual volatile components of the mixture. The present study is only involved the identification and quantification of aroma producing components in tea.

Gas liquid chromatography (GLC) is basically a highly improved form of column chromatography. Instead of a solvent being allowed to drip through a column under gravity, it is forced through under high temperature of up to 400 °C. That makes it much faster. It also allows using a very much smaller particle size for the column packing material, which gives a much greater surface area for interactions between the stationary phase and the molecules flowing past it. This allows a much better separation of the components of the mixture. These methods are highly automated and extremely sensitive. The block diagram of GLC is shown in Fig 2.

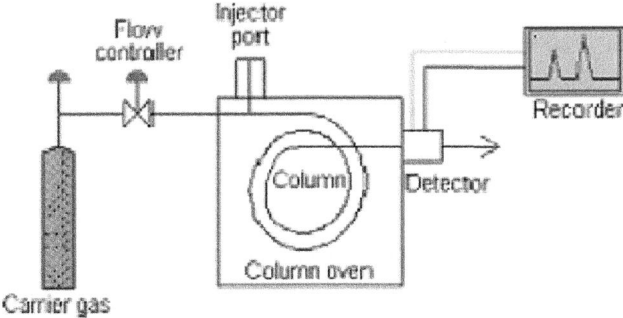

Fig. 2. Block diagram of GLC operation

GLC typically utilizes different types of stationary phases, a pump that moves the mobile phase(s) and analyte through the column. A detector is attached with column to provide a characteristic retention time for the analyte. The detector may also provide additional information related to the analyte, (i.e. mass spectrometric data for analyte if so equipped). Analyte retention time varies depending on the strength of its interactions with the stationary phase, the mobile phase used, and the flow rate of the mobile phase. In present study, there is a form of liquid chromatography, which utilizes higher column size, smaller media inside the column, and gradient of temperature.

In present study identification and quantification of the aroma producing components of tea has been done by a sensitive, fast, and accurate gas liquid chromatography (GLC) technique. Next the same sample was fitted to E-Nose for quality estimation by sensory evaluation. Then one correlation model has been made with sensory response generated by E-Nose and chemical response generated from GLC. Using this model it is also possible to predict the chemical compound of a sample by E-Nose.

2   Experimental Procedure

The experiment was conducted at Institute of Himalayan Bioresource Technology (IHBT), Palampur. The samples were Kangra orthodox black tea of IHBT. There ware total twenty samples in number. From each sample 50 gm ware taken for the E-Nose experiment and the experiment was conducted as above-mentioned condition i.e. heating time=65 sec, headspace time=30 sec, sampling time=50 sec, purging time=100 sec. Then the GLC sample was prepared from that particular finished tea sample and that was fitted to GLC for analysis. The response of the components are measured by the GLC equipped with FID and GC/MS. This technique was applied for each sample (i.e. 20) and all the response were noted.

3   Data Analysis and Results

3.1   Data Normalization

In this data set we obtained one instantaneous response & one purging response for each tea sample. Instantaneous response is a matrix of 800X8(since head space time 30 sec and sampling time 50 sec, so total time is 80 sec (30+50). In one sec 10 data are captured and there are 8 MOS sensors, so total data set is (800X8) & purging response is a vector of 1X8 (when the process shifts from headspace to sampling, i.e. the response of 30th sec).

If V_I is the instantaneous response and V_P is the purging response then the normalization response V_M is described as in (1) for all sensors.

$$\frac{V_I - V_P}{V_P} \tag{1}$$

3.2   Data Matrix Preparation

Form the normalized matrix the maximum value is selected. For 8 sensors 8 value obtained. So finally it is vector of 1X8 and for 20 samples the matrix is 20X8. Also we have the chemical analysis values of the instrument like GLC.

3.3   Data Analysis

For analyzing these data two type of approach were adopted

   a) Cluster analysis b) Classification analysis

3.4   Cluster Analysis

For each tea samples we have one set of Electronic Nose data and also the tea taster score given by human and aroma generated from E-Nose data of that sample based on aroma. Here first all the data (20) sets are grouped as per the aroma score. For example the aroma score <7.5 data sets are grouped in one and the other groups are of aroma score between 7.5 to 8 and more than 8.5. Then these data sets were applied in Principal Component Analysis (PCA) to visualize whether there are true 3 clusters (aroma score <7.5, between 7.5 to 8.5 & > 8.5). The clustering plot is given below in Fig 3 where three distinct groups are present.

   Principal Component Analysis[h,I] (PCA) involves a mathematical procedure that transforms a number of possibly correlated variables into a lesser number of uncorrelated variables called principal components and reduces the number of dimensions also. Here first two dimensions (principal components) are plotted to visualize the clusters.

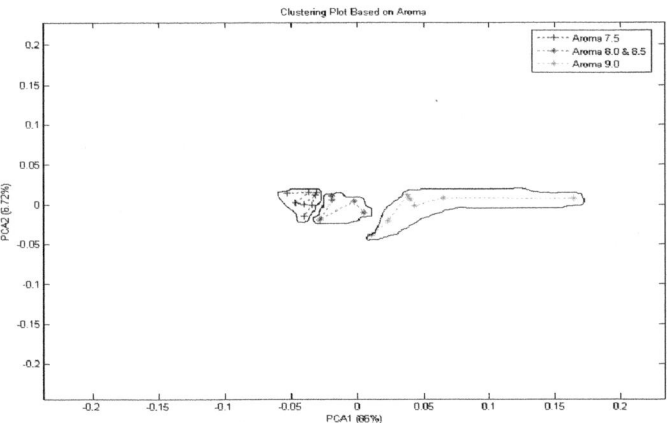

Fig. 3. Clustering analysis of E-Nose data based on Aroma Score

3.5   Classification Analysis

Like all classification analysis[h,I] it is required some data sets as input and the score/output of the corresponding dataset to build the model. Here we have used as output the values of linalool , geraniol , and for all case the input is the maximum normalized value of Electronic Nose response. The algorithms applied for classification are a) Multiple Linear Regression (MLR) and b) Multiple Discriminant

Analysis (MDA). After building the model the same dataset is used as testing data set. The results are given in tabular form.

Multiple Linear Regression (MLR) is one type of statistical algorithms which is used for modeling the relationship between a scalar variable Y (output) and one or more variables denoted by X (E-Nose response). In linear regression, models of the unknown parameters are estimated from the data using linear functions as in (2). Here the equations are

$$Y = MX + C \qquad\qquad\qquad .(2)$$

Where Y is the chemical output or Aroma value and X is the E-Nose sensor response. For this case Y is single column matrix (say Linalool or Geraniol) and X is the matrix of 8-sensor response. So for Table 1 MLR analysis X is a matrix of 19X8(number of sample=19 and number of sensor 8) and Y is 19X1 matrix. (Number of sample=19, no of output=1)

From this first M & C has to estimate. Then for unknown X, Y is calculated using this esteemed M & C.

Multiple discriminant analysis (MDA) used to classify a datasets (E-Nose response), which has more than two categories (output values like 7.5, 8, 9) using distance calculation. First for the same score/output vectors are grouped and mean is calculated. Then the testing vectors distance is calculated from the mean vector for each group. The minimum distance is selected and the final score/output of the testing vector is the score/output mean vector.

The analysis results of classification are described bellow. For each sample there is a vector of E-Nose response and response of volatile flavour compounds geraniol, ionones, linalool, hexenals and pyrazines from GLC. For geraniol, linalool all the E-Nose values we have assigned the response of at the time of training. Then the same sample was given at the time of testing. That prediction result is given next column. Then the difference is calculated between assigned and predicted value. That difference was transformed in percentage. Then the accuracy percentage of prediction is calculated. All the results are tabulated.

In Table 1 regarding MLR portion of the table 'Assigned output (A)' means the assigned value for training as output i.e. Y. 'Predicted output (P)' means after estimation of M&C, using the same input (X) data the new output i.e. Y. The next column describes the difference (abs (A-P)) between assigned & predicted value. The next column gives the % of error in prediction by the formula $\dfrac{abs(A - P)}{A} X100$.

In Table 1 regarding MDA portion of the table 'Assigned output (A1)' means the assigned group/class for training as output. 'Predicted output (P1)' means after training, using the same input (X) data the new output group/class. The next column describes whether there is any difference between assigned and predicted group/class (abs (A-P)). The next column status of prediction. Lastly the average % of error & accuracy is calculated. The Table2 is in same line but only for Geraniol(Y) where the output is Linalool(Y) for Table1.

Table 1. Linalool Prediction by E-Nose

Multiple Linear Regression (MLR)				Multiple Discriminant Analysis (MDA)			
Assigned output (A)	Predicted output (P)	Difference between assigned & predicted	Difference in percentage	Assigned output	Predicted output	Difference between assigned & predicted	Prediction Status
42	39.66	2.34	5.56	42	42	0	Correct
30	35.94	5.94	19.81	30	30	0	Correct
36	29.05	6.95	19.30	36	36	0	Correct
24	28.23	4.23	17.61	24	24	0	Correct
36	37.18	1.18	3.28	36	36	0	Correct
24	29.85	5.85	24.39	24	24	0	Correct
42	44.97	2.97	7.07	42	48	6	Wrong
48	46.41	1.59	3.30	48	48	0	Correct
36	35.14	0.86	2.39	36	36	0	Correct
36	37.92	1.92	5.34	36	36	0	Correct
42	38.79	3.21	7.64	42	42	0	Correct
48	42.33	5.67	11.82	48	42	6	Wrong
48	40.70	7.30	15.21	48	48	0	Correct
42	44.15	2.15	5.12	42	42	0	Correct
48	46.54	1.46	3.05	48	48	0	Correct
42	49.74	7.74	18.43	42	42	0	Correct
48	44.76	3.24	6.76	48	42	6	Wrong
42	41.45	0.55	1.31	42	48	6	Wrong
48	49.19	1.19	2.47	48	48	0	Correct
		Average Difference (%)	9.47			Difference	21.05
		Accuracy of prediction (%)	90.53			Accuracy of prediction (%)	78.95

Table 2. Geraniol Predictions by E-Nose

Multiple Linear Regression (MLR)				Multiple Discriminant Analysis (MDA)			
Assigned output	Predicted output	Difference between assigned & predicted	Difference in percentage	Assigned output	Predicted output	Difference between assigned & predicted	Prediction Status
240.00	268.63	28.63	11.93	240.00	240.00	0.00	Correct
120.00	212.21	92.21	76.84	120.00	120.00	0.00	Correct
280.00	274.19	5.81	2.08	280.00	280.00	0.00	Correct

Table 2. (*Continued*)

240.00	259.61	19.61	8.17	240.00	240.00	0.00	Correct
320.00	314.05	5.95	1.86	320.00	320.00	0.00	Correct
120.00	171.17	51.17	42.65	120.00	120.00	0.00	Correct
280.00	238.73	41.27	14.74	280.00	280.00	0.00	Correct
320.00	280.54	39.46	12.33	320.00	320.00	0.00	Correct
280.00	288.31	8.31	2.97	280.00	280.00	0.00	Correct
360.00	335.37	24.63	6.84	360.00	360.00	0.00	Correct
360.00	211.17	148.83	41.34	360.00	120.00	240.00	Wrong
320.00	315.44	4.56	1.42	320.00	320.00	0.00	Correct
280.00	282.85	2.85	1.02	280.00	320.00	40.00	Wrong
160.00	169.52	9.52	5.95	160.00	160.00	0.00	Correct
280.00	312.99	32.99	11.78	280.00	280.00	0.00	Correct
240.00	233.37	6.63	2.76	240.00	240.00	0.00	Correct
320.00	328.07	8.07	2.52	320.00	320.00	0.00	Correct
320.00	326.85	6.85	2.14	320.00	320.00	0.00	Correct
280.00	233.01	46.99	16.78	280.00	280.00	0.00	Correct
		Average Difference(%)	14.90			Average Difference (%)	10.00
		Accuracy of prediction (%)	85.10			Accuracy of prediction (%)	90.00

4   Conclusions

Here the same data sets were used for both training and testing. Two (MLR & MDA) algorithms ware applied. Here though the accuracy in MLR is less but the accuracy in MDA is very good in both cases. Besides this it is demonstrated the prediction of chemical composition by E-Nose throughout the paper. If this can be proved for more samples then the present scenario of chemical analysis for tea may be changed a lot in future. This work may give a new direction and can open up new paradigms in the field of tea quality analysis.

References

[1] Nabarun, B., Bipan, T., Arun, J., Devdulal, G., Rajib, B., Manabendra, B.: Preemptive Identification of Optimum Fermentation Time for Black Tea Using Electronic Nose. Sensors and Actuators B 131(1), 110–116 (2008)
[2] http://www.tocklai.net
[3] http://www.teaboard.gov.in
[4] http://www.ihbt.res.in/

[5] http://kangravalleytea.com

[6] http://en.wikipedia.org/wiki/Main_Page

[7] Nabarun, B., Sohan, S., Bipan, T., Pradip, T., Arun, J., Devdulal, G., Rajib, B., Manabendra, B., Santanu, S.: Detection of Optimum Fermentation Tim for Black Tea Manufacturing Using Electronic Nose. Sensors and Actuators B 122(2), 627–634 (2007)

[8] Nabarun, B., Rajib, B., Manabendra, B., Bipan, T., Devdulal, G., Arun, J.: Electronic Nose for Black Tea Classification and Correlation of Measurements with Tea Taster Marks. IEEE Transaction on Instrumentation and Measurement 57(7), 1313–1321 (2008)

[9] http://www.statsoft.com

Taste Attributes Profiling in Carrot Juice Using an Electronic Tongue

Zoltán Kovács[1], Dániel Szöllősi[1], András Fekete[1],
Koichi Yoshida[2], Emiko Ishikawa[2], Sandrine Isz[3], and Marion Bonnefille[3]

[1] Department of Physics and Control,
Faculty of Food Science,
Corvinus University of Budapest,
Somlóistreet 14-16, H-1118, Budapest, Hungary
[2] Alpha M.O.S. Japan K.K., JowatakanawaBldg. 8F, 1-5-4 Takanawa,
Minato-ku, 108-0074, Tokyo, Japan
[3] Alpha M.O.S. S.A., 20 Avenue Didier Daurat,
31400, Toulouse, France

Abstract. The taste of five brands of carrot juice was analyzed both by a sensory panel and an electronic tongue. The panelists found significant differences between the carrot juice samples in some appearance and odor attributes and in the relevant taste attributes such as sour taste, sweet taste and taste persistence. Principal component analysis plot calculated from the electronic tongue results showed a clear separation between the sample groups, with a ranking on sourness similar to the one from the panel.

Keywords: sensory analysis, taste analysis, taste profiling, electronic tongue.

1   Introduction

Carrot juice is juice produced from carrots, often consumed as a health drink [1, 2]. Carrot juice, because of its many healthful benefits, is frequently called the "miracle juice". A large number of people suffering from various ailments have found that the inclusion of carrot juice in their diet has greatly improved their health. Countless others have found it to be a valuable "protective" agent in the building and maintenance of health in both children and adults, while its delicious flavor makes it popular with all members of the family as a beverage.

Carrot juice is one of the richest sources of vitamin A that can be used in the daily diet. It also ranks high as a source of the other vitamins, especially those of the B complex. Its mineral content is equally rich, and includes calcium, copper, magnesium, potassium, sodium, phosphorus, chlorine, sulfur, and iron. Carrots have a low yield compared to fruits like apples and oranges in providing juices [3]. Main difficulty in juicing carrots is in separating the pulp, which is very tough, from the juice. Unlike many juices, it is opaque. Carrot juice is usually defined as having a uniquely sweet flavor of concentrated carrots [4, 5].

M.K. Kundu et al. (Eds.): PerMIn 2012, LNCS 7143, pp. 180–186, 2012.

The objective of this study was to perform a taste analysis of carrot juices based on the basic taste attributes using an electronic tongue instrument. Then, the objective was to determine relationship between sensory evaluation and measurement results obtained by electronic tongue ASTREE (Alpha MOS, France), since this analyzer has already been applied to food and beverage evaluation.

2   Material and Method

2.1   Samples

Five different carrot juice brands of 100% carrot content were analyzed with sensory panel and electronic tongue during the experiments. The samples were purchased from different retailers. The samples of different brands were marked by "A", "B", "C", "D", and "E". The specifications of the tested carrot juice samples are shown in Table 1.

Table 1. Specifications of the carrot juice samples (TSS = total soluble solid)

| Sample | Supplier specification | | | | | | Measured | |
	Carrot juice content	Added citric acid	Carbohydrate, g/100 ml	Sugar, g/100 ml	Protein, g/100 ml	Fat, g/100 ml	pH	Conductivity, mS/cm
A	N.A.	N.A.	6.0	N.A.	0.7	0.0	5.21	12.78
B	99.5%	0.5%	8.0	8.0	1.0	<0.1	5.00	12.88
C*	97%	3%	6.7	N.A.	<0.6	<0.1	4.37	9.76
D*	99%	1%	7.0	7.0	1.0	<0.1	4.49	11.74
E**	100%	0%	6.2	6.0	0.6	0.1	4.98	14.57

*heat treated
**lactic fermentation

2.2   Sensory Evaluation

Sensory analysis was performed to evaluate the relationship between the human sensory perception and the electronic tongue measurement on the five carrot juices. Fifteen trained panelists assessed the carrot juices in two replicates (two sessions under the same conditions, but sample codes changed) using profile analysis method, in accordance with international standards (ISO 13299:2003, ISO 11035:1994).

The panelists analyzed the carrot juice samples based on color, odor, taste, and texture. Table 2 summarizes the sensory attributes evaluated and contains the extreme values for each attribute such as: color hue, general odor, sweet odor, acidic odor, carrot odor, off odor, sweet taste, sour taste, carrot taste, off taste, and taste persistence.

Table 2. Sensory attributes used during the sensory analysis

Attributes	Low value	High value
Particles	Low	High
Orange color	Weak	Intense
Fiberness	Fine	Rough
Sweetodor	Weak	Intense
Sour odor	Weak	Intense
Vegetableodor	Othervegetableodor	Carrotodor
Sweet taste	Weak	Intense
Sour taste	Weak	Intense
Bitter taste	Weak	Intense
Off taste	Weak	Intense
Taste persistence	Weak	Intense
Global impression	Bad	Good

2.3   Electronic Tongue

The carrot juice samples were analyzed with ASTREE electronic tongue. This instrument is based on liquid sensor array allowing a measurement of potential difference between each sensor and a reference electrode [6].

The liquid sensors are modified solid electrochemical electrodes on which the active electrode surface is covered by a coating. According to the coating material used, different selectivity can be obtained to various taste substances but also dissolved compounds. One major feature of these liquid sensors is the cross-sensitivity and selectivity so that each sensor could concurrently contribute to the detection of most substances found in the liquid matrix [7].

The ASTREE electronic tongue is equipped with an array of seven different liquid cross-selective sensors. Thus, the use of a cross-sensitive sensor array allows tracking any variation in the liquid matrix. For example, several compounds can contribute to the same taste attribute so that a cross-selective sensor array is needed to provide a global liquid and taste perception. The cross-selectivity of the 7 sensors (SRS, GPS, STS, UMS, SPS, SWS, and BRS) was evaluated on the 5 main tastes: sourness, sweetness, bitterness, saltiness, and the Asian savory sensation known as umami. This specific sensor array allows a relative ranking of attributes intensity of analyzed samples based on a specific methodology [8]. Table 3 shows the analytical parameters applied during the analysis.

Table 3. Electronic Tongue Analytical Conditions

Parameter	Value
Sample volume	90 mL
Time per analysis	120 s
Time per cleaning	20 s
Repeats	9
Sampletemperature	25.0°C (controlled)

Data were processed by one way analysis of variance (ANOVA) and principal components analysis was used to evaluate the sensory and electronic tongue measurement results.

3   Results

3.1   Sensory Evaluation

Cluster analysis was used to evaluate the results of sensory evaluation to identify the best panelists from repeatability point of view. From this analysis, eleven panelists showed acceptable reproducibility and were selected for statistical evaluation. Since no significant difference was observed for attributes evaluation between the two panel sessions (except for global impression), the results from both sessions were taken into account.

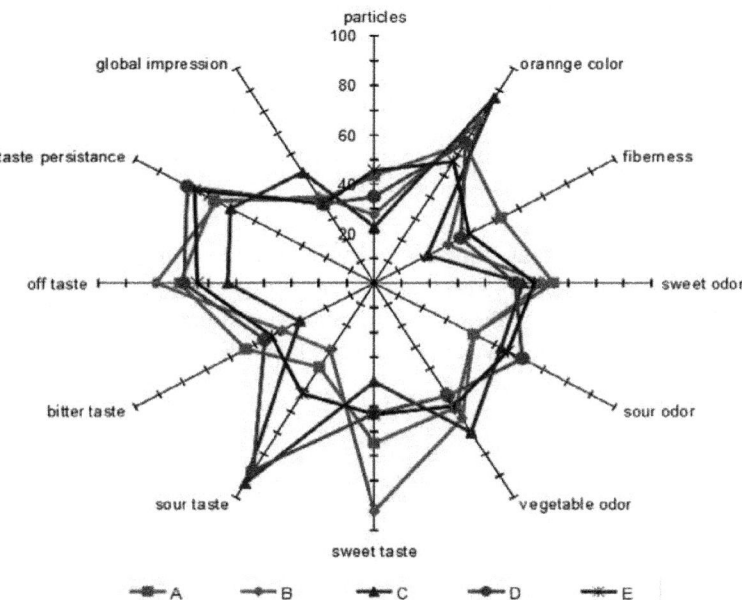

Fig. 1. Sensory profiles of the tested carrot juice samples

Fig. 1 shows that the biggest differences were observed in case of sour, sweet, and off taste. Based on the sensory average score value the sweet taste was the less intense in case of sample "C" and the sweetest one was the sample "B". Reverse order was established in sour taste by the panelist.

3.2   Electronic Tongue

Principal component analysis plot calculated from the electronic tongue results (Fig. 2) shows that there is a good separation between the sample groups. The position of the sample groups based on the first principal component (PC1) is similar to the sour taste results determined by the sensory panel. The arrows on Fig. 2 represent the loadings of the sensors. Sensor SRS, which was developed for sour taste measurement, has the highest influence on PC1.

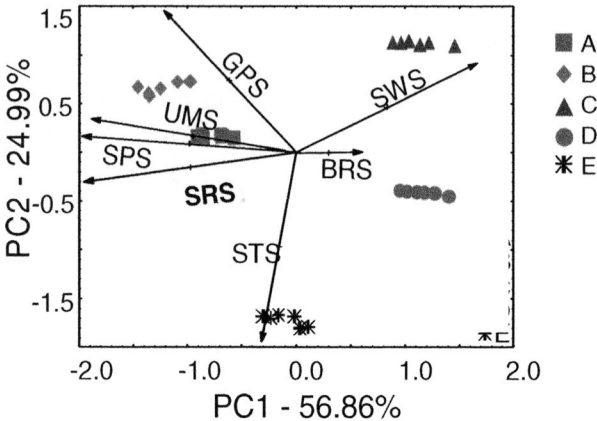

Fig. 2. Principal component analysis score plot of PC1 versus PC2 for electronic tongue measurement of carrot juice samples (sensors: SRS, GPS, STS, SPS, UMS, SWS, and BRS)

A simple data treatment allows comparing samples on an easy relative scale. Corresponding radar representation allows to easily checking differences between samples (Fig 3). Together with a standard addition methodology, it allows to define the sensor that best correlates with a given taste increase.

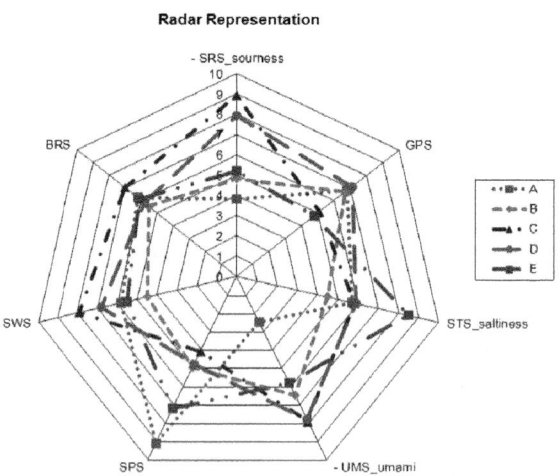

Fig. 3. Radar representation of the different sensors (sensors: SRS, GPS, STS, SPS, UMS, SWS, and BRS) when analyzing the carrot juice samples

The observed sequence of sensor SRS and SWS is similar to the sensory one of sourness intensity and sweetness intensity of the carrot juice samples respectively. Fig. 4 shows the sensory results for "sour taste" with the error bars and the SRS sensor intensity based on electronic tongue measurement results.

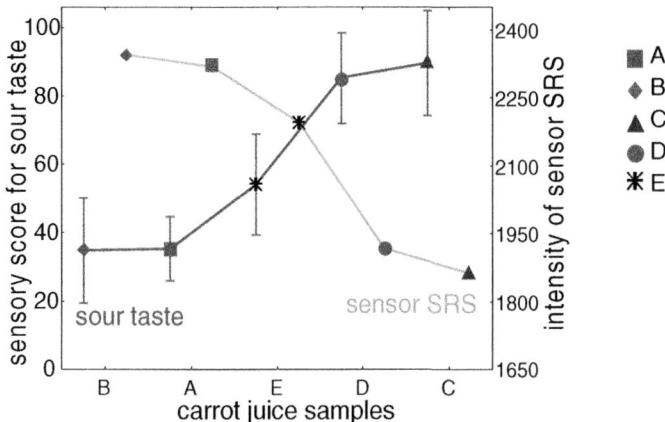

Fig. 4. Plots of sensory scores for "sour taste" with error bars and SRS sensor intensity

Pearson's correlation coefficients were calculated between the average score values of the sour taste evaluated by the sensory panel and the intensity of the electronic tongue sensors. The highest correlation coefficient ($r = -0.998$) was found in the case of the sensor SRS. Similarly, the higher correlation coefficient ($r = -0.762$) to the sweetness intensity was given by the sensor SWS.

4   Conclusion

Carrot juice analysis showed that the panelists found the most significant differences among the samples in sour taste and sweet taste. The determined order based on these two attributes was confirmed by the results of the SRS and SWS sensors of the ASTREE electronic tongue.

References

1. Agricultural Marketing Resource Center (AgMRC). Carrot Profile. Iowa State University, Ames (2011), http://www.agmrc.org
2. Sinha, N.K., Hui, Y.H., Zgl Evranuz, E., Siddiq, M., Ahmed, J.: Handbook of Vegetables and Vegetable Processing. Wiley-Blackwell (November 2010)
3. Rayman, A., Baysal, T., Demirdöven, A.: Optimisation of electroplasmolysis application for increased juice yield in carrot juice production. International Journal of Food Science & Technology 46, 781–786 (2011)

4. Akubor, P.I.: Physicochemical, Microbiological and Sensory Properties of Yoghurt supplemented with Carrot Juice. Nigerian Journal of Nutritional Sciences 32(1) (2011)
5. Munoz, A.M.: Sensory evaluation in quality control: an overview, new developments and future opportunities. Food Quality and Preference 13, 329–339 (2002)
6. Jimenez, C., Bratov, A., Abramova, N., Baldi, A.: ISFET based sensors: fundamentals and applications. In: Encyclodepia of Sensors, vol. X, pp. 1–46 (2006)
7. Major, N., Marković, K., Krpan, M., Šarić, G., Hruškar, M., Vahčić, N.: Rapid honey characterization and botanical classification by an electronic tongue. Talanta 85(1), 569–574 (2011)
8. AM taste ranking leaflet.pdf, http://www.alpha-mos.com

Improvement of Quality Perception
for Black CTC Tea by Means of an Electronic Tongue

Arunangshu Ghosh[1,*], Bipan Tudu[1], Pradip Tamuly[2],
Nabarun Bhattacharyya[3], and Rajib Bandyopadhyay[1]

[1] Department of Instrumentation and Electronics Engineering,
Jadavpur University, Kolkata, India
arunangshu.ghosh@gmail.com
[2] Tea Research Association, Tocklai, Jorhat, Assam, India
[3] Center for Development and Advanced Computing,
Salt Lake, Kolkata, India

Abstract. Electronic tongue has already been used to estimate the quality of tea in terms of tea-tasters scores that are subjective and limited by human sensory organs. It is known that, chemical constituents play significant role to determine the quality of tea. Thus the perception of quality as understood from an electronic tongue can be improved if it can be trained to estimate the amount of major chemicals responsible for quality of tea. An alternate method of rapid quality evaluation of tea is proposed using a voltammetric electronic tongue to determine two major taste descriptors in black tea. The correlation model is developed between the electronic tongue signatures and theaflavins/thearubigins contents of tea using multi-layer perceptrons. The perception of taste is further improved using scaled conjugate gradient as a weight optimization algorithm.

Keywords: Theaflavins, Thearubigins, Voltammetric electronic tongue, Principal component analysis, Multi-layer perceptrons, Scaled conjugate gradient.

1 Introduction

The combined perceptions of taste, olfaction and vision of tea tasters determine the overall quality of finished tea quantified in a scale from 1-10. These scores determine the price of finished tea. The tasters generally ascertain the brighter tea as better than those with darker colours as colour is also an indication of its taste. Another criterion used by tea tasters to describe the quality of tea liquors is the "astringency", which is perceived as a rough and drying sensation in the mouth. Terms such as "strong", "brisk", "harsh" and "dull" are used by professional tea tasters to describe the quality and intensity for the sense of astringency.

However, the segregation of tea based on human perceptions remains highly subjective and market specific. The reproducibility of generating the quality scores are also limited by mental state, fatigue and olfactory-adaptation of tasters.

---

* Corresponding author.

M.K. Kundu et al. (Eds.): PerMIn 2012, LNCS 7143, pp. 187–194, 2012.

The remarkable abilities of biological sensors limited by above factors have been the motivation towards finding instrumental, objective, efficient and inexpensive systems for quality evaluation, like Electronic Nose [1] and Electronic Tongue [2]. These systems mimic the senses of smell and taste of human sensory panel and lead to rapid quality standardization of finished tea. These machines have been used to grade the quality of finished tea [1, 2] and detect optimum fermentation time of tea processing [3]. The rapidity of these instruments aiding the experience and judgments of tea tasters is helpful to keep in pace with the growing production volume. These devices consist of sensor array that generate chemical fingerprints for different samples of tea. The fingerprints are analyzed using an appropriate pattern recognition algorithms and are calibrated with tasters' scores to simulate the generation of quality scores when an unknown tea sample is presented. But, the outputs of these instruments are also susceptible to the uncertainties and limitations of quality scores used for calibration. An approach that may help users to gather improved quality-perception of tea from these instruments could be to train them predict concentrations of biochemical constituents responsible for quality. The generation of target data; in this case concentration of chemical compounds, can be determined by standard instrumental techniques and will be free of organoleptic limitations. The estimation of biochemical compounds in tea also gives a generalized idea of quality Thus a study of biochemical compounds responsible for taste and colour of tea liquor is essential. Polyphenols like catechins, are the most important group of tea components. During the production of black tea, the fermentation (enzymatic oxidation) processes cause green tea catechins to oxidize and polymerize to form oligomeric flavanols, including theaflavins, thearubigin. Theaflavins and thearubigin are two main polyphenols that give black tea its characteristic colour and taste [4]. These polyphenols are thought to reduce the saliva lubrication by reacting with salivary proteins and astringency is perceived as the friction between two non-lubricated surfaces [5].

The taste perception of tea can be considered as a function of its chemical constituents. If an electronic tongue is subjected to tea liquor, the voltage-fingerprints from sensor array shall be a function of its constituents. Thus the data processing module of an electronic tongue could be calibrated with these concentrations so that indications about the same could be obtained for unknown tea samples. In this paper estimations of theaflavin and thearubigin concentrations are done in order to get improved quality perception from an electronic tongue. The usage of voltammetric technique with LAPV waveform generates large amount of information with low detection limit. Literature survey reveals that electronic tongue has been used to evaluate the levels of tea astringency [6, 7]. It has been employed to differentiate among various grades of tea [8, 9]. An electronic tongue is also employed to determine the compositions of electrolytes based on their combined taste [10]. We thus infer that an electronic tongue shall be capable to indicate the concentration of chemical compounds that influences the overall taste.

2   Experimental

The tea samples have been produced under environmentally controlled atmosphere at Tea Research Association, Tocklai, Assam, India. In this experiment a total of 46 different tea samples have been procured over two seasons (June-July and September-October). The TF, TR content of samples has been determined using spectrophotometry [11] and then presented to electronic tongue for collection of responses.

2.1   The Electronic Tongue Setup

An electronic tongue setup has been developed using an array of five working electrodes, made of noble metals – gold, iridium, palladium, platinum, and rhodium; a platinum counter electrode (PH Ionics, India); and an Ag/AgCl reference electrode (saturated KCL, Gamry Instruments Inc., USA). Generation of LAPV pulses and A/D conversion are realized using data acquisition card USB 6008 from National Instruments®. Fig. 1 presents the functional block diagram of the customized electronic tongue setup with the response waveform for LAPV scenario.

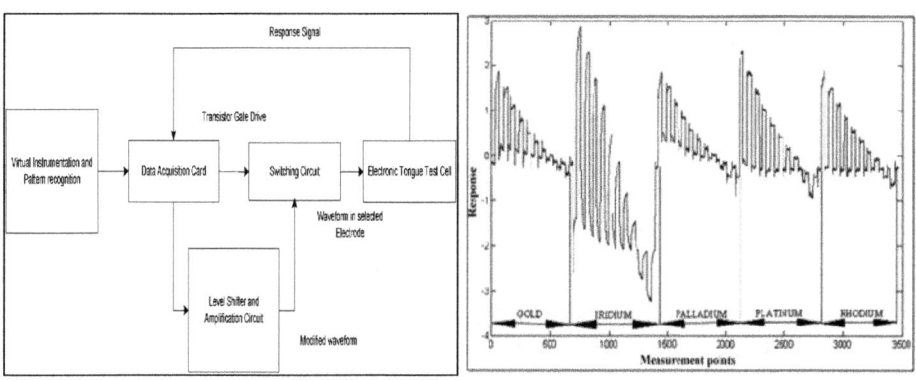

Fig. 1. Functional block diagram and LAPV response of the electronic tongue

The system generates a Large Amplitude Pulse waveform varying from 0 to 500mV in small user-defined steps. A signal of maximum value −0.2V to +0.8V is applied to the sample through working electrodes one at a time. The working electrodes are selected sequentially by a switching circuit. The voltage equivalent of output current from the test sample, after single stage amplification, is applied to the data acquisition card, where it is collected and stored for data analysis. A typical voltammetric response for LAPV is presented in Fig. 1 where 694 data points are collected from each of the five electrodes; the final waveform from single iteration thus consists of 3740 data points.

2.2   Sample Preparation for Electronic Tongue

The tea liquor samples for electronic tongue is prepared by boiling 200ml of de-ionized water poured over 1gm of dry tea. The solution has been allowed to brew for 5 min, after which it is stirred well to uniformly mix the extract with water. The liquor is separated into another beaker carefully, leaving the residual leaves at the bottom.

The separated liquor thus obtained, in above step is filtered and allowed to cool down to 25-28 °C. The samples are then presented to electronic tongue and 38 responses are recorded for each of 46 tea samples. As each of five electrodes produces 694 points, each runs of electronic tongue yields a waveform with 3470 data points. Thus a data matrix of size 3470x1748 is obtained for data analysis.

3   Data Analysis

3.1   Data Preprocessing

Preprocessing stage is very useful as it contributes to feature extraction and increased efficiency of prediction. The preprocessing steps are described below:

i)   The raw data set is normalized with respect to the mean response of each electrode. In this way, only the deviations from mean readings of each electrode are collected for data analysis as shown in equation (1). This step is done in order to remove the effect of sensor drift.

$$M_{i,j} = \sum_{j=0}^{N_o-1} \sum_{e=0}^{N_e-1} \sum_{i=0}^{N_p-1} (M_{(i+e \times N_p),j} - \mu_{e,j})) \tag{1}$$

where, $M_{i,j}$ is i^{th} element of jth observation; N_o, N_e, N_p being the numbers of observations, numbers of electrodes and the number of observations collected for each electrodes respectively and $\mu_{e,j}$ being the mean response of eth electrode over N_p observations, to be presented for j^{th} observation

ii)   Data compression using wavelet transform: The response vectors from electronic tongue has 3470 elements, hence it is desirable to reduce the dimension in order to reduce the complexity during data analysis. In this work the dimension reduction is performed by choosing the approximate coefficients corresponding to 6th level of wavelet decomposition, using "Haar" as a mother wavelet. The above parameters are chosen in support of reference [12].

iii)   In order to improve the training of neural networks the data set is preprocessed with respect to the mean and variance using equation (2). Data set is subjected to mean-variance normalization prior to be presented to neural networks.

$$M_{i,j} = \frac{(M_{i,j} - mean(m_i))}{stdev(m_i)} \tag{2}$$

where M is the input dataset and m_i is i^{th} response vector over all observations.

3.2   Principal Component Analysis (PCA)

The PCA [13] on electronic tongue data transforms the data into information rich, reduced dimension (typically 2) data set. The PCA involves projecting the input data set on the orthogonal axes that are aligned along the direction of maximum variance of the input data set. The data obtained from the multiple electrode array of the voltammetric electronic tongue have been subjected to PCA after mean normalization (eqn. 1) and dimension reduction using wavelets.

3.3   Artificial Neural Networks

A neural network paradigm like back-propagation-multi-layer perceptrons is employed to carry out the function approximation task of predicting the TF and TR content, in a given tea sample.

Multilayer feed-forward neural networks: Multilayer feed-forward neural networks are often preferred, when the relationship between input and output is not known. It exceeds the performance of other function approximators, typically for complex and nonlinear input-output mappings. The weights of the neurons are iteratively updated following some optimization scheme in order to find a global minimum over an error surface (training phase) so as to produce correct response when an unknown input is presented (testing phase). The performance of following training algorithms will be considered.

Gradient descent algorithm [14]**:** In gradient descent (GD) algorithm the weights are updated along the direction of steepest decrease in error function by some user defined steps known as the learning rate. The convergence behavior of network depends significantly on learning rate. It uses first order or linear weight updation scheme due to which GD optimization often shows unsatisfactory and slow convergence on large and complicated problems.

Scaled conjugate gradient algorithm: SCG algorithms are suited for large scale optimizations. They use second order information in error function. The input arguments of the algorithm like step size (σ) and scaling factor (λ) are iteratively determined as the algorithm proceeds. This is a major advantage compared to the line search based algorithms which include sensitive parameters. Details of the algorithm could be found in [15].

4   Results and Discussions

4.1   Observation of Clustering Information Using PCA

The PCA analysis is carried out with 20 tea samples with representative values for TF and 24 tea samples for TR. The colours of markers indicate value of TF/ TR falling in a range specified by the plot legend. The plots are presented in Fig. 2.

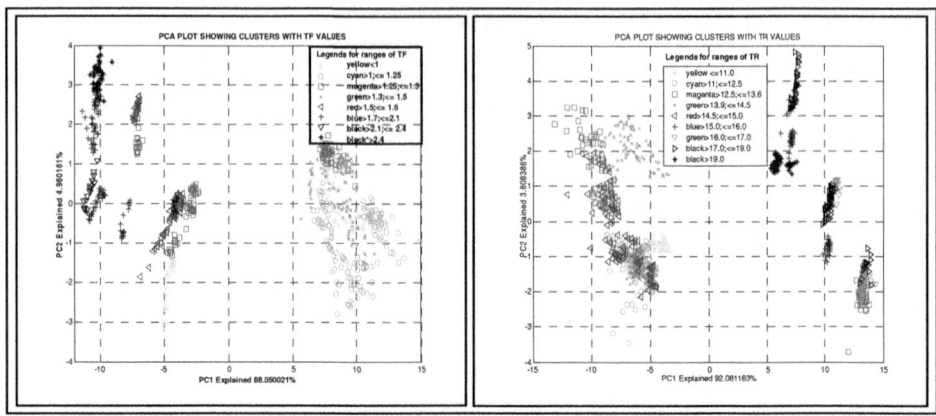

Fig. 2. Plots of electronic tongue responses showing clusters with values of TF and TR

The PC1 and PC2 score plots for TF are 88% and 5% respectively and those for TR are 92% and 3.8% respectively. The plots show non-linear, overlapping and complex relationship among the electronic tongue responses with tendency of cluster formation. Multilayer perceptrons coupled with powerful weight optimization algorithms can be used for model development where such non-linear and complicated relationships exist.

4.2   Prediction of TF and TR Using Neural Network Framework

The total data set obtained is of size 3470x1748. The data-set is mean centered, compressed, mean-variance normalized and is divided into training set of size 55x1398 and test set of size 55x350 i.e. 20% electronic tongue responses over all clones. Two separate models has been considered for prediction of TF and TR. The numbers of input nodes is 55. The number of output node is one. It is known that too small and too large number of hidden nodes may lead to poor generalization. The optimum number of nodes in hidden layer has been selected by trying different architectures with hidden nodes varying from 10 – 90 in steps of 5 nodes. All models are trained for 2000 iterations. The architecture showing best average generalization performances over 10 independent trials are selected for model development. In this experiment the performance of two weight optimization algorithms namely; Gradient descent and Scaled conjugate gradient will be presented. The learning rate and momentum constant for gradient descent is chosen as 0.01 and 0.9 respectively and the values of step size (σ) and scaling factor (λ) for scaled conjugate gradient is chosen as 5×10^{-5} and 5×10^{-7} respectively. These parameters are kept same for all the architectures. Performance summary of the models developed for TF and TR with best testing performance out of those 10 trials is presented in Table 1.

Table 1. Performance summery of best model developed for TF and TR[1]

Target	Algorithm	Architecture	CF	WPA(%)	MPA(%)	MSEP	SDPE
TF	SCG	55-55-1	0.98	78.72	96.50	1.71	0.07
	GD	55-60-1	0.96	68.95	95.60	3.00	0.09
TR	SCG	55-45-1	0.97	87.99	97.96	58.95	0.41
	GD	55-20-1	0.95	87.50	97.17	100.11	0.54

It can be observed that SCG algorithm develops efficient architectures. For model developed for TF a correlation factor of 0.98 is achieved with minimum and mean accuracy of 78.72% and 96.5% respectively. With GD optimization comparable performances could be achieved except some significant decline in values of WPA and MSEP. On the other hand for TR, models developed with GD had significantly smaller structures but had lower CF, MSEP and SDPE than models developed using SCG. The models that yielded best correlation factors of 0.98 and 0.97 for TF and TR respectively were developed using SCG algorithm. SCG thus leads to further improvement in quality perceptions as compared with GD algorithm.

5   Conclusion

Theaflavins and thearubigins are compounds that determine the quality of CTC tea. Use of Electronic tongue simulating generation of quality scores have been reported for quality estimation of tea but has limitations. In this work, perception of quality gathered from electronic tongue has been improved by calibrating the instrument with the amount of TF and TR present in tea. It was presented that the signatures of electronic tongue have a definite relationship with the TF and TR contents in tea. The prediction models were developed using multilayer perceptrons trained with scaled conjugate gradient and gradient descent algorithms. Mapping error for scaled conjugate gradient was observed to be smaller. The rapid measurement of TF and TR may not only present an alternate idea about quality but also help to optimize the production parameters during tea processing so as to maximize taste of tea.

Acknowledgements. The research work has been carried out in collaboration with Tea Research Association Tocklai, Jorhat, Assam and National Tea Research Foundation, Tea Board, India. The work has been financially supported by University Grants Commission and Department of Science and Technology, Government of India.

---

[1] CF: Correlation factor between predicted and actual value
 WPA: Worst prediction accuracy
 MPA: Mean prediction accuracy
 MSEP: Mean square error for prediction
 SDPE: Standard deviation for prediction error

References

1. Bhattacharyya, N., Bandyopadhyay, R., Bhuyan, M., Tudu, B., Ghosh, D., Jana, A.: Electronic nose for black tea classification and correlation of measurements with "Tea Taster" marks. IEEE Transaction on Measurement and Instrumentation 57, 1313–1321 (2008)
2. Palit, M., Tudu, B., Dutta, P.K., Dutta, A., Jana, A., Roy, J.K., Bhattacharyya, N., Bandyopadhyay, R., Chatterjee, A.: Classification of black tea taste and correlation with tea taster's mark using voltammetric electronic tongue. IEEE Transactions on Instrumentation and Measurement 59, 2230–2239 (2010)
3. Bhattacharyya, N., Tudu, B., Jana, A., Ghosh, D., Bandyopadhyay, R., Bhuyan, M.: Preemptive identification of optimum fermentation time for black tea using electronic nose. Sensors and Actuators B: Chemical 131, 110–116 (2007)
4. Roberts, E.A.H.: Economic importance of flavonoid substances: Tea fermentation. In: The Chemistry of Flavonoid Compounds, pp. 468–510. Pergamon, New York (1962)
5. Lyman, B.J., Green, B.G.: Oral astringency: effects of repeated exposure and interactions with sweeteners. Chem. Senses 15, 151–164 (1990)
6. Scampicchio, M., Benedetti, S., Brunetti, S., Mannino, S.: Amperometric electronic tongue for the evaluation of the tea astringency. Electroanalysis 18, 1643–1648 (2006)
7. Hayashi, N., Chen, R.G., Ikezaki, H., Yamaguchi, S., Maruyama, D., Yamaguchi, Y., Ujihara, T., Kohata, K.: Techniques for universal evaluation of astringency of green tea infusion by the use of a taste sensor system. Bioscience Biotechnology Biochemistry 70, 626–631 (2006)
8. Xiao, H., Wang, J.: Discrimination of Xihulongjing tea grade using an electronic tongue. African Journal of Biotechnology 8, 6985–6992 (2009)
9. Ivarsson, P., Holmin, S., Hojer, N., Krantz-Rilcker, C., Winquist, F.: Discrimination of tea by means of a voltammetric electronic tongue and different applied waveforms. Sensors and Actuators B: Chemical 76, 449–454 (2001)
10. Winquist, F., Olsson, J., Eriksson, M.: Multicomponent analysis of drinking water by a voltammetric electronic tongue. Analytica Chimica Acta 683, 192–197 (2011)
11. Ullah, M.R., Gogoi, N., Baruah, D.: The effect of withering on fermentation of tea leaf and development of liquor characters of black tea. Journal of Science Food Agriculture 35, 1142–1147 (1984)
12. Palit, M., Tudu, B., Bhattacharyya, N., Dutta, A., Dutta, P.K., Jana, A., Bandyopadhyay, R., Chatterjee, A.: Comparison of multivariate preprocessing techniques as applied to electronic tongue based pattern classification for black tea. Analytica Chimica Acta 675, 8–15 (2010)
13. Jolliffe, I.T.: Principal Component Analysis, 2nd edn. Springer series in statistics. Springer, New York (1986)
14. Haykin, S.: Neural Networks-A Comprehensive Foundation, 2nd edn. Pearson Education, Asia (2001)
15. Moller, M.F.: A scaled conjugate gradient algorithm for fast supervised learning. Neural Networks 6, 525–533 (1993)

A New Cross-Validation Technique to Evaluate Quality of Recommender Systems

Dmitry I. Ignatov[1], Jonas Poelmans[2,*], Guido Dedene[2,4], and Stijn Viaene[2,3]

[1] National Research University Higher School of Economics, Russia
dignatov@hse.ru
[2] Katholieke Universiteit Leuven, Belgium
{jonas.poelmans,guido.dedene}@econ.kuleuven.be
[3] Vlerick Leuven Management School, Belgium
stijn.viaene@vlerick.be
[4] Amsterdam Business School, Netherlands

Abstract. The topic of recommender systems is rapidly gaining interest in the user-behaviour modeling research domain. Over the years, various recommender algorithms based on different mathematical models have been introduced in the literature. Researchers interested in proposing a new recommender model or modifying an existing algorithm should take into account a variety of key performance indicators, such as execution time, recall and precision. Till date and to the best of our knowledge, no general cross-validation scheme to evaluate the performance of recommender algorithms has been developed. To fill this gap we propose an extension of conventional cross-validation. Besides splitting the initial data into training and test subsets, we also split the attribute description of the dataset into a hidden and visible part. We then discuss how such a splitting scheme can be applied in practice. Empirical validation is performed on traditional user-based and item-based recommender algorithms which were applied to the MovieLens dataset.

Keywords: recommender systems, quality of recommendations, user-behavior modeling, applied combinatorics.

1 Introduction

A modern Internet user rather frequently faces recommender systems. For example, if a user buys a book X in an online book shop she also gets recommendations in the form "other customers who bought book X also bought books Y and Z". There are a lot of web systems which can recommend potentially interesting web sites to a particular user, they are called social bookmarking systems (e.g. http://del.ici.ou.us). Besides consulting the Internet the most popular and non-technological way to get recommendations is still friends' suggestions. However, if a user wants to buy multiple items (to watch, to read etc.) the task

---

* Jonas Poelmans is an aspirant of the Fonds voor Wetenschappelijk Onderzoek Vlaanderen or Research Foundation Flanders.

M.K. Kundu et al. (Eds.): PerMIn 2012, LNCS 7143, pp. 195–202, 2012.

becomes harder, because there may be a lot of different choice options and her
friends may not be informed about latest items in the field or just have a different taste. To cope with these difficulties so-called collaborative filtering can
be used [3]. Recommender algorithms based on collaborative filtering techniques
utilise a fairly simple scheme. They first find users of the system who have similar tastes or preferences as the current user, then compose the list of items the
users selected and rank these items. The results she gets are the Top-N items
of the list. Another less evident but demanded application is recommending key
phrases in web advertising systems, where firms buy advertising phrases from
web search engines to show advertisement by a user's request [4,5]. In this paper
we propose a novel scheme for evaluating the quality of recommendations made.
We empirically show the usefulness of this scheme by applying it to a traditional
user-based and item-based recommender algorithm. These algorithms were using
the well-known MovieLens dataset.The remainder of this paper is composed as
follows. In section 2 we describe in detail the two major groups of recommender
algorithms. In section 3 we zoom in on some popular similarity measures. In
section 4 we present our recommendation quality evaluation scheme. Section 5
details the results of some experiments made. Finally section 6 concludes this
paper.

2   Recommender Models

In this paper without loss of generality we consider only two groups of recommender techniques, which can be called the classical ones, mainly user-based
and item-based approaches [2,1]. A key notion for these techniques is similarity,
which can be expressed as Jacquard measure, Pearson correlation coefficient,
cosine similarity etc. Initial data are usually represented by an object-attribute
matrix, where the rows describe objects (users) and the columns represent attributes (items). A particular cell of the matrix can be either 1 or 0, which stands
for the fact that the item was purchased or not respectively. Also the values can
be rates or marks of items, for example, movie ratings given by users.

User-Based Recommendations. User-based methods find similarity between
a target user u_0 and other users of the recommender system. As a result the
target user has n most frequently bought items by k most similar to u_0 users
(customers). Let u_0 be a target user, u_0^I be items that she evaluated, $sim(u_0, u)$
be a similarity between the target user u_0 and another user u. In this research
we use Pearson correlation coefficient as a similarity measure. Define the set of
nearest neighbors (neighborhood) for the target user by the formula:

$$N(u_0) = \{u | sim(u_0, u) \leq \Theta\}.$$

However, it is appropriate to obtain $Top - k$ nearest neighbors, that is $Top - k$
defines the threshold Θ. Hence the set of nearest neighbors includes k users which
have the similarity with u_0 higher than a certain threshold. After ordering the
users by decreasing similarity, one should select not only $Top - k$ of them, but

also check the similarity value of $(k + 1)$-th user in the list. If this similarity value is equal to the preceding one than one should add $(k + 1)$-th user to the neighborhood $N(u_0)$. One should repeat the procedure until the next similarity value changes. Since we predict the rate of an item i by a specific target user u_0 we are interesting only those users from the neighborhood who have evaluated i:

$$N(u_0|i) = \{u|i \in u^I \& \ u \in N(u_0)\}.$$

Denote by r_{ui} the rate (mark) of an item i by a user u we obtain the formula for the predicting rate

$$\hat{r}_{u_0 i} = \frac{\sum\limits_{u \in N(u_0|i)} sim(u_0, u) \times r_{ui}}{\sum\limits_{u \in N(u_0|i)} sim(u_0, u)}.$$

Item-based recommendations. The idea of the item-based technique is similar to the described user-based method, but similarity is calculated between items. Denote by u_0 again the target user, by u_0^I the items she evaluated, by $sim(i, j)$ the similarity between items i and j. Define the neighborhood for an item i analogously the neighborhood for a target user by $N(i) = \{j|sim(i, j) \geq \Theta\}$. By doing so we have top-k nearest items to i, that is top-k defines Θ. To predict the rate for a target user u_0 one has to compare the items which u_0 evaluated with those that she didn't rate. Therefore we refine the formula for item neighborhood taking into account the target user as follows $N(i|u_0) = \{j|j \notin u_0^I, i \in u_0^I, j \in N(i)\}$.

Denote by r_{ui} the rate of an item i by a user u and by doing so we get

$$\hat{r}_{u_0 i} = \frac{\sum\limits_{j \in u_0^I} sim(i, j) \times r_{u_0 j}}{\sum\limits_{j \in u_0^I)} sim(i, j)}.$$

Then we rank marks in decreasing order and return the first n of them as a recommendation. The main computational advantage of this method is based on the following fact: the number of e-commerce web-site users is usually increasing over time, but new items are added not so frequent. That is why pairwise users' similarity computation while forming a new recommendation may take much time, but items' similarity can be calculated offline in advance and the obtained similarity matrix can be reused many times later. These techniques have some shortcomings, for instance, in case of the so-called cold start problem we don't know user's history and these methods are not able to make recommendations, but they can do it better than some more sophisticated algorithms in case the user's history is known.

3 Similarity Measures

To define similarity between two objects or attributes different similarity measures (or even metrics) are used. Usually, such a measure has the value between 0 and 1 (for absolute similarity). Let us consider some of these measures.

Distance-Based Similarity. To calculate similarity we should find the distance between compared objects or attributes. There are some frequently used ways to calculate the distance. Each initial object is represented by a vector in attribute space (dually for distance between two attributes). Then *Euclidean distance* between two objects x and y is defined as $d(x, y) = \sqrt{\sum_i (x_i - y_i)^2}$. *Hamming distance* is usually used for binary data, which is defined by the formula $d(x, y) = \sum_{x_i \neq y_i} 1$. The simplest way to calculate the similarity then is to apply the following formula $s(x, y) = \frac{1}{1+d(x,y)}$ (see, e.g. [7]).

Let us take a closer look at Hamming distance. In this case d takes only natural values and 0 and the maximal value of s is equal to 1 for $d = 0$. And for the next value $d = 1$ the similarity s is equal to $1/2$; it's a clear drawback of the similarity calculation formula. For example, let x and y be two binary vectors which differ only in one component, according to the previous formula they are only one half similar. This rough character of s values can be easily seen in figure 1.

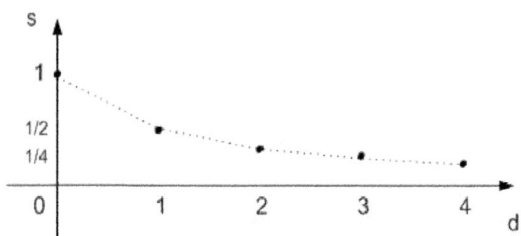

Fig. 1. Similarity versus Hamming distance

Correlation as similarity. In the formula below similarity between two vectors is calculated by means of the well-known Pearson correlation:

$$Pearson(x, y) = \frac{\sum_i (x_i - \overline{x})(y_i - \overline{y})}{\sum_i (x_i - \overline{x})^2 \cdot \sum_i (y_i - \overline{y})^2},$$

where $-1 \leq Pearson \leq 1$.

The main drawback of Pearson correlation as a similarity measure is its undefined value for vectors with constant components. By the way, we have zero denominator for the vector $x = (4, 4, \cdots, 4)$. This is why we may loose some potentially recommended items. For example, let us consider two vectors $a = (0, 5, 5, 4)$ and

$b = (0, 4, 5, 0)$. If one would think on them like tuples of two users' rates then it is intuitively clear that these users are quite similar to each other. However, the correlation will not be calculated because a following constraint: the initial vectors are trimmed to their non-zero components [8]. In our case one should calculate the correlation between (5,5) and (4,5). How it was shown above the correlation is undefined. Some authors proposed to suppose the correlation value equal to 0 [7], but in our opinion it is not correct.

Other similarity measures. There are dozens different measures to find the similarity, for example cosine similarity (very close to Pearson), Jacquard and Tanimoto coefficients, etc.

4   Recommendation Quality Evaluation

In this section we propose the scheme for quality evaluation of an arbitrary recommender system. Let initial data be represented by an object-attribute table (binary relation) $T \subseteq U \times I$, which shows that a user $u \in U$ purchased $i \in I$, i.e. uTi. To evaluate quality of recommendations in terms of precision and recall we can split the initial user set U into training $U_{training}$ and U_{test} test subsets. The size of the test set as a rule should be less than the size of the training set, e.g. 20% and 80% respectively. Recommendation precision and recall is evaluated on the test set. This part of the algorithm looks like one step of the conventional cross-validation. Then each user vector u from U_{test} is divided into two parts which consist of evaluated items $I_{visible}$ and non evaluated items I_{hidden}. I_{hidden} are the items which we intentionally hided. Note that in existing literature the proportion between size of $I_{visible}$ and I_{hidden} is not discussed even in similar schemes [8]. Then, for example, a user-based algorithm makes recommendations according to similarity between users from the test and training sets. Each user from U_{test} gets the recommendations as a set of fixed size $r_n(u) = \{i_1, i_2, \cdots, i_n\}$. Precision and recall defined by

$$recall = \frac{|r_n(u) \cap u^I \cap I_{hidden}|}{|u^I \cap I_{hidden}|},$$

$$precision = \frac{|r_n(u) \cap u^I \cap I_{hidden}|}{|r_n(u) \cap I_{hidden}|},$$

where u^I is a set of all items from I bought by the user u. The values of these measures are calculated for each user and then averaged. The experiment is performed several times, e.g. 100, for different test and training set splits. Then the values are averaged again. In addition there is a possibility to select I_{hidden} set, which can be done at random, but we have to specify the proportion, e.g. 20%. The idea behind the method comes from machine learning where it is called cross-validation, but in case of recommender systems some modifications are needed. We modified m-fold cross-validation, which is performed by splitting the initial set into m disjoint subsets, where each subset is used as a test set and the other subsets are considered as training ones. In addition to standard ways of precision and recall computation we propose original modification of their formulas in case of division by zero. In particular, if $|u^I \cap I_{hidden}| = 0$ then $recall = 1$. If $|r_n(u) \cap I_{hidden}| = 0$ and $u^I = 0$, then $precision = 1$, otherwise $precision = 0$. Experiments have been done on MovieLens datasets about films' rates and synthetical ones which are generated by us.

5   Experiment Results

We have carried out a series of experiments on the movie dataset which contains 1682 movies rated by 943 users and each of the users has evaluated at least 20 movies. All experiments were done on a laptop with Intel Core 2 Duo 2 GHz processor and 3Gb RAM under the operating system Windows Vista. All algorithms were implemented in Python 2.6. We show results of the experiment concerning precision and recall behavior for different number of hidden items (10-fold cross-validation with a neighborhood size of 10).

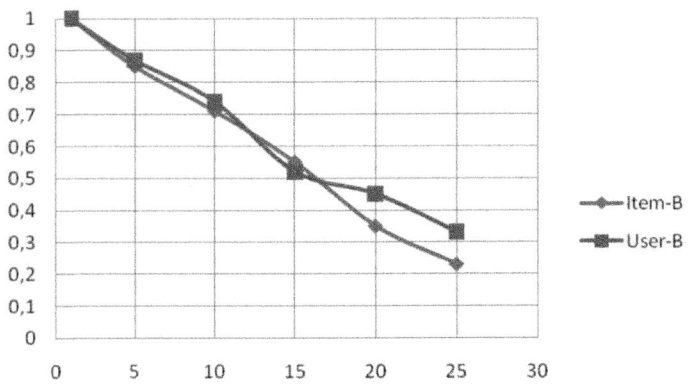

Fig. 2. Recall versus number of hidden items

As we can see from 3 and 4 these methods have almost identical behavior, but the recall of the user-based method is a bit higher in the range from 1 to 10 hidden attributes. In the same way, we conduct experiments on movie rates data where the fraction of hidden attributes was ranging from 1% to 20%. Our diagrams show that the item-based method works better with a rather small number of hidden attributes ($\approx 1\%$). For higher values of $|I_{hidden}|$ the item-based method's quality drastically decreases, while the performance of the user-based method is still quite stable, moreover in our experiments at 6-7% for $|I_{hidden}|$ the recall slightly increases.

We show how the quality of the results is influenced by the number of neighbors and the test set size for our synthetic data set of size 20 $users \times 20$ $items$ with four rectangles 5×5 full of ones (see 4 and 5). We can conclude that precision and recall increase while the number of neighbors grows and the user-based

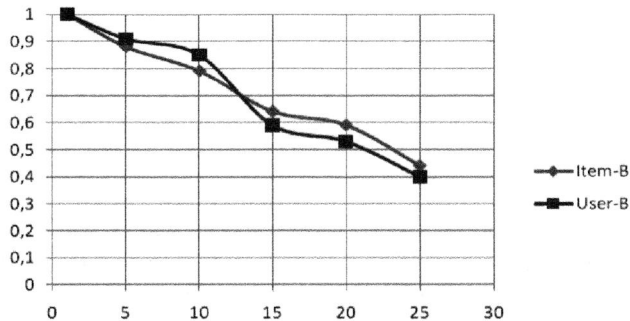

Fig. 3. Precision versus number of hidden items

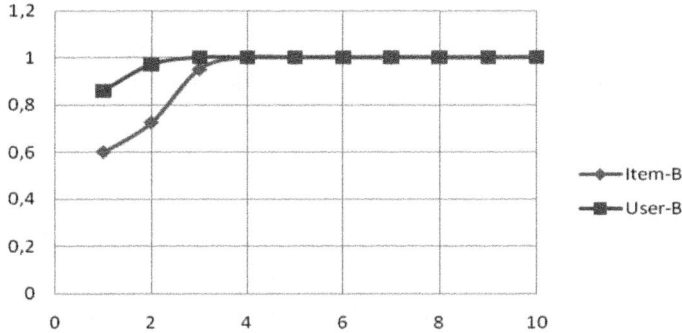

Fig. 4. Recall versus number of nearest neighbors

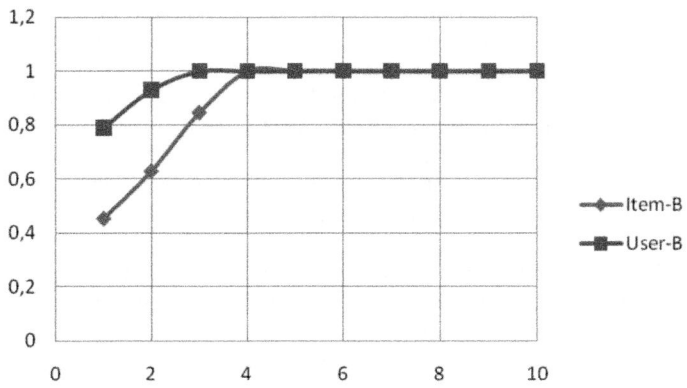

Fig. 5. Precision versus number of nearest neighbors

method needs less number of neighbors than item-based for gaining the same quality. Results for varying test set's size have similar nature, the larger test size the better quality of prediction, and again user-based method shows better quality.

6   Conclusions

The proposed method for recommender systems evaluation makes it possible to compare recommender algorithms and tune their parameters. In the experimentation on real data sets we have found that classical user-based methods are better than item-based in terms of recall and precision for 10 hidden items (Top-10, one of the most typical sizes of recommender lists). Our approach enables the comparison of any other recommender algorithms, e.g. biclustering based algorithms [4,5]. Our future research on recommender systems' quality assessment include a comparative study of biclustering based algorithms and investigation of statistical properties of the approach also taking into account the time parameter. Another potentially interesting avenue is analysing the performance of a Formal Concept Analysis inspired recommender algorithm [9].

References

1. Deshpande, M., Karypis, G.: Item-based top-n recommendation algorithms. J. ACM Transactions on Information Systems 22(1), 143–177 (2004)
2. Sarwar, B.M., Karypis, J., Konstan, J.A., Riedl, J.: Analysis of recommendation algorithms for e-commerce. In: ACM Conference on Electronic Commerce, pp. 158–167 (2001)
3. Goldberg, D., Nichols, D.A., Oki, B.M., Terry, D.B.: Using Collaborative Filtering to Weave an Information Tapestry. Communications of the ACM 35(12), 61–70 (1992)
4. Ignatov, D.I., Kuznetsov, S.O.: Concept-based Recommendations for Internet Advertisement. In: Sixth International Conference on Concept Lattices and Their Applications, pp. 157–166. Palacky University, Olomouc (2008)
5. Ignatov, D.I., Kuznetsov, S.O.: Data Mining techniques for Internet Advertisement Recommender System. In: Proc. of 11th National Conference on Artificial Intelligence, Lenand, Moscow, vol. 2, pp. 34–42 (2008) (in Russian)
6. del Olmo, F.H., Gaudioso, E.: Evaluation of recommender systems: A new approach. J. Expert Systems with Applications 35, 790–804 (2008)
7. Segaran, T.: Programming Collective Intelligence. O'Reilly Media, Sebastopol (2007)
8. Symeonidis, P., Nanopoulos, A., Papadopoulos, A.N., Manolopoulos, Y.: Nearest-biclusters collaborative filtering based on constant and coherent values. J. Information Retrieval 11, 51–75 (2007)
9. Poelmans, J., Elzinga, P., Viaene, S., Dedene, G.: Curbing domestic violence: instantiating C-K theory with formal concept analysis and emergent self-organizing maps. Int. Syst. in Accounting, Finance and Management 17(3-4), 167–191 (2010)

Rough-Fuzzy C-Means for Clustering Microarray Gene Expression Data

Pradipta Maji and Sushmita Paul

Machine Intelligence Unit, Indian Statistical Institute,
203, B.T. Road, Kolkata 700 108, India
{pmaji,sushmita_t}@isical.ac.in

Abstract. Clustering technique is one of the useful tools to elucidate similar patterns across large number of transcripts and to identify likely co-regulated genes. It attempts to partition the genes into groups exhibiting similar patterns of variation in expression level. An application of rough-fuzzy c-means (RFCM) algorithm is presented in this paper to discover co-expressed gene clusters. Selection of initial prototypes of different clusters is one of the major issues of the RFCM based microarray data clustering. The pearson correlation based initialization method is used to address this limitation. It enables the RFCM algorithm to discover co-expressed gene clusters. The effectiveness of the RFCM algorithm and the initialization method, along with a comparison with other related methods, is demonstrated on five yeast gene expression data sets using standard cluster validity indices and gene ontology based analysis.

Keywords: Clustering, Rough Sets, Fuzzy Sets, Microarray.

1 Introduction

Cluster analysis is one of the important techniques for finding natural groups present in the microarray gene expression data set. It divides a given gene set into a set of clusters in such a way that two genes from the same cluster are as similar as possible and the genes from different clusters are as dissimilar as possible [3]. To understand gene function, gene regulation, and cellular processes, clustering techniques have proven to be helpful. The co-expressed genes, that is, genes with similar expression patterns, can be clustered together with similar cellular functions. This approach may further understanding of the functions of many genes for which information has not been previously available.

One of the main problems in microarray gene expression data is uncertainty. Some of the sources of this uncertainty include imprecision in computations and vagueness in class definitions. In this background, the possibility concept introduced by the fuzzy set theory and rough set theory have gained popularity in modeling and propagating uncertainty. Both fuzzy set and rough set provide a mathematical framework to capture uncertainties associated with human cognition process. The clustering of microarray gene expression data using fuzzy c-means (FCM) has been reported in [2].

In this paper, the rough and fuzzy set based rough-fuzzy c-means (RFCM) [4] algorithm has been used for clustering microarray data. While the concept of lower and

M.K. Kundu et al. (Eds.): PerMIn 2012, LNCS 7143, pp. 203–210, 2012.

upper approximations of rough sets deals with uncertainty, vagueness, and incompleteness in class definition, the membership function of fuzzy sets enables efficient handling of overlapping partitions. Each partition is represented by a cluster prototype, a crisp lower approximation, and a fuzzy boundary. The lower approximation influences the fuzziness of the final partition. The cluster prototype depends on the weighting average of the crisp lower approximation and fuzzy boundary [4]. Selection of initial prototypes of different clusters is an important issue of the RFCM based microarray data clustering. Therefore, the pearson correlation based initialization method reported in [5] is used to circumvent the initialization and local minima problems of the RFCM, and enables efficient microarray data clustering. The effectiveness of the RFCM algorithm and the initialization method, along with a comparison with other c-means algorithms, is demonstrated on five yeast microarray data sets using some standard validity indices.

2 Gene Expression Data

In the present research work, publicly available five microarray gene expression data sets are used to compare the performance of different clustering methods. This section gives a brief description of the following five microarray gene expression data sets, which are downloaded from *Gene Expression Omnibus* (www.ncbi.nlm.nih.gov/geo/).

1. **GDS608:** It is a temporal analysis of wild type diploid cells shifted from yeast-form growth in SHAD liquid (plentiful glucose and ammonium) to filamentous-form growth on SLAD agar (low ammonium). The filamentous-form cells were collected hourly for 10 hours. The number of genes and time points of this data are 6303 and 10, respectively.
2. **GDS759:** This data set is related to analysis of gene expression in temperature sensitive pre-mRNA splicing factor mutants prp17 null, prp17-1, and prp22-1 at various time points following a shift from the permissive temperature of $23°C$ to the restrictive temperature of $37°C$. The number of genes and time points of this data are 6350 and 24, respectively.
3. **GDS1013:** It contains the analysis of over-expression of essential ribosomal protein activator IFH1. The cells engineered to express IFH1 from a galactose inducible promoter. The expression was examined at various time points up to 60 minutes following galactose addition. The data set contains 9275 genes with 24 times points.
4. **GDS2347:** It contains the analysis of wild type W303 cells across two cell cycles, a length of 2 hours after synchronization with alpha factor. The number of genes and time points are 6228 and 13, respectively.
5. **GDS2712:** It represents the analysis of Saccharomyces cerevisiae BY4743 cells subjected to controlled air-drying and subsequent rehydration (I) for up to 360 minutes. The data contains 9275 genes and 21 time points.

3 Rough-Fuzzy C-Means Algorithm

Given a set $X = \{x_1, \cdots, x_j, \cdots, x_n\}$ of n objects, the RFCM algorithm of Maji and Pal [4] partitions it into c clusters. Each of the clusters β_i is represented by a centroid v_i, a crisp lower approximation $\underline{A}(\beta_i)$ and a fuzzy boundary $B(\beta_i)$. In the RFCM, following objective function has to be minimized [4]:

$$
J = \begin{cases} w \times \mathscr{A}_1 + (1 - w) \times \mathscr{B}_1 & \text{if } \underline{A}(\beta_i) \neq \emptyset, B(\beta_i) \neq \emptyset \\ \mathscr{A}_1 & \text{if } \underline{A}(\beta_i) \neq \emptyset, B(\beta_i) = \emptyset \\ \mathscr{B}_1 & \text{if } \underline{A}(\beta_i) = \emptyset, B(\beta_i) \neq \emptyset \end{cases}
$$

where $\mathscr{A}_1 = \sum_{i=1}^{c} \sum_{x_j \in \underline{A}(\beta_i)} ||x_j - v_i||^2; \quad \mathscr{B}_1 = \sum_{i=1}^{c} \sum_{x_j \in B(\beta_i)} (\mu_{ij})^{\acute{m}_1} ||x_j - v_i||^2.$

The weight parameter w controls the relative importance of lower and boundary region. Note that, μ_{ij} has the same meaning of membership as that in the FCM. Solving J with respect to μ_{ij}, we get

$$
\mu_{ij} = \left[\sum_{k=1}^{c} \left(\frac{||x_j - v_i||^2}{||x_j - v_k||^2} \right)^{\frac{1}{\acute{m}_1 - 1}} \right]^{-1}. \tag{1}
$$

In the RFCM, each cluster is represented by a centroid, a crisp lower approximation, and a fuzzy boundary. The lower approximation influences the fuzziness of final partition. According to the definitions of lower approximations and boundary of rough sets, if an object $x_j \in \underline{A}(\beta_i)$, then $x_j \notin \underline{A}(\beta_k), \forall k \neq i$, and $x_j \notin B(\beta_i), \forall i$. It implies that the object x_j is contained in β_i definitely and the weights of the objects in lower approximation donot affect other centroids and clusters but they should have similar influence on the corresponding centroid and cluster. Whereas, if $x_j \in B(\beta_i)$, then the object x_j possibly belongs to β_i and potentially belongs to another cluster. Hence, the objects in boundary regions should have different influence on the centroids and clusters. So, in the RFCM, the membership values of objects in lower approximation are $\mu_{ij} = 1$, while those in boundary region are the same as the FCM.

The weighted average of the crisp lower approximation and fuzzy boundary generates new centroid in the RFCM. Modification of the centroid is done by including the effects of fuzzy memberships and lower and upper bounds. The modified centroid calculation for the RFCM is obtained by solving J with respect to v_i:

$$
v_i = \begin{cases} w \times \mathscr{C}_1 + (1 - w) \times \mathscr{D}_1 & \text{if } \underline{A}(\beta_i) \neq \emptyset, B(\beta_i) \neq \emptyset \\ \mathscr{C}_1 & \text{if } \underline{A}(\beta_i) \neq \emptyset, B(\beta_i) = \emptyset \\ \mathscr{D}_1 & \text{if } \underline{A}(\beta_i) = \emptyset, B(\beta_i) \neq \emptyset \end{cases}
$$

$$
\mathscr{C}_1 = \frac{1}{|\underline{A}(\beta_i)|} \sum_{x_j \in \underline{A}(\beta_i)} x_j \; ; \; \mathscr{D}_1 = \frac{1}{n_i} \sum_{x_j \in B(\beta_i)} (\mu_{ij})^{\acute{m}_1} x_j \tag{2}
$$

where $|\underline{A}(\beta_i)|$ represents the cardinality of $\underline{A}(\beta_i)$ and $n_i = \sum_{x_j \in B(\beta_i)} (\mu_{ij})^{\acute{m}_1}$. Thus, the parameter w and fuzzifier $\acute{m}_1$ affect centroids. Since the objects lying in lower approximation definitely belong to a cluster, they are assigned a higher weight w compared to $(1-w)$ of the objects lying in boundary region. Hence, for the RFCM, $0.5 < w < 1$.

Approximate optimization of J by the RFCM is based on Picard iteration through (1) and (2). The process starts by randomly choosing c objects as the centroids of the c clusters. The fuzzy memberships of all the objects are calculated using (1). Let $u_i = (\mu_{i1}, \cdots, \mu_{ij}, \cdots, \mu_{in})$ be the fuzzy cluster β_i associated with the centroid v_i. After computing μ_{ij} for c clusters and n objects, the values of μ_{ij} for each object x_j are sorted and the difference of two highest memberships of x_j is compared with a threshold value δ. Let μ_{ij} and μ_{kj} be the highest and second highest memberships of x_j. If $(\mu_{ij} - \mu_{kj}) > \delta$, then $x_j \in \underline{A}(\beta_i)$, otherwise $x_j \in B(\beta_i)$ and $x_j \in B(\beta_k)$. After assigning each object in lower approximations or boundary regions of different clusters based on δ, membership values μ_{ij} of the objects are modified. The values of μ_{ij} are set to 1 for the objects in lower approximations, while those in boundary regions are remain unchanged. The new centroids of the clusters are calculated as per (2).

Based on the value of δ, the RFCM partitions data set into two classes: lower approximation and boundary. The δ represents the size of granules of the RFCM. In practice, the following definition works well:

$$\delta = \frac{1}{n} \sum_{j=1}^{n} (\mu_{ij} - \mu_{kj}) \tag{3}$$

where n is the total number of objects, μ_{ij} and μ_{kj} are the highest and second highest memberships of x_j. That is, the value of δ represents the average difference of two highest memberships of all the objects in the data set. A good clustering procedure should make the value of δ as high as possible. The source code of the RFCM algorithm written in C language is available at www.isical.ac.in/~pmaji.

The initial choice of the cluster prototypes drives the c-means algorithm to achieve a local optimum solution. Selection of data points from scarce region of data set as initial cluster centers may waste computing resources and may never have the chance to move to new locations where they are needed. To overcome this limitation of the c-means algorithm, an initialization method developed in [5] is used here.

4   Experimental Results

In this section, the performance of hard c-means (HCM), FCM [2], RFCM [4], cluster identification via connectivity kernels (CLICK) [6], and self organizing map (SOM) [8] algorithms on five (GDS608, GDS759, GDS1013, GDS2347, and GDS2712) yeast microarray data sets is presented. The performance of the initialization method reported in [5] is also extensively studied and compared with random initialization method by using aforementioned clustering algorithms. For each data set, the value of c is decided by using CLICK [6] algorithm. The major metrics for evaluating the performance of different algorithms are Silhouette index, Davies-Bouldin index, and Dunn index. The biological evaluation of these methods is also conducted using GO TermFinder, which is developed by using the concept of gene ontology.

4.1   Quantitative Indices

Following quantitative indices are used to evaluate the performance of different gene clustering algorithms.

1. **Silhouette Index:** To assess the quality of clusters, the Silhouette measure proposed by Rousseeuw [7] can be used. For computing the Silhouette value of a gene x_i, first two scalars $a(x_i)$ and $b(x_i)$ are estimated. Let us note β_r the cluster to which gene x_i belongs. The scalar $a(x_i)$ is the average distance between gene x_i and all other genes of β_r. For any other cluster $\beta_s \neq \beta_r$, let $d(x_i, \beta_s)$ denote the average distance of gene x_i to all genes of β_s. The scalar $b(x_i)$ is the smallest of these $d(x_i, \beta_s), r \neq s = 1, \cdots, c$. The Silhouette $s(x_i)$ of gene x_i is then defined as

$$s(x_i) = \frac{b(x_i) - a(x_i)}{\max\{a(x_i), b(x_i)\}}. \tag{4}$$

The Silhouette value lies between -1 and 1. When its value is less than zero, the corresponding gene is poorly classified.

2. **Davies-Bouldin Index:** The Davies-Bouldin (DB) index [7] is a function of the ratio of sum of within-cluster distance to between-cluster separation and is given by

$$\text{DB} = \frac{1}{c} \sum_{i=1}^{c} \max_{i \neq k} \left\{ \frac{S(v_i) + S(v_k)}{d(v_i, v_k)} \right\} \tag{5}$$

for $1 \leq i, k \leq c$. The DB index minimizes the within-cluster distance $S(v_i)$ and maximizes the between-cluster separation $d(v_i, v_k)$. Therefore, for a given data set and c value, the higher the similarity values within the clusters and the between-cluster separation, the lower would be the DB index value. A good clustering procedure should make the value of DB index as low as possible.

3. **Dunn Index:** Dunn's index [7] is also designed to identify sets of clusters that are compact and well separated. Dunn's (D) index maximizes

$$D = \min_{i} \left\{ \min_{i \neq k} \left\{ \frac{d(v_i, v_k)}{\max_l S(v_l)} \right\} \right\} \quad \text{for } 1 \leq i, k, l \leq c. \tag{6}$$

4.2   Random versus New Initialization Method

Table 1 provides comparative results of different c-means algorithms with random initialization of centroids and the pearson correlation based initialization method described in [5] for five yeast microarray data sets. In maximum cases, new initialization method is found to improve the performance in terms of Silhouette index, DB index, and Dunn index of all c-means algorithms. Out of 45 comparisons, the new initialization method is found to provide significantly better results in 36 cases. From the Table 1, it can also be seen that the HCM algorithm with the new initialization method outperforms the RFCM algorithm with random initialization method in four, two, and two cases in terms of Silhouette, DB, and Dunn indices, respectively. The better performance of the new initialization method is achieved due to the fact that it enables the algorithm to converge to an optimum solutions.

Table 1. Performance of Random and New Initialization Methods

Data Sets	Algorithms	Initialization	Silhouette Index	DB Index	Dunn Index
GDS608	HCM	Random	0.078000	1.930995	0.255949
		New	0.086000	1.926900	0.277843
	FCM	Random	0.005000	2.082000	0.000009
		New	0.012000	1.992100	0.000040
	RFCM	Random	0.110000	1.607706	0.271890
		New	0.145000	1.660201	0.253775
GDS759	HCM	Random	0.082000	2.392131	0.034911
		New	0.130000	2.086955	0.070446
	FCM	Random	0.017000	3.614000	0.000000
		New	-0.002000	2.801100	0.000076
	RFCM	Random	0.121000	1.778661	0.081480
		New	0.154000	1.870019	0.077712
GDS1013	HCM	Random	0.220000	0.936899	0.000586
		New	0.249000	0.771935	0.002066
	FCM	Random	0.249000	1.438951	0.002454
		New	0.250000	1.432223	0.002458
	RFCM	Random	0.213000	1.142143	0.002148
		New	0.262000	0.769563	0.003134
GDS2347	HCM	Random	0.134000	2.147014	0.004979
		New	0.214000	1.644646	0.022540
	FCM	Random	0.031000	3.460100	0.000014
		New	0.041000	3.216800	0.000009
	RFCM	Random	0.160000	2.558926	0.007233
		New	0.218000	2.405128	0.042708
GDS2712	HCM	Random	0.250000	0.806405	0.031366
		New	0.251000	0.784470	0.031895
	FCM	Random	0.208000	1.759878	0.012043
		New	0.193000	1.951519	0.012483
	RFCM	Random	0.251000	0.774629	0.039543
		New	0.255000	0.717375	0.057194

4.3 Comparative Performance Analysis

Table 2 compares the performance of different c-means algorithms on five yeast microarray data sets with respect to Silhouette, DB, and Dunn indices. The values of Silhouette, DB, and Dunn indices of the RFCM are better compared to other c-means algorithms in most of the cases. However, the HCM algorithm produces better results compared to the RFCM algorithm only for GDS608 and GDS2347 data sets in terms of Dunn index and DB index, respectively.

4.4 Biological Significance

To interpret the biological significance of the generated clusters, the gene ontology (GO) term finder is used [1]. It finds the most significantly enriched GO terms associated with the genes belonging to a cluster. The GO project aims to build tree structures and controlled vocabularies, also called ontologies, that describe gene products in terms of their associated biological processes (BPs), molecular functions (MFs), or cellular components (CCs). The GO term finder determines whether any GO term annotates a specified list of genes at a frequency greater than that would be expected by chance, calculating the associated p-value by using the hypergeometric distribution and the Bonferroni multiple-hypothesis correction [1]. The closer the p-value is to zero, the more significant the particular GO term associated with the group of genes becomes,

Table 2. Performance of Different C-Means Algorithms

Data Sets	Algorithms	Silhouette Index	DB Index	Dunn Index
	HCM	0.086000	1.926900	0.277843
GDS608	FCM	0.012000	2.012100	0.000040
	RFCM	0.145000	1.660201	0.253775
	HCM	0.130000	2.086955	0.070446
GDS759	FCM	-0.002000	2.961700	0.000076
	RFCM	0.154000	1.870019	0.077712
	HCM	0.249000	0.771935	0.002066
GDS1013	FCM	0.250000	1.432223	0.002458
	RFCM	0.262000	0.769563	0.003134
	HCM	0.214000	1.644646	0.022540
GDS2347	FCM	0.041000	2.867700	0.000009
	RFCM	0.218000	2.405128	0.042708
	HCM	0.251000	0.784470	0.031895
GDS2712	FCM	0.193000	1.951519	0.012483
	RFCM	0.255000	0.717375	0.057194

Table 3. Number of Significant Clusters Generated By Different Algorithms

Ontology	Algorithm	GDS608	GDS759	GDS1013	GDS2347	GDS2712
	CLICK	4	8	11	7	8
	SOM	6	5	11	6	6
MF	HCM	11	18	13	10	9
	FCM	4	7	16	5	9
	RFCM	11	17	15	12	12
	CLICK	4	10	9	9	9
	SOM	4	4	11	8	11
BP	HCM	8	18	15	10	11
	FCM	5	8	15	7	12
	RFCM	11	19	16	9	11
	CLICK	4	11	10	10	8
	SOM	7	5	13	8	8
CC	HCM	12	19	16	10	9
	FCM	7	10	17	6	11
	RFCM	12	18	16	8	11

that is, the less likely the observed annotation of the particular GO term to a group of genes occurs by chance. Hence, the GO term finder is used to determine the statistically significant clusters produced by HCM, FCM, and RFCM algorithms for all the GO terms from the MF, BP, and CC ontologies. If any cluster of genes generates p-value smaller than 0.05, then that cluster is considered as a significant cluster. Table 3 presents the number of significant clusters generated by different algorithms for the BP, MF, and CC for all data sets. All the results reported in this table establish that the RFCM algorithm generates more or comparable number of significant gene clusters than that of

CLICK, SOM, HCM, and FCM. Hence, it justifies the fact that rough sets and fuzzy sets based RFCM discovers groups of co-expressed genes. However, the CLICK algorithm generates more significant clusters than the RFCM for MF ontology in only one case. On the other hand, the HCM produces better results than the RFCM in one, one, and two cases for MF, BP, and CC ontology, respectively. Whereas the FCM provides better result than the RFCM in only one case for MF, BP, and CC each.

5   Conclusion

In this paper, the application of rough-fuzzy c-means (RFCM) algorithm has been demonstrated for clustering microarray data and the performance has been compared with other c-means algorithms. The new initialization method is found to be successful in effectively circumventing the initialization and local minima problems of iterative refinement clustering algorithms like c-means. The effectiveness of the algorithm, along with a comparison with other algorithms, is demonstrated on five yeast microarray data sets. The extensive experimental results show that the RFCM produces better clustering results than do the conventional algorithms in terms of Silhouette index, DB index, Dunn index, and number of biologically significant gene clusters.

Acknowledgement. The work was done when one of the authors, S. Paul, was a Senior Research Fellow of Council of Scientific and Industrial Research, Government of India.

References

1. Boyle, E.I., Weng, S., Gollub, J., Jin, H., Botstein, D., Cherry, J.M., Sherlock, G.: GO: Term Finder Open Source Software for Accessing Gene Ontology Information and Finding Significantly Enriched Gene Ontology Terms Associated with a List of Genes. Bioinformatics 20(18), 3710–3715 (2004)
2. Dembele, D., Kastner, P.: Fuzzy C-Means Method for Clustering Microarray Data. Bioinformatics 19(8), 973–980 (2003)
3. Domany, E.: Cluster Analysis of Gene Expression Data. Journal of Statistical Physics 110, 1117–1139 (2003)
4. Maji, P., Pal, S.K.: Rough Set Based Generalized Fuzzy C-Means Algorithm and Quantitative Indices. IEEE Transactions on System, Man, and Cybernetics, Part B: Cybernetics 37(6), 1529–1540 (2007)
5. Maji, P., Paul, S.: Microarray Time-Series Data Clustering Using Rough-Fuzzy C-Means Algorithm. In: Proceedings of 5th IEEE International Conference on Bioinformatics and Biomedicine, pp. 1–4 (2011)
6. Shamir, R., Sharan, R.: CLICK: A Clustering Algorithm for Gene Expression Analysis. In: Proceedings of the 8th International Conference on Intelligent Systems for Molecular Biology (2000)
7. Theodoridis, S., Koutroumbas, K.: Pattern Recognition, 4th edn. Elsevier (2009)
8. Wang, J., Delabie, J., Aasheim, H.C., Smeland, E., Myklebost, O.: Clustering of the SOM Easily Reveals Distinct Gene Expression Patterns: Results of a Reanalysis of Lymphoma Study. BMC Bioinformatics 3(36), 1–9 (2002)

Topographic Map Object Classification Using Real-Value Grammar Classifier System

Lukasz Cielecki

Institute of Computer Engineering, Control and Robotics
Wroclaw University of Technology
Wybrzeze Wyspianskiego 27
50-370 Wroclaw, Poland
lukasz.cielecki@pwr.wroc.pl

Abstract. Learning Classifier Systems (LCS) became a large branch of machine learning applications that received a lot of attention recently. Our model of LCS - rGCS or real-value Grammar Classifier System - uses grammar inference to classify real-value vectors which may describe range variety of problems. In this paper we utilize the rGCS core in an object recognition task. Our application seeks for certain graphic symbols on a topographic map scan.

1 Introduction

Applications processing digital maps can be divided into two groups: using raster or – more popular in modern software – vector-based digital data. There is still large repository of raster map images acquired mostly by scanning paper documents. These still can be used in navigation software as soon as a calibrations process is completed. This involves obtaining some (two at least) proper coordinates of points in the map and pointing them in the calibration software. That enables the software to interpolate any coordinate in the map and therefore show an actual position recorded by GPS receiver. Calibration is the very first step in the procedure of adapting a raster image map to digital processing but for more sophisticated use some further effort needs to be taken.

Tagging raster map is the most common procedure that results in a "hybrid map" - a map combining raster image background, calibration data and coordinates linked to points of interest (POI) list. Hybrid maps allow a navigation software to search through the list of POIs as well as plot a course to specified point of interest (hill, bridge, tower, etc.) by giving an azimuth directions.

Tagging a raster map makes an association between given coordinates of real object and its raster image. It may be accomplished in two ways: manual and automatic. In manual (interactive) approach human operator simply points out an object in the image. Then coordinates are interpolated based on the calibration data. That requires a lot of attention and work that needs to be done. Another approach - an automatic one - plugs a machine learning algorithm in. It uses an object recognition to classify some parts of the raster map image, consequently ruling the need of a human operator out.

M.K. Kundu et al. (Eds.): PerMIn 2012, LNCS 7143, pp. 211–218, 2012.

It this paper we describe automatic map tagging using rGCS. Its ability to adopt to various problems' environments let us to embed it in an application for locating objects in the raster image maps.

2   Learning Classifier Systems

A Learning Classifier System (LCS) is an evolutionary algorithm that operates on a population of rules used to classify an environmental situation. The first learning classifier system was introduced by Holland [10] shortly after he created Genetic Algorithms (GAs) [9]. Many real-world problems are not conveniently expressed using the ternary representation typically used by LCSs (*true*, *false*, and *don't care* symbol). To overcome this limitation, Wilson [15] introduced real-valued XCS classifier system for problems which can be defined by a vector of bounded continuous real-coded variables.

In [3] we introduced a new model of real-value LCS – the rGCS – to classify real value data. rGCS is based on Grammar-based Classifier System (GCS), which was used to process context free grammar (CFG) sentences [12]. In rGCS terminal rewriting rules were replaced with so-called environment probing rules. That enabled rGCS to explore environment described by real values. First rGCS experiments utilized the checkerboard problem test sets. This simple benchmark proved an ability to solve "real-value input" problems and made new kind of data sets available for our system. Following these preliminary experiments some more complex benchmarks were tested, including 2D data, and function classification [5].

2.1   The GCS

Population of classifiers in the GCS has a form of a CFG rule set in a Chomsky Normal Form (CNF). CNF allows only production rules in the form of $A \rightarrow a$ or $A \rightarrow BC$, where A, B, C are the non-terminal symbols and a is a terminal symbol. The first rule is an instance of terminal rewriting rule. These ones are not affected by GA, and are generated automatically as the system meets unknown (new) terminal symbols. Left hand side of the rule plays a role of classifier's action while the right side a classifier's condition. System evolves only one grammar according to the so-called Michigan approach and classification is considered to be positive for all input examples successfully parsed. In this approach each individual classifier – or grammar rule in GCS – is a subject of GA's operations. All classifiers (rules) form a population of evolving individuals. In each cycle a fitness calculating algorithm evaluates a value of each classifier following the Michigan approach.

Automatic learning of CFG is realized with so-called grammatical inference from text [7]. According to this technique system learns using a training set that in this case consists of sentences both syntactically correct and incorrect (training or learning phase). Grammar which accepts correct sentences and rejects incorrect ones is able to classify unseen so far sentences from a test set (during the test phase). Cocke-Younger-Kasami (CYK) parser, which operates in $\Theta(n^3 \cdot |G|)$ time (where n is the length of the parsed string and $|G|$ is the size of the CNF grammar G) [16], is used to parse sentences from the sets. Environment of classifier system is substituted by an array of CYK parser. Classifier system matches the rules according to the current environmental state (state of parsing) and generates an action (or set of actions in GCS) pushing the parsing process toward the complete derivation of the sentence.

The discovery component of the GCS differs from the standard. It extends LCS with "covering" procedure that adds some rules useful in the current state of parsing (see [13]) and a "fertility" technique which preserves rules' dependencies in the parsing tree [14].

2.2   The rGCS

Despite the fact that the GCS system is able to solve grammar induction problems effectively the area of its usage is strongly limited. Due to the nature of the tagged input data, most tasks it is employed to are connected with formal or natural languages. To overcome that limitation an extension of the GCS that accepts any input data stored as a vector of real values was created.

The rGCS exploits the main idea of the classic GCS system. The CYK table is the environment and the area where the rGCS operates. The learning process is divided into the cycles. During every cycle evolved grammar is tested against each example of the train set, then new rules are evolved or existing ones are modified and another cycle begins. rGCS employs two various kinds of rules - environment probing and regular ones - which are used in different phases of the learning process. Environment probing rules replace GCS standard terminal rewriting rules.

Environment probing rules. Structure of the rules that are used in the very first row of the CYK table during parsing is the main difference between the GCS and the rGCS. Since their role is to sense the input data and then to launch the CYK process we called them the environment probing rules. In the rGCS the input data (environmental situation) is formed by the vector of real numbers that may describe various kinds of data.

Each rule has the form of:

$$A \rightarrow f \,,$$

where:
A is a non-terminal symbol,
f is a real number value.
f value (rule's factor or position) is used during the matching process and the non-terminal A is to put into the first row of the CYK table.

Regular grammar rules. These rules are identical to the ones used in the classic GCS. They are used in the CYK parsing process and the GA phase. They are in the form of:

$$B \rightarrow BC \,,$$

where A, B and C are non-terminal symbols.

Matching phase. During the matching phase a bundle of non-terminals is defined to put into the first row of the CYK table, achieving the goal of translating real input values into the string of symbols capable of parsing.

First a list of distances between the element of an input vector (real number value) and each rule's factor is created and then simply the nearest rule is selected. As the result always one rule is put into the CYK cell. This scheme used during training process uses only a single real value from the rule - a point with no accepting range around it explicitly labeled. That approach differs from the one adopted in Wilson's XCSR [15] where several interval predicates are defined to "catch" input values located inside its boundaries. The main difference is that in the rGCS learning the single value method always chooses at least one rule - no matter where the input value is located. This means that even with limited number of environment probing rules there are no input values that are left unrecognized. This can be referred as some kind of interpolation of an input space.

Strategy where each rule can accept any real value without looking at the distance between them causes some problems however. In many problems only some specific subset of points in the input space (or in the certain dimension of an input space) can exist in the positive examples. Therefore we need to modify the matching phase to stop input values not included in that subset from being accepted. To achieve that we set up a Single Accept Radius parameter which describes every environment probing rule. It is set up and updated (and then not yet used) during the matching phase of the learning process in the rGCS. Simple accept radius is the longest distance between rule's factor and any real value accepted by it that belongs to the positive example. During the test phase we accept only these real values that are located within the learned accept radius. This protects us from accepting values that are outside the area which our terminal rewriting rule is supposed to be employed for.

Matching regular rules used in the CYK parsing process follows the CYK algorithm procedure and is same as in GCS.

Rules adjustments and evolution. Environment probing rules adjustments were widely discussed in [6]. As the environment probing rules match the input vector, some data about the environment is collected to find the best possible value of each rule's real-value factor. The aim is to distribute environment probing rules over the input space. Modified Kohonen neural network adaptation techniques [11] were implemented in the rGCS to allow classifiers' real-value factors to automatically tune to the environment.

Regular grammar rules are evolved just like in the classic GCS system during the evolutionary process. GA is launched at the end of each learning cycle. Fitness evaluation uses a fertility measurement technique (see [14] for discussion), for the rules that were present in any complete parsing tree generated during the cycle. This technique tries to keep all dependencies between rules in the parsing tree by promoting classifiers with large number of descendants.

3   Object Recognition as a Function Classification

One of the most important factors that is a key to effective rGCS application is a proper input data preparation. System's receptors need to be fed with pre-formatted examples from training (and later test) datasets.

In the map tagging problem our goal is to locate and classify small square grayscale bitmaps of size between 3×3 and 8×8 pixels containing accordingly from 9 up to 64 individual pixel points. Each pixel is represented by a real value that holds only luminosity information scaled to $[0, 1]$ interval.

Input data is being preprocessed by "cutting" squares from the map and transforming into an rGCS examples or test vectors of 3 elements: luminosity value of a point and its two integer coordinates inside the cut square. This means that every single square generates as many single examples as the number of pixels its formed out of (i.e. 4×4 square object gives us 16 vectors). In the learning process rGCS core subsystem is assigned to the task of telling whether a luminosity and coordinates of a point in an example fit together. If rGCS assumes they do - than we have a positive classification - otherwise a negative one. Having only an information about one single point is - obviously - not enough. To answer the main question (is the square we test the object we are looking for or isn't?) we need to run a number of independent test for every pixel of the current square. The definite answer is given according to the poll results - we sum the positive and negative classifications of all the pixels and let the majority to decide.

The approach presented above makes the map tagging problem closer to the function classification [4]. Given two coordinate we are about to tell whether the value (luminosity) is correct or not. Preliminary experiments performed on the Butz functions (presented in [2]) proved that that's fair task for the rGCS.

rGCS recognition combines both luminosity- and feature-based approach [1]. The former is provided by environment probing rules while the latter by regular rules and evolved grammars.

3.1   Experiments

Map tagging application was tested on a gray-scale topographic map (scale 1 : 50000) to find survey markers' symbols. Figure 1 shows a symbol image pattern. In actual map scan this has size of only 8×8 pixels (giving us 64 example vectors from each symbol). That can be observed in fig. 1 where processed map fragment with survey markers' symbols highlighted is shown. For experimental purposes we've extracted 1000 example vectors (500 positive and 500 negative ones). Negative examples were randomly chosen from map image data.

During the experiments we estimated following optimal parameters settings: population consisting of 62 individuals (including 12 environment probing rules with three subpopulations – two having 5 and one having 2 individuals), 5000 training cycles.

Environment probing rules are divided into three subpopulations with two of them responsible for translating both pixel coordinates inside an object into

(a)   (b)

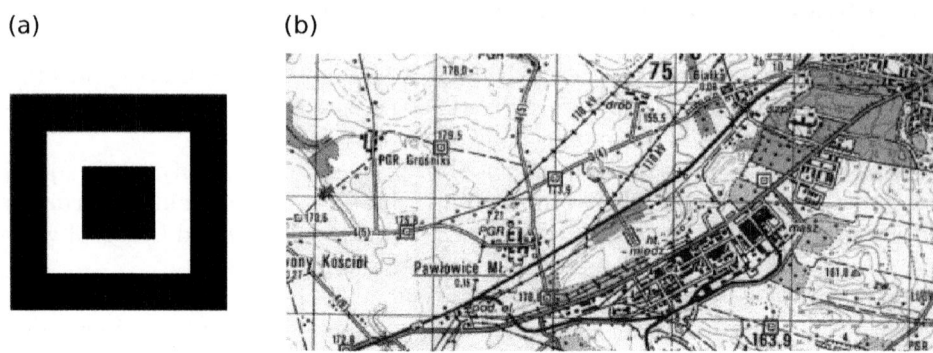

Fig. 1. Single survey marker symbol image (a) and map fragment with survey markers' symbols highlighted (b)

non-terminal symbols. Despite the fact that we classify object that generally have 8×8 pixels size we set up only 5 probing points at each dimension. That's because of the way our survey markers look like (fig. 1) - it can be drawn inside only 5×5 pixel matrix. Due to casting integer coordinates to the real values there is no problem of covering 8 pixels area by 5 rGCS rules - they can reside in not only discrete values but in any point in the input space.

Third input vector's value (luminosity) is pre-classified by two environment probing rules. That's because we only want to know if a point is black or white. In the process of translating input values in to non-terminal symbols these two rules divide luminosity part of input space into two classes and all grays that came out in scanning are included in one of them. Thanks to the rules' adjusting technique in rGCS there is no problem with improper (i.e. to dark) scans since the environment probing rules will find the boundary between two classes automatically.

Most of the grammars induced have reached 69%-78% fitness (average 74,4% at 10 runs). Those grammars then did 68%-75% during testing using sets of previously unseen objects. Best grammars achieved 70% fitness rate at correct classifying positive examples and even 80% at negative ones. That practically means that 3/4 of objects' pixels were recognized properly.

Table 1 compares rGCS results of pixel recognition (percent of correct classifications) with some popular classifiers implemented in *Weka* environment [8]. rGCS scored at least 1% better than other algorithms. Thorough analysis proved that rGCS benefits from its hybrid nature where pixels are recognized in two-stage process, using discretization by environment probing rules and feature learning by context-free grammar.

Table 2 shows results of 10 objects recognition using rGCS system. All recognitions include classification of all 64 pixels inside an object. Each classification gave an answer if a pixel at specified coordinates had proper luminosity or not. Number of positive and negative answers is shown next to the magnified object in the table along with graphical representation of the recognition. The more the "X" sign is located to the left the more pixels are classified as positive.

Table 1. rGCS and other classifiers comparison

Percent of correct classifications of previously unseen examples				
rGCS	OneR	Naive Bayes	C4.5	SVM
71.20%	62.20%	70.45%	69.95%	70.20%

Table 2. Survey markers recognition using rGCS

Image	Poll YES	Recognition	Poll NO	Image	Poll YES	Recognition	Poll NO
	39	--------X-|----------	25		14	----------|----X-----	50
	36	---------X|----------	28		17	----------|---X------	47
	41	--------X-|----------	23		19	----------|---X------	45
	54	----X-----|----------	10		20	----------|--X-------	44
	48	-----X----|----------	16		25	----------|-X--------	39

4 Conclusions and Future Plans

Our map tagging application was able to effectively recognize digitized object images. Proposed way to adopt and pre-format input data along with final result analysis by polling enabled the rGCS core to successfully cope with the problem.

Our future plans include further development of the rGCS core results interpretation like introduction of weights that make central points more important during the final poll. We also consider some improvements to the rGCS environment probing subsystem to let it better fit to the input data and therefore advance grammar evolution.

References

1. Belongie, S., Malik, J., Puzicha, J.: Shape matching and object recognition using shape contexts. IEEE Trans. Pattern Anal. Mach. Intell. 24(4), 509–522 (2002), http://computer.org/tpami/tp2002/i0509abs.htm
2. Butz, M.: Kernel-based, ellipsoidal conditions in the real-valued xcs classifier system. In: Proceedings of the 2005 Conference on Genetic and Evolutionary Computation, pp. 1835–1842. ACM (2005)

3. Cielecki, L., Unold, O.: Real-valued gcs classifier system. International Journal of Applied Mathematics and Computer Science 17(4), 539–547 (2007)
4. Cielecki, L., Unold, O.: 3d function approximation with rgcs classifier system. In: Eighth International Conference on Intelligent Systems Design and Applications, ISDA 2008, vol. 3, pp. 136–141. IEEE (2008)
5. Cielecki, L., Unold, O.: Modified himmelblau function classification with rgcs system. In: Eighth International Conference on Hybrid Intelligent Systems, HIS 2008, pp. 879–884. IEEE (2008)
6. Cielecki, L., Unold, O.: GCS with Real-Valued Input. In: Mira, J., Álvarez, J.R. (eds.) IWINAC 2007. LNCS, vol. 4527, pp. 488–497. Springer, Heidelberg (2007)
7. Gold, E.: Language identification in the limit. Information and Control 10(5), 447–474 (1967)
8. Hall, M., Frank, E., Holmes, G., Pfahringer, B., Reutemann, P., Witten, I.H.: The WEKA data mining software: an update. SIGKDD Explorations 11(1), 10–18 (2009), http://doi.acm.org/10.1145/1656274.1656278
9. Holland, J.: Adaptation in natural and artificial systems: An introductory analysis with applications to biology, control, and artificial intelligence. U Michigan Press (1975)
10. Holland, J.H.: Adaptation. In: Rosen, R., Snell, F. (eds.) Progress in Theoretical Biology. Academic Press (1976)
11. Kohonen, T.: Self–organizing formation of topologically correct feature maps. Biological Cybernetics 43, 59–69 (1982)
12. Unold, O.: Context-free grammar induction with grammar-based classifier system. Archives of Control Science 15(4), 681 (2005)
13. Unold, O., Cielecki, L.: Grammar-based classifier system. Issues in Intelligent Systems: Paradigms, 273–286 (2005)
14. Unold, O.: Playing a Toy-Grammar with GCS. In: Mira, J., Álvarez, J.R. (eds.) IWINAC 2005. LNCS, vol. 3562, pp. 300–309. Springer, Heidelberg (2005)
15. Wilson, S.: Get real! xcs with continuous-valued inputs. Learning Classifier Systems, 209–219 (2000)
16. Younger, D.: Recognition and parsing of context-free languages in time n3*. Information and Control 10(2), 189–208 (1967)

Distance Measures in Training Set Selection for Debt Value Prediction

Tomasz Kajdanowicz, Slawomir Plamowski, and Przemyslaw Kazienko

Wroclaw University of Technology, Wroclaw, Poland,
Faculty of Computer Science and Management,
{tomasz.kajdanowicz,slawomir.plamowski,kazienko}@pwr.wroc.pl

Abstract. A comparative study over six learning scenarios in debt pattern recognition is presented in the paper. There are proposed new approaches for distance measure definitions in training set selection. Using those measures for training set selection the inference models are trained using distinct reference. All proposed approaches are examined in dataset selection during prediction of debt portfolio value. Finally, basic evaluation on prediction performance is conducted.

Keywords: dataset selection, distance measures, probability density function, debt valuation, prediction, supervised learning.

1 Introduction

Supervised machine learning algorithms are required to be able to generalize based on training data. As it may be expected, the characteristic of training dataset utilized in learning algorithm has a great influence on the generalization abilities. Therefore, the selection of training set for learning algorithm should be performed carefully. The most straightforward and clear situation arises when learning concerns data from particular domain and describes always the same stationary object. The statistical dependencies between examples remain unchanged and training may be performed using the same source of training and testing data. Such data, as long as it has appropriate size, may deliver satisfactory generalization ability.

Another situation occurs when generalization needs to be performed for objects for which training data is not available. In such case, learning is performed using data from the same domain but describes other similar objects. An example of such a situation are across-network classification when learning performed on one network adjust models used in generalization on another network[7] or debt portfolio value prediction when value of appraisal of particular portfolio is done using other similar portfolios[6].

The paper considers the problem of training set selection in the prediction task when inference is based on models learnt on data from the same domain but describing other similar objects. Obviously, the greater similarity/smaller distance between objects used in learning and those the inference is applied

M.K. Kundu et al. (Eds.): PerMIn 2012, LNCS 7143, pp. 219–226, 2012.

to, the better performance of inference methods. Similarity/distance identification between training and testing objects can be reduced to similarity/distance measurement between datasets describing their input features, namely similarity/distance between X_{train} and X_{test}. Aforementioned similarity and distance can be invoked interchangeably as similarity can be measured by distance, i.e. two objects are similar if the distance is close to zero. In general, distance is defined as a quantitative degree of how far apart two objects are[2]. The choice of distance measure depends on the representation of objects and type of measurement. Training sets in supervised learning are usually represented by matrices in which columns denote attributes and rows - object instances. A single cell of such matrix contains a value of particular attribute for a given instance. Hence, the the problem of training set selection based on measuring the distance between two datasets X_{train} and X_{test} is actually a matrix distance based selection.

The rest of the paper is organised as follows. In section 2, various approaches and distance measures that may be utilized to training set selection are enumerated. In order to provide a better perspective on the problem, section 3 presents a real-world training set selection problem in debt portfolio value prediction. In section 4 some distance measures for comparison and selection of training datasets are introduced. Evaluation of the impact on the prediction accuracy using proposed distance measures is presented in section 5. Finally, section 6 summarises this work.

2   Related Work

Training set selection from a set of available historical datasets based on the distance between particular testing set and training set may be considered using two equivalent approaches: as selection based on distance between non-equal in size matrices or, better, as calculating measure of goodness of fit between probability density functions. While calculation of probability density for discrete random variables is performed with respect to the counting measure over the sample space, the density of continuous random variables is given by the integral of this variables density. This may imply problems as the exact density is not known and the empirical one can be obtained only. Literature proposes either the estimation of probability density function[9] or, simply, consideration of discrete and finite histogram of random variable[2,12]. The histogram can be considered then as a vector, i.e. coordinates in some space, and numerous distances proposed in the literature can be applied to compare two densities.

There exist a substantial number of distance measures derived from various fields such as computer science, information theory, mathematics, physics, or statistics, etc. Some of them that may be used in distance calculation are standard Euclidean distance and Kullback-Leibler distance. Obviously, these distance measures are only examples and a proper choice of representative distance measure depends on the type of measured data and the measurement itself. For further list of distance measures please refer to [2,13].

The approach of calculating distances between vector version of probability density functions tends to be reasonable but requires estimation of probability density function which sometimes might be troublesome.

The distance of two datasets might be computed by application of other concept - distance matrices. However, this is limited to situation when both datasets have the same size (number of rows) and, what is more, the mapping bijection that states the clear relation of corresponding data examples is known. As the size of compared distinct datasets may differ and the mapping between data examples is not known, it is not always possible to compute distance matrices.

Nevertheless, the distance between datasets may be calculated using matrix norms[8]. The matrix norms are defined in terms of well known vector norms and therefore, one can say, they are induced by vector norms[14]. As some basic norms like (for a given matrix A) matrix 1-norm - returns maximum of A column sums, matrix ∞-norm - returns maximum of A row sums or matrix 2-norm - returns square root of largest eigenvalue of $A \times A$, more sophisticated once needs to be applied to characterize the matrix[8]. One of them can be Frobenius norm. This norm is the sum of the squares of the Euclidean norms of the matrix columns[8]. Thus it is able to model variability of the data. Investigating the literature we can see that norms are not the perfect solution to model distances between matrices.

Summarizing, trying to avoid the situation when a vector version of probability distribution function is required in order to calculate distances between two datasets, a notion of entropy based distance measure is introduced in following sections.

3   Debt Portfolio Value Prediction

Determining the value of debt portfolios and choosing these having the greatest revenue potential is of a great importance for debt traders. Economically crucial decisions are based on the amount of possible repayment of liabilities. As traders (both buyers and sellers) apply distinct collection processes, amount of receivables obtained may be different. This constitutes the area for trading and to establish a transaction price. Therefore debt portfolio assessment is complex task. However, as far as machine learning is concerned, this problem may be understood as a prediction task that assesses the possible repayment value from all debt cases belonging to particular portfolio. The repayment is calculated based on historical data of debts.

The most common routine of debt portfolio trade starts when a seller, usually a bank, telecommunication company, etc. offers a set of debts, called debt package or portfolio, expecting a purchase proposal from buyers. Purchasers, usually a specialized debt recovery entities, offer price and the most suitable offer is chosen. The price proposed by a particular buyer may be obtained in variety of ways, among which the utilization of historical data of debt recovery in order to build a prediction model seems the most reasonable one. Such model provides an estimation of possible return from the package.

In considered situation the valuation of debt portfolio is based on the data of historical claims with their repayment profiles over time. A debt collection company usually assumes that gathered repayment data reflects all important dependencies influencing repayment results like recovery procedures, cash flow plans and other external conditions. Such assumption simplifies the problem as changes in the probabilities caused by evolving business environment are ignored. The model trained on historical data is applied to predict the repayment amount of the offered portfolio. Basing on the obtained results, bids are offered to the seller.

Summarizing, the most significant and sensitive part of debt trade is repayment value prediction process. The accuracy of prediction for offered portfolio relies mainly on model generalization capabilities and quality of training data. As it is very difficult to provide prediction using whole, large historical data, some training dataset selection mechanism needs to be employed. In the further part of the paper we present the method for training set selection for model learning, that is applied to considered business scenario.

4   Distance Measures in Training Set Selection

As previously stated in the paper, training set can be treated as a matrix. Therefore the problem of training set selection is equivalent to the matrix selection using some notion of distance.

In situation when the generalization can be based only on historical datasets of the same domain, describing similar objects with the same attributes, the debt prediction problem is solved by inference from historical portfolios of debts, that have been already repaid. They are used to predict the repayment value of unknown portfolio. Learning could be performed using all historical datasets, but from the practical point of view it would not always be possible (e.g. massive training data) and of high quality (poor inference from complex and non-discriminative data). Therefore some methods for training set selection, reflecting the nature of prediction task, need to be applied. As the selection of appropriate learning data needs to be provided using quantitative measurements, in following subsections there are proposed several distance measurement methods between two datasets.

Training set selection is based on the assumption that there exists set T of k training sets A_i, $i \in \{1, \ldots, k\}$, $k \in \mathbb{N}$. Each training set A_i may, in fact, be matrix of different size, where columns denote attributes and rows - object instances. Suppose there exists testing set B, for which prediction need to be conducted. The actual task is to compose a final training set that will provide the best prediction performance. The final training set may be composed of single dataset A_i or several joined sets from T. Distances between the test set B and each training set $A_i \in T$, namely $dist(B, A_i)$, are computed using their distinct definitions. Based on that, a ranking of the shortest distances between B and all A_i sets is formulated. Few top closest A_i datasets are then combined into final training set. The selection of top closest datasets may be performed in numerous way, e.g. first, three or five closest datasets.

4.1   Histogram Based Distance Measures

Two versions of histogram based distance measures are concerned: equal bins and equal range. Both of measures assume that distance between datasets is calculated using figures describing histograms of datasets' variables. Namely, the distance between dataset A_i and B equals to sum of euclidean distances between discrete version of corresponding variables (histograms) from A_i and B, see equation 1.

The equal bins histogram based measure builds for each variable in each dataset individual histogram of the same number c of beans distributed proportionally to the scope of variable. Therefore while comparing histograms of two distinct datasets only the shape (variance) of histograms is examined and no exact alignment in values of variables is taken into account.

Similarly, the equal range histogram based measure utilizes for each variable in each dataset individual histogram of the same number c of beans but distributed proportionally to the overall scope of variable observed in all datasets. Therefore comparing histograms of two distinct datasets considers the shape (variance) of histograms and exact alignment in values.

The distance between datasets is calculated using figures describing each of c histograms beans for each variable. Namely, the distance between dataset A_i and B equals to sum of euclidean distances between discrete version of each variables (histograms), see equation 1.

$$dist(A_i, B) = \sqrt{\sum_{i=j}^{m} |hist(a_j) - hist(b_j)|^2} \tag{1}$$

where m denotes number of attributes in datasets, a_j, b_j denote jth variable in datasets A_i, B respectively and $hist()$ - one of mentioned above histogram calculation method.

4.2   Mean Variable Distance Measure

Mean variable distance measure calculates simply the euclidean distance between vectors of means of each variable. The distance between A_i and B is calculated according to equation 2.

$$dist(A_i, B) = \sqrt{\sum_{j=1}^{m} |mean(a_j) - mean(b_j)|^2} \tag{2}$$

Unfortunately, while using mean variable distance measure we assume the individual variables come from Gaussian distribution.

4.3   Entropy Based Distance Measure

A calculation of distance between two datasets A_i and B requires a clustering method to be applied on joint A_i and B datasets. It is done in order to obtain number of similar data example groups. Without loss of generality it is assumed that each obtained group contains data examples coming from similar probability distribution. Let $M = M_1, \ldots, M_n$, $n \in \mathbb{N}$ be a set of groups indicated by clustering method. Any non-random grouping algorithm is acceptable. It can be noticed that in each group different number of examples from both input datasets B and A_i may be found. However, if all groups gather data examples from similar distribution, one can assume, that there is similarity between datasets. In other words, the distance between them is relatively small. To quantify that, the method calculates the entropy of share of data examples coming from B and A_i for each groups as follows:

$$S_l = - \sum_{x_j \in M_l} p(x_j) log_2(p(x_j)), \tag{3}$$

where $p(x_j)$ denotes possibility of observing x_j inside M_l group, $l \in \{1, \ldots, n\}$.

Having computed entropy values for all groups, the method calculates variance of these results, which is then used as a distance measure. Employment of variance incorporates some important properties. Desired variance of 0 denotes that all groups obtained in clustering process share the same properties of probability density distribution. This means that for all groups there is the same probability of observing examples from both datasets and in consequence those datasets are very similar.

Using entropy based distance measure requires no assumption in the shape of probability density function of variables.

4.4   Frobenius Norm Distance

Frobenius norm is computed for each of data matrices. Then an euclidean distance between norms of test B and all training datasets A_i is computed to choose the closest matrices. The Frobenius norm is similar to the Euclidean norm and and is derived from an inner product on the space of all matrices [4]. The calculation of the norm value for matrix A with n data examples and m attributes is accomplished according to equation 4.

$$\| A \| = \sqrt{(\sum_{i=1}^{n} \sum_{j=1}^{m} | a_{ij} |^2)} \tag{4}$$

5   Experiments and Results

The main objective of performed experiments was to test and evaluate the impact of proposed distance measures on prediction accuracy using basic ridge regression algorithm[11]. Mean-squared error was used as standard performance measure.

Experiments were carried out on fifteen distinct, real datasets from the same application domain of debt portfolio pattern recognition [6]. Datasets represent

Table 1. Mean square error and Friedman test ranking for debt portfolio value prediction using 5 closest training datasets obtained by application of distinct distance measures and using all 14 remaining datasets

Dataset	Equal bins	Equal range	Mean	Entropy	Frobenius	Remaining datasets
1	0.1677	0.1677	0.0789	0.0800	0.1698	0.1813
2	0.1201	0.1201	0.1221	0.1182	0.1221	0.2181
3	0.0908	0.0998	0.0873	0.0873	0.0831	0.1836
4	0.3808	0.3808	0.0945	0.6847	0.3183	0.4100
5	0.0884	0.0884	0.0956	0.0917	0.0898	0.1911
6	0.0893	0.0884	0.0917	0.0953	0.0955	0.1920
7	0.2136	0.2136	0.2056	0.2064	0.2056	0.3044
8	0.1272	0.1272	0.1328	0.1327	0.1292	0.2321
9	0.0733	0.0732	0.0728	0.0734	0.0733	0.1734
10	0.1640	0.1640	0.1694	0.1616	0.1584	0.2628
11	0.0797	0.0797	0.0725	0.0727	0.0726	0.1730
12	0.1439	0.1439	0.1434	0.1516	0.1439	0.2445
13	0.2295	0.2287	0.2300	0.2344	0.2286	0.3288
14	0.1632	0.1632	0.1597	0.1594	0.1617	0.2621
15	0.0748	0.0748	0.0795	0.0744	0.0786	0.1753
friedmann	3.1333	3.0667	2.8667	3.2000	2.8000	5.9333

the problem of aggregated prediction of sequential repayment values over time for a set of claims.

The experimental procedure works as follows: suppose there exists a debt portfolio B of unknown output, for which prediction needs to be conducted in order to determine value of possible repayment. From among all known portfolios 5 closest ones (according to distance measurement method) are selected. Using selected packages, regression algorithm is trained and eventually basic tests for portfolio B are performed.

Basing on described procedure, the experiment consisting of six rounds, one for each of presented distance measures (equal bins, equal range, mean, entropy, frobenius and final using all remaining datasets) is created. For examined scenarios Friedman test is run. Results are presented in table 1.

As shown during Friedman test, usage of 5 closest datasets for training results in better performance than using all remaining datasets.

Results have been confirmed by Wilcoxon pairwise test. There was no observed significant statistical difference between approaches for selecting training datasets using presented distance measures. However, Wilcoxon signed rank test comparing these methods with Remaining dataset one resulted with p-value in range $[0.000061; 0.0084]$ and therefore there exist significant statistical difference yielding that using training set selection is far better than learning on all remaining datasets.

6   Conclusions

The problem of training set selection was considered in the paper. A comparative study over six learning scenarios was conducted, applying various distance measures in training set selection. All proposed approaches were examined in prediction of debt portfolio value. Finally, basic evaluation on prediction performance was performed.

The results indicate that training set selection is far better than learning based on all available data. Presented distance measures used for training set selection help to provide good choice of learning data to achieve better prediction accuracy and reduce the amount of data needed for prediction process. Both of these advantages are of great importance in many real domain applications as they underlie many bussiness decisions.

Acknowledgement. This work was supported by The Polish Ministry of Science and Higher Education the research project 2011-2012, 2011-2014 and Fellowship co-financed by The European Union within The European Social Fund.

References

1. Cano, J.R., Herrera, F., Lozano, M.: Using evolutionary algorithms as instance selection for data reduction in KDD: an experimental study. IEEE Transactions on Evolutionary Computation 7(6), 561–575 (2003)
2. Cha, S.H.: Comprehensive survey on distance/similarity measures between probability density functions. International Journal of Mathematical Models and Methods in Applied Sciences 1(4), 300–307 (2007)
3. Coifman, R.R., Wickerhauser, M.V.: Entropy-based algorithms for best basis selection. IEEE Transactions on Information Theory 38, 713–718 (1992)
4. Demmel, J.: Applied Numerical Linear Algebra. SIAM (1997)
5. Deza, E., Deza, M.M.: Dictionary of Distances. Elsevier (2006)
6. Kajdanowicz, T., Kazienko, P.: Prediction of Sequential Values for Debt Recovery. In: Bayro-Corrochano, E., Eklundh, J.-O. (eds.) CIARP 2009. LNCS, vol. 5856, pp. 337–344. Springer, Heidelberg (2009)
7. Lu, Q., Getoor, L.: Link-based classification using labeled and unlabeled data. In: ICML 2003 Workshop on The Continuum from Labeled to Unlabeled Data in Machine Learning and Data Mining (2003)
8. Meyer, C.D.: Matrix analysis and applied linear algebra. Society for Industrial and Applied Mathematics (2000)
9. Rencher, A.: Methods of multivariate analysis. John Wiley & Sons (2002)
10. Son, S.-H., Kim, J.-Y.: Data Reduction for Instance-Based Learning Using Entropy-Based Partitioning. In: Gavrilova, M.L., Gervasi, O., Kumar, V., Tan, C.J.K., Taniar, D., Laganá, A., Mun, Y., Choo, H. (eds.) ICCSA 2006. LNCS, vol. 3982, pp. 590–599. Springer, Heidelberg (2006)
11. Theodoris, S., Koutroumbas, K.: Pattern Recognition. Elsevier (2009)
12. Toussaint, G.T.: Bibliography on estimation of misclassification. IEEE Transactions on Information Theory 20(4), 472–479 (1974)
13. Ullah, A.: Entropy, divergence and distance measures with econometric applications, Department of Economics, University of California - Riverside (1993)
14. Zhou, K., Doyle, K., Glover, K.: Robust and Optimal Control. Prentice Hall (1996)

A Second-Order Learning Algorithm for Computing Optimal Regulatory Pathways

Mouli Das[1], C.A. Murthy[1], Subhasis Mukhopadhyay[2], and Rajat K. De[1]

[1] Machine Intelligence Unit, Indian Statistical Institute, Kolkata 700 108, India
{mouli_r,murthy,rajat}@isical.ac.in
[2] Department of Bio-Physics, Molecular Biology and Bioinformatics,
Calcutta University, Kolkata 700 009, India
sm.bmbg@gmail.com

Abstract. Gene regulatory pathways play an important role in the functional understanding and interpretation of gene function. Many different approaches have been developed to model and simulate gene regulatory networks. In this paper we present the results of an iterative new second-order learning algorithm based on the multilayer perceptron (MLP) for generating optimal gene regulatory pathways by using ordinary differential equations. The algorithm based on Newton's method is independent on the learning parameter and overcomes the drawbacks of the standard backpropagation (BP) algorithm. The methodology generates flow vectors which indicate the flow of mRNA and thereby the protein produced from one gene to another gene. A set of weighting coefficients representing concentration of various transcription factors is incorporated. The gene regulatory pathways are obtained through optimization of an objective function with respect to these weighting coefficients. Two gene regulatory networks are used to demonstrate the efficiency of the proposed learning algorithm. A comparative study with the existing extreme pathway analysis (EPA) also forms a part of this study. Results reported in the paper were corroborated by the same reported in the literature.

Keywords: FBA, extreme pathway, backpropagation, MLP, transcription factor.

1 Introduction

The increasing availability of genomic, transcriptomic and related data allows detailed analysis of properties of complex biochemical reaction networks composed of gene networks, protein networks, metabolic networks and signaling networks. Flux balance analysis (FBA) [6] has been useful for large scale analysis of metabolic networks, and methods have been developed to extend this approach for transcriptional regulation. High-throughput technologies allow studying aspects of gene regulatory networks (GRNs) on a genome-wide scale and we will discuss recent advances as well as limitations and future challenges for gene network modelling. GRNs have an important role in every process of life, including cell differentiation, metabolism, the cell cycle and signal transduction. GRNs are

M.K. Kundu et al. (Eds.): PerMIn 2012, LNCS 7143, pp. 227–234, 2012.

concerned with the control of transcription, i.e. how genes are up and down regulated in response to signals [3]. GRNs consist of interactions between proteins, known as transcription factors, and genes, which in turn encode other proteins. By understanding the dynamics of GRNs we can shed light on the mechanisms of diseases that occur when the cellular processes are dysregulated. Inference of gene regulatory pathways is a key goal in the quest for understanding fundamental cellular processes and revealing underlying relations among genes [14].

Optimization by gradient descent is widely used by various machine learning algorithms such as back-propagation (BP) of the error in Multi-Layer Perceptrons (MLPs) and Radial Basis Functions [5]. However, several drawbacks of the BP learning method have been observed; its convergence speed is usually too low, its convergence accuracy is hard to control, it is easily stuck in bad local minima and the choice of proper learning constant largely depends on trial and error [11]. One common approach is to upgrade the normal BP, which is a first-order learning algorithm, to a second-order one [1]. Since the second order method is an optimization algorithm with quadratic convergence speed, it can be used to improve the learning speed and accuracy of the normal BP [13]. We describe an extension of the back propagation algorithm which uses a simple approximation to the second derivative terms. Also, the proposed method is independent of the learning constant in contrary to the difficulty in the choice of a proper learning constant for normal BP.

The proposed method generates the possible flow vectors in the pathway by taking convex combination of the basis vectors spanning the null space of the given node-edge incidence matrix. These flow vectors satisfy the quasi-steady state condition along with other inequality constraints. A set of constraints involving the weighting coefficients representing concentration of various transcription factors is formulated. An objective function, in terms of these weighting coefficients, is formed, and minimized through the new learning technique. The weighting coefficients corresponding to a minimum value of the objective function represent an optimal regulatory pathway yielding the maximal expression of the target gene starting from the initial gene. These optimal pathways determine the gene regulatory routes leading from the transcription of a given gene to the transcription of another gene, and represent the structural and functional properties of the network as a whole. Two benchmark regulatory networks are given to illustrate this approach. The results are biologically validated and compared with the standard extreme pathway analysis (EPA) [12].

2   Second Order Optimization Algorithm

The second order method is derived from Newton's method [2] whose principle is discussed here. The Taylor expansion of a function $E(w)$ of a single variable w in the vicinity of a minimum w^* is given by

$$E(w) = E(w^*) + 1/2(w - w^*)^2 (d^2E/dw^2)_{w=w^*} + O(w^3) \qquad (1)$$

The gradient of the cost function is zero at the minimum. Differentiating the above equation (1) with respect to w gives an approximation of the gradient of the cost function in the neighborhood of a minimum,

$$dE/dw = (w - w^*)(d^2E/dw^2)_{w=w^*} \qquad (2)$$

Therefore, if variable w is in the neighborhood of w^*, the minimum could be reached in a single iteration if the second derivative of the cost function at the minimum were known. w would simply be updated by an amount

$$\Delta w = -\frac{(dE/dw)}{(d^2E/dw^2)_{w=w^*}} \qquad (3)$$

Thus by contrast to simple gradient descent, the direction of motion, in parameter space, is not the direction of the gradient, but a linear transformation of the gradient. Our proposed methodology is an iterative technique that is based on the above formula (equation (3)) with certain modifications in the double derivative term.

3   Proposed Second Order Optimization Methodology

Here we develop a new learning rule based on Newton's method [9] for identification of an optimal regulatory pathway in gene regulatory networks starting from a given gene to a target gene through which the expression level of the target gene becomes maximum. The gene regulatory networks are described by directed graphs [14] with nodes corresponding to genes and edges to regulatory interactions. Genes with outgoing edges are the source genes. For a given source gene, we call the set of all genes with incoming edges from that source gene its target genes. One important concept that we will use below is a representation of a graph by a so-called node-edge incidence matrix $\mathbf{B}$, where the element b_{ij} in a row i and column j equals 1 (i.e., $b_{ij} = 1$), if node i is connected to node j, otherwise $b_{ij} = 0$. Let g_i be the expression level of gene i associated with node i in the graph. There is a flow, associated with each directed edge (i, j) from node i to node j, which indicates the flow of mRNA and thereby protein obtained from gene i transported through the edge (i, j). This protein now binds to gene j and regulates its expression level.

A system boundary is drawn around a gene regulatory network which consists of both internal flows, constrained to be positive and exchange flows, constrained to be either positive, negative or bidirectional depending on the direction. There are n flows/regulatory interactions and m genes in the network. Let n_I be the number of internal flows and n_E be that of exchange flows, and then $n = n_I + n_E$. The i-th internal flow is denoted by v_i and the j-th exchange flow is denoted by b_j. So there are $v_1, \ldots, v_{n_I}$ internal flows and $v_{n_I+1}, \ldots, v_n$ exchange flows where $v_{n_I+l} = b_l$. The target gene can be reached through k biochemical reactions $R_1, R_2, \ldots R_k$ from the starting gene. The algebraic sum of the weighted flows of reactions $R_1, R_2, \ldots R_k$ to reach the target gene is given by

$$z = \sum_{i=1}^{k} c_i v_i \qquad (4)$$

which needs to be maximized for yielding maximum expression level of the target gene. The term c_i denotes the weighting factor, representing concentration of other transcription factors to get the corresponding flow v_i.

The gene flow vectors $\mathbf{v}$ satisfy approximately the quasi-steady state condition

$$\mathbf{Bv} \approx \mathbf{0} \qquad (5)$$

where $\mathbf{B}$ is the $m \times n$ node-edge incidence matrix which can be computed from a given gene regulatory network. As $n > m$, equation (5) is under determined. We generate p number of basis vectors $\mathbf{v}_b$ that span the null space of $\mathbf{B}$. p random numbers a_j, $j = 1, 2, \ldots, p$ are further generated. Finally a vector $\mathbf{v}$ is generated as a linear combination of the basis vectors using a_p i.e., $\mathbf{v} = \sum_{j=1}^{p} a_j \mathbf{v}_{bj}$. The flow vectors $\mathbf{v}$ satisfy the following inequality constraints [12]. All the internal fluxes are positive yielding: $v_i \geq 0, \forall i$. The constraints on the exchange fluxes depending on their direction can be expressed as $\alpha_j \leq b_j \leq \beta_j$ where $\alpha_j \epsilon \{-\infty, 0\}$ and $\beta_j \epsilon \{0, \infty\}$.

All the transcription factors that are not shown in a system may not be expressed at the required level so that the corresponding target genes may not be expressed/inhibited fully. This leads to variation in the concentration of other transcription factors and hence another constraint can be defined as

$$\mathbf{B(Cv)} = \mathbf{0} \qquad (6)$$

where $\mathbf{C}$ is an $n \times n$ diagonal matrix, whose diagonal elements are the components of the vector $\mathbf{c}$. That is, if $\mathbf{C} = [\gamma_{ij}]_{n \times n}$, then $\gamma_{ij} = \delta_{ij} c_i$, where δ_{ij} is the Kronecker delta.

The objective function y can be formulated by using equations (4) and (6)

$$y = 1/z + \mathbf{\Lambda}^T (\mathbf{B(Cv)}) \qquad (7)$$

y has to be minimized with respect to the weighting factors c_i for all i. The term $\mathbf{\Lambda} = [\lambda_1, \lambda_2, \ldots, \lambda_m]^T$ is the regularizing parameter. Initially, a set of random values in $[0, 1]$ corresponding to c_i's are generated. Then c_i's are determined iteratively through a new learning technique based on second order derivatives using equation (3) [5],

$$\Delta c_i = -\frac{\partial y}{\partial c_i} / |\frac{\partial^2 y}{\partial c_i^2}| \qquad (8)$$

Thus by contrast to simple gradient descent, this second order gradient method is independent of the learning parameter. This being a modified version of the Newton's method of weight updating, uses the second-order derivative in addition to the gradient to determine the next updating direction and step size. The modulus of the second order derivative in the denominator of equation (8) indicates the amount of updation necessary to reach the optima and prevents it from converging in the wrong direction. Thus the modified value of c_i is

$c_i(t + 1) = c_i(t) + \Delta c_i,\ \forall i,\ t = 0, 1, 2, \dots\ c_i(t + 1)$ is the value of c_i at iteration $(t + 1)$, which is computed based on the c_i-value at the iteration t.

Regularization parameter λ is chosen empirically from 0.1 to 1.0 in steps of 0.1. The c_i-values for which y attains a minimum value at a particular λ value is observed. c_i attains values between 0 to 1 as mentioned previously corresponding to some values of v_i and is negligible for other values of v_i. We take into account the values of c_i's that are close to 1, corresponding to the minimum value of y. This enables us to identify the optimal regulatory pathway yielding the maximal expression of the target gene starting from the initial gene.

4   Experimental Results and Comparison

T Helper Cell Network

The vertebrate immune system in Fig. 1 is made of diverse cell populations; some of them are antigen presenting cells, natural killer cells, B and T lymphocytes. There is a subpopulation of T lymphocytes, the T-helper, or Th, cells that have received much attention from the modeling point of view. Th cells can be divided into precursor Th0 cells and effector Th1 and Th2 cells, depending on the pattern of secreted molecules. Th1 and Th2 cell types play a central role in cellular immunity and humoral responses, respectively. The regulatory network presented constitutes the most extensive attempt to model the regulatory network controlling the differentiation of Th lymphocytes to date, and it has been implemented both as a discrete and a continuous dynamical system. Here the starting gene is TCR and the target gene is $STAT3$ [8]. There are 33 reactions and 23 genes in the network. The average amount of protein synthesis z for this network is $z = c_{21}v_{21} - c_{33}v_{33}$. The optimal pathway obtained by the new learning rule is $v_1 \rightarrow v_4 \rightarrow v_{10} \rightarrow v_{11} \rightarrow v_{12} \rightarrow v_{22} \rightarrow v_{27} \rightarrow v_{16} \rightarrow v_{17} \rightarrow v_{19} \rightarrow v_{20} \rightarrow v_{21}$. The extreme regulatory pathway obtained by EPA is different from that obtained by the present method and is as follows $v_1 \rightarrow v_4 \rightarrow v_{10} \rightarrow v_{11} \rightarrow v_{12} \rightarrow v_{30} \rightarrow v_{15} \rightarrow v_{16} \rightarrow v_{17} \rightarrow v_{19} \rightarrow v_{20} \rightarrow v_{21}$. The biological significance of the sequence of steps that leads to the optimal path can be found in [4].

The set of all pathways from the starting gene TCR to the target gene $STAT3$ along with c-values and the average amount of the protein synthesized (z) by the target gene are shown in Table 1. The pathway corresponding to serial number 1 yields the highest average z and the corresponding c-values for this pathway is large compared to the c-values of other pathways. The results show that the second order optimization method is able to correctly identify the optimal regulatory pathway.

Transcriptional regulatory network of E. coli

The transcriptional network of *E. coli* is the most complete experimentally characterized network of a single cell [7]. The regulatory network in Fig. 2 is important in oxidative stress response of plant cells and is also an important component in the acid resistance system of *E. coli*. In Fig. 2A, the starting gene is *crp* and

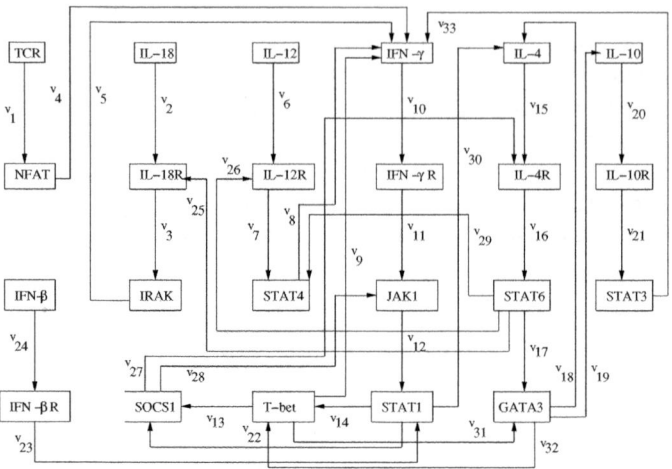

Fig. 1. Th Cell Gene Regulatory Network

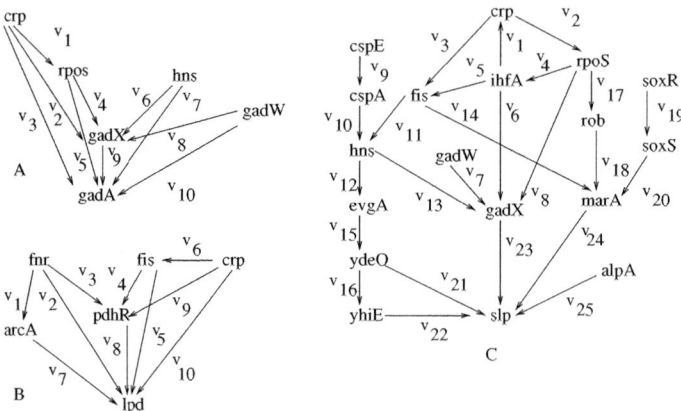

Fig. 2. The three complex regulatory circuits of the extended transcriptional regulatory network of *E. coli*

the target gene is *gadA*. The starting gene in part B, is fnr and the target gene is *lpd*, and in part C the starting gene is *crp* and the target gene is *slp*. The target gene gadA in part A codes for glutamate decarboxylase, an important metabolic enzyme in the gammaaminobutyric acid (GABA) shunt.

The expression of z for the network in Fig. 2A is $z = c_3v_3 + c_5v_5 + c_7v_7 + c_9v_9 + c_{10}v_{10}$. The corresponding expressions for part B is $z = c_2v_2 + c_5v_5 + c_7v_7 + c_8v_8 + c_{10}v_{10}$ and for part C is $z = c_{21}v_{21} + c_{22}v_{22} + c_{23}v_{23} + c_{24}v_{24} + c_{25}v_{25}$. The optimal pathway obtained for Fig. 2A is $p_1 : v_1 \rightarrow v_4 \rightarrow v_9$. Similarly, the optimal pathways are $p_1 : v_3 \rightarrow v_8$ for part B and $p_1 : v_2 \rightarrow v_{17} \rightarrow v_{18} \rightarrow v_{24}$

Table 1. c-values and z-values for the Th regulatory network in Fig. 1

Sl. No.	Some possible paths	Optimal c-values	Average quantity (z) of protein synthesis
1	$v_1 \rightarrow v_4 \rightarrow v_{10} \rightarrow v_{11}$ $\rightarrow v_{12} \rightarrow v_{22} \rightarrow v_{27}$ $\rightarrow v_{16} \rightarrow v_{17} \rightarrow v_{19}$ $\rightarrow v_{20} \rightarrow v_{21}$	$c_1 = 0.97, c_4 = 0.92, c_{10} = 0.89$ $c_{11} = 0.87, c_{12} = 0.81, c_{22} = 0.95$ $c_{27} = 0.96, c_{16} = 0.93, c_{17} = 0.92$ $c_{19} = 0.86, c_{20} = 0.85, c_{21} = 0.84$	53.89
2	$v_1 \rightarrow v_4 \rightarrow v_{10} \rightarrow v_{11}$ $\rightarrow v_{12} \rightarrow v_{30} \rightarrow v_{15}$ $\rightarrow v_{16} \rightarrow v_{17} \rightarrow v_{19}$ $\rightarrow v_{20} \rightarrow v_{21}$	$c_1 = 0.97, c_4 = 0.92, c_{10} = 0.89$ $c_{11} = 0.87, c_{12} = 0.81, c_{30} = 0.52$ $c_{15} = 0.45, c_{16} = 0.93, c_{17} = 0.92$ $c_{19} = 0.86, c_{20} = 0.85, c_{21} = 0.84$	21.45
3	$v_1 \rightarrow v_4 \rightarrow v_{10} \rightarrow v_{11}$ $\rightarrow v_{12} \rightarrow v_{14} \rightarrow v_{13}$ $\rightarrow v_{27} \rightarrow v_{16} \rightarrow v_{17}$ $\rightarrow v_{19} \rightarrow v_{20} \rightarrow v_{21}$	$c_1 = 0.97, c_4 = 0.92, c_{10} = 0.89$ $c_{11} = 0.87, c_{12} = 0.81, c_{14} = 0.25$ $c_{13} = 0.16, c_{27} = 0.96, c_{16} = 0.93$ $c_{17} = 0.92, c_{19} = 0.86, c_{20} = 0.85$ $c_{21} = 0.84$	18.72
4	$v_1 \rightarrow v_4 \rightarrow v_{10} \rightarrow v_{11}$ $\rightarrow v_{12} \rightarrow v_{14} \rightarrow v_{31}$ $\rightarrow v_{19} \rightarrow v_{20} \rightarrow v_{21}$	$c_1 = 0.97, c_4 = 0.92, c_{10} = 0.89$ $c_{11} = 0.87, c_{12} = 0.81, c_{14} = 0.25$ $c_{31} = 0.05, c_{19} = 0.86, c_{20} = 0.85$ $c_{21} = 0.84$	10.92
5	$v_1 \rightarrow v_4 \rightarrow v_{10} \rightarrow v_{11}$ $\rightarrow v_{12} \rightarrow v_{14} \rightarrow v_{31}$ $\rightarrow v_{32} \rightarrow v_{13} \rightarrow v_{27}$ $\rightarrow v_{16} \rightarrow v_{17} \rightarrow v_{19}$ $\rightarrow v_{20} \rightarrow v_{21}$	$c_1 = 0.97, c_4 = 0.92, c_{10} = 0.89$ $c_{11} = 0.87, c_{12} = 0.81, c_{14} = 0.25$ $c_{31} = 0.05, c_{32} = 0.11, c_{13} = 0.16$ $c_{27} = 0.96, c_{16} = 0.93, c_{17} = 0.92$ $c_{19} = 0.86, c_{20} = 0.85, c_{21} = 0.84$	15.56

for part C. The extreme regulatory pathways derived by EPA method for Fig. 2A and B are the same as derived from our proposed second order algorithm. We have obtained a different extreme regulatory pathway by EPA method $v_3 \rightarrow v_{11} \rightarrow v_{12} \rightarrow v_{15} \rightarrow v_{16} \rightarrow v_{22}$ for the network in Fig. 2C.

This application is particularly challenging as the model bacterium $E.coli$ has direct experimental supports. The pyruvate dehydrogenase (PDHR) (the intermediate gene in Fig. 2B) complex of $E.coli$ is a master regulator of the genes involved in the main pathway [10]. PdhR is an important regulator for the steady state maintenance of the central metabolism for energy production. The target gene lpd in Fig. 2B functions as glycine cleavage system L protein. The target gene slp in Fig. 2C is regulated by 17 regulators. These regulators participate in cellular responses to various environmental conditions, such as oxidative stress (soxRS), acid stress (gadW, gadX, evgA, ydeO and yhiE), cold shock (cspE, cspA) and multiple antibiotic resistance (marA). This underlies the importance of this gene in stress response.

5 Conclusions

This paper proposes a novel second-order learning algorithm for exploring gene regulatory networks in which the underlying optimal regulatory pathways from a starting gene to a target gene can be determined in terms of concentration of various transcription factors regulating the genes in the network. The second order system can be shown to have much better convergence properties than the first order gradient descent system. The entire method is based on well known flux balancing approach [6]. The methodology presented here was tested on two biologically significant networks, the T helper cell network and the regulatory network of *E. coli*. The results demonstrate the effectiveness of the methodology in retrieving biologically valid regulatory relations and providing meaningful insights for better understanding the dynamics of gene regulatory networks. We can expect that as more and more gene regulatory networks are reconstructed, the second-order analysis will gradually emerge as an important paradigm for studies of complex biological systems.

References

1. Castillo, E., Berdinas, B.G., Romero, O.F., Betanzos, A.A.: A very fast learning method for neural networks based on sensitivity analysis. Journal of Machine Learning Research 7, 1159–1182 (2006)
2. Dreyfus, G.: Neural Networks: Methodology and Applications. Springer, Heidelberg, Germany (2005)
3. Gardner, T.S., di Bernardo, D., Lorenz, D., Collins, J.J.: Inferring genetic networks and identifying compound mode of action via expression profiling. Science 301, 102–105 (2003)
4. Garg, A., Di Cara, A., Xenarios, I., Mendoza, L., De Micheli, G.: Synchronous versus asynchronous modeling of gene regulatory networks. Bioinformatics 24, 1917–1925 (2008)
5. Haykin, S.: Neural Networks: A Comprehensive Foundation. Macmillan College Publishing Co. Inc., New York (1994)
6. Lee, J.M., Gianchandani, E.P., Papin, J.A.: Flux balance analysis in the era of metabolomics. Briefings in Bioinformatics 7, 1–11 (2006)
7. Ma, H., Kumar, B., Ditges, U., Gunzer, F., Buer, J., Zeng, A.P.: An extended transcriptional regulatory network of escherichia coli and analysis of its hierarchical structure and network motifs. Nucleic Acids Res. 32, 6643–6649 (2004)
8. Mendoza, L., Xenarios, I.: A method for the generation of standardized qualitative dynamical systems of regulatory networks. Theoretical Biology and Medical Modelling 3, 1–18 (2006)
9. Mizutani, E., Dreyfus, S.E.: Second-order stagewise backpropagation for hessianmatrix analyses and investigation of negative curvature. Neural Networks 21, 193–203 (2008)
10. Ogasawara, H., Ishida, Y., Yamada, K., Yamamoto, K., Ishihama, A.: Pdhr (pyruvate dehydrogenase complex regulator) controls the respiratory electron transport system in escherichia coli. Journal of Bacteriology 189, 5534–5541 (2007)
11. Parlos, A.G., Femandez, B., Atiya, A.F., Muthusami, J., Tsai, W.K.: An accelerated learning algorithm for multilayer perceptron networks. IEEE Transactions on Neural Networks 5, 493–497 (1994)
12. Schilling, C.H., Letscher, D., Palsson, B.O.: Theory for the systemic defnition of metabolic pathways and their use in interpreting metabolic function from a pathway-oriented perspective. J. Theor. Biol. 203, 229–248 (2000)
13. Wang, Y.J., Lin, C.T.: A second-order learning algorithm for multilayer networks based on block hessian matrix. Neural Networks 11, 1607–1622 (1998)
14. Xiong, M., Zhao, J., Xiong, H.: Network-based regulatory pathways analysis. Bioinformatics 20, 2056–2066 (2004)

Aggregation of Correlation Measures for the Reverse Engineering of Gene Regulatory Sub-networks

Ranajit Das and Sushmita Mitra

Machine Intelligence Unit, Indian Statistical Institute, Kolkata 700 108, India
{ranajit_r,sushmita}@isical.ac.in

Abstract. This paper presents a simple and novel approach involving the aggregation of some correlation-based techniques for deciphering simple gene interaction sub-networks from biclusters in microarray time series gene expression data. Preprocessing has been used for discarding the weakly interacting gene pairs, *i.e.*, those that are poorly correlated. The proposed technique was successfully applied to public-domain data sets of Yeast and the experimental results were biologically validated based on benchmark databases and information from literature.

Keywords: Biclustering, transcriptional regulatory network, bioinformatics, correlation, gene expression profile, gene interaction network.

1 Introduction

DNA microarray experiments simultaneously monitor the expression levels of thousands of genes, in parallel, and help immensely in the large-scale study of gene expression patterns. It, thus, forms an indispensable tool for exploring gene regulatory networks from the system level. The process of expression of genes is one in which the DNA sequence of genes is transformed to the final functional product, *i.e.*, protein, through a series of steps. Gene expression data is a measure of the amount of messenger RNAs (mRNAs) produced by the gene at different instances of time or under different conditions. Reconstruction of the interaction between co-regulated genes, exploring expression profiles, is crucial for understanding the cell physiology and fundamental cellular processes [9].

An important task while analyzing gene expression profiles, which is inherently noisy and prone to different kinds of uncertainty, imprecision and ambiguity, is the discovery of co-regulated groups of genes. Genes that are simultaneously expressed are highly probable of sharing some common biological pathway(s) [6], [9]. Clustering is an important tool for analyzing and estimating such noisy expression data, by grouping co-expressed genes with the assumption that they are co-regulated. Clustering has been applied to search for co-expressed groups of genes [5] and to reverse engineer interaction/regulatory networks [11].

A genetic interaction network can be conceived as a complex network of proteins, genes and protein complexes, etc. linked to one another, and acting as

M.K. Kundu et al. (Eds.): PerMIn 2012, LNCS 7143, pp. 235–242, 2012.

a complex input-output system for controlling cellular functions. A gene regulatory sub-network, by contrast, is a portion of a gene regulatory network. A subset of genes participates in a cellular process of interest. Again, a gene may be involved in several cellular processes, simultaneously. The set of co-expressed genes in a network form a coherent group that can encode proteins and take part in common biological processes. Biclustering often helps to find a subset of co-expressed genes under a subset of experimental conditions.

Evolutionary biclustering [7] is one such approach that has been used in this paper. It is followed by simple extraction of gene interaction pairs using the aggregation of some correlation-based techniques, for an automated generation of genetic regulatory sub-networks. To study the similarity pattern between gene expression vectors in a bicluster we have employed several correlation-based measures. Preprocessing, followed by the elimination of weak correlation links, helps to retain strongly regulated (up-regulated (activated) or down-regulated (repressed/ inhibited)) gene pairs. The different sections are organized as follows. In Section 2 the reverse engineering of gene regulatory sub-networks is discussed. The proposed aggregation technique is described in Section 3, which briefly introduces the different correlation based measures. A gene pair having an aggregation correlation magnitude above a detection threshold was considered to be interacting or regulating each other. The final adjacency matrix is formed after the resulting aggregation of the correlation matrices followed its discretization. Based on this the regulatory sub-network is generated and biologically validated. The usefulness of the model is demonstrated in Section 4, using time-series gene expression data from Yeast. Finally, Section 5 concludes the article.

2   Reconstruction of Gene Interaction Sub-network: An Aggregation of Correlation-Based Approaches

The process of gene expression constitutes the central dogma of molecular biology. A gene produces a protein by *transcription* followed by *translation*. The reaction is mediated by an enzyme, which is responsible for protein production. Extraction of biological networks involving gene pairs, which demonstrate transcription factor (TF)-target relationship, is an important research problem. A gene interaction network is a system which comprises of proteins and genes binding to each other, and acting as a complex input-output system for controlling cellular functions. A TF is a gene product that regulates the expression of other genes by interacting with their promoter regions, while the gene being regulated is called its target. TFs that up-regulate (or down-regulate) the same target gene may be found to demonstrate similar gene expression patterns along time [6], [9]. A proper understanding of gene interaction networks is essential for the understanding of fundamental cellular processes pertaining to growth and decay, development, secretion of hormones, etc.

Biclustering refers to the simultaneous clustering involving both attributes and samples [7]. In this paper an attempt has been made to model the relationship between a TF and its target's expression level variation over time in the framework of the generated biclusters. Similarity measures like correlation has been widely used in literature for the analysis of gene expression data. Here, we use the aggregation of some correlation-based measures while constructing the gene interaction sub-network.

3   Correlation between Gene Pairs

A gene expression profile E is represented over a series of t time points. Since the genes in a bicluster are co-expressed, the concept of correlation is used to quantify their similarity.

3.1   Pearson's Correlation

The *Pearson's correlation coefficient*, $M_1(E_x, E_y)$ between two gene expression profile vectors E_x and E_y provides a similarity measure between the two time-series curves, sampled at E_{xi} and E_{yi} over t time intervals [8]. This is expressed as

$$M_1(E_x, E_y) = \frac{\sum E_{xi}E_{yi} - \sum E_{xi}\sum \frac{E_{yi}}{t}}{\sqrt{(\sum E_{xi}^2 - \frac{(\sum E_{xi})^2}{t})(\sum E_{yi}^2 - \frac{(\sum E_{yi})^2}{t})}}, \tag{1}$$

where i = 1, ..., t. M_1 is commonly used for quantifying the co-expression similarity.

3.2   Time-Lagged Correlation/Cross Correlation

To quantify the similarity between gene expression profiles time-lagged correlation or cross-correlation can be employed for analyzing the positive or negative correlation between time-lagged profiles of gene pairs. We have allowed for the delay, $d = \Delta t$, of maximum two time point-shifts as longer time point shifts are difficult to be explained biologically [4]. The cross correlation $TC_d(E_x, E_y)$ between the gene expression profile pair is expressed as

$$TC_d(E_x, E_y) = \frac{\sum E_{xi}E_{yi-d} - \sum E_{xi}\sum \frac{E_{yi-d}}{t}}{\sqrt{(\sum E_{xi}^2 - \frac{(\sum E_{xi})^2}{t})(\sum E_{yi-d}^2 - \frac{(\sum E_{yi-d})^2}{t})}}, \tag{2}$$

where i = 1, ..., t. Cross correlation, thus, describes the normalized cross covariance function. The delay d is chosen to maximize the absolute value of the correlation as

$$M_2(E_x, E_y) = \max |TC_d(E_x, E_y)| \qquad\qquad where -2 < d < 2. \tag{3}$$

3.3   Leave-One-Out Correlation

The *Leave-one-out correlation*, $M_3(E_x, E_y)$ is the Pearson's correlation coefficient (eqn. (1)) computed between two gene expression profile vectors E_x and E_y, sampled over $t-1$ time points, where the E is represented over t time points. So there are $t-1$ computations of M_3, with one time point being left out every time during the computation. Then we choose the best absolute Leave-one-out correlation value from these $t-1$ measurements.

3.4   Partial Correlation

The *Partial correlation* is the correlation (eqn. (1)) that remains between two variables if the effect of other variables has been regressed away. The Partial correlation coefficient, $M_4(E_x, E_y)$ between two gene expression profile vectors, conditioned on all the other variables (other gene expression profile vectors in the bicluster), can be computed in a straightforward manner from the covariance matrix provided the inverse of the covariance matrix exists.

3.5   Spearman's Rank Correlation

The *Spearman's rank correlation coefficient* $M_5(E_x, E_y)$ provides a local, shape-based similarity measure between the two time-series curves [3]. M_5 is expressed as

$$M_5(E_x, E_y) = 1 - \frac{6}{t(t^2 - 1)} \sum [r_{E_x}(E_{xi}) - r_{E_y}(E_{yi})]^2, \tag{4}$$

where i = 1, ..., t, $r_{E_x}(E_{xi})$ denotes the rank of E_{xi}. We have employed an extended version of M_5 which takes into consideration the resolving of ties, *i.e.*, $E_{xj} = E_{xi}$ for $i \neq j$.

During the computation of the different correlation-based measures we have assumed the absence of self correlations among the genes.

3.6   Aggregation Index

The final correlation similarity value between a pair of genes is computed by taking an aggregation of these five correlation-based approaches. This is done by computing the average of the pairwise correlation value, $M(E_x, E_y)$ resulting from the five measures above and is used for deciphering simple gene interaction sub-networks from biclusters in microarray data.

$$M(E_x, E_y) = \frac{1}{5} \sum_{j=1}^{5} M_j(E_x, E_y), \tag{5}$$

where $M(E_x, E_y)$ denotes the *Aggregation Index* which provides the aggregation of the five correlation measures.

Preprocessing is done to filter out the weaker aggregation correlation coefficients M, which presumably contribute less towards regulation. This allows us to avoid an exhaustive search of all possible interactions between genes. The remaining coefficients, having absolute values above a detection threshold, imply a larger correlation between gene pairs. In this manner we are able to focus on a few strongly connected genes, that possibly link the remaining sparsely connected genes.

The correlation range $[M_{\max}, M_{\min}]$ is divided into three partitions each, using *quantiles*[1] [8] so that the influence of extreme values or noisy patterns are

---

[1] Quantiles are partition values which divide the distribution such that there is a given proportion of observations below the quantile.

lessened. Following this procedure the second positive quantile (Q_2^+) can be computed, which gives us the value of M^+ that exceeds two-thirds of the positive measurements and is less than the remaining one-third. Analogously the negative quantile pair Q_2^- can be computed.

It is to be noted that negative correlation between two gene profiles is essentially not zero correlation between them.

An adjacency matrix is computed from the eventual aggregation correlation matrix, based on

$$A(i,j) = \begin{cases} -1 \text{ if } & M \leq Q_2^- \\ +1 \text{ if } & M \geq Q_2^+ \\ 0 & \text{otherwise.} \end{cases} \tag{6}$$

Finally, a sub-network connecting the various genes is generated and biological validation is made in terms of ontology study[2].

3.7   The Algorithm

The concept of aggregation of correlation is incorporated to take into account the regulation between genes. This allows a more realistic modeling of gene interactions within the reduced localized domain of biclusters. In this work we extend our earlier network extraction algorithm [3], [4], [8] to include an overall influence. The main steps of the algorithm are outlined as follows:

1. Extraction of biclusters by multi-objective genetic algorithm.
2. Determination of different pairwise correlations between gene pairs.
3. Aggregation of the correlation similarity for the five correlation-based approaches, as discussed in Sections 3.1– 3.5.
4. Discretization of the eventual correlation matrix for eliminating the weaker interactions.
5. Network generation from adjacency matrix.
6. Biological validation.

4   Experimental Results

We used the Yeast cell-cycle $CDC28$ data [2] which is a collection of 6178 genes (features/attributes) for 17 conditions (time points/samples), taken at an interval of 10-minutes covering nearly two cycles, with the experiments being performed using Affymetrix oligonucleotide array. The missing values present in the data set were imputed following the approach discussed in Ref. [1]. Biclusters were extracted to detect sets of co-regulated genes. This allowed us to focus on reduced modules for subsequent processing.

A sample network comprising four biclusters (modules or sub-networks) of sizes 6, 7, 10 and 14, respectively, is depicted in Fig. 1. A transcription factor is connected to its target gene by an arrow when such a TF-target pair is found to

---

[2] http://db.yeastgenome.org/cgi-bin/GO/goTermFinder

exist within any of the biclusters. Gene pairs connected by solid lines depict positive correlation, while those connected by dashed lines are correlated negatively.
It is interesting to note that this aggregation of the five different correlation
measures resulted in the elimination of outliers and retention of significant links.
This results in the generation of a sparse and meaningful sub-network. The TF
named $YHR084W$ (encircled with solid lines) depicted in Fig. 1, as an example, is a member of the network of 10 genes and has targets in all the four
networks. These biclusters were biologically validated from gene ontology study,
based on the statistically significant Gene Ontology (GO) annotation database
as discussed below.

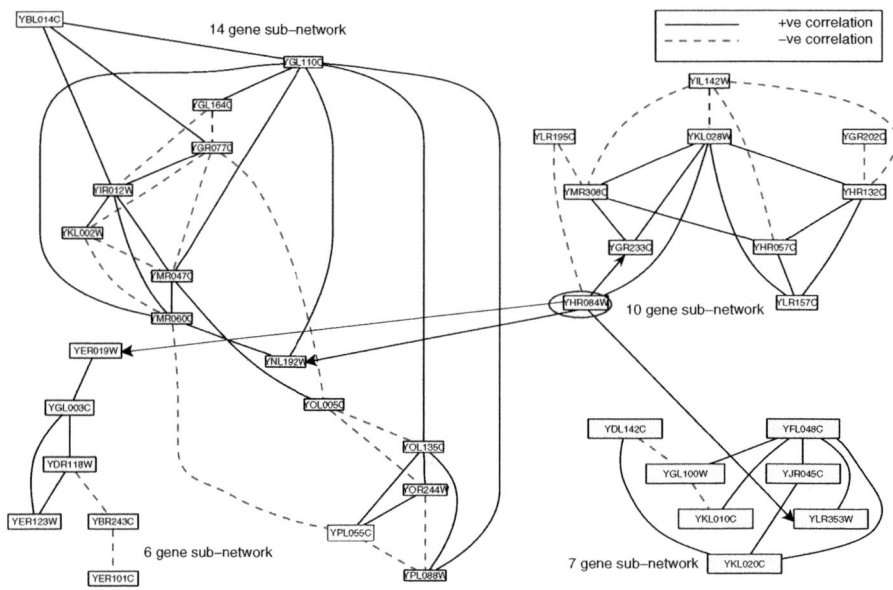

Fig. 1. Sub-network (bicluster) of 10 genes connected by transcription factor
$YHR084W$ to sub-networks (biclusters) of 6, 7 and 14 genes

We tried to explain and biologically validate the relationship between the
expression level variation over time of a TF and its target as predicted by our
system. It has been reported during the prediction of regulatory networks [10]
that the gene pair $YHR084W$-$YNL192W$ (where TF belongs to the 10-node
network while its target lies in the 14-node network) form a TF-target pair.
We further verified the summary of the pair (in Fig. 1) in terms of *Molecular
Function*, *Biological Process* and *Cellular Component* from the Saccharomyces
Genome Database (SGD). Computation of the Aggregation Index indicated that
$YHR084W$ interacts with $YNL192W$. Such strong interaction, as obtained by
us, may be due to mating-specific binding behaviour or, they may belong to an
additional mechanism for cell fusion. Our findings are further corroborated in

the literature [12]. One can also arrive at similar conclusions, for the remaining TF-target pairs, with a certain definite degree of confidence. The results are found to be consistent with the information available in the literature as well as that in the databases.

5   Conclusions and Discussion

In this paper we have described an approach for the extraction of correlated gene pairs after the aggregation of five pairwise correlation measures, for the generation of gene interaction networks. The use of multiobjective biclustering helped us to initially focus on a smaller search space. Biologically relevant biclusters were obtained, using time-series gene expression data from Yeast. These were validated using the statistically significant GO annotation database. Sample TF-target gene pairs in the network of Fig. 1 depict strong aggregation correlations. We tried to model the interaction between them from information available in the literature/databases *viz.*, Saccharomyces Genome Database. In future, an attempt can be made to apply this methodology to other categories of biological networks, *viz.* metabolic and signaling networks, and also to more complex organisms, *viz.* humans. It also needs to be mentioned that we have not considered microarray time-series experiments involving unequal time intervals, *i.e.*, while computing the different correlations between gene profiles, experiments with equal time intervals were only considered. This aspect can also be looked into, for future.

References

1. Bo, T., Dysvik, B., Jonassen, I.: LSimpute: accurate estimation of missing values in microarray data with least squares methods. Nucleic Acids Research 32, 1–8 (2004)
2. Cho, R.J., Campbell, M.J., Winzeler, L.A., Steinmetz, L., Conway, A., Wodicka, L., Wolfsberg, T.G., Gabrielian, A.E., Landsman, D., Lockhart, D.J., Davis, R.W.: A genome-wide transcriptional analysis of the mitotic cell cycle. Molecular Cell 2, 65–73 (1998)
3. Das, R., Mitra, S., Banka, H., Mukhopadhyay, S.: Evolutionary Biclustering with Correlation for Gene Interaction Networks. In: Ghosh, A., De, R.K., Pal, S.K. (eds.) PReMI 2007. LNCS, vol. 4815, pp. 416–424. Springer, Heidelberg (2007)
4. Das, R., Mitra, S., Mukhopadhyay, S.: Cross-Correlation and Evolutionary Biclustering: Extracting Gene Interaction Sub-networks. In: Chaudhury, S., Mitra, S., Murthy, C.A., Sastry, P.S., Pal, S.K. (eds.) PReMI 2009. LNCS, vol. 5909, pp. 199–204. Springer, Heidelberg (2009)
5. Eisen, M.B., Spellman, P.T., Brown, P.O., Botstein, D.: Cluster analysis and display of genome-wide expression patterns. Proceedings of National Academy of Sciences USA 95, 14863–14868 (1998)
6. Jong, H.d.: Modeling and simulation of genetic regulatory systems: A literature review. Journal of Computational Biology 9, 67–103 (2002)
7. Mitra, S., Banka, H.: Multi-objective evolutionary biclustering of gene expression data. Pattern Recognition 39, 2464–2477 (2006)

8. Mitra, S., Das, R., Banka, H., Mukhopadhyay, S.: Gene interaction - An evolutionary biclustering approach. Information Fusion 10, 242–249 (2009)

9. Mitra, S., Das, R., Hayashi, Y.: Genetic networks and soft computing. IEEE/ACM Transactions on Computational Biology and Bioinformatics 8, 94–107 (2011)

10. Qian, J., Lin, J., Luscombe, N.M., Yu, H., Gerstein, M.: Prediction of regulatory networks: Genome-wide identification of transcription factor targets from gene expression data. Bioinformatics 19, 1917–1926 (2003)

11. Tavazoie, S., Hughes, J.D., Campbell, M.J., Cho, R.J., Church, G.M.: Systematic determination of genetic network architecture. Nature Genetics 22, 281–285 (1999)

12. Zeitlinger, J., Simon, I., Harbison, C., Hannett, N., Volkert, T., Fink, G., Young, R.: Program-specific distribution of a transcription factor dependent on partner transcription factor and MAPK signaling. Cell 113, 395–404 (2003)

Interactive Content Based Image Retrieval Using Ripplet Transform and Fuzzy Relevance Feedback

Manish Chowdhury, Sudeb Das, and Malay Kumar Kundu

Machine Intelligence Unit, Indian Statistical Institute, Kolkata 700 108, India
{st.manishc,to.sudeb}@gmail.com, malay@isical.ac.in

Abstract. In this article, a novel content based image retrieval (CBIR) system based on a new Multiscale Geometric Analysis (MGA)-tool, called Ripplet Transform Type-I (RT) is presented. To improve the retrieval result, a fuzzy relevance feedback mechanism (F-RFM) is also implemented. Fuzzy entropy based feature evaluation mechanism is used for automatic computation of revised feature's importance and similarity distance at the end of each iteration. Experimental results on a large image database demonstrate the efficiency and effectiveness of the proposed CBIR system in the image retrieval paradigm

Keywords: Ripplet Transform, Relevance Feedback, Content Based Image Retrieval, Fuzzy logic.

1 Introduction

The tremendous growth in quantity of images stored in digital form in the internet, have raised many demanding issues regarding effective digital data management. The task of retrieving relevant images from a large image database (DB), by measuring similarities between the query image and the database images, based on automatically derived features like color, texture, shape etc. has became a potential area of research. The performance of a CBIR system, strongly depends both on the availability of suitable features, for proper representation of the semantic aspects of the images automatically, and also the effectiveness of the used similarity measure [1]. High retrieval efficiency and less computational complexity, are the desired characteristics of an efficient CBIR system.

Wavelet transform (WT) based low level features, provide a unique representation of an image, and are highly suitable for characterizing textures of the image [2]. Many WT based CBIR systems have been proposed in the literature [3,2]. But WT is inherently non-supportive to directionality and anisotropy. As a result, CBIR system based on WT provide limited performance. To overcome these limitations of WT, recently a theory called Multi-scale Geometric Analysis (MGA) for high-dimensional signals has been developed, and several MGA tools were proposed like Ridgelet, Curvelet, Bandlet and Contourlet etc.[4,5,6].

Relevance feedback mechanism (RFM) has been used as an effective tool to provide significant performance boost in CBIR systems through continuous

M.K. Kundu et al. (Eds.): PerMIn 2012, LNCS 7143, pp. 243–251, 2012.

learning and interaction with the end-users. Most of the RFM, employ two approaches namely, query vector moving technique and feature re-weighting technique to improve the retrieval results [7]. Feature re-weighting technique utilizes both the relevant and the irrelevant result's information, to obtain more effective result [2,8]. But in all these cases time complexity per iteration are high and the accuracy of the relevant images are low.

In this paper, we have used the type-I Ripplet Transforms (RT) coefficients to represent the images at different scales and different directions. RT coefficients of intensity and chromaticity planes are used as the primitive features for computation of mean and standard deviation. To improve the performance of the retrieval system, a simple fuzzy based relevance feedback mechanism (F-RFM) with Euclidian similarity measure is used.

The rest of the paper is organized as follows. RT is described in section 2. Section 3, presents the proposed CBIR system. Experimental results and comparisons are given in section 4, and the conclusion is drawn in section 5.

2   Ripplet Transform Type-I (RT)

Conventional transforms like (Fourier Transform) FT and Wavelet transform (WT) suffer from discontinuities such as edges and contours in images. To address this problem, Jun Xu et al. proposed a new MGA-tool called RT. RT is a higher dimensional generalization of the Curvelet Transform (CVT), capable of representing images or $2D$ signals at different scales and different directions. To achieve anisotropic directionality, CVT uses a parabolic scaling law. From the perspective of microlocal analysis, the anisotropic property of CVT guarantees resolving $2D$ singularities along C^2 curves. On the other hand, RT provides a new tight frame with sparse representation for images with discontinuities along C^d curves [9].

There are two questions regarding the scaling law used in CVT: 1) Is the parabolic scaling law optimal for all types of boundaries? and if not, 2) What scaling law will be optimal? To address these questions, Jun Xu et al. intended to generalize the scaling law, which resulted in RT. RT generalizes CVT by adding two parameters, i.e., support c and degree d. CVT is just a special case of RT with $c = 1$ and $d = 2$. The anisotropy capability of representing singularities along arbitrarily shaped curves of RT, is due to these new parameters c and d.

2.1   Discrete Ripplet Transform (DRT)

As digital image processing needs discrete transform instead of continuous transform, here we describe the discretization of RT [9]. The discretization of Continuous RT (CRT) is based on the discretization of the parameters of ripplet functions. The scale parameter a is sampled at dyadic intervals. b (position parameter) and θ (rotation parameter) are sampled at equal-spaced intervals. a_j, $\overrightarrow{b}_k$ and θ_l substitute a, $\overrightarrow{b}$ and θ respectively, and satisfy that $a_j = 2^{-j}$, $\overrightarrow{b}_k = [c \cdot 2^{-j} \cdot k_1, 2^{-j/d} \cdot k_2]^T$ and $\theta_l = \frac{2\Pi}{c} \cdot 2^{-\lfloor j(1-1/d) \rfloor} \cdot l$, where $\overrightarrow{k} = [k_1, k_2]^T$, and j, k_1, k_2, $l \in \mathbb{Z}$. $(\cdot)^T$ denotes the transpose of a vector. $d \in \mathbb{R}$, since any real number can be approximated by rational numbers, so we can represent d with $d = n/m$, $n, m \neq 0 \in \mathbb{Z}$. Usually, we prefer $n, m \in \mathbf{N}$ and n, m are both primes. In the frequency domain, the corresponding frequency response of ripplet function is in the form

$$\widehat{\rho}_j(r, \omega) = \frac{1}{\sqrt{c}} a^{\frac{m+n}{2n}} W(2^{-j} \cdot r) V(\frac{1}{c} \cdot 2^{-\lfloor j\frac{m-n}{n}\rfloor} \cdot \omega - l) \tag{1}$$

where W and V are the 'radial window' and 'angular window', respectively and satisfy the following admissibility conditions:

$$\sum_{j=0}^{+\infty} |W(2^{-j} \cdot r)|^2 = 1 \tag{2}$$

$$\sum_{l=-\infty}^{+\infty} |V(\frac{1}{c} \cdot 2^{-\lfloor j(1-1/d)\rfloor} \cdot \omega - l)|^2 = 1 \tag{3}$$

given c, d and j.

The 'wedge' corresponding to the ripplet function in the frequency domain is

$$H_{j,l}(r, \theta) = \{2^j \leq |r| \leq 2^{2j}, |\theta - \frac{\pi}{c} \cdot 2^{-\lfloor j(1-1/d)\rfloor} \cdot l| \leq \frac{\pi}{2} 2^{-j}\} \tag{4}$$

The DRT of an $M \times N$ image $f(n_1, n_2)$ will be in the form of

$$R_{j, \overrightarrow{k}, l} = \sum_{n_1=0}^{M-1} \sum_{n_2=0}^{N-1} f(n_1, n_2) \overline{\rho_{j, \overrightarrow{k}, l}(n_1, n_2)} \tag{5}$$

where $R_{j, \overrightarrow{k}, l}$ are the ripplet coefficients and $\overline{(.)}$ denotes the conjugate operator.

The image can be reconstructed through Inverse Discrete Ripplet Transform (IDRT)

$$\widetilde{f}(n_1, n_2) = \sum_{j} \sum_{\overrightarrow{k}} \sum_{l} R_{j, \overrightarrow{k}, l} \rho_{j, \overrightarrow{k}, l}(n_1, n_2) \tag{6}$$

3   Proposed CBIR System

The proposed CBIR system consists of two main parts. First part is the feature extraction using RT and second part is the F-RFM. In the following subsections each of the aforementioned parts are explained thoroughly.

3.1   Feature Extraction Using Ripplet Transform Type-I

RT is a new MGA-tool, which satisfies the multiresolution, good localization, high directionality, general scaling and support, anisotropy and fast coefficient decay properties. This makes RT as an effective tool to represent images or 2D signals, and motivated us to use it, to represent the images in the DB.

The images in the DB prior to RT based decomposition, are transformed to YCbCr color space. This ensures that the textural characterization of the image are independent of the color characterization. RT decomposition over the intensity plane (Y) characterizes the texture information, while the RT decomposition over chromaticity planes (Cb & Cr) characterize color. Texture and color information are extracted by using RT on each color plane with a 4 level (1, 2, 4, 4) decomposition. This decomposition configuration provides 11 ($= 1 + 2 + 4 + 4$) subbands for each image of the DB, for each color plane. As, there are 3 color planes, so altogether we get 33 ($= 3 \times 11$) subbands for each image of the DB. For each subband S_j, its mean (f^j_{mean}) and standard deviation (f^j_{std}) are computed, and used as the representative features of the image (I):

$$f^j_{mean}(I) = \frac{1}{M \times N} \sum_{m=1}^{M} \sum_{n=1}^{N} |S^I_j(m, n)| \tag{7}$$

$$f^j_{std}(I) = \sqrt{\frac{1}{M \times N} \sum_{m=1}^{M} \sum_{n=1}^{N} (S^I_j(m, n) - f^j_{mean}(I))^2} \tag{8}$$

where, $S^I_j(m, n)$ represents coefficient at (m, n) of the subband S_j of size $M \times N$ of the image I and $j = 1, 2, ..., 33$. The final feature vector of an image I in the DB is as follows:

$$f_{vec}(I) = [f^1_{mean}(I), f^2_{mean}(I), ..., f^{33}_{mean}(I), f^1_{std}(I), f^2_{std}(I), ..., f^{33}_{std}(I)]$$

3.2   Fuzzy Based Relevance Feedback

The retrieval result of the first pass of the proposed CBIR system is obtained by measuring the Euclidean distance between the RT based features of the query image (provided by the user) and the images stored in the database (DB). If the user are not satisfied with the result, then the user will select a set of relevant and irrelevant images from the top 20 ranked displayed images.

The features of the image I of the DB, is computed using RT and is represented by a set of features, $F = \{f_q\}_{q=1}^{N}$, where f_q is the qth feature component in the N dimensional feature space. We have used Euclidean distance with weight w_q for measuring the similarity between the query image I_{qr} and other images I in the DB:

$$D(I, I_{qr}) = \sum_{q=1}^{N} w_q ||f_q(I) - f_q(qr)|| \tag{9}$$

where $||f_q(I) - f_q(qr)||$ is the Euclidean distance between the qth feature component and w_q is the weight assigned to the qth feature component. The weights should be adjusted such that, the features have small variation over the relevant images and large variation over the irrelevant images. Let k similar images $I_s = \{I_1, I_2, ..., I_k\}$ where, $I_k \epsilon I_s$, are returned to the user. Let I_r be the set of relevant images and I_{ir} be the set of irrelevant images as marked by the user. $\{I_r = I_j | I_j$ relevant, for $I_j \epsilon I_s\}$ and $\{I_{ir} = I_j | I_j$ irrelevant, for $I_j \epsilon I_s\}$. The information from relevant images (I_r) and irrelevant images (I_{ir}) are combined to compute the relative importance of the individual features, by using fuzzy feature evaluation index (FEI) of pattern classification problems [10].

The FEI is defined from interclass and intraclass ambiguities as follows : let $C_1, C_2,.. C_j ... C_m$ be the m pattern classes in an N dimensional $(f_1, f_2, f_q, ...f_N)$ feature space where class C_j contains n_j number of samples. The features values along the qth co-ordinate along class C_j are assigned as standard S-type membership function between 0 and 1 [11] . The entropy of a fuzzy set gives a measure of *intraset ambiguity* along the qth co-ordinate axis in C_j and is computed as follows:

$$H(A) = (\frac{1}{n_j \ln 2}) \sum_i S_n(\mu(f_{iqj})); i = 1, 2...n_j \qquad (10)$$

where the Shannon's function is,

$$S_n(\mu(f_{iqj})) = -\mu(f_{iqj})ln(\mu(f_{iqj})) - \{1 - \mu(f_{iqj})\}ln\{1 - \mu(f_{iqj})\} \qquad (11)$$

Entropy (H) is dependent on the absolute values of membership (μ). $H_{min} = 0$ for $\mu=0$ or 1, $H_{max} = 1$ for $\mu=0.5$.

The criteria of a good feature is that, it should be nearly invariant within class, while emphasizing differences between patterns of different classes [10]. The value of H would therefore decreases, after combining the class C_j and C_k, as the goodness of the qth feature in discriminating pattern classes C_j and C_k increases. The measure denoted as H_{qjk} is called *"interset ambiguity"* along q^{th} dimension between classes C_j and C_k. Considering these two types of ambiguities, the FEI for the qth feature is given:

$$FEI_q = \frac{H_{qjk}}{H_{qj} + H_{qk}}. \qquad (12)$$

Lower value of FEI_q, indicates better quality of importance of the qth feature in recognizing and discriminating different classes. The precision of retrieval can be improved with these values.

In the proposed CBIR system, the number of classes are two. The relevant/positive images constitute the 'intraclass' and the irrelevant/negative images constitute the 'interclass' image features. To evaluate the importance of the qth feature, the qth component of the retrieved images is considered. i.e., $I^{(q)} = \{I_1^{(q)}, I_2^{(q)}, I_3^{(q)},, ...I_k^{(q)}\}$. H_{qj} is computed from $I_r^{(q)} = \{I_{r1}^{(q)}, I_{r2}^{(q)}, I_{r3}^{(q)},, ...I_{rk}^{(q)}\}$. Similarly H_{qk} is computed from the set of images, $I_{ir}^{(q)} = \{I_{ir1}^{(q)}, I_{ir2}^{(q)}, I_{ir3}^{(q)},, ...I_{irk}^{(q)}\}$. H_{qkj} is computed combining both the sets. Images are ranked according to Euclidean distance. The user marks the relevant and irrelevant set from 20 returned images, for automatic evaluation of (FEI). The weight w_q is a function of the evaluated (FEI_q) as shown as,

$$w_q = F_q(FEI_q) \qquad (13)$$

In the first pass, all features are considered to be equally important. The feature space of the relevant images are therefore altered in a similar fashion after updating the components with w_q. As a result, the ranks of the relevant images are not affected much. For irrelevant images, one feature component may be very close to the query, whereas other feature component may be far away from the query feature. But the magnitude of the similarity vector may be close to the relevant ones. Multiplying by w_q increases the feature separation between the irrelevant component, such that due to the combined effect the irrelevant image may be pulled down.

4   Experimental Results and Comparisons

To prove the effectiveness of the proposed system, extensive experiments were performed on 1000 images of SIMPLIcity database [3] with 10 different classes (African, Ocean, Building, Bus, Dinosaurs, Elephant, Flower, Horse , Mountain, Food) of images. The retrieval results obtained using the proposed CBIR system, are compared with some of the existing retrieval systems [12,13,14]. The experiments were carried out on a Dell Precision T7400 PC with 4GB RAM and was implemented using MATLAB R2008a.

Two commonly used statistical measures were computed to assess the proposed system's performance, namely precision and recall, which are defined:

$$Precision \ (P) = \frac{N_{RIR}}{N_{RIR} + N_{IRIR}} \tag{14}$$

$$Recall \ (R) = \frac{N_{RIR}}{T_{RID}} \tag{15}$$

where, N_{RIR} is the Number of relevant images retrieved, N_{IRIR} is the Number of irrelevant images retrieved and T_{RID} is the Total number of relevant images in the database.

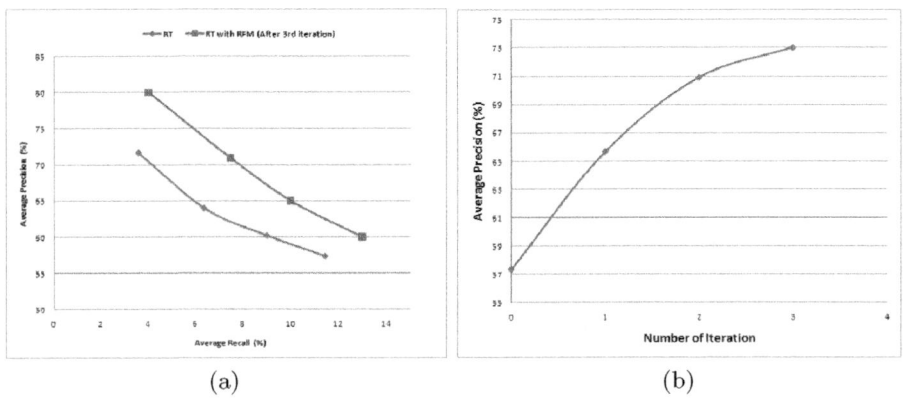

(a)   (b)

Fig. 1. (a) Average Precision vs. Average Recall (b) Average Precision vs. Number of Iteration

If the user is satisfied with the retrieved results without using RFM then the retrieval process is ended in the first pass. If, however, the user is not satisfied, he/she can select top query based relevant images as positive feedbacks and the remaining as negative examples for updating the weight parameters and revising the features. Using these feedbacks, FEIs and weights of the features are computed as described in Section.3.2. Then, all the images are re-sorted based on the weighted similarity metric. If the user is still not content with the result, he/she can repeat the process.

The graph of the Fig.1(a), shows the performance (in terms of average precision vs. average recall) of the proposed system. It clearly shows that, the performance of RT based features with F-RFM (considering only 3rd iteration's results) is better than the RT based features without F-RFM. The graph of the Fig.1(b), shows the improvement in performance with each iteration of the F-RFM.

As an example, using one of the image from the '*Flower*' class of SIMPLIcity DB as the query image, the retrieval results are shown in Fig.2(a). There is one irrelevant image in the retrieval result at the first pass. But with every iteration of the F-RFM as shown in Fig.2(b), the ranking of the retrieved images got changed, and more and more similar images came up as the improved retrieval result.

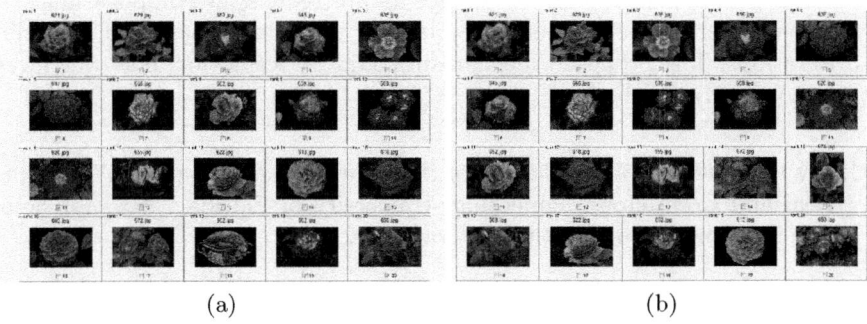

(a)   (b)

Fig. 2. Performance of the proposed CBIR system (top left side image is the query image) (a) First pass of the retrieval result (b) First Iteration

Table.1, shows the performance comparisons between our proposed CBIR system with some of the existing CBIR methods. From Table.1, it can be easily seen, that the proposed CBIR system provide improved retrieval performance over other existing CBIR algorithms namely, SIMPLIcity [12], FIRM [13], using salient points (salient points detected by Harris Comer Detector (SP by HCD), color salient points (CSP)) [14]. The '*Bold*' values indicate the highest retrieval performance.

Table 1. Comparison with other existing CBIR systems in terms of Average Precision

Class	Wang[12]	FIRM[13]	SP by HCD[14]	CSP[14]	Proposed Method
Africans	0.48	0.47	0.40	0.48	**0.49**
Sea	0.32	0.35	0.31	0.34	**0.40**
Building	0.35	0.35	0.32	0.33	**0.39**
Buses	0.36	**0.60**	0.44	0.52	0.58
Dinosaur	0.95	0.95	0.92	0.95	**0.96**
Elephant	0.38	0.25	0.28	0.40	**0.50**
Flower	0.42	0.65	0.58	0.60	**0.75**
Horse	0.72	0.65	0.68	0.70	**0.80**
Mountain	0.35	0.30	0.32	0.36	**0.40**
Food	0.38	0.48	0.44	0.46	**0.51**
Average	0.47	0.51	0.47	0.51	**0.55**

5   Conclusions

From our experiments, we have noticed that ripplet transform based image coding is suitable for representing low level features (color, texture, edge etc.) of the images. The proposed CBIR system based on RT features is able to improve the accuracy of the retrieval performance and to reduce the computational cost. The retrieval performance is improved further using fuzzy based RFM within 2 to 3 iterations. The proposed mechanism could be tested for video retrieval as future scope of research.

Acknowledgment. We would like to thank Jun Xu and Depeng Wu (Dept. of Electrical and Computer Engineering, University of Florida, USA) for helping us in the implementation of Ripplet Transform.

References

1. Heesch, D.: A survey of browsing models for content based image retrieval. Multimedia Tools Application 40, 1380–7501 (2008)
2. Kundu, M.K., Chowdhury, M., Banerjee, M.: Interactive Image Retrieval with Wavelet Features. In: Kuznetsov, S.O., Mandal, D.P., Kundu, M.K., Pal, S.K. (eds.) PReMI 2011. LNCS, vol. 6744, pp. 162–172. Springer, Heidelberg (2011)
3. Wang, J.Z., Li, J., Wiederhold, G.: SIMPLIcity: Semantics-sensitive integrated matching for picture libraries. IEEE Transactions on Pattern Analysis and Machine Intelligence 23, 947–963 (2001)
4. Do, M.N., Vetterli, M.: The finite ridgelet transform for image representation. IEEE Transactions on Image Processing 12, 16–28 (2003)
5. Candes, E., Donoho, D.: Continuous curvelet transform: I. resolution of the wavefront set. Applied and Computational Harmonic Analysis 19, 162–197 (2005)
6. Do, M.N., Vetterli, M.: The contourlet transform: An efficient directional multiresolution image representation. IEEE Transactions on Image Processing 14 (2005)

7. Rui, Y., Huang, T.S., Mehrotra, S.: Relevance feedback: a power tool for interactive content-based image retrieval. IEEE Transactions on Circuits and Systems for Video Technology 8, 644–655 (1998)
8. Jin, Z., King, I., Li, X.: Content-Based Image Retrieval by Relevance Feedback. In: Laurini, R. (ed.) VISUAL 2000. LNCS, vol. 1929, pp. 521–529. Springer, Heidelberg (2000)
9. Xu, J., Yang, L., Wu, D.: Ripplet: A new transform for image processing. Journal of Visual Communication and Image Representation 21, 627–639 (2010)
10. Pal, S.K., Chakraborty, B.: Intraclass and interclass ambiguities (fuzziness) in feature evaluation. Pattern Recognition Letters 2, 275–279 (1984)
11. Pal, S.K., Majumder, D.D.: Fuzzy Mathematical Approach To Pattern Recognition. Willey Eastern Limited, New York (1985)
12. Li, J., Wang, J.Z., Wiederhold, G.: IRM: Integrated region matching for image retrieval. In: Proceeding of the 8th ACM Int. Conf. on Multimedia, pp. 147–156 (2000)
13. Chen, Y., Wang, Z.: A Region-based fuzzy feature matching approach to content-based image retrieval. IEEE Transactions on Pattern Analysis and Machine Intelligence 24, 1252–1267 (2002)
14. Hiremath, P.S., Pujari, J.: Content based image retrieval using color boosted salient points and shape features of an image. International Journal of Image Processing (IJIP) 2, 10–17 (2008)

Fast Computation of Edge Model Representation for Image Sequence Super-Resolution

Malay K. Nema[1], Subrata Rakshit[1], and Subhasis Chaudhuri[2]

[1] Computer Vision Group, CAIR, DRDO, Bangalore, India
{malay,srakshit}@cair.drdo.in
[2] VIP Lab, Dept. of EE, IIT Bombay, Mumbai, India
sc@ee.iitb.ac.in

Abstract. Edge model based representation of Laplacian subbands has been demonstrated to be useful in single frame high resolution image generation. A reconstruction based multiframe super-resolution algorithm yields a better super-resolved image if high resolution estimate of individual frame is given as input, instead of original low resolution frames. Fast computation of edge-model based representation enables fast single frame high resolution image generation for multiple frames and in turn helps in speeding up reconstruction based super resolution. In the present work, efficient multiframe edge model computation is achieved by computing edge model for the reference frame and then computing successive models by adapting it on the remaining frames.

Keywords: Laplacian subbands, Subband modelling, edge model, edge model adaptation, super-resolution(SR).

1 Introduction

It is desirable to have a fast method for generation of super-resolved images in order to make them usable in systems of limited resources or for SR in the context of videos. Earlier algorithms [7][15][6] have been improved upon from the point of view of speed enhancement, robustness and attainable resolution limits by researchers time to time in [4][13][5][1][2]. All these techniques consider motion among the successive frames. Motion free super resolution algorithms using various cues have also been developed [3][8][16]. Multi-frame SR methods perform better when the input provided are high resolution (HR) estimates of low resolution (LR) frames instead of LR frames themselves. The overhead in this process is to get HR estimates of LR frames. We take the edge model based representation [12] as our framework and exploit its usage in HR image generation [11]. The primitive set (PS) based HR image generation technique is similar in essence, to the one proposed in [16], but the ease of access to individual locations is greater and the model adaptation technique (proposed in this paper) is also feasible through the PS based technique. In this paper, we speed up the process of generating individual HR images for each LR frame by efficiently adapting the edge model based representation for subpixel shifted frames. Subsequently the HR estimates are utilised as input to reconstruction based SR method. The model adaptation approach drastically reduces the average computation cost per frame.

M.K. Kundu et al. (Eds.): PerMIn 2012, LNCS 7143, pp. 252–259, 2012.

This paper is arranged as follows. We briefly explain the edge-model based representation [12] in the following section and adaptation of model in Sec.2.1. We also analyse the gain and losses of model adaptation technique. Subsequently, we apply the model adaptation technique to SR in Sec. 3. We demonstrate the results using model adaptation and give our conclusions in Sec.4

2 Edge-Model Based Representation and Model Adaptation

The edge model based representation of Laplacian subbands is a descriptive representation which provides information about location and nature of any edge. The model employs superposition of a small set of primitives to effectively approximate edges of interest. We call this set as PS and the representation as PS model. The PS is shown in the Fig. 1. In the text we use 'edge model based representation' and 'PS model' interchangeably. Considering the source vector $\mathbf{x}_m$ of dimension d such that $\mathbf{x}_m =$

Fig. 1. Primitive Set PS28. Top row model elements are for sharp edges (PS14), bottom row model elements for blurred edges. Due to the bandwidth of the Laplacian subbands, both types of edges may be present. PS14 augmented by bottom row constitutes PS28

$(x_{m,1}, x_{m,2}, \ldots, x_{m,k})$: $m = 1, 2, \ldots M$; $d = d_1 \times d_2$. i.e. $\mathbf{x}_m$ is a sub-image of dimension $d_1 \times d_2$, M is the number of qualified partition to be represented. Let N be the number of code vectors and let $\mathbf{PS} = \{\mathbf{p}_1, \mathbf{p}_2, \ldots, \mathbf{p}_i, \ldots, \mathbf{p}_N\}$: $N < d$ represent the code book in which each code vector $\mathbf{p}_i$ is of the dimension d such that $\mathbf{p}_i = (p_{i,1}, p_{i,2}, \ldots, p_{i,d})$: $i = 0 \ldots N$, $d = d_1 \times d_2$. Let l_i be the encoding region of dimension d, associated with code vector $\mathbf{p}_i$ and let the Laplacian sub-band image (**L**) be an ensemble of all l_is and ψ as $\mathbf{L} = l_1 \cup l_2 \cup \ldots \cup l_i \cup \ldots \cup l_N \cup \psi$, where ψ represent the area with no or low energy signal. The approximation to $\mathbf{x}_m$, $Q(\mathbf{x}_m)$ is given by $Q(\mathbf{x}_m) = \mathbf{p}_i$ if $\mathbf{x}_m \in l_i$. The representation for any source vector $\mathbf{x}_m$ is carried out iteratively as

$$Q^0(\mathbf{x}_m) = \alpha_0 \mathbf{p}_{i,0},$$
$$Q^1(\mathbf{x}_m) = \alpha_0 \mathbf{p}_{i,0} + \alpha_1 \mathbf{p}_{i,1},$$
$$\vdots \tag{1}$$
$$Q^n(\mathbf{x}_m) = Q^{n-1}(\mathbf{x}_m) + \alpha_n \mathbf{p}_{i,n},$$

where α are the projection coefficients, $\alpha_0 \mathbf{p}_{i,0} = \arg\min_{\alpha, \mathbf{p}_i} \|\mathbf{x}_m - \alpha_0 \mathbf{p}_{i,0}\|$ and $Q(\mathbf{x}_m - Q^{n-1}(\mathbf{x}_m)) = \alpha_n \mathbf{p}_{i,n}$. The modelling (quantisation) error is defined as $J_{Q,n} = \sum \|\mathbf{x}_i - Q^n(\mathbf{x}_i)\|$. The projection coefficient α for minimal reconstruction error for any given PS element $\mathbf{p}_i$ is defined as

$$\alpha_{opt} = \frac{\mathbf{p}_i.\mathbf{x}}{\|\mathbf{p}_i\|}. \tag{2}$$

Further detail on modelling can be obtained from [12]. We get full representation in the form of description about any $\mathbf{p}_i$ being present at row, column location and α_i (projection coefficient). A Laplacian image can be reconstructed by adding all the $\alpha_i * \mathbf{p}_i$ at their respective locations. Though the PS is not a basis for Laplacian subbands, it has been shown to be a satisfactory representation from the point of intended image manipulation. It can be seen in Eqn. 1, the PS model generation involves nested searches in model computation. For a set of sub-pixel shifted frames, individual PS model generation can be seen as consumption of time for some thing which has already been computed. We try to minimise the computation overhead of repeated nested search by model adaptation.

2.1 Model Adaptation

We establish the feasibility of adapting PS model of a frame to other sub-pixel shifted frames. Experimental set is simulated from the same image using cubic interpolation with sub-pixel shifts of $[0.0 \ldots 0.7]$. Let the reference frame be F_R and other (dependent) frames are denoted by $F_k : k = 1 \ldots K$; K being the number of available frames. Let the Laplacian subbands of frames be denoted by $\mathbf{L}_R$ and $\mathbf{L}_k$ respectively. Let the reference frame model be $Q(\mathbf{x}_{mR})$. For model adaptation we take the $Q(\mathbf{x}_{mR})$ and recompute the projection coefficients for the sub-pixel shifted frame to get it's model

$$\hat{Q}(\mathbf{x}_{m,k}) = PSA(\mathbf{L}_k)|Q(\mathbf{x}_{m,R}) : \mathbf{x}_{m,k} \in \mathbf{L}_k; \text{ iff } \mathbf{L}_k \in \mathbf{L}_R \quad (3)$$

Where $PSA(\mathbf{L}_k)|Q(\mathbf{x}_{m,R})$ is the PS model adaptation for k^{th} frame F_k assuming the presence of reference frame model: $Q(\mathbf{x}_{mR})$. Taking help from Eqn. 1 and Eqn. 2, we define $PSA(\mathbf{L}_k)|Q(\mathbf{x}_{m,R})$ as

$$\begin{aligned}
\hat{Q}^0(\mathbf{x}_{m,k}) &= \alpha_{0_{opt},k}\mathbf{P}_{i,0} \\
\hat{Q}^1(\mathbf{x}_{m,k}) &= \alpha_{0_{opt},k}\mathbf{P}_{i,0} + \alpha_{1_{opt},k}\mathbf{P}_{i,1} \\
&\vdots \\
\hat{Q}^n(\mathbf{x}_{m,k}) &= Q^{n-1}(\mathbf{x}_{m,R}) + \alpha_{n_{opt},k}\mathbf{P}_{i,n}.
\end{aligned} \quad (4)$$

where $\mathbf{p}_{i,n} = \arg\min_{\mathbf{p}_i}(J_{Q_R,n})$ and $\alpha_{n_{opt},k}$ for any given $\mathbf{p}_i$ and $\mathbf{x}_{m,k}$ is given by $\alpha_{n_{opt},k} = \mathbf{p}_{i,n}.\mathbf{x}_{m,k}/\|\mathbf{p}_{i,n}\|$.

The PS models for sub-pixel shifted images can be approximated by changes in the projection coefficients only. This eliminates the nested search for model elements and their placements, which is the primary cost of the original model computation process. We analyse the gains and losses associated with the model adaptation now.

2.2 Model Adaptation: Error Analysis

Model adaptation errors were calculated based on $\mathbf{L}_k - \mathbf{L}_{a,k}$. Where $\mathbf{L}_{a,k}$ is the Laplacian images reconstructed through $\hat{Q}(\mathbf{x}_{m,k})$ and $\mathbf{L}_k$ is the true Laplacian subband image of the frame. The normalised errors for all the experimental set frames were computed.

The error plot is shown in Fig. 2, where a cubic spline has been fit to the individual data points to highlight the general trend. The model adaptation error increases with the increase in sub-pixel shift, while the PS modelling error remains more or less flat, which is according to expectation. The error for 0.6 pixel shift is not more than $0.5dB$ w.r.t. the case when dedicated modelling is done for the individual frame. The gain in computation time is shown in Fig. 3. The computation time for PS model generation for sub-pixel shifted frames is phenomenally less compared to that for individual model for each frame. For the experimental sequence of 64 frames, it took nearly 3 hrs on a SUNBlade machine, whereas by using the proposed model adaptation technique it took 3min and 10sec. only. Over all, the gain in computation time compared to a tolerable loss of accuracy makes the PS model adaptation scheme a viable means of generating models for image sequence/video frames.

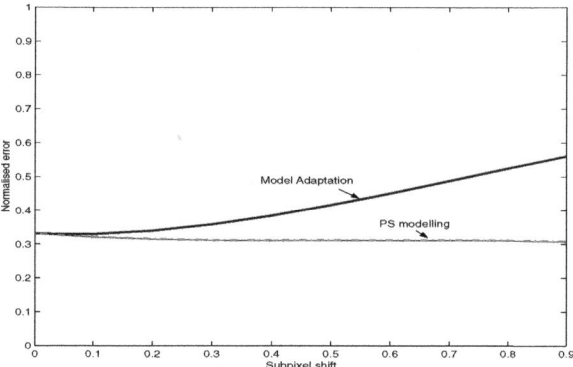

Fig. 2. Normalised error plot for true PS model and PS model adaptation. A synthetic frame set based on Lena image was used for this experiment.

3   PS Adaptation for Super-Resolution

A multi-frame reconstruction based SR algorithm generates better SR images when HR estimates of LR frames are given as inputs instead of LR frames themselves. It is mainly due to two factors (a) sub-pixel registration errors reduce at HR grid and (b) there is an extra element of resolution enhancement (LR frame specific) in the HR estimates. A single frame super-resolution output using edge model representation compares well with other state of art methods. A sample result is given in Fig. 4, and others are available in [10]. The fact that the PS model based super-resolution method has access to edges in a piecewise manner, makes the model adaptation possible at ease. We generate HR estimates for the sub-pixel shifted LR frames using PS-model adaptation. It is observed in Sec. 2.2, that the adapted model comes close to the one generated through dedicated modelling. This opens the possibility of exploiting it for single frame HR image generation for a sequence.

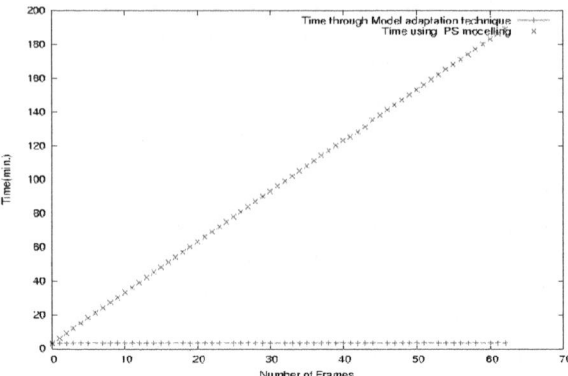

Fig. 3. Computational time for the approach of multi-frame PS model adaptation. The experiment ensured availability of sub-pixel shifted frames. For a lengthy video a preliminary pass is required to assess relevant motion vectors of a uniform environment.

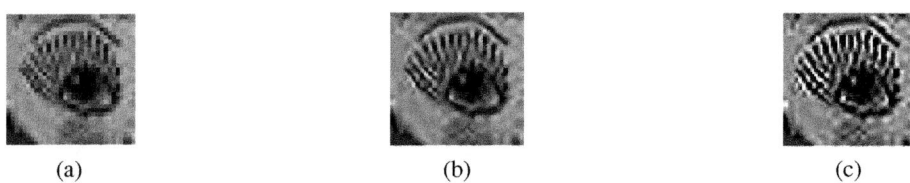

(a)   (b)   (c)

Fig. 4. Single frame image super-resolution comparison. (a) LR sample (b) output from [9] (c) result from PS based method.

3.1 Single Frame HR for Image Sequence

Considering the standard notations for Laplacian pyramids, initial image is $\mathbf{G}_0$, its first sub-band is $\mathbf{L}_0$, the HR image is denoted by $\mathbf{G}_{-1}$ and its first sub-band is $\mathbf{L}_{-1}$. The model adaptation usage will essentially replace the high resolution estimate of Laplacian subband $\hat{\mathbf{L}}_{-1}$ in single frame high resolution image generation algorithm [11] with $\mathbf{L}_{ia}$. Our proposed algorithm for single frame HR generation for a sequence of images is as follows.

1. $\forall \mathbf{G}_{0,k}$ (LR frames), generate $\hat{\mathbf{L}}_{-1,k}$ using Symmetric Residue Pyramids (SRP) [14] without prior ($\mathbf{0}$ image). This gives an estimate of $\mathbf{L}_{-1,k}$ with edges at correct locations but with improper widths.
2. Generate an edge model description of reference frame (say 0th) $\mathbf{L}_{1,0} : Q(\mathbf{x}_{m,R})$.
3. Use the $Q(\mathbf{x}_{m,R})$ for generating $\hat{Q}^n(\mathbf{x}_{m,k})$ as in Eqn. 4.
4. Reconstruct $\tilde{\mathbf{L}}_{-1a,k}$ from $\hat{Q}^n(\mathbf{x}_{m,k})$ with model switch ($\mathbf{p}_i = \mathbf{p}_{(i-14)} \forall \mathbf{p}_i, i > 14$).
5. $\forall \mathbf{G}_{0,k}$ obtain $\mathbf{L}_{-1a,k}$ through SRP with $\tilde{\mathbf{L}}_{-1a,k}$ as prior.
6. Obtain HR image $\mathbf{G}_{-1a,k} = \mathbf{U}(\mathbf{G}_{0,k}) + \mathbf{L}_{-1a,k}$.

We now check for the **effect on single frame HR generation**. The following experiment has been done to analyse the behavior of the process. The HR images were created using the proposed algorithm. It was observed that the extra PSNR error incurred is *less than 0.5dB*. The comparative error plots are shown in Fig. 5. In the plots it can be observed that the plot for PSNR for model adaptation-based HR image generation follows the trend of PSNR for PS-based HR image generation. This indicates that the model adaptation process can be used for HR image generation for a sequence, thus exploiting the enormous gain in computation time with a very marginal loss in PSNR. This paves the way for using PS model adaptation for multi frame SR.

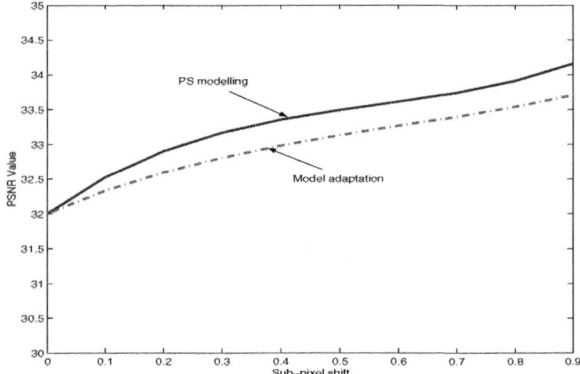

Fig. 5. PSNR plots: The HR error plot for model adaptation scheme does differ less then $0.5dB$ from the plot that of for PS-based HR image generation

3.2 PS Model Adaptation for Reconstruction Based SR

Considering the gain in computation time for achieving model adaptation based HR imagery, it is viable to use this technique for reconstruction-based multiframe super-resolution. The input low resolution frame will be replaced by individual HR estimates obtained through model adaptation. We assume that for the selection of relevant frames the motion vectors are known to the extent of integer pixel accuracy. Proposed scheme for multi-frame SR is as follows.

step 1: Generate the HR images using model adaptation as mentioned in Sec. 3.1.
step 2: Use these HR frames as inputs to a reconstruction based SR method to get an SR reconstruction of subset. We use the method given in [5].
step 3: For long sequences, use a moving window on the HR estimates to generate a sequence of SR frames.

The above steps are with the assumption that the frames are at sub-pixel shifts. In case of videos, one would have to occasionally redefine the reference frame and compute a PS model *ab initio*.

4   Results and Conclusions

The result for the proposed method are given in Fig. 6. While the model adaptation drastically reduces the computation time, we achieve better SR image due to the factors pointed out in Sec. 3. Our results are generated using 128×128 dimension LR sequences. While the results of proposed method is better, it took less time/frame to generate individual HR estimates. The input is super-resolved to $4\times$ to achieve 512×512 images. The output from the proposed method stands out clearly, especially areas of eye-lashes and cross-hatches depicting the hat of the doll and the letters on the number plate are more clear.

Conclusively, this paper proposed a fast method to generate PS model for multiple sub-pixel shifted frames through model adaptation. The model adaptation is shown to be useful in multi-frame single image HR and reconstruction based SR generation. Experiments of the proposed scheme shows good results. While the quality of results are good, the per frame model generation cost is mitigated. The proposed method can be extended for generating higher resolution clips from SD videos.

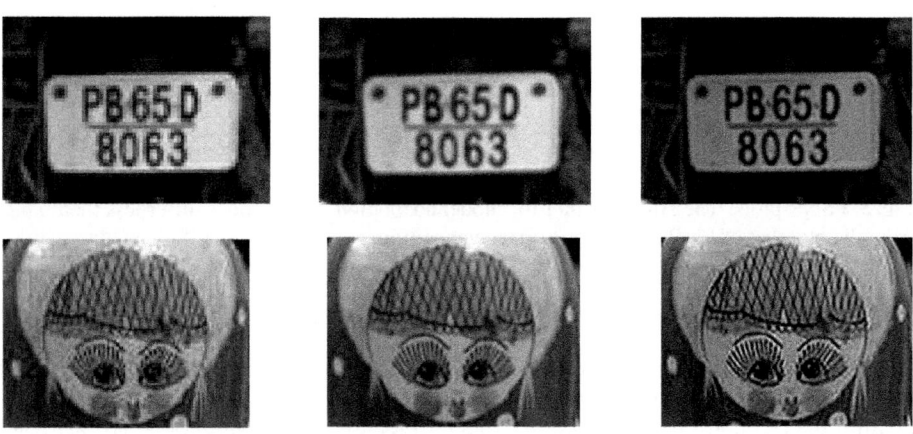

Fig. 6. Output of the proposed scheme on vehicle registration number plates and Matryoshka doll respectively. The left image is low resolution frame, Middle image is the output using LR frames as input, and the right image is the output from proposed method using the same number of frames(6 and 8 respectively). The clarity in the output from proposed method is noticeable.

References

1. Baker, S., Kanade, T.: Hallucinating faces. In: International Conference on Automatic Face and Gesture Recognition (2000)
2. Baker, S., Kanade, T.: Limits on super-resolution and how to break them. IEEE Trans. PAMI 24(1) (September 2002)
3. Chaudhuri, S., Joshi, M.: Motion-Free Super-Resolution. Springer, Heidelberg (2005)
4. Elad, M., Or-Hel, Y.: A fast super-resolution reconstruction algorith for pure translational motion and common space-invariant blur. IEEE Trans. Image Processing 10(8) (2001)

5. Farsiu, S., Robinson, S., Elad, M., Milanfar, P.: Fast and robust multi-frame superresolution. IEEE Trans. Image Processing (2004)
6. Ur, H., Gross, D.: Improved resolution from sub-pixel shifted pictures. CVGIP:Graphical models and Image Processing 54, 181–186 (1992)
7. Irani, M., Peleg, S.: Improving resolution by image registration. CVGIP: Graphical Models and Image Proc. 53, 231–239 (1991)
8. Jiji, C.: Single-Frame Image Super-resolution. Ph.D. thesis, IIT Bombay (2007)
9. Kim, K., Kwon, Y.: Single-image super-resolution using sparse regression and natural image prior. IEEE Transactions on Pattern Analysis and Machine Intelligence (2010)
10. Nema, M.: Edge model based representation of Laplacian subbands and its applications. Ph.D. thesis, IIT Bombay (2010)
11. Nema, M.K., Rakshit, S., Chaudhuri, S.: Edge Model Based High Resolution Image Generation. In: Kalra, P.K., Peleg, S. (eds.) ICVGIP 2006. LNCS, vol. 4338, pp. 1–12. Springer, Heidelberg (2006)
12. Nema, M.K., Rakshit, S.: Edge-Model Based Representation of Laplacian Subbands. In: Narayanan, P.J., Nayar, S.K., Shum, H.-Y. (eds.) ACCV 2006. LNCS, vol. 3851, pp. 80–89. Springer, Heidelberg (2006)
13. Nguyen, N., Milanfar, P., Golub, G.: A computationally efficient superresolution image reconstruction algorithm. Transactions in Image Processing (2000)
14. Rakshit, S., Nema, M.: Symmetric residue pyramids: An extension to burt laplacian pyramids. In: Proc. IEEE ICASSP (2003)
15. Schultz, R.R., Stevenson, R.L.: Extraction of high-resolution frames from video sequences. IEEE Trans. Image Processing (1996)
16. Sun, J., Sun, J., Xu, Z., Shum, H.: Gradient profile prior and its applications in image super-resolution and enhancement. IEEE Transaction on Image Processing (2011)

Detection of Structural Concavities in Character Images—A Writer-Independent Approach

Soumen Bag[1], Partha Bhowmick[1], and Gaurav Harit[2]

[1] Department of Computer Science and Engineering, IIT Kharagpur, India
{bagsoumen,bhowmick}@gmail.com
[2] Department of Computer Science and Engineering, IIT Rajasthan, India
gharit@iitj.ac.in

Abstract. In this paper, we present a novel technique for detection of concave regions as a structural information of character images. The problem difficulty lies in reporting all concavities irrespective of the viewing direction on the 2D plane. In our approach, we detect concave regions by analyzing the sequence of discrete turns taken to describe the character stroke; hence, it becomes view-invariant. The proposed method has the added advantage of detecting same concave regions of a particular character written by different individuals. We have tested our method on printed and handwritten Bangla and Hindi isolated character images. Initial results demonstrate the efficacy of our approach.

Keywords: Bangla and Hindi characters, concavity and convexity analysis, handwritten character recognition, writer-independent approach.

1 Introduction

Concavity or convexity acts as a major structural feature of an object in general. Hence, the interplay of concave and convex parts, in some form or the other, has been used in many works to derive and use the shape information of an object. For example, it is important for the recognition of objects by comparing with given shapes from a database. Depending on the requirement, several works have been reported in the literature on concavity and convexity detection of digital objects [6,13].

In this paper, our focus is mainly on the detection of structural concavity of character images, particularly for Bangla and Hindi languages. For last few decades, different structural-property extraction methods are reported for Indian OCR systems [12]. Chaudhury and Pal [5] proposed a method to extract different character strokes with different orientations in a character image. Dutta and Chaudhuri [7] detected different structural properties, such as junction points, holes, stroke segments, curvature maxima, curvature minima, and inflexion points of character images. To detect convexity of Bangla numerals, Pal and Chaudhuri [11] used water-flow model. Methods for the detection of similar type of structural properties are also reported for Devanagari script in the literature [3,8,9].

M.K. Kundu et al. (Eds.): PerMIn 2012, LNCS 7143, pp. 260–268, 2012.

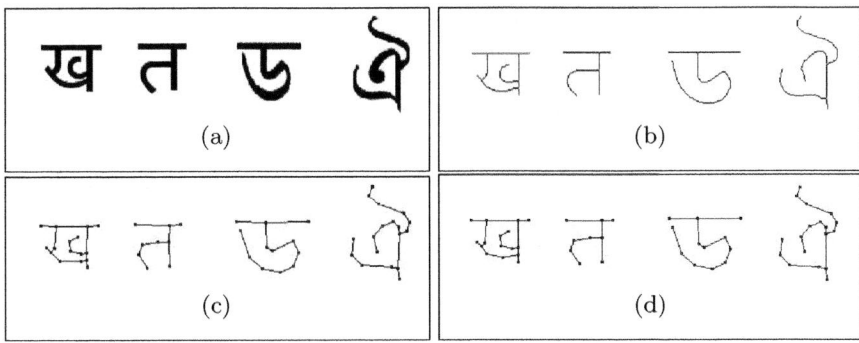

Fig. 1. Straight line approximation and junction point refinement of thinned character image. (a) Input image; (b) Thinned image; (c) Straight line approximation result; (d) Improved result after junction point refinement. Notice that the horizontal pieces (headline) and the vertical pieces have been straightened after junction point refinement.

We see that for Indian scripts there exist a large-scale shape variations in the same character written by various persons. The main challenge is to detect the same structural properties of a character written by different individuals. From this point of view, we propose a method to extract different structural concave regions of printed and handwritten character images. The method has the novelty to detect same concave regions of a character written by different persons.

This paper is organized as follows. Section 2 describes the proposed methodology for detection of structural concave regions. Section 3 contains the experimental results. Concluding remarks and future work are given in Section 4.

2 Proposed Methodology

In this section, we propose a novel methodology for extracting structural concave regions of isolated character images by analyzing the concavity and convexity features of character strokes irrespective of the writer and the viewing direction.

2.1 Preprocessing

Given a scanned document image, we first binarize it using Otsu's algorithm [10]. Currently we are working with isolated character images. Before extracting the concave regions, character images are converted to single-pixel-thick images using a medial-axis based thinning strategy proposed by Bag and Harit [2]. Few sample thinning results are shown in Fig. 1(b). We observed that for noisy images, the proposed medial-axis based thinning results in undesired small concave and convex regions. To solve this problem, we apply a straight line approximation method, proposed by Bhowmick and Bhattacharya [4], on thinned images.

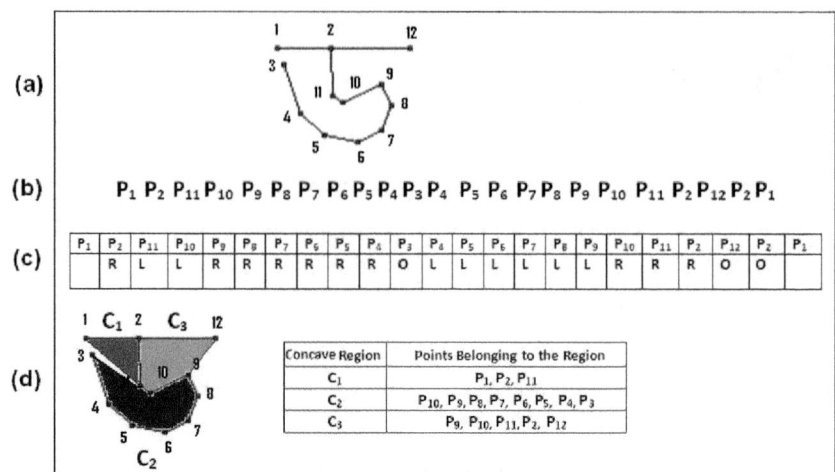

Fig. 2. Concavity/convexity detection of a thinned image. (a) Image with approximation points; (b) Sequence of traversed points; (c) Concavity/convexity of points (L: Concave, R: Convex, O: Endpoint); (d) Concave regions (filled by different colors) and set of points belonging to these regions.

The results of straight line approximation for Fig. 1(b) are shown in Fig. 1(c). We observe that the approximation results often contain deviation of thinned images at the junction points. So, to preserve the true shape at the junction points during approximation, we perform *junction point refinement*. The detailed methodology is reported in [1]. Fig. 1(d) shows the improved results after straight line approximation.

2.2   Concavity and Convexity Detection

After applying straight line approximation on the thinned image, we get an ordered set of approximation points, $V = \{p_1, p_2, \ldots, p_n\}$, and a set of edges, $E = \{e_1, e_2, \ldots, e_m\}$, connecting approximation points according to the structural shape of the original character image (Fig. 2(a)). Now, we visit all the points starting from an endpoint p_1 in such a manner that endpoints (excepting the

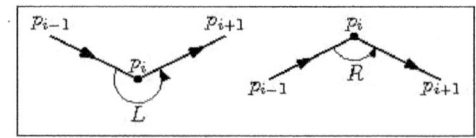

Fig. 3. Detection of concavity and convexity of a point with respect to its neighbor points. *left:* Concave shape; *right:* Convex shape.

start point of the traversal) are visited exactly once, junction points are visited a number of times depending on its number of branches, and remaining points are visited for exactly two times. Finally, the traversal ends at the start point p_1 (Fig. 2(b)). Next, we detect the concavity and convexity of all these points (except the start and endpoints of traversal) by calculating the value of twice the signed area of a triangle formed by the point $p_i(x_i, y_i)$ and its two adjacent points, $p_{i-1}(x_{i-1}, y_{i-1})$ and $p_{i+1}(x_{i+1}, y_{i+1})$ using Eq. 1. The concavity/convexity of a point p_i indicates the concavity/convexity nature of a region bounded by the adjacent points, p_{i-1}, p_i, and p_{i+1} as shown in Fig. 3.

$$\Delta(p_{i-1}, p_i, p_{i+1}) = \begin{vmatrix} 1 & 1 & 1 \\ x_{i-1} & x_i & x_{i+1} \\ y_{i-1} & y_i & y_{i+1} \end{vmatrix} \quad (1)$$

If $\Delta(\cdot)$ yields a negative value, then the point p_i has a concave property and is marked as L. If the value is positive, then p_i has a convex property and is marked as R (Fig. 3). If the value is equal to 0, then the point p_i has the same property as its previous point p_{i-1}. We mark endpoints as O to exclude them from concavity/convexity detection.

After detecting the concavity/convexity of all the points, we get a sequence such as $\{R_2, R_3, L_4, L_5, R_6, R_7, \ldots, R_i, \ldots, R_N\}$ where L_i/R_i indicates the concavity/convexity of point p_i (Fig. 2(c)).

2.3   Algorithm DETECT-CONCAVE-REGION

Algorithm 1 outlines the specific steps used in concave region detection for character images. The input is a set of points, $\mathcal{T}$, and the number of total points in the set $\mathcal{T}$ is N. The set $\mathcal{T}$ is a structure with two members: concavity/convexity of a point, C_{id}, and its coordinate values, *point*. We define another structure CR to store the points belonging to the detected concave regions. In the algorithm, Step 5 detects the first R to start concave region detection. Steps 5–23 detect all the points of a concave region and store them in CR. The whole process repeats to detect all remaining concave regions until $\mathcal{T}$ is finished. Steps 2–4 exclude the sequence of L or O for detecting the concave region. Finally, this procedure returns a set of concave regions and a set of points belonging to these regions (Fig. 2(d)).

3   Experimental Results

We collected characters from several heterogeneous printed documents of Bangla and Hindi. All the characters were collected in a systematic manner from printed pages scanned on a HP scanjet 5590 scanner at 300 dpi. The algorithm has been implemented with C programming language using OpenCV 2.0 on Unix/Linux platform. At first, images were thinned by Bag and Harit thinning method [2].

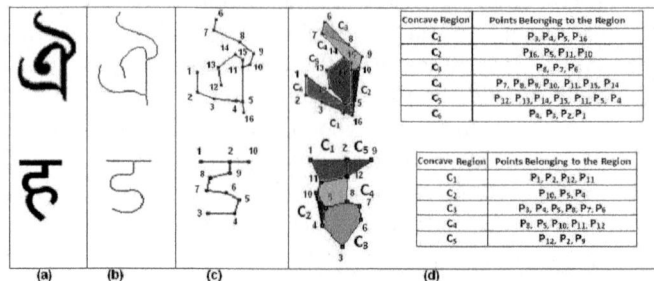

Fig. 4. Concave regions of character images. (a) Character image; (b) Thinned image; (c) Image with approximation points; (d) Concave regions filled by different colors and set of points belonging to these regions.

Algorithm 1. Procedure DETECT-CONCAVE-REGION to detect concave regions of a character image

---

Procedure DETECT-CONCAVE-REGION (T, N)

Steps:

1: $i \leftarrow 2$
2: **if** $T[i].C_{id} = L$ **OR** $T[i].C_{id} = O$ **then**
3:    $i \leftarrow i + 1$
4: **end if**
5: **if** $T[i].C_{id} = R$ **then**
6:    $j \leftarrow i$, $count \leftarrow 0$, $startflag \leftarrow 0$
7:    **while** $T[i].C_{id} \neq L$ **AND** $T[i].C_{id} \neq O$ **do**
8:       **if** $startflag = 0$ **then**
9:          $CR[index].storage[count] \leftarrow T[j - 1].point$
10:          $count \leftarrow count + 1$
11:          $CR[index].storage[count] \leftarrow T[j].point$
12:          $count \leftarrow count + 1$
13:          $startflag \leftarrow 1$
14:       **else**
15:          $CR[index].storage[count] \leftarrow T[j].point$
16:          $count \leftarrow count + 1$
17:       **end if**
18:       $j \leftarrow j + 1$
19:    **end while**
20:    $CR[index].storage[count] \leftarrow T[j].point$
21:    $index \leftarrow index + 1$
22:    $i \leftarrow j + 1$
23: **end if**
24: *Repeat from step 2 until T is finished (i.e., $i > N$)*

Then the proposed method was applied on these thinned images to detect concave regions and set of points belonging to these regions. The outputs are the

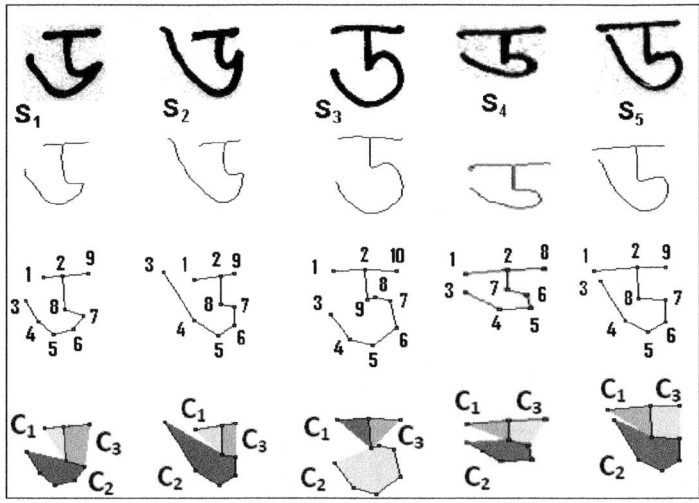

Fig. 5. Detected concave regions of a Bangla character written by different persons. 1st row: Handwritten characters; 2nd row: Thinned images; 3rd row: Images with approximation points; 4th row: Concave regions filled by different colors.

set of concave regions filled by different colors and the set of points belonging to these regions. Fig. 4 shows sample results of concave region detection on Bangla and Hindi character images.

We applied this method on different Bangla and Hindi characters written by various persons. For experimental purpose, we took the database of ISI Kolkata [14] and our own dataset for handwritten Bangla and Hindi characters respectively. We have compared the detected concave regions for different samples of a character written by different individuals based on the number of detected concave regions and the set of points belonging to these regions. In Fig. 5, there is a set of 5 samples of a Bangla character written by different persons. After applying the procedure *DETECT-CONCAVE-REGION* on these 5 samples, we get a set of concave regions and points belonging to these regions. Table 1 gives a detailed information of the different concave regions of these samples by indicating the number of concave regions and their corresponding sets of points. By comparing them, we can conclude that the detected concave regions are same for different samples of a character. A set of results of different handwritten characters are shown in Fig. 6.

4   Concluding Remarks

In this paper, we have proposed a novel structural concave region detection method for Indian character images. We have analyzed concavity/convexity of character strokes irrespective of the writer and the viewing direction to detect different concave regions bounded by character strokes. The proposed method

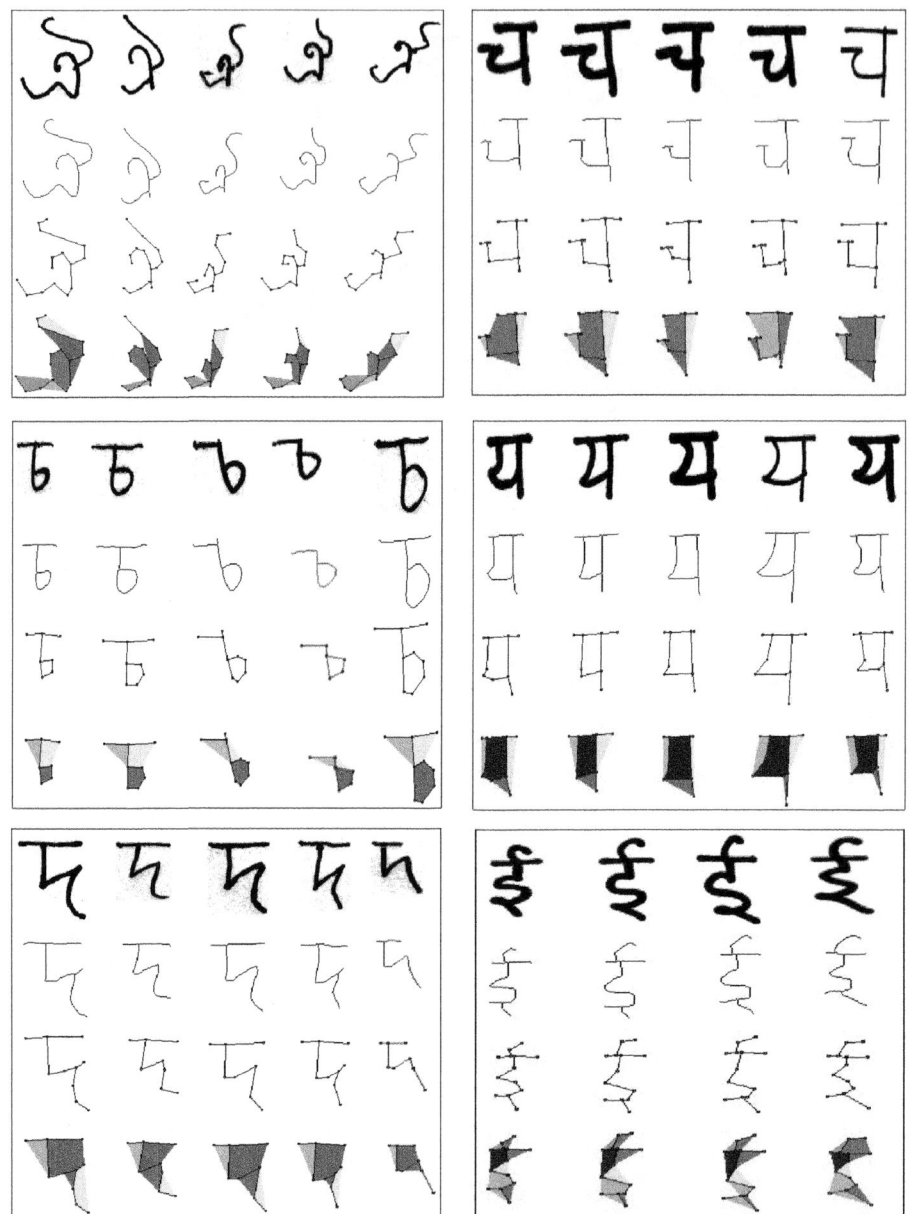

Fig. 6. Detection of concave regions of different samples of same character (Bangla and Hindi) written by different individuals. 1st *row*: Handwritten characters; 2nd *row*: Thinned images; 3rd *row*: Images with approximation points; 4th *row*: Concave regions filled by different colors.

Table 1. Comparison of detected concave regions for different samples of a character written by different individuals

Sample ID	# Concave regions	Concave region ID	Set of points
S_1	3	C_1	$C_1 : \langle 1,2,8 \rangle$
		C_2	$C_2 : \langle 3,4,5,6,7,8 \rangle$
		C_3	$C_3 : \langle 7,8,2,9 \rangle$
S_2	3	C_1	$C_1 : \langle 1,2,8 \rangle$
		C_2	$C_2 : \langle 3,4,5,6,7,8 \rangle$
		C_3	$C_3 : \langle 7,8,2,9 \rangle$
S_3	3	C_1	$C_1 : \langle 1,2,9 \rangle$
		C_2	$C_2 : \langle 3,4,5,6,7,8,9 \rangle$
		C_3	$C_3 : \langle 9,2,10 \rangle$
S_4	3	C_1	$C_1 : \langle 1,2,7 \rangle$
		C_2	$C_2 : \langle 3,4,5,6,7 \rangle$
		C_3	$C_3 : \langle 6,7,2,8 \rangle$
S_5	3	C_1	$C_1 : \langle 1,2,8 \rangle$
		C_2	$C_2 : \langle 3,4,5,6,7,8 \rangle$
		C_3	$C_3 : \langle 7,8,2,9 \rangle$

is tested on printed and handwritten Bangla and Hindi characters and we have obtained promising results. It has the potentiality to detect same concave regions of a character written by different persons. The main challenge for the handwritten optical character recognition (OCR) is to handle cursive character images with large-scale structural shape variations of same character written by different persons. In future, we shall extend this unique characteristic of our proposed method to make it applicable to detect invariant feature set to character classification for printed and handwritten OCR systems.

References

1. Bag, S., Bhowmick, P., Harit, G.: Recognition of Bengali handwritten characters using skeletal convexity and dynamic programming. In: Proc. EAIT, pp. 265–268 (2011)
2. Bag, S., Harit, G.: A medial axis based thinning strategy and structural feature extraction of character images. In: Proc. ICIP, pp. 2173–2176 (2010)
3. Bansal, V., Sinha, R.M.K.: Integrating knowledge sources in Devanagari text recognition system. IEEE Trans. SMC 30(4), 500–505 (2000)
4. Bhowmick, P., Bhattacharya, B.B.: Fast polygonal approximation of digital curves using relaxed straightness properties. IEEE Trans. PAMI 29(9), 1590–1602 (2007)
5. Chaudhuri, B.B., Pal, U.: A complete printed Bangla OCR system. Patt. Rec. 31(5), 531–549 (1998)
6. Dorksen-Reiter, H., Debled-Rennesson, I.: Convex and concave parts of digital curves. Geometric Properties for Incomplete Data 2, 145–159 (2006)
7. Dutta, A., Chaudhury, S.: Bengali alpha-numeric character recognition using curvature features. Patt. Rec. 26(12), 1757–1770 (1993)

8. Kompalli, S., Setlur, S.: Design and comparison of segmentation driven and recognition driven Devanagari OCR. In: Proc. DIAL, pp. 96–102 (2006)
9. Ma, H., Doermann, D.: Adaptive Hindi OCR using generalized Hausdorff image comparison. ACM Trans. Asian Lang. Info. Processing 2(3), 193–218 (2003)
10. Otsu, N.: A threshold selection method from gray-level histogram. IEEE Trans. SMC 9(1), 62–66 (1979)
11. Pal, U., Chaudhuri, B.B.: Automatic recognition of unconstrained off-line Bangla handwritten numerals. In: Proc. ICML, pp. 371–378 (2000)
12. Pal, U., Chaudhuri, B.B.: Indian script character recognition: A survey. Patt. Rec. 37, 1887–1899 (2004)
13. Roussillon, T., Tougne, L., Sivignon, I.: Robust decomposition of a digital curve into convex and concave parts. In: Proc. ICPR, pp. 1–4 (2008)
14. Bhattacharya, U.: Handwritten character databases of Indic scripts, http://www.isical.ac.in/~ujjwal/download/database.html

Semi-supervised Fuzzy Clustering Algorithms for Change Detection in Remote Sensing Images

Niladri Shekhar Mishra[1], Susmita Ghosh[2], and Ashish Ghosh[3]

[1] Department of Electronics and Communication Engineering
Netaji Subhash Engineering College, Kolkata, 700152, India
niladrimishra@gmail.com
[2] Department of Computer Science and Engineering
Jadavpur University, Kolkata, 700032, India
susmitaghoshju@gmail.com
[3] Center for Soft Computing Research
Indian Statistical Institute, 203 B.T. Road, Kolkata, 700108, India
ash@isical.ac.in

Abstract. For the problem of *change detection* it is difficult to have sufficient amount of ground truth information that is needed in supervised learning. On the contrary it is easy to identify *a few* labeled patterns by the experts. In this situation to avoid wastage of available information semi-supervision is suggestible to enhance the performance of unsupervised ones. Here we present the fuzzy clustering based semi-supervised technique to detect the *changes* in remote sensing images that takes care of spatial correlation between neighboring pixels of the difference image produced by comparing two images acquired on the same geographical area at different times. To do so two classical fuzzy clustering algorithms, namely fuzzy c-means (FCM) and Gustafson Kessel clustering (GKC) algorithms have been used in semi-supervised way. For clustering purpose various image features are extracted using the neighborhood information of pixels. To show the effectiveness of the proposed technique, experiments are conducted on two multispectral and multitemporal remote sensing images. Results are compared with those of existing unsupervised fuzzy clustering based technique, Markov random field (MRF) & neural network based algorithms and found to be superior.

Keywords: Semi-supervision, remote sensing, change detection, multitemporal images, fuzzy clustering, fuzzy c-means clustering, Gustafson Kessel clustering.

1 Introduction

In remote sensing applications, change detection is the process of identifying differences in the state of an object or phenomenon by analyzing a pair of images acquired on the same geographical area at different times. This is useful to identify vegetation changes [6], monitoring shifting cultivations, studies on land-use/land-cover dynamics, burned area assessment [4], monitoring urban growth *etc.*

M.K. Kundu et al. (Eds.): PerMIn 2012, LNCS 7143, pp. 269–276, 2012.

Before performing *change detection* between two multitemporal images, a certain degree of pre-processing is needed because of co-registration error, radiometric and geometric errors [8]. After pre-processing, the multitemporal images are taken as input and compared pixel by pixel to generate another image, called the difference image (DI), using different spectral bands. Among various methods, CVA (*i.e.* Change Vector Analysis) is the most popular one [8] and is used in our study also.

In literature mainly two directions are suggested to detect the *changes* in remotely sensed data, in supervised and unsupervised [1,5,6,8,9] manner. In supervised ones a set of *training patterns* is required for learning the classifier. In real-life it is difficult to have data containing spectral signatures of changes from which *training patterns* can be generated. In such situations (in absence of ground truth information) unsupervised techniques are opted as there is no need of *training data.*

Unsupervised *change detection* can be done either using context-insensitive or context-sensitive procedures. Histogram thresholding [4] is of the first kind. The threshold value may be selected by *manual trial-and-error* (MTET) process or by automatic techniques to analyze the statistical distribution of the DI, where spatial correlation between the neighboring pixels is not taken into account. To remove this bottleneck, context-sensitive techniques [1] based on MRF are proposed where selection of a proper model for the statistical distributions of *changed* and *unchanged* classes are required. In order to overcome the limitations imposed by the need of selecting or estimating a statistical model for *changed* and *unchanged* class distributions, unsupervised, distribution free and context-sensitive change detection techniques based on neural networks [8,9] and fuzzy clustering [7] have been proposed. It was analyzed in [7] that techniques based on fuzzy clustering are less time & computation intensive (than all existing techniques) but comparable in terms of efficiency. An attempt was made [7] to recover the *changed* and *unchanged* regions of the DI by constructing two clusters. Normally the pixels of the DI belonging to two clusters *changed* and *unchanged* are not separable by sharp boundaries (as they are highly overlapped). As fuzzy clustering technique is more appropriate and realistic to separate overlapping clusters, fuzzy clustering techniques had been chosen (in [7]) to have a better judgement of the two groups. In this regard two fuzzy clustering algorithms namely fuzzy c-means [3] and Gustafson Kessel [10] were used.

For the problem of *change detection* in remotely sensed images experts can collect a small amount of information (in the form of labeled patterns) about the two classes easily. This less amount of collected labeled patterns is not sufficient for choosing supervised methods. Then to utilize the available information semi-supervision is fruitful. In the present work we have integrated semi-supervision with the unsupervised methodology (proposed in [7]) to detect the *changes*. It has been seen [2,11] that by supplying a minimum knowledge (by means of a few labeled patterns) the outcome of fuzzy clustering can be improved. The supplied labeled data steer the partitioning to a more (than the unsupervised version) appropriate one to yield better result.

To assess our proposed technique, experiments are carried out on three real world data sets and compared the results with those obtained by already published work. The proposed technique has an edge with respect to both error and time requirement.

2   Clustering

Cluster analysis partitions a data set into a reasonable number of disjoint groups, where each group contains similar patterns. The partitions are such that patterns are "homogeneous" within the clusters and "heterogeneous" between the clusters.

2.1   Hard C-Means (HCM) Clustering

In this simplest clustering technique, from a set of patterns, c number of patterns are randomly chosen as initial cluster centers. In each iteration the patterns are assigned to the cluster having the nearest center; and the centers are updated accordingly. The centers are arithmetic mean of the patterns assigned to a cluster at the previous iteration. Thus, if $\mathbf{V} = [\mathbf{v}_1, \mathbf{v}_2, .., \mathbf{v}_c]$, includes c number of vectors $\mathbf{v}_i$, $(\mathbf{v}_i, 1 \leq i \leq c)$ of cluster centers, then after the first iteration $\mathbf{v}_i$ becomes the arithmetic mean of the patterns assigned to the ith cluster. This process continues until the centers become stable (the difference of the values in two successive iterations becomes less than ϵ, a predefined small positive constant) *i.e. no changes* occur from the *partitioning* point of view.

The HCM algorithm basically minimizes the following objective function

$$J(\mathbf{X}; \mathbf{V}) = \sum_{i=1}^{c} \sum_{k=1}^{n} ||(\mathbf{x}_k - \mathbf{v}_i)||^2, \tag{1}$$

where $\mathbf{X} = [\mathbf{x}_1, \mathbf{x}_2, .., \mathbf{x}_n]$,   i.e., $\mathbf{X}$ includes n unlabeled objects and $\mathbf{x}_k$ is the kth unlabeled object with $||(\mathbf{x}_k - \mathbf{v}_i)||^2$ (Euclidean norm) as the dissimilarity measure between $\mathbf{x}_k$ and the ith cluster.

2.2   Fuzzy Clustering

In fuzzy clustering the elements are assigned not only to one cluster, but to all the clusters with certain degree of belonging. This belongingness to groups is not hard/crisp, rather soft and gradual and is represented by a numeric value between 0 to 1 (called, "membership grade"). Amongst various fuzzy clustering algorithms, Fuzzy C-Means (FCM) [3] is the basic one. As it has some limitations, several algorithms have been developed further to improve its performance [10].

Fuzzy C-Means Clustering (FCM). FCM attempts to find fuzzy partition-ing of a given pattern-set by minimizing the following objective function

$$J_m(\mathbf{X}; U, \mathbf{V}) = \sum_{i=1}^{c} \sum_{k=1}^{n} (\mu_{ik})^m ||(\mathbf{x}_k - \mathbf{v}_i)||^2 \tag{2}$$

where U, the fuzzy partition matrix, is computed as
U = $[\mu_{ik}] \in M_{fcn}$,

$$\mathbf{v}_i = \frac{\sum_{k=1}^{n} (\mu_{ik})^m x_k}{\sum_{k=1}^{n} (\mu_{ik})^m} \tag{3}$$

and the membership value of the kth element belonging to the ith cluster, μ_{ik}, is expressed as

$$\mu_{ik} = \frac{1}{\sum_{j=1}^{c} \left(\frac{d_{ik}}{d_{jk}}\right)^{\frac{2}{(m-1)}}}, \tag{4}$$

with $d_{ik} = \sqrt{||(\mathbf{x}_k - \mathbf{v}_i)||^2}$ and $m(> 1)$ as a parameter, called fuzzifier. Efficiency of FCM is highly dependent on the proper selection of the fuzzifier. For $m >> 1$ the process is more fuzzy. During optimization of $J_m(X; U, V)$, following two constraints must be satisfied, (i) $\sum_{i=1}^{c} \mu_{ik} = 1$ and (ii) $\mu_{ik} \in [0, 1]$. Note that, HCM is a special case of FCM with $\mu_{ik}=0$ or 1, $\forall$ i and k.

Though FCM is famous for its simplicity, it tends to recover clusters with simi-lar sizes and circular shapes. When clusters have non-spherical (ellipsoidal/linear varieties) shapes, FCM fails to provide good performance.

Gustafson-Kessel Clustering (GKC). Since FCM employs Euclidean norm to measure the dissimilarity between patterns and cluster centers, only spherical shapes can be recovered using FCM. Gustafson and Kessel introduced [10] adap-tive distance norm to measure the distance between clusters using covariance matrix of the cluster centers. Using GKC ellipsoidal shapes could be detected. Each cluster has its own norm-inducing matrix A_i, a positive definite symmetric one, for automatically adapting the shapes of the clusters. The fuzzy covariance matrix F_i of the ith cluster is expressed as

$$F_i = \frac{\sum_{k=1}^{n} (\mu_{ik})^m (\mathbf{x}_k - \mathbf{v}_i)(\mathbf{x}_k - \mathbf{v}_i)^T}{\sum_{k=1}^{n} (\mu_{ik})^m}. \tag{5}$$

The distance, D_{ikA_i} is represented as

$$D_{ikA_i} = \sqrt{(\mathbf{x}_k - \mathbf{v}_i)^T A_i (\mathbf{x}_k - \mathbf{v}_i)}, \tag{6}$$

where $A_i = [\rho_i det(F_i)]^{1/\eta} F_i^{-1}$, η is the dimension of patterns and ρ_i is a prede-fined constant which controls the shape of the corresponding cluster restraining its size.

Thus

$$\mu_{ik} = \frac{1}{\sum_{j=1}^{c} \left(\frac{d_{ikA_i}}{d_{jkA_i}} \right)^{\frac{2}{(m-1)}}}. \tag{7}$$

It is noticeable that in the first step of the algorithm, though U is initialized randomly, ρ_i has to be set reasonably to catch up proper shapes of the clusters during optimization.

3   Proposed Semi-supervised Change Detection Technique

Several techniques (*e.g.* [2,11]) have been proposed to enhance the performance of fuzzy clustering with the aid of semi-supervision. The present work is inspired by [2]. Here we have incorporated semi-supervision to the already existing *unsupervised change detection* technique [7]. It has been observed from the results that the present concept can boost up the performance of the existing one.

The labeled patterns can be collected in many ways. Here, for experimental purpose labeled patterns from both the classes (*changed* & *unchanged*) are acquired randomly (5% from *changed* & 1% from *unchanged*) from the ground truth . The ground truth is generated by manual analysis of two multitemporal images of the same geographical area at different times.

Memberships (μ_{ik}^l) are known & hard for the labeled patterns $(\mathbf{x}^l)$. The initial locations of the cluster centers are computed by (8),

$$\mathbf{v}_{i,l} = \frac{\sum_{k=1}^{n_l} (\mu_{ik}^l)^m \mathbf{x}_k^l}{\sum_{k=1}^{n_l} (\mu_{ik}^l)^m}. \tag{8}$$

The memberships (μ_{ik}^{nl}) for the unlabeled ones $(\mathbf{x}^{nl})$ are initialized using this $\mathbf{v}_{i,l}$ by (4). For calculating cluster centers afterwards labeled patterns also participate along with unlabeled ones. This is done using (9). At the subscript of (9), "semi" denotes the effect of semi-supervision while evaluating cluster means at every iteration.

$$\mathbf{v}_{i,semi} = \left(\frac{\sum_{k=1}^{n_l} (\mu_{ik}^l)^m \mathbf{x}_k^l + \sum_{k=1}^{n_{nl}} (\mu_{ik}^{nl})^m \mathbf{x}_k^{nl}}{\sum_{k=1}^{n_l} (\mu_{ik}^l)^m + \sum_{k=1}^{n_{nl}} (\mu_{ik}^{nl})^m} \right). \tag{9}$$

For a clear comparison we have applied the same concept in hard clustering (HCM) also and named the process as SEMI_HCM. As in fuzzy ones the cluster centers are initialized using the labeled patterns only and the labeled & unlabeled patterns both participate while updating them. The assignment (and reassignment) of patterns during optimization is done only for the unlabeled ones.

4   Experimental Results

To assess the effectiveness of the proposed approach, we considered three multi-temporal remote sensing data sets corresponding to geographical areas of Mexico,

Sardinia island, Italy and Peloponnesian Peninsula, Greece [8]. Similar findings were obtained for all these data sets. Considering the space limitations, here we have presented results for only Mexico data set.

We have presented comparative analysis of the performances of our proposed semi-supervised algorithms with their corresponding unsupervised variants and one context-insensitive technique (namely MTET) & two context-sensitive techniques. MTET produces a minimum error change detection map by finding an optimal decision threshold for DI assuming pixels are independent in spatial domain. The change detection technique presented in [4], where EM is combined with MRF (in this article it will be referred as EM+MRF) and a technique based on 'Hopfield-Type Neural Networks' [8] (HTNN) are considered as context-sensitive techniques for comparison.

The data set used is made up of two multispectral images acquired in an area of Mexico on 18th April 2000 and 20th May 2002 (Fig. 1). The corresponding difference image and the reference map are also shown in Fig. 1. The change detection maps obtained by the SEMI_HCM, SEMI_FCM and SEMI_GKC are shown in Figs. 2 (a), 2 (b), 2 (c) respectively.

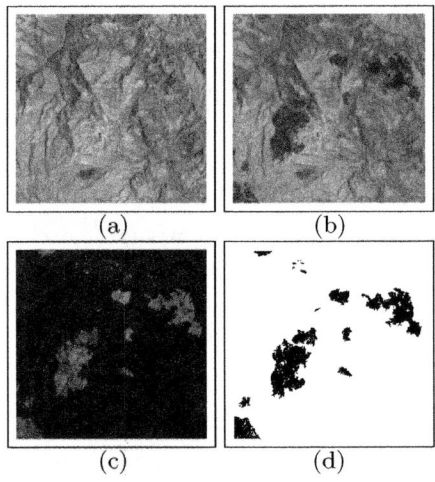

Fig. 1. Band 4 image of Mexico area. (a) acquired in April 2000, (b) acquired in May 2002, (c) corresponding difference image and (d) reference map of the changed area.

Quantitative analysis is carried out in terms of **overall error (OE)**, number of **false alarms** (i.e., unchanged pixels identified as changed ones -**FA**) and **missed alarms** (i.e., changed pixels categorized as unchanged ones -**MA**). It is better to have less **missed alarms** because it denotes the actual changes that the algorithm failed to detect. Also **overall error** should be minimum.

We have compared the *change detection* map created by SEMI_HCM, SEMI_FCM and SEMI_GKC with the ground truth image (used as reference

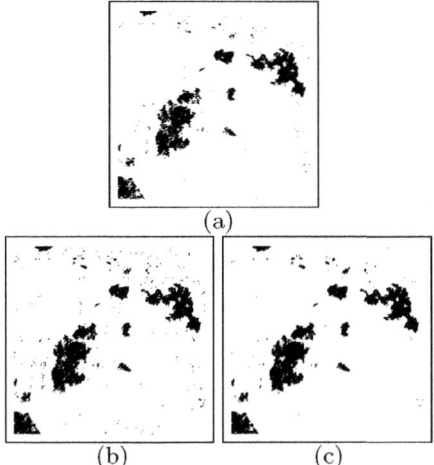

Fig. 2. Change detection maps obtained by (a) SEMI_HCM, (b) SEMI_FCM, and (c) SEMI_GKC

map) and put the results in Table 1. For fuzzy techniques, the value of m affects the results. Here we have presented the best results, obtained by varying m. For GKC algorithm ρ_is affect the results and we set them accordingly. For all the experiments, ϵ is set to 0.0000001.

Table 1. Missed alarms, false alarms and overall error for Mexico data set

Techniques used	MA	FA	OE
MTET	2404	2187	4591
HCM	3425	734	4159
SEMI_HCM	3200	706	3906
HTNN	558	2707	3265
EM+MRF ($\beta = 1.5$)	946	2257	3203
FCM ($m = 14$)	1178	1734	2912
SEMI_FCM ($m = 14$)	1059	1651	2710
GKC ($m = 15.5$, $\rho_1 = 1$, $\rho_2 = 2.2$)	1452	1076	2528
SEMI_GKC ($m = 15.5$, $\rho_1 = 1$, $\rho_2 = 2.2$)	1336	1084	**2420**

From Table 1 it is seen that by using semi-supervised fuzzy clustering (SEMI_FCM or SEMI_GKC) we can attain better performance than all the pre-suggested techniques. Also the proposed algorithms are better than their crisp version (SEMI_HCM). Overall error incurred by SEMI_FCM is less than that obtained by SEMI_HCM; and SEMI_GKC incurred the least error. GKC produced better results as it can handle non-spherical clusters also [7]. As SEMI_GKC produced even better than that we can state that semi-supervision can handle the situation well.

Although the existing techniques produced reasonable performance, they require either the assumption of distributions of classes and is very time consuming (in EM+MRF and HTNN) or needs much more effort to implement (in HTNN). On the other hand, the proposed technique does not require any a priori knowledge of the data distributions and is very fast.

5   Discussion and Conclusion

Semi-supervised fuzzy clustering algorithms for detecting changes in multitemporal, multispectral remote sensing images have been proposed. The proposed context-sensitive techniques can enhance the performance of the corresponding unsupervised versions. They do not require explicit assumption about the underlying classes like context-sensitive process presented in [4] (EM+MRF) as they are distribution free as well as they are less computation intensive. Compared to another context-sensitive technique proposed in [8] (HTNN), they are very simple, easy to implement and have improved performance.

References

1. Bazi, Y., Bruzzone, L., Melgani, F.: An unsupervised approach based on the generalized Gaussian model to automatic change detection in multitemporal SAR images. IEEE Transactions on Geoscience and Remote Sensing 43(4), 874–887 (2005)
2. Bensaid, A.M., Hall, L.O., Bezdek, J.C., Clarke, L.P.: Partially supervised clustering for image segmentation. Pattern Recognition 29(5), 370–379 (1996)
3. Bezdek, J.C.: Pattern Recognition with Fuzzy Objective Function. Plenum Press, New York (1981)
4. Bruzzone, L., Prieto, D.F.: Automatic analysis of the difference image for unsupervised change detection. IEEE Transactions on Geoscience and Remote Sensing 38(3), 1171–1182 (2000)
5. Canty, M.J.: Image Analysis, Classification and Change Detection in Remote Sensing. CRC Press, Taylor & Francis (2006)
6. Chavez Jr., P.S., MacKinnon, D.J.: Automatic detection of vegetation changes in the southwestern United States using remotely sensed images. Photogrammetric Engineering and Remote Sensing 60(5), 1285–1294 (1994)
7. Ghosh, A., Mishra, N.S., Ghosh, S.: Fuzzy clustering algorithms for unsupervised change detection in remote sensing images. Information Science 181(4), 699–715 (2011)
8. Ghosh, S., Bruzzone, L., Patra, S., Bovolo, F., Ghosh, A.: A context-sensitive technique for unsupervised change detection based on Hopfield-type neural networks. IEEE Transactions on Geoscience and Remote Sensing 45(3), 778–789 (2007)
9. Gopal, S., Woodcock, C.: Remote sensing of forest change using artificial neural networks. IEEE Transactions on Geoscience and Remote Sensing 34(2), 398–404 (1996)
10. Gustafson, D.E., Kessel, W.C.: Fuzzy clustering with a fuzzy covariance matrix. In: IEEE Conference on Decision and Control, San Diego, CA, pp. 761–766 (1979)
11. Pedrycz, W., Waletzky, J.: Fuzzy clustering with partial supervision. IEEE Transactions Systems Man and Cybernetics-Part B 27(5), 787–795 (1997)

SLAR (Simultaneous Localization And Recognition) Framework for Smart CBIR

Gyanesh Dwivedi[1], Sukhendu Das[1], Subrata Rakshit[2],
Megha Vora[1], and Suranjana Samanta[1]

[1] V.P. Lab, IIT Madras, Chennai- 600036, India
{gyaneshd,sdas,ssamanta}@cse.iitm.ac.in, meghavora25@gmail.com
[2] CAIR (DRDO), Bangalore- 560093, India
srakshit@cair.drdo.in

Abstract. In traditional content-based image retrieval (CBIR) methods, features are extracted from the entire image for computing similarity with query. It is necessary to design a smart object-centric CBIR to retrieve images from the gallery, having objects similar to that present in the foreground of the query image. We propose a model for a novel SLAR (Simultaneous Localization And Recognition) framework for solving this problem of smart CBIR, to simultaneously: (i) detect the location and (ii) recognize the type (ID or class) of the foreground object in a scene. The framework integrates both unsupervised and supervised methods of foreground segmentation and object classification. This model is motivated by the cognitive models of human visual perception, which generalizes from examples to simultaneously locate and categorize objects. Experimentation has been done on six categories of objects and the results have been compared with a contemporary work on CBIR.

Keywords: SLAR, smart CBIR, SVM, Graph-cut, MTH, HOG, Cognitive model.

1 Introduction

Content-based image retrieval (CBIR) [11], [14], [10], [15], [12], involves the process of retrieving digital images from a large database based on similarity in content. In traditional CBIR, global features such as, color, shape, texture and interest points are extracted from the entire query image. The desired content of an image is however not holistic but often localized, thus requiring object-centric Content Based Image Retrieval [10]. In order to design such a 'smart' CBIR, one needs to automatically focus on the (foreground) object of interest and retrieves features only from it. The main problem with smart CBIR is to automatically find the area of interest and segment the foreground object from the image.

To facilitate the above, one may rely on two inter-related processes: (i) Object (or target) Recognition and (ii) Detection (Localization) of a foreground object appearing as a distinct part of a scene. Each one of these problems, when solved in isolation, assumes that the other has been solved independently. Object

M.K. Kundu et al. (Eds.): PerMIn 2012, LNCS 7143, pp. 277–287, 2012.

recognition assumes that the object is pre-segmented from the background, while foreground segmentation operation assumes that the object class and features are known a priori. With the basic motivation of solving the complex problem of smart CBIR, we need to integrate these two complimentary processes in a unified framework. This motivated us to propose a SLAR (Simultaneous Localization and Recognition) framework to address the issues in smart CBIR.

The human brain [1] has two distinct parts, where: (i) the temporal (ventral) lobe solves the problem of object recognition, while (ii) the dorsal (parietal) part solves the problem of localization and mapping. It is the mutual collaborative exchange of information between the two intelligent parts of the brain, which helps humans to solve this problem with effortless ease. As a first step towards building such a computational model, we concentrate on designing an integrated framework for SLAR combining supervised classifiers, feature detection modules and similarity measures, which can learn from examples to retrieve images for an object-centric smart CBIR.

For SLAR, one needs to simultaneously detect (localize) the position of the object as well as identify its class (category) in an image. We first employ Graph-cut [2] on the given query image to extract the potential foreground region. Pruning is used to clean the Graph-cut output, followed by a K-Medoid based part-segmentor. A set of candidate foreground (object) regions are formed by creating groups of prominent segments obtained from the pruned graph-cut output. Using features from these regions a set of trained SVMs decide the category of the foreground object. Finally, Distance Transform (DT) based correlation is used as a shape similarity measure to retrieve rank-ordered outputs from the training gallery. Results are shown using six (6) categories of objects in the database, created using image samples from the Microsoft Research database [7] and samples collected from internet.

2   Literature Review

Some of the popular image Content Based retrieval systems [14], [10], [15], [12] are QIBC, MARS, Virage, Photobook, FIDS, Netra, Cortina etc. Low-level features, extracted from the whole image has been used for rank-ordered retrieval based on some similarity measure. In the work done by Lui et al. [11], Multi-Texton Histogram (MTH) has been used for image retrieval. MTH integrates the advantages of co-occurrence matrix and histogram. MTH is an improved version of Texton Co-occurance Matrix (TCM). Results have been shown on Corel 500 and Corel 1000 datasets using precision/recall measure.

Leibe et. al [8] presents a novel method for localizing objects of a visual category in cluttered real-world scenes. The core part of the approach is a highly flexible learned representation for object shape that can combine the information observed on different training examples in a probabilistic extension of the Generalized probabilistic Hough Transform. In addition, a Minimum Description length (MDL) based hypothesis verification stage is also used to resolve ambiguities between overlapping hypotheses and factor out the effects of partial occlusion. Efficient algorithms (codebook generation, Agglomerative clustering, ISM, Probabilistic Hough vote, Scale-adaptive hypothesis search, MDL formulation for top-down segmentation etc.) have been provided for the design of a six stage framework and the performance of the resulting recognition has been evaluated on dataset of six categories of objects. The work by Levin et al. [9] used discriminative and part-based methods for supervised object segmentation. They use both top-down and bottom-up cues simultaneously which has been formulated in the context of convex optimization problem of a Conditional Random Field. Results have been shown on synthetic octopus dataset and real world datasets of horses, cars and cows. Pedro et al. [6] described an object detection system based on a mixture of multi-scale deformable part model. They model objects using visual grammars. Results have been shown using precision/recall curves on PASCAL VOC and INRIA person dataset.

In all the aforementioned papers the problems have been solved as an object detection problem, with an assumption that the class of query image is known. Literature published in the recent past have shown that most researchers have solved the problem of detection (or localization) of an object within a scene, with a limited set of objects [8], [9]. When the number of classes or categories of objects involved is large the problem generally becomes intractable. The problem of object recognition assumes that the object has been accurately pre-segmented (detection solved separately). Simultaneous object detection and recognition is a complex problem, and appears to be unsolvable in the presence of background clutter, noise and occlusion. In this paper, an attempt has been made to simultaneously solve the problem of recognition and localization. To achieve this Graph-cut [2] and SVM [5] are used for help in localization and recognition.

3   Description of the Framework

The problem of SLAR framework (**"What is Where?"**) involves solving localization and recognition problems simultaneously, where the uncertainty involves in both. The present work assumes less noise in image/scene, no intermixing of foreground and background textures, no partial object and less variations in affine transformations of shape. We do not model the effect of shadows, allow only minor shading variations on the surface of the target objects, and ignore partial objects as well as occlusion. The following subsections describe the steps and issues of the proposed framework.

3.1   Proposed Stages of Framework

The problem of the design of a SLAR for a smart CBIR can be defined as: Given a gallery of different categories of object shapes, find the similar set of samples in a given category, which closely resemble the object present in the test scene.

Input: Gallery of sample object templates, and a test image sample.

Output : Retrieved gallery samples, based on rank-ordered similarity.

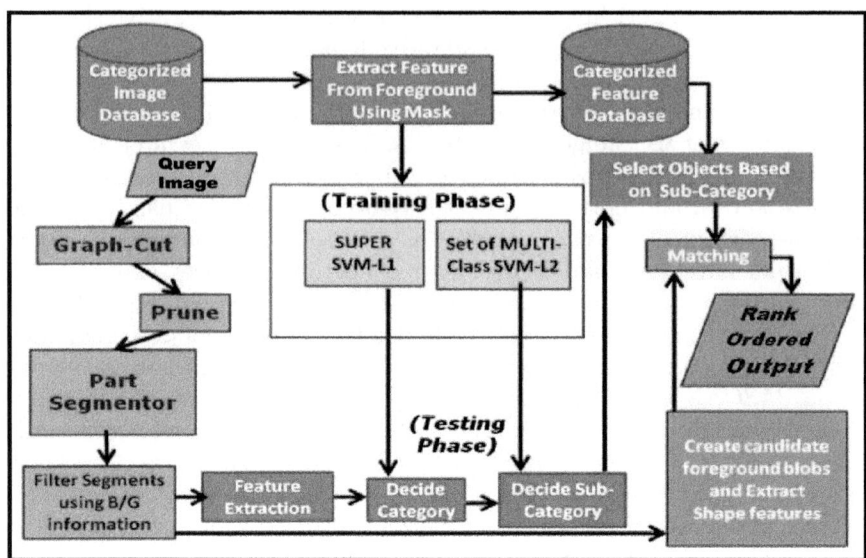

Fig. 1. Proposed SLAR framework for object-centric 'smart' segmentation

Our proposed method is motivated by the cognitive model [1] of the human brain. The temporal (ventral) lobe of the brain solves the problem of object recognition, while the dorsal (parietal) lobe solves the problem of localization. It is the exchange of mutual information (forward and backward) between these two lobes which enables the human brain to simultaneously identify and recognize objects in a complex scene. As a first step to solve the complex SLAR problem, we implement a framework combining detection and identification, which gets mutually benefitted from each other. The technology proposed is semi-supervised - a judicial mixture of supervised (SVM classifier) and unsupervised techniques (Graph-cut and K-medoids clustering). The entire framework for training and testing is given in Fig. 1. The steps to be followed for the design of a smart method for intelligent image segmentation is briefly outlined in two parts: training and testing phases. These are described in the following:

Training Phase

1. For each training image, $i = 1, 2, ..., N$ perform:
   (a) Manually create a foreground mask.
   (b) Extract features (texture, color, HOG (Histogram of Oriented Gradient) [6], MTH [11]) from foreground object in an image using mask.
   (c) Compute the distance transform (DT) of each foreground mask.
2. Train super SVM-L1 using HOG feature and multi-class SVM-L2 using HOG and MTH, to decide the category and sub-category of the test image, in order to reduce the search space.

Sample training images and their respective hand-drawn foreground masks are given in Fig. 2.

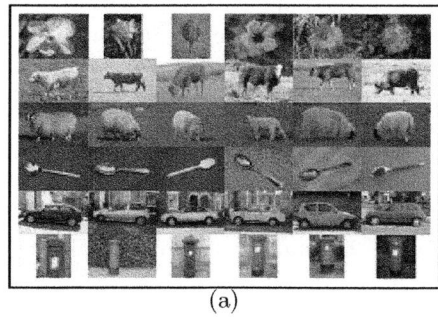 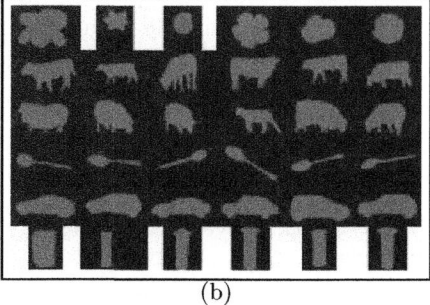

(a)   (b)

Fig. 2. (a) Sample training images one row for each category, (b) corresponding foreground masks

Testing Phase

1. Segment the query image using Graph-cut (Unsupervised) [13].
2. Prune the output to remove small, insignificant disconnected regions.
3. Segment pruned Graph-cut output using K-medoid and delete small segments.
4. Extract features from output of Step 3 and use SVMs to decide the category and sub-category of the object in the test image.
5. Create a set of foreground candidate blobs using the significant sub-segments obtained from Step 3. For each such combination of parts, perform:
   (a) Extract contour map using Canny edge operator [3].
   (b) Compute the Convolution function between edge map and Distance Transform (DT) map (in step 1(c) of training stage), for the set of foreground gallery samples belonging to the category detected in Step 4.
6. Merge the results retrieved by all candidate blobs and rank order the outputs using Convolution values.

3.2   Details and Issues in the Design

In the following, we describe a few issues and design details involved in the implementation of the framework given in Fig. 1.

1. The initialization of Graph-cut process on the query image is done leaving a set of border pixels of constant width (≥ 5) as background.
2. Pruning uses morphological processing (cleaning, filling) to remove small isolated patches in Graph-cut output.
3. K-medoid with K $= 4$ is used for part segmentation. Feature used are mean (μ) of R, G and B pixels over a 3*3 window.
4. Features used for different stages are given in Table 1.
5. The training of SVMs (using linear kernel) [4] are done using a set of gallery samples (see Fig. 2 for a few samples). The performances using testing set in Table 2 are given in Table 3.

6. Currently, filtering the background segments is done using a hypothesis that the smallest part (identified by K-medoid) belongs to the background.
7. A set of blobs are formed using different combinations of k-subregions, as: (i) all the blobs, (ii) leaving smallest one out, and (iii) the largest two blobs. The set of blobs form candidate foreground objects in the query scene.

Table 1. Processes and corresponding features used

Process	Features
Graph-Cut	color
SUPER SVM-L1	HOG
MULTI CLASS SVM-L2	HOG + MTH
Part Segmentor	color intensity mean
Matching	DT

Table 2. Number of training and testing samples per category

Classes	Training Set		Testing Set	
Animate	Cow(25) Flower(25) Sheep(25)	75	Cow(17) Flower(14) Sheep(17)	48
Inanimate	Car(25) Spoon(25) Postbox(25)	75	Car(26) Spoon(20) Postbox(15)	61

Table 3. Confusion matrices for classification results: (a) Animate vs. Inanimate (using SUPER SVM-L1), (b) Cow, Flower and Sheep (using MULTI Class SVM-L2), (c) Car, Spoon and Postbox (using MULTI Class SVM-L2)

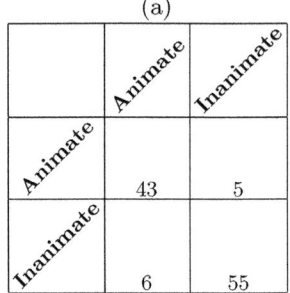

(a)

	Animate	Inanimate
Animate	43	5
Inanimate	6	55

(b)

	Cow	Flower	Sheep
Cow	12	4	1
Flower	3	10	1
Sheep	4	0	13

(c)

	Car	Spoon	Postbox
Car	26	0	0
Spoon	6	13	1
Postbox	1	4	10

In the following section, the intermediate results of proposed framework and visual comparative study with a state-of-the-art work [11] is presented.

4 Experimental Results

We have obtained image databases from various sources - Berkeley (301 images), Microsoft research (4474), PASCAL object recognition database collection (27,160) etc. We have filtered the same, and selected those which only have a predominant foreground object, in the presence of smooth background texture, less clutter etc. In order to incorporate semantic information, the gallery has been categorized as shown in Fig. 3.

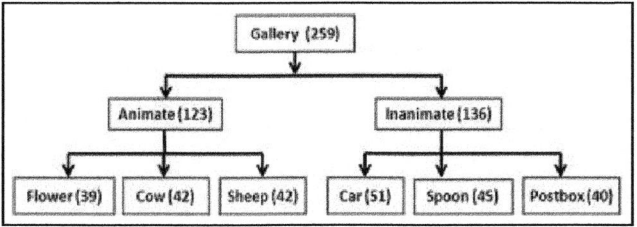

Fig. 3. A dendogram of library of real-world gallery samples/objects, to be used for smart Image Segmentation

Fig. 4. (a) Query Sample, (b) Graph-cut and (c) Pruned graph-cut outputs

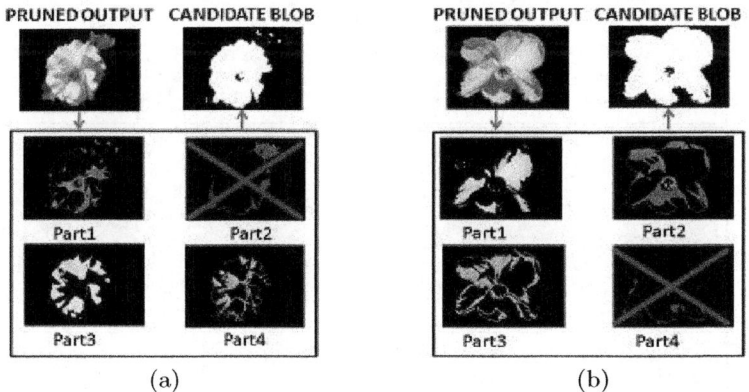

Fig. 5. Part segmented output; (a) Part2 is shown to be discarded as the least area, (b) Part4 is shown to be discarded as the least area

During training, HOG and MTH features are extracted from the foreground objects in the training set using manually created foreground masks. HOG is used for training the super-SVM-L1 to distinguish between animate and

I - ANIMATE

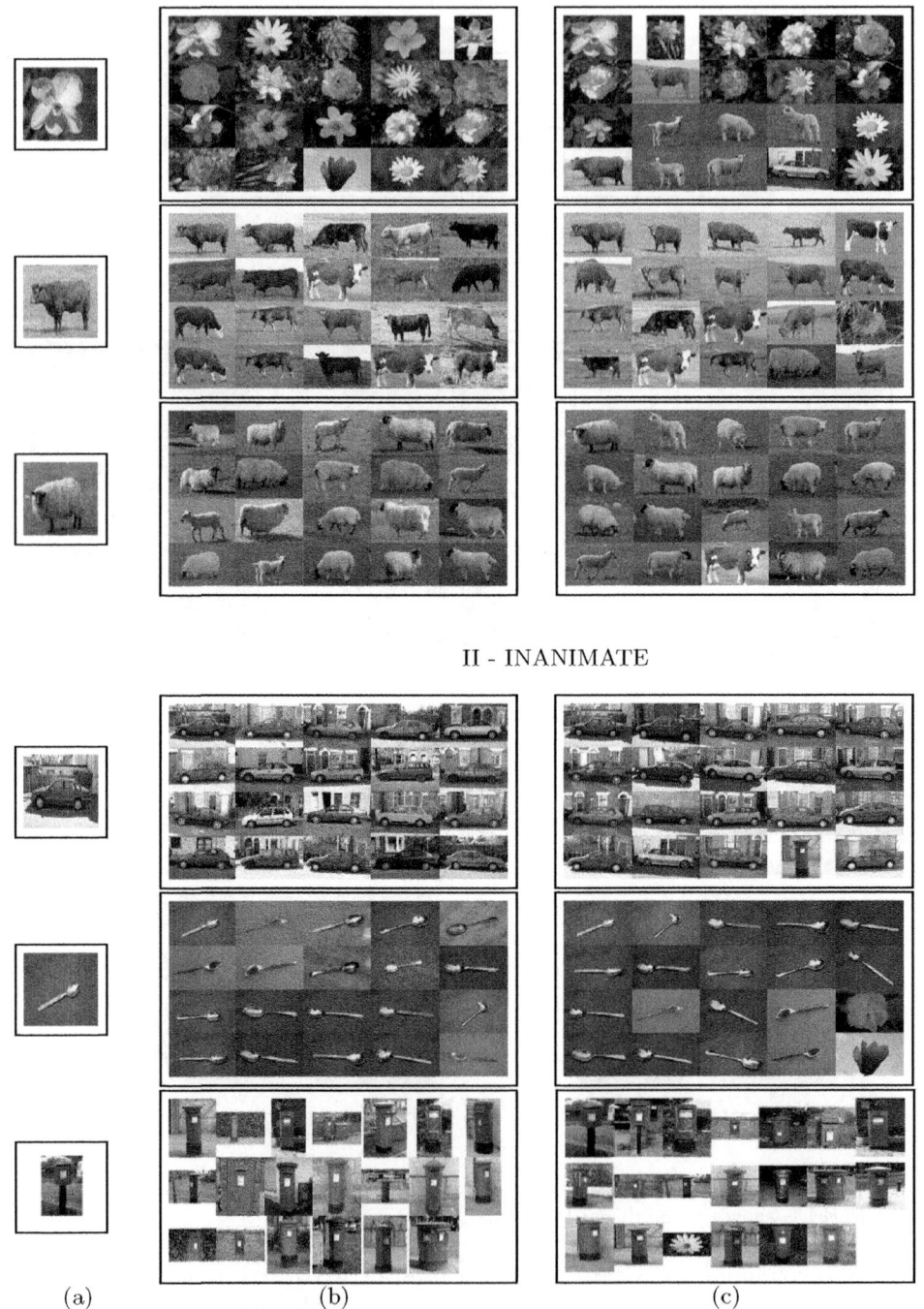

II - INANIMATE

(a)   (b)   (c)

Fig. 6. (a) Sample queries, (b) Corresponding CBIR outputs of proposed framework, (c) Output of an existing method of CBIR, based on MTH [11] for I - animate, II - inanimate class of objects

inanimate category. HOG and MTH features are used to train multi-class SVM-L2 to distinguish within animate (Cow, Flowers and Sheep) and inanimate (Car, Spoon and Postbox) sub-category. For each image in the categorized image database (gallery) distance transform (DT) corresponding to its foreground mask is stored in the categorized feature database, which is later used for template matching.

Graph-cut is applied (see Fig. 4(a)) to extract the foreground object (see Fig. 4b) from the given query image. In order to remove isolated patches first pruning is performed (see Fig. 4c), followed by K-medoid based part segmentor.

The segment with the least area is discarded from the output of part segmentor, using an assumption that it may contain background information (see Fig. 5). Next, we use the remaining $K - 1$ segments to get a set of candidate foreground blobs. In order to decide the sub-category of an object in the query image HOG feature is extracted from the cleaned graph-cut output and given to the trained super-SVM-L1 to decide the super-category. HOG and MTH features are given to multi-class SVM-L2 to determine its sub-category. Edge map of the candidate foreground blob, obtained by Canny edge operator [3], is now matched with the DTs of foreground samples within sub-category of objects in gallery (given by multiclass SVM) to give rank ordered output.

Figure 6 (a) shows sample query images. Results of our proposed methodology on these query images are shown in Fig. 6 (b), while the result of the state-of-the-art Multi-Texton Histogram [11] for the same is shown in Fig. 6 (c). Part I and II of Fig. 6 show results for animate and inanimate class of objects. It is apparent from Fig. 6 that the proposed method outperforms MTH. From the results shown in Fig. 6, it is clear that similar object (say, for example spoon) even with different color and texture background are retrieved by our proposed methodology which is not possible with MTH. Moreover, with MTH different objects with similar color and texture as that of the query image are also retrieved (see Figs. 6 (c)). The reason for this is that MTH is non-object centric, whereas our method is object centric (extracts features from the probable foreground region).

In general, over 109 test cases were observed, within which failure occurred in 27 cases. Performance analysis using precision/recall metric shows promising results when compared with the same for the method presented in [11]. Table 4 shows the computational time required for different modules of our framework.

Table 4. Computational time (in secs.) for different modules in the framework (with a Pentium 4, 3.40 GHz CPU, 2 GB RAM), averaged over 50 samples

Graph-cut	Part-Segmentor	SVM-Testing	Matching	Total Time
88.51	6.92	2.1	9.5	107.03

5   Conclusions

We have proposed a framework for simultaneously solving the problem of object recognition and detection, using a SLAR framework. The design of the framework is motivated by cognitive model of the human brain. The SLAR framework is semi-supervised, combining supervised classifier for object recognition and unsupervised processes used for detection/localization. Performance is better than a texton based CBIR technique proposed in the recent past.

The classification performance at each stage can be improved by using Probabilistic SVM. Segmentation can be improved using background information and rich shape features like CSS. Experimentation, may be extended for a large set of different image categories. The framework can be improved by utilizing state-of-the-art cognitive science driven algorithms, like saliency detection in an image and Active learning or Transfer learning methods. Extension of this work for objects with hole, occlusion of foreground objects and shading variations of target objects form a nice scope of future work.

Acknowledgements. A part of this work was sponsored by CAIR (DRDO), Bangalore, India.

References

1. Baars, B.J., Gage, N.M.: Cognition, Brain, and Consciousness, Introduction to Cognitive Neuroscience. Academic Press (2010)
2. Boykov, Y., Funka-Lea, G.: Graph cuts and efficient n-d image segmentation. International Journal of Computer Vision 70, 109–131 (2006)
3. Canny, J.: A computational approach to edge detection. IEEE Transactions on Pattern Analysis and Machine Intelligence 8(6), 679–698 (1986)
4. Chang, C.C., Lin, C.-J.: Libsvm: A library for support vector machines (2001)
5. Cortes, C., Vapnik, V.: Support vector network. Machine Learning 20, 1–25 (1995)
6. Felzenszwalb, P.F., Girshick, R.B., McAllester, D.A., Ramanan, D.: Object detection with discriminatively trained part-based models. IEEE Transactions on Pattern Analysis and Machine Intelligence 32, 1627–1645 (2010)
7. http://research.microsoft.com/enus/projects/objectclassrecognition/
8. Leibe, B., Leonardis, A., Schiele, B.: Robust object detection with interleaved categorization and segmentation. International Journal of Computer Vision 27(1-3), 259–289 (2007)
9. Levin, A., Weiss, Y.: Learning to combine bottom-up and top-down segmentation. International Journal on Computer Vision 81, 105–118 (2009)
10. Lin, C.H., Chen, R.-T., Chan, Y.K.: A smart content-based image retrieval system based on color and texture feature. Image and Vision Computing 27(6), 658–665 (2009)
11. Liu, G.-H., Zhang, L., Hou, Y.-K., Li, Z.-Y., Yang, J.-Y.: Image retrieval based on multi-texton histogram. Pattern Recognition 43, 2380–2389 (2010)
12. Rahman, M. M., Bhattacharya, P., Desai, B.C.: A unified image retrieval framework on local visual and semantic concept-based feature spaces. Journal of Visual Communication and Image Representation 27, 658–665 (2009)

13. Rother, C., Kolmogorov, V., Blake, A.: Grabcut: Interactive foreground extraction using iterated graph-cuts. ACM Transactions on Graphics 23(3), 309–334 (2004)
14. Wang, J.Z., Li, J., Wiederhold, G.: SIMPLICITY: semantics sensitive integrated matching for picture libraries. IEEE Transactions on Pattern Analysis and Machine Intellegence 23, 947–963 (2001)
15. Wu, Y., Wu, Y.: Shape-based image retrieval using combining global and local shape features. In: 2nd International Congress on Image and Signal Processing, pp. 1–5 (October 2009)

A Novel Statistical Model to Evaluate the Performance of EBGM Based Face Recognition

Munmun Chakraborty, Kunal Chanda, and Debasis Mazumdar

CDAC, Kolkata
{munmun.chakraborty,kunal.chanda,
debasis.mazumdar}@cdackolkata.in

Abstract. Pose, illumination, expression and other transitive and demographic variates present in the facial images have significant effects on the performance of face recognition system. A Gibbs sampler based statistical simulation algorithm is presented to evaluate the performance of EBGM based face recognition system. A new set of microscopic and stochastic image features are proposed which takes key role in determining the quality of facial images. Effects of these features on the performance of the EBGM based face recognition system are evaluated using an algorithm based on random effects model and Gibbs sampler.

Keywords: Face Recognition, Random Effects Model, Elastic Bunch Graph.

1 Introduction

Computerized face recognition systems are now a day's available as a commercial product. When designing a face recognition system it is very important to know how to measure the accuracy of the system. The performance evaluation of any face recognition system plays a key role to assess how well it serves its purpose of matching facial images obtained from people to stored templates synthesized from sample data. In the literature several statistical methods have been proposed to date, exploiting the correspondence between the authentication problem and statistical decision theory [12], [13]. Shen et al defined performance metrics of biometric authentication system in terms of error rates. The present paper addresses the issue of performance evaluation of elastic bunch graph matching (EBGM) based face recognition system using random effects model. Our contribution can be quantified as (i) Analysis of effects of different covariates which affect the performance of an EBGM face recognition system based on experimental data and supplemented with human perceptual data.(ii) Simulation of the score distributions for authentic and imposters, based on these image properties and (iii) What error rates of false acceptance (FAR) and false rejection (FRR) can be expected when an EBGM based Face Recognition System is applied to a large unknown database. The rest of the paper is organized as follows:

M.K. Kundu et al. (Eds.): PerMIn 2012, LNCS 7143, pp. 288–297, 2012.

Section 2 describes different covariates and their effects on facial features. A brief description of the random effects model and its application for performance evaluation of EBGM based face recognition system is presented in section 3.

2 Different Covariates and Their Effects on Facial Features

Any biometric authentication systems developed are expected to offer quite high level of performance even when used with databases containing information on millions of people [2]. In the deployment scenario, the situation becomes further complicated because of different levels of variations introduced between the database image and the query image of the same person. The most common causes of variations between the query and database image are as follows: (i) variations due to the difference of pose, illumination, expressions, age etc. (ii) degraded image quality. (iii) internal and external ornamentation like growth of beard, moustache, use of spectacles or even application of loud make up etc. The present study is intended to result in a comparative description of the effects of image properties on different components of the feature vector. The obtained result is utilized to develop a model of feature prioritization. Finally the effect of these covariates on the performance of EBGM based face recognition system[1] is modeled using statistical random effects model [3] ,[4], [5]. In light of the model the following issues are analyzed:

- Effects of different covariates, which affect the performance of an EBGM, based face recognition system.
- Prediction of the score distributions for authentic and imposters, based on these image properties.
- Error rates of false acceptance (FAR) and false rejection (FRR) which can be expected when an EBGM based face recognition system is applied to a large unknown database?

The effect of image properties on the performance of biometric authentication system has been studied by many researchers [6], [7], [8]. Our study is a bit different from them, in the sense that, it analyzes the effects of different image covariates, transitive subject covariates (like pose, expression, illumination variations) and demographic covariates (like age, ethnicity etc.) on the low level feature properties. For example, in EBGM, a set of Gabor jets of different orientations and resolutions are employed to collect textural information around each fiducial point. These information are ultimately converted into feature vector to represent the unique biometric property of any face. One important issue is how unique these feature vectors are across the different variations expected in any deployment scenario. In the following sections we will present experimental data showing the variations occurring in the feature vectors across the different image properties, demographic parameters and transitive subject covariates. The result obtained is used to develop a model to validate face images and to check whether the images are suitable for use in identification documents. Validated face images should allow automatic face recognition to be successfully performed. The parameters of the face image concerned are numerous and are dealing with image resolution, sharpness and focus, image tonal range and color, lighting, subject and scene composition. The set of parameters, chosen in our experiment, falls under two categories. The parameters related to the image properties are the following: image resolution, image brightness, image sharpness. The parameters related to the demographic and transitive subject covariates are: age, pose variations, expression variations. In the following we present some results to show the variations of the feature vectors caused by different parameters. Our study is focused on the key parameters like image covariates, transitive subject covariates and demographic covariates having major role in affecting the performance of an EBGM based face recognition system.

2.1   Image Parameters and Their Influence on Feature Vectors

Automatic face recognition systems are expected to operate in various field conditions where the imaging environment is unconstrained. Low contrast or blurring, poor ambient illumination conditions are the common factors in the deployment scenario, which deteriorates the performance of the system. To classify images among the good, average and poor quality a set of image parameters are chosen as described below: (i)Mean intensity (In) across an image computed in the HSI plane. Any image captured in good ambient illumination possesses the value within a range having distinct lower and upper limit. Any value smaller than the lower limit corresponds to an image with poor intensity. High values correspond to good ambient illumination. It should further be noted that the value beyond certain upper limit resulted in an abnormal flashed image which falls under the poor category. (ii) Ratio (r) of the average value of the high frequencies to the average value of the low frequencies present in the Fourier spectrum of the image. Larger values of r corresponds to the presence of higher frequencies in the image. Higher frequencies indicate the presence of sharper features of the image like edge, corner etc. Stated macroscopically, the variable r quantifies the relative proportion of the sharp features in the image. Physically it is an index for measuring the level of image focus. It should also be noted here that some images posses the value of r abnormally high although the image quality falls under the poor class. Scanned images, images from the newsprint are sometimes grainy in appearance. The grain boundaries introduce higher frequencies and make the value of r abnormally high although the image over all quality is bad. (iii) Coefficient of kurtosis (k) of the distribution of frequencies in the Fourier spectrum of the image. High value of k will corresponds to a sharply peaked distribution containing a few frequencies. In the spatial domain it corresponds to an image of homogeneous pixel values i.e. less contrastive. Less value of k on the other hand represents contrastive images. In the present work the scheme of classification of images into poor, average and good category has two steps. In the beginning the classification is made by humans of different age groups. This categorization is used in the next step to prepare the example sets and the corresponding learning rules for a decision tree [12], [13]. to ultimately classify the facial image dataset hierarchically into three classes based on the aforementioned image covariates . In the first part of the experiment human subjects were chosen from three age groups, namely, the age group of (8-12) years, (18-22) years and (34-50) and designated as young, adult and old respectively. Table 1 represent the number of samples classified into three groups (column wise) by the human subjects taken from three age groups (row wise). The total number of sixty face was chosen to prepare the sample set.

Table 1.

	Poor	Average	Good
Child	17	22	21
Adult	20	21	19
Old	19	20	21

Table 2.

Variations	Degrees of Freedom	Mean Square Variations	F Statistics
Row Variation $V\gamma^2 = 0.0144$	No. of row=a $d.f.r = (a - 1)= 2$	Across row S2 $\gamma = V\gamma(a -1)$ $= 0.0072(a- 1)$	$F_{df}=2,4$ $=0.00323$
Column Variation $Vc = 9.1068$	No. of col=b $d.f.c = (b- 1) =2$	Across column $S2c =$ $Vc(b-1)$ $= 4.5534$	$F_{df}=2,4$ $=2.0487$
Total Variation $Vtotal = 18.0112$	$d.f.t = (a.b - 1)$ $= 8$		

Table 2 shows the statistical result of the ANOVA test conducted on this data set. It should be noted here that the value of F = 1.88 being smaller than both $F0.95,2,6 = 5.14$ and $F0.99,2,6 = 10.9$ ensures the null hypothesis that the mean of the three classes are the same [13]. Images classified by the decision tree trained on this data set and learned the class boundaries based on judgment into good, average and poor qualities are shown in Table 3 along with the corresponding values of the image covariates and the class name. The schematic representation of the decision tree and the different classes are shown in Fig.1.

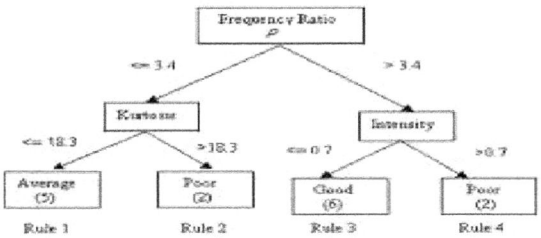

Fig. 1. Schematic representation of the decision tree

It is to be noted here that the attribute ρ in Fig.1 has the maximum information gain as it represent the root node of the decision tree. This is a very trivial fact describing the truth that contrastive image brings more clarity to the human perception. At the end of the classification we find that the good images belong to the class having larger value of ρ (<3.4), moderate value of the illumination ≤ 0.7). Image under the average class has lower values of ρ ($\leq$3.4) and lower value of $K \leq$ 18.3 . One leaf node ($\rho \leq 3.4$ and $K > 18.3$) of the decision tree corresponds to less contrastive blur images and falls under the poor class. Another leaf node ($\rho > 3.4$ and In > 0.7) presents the over lighted and hyper flashed images that are again categorized as poor class. In the following sections we will describe how the feature vectors changes under the influence of transitive subject covariates.

Table 3.

Image	Mean intensity (I_a)	Ratio of average high frequency to low frequency $\rho = \dfrac{\langle f_{high} \rangle}{\langle f_{low} \rangle}$	Coefficient of kurtosis of the Fourier spectrum (κ)	Quality of the image
	0.5	4.4	8.6	good
	0.5	4.8	6.3	good
	0.4	3.4	9.2	average
	0.7	2.7	9.4	average
	0.6	2.9	14.8	poor
	0.7	2.7	83.0	poor

2.2   Variations of Feature Vectors Across the Transitive Subject Covariates

Recognizing a face across pose, illumination and expression is a well-researched subject. Many significant and effective algorithms are already available for this purpose [11], [14]. Currently many researchers have reported their work in the area of face recognition across age variation [15]. In this section we will present some experimental results to show how the feature vector representing the textures in the feature space changes with different transitive subject covariates like pose, illumination, expression and age in case of face recognition using EBGM algorithm. Given an image patch I(x,y) around any fiducial point in a face, its Gabor transformation is given by eqn.(1):

$$W_{mn}(x,y) = \int I(x_1,y_1) g^*_{mn}(x - x_1, y - y_1) dx_1 dy_1 \qquad (1)$$

The coefficients represents the projection of the image patch along the Gabor filter of resolution index m (varies 1 to 5 in our case) and orientation index n (varies 1 to 8 in an interval of 22.5° to include 180°). The integral in the right hand side of the equation represents the convolution of the image function I with the complex conjugate of the Gabor filters represented by g^*_{mn}. We assume that the local texture regions are spatially homogeneous. A feature vector of dimension 40 is now constructed using the coefficients of all Gabor coefficients W_{mn} (m=1....5 and n=1....8). Let $\bar{f}_r^i$ represents the feature vector at the i th fiducial point (i=1....14) of a face at reference condition (i.e. a pure mugshot taken at constrained illumination condition and without any pose or expression).Further we assume that $\bar{f}_t^{\,i}$ represent the feature vector at the same fiducial point of the same face having variation in terms of pose illumination or expression. The distance between the two feature vectors $\bar{f}_r^{\,i}$ and $\bar{f}_t^{\,i}$ in the feature space is measured using a correlation distance metric $d_c(r,t)$ analogous to the similarity function defined in eqn (2) as follows:

$$d_c(r,t) = \frac{(\bar{f}_r^{\,i})(\bar{f}_t^{\,i})^T}{\sqrt{(\bar{f}_r^{\,i})^2\,(\bar{f}_t^{\,i})^{T^2}}} \tag{2}$$

The correlation metric $d_c(r,t)$ being a measure of the variation of the textural property has a strong influence on the accuracy of the face recognition system. Larger value of it will lead towards poor identification performance. The function $d_c(r,t)$ is measured separately for illumination, pose, expression and age variation. In the next section we describe the significance of different covariates on the statistical performance evaluation of EBGM based system.

3   Relating Performance Evaluation to Covariates

Performance evaluation of any face recognition system is important to assess how well it serves its purpose of matching facial image obtained from a subject to templates stored in the database. Present section addresses the issues of performance evaluation of an EBGM based face recognition system using random effects model The model was successfully used in many stochastic problems like analysis of the weights of young laboratory rats . Unlike the fixed effects models like regression or ANOVA, which are restricted to make inference about the covariate effects only to the database in hand, the random effects model can provide a general inference to a larger or even different database drawn from the same population. A random effects model assumes that a particular subset of subjects present in a database is a random sample from a bigger population, so that the inference easily extends to that bigger population. The model has the capability to make valid inference about the effects of the covariates and predicted error rates if another subset of individuals (even different from the current sample) is drawn from this population. Another advantage of the random effects model is that it takes into account heterogeneity across individuals in their regression coefficients with the help of a probability distribution unlike fixed effects models, thus capturing more inherent variability in the data that involve repeated measures or multilevel data structures. Several works has already been conducted in this direction. Givens used random effects in a Generalized Linear Mixed Models (GLMM) framework for evaluating the performance of PCA based face recognition algorithm. Sinjini used the model for performance evaluation of biometric authentication systems in general and in specific they reported the result for three face recognition system based on (i) MACE filter system , (ii) GMM based face recognition system and (iii) Facial asymmetry - Based system. In the present work we apply the random effects model in the context of performance evaluation of EBGM based face recognition system in terms of different covariates. In the following two consecutive section we describe the basics of the random effects model and its application in evaluating the performance of EBGM based face recognition system.

3.1   The Random Effects Model (REM) for Face Recognition

A face recognition system based on EBGM algorithm is considered and we wish to develop a random effects model (REM) to evaluate the performance of the system. We would further like to incorporate the effects of different covariates like image parameters, pose, illumination etc. into our model. Let the database be considered as a subset of face images randomly collected from a larger universal population of face images. Let there be p people in the database, i.e. the cardinality of the subset is p. Further we suppose that there are n number of query images for the i th person, = 1,2,....,p which gives a total number of np query images for the entire database. Besides we also have a template bank where a template for each of these p individuals is stored in the training stage. In the authentication stage, each of the n images is matched to each of these p templates. Let Yij denote the match score for the j th query image of the i th subject in the database, when tested against one of the templates stored in the database. If $Yij > \tau$ (where τ is a predefined threshold), the system declares the person tested as an " authentic", otherwise, if $Yij < \tau$,the system decides that a match has not been found and the person tested is declared as an "imposter". Then the false rejection rate (FRR) and the false acceptance rate (FAR) are defined in eqn (3) and (4) as follows:

$$FRR = P(Y_{ij} \leq \tau | Y_{ij} \in authentic) = \int_{-\infty}^{\tau} \xi_A(x)dx,$$

$$FAR = P(Y_{ij} > \tau | Y_{ij} \in imposter) = \int_{\tau}^{\infty} \xi_I(x)dx$$

(3) and (4)

where $\xi_A(.)$ and $\xi_I(.)$, denote the distribution of the match scores for the authentic and the imposters respectively. Let $x_{ij}^{(m)}$ m , = 1,2,..,M be a collection of covariates associated with the image which affect the matching score. In the set of covariate, one of the members assumes value one if the subject is matched against the peer matched pair and equal to zero otherwise. Other members of the set correspond to the image covariates, transitive subject covariates and demographic covariates. Under these assumptions The random effects model for the EBGM based face recognition system is given by eqn (5) and eqn (6) as follows:

$$\zeta(Y_{ij}) \stackrel{ind}{\sim} N(\alpha_i + \sum_{m=1}^{M} \beta_i^m x_{ij}^m, \sigma^2), i = 1.........,k, j = 1,......n_i$$

(5)

$$\theta_i = (\alpha_i, \beta_i^m, \ldots\ldots\ldots, \beta_i^M)^T \overset{ind}{\sim} MVN(\theta_0, \Sigma), i = 1, \ldots\ldots, k, \tag{6}$$

where $\zeta(.)$ is called the link function. It is a monotonic function capable of transforming the scores to ensure conformity of the response variable to the underlying assumptions of the model, such as, normality, homoscedasticity, etc $\theta_0 = (\alpha_0, \beta_0^1 \ldots\ldots \beta_i^M)$ is an (M+1)- dimensional vector and Σ is an (M+1) X (M+1) covariance matrix. We further represent our observed match scores, after transforming using the link function $\zeta(.)$ as y $= (\zeta(y_{ij})$, i= 1\ldots\ldots p and j = 1\ldots\ldots n_i). The (conjugate) prior distribution assigned to σ^2, θ_0 and Σ in the model described by Givens et al.[23] , Sinjini et al. are as follows:

σ^2 = IG (a,b), $\theta_0 \sim N((\eta, C)$ and $\Sigma^{-1} \sim$ Wishart $((\rho R)^{-1}, \rho)$,where IG denotes the inverse gamma distribution. R is a matrix and $\rho \geq 2$ is a scalar degrees of freedom parameter characterizing the Wishart distribution. All the hyper parameters in the model a , b, η, C, ρ, R are assumed known. The parameters to be estimated are $\theta_i, \theta_0, \Sigma$ and . Gibbs sampling is used to simulate from the conditional posterior distributions of each of the four unknown parameters given the remaining three termed full conditional. The closed-form expressions of posterior distributions are given by eqn (7),(8),(9),(10)and(11) as follows:

$$\theta_i | y_i, \theta_0, \Sigma^{-1}, \sigma^2 \sim N(D_i(\frac{1}{\sigma^2} X_i^T y_i + \Sigma^{-1}\theta_0), D_i), i = 1, \ldots, p, \tag{7}$$

where

$$D_i^{-1} = \frac{1}{\sigma^2} X_i^T X_i + \Sigma^{-1}, \qquad y_i = (y_{i1}, y_{i2}, \ldots\ldots, y_{ini})^T, \tag{8}$$

$$X_i = \begin{pmatrix} 1 & x_{i1}^1 & \cdots & x_{i1}^M \\ \vdots & & & \\ \vdots & & & \\ 1 & x_{ini}^1 & \cdots & x_{ini}^M \end{pmatrix}, \theta_0 | y_i, \theta_i, \Sigma^{-1}, \sigma^2 \sim N(V(p\Sigma^{-1}\overline{\theta} + C^{-1}\eta), V) \tag{9}$$

where $V = (p\Sigma^{-1} + C^{-1})^{-1}$ and $\overline{\theta} = \frac{1}{p}\sum_{i=1}^{p}\theta_i$

$$\Sigma^{-1} | y, \theta_i, \theta_0, \sigma^2 \sim Wishart \left(\left[\sum_{i=1}^{p}(\theta_i - \theta_0)(\theta_i - \theta_0)^T + \rho R \right]^{-1}, p + \rho \right) \tag{10}$$

$$\sigma^2 \big| y, \theta_i, \theta_0, \Sigma^{-1} \sim IG\left(\frac{n}{2} + a, \frac{1}{2}\sum_{i=1}^{p}(y_i - X_i\theta_i)^T(y_i - X_i\theta_i) + b\right), \qquad (11)$$

where $n = \sum_{i=1}^{p} n_i$ and IG denotes an inverse Gamma distribution. Following Sinjini et al. The values of the hyperpriors are chosen, namely, $C^{-1} = 0$, $a = b = \frac{1}{\varepsilon}$ where $\varepsilon = 0.001$. To ensure proper mixing of the Markov chains different starting values of the chains are generated using a random number generator. The convergence of the Gibbs sampler is shown using trace plots . Let $\chi \equiv \{\theta_i, \theta_0, \Sigma, \sigma^2\}$ be the set of parameters to be estimated for the model. The Gibbs sampler yields a Markov chain $(\chi^{(i)}, i = 1, 2, \ldots)$ whose distribution converges to the true posterior distribution of the parameters beyond the burn-in period described as in eqn (12):

$$\chi = \frac{1}{(n - n_1)} \sum_{i=n_1+1}^{n} \chi^{(i)} \cong E\{\chi|y\} \qquad (12)$$

Once the marginal posteriors for the population parameters and the posterior predictive distributions of the match scores are obtained, we can estimate the predictive distribution of the link function-transformed match score $\zeta(y)$ for a score of a new individual using a kernel density of the form as in eqn (13)

$$p(\zeta(y)|y) = \int p(\zeta(y)|\theta_i, \sigma^2) p(\theta_i, \sigma^2|y) \partial\theta_i \, \partial\sigma^2 \qquad (13)$$

Since the authentic and imposter score distributions are expected to be well separated; a mixture of Gaussian kernels are fitted to the posterior predictive distributions of score. The simulated score distribution for authentic and imposter are shown in Fig. 2. The simulated FAR and FRR curve is given in Fig. 3.

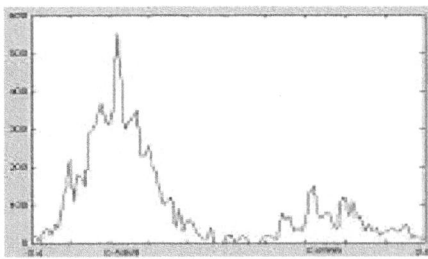   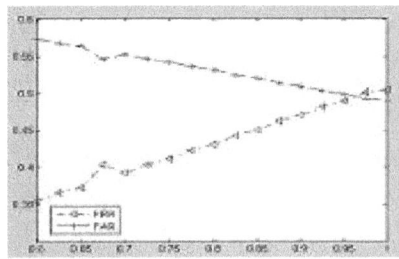

Fig. 2. Simulated score distribution   **Fig. 3.** Simulated FAR and FRR curve

4   Conclusion

In the present paper a simulation algorithm is described to test and evaluate the performance of EBGM based Face Recognition System. The algorithm analyzes the effects of different covariates causing derogatory effects on the overall performance of the system. The macroscopic features of facial images like contrast, blurriness etc are mapped in terms of microscopic and statistical image properties.

References

1. Wiskott, L., Fellous, J.M., Kruger, N., Malsburg, C.V.D.: Face Recognition by Elastic Bunch Graph Matching. In: Intelligent Biometric Techniques in Fingerprint and Face Recognition, ch. 11, pp. 355–396 (1999)
2. Phillips, P.J., Scruggs, W.T., O'Toole, A.J.F., Patrick, J., Bowyer, K.W., Schott, C.L., Sharpe, M.: FRVT 2006 and ICE 2006 Large-Scale Results. NISTIR 7408 National Institute of Standards and Technology Gaithersburg, MD 20899,
   http://www.frvt.org
3. Gelfand, A.E., Hills, S.E., Racine-Poon, A., Smith, A.F.M.: Illustration of Bayesian Inference in Normal Data Models Using Gibbs Sampling. J. Am. Statistical Assoc. 85(412), 972–985 (1990)
4. Gelman, A., Carlin, J.B., Stern, H.S., Rubin, D.B.: Bayesian Data Analysis. Chapman and Hall (1995)
5. Mitra, S., Savvides, M., Brockwell, A.: Statistical Performance Evaluation of Biometric Authentication Systems Using Random Effects Models. IEEE Trans. PAMI 29, 517–530 (2007)
6. McLachlan, G., Peel, D.: Finite Mixture Models. John Wiley and Sons (2000)
7. Givens, G.H., Beveridge, J.R., Draper, B.A., Bolme, D.: A Statistical Conf. Assessment of Subject Factors in the PCA Recognition of Human Faces. In: Proc. IEEE Computer Vision and Pattern Recognition (2003)
8. Givens, G.H., Beveridge, J.R., Draper, B.A., Grother, P., Phillips, P.J.: How Features of the Human Face Affect Recognition: A Statistical Comparison of Three Face Recognition Algorithms. In: Proc. IEEE Conf. Computer Vision and Pattern Recognition, pp. 381–388 (2004)
9. Phillips, P.J., Grother, P., Ross, J., Blackburn, D., Tabassi, E., Bone, M.: Face recognition vendor test 2002: Evaluation report (March 2003)
10. Blackburn, D., Bone, M., Philips, P.J.: Facial recognition vendor test 2000: evaluation report (2000)
11. Gross, R., Shi, J., Cohn, J.: Quo vadis face recognition? In: Third Worhshop on Empirical Evaluation Methods in Computer Vision (2001)
12. Pao, Y.H.: Adaptive Pattern Recognition and Neural Networks. Addison-Wesley Publishing Co.
13. Quinlan, J.R.: C45 Programs For Machine learning. Kaufmann Publishers,
    http://www.rulequest.com
14. Zhao, W., Chellapa, R., Phillips, P.J., Rosenfield, A.: Face Recognition: A Literature Survey. ACM Computing Surveys (CSUR) 35(4), 399–458 (2003)
15. Unsang, P., Yiying, T., Jain, A.K.: Age Invariant Face Recognition. PAMI 32(5), 947–954 (2010)

A New Proposal for Locality Preserving Projection

Gitam Shikkenawis and Suman K. Mitra

Dhirubhai Ambani Institute of Information and Communication Technology,
Gandhinagar, Gujarat, India-382007
{201011049,suman_mitra}@daiict.ac.in

Abstract. Locality Preserving Projection (LPP) is the recently proposed approach for dimensionality reduction to preserve the neighbourhood information. It is widely used for finding the intrinsic dimensionality of data. As LPP preserves the information about the nearest neighbours of data points, it may lead to misclassification in the overlapping regions of two or more classes. The conventional method works on a graph based technique where weights given to the edges are used to emphasize the local information. In this paper, we propose a new weighing scheme for the neighbourhood preserving graph which also gives importance to the data points that are at a moderate distance, in addition to the nearest points. This helps in resolving the ambiguity occurring in the overlapping regions. The proposal is tested on varying datasets.

Keywords: Dimensionality Reduction, Principal Component Analysis, Locality Preserving Projection.

1 Introduction

There are many cases in Image Recognition where intrinsically lower dimensional data lies in a higher dimensional space and in such cases it is advantageous to work in the subspace instead of the full image space. The goal of subspace analysis is to determine the intrinsic dimensionality of the data point and extract the principal components referred to as the basis functions of the manifold. There are different ways of finding the basis depending upon the required structure. In these subspace based methods, the basis vectors found from the training set of images are used as the projection vectors. Each image in the training set is projected on the new less dimensional subspace of the original high dimensional one. Recognition is performed by projecting the input image into subspace and then classifying it by comparing its position in the newly created subspace with the position of known (trained) data points.

LPP [1] (Locality Preserving Projection) is the recently proposed approach for dimensionality reduction. In many real world problems, local manifold structure is more important than the global Euclidean structure [2]. LPP finds an embedding that preserves local information, and obtains a subspace that best detects the essential data manifold structure. In LPP, neighbourhood information is stored in a graph and basis vectors are found using the notion of Laplacian of the graph. A weighing function is used to assign weights to the edges of the

M.K. Kundu et al. (Eds.): PerMIn 2012, LNCS 7143, pp. 298–305, 2012.

graph. This function incurs heavy penalty if data points are mapped far apart hence giving more emphasis to the nearest neighbours.

LPP has been applied in a variety of areas for both dimensionality reduction and recognition purpose. Laplacianfaces [2] is the technique based on LPP which finds the face subspace that best describes the manifold structure. It is a widely used approach for human face recognition. He et al. [3] extended the idea of LPP for document representation and indexing known as locality preserving indexing (LPI). Locality preserving clustering (LPC) [4] was constructed using the concepts of LPP for image database clustering. Incremental LPP [5], [6] was used for information retrieval in which relevance feedback was used to enhance the performance. A two dimensional extension of LPP was also proposed by Sibao et al. [7] in which 2D matrices were directly used instead of the conventional 1D vector based approach.

Many other dimensionality reduction techniques have also been proposed in literature.PCA (Principal Component Analysis) [8] is the most widely used method for dimensionality reduction. In this approach, eigenvectors of the covariance matrix that capture the maximum variance in the given data set are considered as the basis function. By choosing appropriate number of eigenvectors that best describe the data, dimensionality can be reduced without loosing much information. It is a global structure preserving technique.

LDA (Linear Discriminant Analysis) [9] encodes discriminating information in a linearly separable space using basis that are not necessarily orthogonal [2]. The project axes are searched on which, the data points of different classes are far apart from each other while the data pints from the same class are closer i.e. maximizing the between class scatter and minimizing the within class scatter. LDA again is a global structure preserving projection. If the training samples are sufficient, LDA performs better than PCA[7].

The study of LPP reveals that it takes care of local manifolds, paying no attention in the regions where two classes are overlapping. With this in mind, to improve the performance of LPP in overlapping regions between two classes, we have proposed a new weighing function which is a mixture of the conventional Heat Kernel approach[1] and the Cauchy distribution. Here,in contrast to the conventional approach, the data points that are at a moderate distance from the point of interest are also given more emphasis. The technique has been tested on the synthetically generated datasets as well as the real datasets of hand written digits and faces. Various dimensionality reduction methods are explained in Section 2. In Section 3, the proposed approach is described. Section 4 contains the experimental results and comparisons of the proposed approach and conventional LPP.

2   Dimensionality Reduction Methods

Given labeled training data, our aim is to classify the unlabeled testing samples to the appropriate class. Samples are usually vector valued. In case the data is not a vector, such as image, it is first transformed into the vector form. Let the image $I(i,j)$ be a two dimensional array of size $N \times N$. Each image is transformed to a one dimensional vector of size N^2. Hence each image becomes a point in N^2 dimensional space. Let there be m training images in the set and they are represented as rows of matrix X. To project the set of training images to the subspace, we need to find the transformation matrix W. The transformation can be represented by $Y = W^T X$ where Y is the mapping of X in the subspace. Two most common dimensionality reduction processes are PCA and LDA[8],[12],[9]. Now let us look at Locality Preserving Projection(LPP).

LPP is obtained by finding the optimal linear approximations to the eigenfunctions of the Laplace Beltrami operator on the manifold [1]. It aims to preserve the neighbourhood information. The objective function is:

$$min \sum_{ij} (y_i - y_j)^2 S_{ij} \qquad (1)$$

S is a symmetric matrix representing the weights of edges of the adjacency graph. The data points are considered as the nodes of the graph while existence of edges depend on whether two nodes are considered as neighbours or not. The procedure of calculating S_{ij} as given in He et al. [5] consists of two steps:

Step 1: Constructing the adjacency graph - Let G be the graph with the same number of nodes equal to the number of images in the training dataset. We put an edge between nodes i and j if x_i and x_j are close. The closeness can be determined in two different ways.

- ϵ - neighbourhood: The nodes i and j are connected by an edge if $\|x_i - x_j\|^2 < \epsilon \in R$. Here the norm is the usual Euclidian norm in R^n.
- k - nearest neighbours: The nodes i and j are connected by an edge if i is among k nearest neighbours of j or vice versa, $k \in N$.

Once the adjacency graph is obtained, LPP will try to optimally preserve it in choosing projection.

Step 2: Estimation of weights - S is a sparse symmetric matrix of $m \times m$ with S_{ij} having the weight of the edge connecting vertices i and j and 0 if no such edge is there. Again we have two variations for weighing the edges.

- No parameter: $S_{ij} = 1$ if nodes i and j are connected by an edge.
- Heat kernel: $S_{ij} = e^{\frac{-\|x_i - x_j\|^2}{t}}$ if nodes i and j are connected by an edge. $t \in R$.

The objective function with this choice of symmetric weights incurs a heavy penalty if neighbouring points x_i and x_j are mapped far apart. This is an attempt to ensure that if x_i and x_j are close then their mappings in the projection space are close as well. The objective function can be reduced to the matrix form as:

$$\frac{1}{2} \sum_{ij} (y_i - y_j)^2 S_{ij} = W^T X L X^T W \qquad (2)$$

where W is the transformation matrix and $L = D - S$ is the Laplacian matrix[11] and $D_{ii} = \sum_i S_{ij}$, a diagonal matrix which provides a natural measure on the data points. The transformation vector W that minimizes the objective function is given by the solution to the generalized eigenvalues problem[2]: $XLX^TW = \lambda XDX^TW$.

where, XLX^T and XDX^T are symmetric and positive semi definite. W^TX gives the projection to the locality preserving subspace. The directions preserving locality are those minimizing the local variance [2].

3   Proposed Improvement for LPP

Conventional LPP though well preserves the local information within the data, however, pays a little or no attention in the region of overlap of two classes. It discriminates the variability within class again paying no attention in the overlapping regions of the sub manifold. Our aim, in this section, is to suggest a mechanism that takes care of the variability in the overlapping region. Emphasis is given on the regions where two classes are overlapping or are very close to each other. In these cases, many a times it happens that nearest neighbour of a data point is a data point from the other class. In LPP these two data points even being included in two different classes could be connected. We focus on preserving the local manifold and at the same time discriminating the points in the overlapping regions. In LPP, similarity function $e^{\frac{-(x_i - x_j)^2}{t}}$ is used. It is applied to few nearest neighbours of the data point of interest. In overlapping region, if only the nearest neighbours are used for classification, it may lead to wrong classification.

The point on which the present proposal evolved is that the data points that are at a moderate distance from the data point of interest should be given some emphasis as this would be helpful in resolving the problem occurring within the overlapping region. For constructing the adjacency graph, the decision whether to consider two data points as neighbours or not is taken by applying K-means classifier on the entire dataset. If class assigned to the two points is same then they are connected by an edge and a weight is assigned in the similarity matrix S_{ij} according to a newly proposed penalty function. In particular, a Cauchy PDF is used for penalty function.

A dataset is generated synthetically to test the above mentioned two proposals. A 7-class data is generated from the Gaussian pdf with different mean vectors and variance-co-variance matrices such that we get overlapping in some of the classes. Projections of synthetically generated data points using the conventional LPP and with the proposed Cauchy function are shown in Figure 1. Using only Cauchy distribution as penalty function for weighing, a little less compactness in the local information is observed. Hence, to preserve closeness among the neighbours and also resolve the overlapping region ambiguities, a similarity function as mentioned below is used.

$$S_{ij} = \begin{cases} e^{-\frac{\|x_i - x_j\|^2}{t}}; & \text{if } \|x_i - x_j\| < D \text{ and } x_i, x_j \text{ belong to same class} \\ \frac{1}{\pi}\left(\frac{1}{(\|x_i - x_j\| - x_0)^2 + 1}\right); & \text{if } \|x_i - x_j\| > D \text{ and } x_i, x_j \text{ belong to same class} \\ 0; & \text{Otherwise} \end{cases} \quad (3)$$

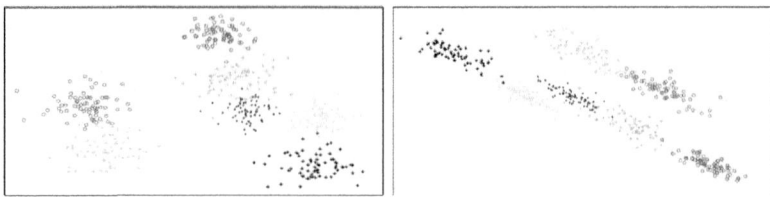

Fig. 1. First plot shows the projection of the dataset using the conventional LPP and second one is the projection using the Cauchy weighing function

4   Experiments and Results

When image data is transformed into vector and all such image vectors form the data matrix, it may turn out to be singular [2] To overcome the problem of singularity, PCA is applied on the images before LPP [2]. As suggested in Turk et al. [8], only first m eigenvectors of the covariance matrix carry meaningful information rather than N^2. We are choosing first m eigenvectors for representing the images for further experiments. First the method was tested on the synthetically generated data and after that the tests were performed on MNIST hand written digit dataset and YALE face database B.

For initial experimentation purpose, two and three dimensional datasets containing different number of classes were generated from Gaussian pdfs. For each class, 100 random samples were taken. One synthetic dataset and results after applying LPP and proposed approach are given in Figure 2. The quantitative measure of the results is shown in Table 1. Out of all the samples, 43 samples, mostly from overlapping regions, are tested. From Figure 2 and Table 1, it can be concluded that in the overlapping region, proposed approach is able to give more accurate classifications. $2D$ dataset containing 12 classes and $3D$ dataset containing 6 classes were also generated in the same manner. Experimental results are also shown in Table 1.

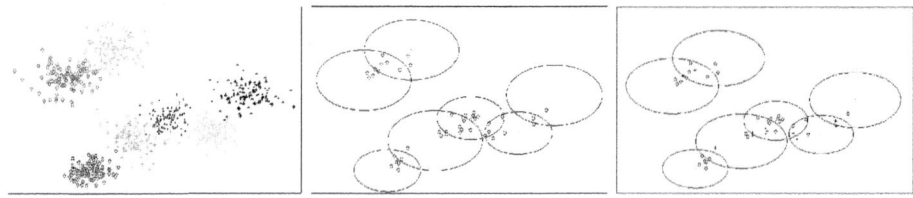

Fig. 2. First plot shows the generated dataset. Class boundaries of all the classes and the selected testing samples are shown in the second plot. Third plot shows results of LPP and the proposed method. Circles are the correctly classified data points. Data points with plus sign are the wrongly classified points using both the methods and dots are wrongly classified using only LPP.

Table 1. Comparison of results on Synthetic data

Synthetic Dataset	Classes	Dimensions	Error Rate (%)	
			LPP	Proposed Approach
1	7	2	30.23	18.6
2	12	2	24	17
3	6	3	31.66	25

The MNIST database [13] of handwritten digits was constructed from NIST's Special Database 3 and Special Database 1 which contain images of handwritten digits. The digits have been size-normalized and centered in a fixed-size image of 20 × 20 pixels. This dataset has also been used in [7]. For the experimentation purpose, 200 images per digit were selected randomly from the database. There is a lot of structural similarity between digits 3, 8 and 1, 7. Hence, possibility of overlapping is very high. Performance of the present proposal has been compared with that of conventional LPP using a few pairs of digits. Out of 400 dimensions, only 2 strongest dimensions are projected in Figure 3. It has been observed that proposed technique has a better projection and it takes care of intrinsic characteristics even within single digit.

The Yale face database [14] contains 5760 single light source images of 10 subjects each seen under 576 viewing conditions. A subset with 36 images per person was created to perform the experiments. All the images were cropped and resized to 100 × 100 pixels. Conventional LPP and the proposed approach is

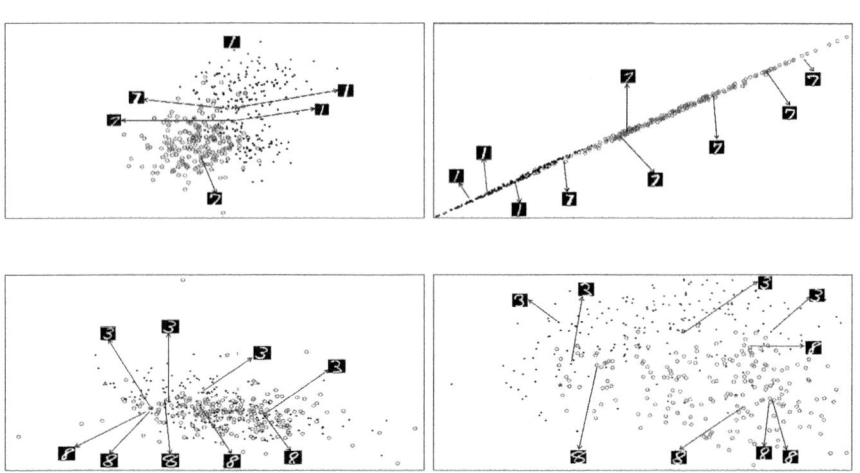

Fig. 3. Digit pair 1 − 7 and pair 3 − 8 are projected in 2D space. Dots represent 1 in first row and 3 in second row whereas circle represents 7 and 8 in respective rows. In first column, the projection is taken using LPP and second shows the projection using proposed method.

used taking a pair of persons at a time. In first experiment, a male and a female are selected while in the second experiment two male personals are selected. The selection has been done by visual inspection such that there are similarities in faces. The results are shown in Figure 4. Here, two strongest projections are plotted. The result in first row shows, in conventional LPP, there are many cases where two different faces are projected close by. In case of improved method, the classes are not only well separated, but also none of the data points are mapped closer to the points from other class. In case of male-male experiment, cases of two data points from different classes projected close by is drastically reduced. To justify the results quantitatively, K-nearest neighbors of all the data points of these 2D projections are computed and validated with the known labels. This result is given in Table 2.

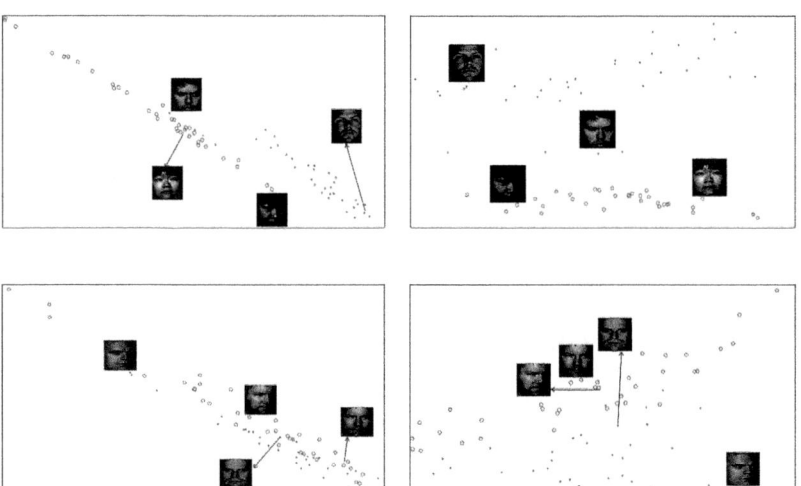

Fig. 4. Projection of face images from Yale face database using two strongest dimensions of LPP in first column and Proposed method in second column

Table 2. Comparison of both the methods on MNIST and YALE datasets (best two dimensions are selected and then KNN is used to classify the projected points)

Dataset	Selected Classes	Error Rate (K=1) (%)		Error Rate (K=3) (%)	
		LPP	Proposed Approach	LPP	Proposed Approach
MNIST Hand written digit Dataset	digit 3 & 8	42.25	19	37.75	16.5
	digit 1 & 7	12.5	8.75	10.25	6.25
	digit 1 & 5	40.5	13.75	35.75	9.75
YALE Face Dataset	Person 1 & 5	1.67	0	1.38	0
	Person 3 & 4	6.38	2.5	7.5	1.67

5 Conclusion

A modification to the weighing function of LPP is proposed here to resolve the problem of ambiguity in the overlapping region of two or more classes. In addition to the neighbouring points, emphasis is also given to the points at a moderate distance from the point of interest. The results of the experiments show that the proposed method provides better results as compared to the conventional LPP approach, specially in the regions of overlapping.

References

1. He, X., Niyogi, P.: Locality Preserving Projections. In: Proc. Conf. Advances in Neural Information Processing Systems (2003)
2. He, X., Yan, S., Hu, Y., Niyogi, P., Zhang, H.: Face Recognition using Lapacianfaces. IEEE Transactions on Pattern Analysis and Machine Intelligence 27(3), 328–340 (2005)
3. He, X., Cai, D., Liu, H.F., Ma, W.Y.: Locality preserving indexing for document representation. In: Proceedings of the 27th Annual International ACM SIGIR Conference on Research and Development in Information Retrieval, pp. 96–103 (2004)
4. Zheng, X., Cai, D., He, X.F., Ma, W.Y., Lin, X.Y.: Locality preserving clustering for image database. In: Proceedings of the 12th Annual ACM International Conference on Multimedia, pp. 885–891 (2004)
5. He, X.F.: Incremental semi-supervised subspace learning for image retrieval. In: Proceedings of the 12th Annual ACM International Conference on Multimedia, pp. 2–8 (2004)
6. Lu, K., He, X.F.: Image Retrieval based on incremental subspace learning. Pattern Recognition 38, 2047–2054 (2005)
7. Chen, S., Zhao, H., Kong, M., Luo, B.: 2D-LPP: A two-dimensional extension of locality preserving projections. Neurocomputing 70, 912–921 (2007)
8. Turk, M., Pentland, A.: Eigenfaces for Face Recognition. Journal of Cognitive Neuroscience 3(1), 71–86 (1991)
9. Belhumeur, P.N., Hespanha, J.P., Kriengman, D.J.: Eigenfaces vs. Fisherfaces: Recognition using class specific linear projection. IEEE Trans. Pattern Analysis Machine Intelligence 19(7), 711–720 (1997)
10. Chung, F.R.K.: Spectral Graph Theory. Proc. Regional Conf. Series in Math., vol. (92) (1997)
11. Belkin, M., Niyogi, P.: Laplacian Eigenmaps and Spectral Techniques for Embedding and Clustering. In: Advances in Neural Information Processing Systems, Vancouver, British Columbia, Canada, vol. 14 (2002)
12. Jolliffe, I.T.: Principal Component Analysis, 2nd edn. Springer, Berlin (2002)
13. The MNIST database of Hand Written Digits,
    http://yann.lecun.com/exdb/mnist/
14. The Yale Face Database,
    http://vision.ucsd.edu/ leekc/ExtYaleDatabase/Yale20Face20Database .html

Self-similarity and Points of Interest
in Textured Images

Shripad Kondra[1,2,*] and Alfredo Petrosino[2]

[1] Neuroimaging Lab, National Brain Research Centre, India
[2] Department of Applied Science, University of Naples "Parthenope", Italy
`alfredo.petrosino@uniparthenope.it`

Abstract. We propose the application of symmetry for texture classification. First we propose a feature vector based on the distribution of local bilateral symmetry in textured images. This feature is more effective in classifying a uniform texture versus a non-uniform texture. The feature when used with a texton-based feature improves the classification rate and is tested on 4 texture datasets. Secondly, we also present a global clustering of texture based on symmetry.

1 Introduction

Symmetry is a prevalent perceptive feature for humans. For instance, the human face or body is approximately symmetric, a quality that is exploited to assist in face recognition and facial feature detection. Symmetry is said to be important in perception. Several psychological studies have been performed to show it. Psychologists of the Gestalt school have assigned a relevant role to symmetry in attentive mechanism both in visual and auditory systems [6]. For example, psycho-physical experiments show that infants (1-2 years old) tend to fixate symmetrically around an arbitrary single distinctive stimulus (i.e. corners of a triangle).

Where has symmetry been used? It has been used to find interest points, to determine symmetry axis [14,12,10,9,5]. Classification was done based on global symmetry of the image, but never on the distribution of the local symmetries. Detected symmetry has been used in finding lines in images [4]. Recently a global model based on affine symmetry between structural textures at a local level has been developed in a multiresolution framework for multiscale analysis, by which the self similarity of the image is exploited across space and scale [11].

What is meaningful in textured man-made structures is the property of being symmetrical, like correspondence in size, shape, and relative position of parts on opposite sides of a dividing line or median plane or about a center or axis. Figure 1 shows some examples of man-made structures which have symmetry.

Zavidovique et al. [14] have proven that, in any direction, the optimal symmetry axis corresponds to the maximal correlation of a pattern with its symmetric

---

* This work was done when Shripad Kondra was at University of Naples.

M.K. Kundu et al. (Eds.): PerMIn 2012, LNCS 7143, pp. 306–313, 2012.
© Springer-Verlag Berlin Heidelberg 2012

Fig. 1. Symmetry in famous Man-made structures

version. In particular, in this paper we deal with bilateral symmetry, a measure obtained by using correlation with the flipped image around a particular axis.

The paper consists of two parts: the first one about using symmetry for texture classification and the second one about using symmetry for clustering textures. Symmetry can be used to distinguish between texture which are uniform and textures which are complex. We will discuss first about single-scale symmetry distribution and extend it to multi-scale. We shall then mention about a new symmetry based feature vector. The symmetry is extracted from different patches over the image and the feature vector is formed using the symmetry, angle distribution and other patch properties. We used our symmetry based feature in combination with a texton–based method [7] for texture classification on four standard texture datasets. We also present a new feature vector based on symmetry. The symmetry is extracted from different patches over the image and the feature vector is formed using the symmetry, angle distribution and other patch properties.

2 Texture Classification Using Symmetry

2.1 Single Scale Symmetry

Symmetry of a patch around each pixel is found as follows. Any image is resized to have diagonal size of 256 pixels and the patch size is 12×12. The symmetry is calculated by the following steps shown in Algorithm 1.

Input: Set of points
Output: Symmetry distribution
foreach 12×12 *Patch around a point i* **do**
  foreach *Rotation theta* **do**
    1. Normalize the patch;
    2. Find the correlation between the rotated patch and its reflected patch around y–axis;
  end
  Find the maximum symmetry value and corresponding angle;
end

Algorithm 1: Calculation of single scale symmetry distribution

The range of the symmetry value is between 0 and 1, with 1 as maximum symmetry. In order to use symmetry to represent texture, it is necessary to see if the symmetry distribution for an image is rotation invariant. To see this we tested the symmetry distribution of some images with their rotated versions. This can be seen from the following figures. The symmetry is obtained as the maximum over 8 different patch rotations. Figure 2 shows the distribution of symmetry and the corresponding angle at which maximum symmetry is detected. The angle distribution is further sorted to make it rotation invariant.

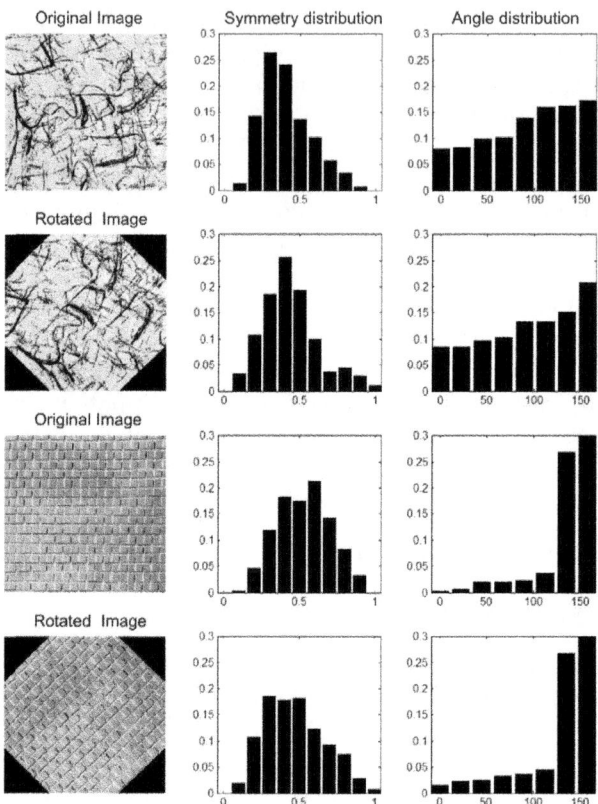

Fig. 2. Single scale symmetry distributions for some textures

2.2   The New Multiscale Feature Vector

Firstly, the image is whitened in the range $[0, 1]$ by removing the mean. Next for every point in the image, the following four different parameters are extracted from three different patch sizes (12×12, 24×24, 36×36).

1. Multiscale symmetry for the patch at three scales
2. The maximum direction for the symmetry along each of the three scales

3. The mean intensity of the patch for each scale
4. The entropy of the patch for each scale (calculated in terms of dit (log10))

Two feature vectors are then constructed:

1. One for the points having mean intensity <0 and
2. Another having mean intensity>=0.

Each feature vector consists of

1. Distribution of symmetry with 11 histogram bins in the range [0, 1], with bin width 0.1.
2. Sorted distribution of symmetry directions. (14 different directions are used)
3. Distribution of entropy with 5 bins in the range [0, 0.6], with bin width 0.15

Thus, the dimension of feature vector is $3 \times (11 + 14 + 5) \times 2 = 180$ (3 is the number of scales). The details of the feature vector are shown in figure 3. The parameters such as the histogram bins, number of directions and weight for each feature are selected from experiments on a small subset of Brodatz texture dataset.

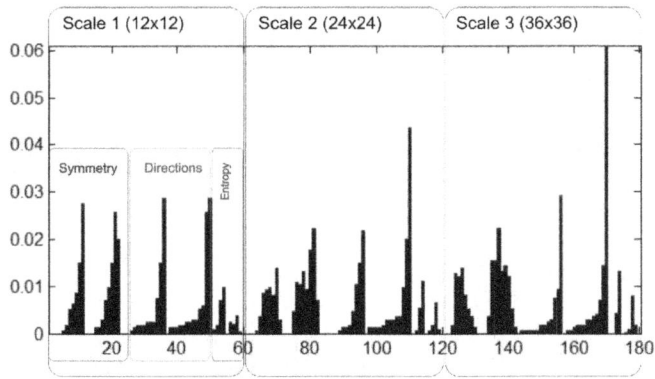

Details of the Model (Feauture Vector)

Fig. 3. Multiscale scale feature vector used for texture classification

2.3 Image Representation for Textons

For texton representation, we use the method of [7]. The method uses 3 circular filters. Images are first filtered using these filters, then thresholded and averaged over two small neighborhoods (3 × 3 and 6 × 6). Eighty universal textons are used for each neighborhood. The feature space is reduced in one neighborhood by grouping into 4 bins. Each image is thus represented by a 2D histogram giving a 320 (80 × 4) dimensional feature vector (indicated as *Model*).

2.4   Textons and Symmetry Combined

From the experiments done on the small subset of Brodatz texture dataset (see table 1), it was found that the symmetry based feature vector gives alone poor performance as can be seen from the recognition rate. But the performance improve when the feature vector it was combined with the texton distribution [7]. A combined feature vector is formed using the texton and symmetry distribution. For each image we have two representations: one for textons and another for symmetry. The combined model for different images is shown in Figure 4. In the first two cases texton distribution is different but the symmetry distribution is nearly the same. Whilst, in the last two images texton distribution is nearly the same but the symmetry distribution is different.

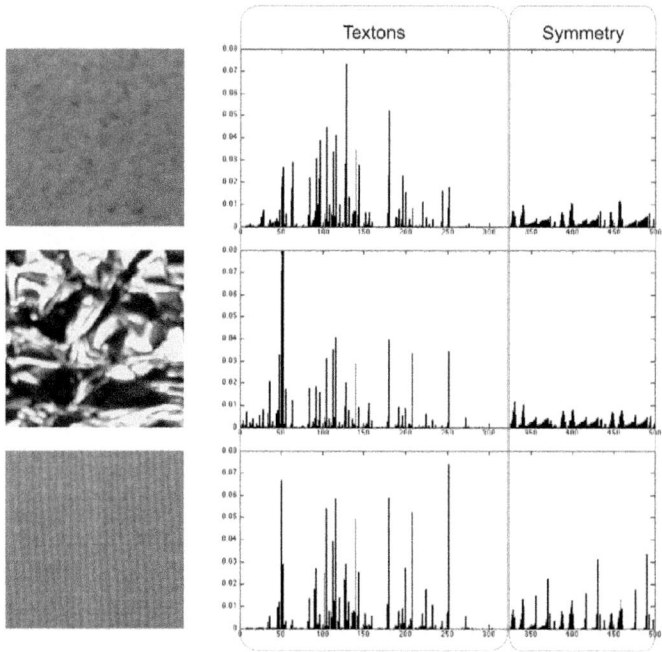

Fig. 4. Combined feature vector Textons plus Symmetry

2.5   Texture Dataset Benchmarking

The experimental setup is the same as mentioned in [7]. The model is trained with SVM using chi-square kernel. The weight of symmetry vector was chosen as 0.4 for this experiment.

The results from Table 1 indicate that symmetry alone is not a good feature for classification. Symmetry can be used to help the classification results between uniform and non-uniform textures. Using the parameters tuned from this small dataset, the recognition was done on four different datasets giving the following

Table 1. Parameter tuning on a small subset of Brodatz dataset

Feature	Recognition rate (%) on subset of Brodatz dataset
Symmetry	72.98 ±1.8
Textons [8]	95.97 ± 0.72
Textons + Symmetry	98.27 ± 1.4

results. For the experimental evaluation, four texture datasets were used. The texture datasets are UIUCTex [8], KTH-TIPS [3], Brodatz [1], and CUReT [2].

Table 2. Comparison with other state of art methods

Database	UIUCTex	KTH-TIPS	Brodatz	CUReT
Proposed	96.9 ±0.8	**98.1 ±1.1**	94.0 ±0.9	98.5 ±0.2
Kondra [7]	92.9 ±1.2	97.7 ±0.8	92.3 ±1.0	97.0 ±0.4
Zhang [15]	**98.3 ±0.5**	95.5 ±1.3	**95.4 ±0.3**	95.3 ±0.4
Hayman [3]	92.0 ±1.3	94.8 ±1.2	95.0 ±0.8	**98.6 ±0.2**
VZ-joint [13]	78.4 ±0.9	92.4 ±1.4	92.9 ±1.0	96.0 ±0.7
Lazebnik [8]	96.4 ±2.0	91.3 ±2.1	89.8 ±0.8	72.5 ±0.4
G. Gabor	65.2 ±2.0	90.0 ±2.0	87.9 ±1.0	92.4 ±0.5

The combination of textons and symmetry thus improves the results as can be seen from Table 2. As it can be evidenced (rows 1 and 2 in the table), for UIUC-Tex dataset the recognition rate increased by 4% considering that UIUCTex dataset has more non-uniform textures.

3   Texture Clustering Using Symmetry

Using only the symmetry and direction vector (single scale of the new feature vector), we clustered the 111 Images in the Brodatz dataset into 4 separate clusters using K–means algorithm with correlation based distance. We named the clusters as Coarse, Directional, Fine, Complex as shown in figure 5. This type of clustering was never done before to our knowledge. The visual meaning captured from the clusters is that symmetry is indeed a human visual phenomenon and there must be a local symmetry evaluation inside the visual system.

Taking into account the mean feature vector of the clusters, it can be seen that the directional textures have high symmetry and the angle distribution has one prominent angle. The other clusters have a wide angle distribution. Fine textures have less symmetry. Complex textures have medium symmetry, while Coarse textures have the highest symmetry.

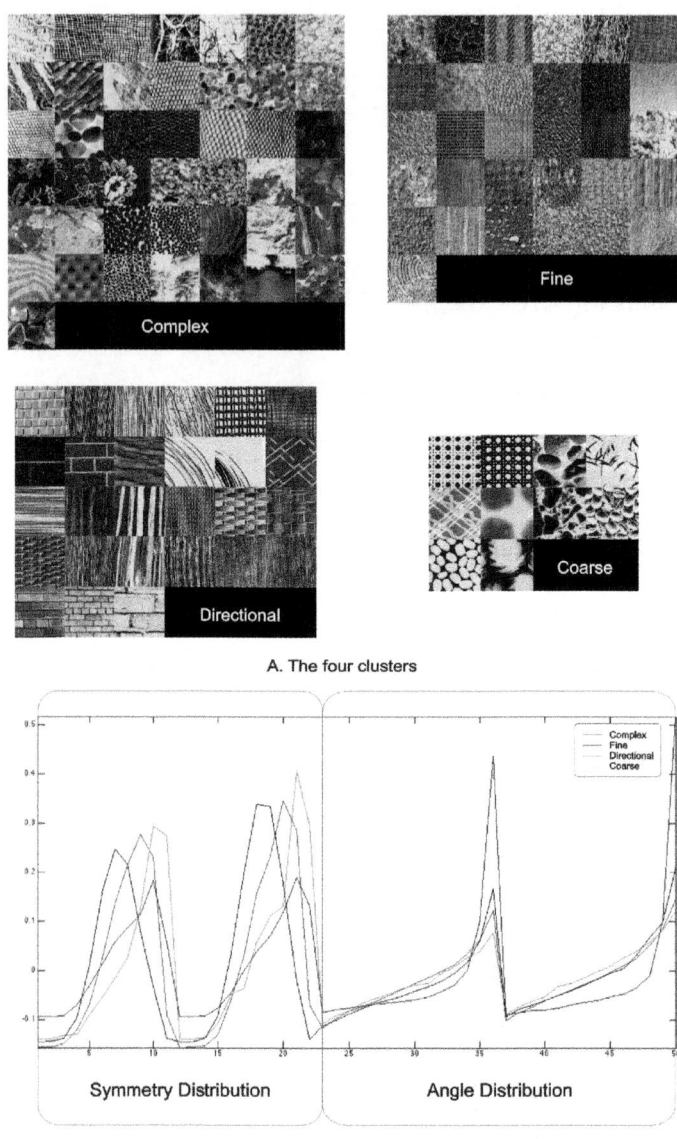

A. The four clusters

B. The mean normalized feature of the above four clusters

Fig. 5. Texture clusters

4   Discussion

In this work we have proposed a feature vector based on symmetry. The conducted experiments fix that symmetry is more effective in classifying a uniform texture versus a non-uniform texture; when used with a texton-based feature, symmetry improves the classification rate. We tested the classification performance on four texture datasets and achieved increase in performance over the previous texton based approaches. We also present a global clustering of texture based on the symmetry. The textures are clustered into more meaningful sets, which shows the importance of symmetry in humans. The method may be more suitable for biomedical images where objects of interest are mostly symmetric and images are usually captured under restricted geometric pose. Ongoing work consists into constructing an affine invariant symmetry descriptor. The algorithm reported here can be tweaked to detect multiple reflection and rotation symmetries.

References

1. Brodatz, P.: Textures: A Photographic Album for Artists and Designers. Dover, New York (1996)
2. Dana, K.J., Ginneken, B.V., Nayar, S.K., Koenderink, J.J.: Reflectance and texture of real-world surfaces. ACM Transactions on Graphics (TOG) 18(1), 1–34 (1999)
3. Hayman, E., Caputo, B., Fritz, M., Eklundh, J.-O.: On the Significance of Real-World Conditions for Material Classification. In: Pajdla, T., Matas, J(G.) (eds.) ECCV 2004. LNCS, vol. 3024, pp. 253–266. Springer, Heidelberg (2004)
4. Huebner, K.: A Symmetry Operator and Its Application to the RoboCup. In: Polani, D., Browning, B., Bonarini, A., Yoshida, K. (eds.) RoboCup 2003. LNCS (LNAI), vol. 3020, pp. 274–283. Springer, Heidelberg (2004)
5. Keller, Y., Shkolnisky, Y.: An algebraic approach to symmetry detection. In: Proceedings of the 17th International Conference on Pattern Recognition, ICPR 2004, vol. 3 (2004)
6. Koehler, W., Wallach, H.: Figural after-effects: an investigation of visual processes. Proc. Amer. Phil. Soc. 88, 269–357 (1944)
7. Kondra, S., Torre, V.: Texture classification using three circular filters. In: Sixth Indian Conference on Computer Vision, Graphics & Image Processing, ICVGIP 2008, pp. 429–434 (2008)
8. Lazebnik, S., Schmid, C., Ponce, J.: A sparse texture representation using local affine regions. IEEE Transactions on Pattern Analysis and Machine Intelligence, 1265–1278 (2005)
9. Loy, G., Eklundh, J.O.: Detecting Symmetry and Symmetric Constellations of Features. In: Leonardis, A., Bischof, H., Pinz, A. (eds.) ECCV 2006. LNCS, vol. 3952, pp. 508–521. Springer, Heidelberg (2006)
10. Manmatha, R., Sawhney, H.: Finding symmetry in intensity images. Tech. rep., University of Massachusetts Amherst MA USA (1997)
11. Park, H., Martin, G.R., Bhalerao, A.: An affine symmetric image model and its applications. IEEE Transactions on Image Processing 19(7), 1695–1705 (2010)
12. Stentiford, F.: Attention Based Facial Symmetry Detection. In: Singh, S., Singh, M., Apte, C., Perner, P. (eds.) ICAPR 2005. LNCS, vol. 3687, pp. 112–119. Springer, Heidelberg (2005)
13. Varma, M., Zisserman, A.: A statistical approach to texture classification from single images. International Journal of Computer Vision 62(1), 61–81 (2005)
14. Zavidovique, B., Ges, V.D.: The s-kernel: A measure of symmetry of objects. Pattern Recognition 40(3), 839–852 (2007)
15. Zhang, J., Marszalek, M., Lazebnik, S., Schmid, C.: Local features and kernels for classification of texture and object categories: A comprehensive study. In: 2006 Conference on Computer Vision and Pattern Recognition Workshop, p. 13 (2006)

Ordinal Incremental Data in Collaborative Filtering

Elena Polezhaeva

Lomonosov Moscow State University, Moscow
lena_polejaeva@mail.ru

Abstract. In modern collaborative filtering applications initial data are typically very large (holding millions of users and items) and come in real time. In this case only incremental algorithms are practically efficient. The additional complication in using standard methods for matrix decompositions appears when the initial data are ratings, i.e. they are represented in the ordinal scale. Standard methods are used for quantitative data. In this paper a new incremental gradient method based on Generalized Hebbian Algorithm (GHA) is proposed. It allows to find matrix decompositions for ordinal data bulks. The functional for ordinal data is worked in. The algorithm does not require to store the initial data matrix and effectively updates user/item profiles when a new user or a new item appears or a matrix cell is modified. The results of experiments show the better RMSE when applying an algorithm adjusted to ordinal data.

Keywords: Collaborative filtering, Generalized Hebbian algorithm, sparse matrix, large data, ordinal data, incremental data, matrix factorization.

1 Introduction

Collaborative Filtering (CF) is used in recommender systems and Customer Relationship Management System (CRM) for personalization. Initial data are represented by a sparse matrix $Y = (y_{ur})_{n \times d}$, in which rows correspond to n users, columns — to d items (documents, films, etc.). Each matrix cell contains information about the usage of an item by a user. So matrix cell may be a rating, a sum paid by user, a mark about visiting site (0 or 1), etc.

The aim is to predict for any user his preferences towards items or, in other words, to fill any empty cell in the initial matrix.

A proposed method should meet the main requirements lodged to CF methods. It should effectively add rows, columns and elements in the matrix Y (the requirement of incrementality), considering the type of initial data and the matrix sparseness.

In this paper the matrix factorization is used. The idea behind the matrix factorization techniques is the following: the matrix Y is approximated by a product of two low-rank matrixes $Y = UR$. Each row of the matrix $U_{n \times L}$ is

M.K. Kundu et al. (Eds.): PerMIn 2012, LNCS 7143, pp. 314–320, 2012.

a user's profile, each column of the matrix $R_{L \times d}$ is an item's profile, L is the number of features. Matrixes which can be approximated in such a way have the rank no more than L.

The thin singular value decomposition (SVD) [1] is effective because it uses a compressed representation of the data. Reduced data (profiles) are formed for users and items, then not all data are held. In modern collaborative filtering applications initial data are typically very large (holding millions of users and items), sparse and come in real time. So the requirement of incrementality is very important. It should be possible to update stored data is case of appearing of a new user/item (1) or a new value in a matrix cell (2). Usually it is proposed to solve only one of these incremental problems. In works of Brand [1], [2] new items and ratings are added efficiently. In paper [3] algorithm efficiently incorporates into the model new users or new ratings but doesn't handle the addition of new items.

In this paper an algorithm is proposed which updates stored data in both cases of incrementality. It is based on Generalized Hebbian algorithm (GHA) [4]. The advantage of using GHA is that only known elements of the initial matrix are involved in calculations. The situation is considered, when Y contains ordinal data (for example, ratings), where $\Omega \subseteq \{1, ..., n\} \times \{1, ..., d\}$ is a set of non-empty elements in Y.

Section 2 describes main notations. Section 3 outlines a GHA algorithm for ordinal data. The functional for ordinal data is worked in. Section 3 presents experiments which show how root-mean-square error (RMSE) [3] depends on the number of the algorithm's iterations, the number of users and the number of known elements in the initial matrix. When the number of users increases the rate of convergence also increases (from 1000 iterations on 600 users to 40 iterations on 940 users). When a data amount increases the number of iterations decreases thus minimizing the working time of the algorithm.

2   Main Notations

The following notations are used:
n — the number of users;
d — the number of items;
$Y_{n \times d} = (y_{ij})_{i=1}^{n}{}_{j=1}^{d}$ — the sparse initial data matrix;
$\widehat{Y}_{n \times d} = (\widehat{y}_{ij})_{i=1}^{n}{}_{j=1}^{d}$ — the low-rank matrix which approximates the matrix Y;
$U_{n \times L} = (u_{il})_{i=1}^{n}{}_{l \in L}$ — the user feature matrix;
$R_{L \times d} = (r_{lj})_{l \in L}{}_{j=1}^{d}$ — the item feature matrix;
L — the number of features;
$\Omega \subseteq \{1, ..., n\} \times \{1, ..., d\}$ — a set of only non-empty elements of the matrix Y.

3   Generalized Hebbian Algorithm

Algorithm GHA used in [4] calculates SVD for the sparse quantitative data matrix Y. A minimization problem of root-mean-square error (RMSE) is used for finding matrixes U and R [3]:

$$\text{MSE} = \frac{1}{|\Omega|} \sum_{(i,j)\in\Omega} (y_{ij} - \hat{y}_{ij})^2 \rightarrow \min_{U,R},$$

where $\hat{y}_{ij}$ is a result of an algorithm's work:

$$\hat{y}_{ij} = u_i r_j = \sum_{l=1}^{L} u_{il} r_{lj},$$

where u_i denotes the row (vector) of U, r_j denotes the column (vector) of R. In case of $\Omega = \{1, ..., n\} \times \{1, ..., d\}$ there is a classical SVD problem for the matrix Y not including empty elements.

In case of the ordinal initial data matrix Y it is proposed to turn to a quantitative scale. Let, without loss of generality, the elements of the matrix Y possess the values from the set $M = \{1, ..., \bar{m}\}$. Let $\beta_m \in \mathbb{R}$ is assigned to every $m \in M$, and the following conditions are imposed: $\beta_1 \leq \cdots \leq \beta_{\bar{m}}$.

For finding matrixes U and R not only RMSE is minimized but also a set of values $\beta = (\beta_1, \ldots, \beta_{\bar{m}})$ is defined:

$$\text{MSE} = \frac{1}{|\Omega|} \sum_{(i,j)\in\Omega} (\beta_{y_{ij}} - u_i r_j)^2 \rightarrow \min_{U,R,\beta}.$$

For excluding a trivial solution $\beta = 0$, $U = 0$, $R = 0$, additional normalization conditions are imposed:

$$\frac{1}{n} \sum_{i=1}^{n} \|u_i\|^2 = 1; \quad \frac{1}{d} \sum_{j=1}^{d} \|r_j\|^2 = 1.$$

The best value of β_m is found analytically:

$$\beta_m = \frac{\sum\limits_{(i,j)\in\Omega} [y_{ij} = m] u_i r_j}{\sum\limits_{(i,j)\in\Omega} [y_{ij} = m]}.$$

Let us introduce dual variables λ_1 and λ_2 corresponding to normalization conditions.

The optimization task for Lagrangian is:

$$\sum_{(i,j)\in\Omega} (\beta_{y_{ij}} - u_i r_j)^2 + \lambda_1 \sum_{i=1}^{n} (\|u_i\|^2 - 1) +$$

$$+ \lambda_2 \sum_{j=1}^{d} (\|r_j\|^2 - 1) \rightarrow \max_{\lambda_1,\lambda_2} \min_{u,r,\beta}.$$

An enumeration procedure of value grid is used for λ_1 and λ_2 optimization . The stochastic gradient descent iterations are made for U and R optimization.

A random pair $(i, j) \in \Omega$ is chosen on every step of the iteration process and then the incremental gradient descent step is used for all $l = 1, \ldots, L$:

$$u'_{il} = (1 - \eta\lambda_1)u_{il} + \eta \sum_{j:\ (i,j)\in\Omega} r_{lj}(\beta_{y_{ij}} - u_i r_j),$$

$$r'_{lj} = (1 - \eta\lambda_2)r_{lj} + \eta \sum_{i:\ (i,j)\in\Omega} u_{il}(\beta_{y_{ij}} - u_i r_j),$$

where η is a learning rate, u'_{il}, r'_{lj} are new values of variables u_{il}, r_{lj}.

Let us introduce an onto function from the estimation $\hat{y}_{ij} = u_i r_j$ received by the algorithm back to the set M for finding RMSE:

$$R(\hat{y}_{ij}) = \begin{cases} 1, & \hat{y}_{ij} \leq \frac{\beta_1 + \beta_2}{2}, \\ m, & \frac{\beta_{m-1} + \beta_m}{2} < \hat{y}_{ij} \leq \frac{\beta_m + \beta_{m+1}}{2}, \\ \bar{m}, & \frac{\beta_{\bar{m}-1} + \beta_{\bar{m}}}{2} \leq \hat{y}_{ij}. \end{cases} \tag{1}$$

The quality of decomposition is defined by RMSE:

$$\text{RMSE} = \sqrt{\frac{1}{|\Omega|} \sum_{(i,j)\in\Omega} (y_{ij} - R(\hat{y}_{ij}))^2}.$$

The advantage of the gradient descent method is that it makes it possible to add new values in the matrix Y straight during the iterations.

Algoritm 1. *The stochastic gradient descend method for ordinal data* of searching U, R is below. The result of the algorithm is a fully populated matrix Y.

Require: $Y = \{y_{ij}\} \in \mathbb{M}^{n\times d}, (i,j) \in \Omega; \lambda_1; \lambda_2; \eta;$
Ensure: U, R;
  1: Initialization: $\beta_m = m$ for all $m \in M$; elements U, R are from the interval $[0, 0.7]$;
  2: $\bar{y}_m = \sum_{(i,j)\in\Omega} [y_{ij} = m];$
  3: **for** $t = 1, \ldots, T$ **do**
  4:     **for all** $(i,j) \in \Omega$ *in random order* **do**
  5:        **for all** $l = 1, \ldots, L$ **do**
  6:           $\tilde{u}_{il} = (1 - \eta\lambda_1)u_{il} + \eta\sum_j r_{lj}(\beta_{y_{ij}} - u_i r_j);$
  7:           $\tilde{r}_{lj} = (1 - \eta\lambda_2)r_{lj} + \eta\sum_i u_{il}(\beta_{y_{ij}} - u_i r_j),$
  8:     $\beta_m = (\bar{y}_m)^{-1} \sum_{(i,j)\in\Omega} [y_{ij} = m]u_i r_j,$
  9:     Find $RMSE$.
10:     **If** $RMSE$ didn't decrease on the last two iterations **then stop**.
11:     Add new elements (i, j).

The result of GHA is data without empty elements. L_1 and L_2 norms are used below in experiments.

4 Experiments

Experiments were made on MovieLens data: 943 users, 1682 items, 10^5 known ratings (all ratings are ordinal from 1 to 5). The matrix Y was modified during iterations: the rows (users) and columns (items) were added, the values in the cells were added and modified. An experiment showed that when the data amount increased the RMSE decreased.

When the number of users increases the rate of convergence also increases (from 1000 iterations on 600 users to 40 iterations on 940 users).

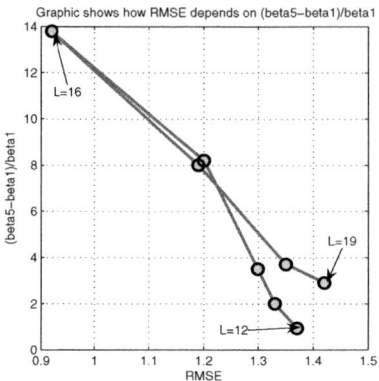

Fig. 1. Graphic shows how RMSE depends on the ratio $\frac{\beta_5 - \beta_1}{\beta_1}$

The least value of $RMSE = 0.92$ was achieved on rank-16 basis. Simultaneously the greatest dispersion of β_m was reached, $\frac{\beta_5 - \beta_1}{\beta_1} = 13.8$ (Fig. 1). Other parameters were $\lambda_1 = \lambda_2 = 0.18$, $\eta = 0.25$.

RMSE of the Algorithm ($RMSE = 0.92$, 5 iterations) is better than the result achieved by Takacs [3], not considering that data are ordinal: RMSE = 0.93, 7 iterations (Fig. 2).

The results of testing the Algorithm in the incremental mode are shown on Fig. 3. RMSE after different modifications (additions of the elements in empty cells of Y, additions of rows, columns in Y) depends on:

- the type of modifications;
- the epoch in which the modifications are made.

With the chosen stopping criterion (RMSE doesn't decrease on the last two iterations) when several elements (i, j) are added RMSE doesn't increase a lot, as the i-th user and the j-th item already exist in the sample, so the profiles u_i and r_j were modified on the previous epochs of the Algorithm (steps 7, 8 in **Algorithm 1**).

RMSE increases when new rows or columns are added in Y. The addition of items have a more influence on the increase of RMSE than the addition of

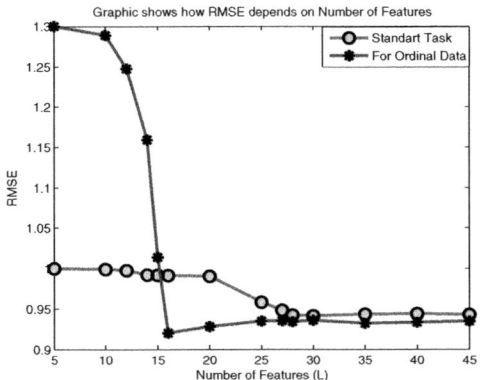

Fig. 2. Graphic shows how RMSE depends on the number of features (L)

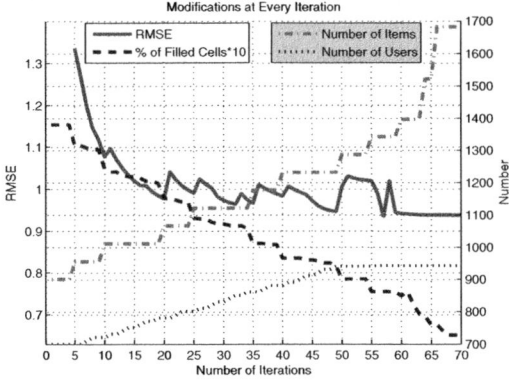

Fig. 3. Modifications on every iteration

users. Though the algorithm converges even if there are modifications on every iteration. Although new users and items are added (new values in cells of Y) even on the late iterations RMSE also changes a lot. It can be explained by the fact that the percent of filled cells in the matrix Y decreases on every iteration (Fig. 3). The curve of the percent of filled cells decreases: users and items are added but users are not very active and items are not popular. So there are many empty cells in added rows and columns.

It is very interesting that all $\beta_{y_{ij}}$ increase (even if we don't impose conditions on $\beta_{y_{ij}}$): $\beta_1 = 0.088$; $\beta_2 = 0.45$; $\beta_3 = 0.680$; $\beta_4 = 0.822$; $\beta_5 = 0.897$.

The working time measurement of the Algorithm showed that a proposed method scaled well and could be applied to the large data amount.

5   Results

The gradient computing techniques of matrix decompositions may be applied for solving practical tasks in Collaborative Filtering in which the initial data are very large and sparse. The data are modified and dynamically increase. The data are measured in quantitative or ordinal scale. The results of experiments show that with an account taken of the scale of measurement an accuracy of the decomposition may be increased.

References

1. Brand, M.: Fast Low-rank modifications of the thin singular value decomposition. Linear Algebra and Its Applications 415(1), 20–30 (2006)
2. Brand, M.: Fast online SVD revisions for lightweight recommender systems. In: SIAM International Conference on Data Mining, SDM (2003)
3. Takacs, G., Pilaszy, I., Nemeth, B., Tikk, D.: Scalable Collaborative Filtering Approaches for Large Recommender Systems. The Journal of Machine Learning Research 10, 623–656 (2009)
4. Gorrell, G.: Generalized Hebbian Algorithm for Incremental Singular Value Decomposition in Natural Language Processing. In: Proceedings of EACL (2006)

Combining Evidence from Temporal and Spectral Features for Person Recognition Using Humming

Hemant A. Patil[1], Maulik C. Madhavi[1], Rahul Jain[2], and Alok K. Jain[3]

[1] Dhirubhai Ambani Institute of Information and Communication Technology, Gujarat, India
[2] Hindustan Institute of Technology and Management, Keetham, Agra, Uttar Pradesh, India
[3] Nikhil Institute of Engineering and Management, Mathura, Uttar Pradesh, India
{hemant_patil,madhavi_maulik}@daiict.ac.in,
{rahuljn298,alok.sachit}@gmail.com

Abstract. In this paper, hum of a person is used to identify a speaker with the help of machine. In addition, novel temporal features (such as zero-crossing rate & short-time energy) and spectral features (such as spectral centroid & spectral flux) are proposed for person recognition task. Feature-level fusion of each of these features with state-of-the art spectral feature set, *viz.*, Mel Frequency Cepstral Coefficients (MFCC) is found to give better recognition performance than MFCC alone. In addition, it is shown that the person identification rate is competitive over baseline MFCC. Furthermore, the reduction in equal error rate (EER) by 1.46 % is obtained when a feature-level fusion system is employed by combining evidences from MFCC, temporal and proposed spectral features.

Keywords: Humming, Mel cepstrum, zero-crossing rate, short-time energy, spectral centroid, spectral flux and polynomial classifier.

1 Introduction

Due to global security concern, recognition of a person's voice with the help of machines is now an emerging field and an active research area for the past 4-5 decades. As humming contains no linguistic information, voice biometrics based on humming is a challenging research issue. It is similar to other biometrics, the process of identifying a specific individual, often used for security and forensic applications. In this paper, an attempt is made to extract the different temporal features like zero-crossing rate (ZCR) and short-time energy (STE) along with the spectral features including spectral centroid (SC), spectral flux (SF) and Mel Frequency Cepstral Coefficients (MFCC) from the hum signal recorded in a natural environment including a little amount of noise.

While producing hum oral cavity is closed and vocal tract is coupled with nasal cavity. While it is possible many people keep their mouth open while singing or humming, however, without significant coupling of nasal cavity, it is difficult to produce hum. Hence, hum produced by various speakers is nasalized sound. The nasal cavity remains steady during hum production and is known to be speaker-specific. Several experiments conducted by Amino and Arai *et. al.* [1] shows that nasal sounds

M.K. Kundu et al. (Eds.): PerMIn 2012, LNCS 7143, pp. 321–328, 2012.

have more inter-speaker variability and less intra-speaker variability. This motivated authors to use hum for person recognition task.

1.1   Prior Work Related to This Field

To the best of the authors' knowledge, person recognition using humming was first proposed in [2] using Linear Prediction Coefficients (LPC), Linear Prediction Cepstral Coefficients (LPCC) and MFCC [2]. Jin *et. al.* found that pitch, which is conducive to humming-based music retrieval, is not conducive to human verification and identification (as the pitch in humming is highly dependent on the melody and not on the target speaker) [3]. Recently, a new feature set, *viz.*, Variable Length Teager Energy based Mel Frequency Cepstral Coefficients (VTMFCC) is proposed for this problem [4]. In this paper, we propose novel temporal and spectral features for the person recognition task. These features are discussed in brief in next section.

Rest of the paper is organised as follows, Section 2 describes the temporal and spectral features proposed in this work. Section 3 presents the experimental set up. Section 4 presents the experimental results and Section 5 concludes the paper and give summary of our future research work.

2   Features Used

In this section, we describe computational details of temporal and spectral features proposed for person recognition task.

2.1   Temporal Features

In this work, various temporal features such as zero crossing rate and short-time energy are used.

Zero-Crossing Rate (ZCR). It is the rate of sign changes along the signal, i.e., the rate at which signal changes from positive to negative or vice-versa. This feature is more likely to be used in speaker recognition and music information retrieval (MIR) system. ZCR is more for unvoiced speech than the voiced speech. Thus, ZCR is an indication of quasi-periodicity value of humming signal. For a complex signal ZCR is a measure of noisiness [5], [6].It is defined as,

$$zcr = \frac{1}{N-1} \sum_{n=1}^{N-1} \mathbb{I}\{s(n)s(n-1) < 0\}, \qquad (1)$$

where $s(n)$ is a hum signal of length N and indicator function $\mathbb{I}\{A\}$ is 1 if its argument A is true and 0 otherwise.

Short-Time Energy (STE). Usually intelligible speech consists of voiced and unvoiced regions. In this work, short-time energy is used to determine the energy of these regions of the signal. Short-time energy can also be used to detect the transition from unvoiced to voiced regions and vice-versa. The energy of voiced region is greater than unvoiced region. The equation for STE is given by,

$$E_n = \sum_{m=-\infty}^{\infty} \{s(m)h(n-m)\}^2 ,$$

(2)

where $s(m)$ is the signal and $h(m)$ is the Hamming window function of duration equal to the frame of humming signal.

2.2   Spectral Features

In this subsection, brief computational details of various spectral features such as spectral centroid, spectral flux and state-of-the art spectral feature set, i.e., MFCC are given.

Spectral Centroid (SC). It is a measure that indicates where most of the power of a speech segment is *spectrally* located. It indicates where the "center of the mass" of the spectrum lies. It is calculated as a weighted mean of the frequencies present in a signal, determined using Fourier transform with their magnitudes as the weights, i.e.,

$$SC = \frac{\sum_{k=0}^{N-1} X(k)F(k)}{\sum_{k=0}^{N-1} X(k)} ,$$

(3)

where X(k) represents the weighted frequency value, or magnitude of bin number k, and F(k) represents the center frequency of that bin. Higher values of SC correspond to spectra in the range of higher frequencies [7].

Spectral Flux (SF). It is a measure of how quickly the power spectrum of a signal is changing, calculated by comparing the power spectrum for one frame with the power spectrum from the previous frame. It is used to determine the timbre of an audio signal, or in onset detection, among other things. Intuitively, spectral density captures the frequency content of a stochastic process and help in recognizing periodicity of a hum signal. If there is a transient attack at some location in signal, the change in energy will be denoted by a jump in the difference of energy between short-time spectrum of two consecutive frames of humming signal, i.e.,

$$SF(n) = \sum_{k=-\frac{N}{2}}^{\frac{N}{2}-1} H(|X(n,k)|-|(X(n-1,k)|) ,$$

(4)

where $X(n,k)$ is the kth frequency bin of the nth frame and $H(x) = \frac{x+|x|}{2}$ is the half-wave rectifier function.

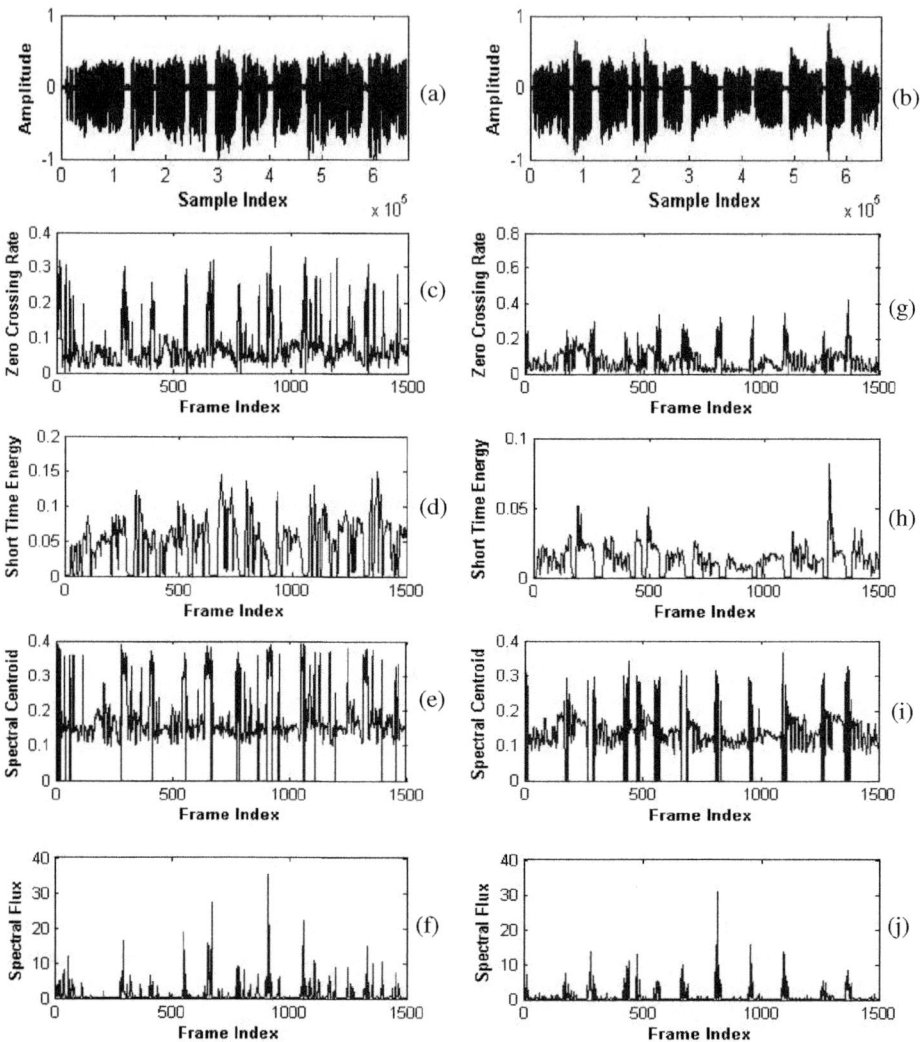

Fig. 1. Hum for a song by a (a) male speaker A, (b) male speaker B, plot for speaker A's (c) ZCR, (d) STE, (e) SC and (f) SF per frame and plot for speaker B's (g) ZCR, (h) STE, (i) SC and (j) SF per frame

Fig.1 shows plot of hum signal produced by two male speakers of same age and their corresponding frame wise ZCR, STE, SC and SF. It is evident that the pattern of variation of all these four features is quite distinct for each speaker and gives evidence of combining speaker-specific information.

Mel Frequency Cepstral Coefficients (MFCC). For MFCC calculation, first input humming signal is passed via pre-processing block (framing, Hamming windowing and pre-emphasis). Then, pre-processed frame is passed through Mel filterbank, followed by subband energy and logarithm operation is performed. Finally, Discrete Cosine Transform (DCT) is applied to obtain MFCC feature vectors [8].

3   Experimental Setup

The database is prepared from 50 subjects (36 males and 14 females) in the radio room of DA-IICT Gandhinagar (India). Table 1 shows the details of corpus used in this paper, where the same set of songs were used to train the system across all the subjects, while another sets of songs (these songs are different than the songs used in training) were used to test across all the subjects.

Table 1. Detail of Humming Corpus

Item	Details
No. of subjects	50 (36 males & 14 females)
Sampling rate	22050 Hz
Sampling format	16-bit resolution, mono channel
Training segments	30 s, 60 s, 90 s (3 training segments)
Testing segments	1 s,2 s, … 30 s (30 testing segments)
Genuine trials	50 x3 (no. of training segments) x 30 (no. of testing segments) =4,500
Impostor trials	(50 x 50 x 30 x 3) (total trials) – 4,500(genuine trials) =2,25,000- 4,500 =2,20,500

In this paper, a discriminatively-trained polynomial classifier is used as the basis for all experiments. This classifier is the best approximation to the optimal Bayes classifier. It has capability of new class addition and efficient multiply and add DSP structure. It uses out-of-class data to optimize performance (as opposed to other statistical methods such as HMM, GMM, etc.). For example, for a 2 dimensional (i.e. 2-D) feature vector $\mathbf{x} = [x_1 \ \ x_2]^T$ and second order polynomial function, $p(\mathbf{x})$ is given by

$$p(\mathbf{x}) = \begin{bmatrix} 1 & x_1 & x_2 & x_1^2 & x_1 x_2 & x_2^2 \end{bmatrix}^T \qquad (5)$$

This can be approximated using the training feature set as

$$\mathbf{w}_{spk} = \arg\min_{\mathbf{w}} \left[\sum_{i=1}^{N_{spk}} \left| \mathbf{w}^T p(\mathbf{x}_i) - 1 \right|^2 + \sum_{i=1}^{N_{imp}} \left| \mathbf{w}^T p(y_i) \right|^2 \right], \tag{6}$$

where $x_{1,}......,x_{N_{spk}}$ are speaker's training data and $y_{1,........,}y_{N_{imp}}$ is the impostor data. The details of classifier structure and training algorithm are given in [9].

4   Experimental Results

In this work, 12-*D* MFCC per frame (of duration 20 ms) was extracted. A single scalar value of ZCR, STE, SC, and SF from the same frame were extracted and concatenated with 12-*D* MFCC to form 13-*D* feature vectors, i.e., 12-*D* MFCC + 1-*D* ZCR, 12 -*D* MFCC + 1-*D* STE, 12-*D* MFCC + 1-*D* SC and 12-*D* MFCC + 1-*D* SF. In addition, 12-*D* MFCC were also concatenated with all the four features taken together, i.e., MFCC+ ZCR+ STE+ SC+ SF to form 16-*D* feature vector. In this paper, Detection Error Tradeoff (DET) curves are used to show the overall system performance in statistically meaningful way. In particular, EER and opt. DCF are used for person verification [10] whereas Identification Rate (% ID) is used for person identification and 95 % confidence interval (CNF) are shown in the bracket to quote statistical significance of our results. The DET curves for various recognition systems with feature-level fusion and MFCC alone are shown in Fig. 2. For calculation of Detection Cost Function (DCF), costs associated with False Acceptance (FA) and False Rejection (FR) are taken as 1 and prior probabilities of genuine and impostor trials are assumed to be equal, i.e., 0.5. Table 2 shows corresponding EER, Opt. DCF and % ID (along with 95 % confidence interval).

Table 2. EER (%) and %ID rate for person recognition task

Features	EER (in %)	Opt. DCF	% ID	95% CNF
MFCC	12.95	0.1268	77.71	(76.49,78.93)
MFCC+ZCR	12.82	0.1247	78.68	(77.48,79.87)
MFCC+STE	11.91	0.1172	83.17	(82.08,84.26)
MFCC+SF	12.84	0.1254	79.62	(78.44,80.79)
MFCC+SC	12.75	0.1245	80.35	(79.19,81.51)
MFCC+ZCR+ STE+SF+SC	**11.49**	0.1123	**86.29**	(85.28,87.29)

Fig. 2 (a)-(e) shows DET curves for feature-level fusion of ZCR, STE, SC & SF with MFCC and MFCC alone. It is evident from Fig. 2(e) that the EER is decreased significantly by 1.46 % when we fused the four features, *viz.*, ZCR, STE, SC and SF with the MFCC. This indicates that ZCR, STE, SC & SF carry equivalent complementary information than MFCC alone and hence better recognition performance at *all* the operating points of DET curves. Finally, 95 % confidence intervals are not varying wider indicating greater confidence in statistical sense obtained from experimental results.

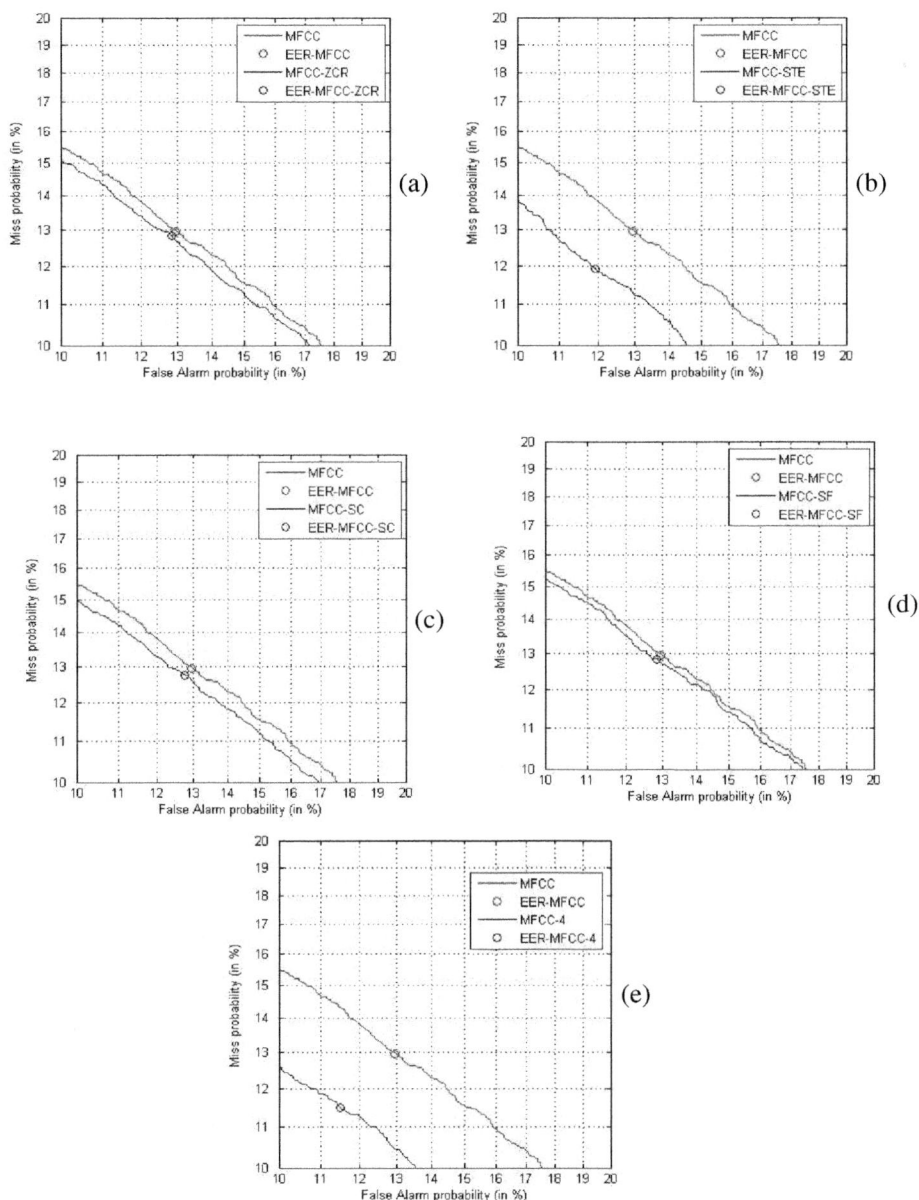

Fig. 2. DET curves for feature-level fusion of MFCC with (a) ZCR, (b) STE, (c) SC, (d) SF, (e) ZCR+STE+SC+SF

5   Summary and Conclusion

In this paper, a novel approach to person recognition using humming is presented by combining evidence from several temporal (i.e., ZCR & STE) and spectral (i.e., SF & SC) features with state-of the art MFCC. This resulted in reduced EER and increased % ID over large population size. One of the limitations of the present work is that results are on single session data and humming data is considered with closed mouth. Our future work will be directed to perform person recognition experiments on intersession humming data including large number of subjects.

Acknowledgements. Authors would like to thank the authorities of DA-IICT Gandhinagar and Prof. Ashish Chandiok of BMAS Engineering College, Agra for his kind help during this research work.

References

1. Amino, K., Arai, T.: Perceptual Speaker Identification Using Monosyllabic Stimuli-Effects of the Nucleus Vowels and Speaker Characteristics Contained in Nasals. In: INTERSPEECH 2008, Brisbane, Australia, pp. 1917–1920 (2008)
2. Patil, H.A., Jain, R., Jain, P.: Identification of Speakers from their Hum. In: Sojka, P., Horák, A., Kopeček, I., Pala, K. (eds.) TSD 2008. LNCS (LNAI), vol. 5246, pp. 461–468. Springer, Heidelberg (2008)
3. Jin, M., Kim, J., Yoo, C.D.: Humming-based Human Verification and Identification. In: Proc. Int. Conf. on Acoustic, Speech and Signal Processing, ICASSP 2009, Taipei, Taiwan, pp. 1453–1456 (2009)
4. Patil, H.A., Parhi, K.K.: Novel Variable Length Teager Energy based Features for Person Recognition from Their Hum. In: Proc. Int. Conf. on Acoustic, Speech and Signal Processing, ICASSP 2010, Dallas, Texas, USA, pp. 4526–4529 (2010)
5. Huang, R., Hansen, J.H.L.: Advances in Unsupervised Audio Classification and Segmentation for the Broadcast News and NGSW Corpora. IEEE Transactions on Audio, Speech, and Language Processing 14(3), 907–919 (2006)
6. Kedem, B.: Spectral Analysis and Discrimination by Zero-Crossings. Proc. IEEE 74(11), 1477–1493 (1986)
7. Schubert, E., Wolfe, J., Tarnopolsky, A.: Spectral Centroid and Timbre in Complex, Multiple Instrumental Textures. In: Proceedings of the 8th International Conference on Music Perception & Cognition, Evanston, IL, pp. 654–657 (2004)
8. Davis, S.B., Mermelstein, P.: Comparison on Parametric Representation for Monosyllabic Word Recognition in Continuously Spoken Sentences. IEEE, Transactions on Acoustics, Speech, And Signal Processing ASSP-28(4), 357–366 (1980)
9. Campbell, W.M., Assaleh, K.T., Broun, C.C.: Speaker Recognition with Polynomial Classifiers. IEEE Transactions on Speech and Audio Processing 10(4), 205–212 (2002)
10. Martin, A.F., Doddington, G., Kamm, T., Ordowski, M., Przybocki, M.: The DET Curve in Assessment of Detection Task Performance. In: Proc. EUROSPEECH 1997, Rhodes, Greece, vol. 4, pp. 1895–1898 (1997)

Novel Interleaving Schemes for Speaker Recognition over Lossy Networks

Hemant A. Patil[1], Parth A. Goswami[2], and Tapan Kumar Basu[3]

[1] Dhirubhai Ambani Institute of Information and Communication Technology (DA-IICT),
Gandhinagar, Gujarat, India
[2] A.V. Parekh Technical Institute (AVPTI), Rajkot, Gujarat, India
[3] Institute of Technology and Marine Engineering (ITME), Jhinga, Amira, West Bengal, India
{hemant_patil,goswami_parth}@daiict.ac.in, basutk02@yahoo.co.in

Abstract. Cases of cybercrime & terrorism on IP network is increasing day by day. In addition, there is a tendency to fraud phone-banking systems, and gain access to secure premises or accounts, which may be protected through the voice-based biometric system. To minimize these problems, we need a voice/speaker recognition system with utmost accuracy. Number of users of internet applications is also increasing, causes heavy traffic over IP channel almost round the clock. In this paper, the effect of packet loss on the performance of speaker recognition system is demonstrated and to alleviate this degradation we propose novel interleaving schemes. The proposed interleaving schemes help to spread the risk of burst loss in the network which is expected to improve speech quality and hence performance of the speaker recognition system.

Keywords: Internet protocol (IP) network, automatic speaker recognition, packet loss, interleaving, Mel cepstrum, polynomial classifier.

1 Introduction

Speaker Recognition (SR) Systems has been an active area of research for past four decades with speech collected mostly in research laboratory environments. Real-time voice communication over IP network, i.e., VoIP is becoming very popular in recent years because of its ease of use, simplicity and cost effectiveness [5],[9]. However, due to growing applications and possible misuses of Voice over Internet Protocol (VoIP) networks, there is a need to employ SR system over VoIP network (in the context of internet security and law enforcement agencies). However, real-time packet switched data communication networks are affected by many Quality of Service (QoS) related challenges such as packet loss, packet reordering, delay, network jitter, far-end cross-talk, etc. [1]. So it is important to study the effect of these artifacts of VoIP on SR system performance.

VoIP uses User Datagram Protocol (UDP) [5]. UDP does not employ any error recovery technique, neither it guarantees the delivery of a packet to host at other end of IP network nor it handles the congestion on the channel [5]. Because of these the packets which are lost or rather dropped by the channel are not sent again by the

M.K. Kundu et al. (Eds.): PerMIn 2012, LNCS 7143, pp. 329–337, 2012.

sender. In this paper, packet loss issue is chosen to study, because it is one of the artifacts which occur frequently in VoIP network [1],[5]. Moreover, it is proven that packet loss degrades the performance of speech recognition system [7] and hence it was felt to investigate how it affects the performance of SR system. Next, a brief overview of related work in this area is discussed.

Hassan *et. al.* observed that perceptual quality of the speech is a function of packet loss rate and it decreases drastically as the packet loss rate increases [8]. Borah and DeLeon observed significant performance degradation of SR system for test utterances acquired from VoIP which may havs dropouts due to packet loss. They improved the performance by training SR system with lossy speech packets corresponding to the loss rate experienced by the speaker to be identified while testing [2]. Pedro *et. al.* shown in their experiments that speech recognition performance is more sensitive and dependent on the packet loss and they have used packet interleaving, packet repetition and packet interpolation techniques for improving performance of speech recognition system [7]. Agrawal *et. al.* have presented the work on speaker recognition from compressed VoIP packet stream [3]. Recently, Keller *et. al.* proposed several interleaving schemes to improve speech quality of mixed excitation linear prediction (MELP) coded voice over lossy network [11]. In this paper, we propose application of these novel interleaving schemes (in addition to incorporation of lossy training with and without redundancy) for performance improvement of SR system over lossy VoIP network.

2   Quality of Service (QoS) and Problem Formulation

There are various reasons because of which packets are lost or rather dropped by the channel over the network. Major factors which are responsible for the packet loss are the following [5]

- Signal degradation due to multipath fading
- Channel congestion,
- Faulty network hardware,
- Buffer overload.

Now let us examine the effect of packet loss on the acoustic features (such as spectrogram and formants) of the speech signal. Arrows in the speech waveform shown in Fig. 2(a) are marked against location of lost packets whereas arrows at corresponding location in Fig. 2(b) are marked in the spectrogram to indicate the estimation of formants in the duration of packet loss, while dotted arrows in Fig. 2(b) indicate the estimation of formants in regions of silence. In computer simulation, zeros have been inserted at the places of packet loss. It is evident from Fig. 2 that there is improper estimation of formants in the region when packets are lost. In addition, formant estimation is good in silence periods and it is not flat, while in the duration of a lost packet estimation of all formants are more or less flat and packet loss affects all the formants. Therefore, it is expected that packet loss can affect *perceptual quality* of speech and also affects extraction of its acoustic features. When one packet is lost we may consider this as if one phoneme is lost within a speech utterance [8].

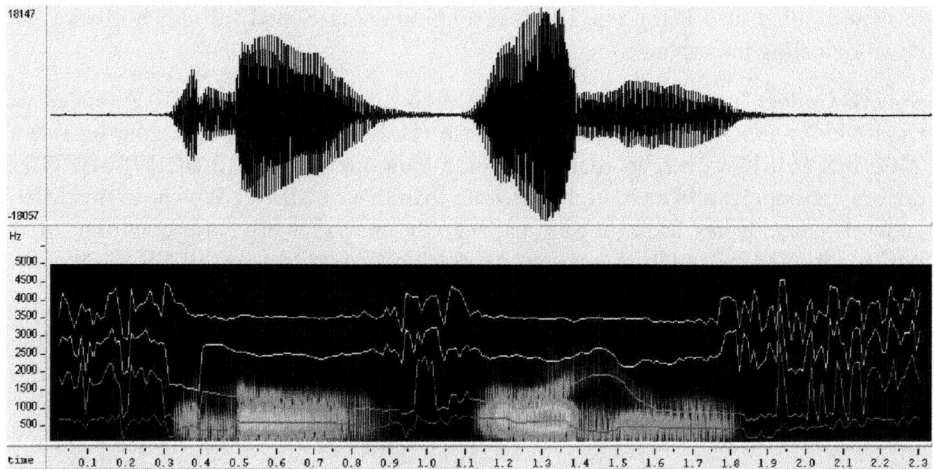

Fig. 1. (a) Speech utterance 'Hello, how are you?' without packet loss (b) corresponding spectrogram and formant contour for first four formants

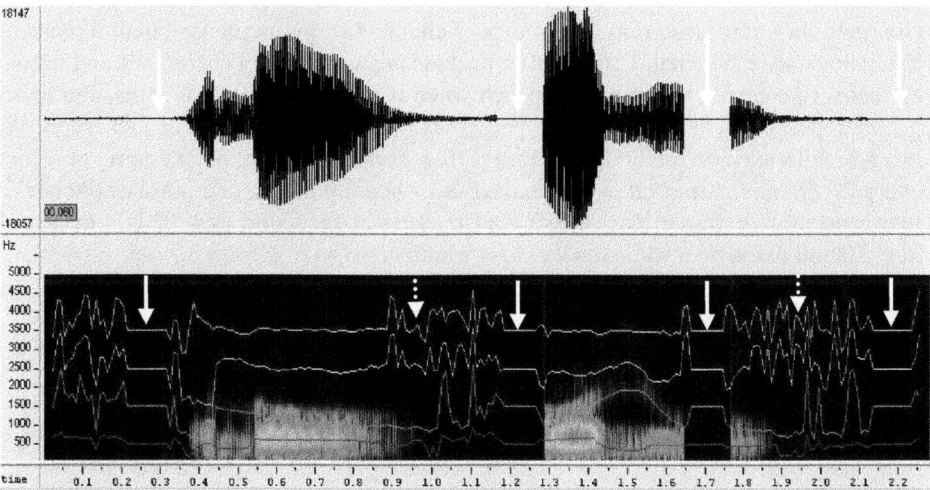

Fig. 2. Effect of packet loss. (a) same speech utterance (as shown in Fig.1(a)) with random packet lost (b) corresponding spectrogram and formant contour for first four formants

3   Experimental Setup

In this section, a brief detail of experimental setup used for SR is presented.

Speech Corpus: In this work, database of 100 speakers (46 male and 54 female, with age range 18-22 years) recorded in English language is used. The recording was done with the help of Creative Headset HS-300 with 22050 Hz sampling frequency (down-sampled to 8 kHz) and 16-bit resolution using Sound Editing Software with noise canceling microphone.

Speech Codec: In this paper, Mixed Excitation Linear Prediction (MELP) codec was used which is U.S. Department of Defense (DoD) standard and has the bit-rate of 2400 bps [6]. However, in real-time voice data applications, iLBC [9] and G.729 codecs are popular and have higher bit-rate than that of MELP. We chose this MELP codec because it has least bit-rate and we can analyze worst case condition of the packet loss and by intuition, we can expect higher performance of SR system over lossy network employing above mentioned codecs.

Spectral Features: In SR, cepstral-based features are dominantly used due to their property of capturing vocal tract-based spectral information. Hence, spectral features such as Mel frequency Cepstral Coefficients (MFCC) are used.

4 Novel Interleaving Schemes for Speaker Recognition [11]

As discussed in Section 2, zeros are replaced in the place of a lost packet, which is a popular scheme known as *silence insertion* [14]. By inserting zeros in speech packets (we call this zero insertion scheme as Scheme-1a) we perceive small breaks in continuous speech signal. Consecutive packets are *statistically correlated* and human ear cannot perceive change in the speech when it is of the order of few *ms*, and hence packet repetition scheme has higher perceptual quality than that of zero insertion. We propose interleaving method to improve the performance of SR system, in which every 2nd frame of a packet is interleaved. So when a packet is lost, this whole packet loss reduces to a frame loss in different packets at reception end. This reduces the degradation made by a whole packet loss which consists of 4 frames.

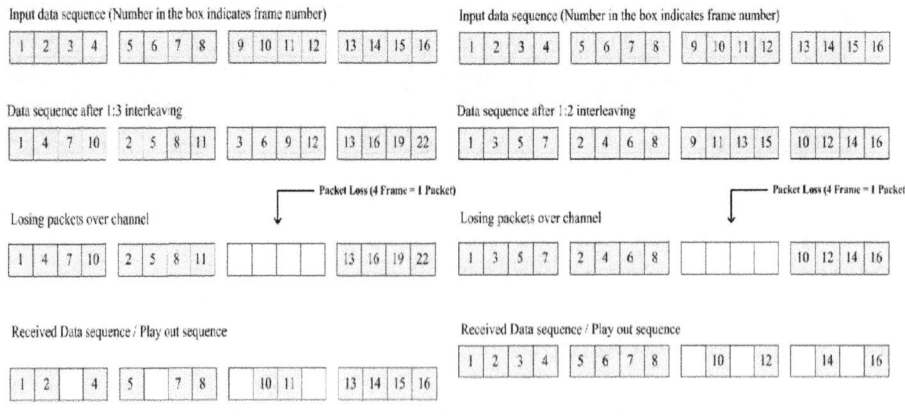

Fig. 3. 1:2 Interleaving scheme (4 frames/packet) [11]

Fig. 4. 1:3 Interleaving scheme (4 frames/packet) [11]

We will call this scheme as Scheme 2-a. If lost frames are replaced by previously received frame then we call that modified scheme as Scheme 2a-fr [11]. Next interleaving scheme interleaves every 3rd frame we call it as Scheme 3-a.

The scheme which incorporates redundancy are denoted with suffix 'b', i.e., Scheme 2-b, in which 1:2 interleaving is done with 100% redundant data transmitted. Thus, we will call 1-b as zero insertion with 100 % redundancy. These interleaving schemes have been simulated in MATLAB environment with the assumption of *statistically independent* packet loss rates.

5   Experimental Results

In this paper, polynomial classifiers of 2nd order approximation are used as basis for all the experiments [12]. Various interleaving schemes discussed in section 4 were applied on database of 100 speakers. Header information of IP packet and its processing has not been considered for the SR experiments considering the fact and intuition that it will not affect the performance. Then packet loss rates of 5%, 10%, 15% and 20% have been simulated. Higher packet loss rates are omitted in these experiments because of its less probability of occurrence in realistic scenarios of VoIP network. There is a trade off between two errors of recognition task *viz.* False Alarm (FR) and False Rejection (FR) and this trade off curve is known as Detection Error Trade-off (DET) curve, which is a standard of performance evaluation recommended by NIST [13]. Selection of operating point (threshold) where FA and FR are equal is referred to equal error rate (EER). Detection cost function (DCF) gives the cost of FA and FR. Table 1 shows EER and optimal DCF values for baseline scheme 1-a and various proposed interleaving schemes. It is evident from Table 1 that proposed interleaving performs better than the baseline scheme 1-a in majority of the cases of packet loss rates.

Table 1. EER (%) and opt. DCF comparison for different schemes for lossy training method

Scheme	5% PL		10% PL		15 %PL		20% PL	
	EER	DCF	EER	DCF	EER	DCF	EER	DCF
1a	24.2667	0.2354	24.6000	0.2396	24.8333	0.2410	25.2000	0.2446
2a-fr	24.2000	0.2344	24.5000	0.2371	24.6667	0.2389	24.8000	0.2402
2b-fr	24.2000	0.2351	24.3667	0.2372	24.4333	0.2374	24.5000	0.2383
3a-fr	24.2667	0.2346	24.5333	0.2377	24.6333	0.2389	24.6667	0.2400
3b-fr	24.1333	0.2342	24.3333	0.2360	24.4333	0.2371	24.6333	0.2386

Fig. 5 shows DET curves for performance of SR system with and without packet loss simulation using scheme 1-a. It is very clear from Fig.5 that as packet loss rate increases, EER also increase which is as expected, however, not desirable. This implies degradation in SR system performance due to lossy network. By employing the interleaving schemes with the frame replication method and packet repetition method, we get the improvement in SR system performance (as shown in Table 1). It is evident from Table-1 that every proposed interleaving schemes are performing well than baseline scheme-1a (i.e., zero insertion).

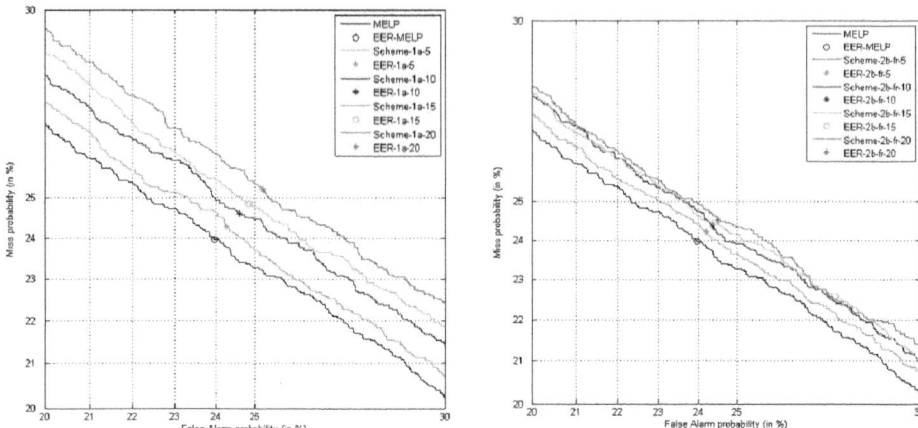

Fig. 5. DET curves to illustrate effect of packet loss on speaker recognition (Scheme 1-a)

Fig. 6. DET curves to illustrate effectiveness for Scheme 2b-fr with lossy training

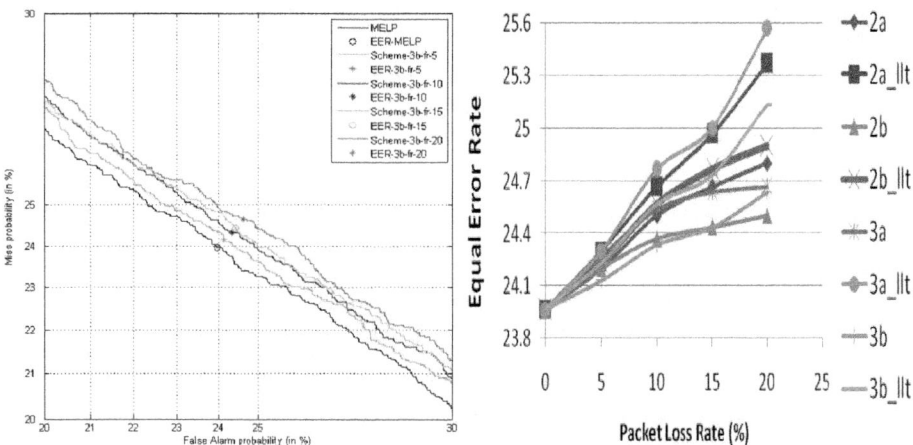

Fig. 7. DET curves to illustrate effectiveness for Scheme 3b-fr with lossy training

Fig. 8. EER comparison for lossy and loseless training methods

Conventionally, training data has no packet loss because they are recorded in good acoustic environment and they are not passed through actual IP network, while testing data will always travel through IP channel and we have to audit VoIP channel testing speech utterances, it has many lost packets in them based on the network condition and traffic onto it at that time [4]. So, to get a better match training and testing speech we have considered the lossy training method, abbreviated as *llt,* (which was proposed in [2]) to be applied on the different interleaving schemes discussed in Section 4.

It is evident from Fig.5-7 (i.e., DET curves for proposed interleaving schemes) that EER for consecutive packet loss rate has been decreased significantly and it indicates that all proposed interleaving schemes have performed well as compared to baseline scheme-1a. In addition, 3b-fr scheme gave best relative performance. From Table-2 we can infer that when packets are lost artificially on training data then it performs significantly well in most of the case. Table 2 shows the performance of SR with lossless training (i.e., *llt*). And from that we can infer that with lossy training better performance can be achieved even at higher packet loss rates.

Table 2. EER(%) and opt. DCF for conventional training (lossless training, i.e., llt)

Scheme	5% PL		10% PL		15 %PL		20% PL	
	EER	DCF	EER	DCF	EER	DCF	EER	DCF
2a-fr_llt	24.3000	0.2343	24.6667	0.2388	24.9667	0.2411	25.3667	0.2446
3a-fr_llt	24.3000	0.2343	24.7667	0.2403	25.0000	0.2426	25.5667	0.2469
2b-fr_llt	24.2333	0.2348	24.5667	0.2378	24.7667	0.2391	24.9000	0.2410
3b-fr_llt	24.2333	0.2350	24.5667	0.2380	24.7333	0.2392	25.1333	0.2428

Table 3. Comparisons of Differential EER and Differential DCF for Novel Interleaving Schemes

	5% PL		10% PL		15 % PL		20% PL	
Scheme	EER	DCF	EER	DCF	EER	DCF	EER	DCF
1a	0.3000	0.0030	0.6333	0.0072	0.8666	0.0086	1.2333	0.0122
2a-fr	0.2333	0.0020	0.5333	0.0047	0.7000	0.0065	0.8333	0.0078
3a-fr	0.3000	0.0022	0.5666	0.0053	0.6666	0.0065	0.7000	0.0076
2b-fr	0.2333	0.0027	0.4000	0.0048	0.4666	0.0050	0.5333	0.0059
3b-fr	0.1666	0.0018	0.3666	0.0036	0.4666	0.0047	0.6666	0.0062

Fig.8 shows comparison of performance of proposed interleaving schemes for conventional (loseless) training and lossy training. In order to investigate the effectiveness of different interleaving schemes to improve SR system performance and to ignore (normalize) the degradation due to the use of very low bit-rate MELP codec, differential EER and DCF are calculated (by taking EER and DCF for baseline MELP-based SR as the reference). Table 3 shows the comparison of differential EER and differential DCF for the proposed interleaving schemes. For the differential EER, as the value tends to zero indicates the performance improvement of a SR system with that particular scheme is good. It can be observed that for the scheme 3b-fr value of differential EER and differential DCF is less for all the cases of PLRs. This implies that this scheme succeed to a larger extent in alleviating the degradation in the performance of SR system over lossy network.

6   Summary and Conclusion

In this study, it was observed that performance of a SR system is sensitive to the rate of packet loss rates over the IP network channel. From experimental results, we observe that EER decreases with proposed interleaving schemes and performs well with lossy training method and frame redundancy. Proposed schemes perform well for SR but at the cost of an additional algorithmic delay and reduced data rate. Future research can be directed towards variation of number of frames in a packet, number of frames to be interleaved with burst loss. One of the limitations of the present work is, SR has large EER primarily due to use of very less bit-rate speech codec (i.e., 2.4 kbps). Our future work will be directed towards using internet Low Bit-rate Codec (iLBC) for the VoIP system.

References

1. Mehta, P., Udani, S.: Voice over IP. IEEE Potentials 20, 36–40 (2001)
2. Borah, D.K., DeLeon, D.: Speaker Identification in the Presence of Packet Loss. In: IEEE 11th Digital Signal Processing Workshop and IEEE Signal Processing Education Workshop, pp. 302–306 (2004)
3. Aggarwal, C., Olshefski, D., Saha, D., Shae, Z., Yu, P.: CSR: Speaker Recognition from Compressed VoIP Packet Stream. In: IEEE International Conference on Multimedia and Expo, ICME Amsterdam, Netherlands, pp. 970–973 (2005)
4. Wang, X., Lin, J.: Applying Speaker Recognition Over VoIP Auditing. In: Proceedings of the 6th International Conference on Machine Learning and Cybernetic, Hong Kong, pp. 3577–3581 (2007)
5. Davidson, J., Peters, J.: Voice Over IP Fundamentals. Cisco Press (2000)
6. McCree, A., Truong, K., Bryan, G., Barnwell, T.P., Vzswanathanl, V.: A 2.4 kbit/s MELP Coder Candidate for the New U.S. Federal Standard. In: Proceedings International Conference Acoust., Speech and Signal, ICASSP, Atlanta Georgia, pp. 200–203 (1996)
7. Mayorga, P., Besacier, L., Hernandez, A.: Packet Loss and Compression Effects on Vocal Recognition. In: Proceedings of CERMA (2006)
8. Hassan, M., Nayandoro, A., Atiquzzaman, M.: Internet Telephony: Services, Technical Challenges, and Products. IEEE Communications Magazine 38, 96–103 (2000)
9. Sat, B., Wah, B.W.: Analysis and Evaluation of the Skype and Google-talk VoIP Systems. In: ICME, pp. 2153–2156 (2006)
10. Davis, S.B., Mermelstein, P.: Comparison of Parametric Representations for Monosyllabic Word Recognition in Continuously Spoken Sentences. IEEE Trans. Acoustic, Speech and Signal Processing 28(4), 357–366 (1980)

11. Keller, H., George, S., Keith, T.: A Multilanguage Study of the Quality of Interleaved MELP Voice Traffice Over a Lossy Network. IEEE Signal Processing Letters 16, 565–568 (2009)
12. Campbell, W.M., Assaleh, K.T., Broun, C.C.: Speaker Recognition with Polynomial Classifiers. IEEE Transactions on Speech and Audio Processing 10(4), 205–212 (2002)
13. Martin, A.F., Doddington, G., Kamm, T., Ordowski, M., Przybocki, M.: The DET Curve in Assessment of Detection Task Performance. In: Proceeding Eurospeech 1997, Rhodes, Greece, vol. 4, pp. 1899–1903 (1997)
14. Wasem, O., Goodman, D., Dvorak, C., Page, H.: The Effect of Waveform Substitution on the Quality of PCM Packet Communications. IEEE Transactions on Acoustics, Speech, and Signal Processing 36, 342–348 (1988)

Class Dependent 2D Correlation Filter for Illumination Tolerant Face Recognition

Pradipta K. Banerjee[1], Jayanta K. Chandra[1], and Asit K. Datta[2]

[1] Department of Electrical Engineering
Future Institute of Engineering and Management
Kolkata-700150
pradiptak.banerjee@gmail.com
[2] Department of Applied Optics and Photonics
University of Calcutta, Kolkata
asitdatta@gmail.com

Abstract. This paper proposes a class dependent 2D correlation filtering technique in frequency domain for illumination tolerant face recognition. The technique is based on the frequency domain correlation between phase spectrum of reconstructed image and the phase spectrum of optimum correlation filter. The optimization is achieved by minimizing the energy at the correlation plane due to resonstructed image and maximizing the corelation peak. The synthesis of optimum filter is developed by using the projecting image. Peak to side lobe ratio (PSR) is taken as the metric for recogntion and classification. The performance evaluation of this technique is validated by comparing performance of other unconstrained filtering techniques using benchmark databases (Yale B and PIE) and better results are obtained.

Keywords: Correlation Filter, Illumination Tolerant, Face Recognition.

1 Introduction

In majority cases of illumination invariant face recognition techniques, the analysis and processing are carried out on the spatial representation of the face images i.e., the intensity values of the face images[3,10,12]. While there has been varying and significant levels of performance achieved through the use of spatial 2-D data, the use of a frequency domain representation, sometimes achieves better performance [7,9,8]. The use of the Fourier transform allows to quickly and easily obtain raw frequency data which are significantly more discriminative (after appropriate data manipulation) than the raw spatial data from which it is derived. One can further increase discrimination capability through the use of correlation filters for classification and recognition,so as to achieve significant improved performance and tolerance compared to their spatial domain counterparts. Correlation filters offer several advantages such as built-in shift-invariance and degrade gracefully in any impairment in the test image. Thirdly, while building frequency domain correlation filters, the phase spectrum of face images can

M.K. Kundu et al. (Eds.): PerMIn 2012, LNCS 7143, pp. 338–345, 2012.

be exploited to improve upon the recognition performance since the phase information of an image holds much more significant information than the amplitude
[10]. Frequency domain correlation (Fig.(1(a)) is performed by cross correlating
test face image with a pre-synthesized filter generated from the stored face image
database and then the resulting correlation output is obtained in space domain
after inverse Fourier transform. The correlation output is searched for peaks and
the relative heights of these peaks are used to determine whether the test face
is authentic or impostor. Of many types of correlation filters available, the unconstrained minimum average correlation energy (UMACE) filter [4], maximum
average correlation height (MACH) filter [4] and its variants are few much used
prominently in many applications.

In this paper, a frequency domain correlation technique is developed from the
phase only information of reconstructed image, termed as PORI, obtained by
class specific principal component analysis (CS-PCA) and the phase spectrum of
an optimum performance filter obtained from the projecting image. In subspace
analysis, a truncated subspace is derived from the original one by keeping only
those eigenvectors which are associated with useful information of the training
images[11]. The synthesis of optimum performance filter, termed as OPICF, is
done by minimizing the projecting image correlation energy (PICE) and maximizing the height of projecting image correlation peak (basically the peak
energy). The frequency domain correlation between PORI and phase spectrum
of OPICF produces a response surface, the nature of which is totally depended
on the face class involved. Ideally a delta type response at correlation plane is
obtained if PORI and OPICF are generated from the same face class. A peak
based metric, termed as peak to side-lobe ratio (PSR) [5] measured from the
correlation plane is used for authentication purpose. Two benchmark databases
PIE[1] and YaleB (extended)[2] are used for system performance verifications.

2   Formulation of Phase Only Reconstructed Image (PORI)

Each training face image is of size $(p \times q)$. Class specific PCA (CS-PCA) is applied
over a certain class C_k out of M number of classes $(k = 1, 2, \cdots, M)$ where
each class contains N number of lexicographically ordered training vectors x_i of
dimension $d \times 1$, where $d = p \times q$. It has been suggested that by withdrawing first
three principal components, the variation due to light is reduced [10]. Moreover,
the least significant eigenvector is more sensitive to noise. Hence the truncated
subspace $E_t^{C_k}$ is obtained by withdrawing first three and last one eigenvectors
and given as

$$E_t^{C_k} = [e_4, e_5, e_6, \cdots, e_{(N-1)}]_{d \times (N-4)}^{C_k} \qquad (1)$$

where e_i's are the orthonormal vectors.

During reconstruction of face images, for any test image T^{C_k} (of dimension
$p \times q$) and corresponding vector τ^{C_k} of $d \times 1$ dimension, the difference vector is
obtained as,

$$\tau_d^{C_k} = \tau^{C_k} - m \qquad (2)$$

where m is the average image vector. Projecting $\tau_d^{C_k}$ into the subspace $E_t^{C_k}$, the projected vector ω^{C_k} (of dimension $(N-4) \times 1$) is obtained as,

$$\omega^{C_k} = [E_t^{C_k}]^T \tau_d^{C_k} \tag{3}$$

The reconstructed version r^{C_k} of the test vector τ^{C_k} can be formulated as,

$$r^{C_k} = m + \sum_{i=1}^{N-4} e_i^{C_k} \omega_i^{C_k} \tag{4}$$

The reconstructed image R^{C_k} (of dimension $p \times q$) in space domain can be reconstructed from the eq.(4) by reshaping the vector r^{C_k} (of dimension $d \times 1$) in row-column order.

Phase-only-reconstructed-image (PORI) is formed by taking the phase spectrum of R^{C_k}. The 2D Fourier transform of R^{C_k} and its phase spectrum $\mathbf{R}_\phi^{C_k}$ are given by,

$$\mathbf{R}^{C_k} = \sum_{x=0}^{p-1} \sum_{y=0}^{q-1} R^{C_k}(x, y) e^{-\frac{j2\pi ux}{p}} e^{-\frac{j2\pi vy}{q}} \tag{5}$$

$$and, \qquad \mathbf{R}_\phi^{C_k} = e^{j\angle \mathbf{R}^{C_k}} \tag{6}$$

3 Formulation of Optimum Projecting Image Correlation Filter (OPICF)

Since a sharp and distinct correlation peak reduces the chances of misclassification, minimization of energy at the correlation plane containing undesired side lobes and maximization of correlation peak height are necessary. The projecting image correlation energy (PICE) at the correlation plane $g_T^{C_k}(m, n)$ in response to input image T^{C_k} of class C_k and its frequency domain representation are given by

$$PICE = \sum_{m=1}^{p} \sum_{n=1}^{q} |g_T^{C_k}(m, n)|^2 \tag{7}$$

$$\mathbf{PICE} = \sum_{k=1}^{p} \sum_{l=1}^{q} |\mathbf{G}_T^{C_k}(k, l)|^2 \tag{8}$$

where, $\mathbf{G}_T^{C_k}(k, l)$ is the Fourier transform (FT) of correlation surface $g_T^{C_k}(m, n)$. Let the desired optimum filter is $\mathbf{H}_T^{C_k}(k, l)$. The frequency domain correlation surface $\mathbf{G}_T^{C_k}(k, l)$ is obtained by correlating the Fourier transformed test face image $\mathbf{F}_T^{C_k}(k, l)$ (FT of T^{C_k}) and the desired filter $\mathbf{H}_T^{C_k}(k, l)$. Hence $\mathbf{G}_T^{C_k}(k, l)$ can be mathematically reformulated as

$$\mathbf{G}_T^{C_k}(k, l) = \mathbf{H}_T^{C_k}(k, l) [\mathbf{F}_T^{C_k}(k, l)]^*$$
$$= \sum_{k=1}^{p} \sum_{l=1}^{q} |\mathbf{H}_T^{C_k}(k, l)|^2 |\mathbf{F}_T^{C_k}(k, l)|^2 \tag{9}$$

If $\mathbf{H}_T^{(C_k)}$ is expressed by vector $\mathbf{h}_T^{C_k}$ and a diagonal matrix $\mathbf{F}_{TD}^{C_k}$ containing $\mathbf{F}_T^{C_k}(k,l)$ along its diagonal, then **PICE** can be expressed by matrix-vector equation as

$$\mathbf{PICE} = ([\mathbf{h}_T^{C_k}]^+ \mathbf{F}_{TD}^{C_k})([\mathbf{F}_{TD}^{C_k}]^* \mathbf{h}_T^{C_k}) = [\mathbf{h}_T^{C_k}]^+ \mathbf{P}_{TD}^{C_k} \mathbf{h}_T^{C_k} \tag{10}$$

where $\mathbf{P}_{TD}^{C_k} = \mathbf{F}_{TD}^{C_k}[\mathbf{F}_{TD}^{C_k}]^*$ is a $d \times d$ diagonal matrix containing power spectral density of T^{C_k} along its diagonal.

In addition of suppressing side lobes of the correlation peak, it is also needed that the required optimum filter must yield large peak values at the origin at the correlation plane. This condition is met by maximizing projecting image correlation height (**PICH**). The frequency domain expression for **PICH** for T^{C_k} is obtained as,

$$\mathbf{PICH} = [\mathbf{F}_{TD}^{C_k}]^+ \mathbf{h}_T^{C_k} \tag{11}$$

where $+$ sign indicates conjugate transpose. To make **PICH** large while reducing **PICE** the optimum filter $\mathbf{h}_T^{C_k}$ is synthesized as,

$$\mathbf{OPICF} = \frac{|\mathbf{PICH}|^2}{\mathbf{PICE}} = \frac{[\mathbf{h}_T^{C_k}]^+ \mathbf{F}_{TD}^{C_k}[\mathbf{F}_{TD}^{C_k}]^+ \mathbf{h}_T^{C_k}}{[\mathbf{h}_T^{C_k}]^+ \mathbf{P}_{TD}^{C_k} \mathbf{h}_T^{C_k}} \tag{12}$$

where, $|\mathbf{PICH}|^2$ represents the energy of correlation plane peak value. The optimum filter $\mathbf{h}_T^{C_k}$ that maximizes the ratio of quadratics (eq.12) is the dominant eigen vector [4] of $[\mathbf{P}_{TD}^{C_k}]^{-1} \mathbf{F}_{TD}^{C_k}[\mathbf{F}_{TD}^{C_k}]^+$ or it can be written as

$$\mathbf{OPICF} = h_T^{C_k} = [\mathbf{P}_{TD}^{C_k}]^{-1} \mathbf{F}_{TD}^{C_k} \tag{13}$$

Hence the desired 2-D OPCIF, $\mathbf{H}_T^{C_k}$ is formed by reshaping the vector $\mathbf{h}_T^{C_k}$ in proper row-column order. The phase extension of $\mathbf{H}_T^{C_k}$ can be simply obtained by

$$\mathbf{H}_\phi^{C_k} = e^{j \angle \mathbf{H}_T^{C_k}} \tag{14}$$

4   Face Classification and Recognition Analysis

The detail process of face classification and /or recognition is given in Fig.(1(b)). At first, the CS-PCA is computed and truncated over the total population of M-classes of face images. Hence M numbers of class specific subspaces $E_t^{C_k}$ are formed. A test face image T^{C_k} (treated as projecting image) from any class, $C_k, k \in M$ is projected onto the M numbers of subspaces resulting M-numbers of reconstructed images $R^{C_k}, k \in M$. From these R^{C_k} PORI for each class is formed according to equation (6). Hence M-numbers of PORI in frequency domain are formed. Along with this operation, OPICF is formed from test face image T^{C_k}.

For face recognition of a particular class, each PORI thus obtained is correlated with phase only OPICF. For authentication a sharp and distinct peak in the correlation plane is needed. Ideally a delta type correlation plane is desired for reducing classification errors. A delta function $\delta(m,n)$ is represented by a

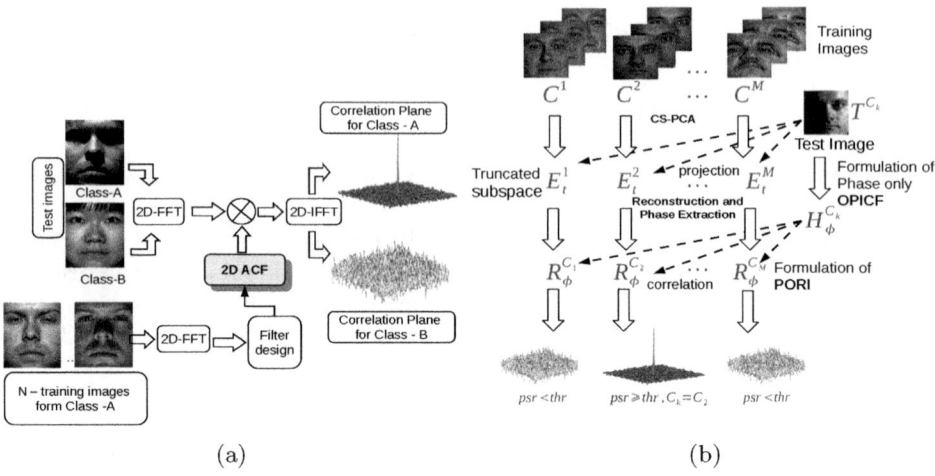

$$(a) \qquad\qquad\qquad\qquad (b)$$

Fig. 1. (a) Basic correlation technique in frequency domain (b) Shows the detail process of the proposed system

constant flat Fourier transform. This can be achieved if and only if PORI is identical to phase only OPICF i.e. all the phases are canceled out resulting in a constant flat spectrum. The spatial domain correlation output obtained from $\mathbf{R}_\phi^{C_a}$ of say a face image from class **a** and $\mathbf{H}_\Phi^{C_b}$ of face image from class **b** is given by

$$c(m,n) = FFT^{-1}\{\mathbf{R}_\phi^{C_a} \otimes [\mathbf{H}_\Phi^{C_b}]^*\} \qquad (15)$$

Decision of authentication could be made in an ideal situation by the following relation,

$$c(m,n) = \begin{cases} \delta(m,n) & \text{if } a = b \\ 0 & \text{if } a \neq b \end{cases}$$

In a practical situation, peak to side lobe ratio (PSR) of the peak at the correlation plane $c^{C_k}(m,n)$ is calculated. The test face image T^{C_k} is classified into a class for which the PSR value is greater than the preset-set threshold value denoted by `thr`, usually taken as 10[5].

5 Results

Based on the PIE face database and YALE B database, the comparative performance of the proposed frequency domain correlation filtering technique is compared with the available correlation techniques. The proposed frequency domain correlation does not have any pre-defined constraint in the correlation plane during its synthesis and hence it's performance is compared only with the unconstrained filters, such as, UMACE filter[4], MACH filter [4], unconstrained optimal trade off synthetic discriminant function (UOTSDF) filter [6] and optimal trade off MACH (OTMACH) filter [5]. Three sets of training images are taken (randomly) from both PIE and Yale databases to synthesize the five filters. Table.(1) summarizes the results obtained after performing the experiments over the whole database (both PIE and Yale B). From two confusion matrices, the mean recognition and mean error are calculated and presented in Table.(1). It is established that the performance of the proposed method outperforms the other techniques.

Table 1. Summarizes the %mean recognition and %mean error rate comparison of all filters while experiments are performed with both the databases. Bold numerics shows the improved results obtained by the proposed method.

Methods	Yale Train-1		Yale Train-2		Yale Train-3	
	% rec	% error	% rec	% error	% rec	% error
UMACE	89.06	3.716	96.87	0.42	95.3125	5.405
UOTSDF	87.5	6.33	96.87	1.82	96.87	7.51
MACH	90.62	5.02	96.87	1.65	96.8	6.37
OTMACH	89.06	3.97	96.87	0.55	95.317	5.82
Proposed	**96.87**	**0.211**	**100**	**0.38**	**100**	**0.2534**
Methods	PIE Train-1		PIE Train-2		PIE Train-3	
	% rec	% error	% rec	% error	% rec	% error
UMACE	100	1.2698	100	1.507	100	0.9524
UOTSDF	100	1.2698	100	1.5079	100	0.9524
MACH	100	1.4286	100	1.9048	100	1.1905
OTMACH	100	1.4286	100	1.9841	100	1.1905
Proposed	100	**0.92**	100	**1.03**	100	**0.1587**

Further, the performance of the proposed and other existing techniques are compared for impostor classes. The correlation surface is set at standard PSR value of 10. The performance for impostor classes are only shown and compared with the existing filters in Fig.(2). It is observed that the proposed filter outperforms the other unconstrained filter based correlation techniques as this has less number of misclassification for impostor classes.The performance of correlation filters can further be characterized, in terms of the probabilities of correct detection (P_D) and false alarm (P_{FA}) with the help of receiver operation characteristic (ROC) curves. Fig.(2)(e) the ROC curve for the proposed filter is approaching to a step function and hence it has the best possible detection performance comparing to the other filters. The detail view of the left upper corner of the ROC curves (Fig.2(f)) are cropped and zoomed for better visibility. From the above figures it is clear that the proposed system has better ability to recognize the person even under wide variations in illumination conditions.

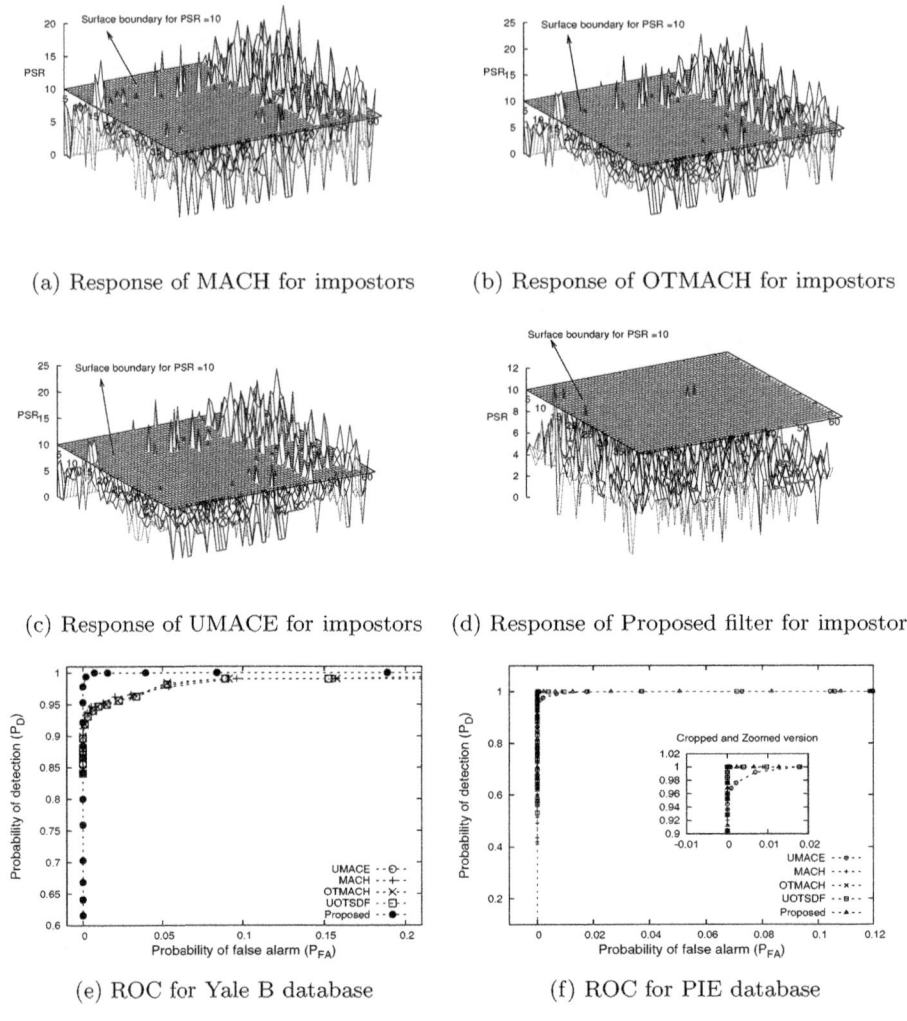

(a) Response of MACH for impostors   (b) Response of OTMACH for impostors

(c) Response of UMACE for impostors   (d) Response of Proposed filter for impostors

(e) ROC for Yale B database   (f) ROC for PIE database

Fig. 2. (a)-(d) represnt the correlation surfaces for different filters. Minimum number of misclassifications is occured for proposed method. (e)-(f) ROC curves show the performance of different filters along with the proposed method.

6   Conclusion

In this paper a new frequency domain class dependent 2D correlation technique for robust and effective face recognition is presented. Sharp peak with suppressed side lobe is obtained in the response surface of proposed system due to the synthesis of phase spectrums of projecting image correlation filter. The filter is optimized by considering the minimum energy of the correlation surface and maximum height of the correlation peak. Thus obtained sharp peak with suppressed side lobe makes the proposed system more responsive with respect to enhanced recognition accuracy of true class images and reduced misclassification error of impostor classes. The results of the proposed method is compared with other correlation filter based classifier in frequency domain and in each cases the proposed system outperforms the other. In this study all the experiments are performed with differently illuminated frontal face images and no pose variation is considered. How to extend the proposed system for both pose and illumination invariant face recognition needs further investigation.

References

1. Sim, T., Baker, S., Bsat, M.: The CMU pose, illumination, and expression database. IEEE Transactions on Pattern Analysis and Mlachine Intelligence 25(12), 1615–1618 (2003)
2. Georghiades, A.S., Belhumeur, P.N., Kriegman, D.J.: From few to many: Illumination cone models for face recognition under variable lighting and pose. IEEE Trans. Pattern Anal. Mach. Intelligence 23(6), 643–660 (2001)
3. Adini, Y., Moses, Y., Ullman, S.: Face recognition: The problem of compensating for changes in illumination direction. IEEE Transaction of Pattern Analysis and Machine Intelligence 19(7) (1997)
4. Mahalanobis, A., Vijaya Kumar, B.V.K., Song, S., Sims, S., Epperson, J.: Unconstrained correlation filter. App. Opt. 33, 3751–3759 (1994)
5. Vijaya Kumar, B.V.K., Mahalanobis, A., Juday, R.: Correlation Pattern Recognition. Cambridge University Press (2005)
6. Vijaya Kumar, B.V.K., Savvides, M., Xie, C.: Correlation pattern recognition for face recognition. Proc. IEEE 94 (2006)
7. Savvides, M., Vijaya Kumar, B.V.K.: Illumination Normalization using Logarithm Transforms for Face Authentication. In: Kittler, J., Nixon, M.S. (eds.) AVBPA 2003. LNCS, vol. 2688, pp. 549–556. Springer, Heidelberg (2003)
8. Savvides, M., Heo, J., Abiantun, R., Xie, C., Vijaya Kumar, B.V.K.: Partial and holistic face recognition on frgc-ii data using supportvector machines. In: Proc. of IEEE ICCVPR, vol. 48 (2006)
9. Savvides, M., Heo, J., Abiantun, R., Xie, C., Vijaya Kumar, B.V.K.: Class dependent kernel discrete cosine transform features for enhanced holistic face recognition in frgc-ii. In: Proc. of IEEE Int. Conf. on Acoustics, Speech and Signal Processing, vol. II, p. 185 (2006)
10. Belhumeur, P.N., Kreigman, D.J.: Eigenfaces vs fisherfaces: recognition using class specific linear projection. IEEE Tran. Pattern Analysis and Machine Intelligence 20(7) (1997)
11. Wang, S., Draper, J., Ross, J.: Analyzing pca-based face recognition algorithms: Eigenvector selection and distance measures. ABCD (July 2001)
12. Sim, T., Kanade, T.: Combining models and exemplars for face recognition: An illumination example. In: Proceedings of the CVPR (December 2001)

Removing EEG Artifacts Using Spatially Constrained Independent Component Analysis and Daubechies Wavelet Based Denoising with Otsu' Thresholding Technique

G. Geetha[*] and S.N. Geethalakshmi[**]

Department of Computer Science, Avinashilingam Institute for Home Science and Higher Education for Women

Abstract. ElectroEncephaloGram (EEG) records contains data regarding abnormalities or responses to some stimuli in the human brain. Such rhythms are examined by physicians for the purpose of detecting the neural disorders and cerebral pathologies. Because to the occurrences of artifacts, it is complicated to examine the EEG, for they introduce spikes which can be confused with neurological rhythms. Therefore, noise and undesirable signals must be removed from the EEG to guarantee a correct examination and diagnosis. This paper presents a novel technique for removing the artifacts from the ElectroEncephaloGram (EEG) signals. This paper uses Spatially-Constrained Independent Component Analysis (SCICA) to separate the exactly the artificate Independent Components (ICs) from the initial EEG signal. Then, Wavelet Denoising is applied to eliminate the brain activity from extracted artifacts, and finally project back the artifacts to be subtracted from EEG signals to get clean EEG data. This paper uses Daubechies wavelet transform for wavelet denoising. Here, thresholding plays an important role in deciding the artifacts. Therefore, a better thresholding technique called Otsu', thresholding is applied. Experimental result shows that the proposed technique results in better removal of artifacts.

Keywords: Artifact Removal, ElectroEncephaloGram (EEG), Wavwlet Denoising, Spatially-Constrained Independent Component Analysis (SCICA).

1 Introduction

Human brain human brain possesses rich spatiotemporal dynamics because of its complicated nature. Electroencephalography (EEG) provides a direct determination of cortical behavior with millisecond temporal resolution when compared to other techniques. Electroencephalogram (EEG) is multivariate time series data measured at multiple sensors positioned on scalp that imitates electrical prospective produced by

---

[*] Research Scholar.
[**] Associate Professor.

M.K. Kundu et al. (Eds.): PerMIn 2012, LNCS 7143, pp. 346–357, 2012.
© Springer-Verlag Berlin Heidelberg 2012

behaviors of brain and is a record of the electrical potentials created by the cerebral cortex nerve cells. There are two categories of EEG, based on where the signal is obtained in the head: scalp or intracranial. Scalp EEG being the focus of the research, small metal discs, also called as electrodes, are kept on the scalp with good mechanical and electrical touch. Intracranial EEG is obtained by special electrodes placed in the brain during a surgery. For the purpose of affording an exact finding of the voltage of the brain neuron, the electrodes are of low impedance. The variations in the voltage difference among electrodes are sensed and amplified before being transmitted to a computer program. EEG offers a continuous graphic display of the spatial sharing of the varying voltage with time.

However, the captured EEG [4-7] includes artifacts in their wave form. Several researches have been conducted to remove those in the EEG signal and various techniques are resulted because of this research. This paper proposed a new technique for removing the artifacts [8, 9] from the EEG signal which uses Spatially-Constrained ICA (SCICA) [12, 13] and wavelet denoising techniques. The wavelet used in this paper is Daubechies wavelet transform [19]. Threshold plays an important role in separating the artifacts from the non artifact EEG [17]. For this purpose this paper uses Otsu's Thresholding Method. This method assumes that EEG contains two classes namely, artifact and non artifact signal and then it calculates the optimum threshold separating those two classes.

2   Related Works

Shao *et al.,* [1, 2] proposed an automatic EEG Artifact removal: A Weighted Support Vector Machine approach with error correction. An automatic electroencephalogram (EEG) [15. 16] artifact removal method is presented in this paper. Compared to past methods, it has two unique features: 1) a weighted version of support vector machine formulation that handles the inherent unbalanced nature of component classification and 2) the ability to accommodate structural information typically found in component classification. The advantages of the proposed method are demonstrated on real-life EEG recordings with comparisons made to several benchmark methods. Results show that the proposed method is preferable to the other methods in the context of artifact removal by achieving a better tradeoff between removing artifacts and preserving inherent brain activities. Qualitative evaluation of the reconstructed EEG epochs also demonstrates that after artifact removal inherent brain activities are largely preserved.

Kavitha *et al.,* [3] suggested a modified ocular artifact removal technique from EEG [10, 11] by adaptive filtering. Electroencephalogram (EEG) is the reflection of brain activity and is widely used in clinical diagnoses and biomedical researches. EEG signals recorded from the scalp contain many artifacts that make its interpretation and analysis very difficult. One major source of artifacts is from eye movements that generate the Electrooculogram (EOG). Many applications of EEG such as brain computer interface (BCI) need real time processing of EEG [14]. Adaptive filtering is one of the most efficient methods for removal of ocular artifacts which can be applied in real time. In conventional adaptive filtering, the primary input is measured EEG and the reference inputs are vertical EOG (VEOG) and horizontal EOG (HEOG) signals. In this paper, we have proposed an adaptive filtering approach which includes radial EOG (REOG) signal as a third reference input. We have analyzed the performance of adaptive algorithms using two reference inputs i.e. VEOG and HEOG and three reference inputs i.e. VEOG, HEOG and REOG and it is found that the proposed 3 reference method gives more accurate results than the existing two reference method.

3   Methodology

The architecture of the proposed method for preprocessing of EEG data is presented in figure 1 [17]. As represented, EEG data is implicited to be generated based on ICA model as

$$x(t) = As(t) + v(t) \tag{1}$$

where $x(t) = [x_1(t), x_2(t), \cdots, x_M(t)]^T$ which is a linear mixture of N sources $s(t) = [s_1(t), s_2(t), \cdots, s_N(t)]^T$, A is M×N mixing matrix, and $v(t) = [v_1(t), v_2(t), \cdots, v_M(t)]^T$ is nothing but the additive noise at the EEG sensors. Here the number of sources is represented as N, there is represented waveforms $s_i(t)$, and mixing matrix A are all unknown. In order to make the problem simple, the square mixing problem is considered, i.e., M = N. The source signals $s_i(t)$ can be regarded as being created from various brain regions and artifacts. These artifacts mask the brain activity data, and are dangerous for further examination and processing. Thus it is especially vital to process EEG data x(t) so that contribution of artifacts is separated, without damaging the brain-activity data, and is the key focus of the technique provided by the author. As represented in figure 1, the proposed technique consists of following key process:

- Preprocessing with the help of existing filtering.
- Use SCICA to obtain SC-ICs representing artifacts in EEG data.
- Use WD to separate any brain activity leaked to these artifact ICs.
- The extracted artifact-only signals are projected back, and subtracted from, EEG data to get clean EEG for further examination and processing.

The purpose of conventional filtering is to process raw EEG data x(t) to eliminate 50 Hz line noise, baseline values, artifacts inhabiting in very low frequencies and high frequency sensor noise v(t), and this phase may include mixture of different existing notch, lowpass, and/or highpass filters.

Spatially-Constrained ICA (SCICA)
The main process in the proposed technique is the application of SCICA to obtain artifact ICs from filtered and baseline corrected EEG data y(t). Here SCICA is described in detail. The key intention is to describe a Spatial Constraint (SC) on the mixing matrix A to symbolize specific prior knowledge or prior assumptions concerning the spatial topography of some source sensor projections, i.e., the SC

operates on chosen columns of A and is enforced with reference to a set of predetermined constraint sensor projections, represented by A_c. Thus, the spatially constrained mixing matrix consists two kinds of columns

$$A = [\hat{A}_c, A_u] \tag{2}$$

Where $\hat{A}_c \approx A_c$ are columns regarded as constraint, and A_u are otherwise regarded as unconstrained columns. Based on the usage, the predetermined sensor projections could be gathered by manual choice of sources extracted from a previous information segment with the help of existing ICA technique or derived from the predictions of some mathematical model of the signal obtaining procedure under examination. Based upon the confidence level regarding the accuracy of the constraint topographies A_c, and the level to which constrained columns $\overline{A}_c$ may diverge from reference A_c, there are three kinds of constraints: 1) hard constraints representing fixed column, 2) soft constraints permitting divergence within a small angular threshold α, and 3) weak constraints that only afford an initial approximation for otherwise unconstrained assessment. The spatially-constrained-FastICA (SCFastICA) technique is considered with soft SCs.

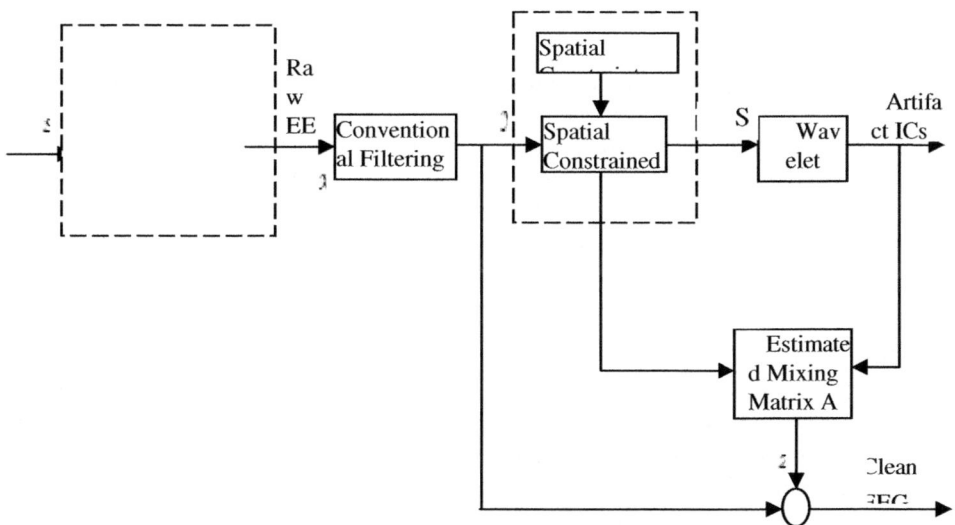

Fig. 1. Overall Process of Artifact Removal

The purpose of conventional filtering is to process raw EEG data x(t) to eliminate 50 Hz line noise, baseline values, artifacts inhabiting in very low frequencies and high frequency sensor noise v(t), and this phase may include mixture of different existing notch, lowpass, and/or highpass filters.

Spatially-Constrained ICA (SCICA)
The main process in the proposed technique is the application of SCICA to obtain artifact ICs from filtered and baseline corrected EEG data y(t). Here SCICA is

described in detail. The key intention is to describe a Spatial Constraint (SC) on the mixing matrix A to symbolize specific prior knowledge or prior assumptions concerning the spatial topography of some source sensor projections, i.e., the SC operates on chosen columns of A and is enforced with reference to a set of predetermined constraint sensor projections, represented by A_c. Thus, the spatially constrained mixing matrix consists two kinds of columns

$$A = [\hat{A}_c, A_u]$$ (2)

Where $\hat{A}_c \approx A_c$ are columns regarded as constraint, and A_u are otherwise regarded as unconstrained columns. Based on the usage, the predetermined sensor projections could be gathered by manual choice of sources extracted from a previous information segment with the help of existing ICA technique or derived from the predictions of some mathematical model of the signal obtaining procedure under examination. Based upon the confidence level regarding the accuracy of the constraint topographies A_c, and the level to which constrained columns $\hat{A}_c$ may diverge from reference A_c, there are three kinds of constraints: 1) hard constraints representing fixed column, 2) soft constraints permitting divergence within a small angular threshold α, and 3) weak constraints that only afford an initial approximation for otherwise unconstrained assessment. The spatially-constrained-FastICA (SCFastICA) technique is considered with soft SCs.

The SCFastICA technique aims to maximize the statistical independence of the unconstrained sources and at the same time reducing the divergence among the spatially constrained source sensor projections and their corresponding reference topographies. A deflationary technique is implemented to take out only desired components, and therefore the output of the SCFastICA technique is SC-ICs (which are artifact signals in our case), and an estimate of corresponding mixing matrix. This results in fast computational time, as compared with if all ICs are extracted.

Wavelet Denoising (WD) of SC-ICs
It is significance mentioning that SC-ICs determined by SCFastICA are expected to correspond to artifacts only; on the other hand, some brain action might escape to these gathered signals. As artifacts have a frequency overlap with the brain signals, conventional filtering technique cannot be utilized, and therefore this paper focuses on using Wavelet Denoising to take away any brain activity from gathered SC-ICs.

Daubechies wavelet transform [19] is used in this paper which has the ability to remove the noise in better manner.

When processing signals, the prime consideration is the localization, i.e., the characterization of local properties, of a given basis function in time and frequency. Daubechies Wavelet Transform will help in better detection of local properties. For each integer r, Daubechies' orthonormal basis for $L^2(R)$ is defined as

$$\phi_{r,j,k}(x) = 2^{j/2}\phi_r(2^j x - k), j, k \in \mathbf{Z}$$ (3)

where the function $\phi_r(x)$ in $L^2(R)$ has the property that $\{\phi_r(x - k)|k \in Z\}$ is an orthonormal sequence in $L^2(R)$. Then the trend f_j, at scale 2^{-j}, of a function $f \in L^2(R)$ is defined as

$$f_j(x) = \sum_k \langle f, \phi_{r,j,k} \rangle \phi_{r,j,k}(x) \tag{4}$$

The details or fluctuations are defined by

$$d_j(x) = f_{j+1}(x) - f_j(x) \tag{5}$$

To analyze these details at a given scale, we define an orthonormal basis $\psi_r(x)$ having properties similar to those of $\phi_r(x)$ described above.

$\phi_r(x - k)$ and $\psi_r(x)$ called the father wavelet and the mother wavelet, respectively, are the wavelet prototype functions required by the wavelet analysis.

Daubechies' orthonormal basis has the following properties:

- ψ_r has the compact support interval $[0, 2r + 1]$
- ψ_r has about $r/5$ continuous derivatives
- $\int_{-\infty}^{\infty} \psi_r(x) dx = \cdots = \int_{-\infty}^{\infty} x^r \psi_r(x) dx = 0$

Daubechies' wavelets give remarkable results in signal analysis and synthesis due to the above properties. In fact, a wavelet function with compact support can be easily implemented by finite length filters. This finite length property is important for spatial domain localization. Furthermore, functions with more continuous derivatives analyze continuous functions more efficiently and avoid the generation of edge artifacts. Since the mother wavelets are used to characterize details in the signal, they should have a zero integral so that the trend information is stored in the coefficients obtained by the father wavelet. A Daubechies' wavelet representation of a function is a linear combination of the wavelet function elements.

The Daubechies Wavelet Transform examines a finite length time domain signal by breaking up the initial domain in two phases: the detail and approximation data. The approximation domain is sequentially decomposed into detail and approximation domains. The basic principle is that the decomposition of a noisy signal on a wavelet basis (by Daubechies Wavelet Transform) have the property to "concentrate" the informative signal in few wavelet coefficients having large absolute values without altering the noise random distribution. After performing these operations, the noise coefficients have minimum values, inversely to the informative signal (normal or pathologic neural activity and artifacts). Consequently, denoising can be attained by thresholding the wavelet coefficients using Otsu's thresholding method. The implementation is as follows:

- Choosing the value of the threshold using Otsu's Thresholding Method
- Then Daubechies Wavelet Transform is performed to the SC-IC signal to obtain details and approximations

- Threshold the detailed components obtained in the previous step
- Finally inverse Daubechies Wavelet Transform is utilized to obtain only the artifact signal

Otsu's Thresholding Method
A signal consists of N values with levels from 1 to L. The number of values with gray level i is represented by f_i, giving a probability of level i in the given signal is

$$p_i = \frac{f_i}{N} \tag{6}$$

In the case of bi-level thresholding, the values are aeperated into two classes, C_1 with levels [1, …, t] and C_2 with levels [t+1, …, L]. Then, the level probability distributions for the two classes are

$$C_1 : \frac{p_1}{\omega_1(t)}, …, \frac{p_t}{\omega_1(t)} \text{ and}$$
$$C_2 : \frac{p_{t+1}}{\omega_2(t)}, \frac{p_{t+2}}{\omega_2(t)}, …, \frac{p_L}{\omega_2(t)},$$

where

$$\omega_1(t) = \sum_{i=1}^{t} p_i \tag{7}$$

and

$$\omega_2(t) = \sum_{i=t+1}^{L} p_i \tag{8}$$

Also, the means for classes C_1 and C_2 are

$$\mu_1 = \sum_{i=1}^{t} \frac{ip_i}{\omega_1(t)} \tag{9}$$

and

$$\mu_1 = \sum_{i=t+1}^{L} \frac{ip_i}{\omega_2(t)} \tag{10}$$

Let μ_T be the mean intensity for the whole values. It is easy to show that

$$\omega_1\mu_1 + \omega_2\mu_2 = \mu_T \tag{11}$$

$$\omega_1 + \omega_2 = 1 \tag{12}$$

Using discriminant analysis, Otsu defined the between-class variance of the thresholded data

$$\sigma_B^2 = \omega_1(\mu_1 - \mu_T)^2 + \omega_2(\mu_2 - \mu_T)^2 \tag{13}$$

For bi-level thresholding, Otsu verified that the optimal threshold t* is selected so that the between-class variance σ_B^2 is maximized; that is,

$$t^* = \text{ArgMax}\{\sigma_B^2(t)\}.$$
$$1 \leq t < L \tag{14}$$

The previous formula can be easily extended to multilevel thresholding of a signal. Assuming that there are M-1 thresholds, $\{t_1, t_2, ..., t_{M-1}\}$, which seperates the original image into M classes: C_1 for $[1,..., t1]$, C2 for $[t_1+1, ..., t_2]$, ... , C_i for $[t_{i-1}+1, ..., t_i]$, ..., and C_M for $[t_{M-1}+1, ..., L]$, the optimal thresholds $\{t_1^*, t_2^*, ..., t_{M-1}^*\}$ are chosen by maximizing σ_B^2 as follows:

$$\{t_1^*, t_2^*, ..., t_{M-1}^*\} = \text{ArgMax}\{\sigma_B^2(t_1, t_2, ..., t_{M-1})\}$$
$$1 \leq t_1 < \cdots < t_{M-1} < L \tag{15}$$

where

$$\sigma_B^2 = \sum_{k=1}^{M} \omega_k(\mu_k - \mu_T)^2 \tag{16}$$

with

$$\omega_k = \sum_{i \in C_k} p_i \tag{17}$$

$$\mu_k = \sum_{i \in C_k} i p_i / \omega(k), \tag{18}$$

The ω_k in equation (12) is regarded as the zeroth-order cumulative moment of the kth class C_k, and the numerator in equation (15) is regarded as the first-order cumulative moment of the kth class C_k; that is,

$$\mu(k) = \sum_{i \in C_k} i p_i \tag{19}$$

Once "clean" artifacts are obtained, these are projected back to EEG sensors with the help of mixing matrix A obtained by SCFastICA, and artifacts in the EEG data are obtained, as represented by z(t) in figure 1. At last, the clean EEG data $\hat{x}(t)$ is obtained by subtracting artifacts z(t) from EEG data y(t).

4   Experimental Results

This section presents the evaluation of the proposed artifact removal technique. Initially, EEG signals are captured with occurrence of artifacts. The captured EEG signal is shown in figure 2(a) and 3(a).

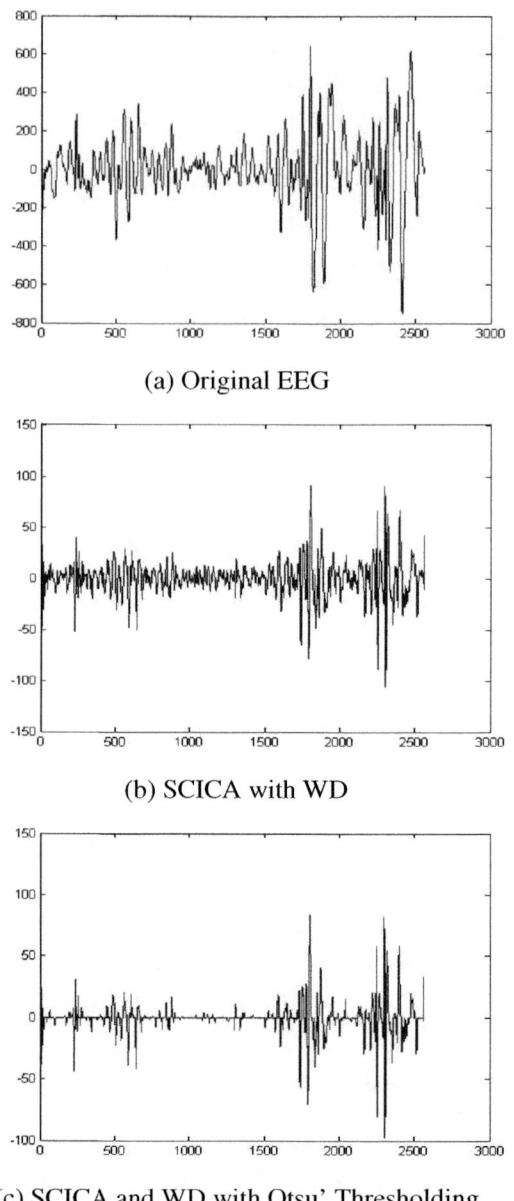

(a) Original EEG

(b) SCICA with WD

(c) SCICA and WD with Otsu' Thresholding

Fig. 2. Results Obtained for Artifact Removal with a Sample Signal 1

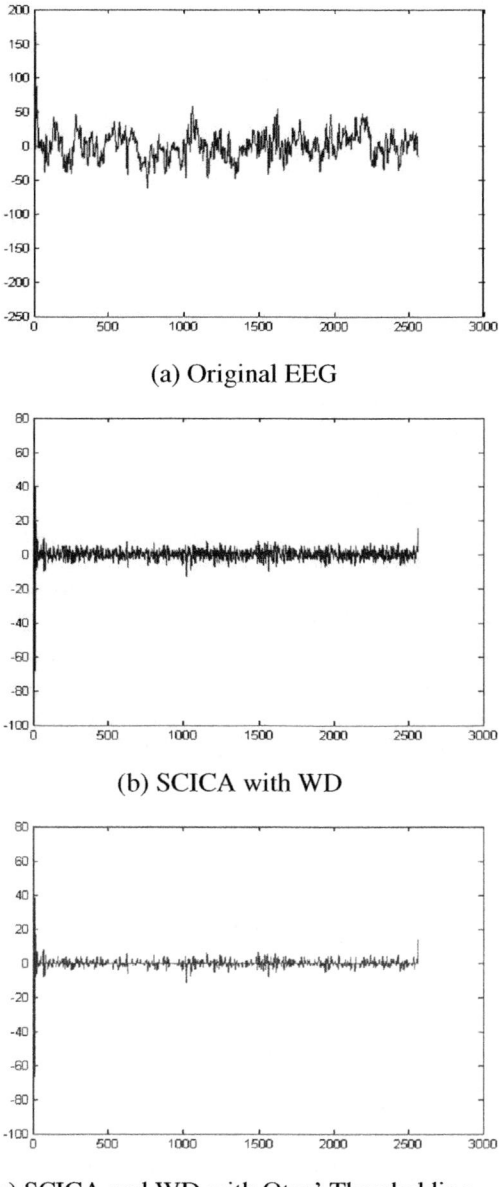

(a) Original EEG

(b) SCICA with WD

(c) SCICA and WD with Otsu' Thresholding

Fig. 3. Results Obtained for Artifact Removal with a Sample Signal 2

The results obtained are depicted in figure 2 and figure 3. The signal resulted after the usage of wavelet filtering and Spatially-Constrained ICA is shown in figure 2(b) and 3(b). Final signal obtained by using the otsu's thresholding technique is shown in figure 2(c) and 3(c). From the figures, it can be observed that the proposed artifact removal technique results in better removal of artifacts when compared to the existing technique. The resulted EEG signal after removing the artifact is better for the proposed technique as seen in figure 3(c) i.e., the unnecessary artifacts are removed from the signal and clear signal which represents the peaks are resulted whereas the usage of SCICA and WD (refer figure 3(c))alone does not result in clear separation of peak signals.

This will help in improving the performance of the further processing with this obtained EEG signal.

5   Conclusion

This paper focuses on removing the artifacts from ElectroEncephaloGram (EEG) signals. This is an important process before analyzing the EEG signal which is useful obtaining the only the necessary data in EEG signal. Various researchers focused on this process and developed their own technique. This paper intends on developing a new technique to remove the artifact from EEG. The proposed approach uses Spatially-Constrained Independent Component Analysis (SCICA) to separate the exactly the artificate Independent Components (ICs) from the initial EEG signal. Then, Daubechies Wavelet Transform based Wavelet Denoising is applied to eliminate the brain activity from extracted artifacts, and finally project back the artifacts to be subtracted from EEG signals to get clean EEG data. The thresholding technique used in this paper is otsu's thresholding. Experimental result suggests that the proposed approach results in better removal of artifact when compared to the existing techniques.

References

[1] Shao, S.-Y., Shen, K.-Q., Ong, C.J., Wilder-Smith, E., Li, X.-P.: Automatic EEG Artifact Removal: A Weighted Support Vector Machine Approach with Error Correction. IEEE Transactions on Biomedical Engineering 56, 336–344 (2009)
[2] Shao, S.-Y., Shen, K.-Q., Ong, C.-J., Li, X.-P., Wilder-Smith, E.P.V.: Automatic identification and removal of artifacts in EEG using a probabilistic multi-class SVM approach with error correction. In: IEEE International Conference on Systems, Man and Cybernetics, pp. 1134–1139 (2008)
[3] Kavitha, P.T., Lau, C.T., Premkumar, A.B.: Modified ocular artifact removal technique from EEG by adaptive filtering. In: International Conference on Information, Communications & Signal Processing, pp. 1–5 (2007)
[4] Kim, K.H., Yoon, H.W., Park, H.W.: Improved algorithm for ballistocardiac artifact removal from EEG simultaneously recorded with fMRI. In: 26th Annual International Conference of the IEEE Engineering in Medicine and Biology Society, vol. 1, pp. 936–939 (2004)
[5] LeVan, P., Urrestarrazu, E., Gotman, J.: A system for automatic artifact removal in ictal scalp EEG based on independent component analysis and Bayesian classification. Clinical Neurophysiology 117(4), 912–927 (2006)

[6] Croft, R.J., Barry, R.J.: Removal of ocular artifact from the EEG: a review. Clinical Neurophysiology 30(1), 5–19 (2000)

[7] Joyce, C., Gorodnitsky, I., Kutas, M.: Automatic removal of eye movement and blink artifacts from EEG data using blind component separation. Phychophysiology 41(2), 313–325 (2004)

[8] Krishnaveni, V., Jayaraman, S., Aravind, S., Hariharasudhan, V., Ramadoss, K.: Automatic identification and Removal of ocular artifacts from EEG using Wavelet transform. Measurement Science Review 6(4), 45–57 (2006)

[9] Krishnaveni, V., Jayaraman, S., Malmurugan, N., Kandasamy, A., Ramadoss, D.: Non adaptive thresholding methods for correcting ocular artifacts in EEG. Academic Open Internet Journal 13 (2004)

[10] Yuval-Greenberg, S., Tomer, O., Keren, A.S., Nelken, I., Deouell, L.Y.: Transient Induced Gamma-Band Response in EEG as a Manifestation of Miniature Saccades. Neuron 58(3), 429–441 (2008)

[11] Verobyov, S., Cichocki, A.: Blind noise reduction of multisensory signals using ICA and subspace filtering, with application to EEG analysis. Biological Cybernetics 86, 293–303 (2002)

[12] Potter, M., Gadhok, N., Kinsner, W.: Separation performance of ICA on simulated EEG and ECG signals contaminated by noise. Canadian Journal of Electrical and Computer Engineering 27(3), 123–127 (2002)

[13] Choi, S., Cichocki, A., Park, H., Lee, S.: Blind Source Separation and Independent Component Analysis: A Review. Neural Information Processing – Letters and Reviews 6(1) (January 2005)

[14] Cichocki, A., Amari, S.-I.: Adaptative blind Signal and Image Processing Learning Algorithms and Applications. John Wiley & Sons, Ltd. (2002)

[15] Sutherland, M.T., Tang, A.C.: Blind source separation can recover systematically distributed neuronal sources from "resting" EEG. In: Proceedings of the Second International Symposium on Communications, Control, and Signal Processing (ISCCSP 2006), Marrakech, Morocco, March 13-15 (2006)

[16] Kierkels, J.J.M., Van Botel, G.J.M., Vogten, L.L.M.: A Model-Based Objective Evaluation of Eye Movement Correction in EEG Recordings. IEEE Transactions on Biomedical Engineering 53(2) (February 2006)

[17] Akhtar, M.T., James, C.J.: Focal Artifact Removal from Ongoing EEG – A Hybrid Approach Based on Spatially-Constrained ICA and Wavelet De-noising. In: Annual International Conference of the IEEE EMBS Minneapolis, pp. 4027–4030 (2009)

[18] Castellanos, N.P., Makarov, V.A.: Recovering EEG brain signals: Artifact suppression with wavelet enhanced independent component analysis. J. Neuroscience Methods 158, 300–312 (2006)

[19] Wang, J.Z., Wiederhold, G., Firschein, O., Wei, S.X.: Content-based image indexing and searching using Daubechies' wavelets. Int. J. Digit. Libr. 1, 311–328 (1997)

Performance Evaluation of PBDP Based Real-Time Speaker Identification System with Normal MFCC vs MFCC of LP Residual Features

Soma Khan, Joyanta Basu, and Milton Samirakshma Bepari

Centre for Development of Advanced Computing (C-DAC), Kolkata
Plot – E2/1, Block – GP, Sector – V, Salt Lake Electronics Complex, Bidhannagar,
Kolkata – 700 091, West Bengal, India
{soma.khan,joyanta.basu,milton.bepari}@cdac.in

Abstract. Present study compares, Mel Frequency Cepstral Coefficients (MFCC) of Linear Predictive (LP) Residuals with normal MFCC features using both VQ and GMM based speaker modeling approaches for performance evaluation of real- time Automatic Speaker Identification systems including both co-operative and non co-operative speaking scenario. Pitch Based Dynamic Pruning (PBDP) technique is applied regarding optimization of Speaker Identification process. System is trained and tested with voice samples of 62 speakers across different age groups. Residual of a signal contains information mostly about the source, which is speaker specific. Result shows that, in co-operative speaking, MFCC of LP residuals outperform normal MFCC features for both VQ and GMM based speaker modeling with an improvement of 7.6% and 6.8% in average accuracy respectively. But combined modeling of both features (source and vocal tract) is required for non co-operative speaking in real-time as it enhances the highest identification accuracy from 67.7% to 83%.

Keywords: Linear Predictive Residual, Mel Frequency Cepstral Coefficients, Pitch Based Dynamic Pruning, Vector Quantization, Gaussian Mixture Model.

1   Introduction

Automated Biometrics-based Personal Identification systems replace all the existing user authentication methods by recognizing a person from some unique distinguishing traits like Fingerprint, Face, Voice, Iris etc. which are inseparable part of that individual. Human voice is one of the principle Biometric data used in these types of systems for its wide availability, easy transmission, low storage cost and ease of use. In these days, Voice based Authentication or Speaker Recognition (SR) techniques with real time usability have become an active research area under Speech processing. Speaker recognition encompasses both speaker verification (ASV) and identification (ASI) where input speech can be constrained to a known phrase (text-dependent) or totally unconstrained (text-independent).

M.K. Kundu et al. (Eds.): PerMIn 2012, LNCS 7143, pp. 358–366, 2012.

Since last decade, Gaussian Mixture Models (GMM) [1] has become the dominant approach in text-independent SR applications. However, the ease of implementation, numerical stability and lower memory usage make Vector Quantization (VQ) [2] approach also attractive for practical systems. Apart from these two basic types of modeling technique, selection of proper acoustic features for comparison seems to be important from performance evaluation point of view. Most of the present Speaker recognition studies focus on speaker information due to vocal tract modeling of individual speakers and use Mel-Frequency Cepstral Coefficients (MFCC) or Linear Predictive Cepstral Coefficients (LPCC) as input speech features. Relatively less number of studies are reported so far on excitation source information present within human speech. Among this, some studies [3, 4] have revealed the usefulness of Linear Predictive (LP) Residual feature for source modeling with appropriate measure. However, Mel Frequency Cepstral representation of LP residual is not yet studied well and neither comparatively tested in real time Speaker Recognition experiments with different (co-operative and non co-operative) speaking situations.

Present study compares, MFCC of LP Residuals with normal MFCC using both VQ and GMM based speaker modeling separately for co-operative and non co-operative speaking scenario. Pitch Based Dynamic Pruning (PBDP)[5] technique is applied regarding optimization of Speaker Identification process which uses speaker specific normal pitch range for pruning unlikely speakers before matching. Present study results will be used in building a text-independent ASI system for voice based automation of office attendance where an employee will simply utter his office id for daily attendance.

2   System Description

Fig. 1 represents the overall system design and data flow of the proposed ASI model. It consists of three main modules; Speech signal processing, Training and Testing

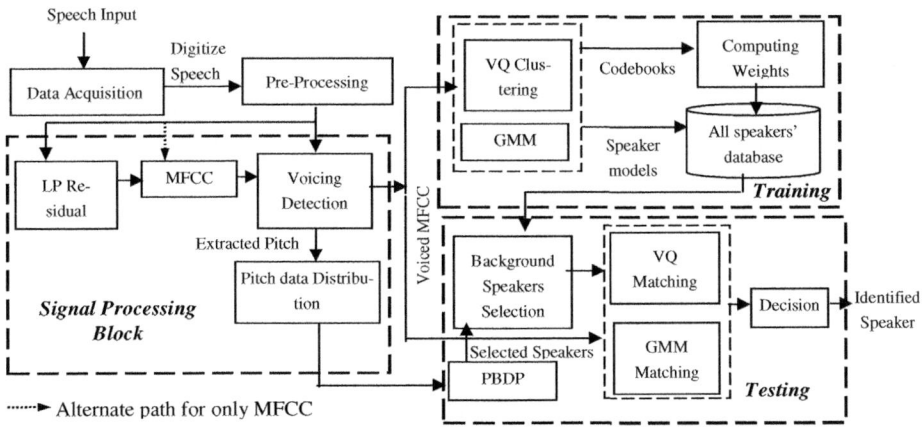

Fig. 1. Modules and data flow diagram of the Voice based Office Attendance system

2.1   Signal Processing

After Pre-Processing (noise reduction, DC normalization etc.) the digitized speech is sent for Voicing-Detection and Extraction of normal MFCC feature or extraction of **MFCC of LP Residuals.** Speech signal production is result of an interactive process between the glottal excitation (source) and the vocal tract (system). LP Residual of a signal contains information mostly about the source, which is speaker specific.

In Linear Predictive Coding (LPC) analysis (Fig. 2), from the input speech signal, we get the filter coefficients a_i and the appropriate excitation signal.

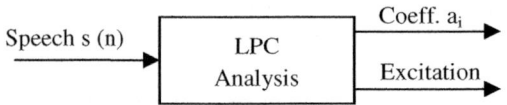

Fig. 2. Block diagram of the linear prediction analysis

After estimating the coefficients of the linear predictor for a given speech frame, we can compute the error using the formula $e(n) = s(n) - \sum_{i=1}^{k} a_i s(n-i)$.

Here, k is the LPC order. This residual, *e(n)*, represents essentially the part of the speech that was not predicted by the linear combination of previous samples. This residue *e(n)* is then send for MFCC computation to emphasize low frequency components and capture features corresponds to source excitation. Thus source information of the input speech is represented as a sequence of Cepstral vectors.

The YIN algorithm [6], based on well-known autocorrelation method is used here for voicing detection, and then, only voiced MFCC frames are used for Training and Testing. From the extracted pitch values, pitch occurrence frequency distributions are prepared within normal human voicing range (generally 80 Hz to 420 Hz). Later, at the time of testing, these distributions are used for pruning (PBDP) unlikely speakers.

2.2   Training

VQ based speaker modeling. Training feature vectors are clustered in m separate clusters represented by a *centroid* called *Code vector*. The resulting set C = {C1, C2 …Cm} of code vectors is called a Codebook. LBG clustering Algorithm [2] is used here for its efficiency and simple implementation. Then, some weights are assigned to all code vectors by using a Speaker Discriminative Weighting scheme [7], so that code vectors with higher discriminating power can get larger weights and vice-versa. So, the result of VQ based training is a database of all speakers' weighted codebooks.

GMM based speaker modeling. The distribution of feature vectors extracted from a person's speech is modeled by a Gaussian mixture density which is a weighted linear combination of M component uni-modal Gaussian densities, each parameterized by a mean vector, and covariance matrix and a mixture weight distributed over M components such that their sum should be unity. Maximum likelihood estimation of speaker model parameters are done using Expectation-Maximization (EM) algorithm [8]. Gaussian components can be assumed as modeling the underlying broad phonetic sounds that characterize a person's voice [1].

2.3   Testing

In testing, first PBDP is applied to reduce the search space and time by pruning out some of the unlikely speakers before matching.

Pitch Based Dynamic Pruning (PBDP) Algorithm. Fundamental frequency (frequency at which vocal folds vibrate) or Pitch is an important prosodic feature. As one speaks something, his/her pitch (along with other features like tone, duration, amplitude, emphasis etc) changes continuously following appropriate intonation pattern to convey the information of the speech. Though one may speak in different Pitch levels but gender wise a wide classification is there, as male speakers are reported to have lower Pitch levels than female speakers [9]. However, this criterion may not work for age or emotional variations. Generally in normal conditions, every individual speaks within some specific Pitch range. Pitch Based Dynamic Pruning (PBDP) algorithm is being designed to use this Normal Pitch range. Here, selection of training text is important. It should be same for all speakers and should cover almost all kind of pitch variations. The algorithm includes the following steps:

Step 1. From each speaker's training speech data, detect the voicing zones and get the Pitch values for a small time-stamp interval (here, it is 10ms).
Step 2. Find the minimum and maximum Pitch values from whole training pitch data. Also find the standard deviation of the pitch values for each speaker.
Step 3. For each speaker, calculate the frequency distribution of the training data pitch values, with *start value* nearly equal to minimum (its immediate lower multiple of ten in our study) pitch, *stop value* nearly equal to maximum (its immediate higher multiple of ten in our study) pitch and a suitable *step value* analyzing the standard deviations calculated in step 2 above (step value should be higher, if most of the speakers have higher standard deviation values and vice-versa).
Step 4. In the testing phase, the activities of step 1 and 3 are repeated for test speech data of the unknown speaker with same start value, stop value and step value already set for training data.
Step 5. From the frequency distribution of the test data pitch values, select the *Frequent Voicing Activity Zones (FVAZ)* where pitch occurrence frequencies are significantly higher and above Occurrence Discarding Threshold or ODT (Here, ODT = 5% of total occurrence).
Step 6. Now, for each speaker in the training database, find the *Voicing Occurrence Frequency Rate (VOFR)* within that particular FVAZ of the test data from unknown speaker by using the following formula:

$$\frac{\text{(Sum of the pitch occurrence Frequencies within the test data FVAZ)} * 100}{\text{(Total number of pitch occurrence frequencies in the whole distribution of the training speaker)}}$$

Step 7. Select the speakers having higher VOFR values. The rest of the speakers are pruned out from the matching list for that test data.

Thus the speakers, who have significant portions of their normal pitch range matching with the FVAZ of the unknown speaker, are the most likely speakers for matching. And the pruning is dynamic, because VOFR of each training speaker will change for different FVAZ of the test data, and pitch wise no Static Pruning threshold is set among the training speakers. First 20 speakers having higher *VOFR* values are selected here as background speakers for matching which is done in the following ways:

VQ based approach. Matching scores are calculated using the following formula [7]:

$$s_w(X, C_i) = \frac{1}{T} \sum_{t=1}^{T} \frac{1}{d(x_t, c_{min}^{i,t})} \cdot w(c_{min}^{i,t}) \tag{1}$$

Here, $s_w(X, C_i)$ is the weighted matching function, $X = \{x_1, x_2, ..., x_T\}$ is the sequence of test vectors, $d(x_t, c_{min}^{i,t})$ is the General Euclidian distance function between a test vector x_t and its nearest code vector $c_{min}^{i,t}$ in the codebook C_i of ith speaker in the database and $w(c_{min}^{i,t})$ is the associated weight of that code vector. The codebook getting highest matching score is the best match or Identified Speaker.

GMM based approach. Given a reference group of S background speakers R = {1, 2,..., S} represented by models $\lambda_1, \lambda_2 ....., \lambda_s,$, the speaker model which get the maximum posterior probability for the test feature vector sequence, $X = \{x_1, x_2, ..., x_T\}$, is the identified speaker.

3   Experimental Setup

Experiments are done in three sessions and two languages (Bengali & English). In each session, training text is same for all speakers and it is phonetically rich. Testing is done in two modes. Co-operative mode testing is done in first two sessions, where all speakers are said to normally utter their name and office-id, in 5 repetitions before they readout the training text material. In the last session, Non co-operative mode testing is designed specially to face the real-time speaking. Here, 10 test utterances are collected for each speaker, no specific text is given and enough pitch variations are allowed only a time-limit of 4 sec is maintained.

All data are collected in lab environment. Recording format is 16-bit PCM mono. Table 1 shows specifications for acoustic feature extraction. In voicing detection, analysis frame timing is 0.025 sec with a shifting of 0.01 sec. Voiced zones of length less than 0.030 sec is discarded here.

Table 1. Specifications for acoustic feature extraction

Parameter	Values	Parameter	Values
Sampling Rate (Hz)	22050	DFT Size	1024
Frame Rate (Frames/sec)	100	Pre-emphasis factor	0.97
Window Length (sec)	0.025625	LPC Frame Length (no. of samples)	512
Number of Cepstra	13		
Number of Mel Filters	40	LPC order	20

4   Result and Observations

Though in general, male and female speakers are having different normal pitch range, but pitch occurrence frequency distribution (POFD) of co-operative speaking shown in figure 3 and 4 makes it clear that 180 Hz to 260 Hz is common for both. Figure 5 and 6, shows that, for abrupt pitch variations, normal POFD of the same male and female speakers are getting distorted in non co-operative speaking apart from shifting and extending of normal pitch range on both sides. Especially in case of lower age group (below 30 or a2 group) speakers, it is quite noticeable that, the concentrated occurrence distribution in co-operative speaking is getting randomly distributed over different pitch levels in non co-operative speaking which represents the true pattern and uncertainty of real time speech.

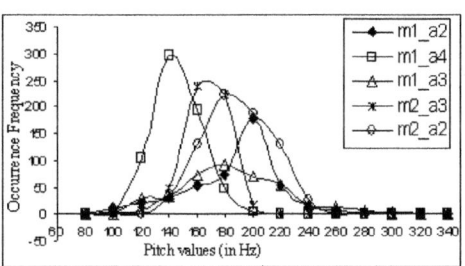
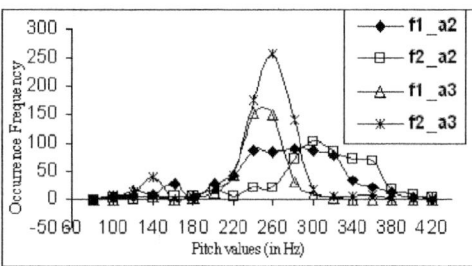

Fig. 3. Co-operative mode, POFD of 5 males   **Fig. 4.** Co-operative mode, POFD of 4 females

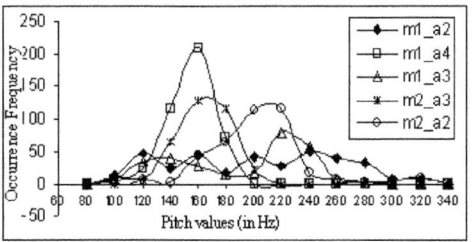

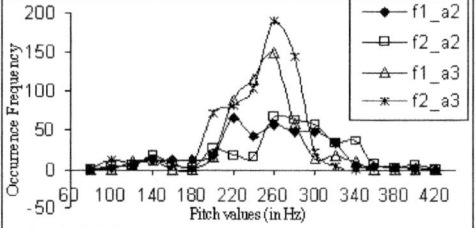

Fig. 5. Non Co-operative, POFD of 5 males   **Fig. 6.** Non Co-operative, POFD of 4 females

For depicting comparative results, Percentage of identification accuracy is plotted against different codebook size (in case of VQ) and varying number of mixtures (in case of GMM). Figure 7 and 8 shows the result of co-operative speaking scenario and identification accuracy is calculated after accumulating all test data collected in first two sessions. From figure 7 and 8 it is observed that, MFCC of LP Residue features outperform normal MFCC for both VQ and GMM with highest identification accuracy of 94% and 93%. An improvement of 7.6 % and 6.8% in average accuracy is noticed respectively. VQ attains highest accuracy at codebook size 256 and then gets stable while GMM attains highest accuracy using 16 mixture and then decreases with higher number of mixtures. For MFCC, a slight 2% increase of average accuracy is noticed in case of GMM than VQ.

Figure 9 and 10 depicts the result of last session testing with unrestricted text and pitch variations. It is specially meant for non co-operative speaking, the unavoidable situation for any text independent real-time ASI system. Results revealed the impact of source modulation due to abrupt pitch variations. Here, MFCC gets better performance accuracy in both VQ and GMM approach with 77.5% and 75.5% respectively. MFCC of LP residue attains a highest accuracy of 67.7% using 8 mixtures GMM. But this performance is still below the acceptable level.

Figure 11 and 12 represents the result of combined modeling of the above two types of features both for VQ and GMM modeling where average accuracy is increased. For Co-operative mode test data, highest accuracy achieved is 96% and 95% and for Non co-operative mode test data, accuracy increased to 83% and 82% for VQ and GMM respectively. These results are quite encouraging for acceptable performance level of real time speaker recognition system.

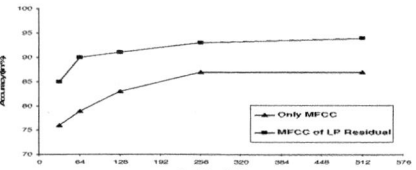

Fig. 7. Co-operative mode, Codebook size Vs Accuracy (in %)

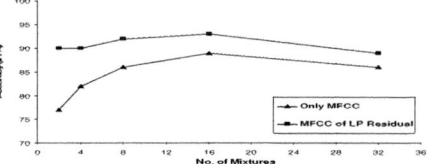

Fig. 8. Co-operative mode, no. of mixtures Vs Accuracy (in %)

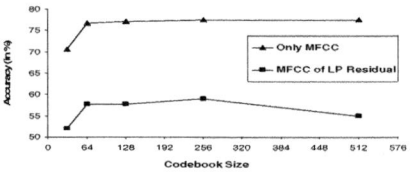

Fig. 9. Non co-operative mode, Codebook size Vs Accuracy (in %)

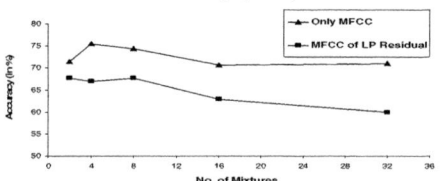

Fig. 10. Non co-operating mode, no. of mixtures Vs Accuracy (in %)

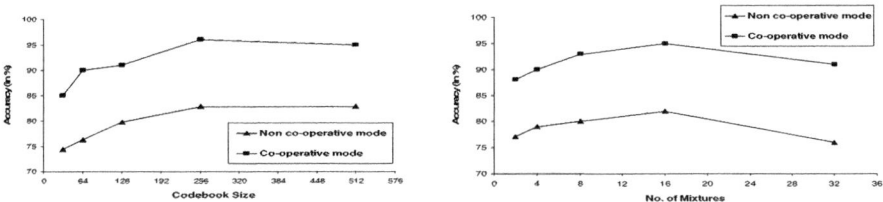

Fig. 11. Combined modeling, Codebook size **Fig. 12.** Combined modeling, no. of mixtures
Vs Accuracy (in %)   Vs Accuracy (in %)

    In Fig. 13, the overall system performance (for combined modeling with co-
operative speaking) is shown in terms of percentage Accuracy vs. Total Identification
time (time for Matching + PBDP) over varying codebook sizes, using and without
using PBDP. Problem occurring for speakers who have common FVAZ of 180 Hz to
260 Hz in their test speech sample are easily distinguished by using PBDP and hence,
5% increment in accuracy is noticed. In average, 42.56% of the total identification
time is reduced using PBDP. A same phenomenon is observed for varying number of
mixtures (in case of GMM).

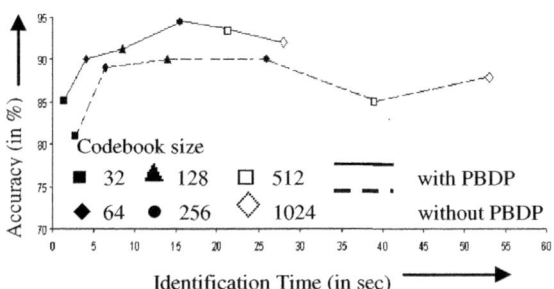

Fig. 13. System Performance on varying Codebook size

5   Conclusion

Source information present in MFCC of LP residue feature is sufficient enough for
building real-time ASI systems with co-operative speaking. But combined modeling
of source and vocal tract information is required to deal with non co-operative
speaking in real-time. Without changing the study framework, present work can be
further extended by verifying the results after including more number of speakers in
the database with appropriate combined modeling of similar source and system
features. This is necessary for building a high performance practical ASI system to
deal with different real world situations within optimal time-storage requirements.

References

1. Reynolds, D.A., Rose, R.C.: Robust text-independent speaker identification using Gaussian mixture speaker models. IEEE Trans. on Speech and Audio Processing, 72–83 (1995)
2. Linde, Y., Buzo, A., Gray, R.M.: An algorithm for vector quantizer design. IEEE Trans. on Comm. 28(1), 84–95 (1980)
3. Thevenaz, P., Hugli, H.: Usefulness of the LPC-residue in text-independent speaker verification. Speech Commun. 17(1-2), 145–157 (1995)
4. Hayakawa, S., Takeda, K., Itakura, F.: Speaker Identification Using Harmonic Structure of LP-residual Spectrum. In: Bigün, J., Borgefors, G., Chollet, G. (eds.) AVBPA 1997. LNCS, vol. 1206, pp. 253–260. Springer, Heidelberg (1997)
5. Khan, S., Basu, J., Das Mandal, S.K.: Applying Pitch Based Dynamic Pruning in Designing Real time Speaker Identification System. In: O-COCOSDA, Kathmandu, Nepal (2010)
6. De Cheveigné, A., Kawahara, H.: YIN, a fundamental frequency estimator for speech and music. The Journal of the Acoustical Society of America 111(4), 1917–1930 (2002)
7. Kinnunen, T., Fränti, P.: Speaker Discriminative Weighting Method for VQ-Based Speaker Identification. In: Bigun, J., Smeraldi, F. (eds.) AVBPA 2001. LNCS, vol. 2091, pp. 150–156. Springer, Heidelberg (2001)
8. Dempstar, A., Larid, N., Rubin, D.: Maximum likelihood from incomplete data via the EM algorithm. Royal Statistical Society B 39, 1–38 (1977)
9. Simpson, A.P.: Phonetic differences between male and female speech. Language and Linguistics Compass 3(2), 621–640 (2009)

Investigation of Speech Coding Effects on Different Speech Sounds in Automatic Speech Recognition

A.V. Ramana[1], P. Laxminarayana[2], and P. Mythilisharan[1]

[1] Department of ECE, Osmania University
[2] Research and Training Unit for Navigational Electronics,
Osmania University
avramana_9@yahoo.com,
laxminarayana@osmania.ac.in,
mythilisharan@gmail.com

Abstract. Automatic Speech Recognition (ASR) systems are increasing in usage for voice centric applications in mobile handheld and Voice over Internet Protocol (VoIP) based devices. The necessity is also increasing to find out the ASR performance under different network impediments when the recognition is performed in the remote servers, in real sense. Among the major impediments, speech coding is the one, which affects the ASR performance greatly, when using it with different sampling rates and bit rates in the practical systems. The speech codecs which use different algorithms for generating different bit rates will affect the speech sounds, i.e. vowels and consonants, differently, and cause the critical sounds in the words to be changed and in-turn affects the overall word recognition performance of the ASR systems. In this paper, the influence of the sampling rate and bit rate changes with different narrowband and wideband codecs on the speech sounds is analyzed. Investigation is carried out to see how the speech sounds are changing while using different codecs operating at different bit rates.

Keywords: ASR, VoIP, GSM wireless networks, HMM, NB, WB.

1   Introduction

Automatic Speech Recognition (ASR) systems are slowly becoming part of the Wireless and Voice over Internet Protocol (VoIP) based systems, which use the combinations of various speech codecs for the ASR recognition, through remote servers to reduce the computational load on the client devices or handheld devices [1] [2]. The speech codecs are used for compressing the speech data for achieving the lower bit rates. Wireless and VoIP systems are using different narrowband (NB) and wideband (WB) speech codecs for voice compression with various bit rates. It is also a known fact that the quality of speech will be degraded when it is being encoded-decoded in several phases, over a transmission channel, and in-turn affects the ASR recognition performance when conducting the recognition in remote servers [3].

M.K. Kundu et al. (Eds.): PerMIn 2012, LNCS 7143, pp. 367–377, 2012.

Any ASR system based on Hidden Markov Models (HMM) is generally developed with the speech database sampled at 16-kHz. Mostly, HMMs also will be created using the same 16-kHz speech database in training phase and are stored in the servers for recognition. Naturally, when 16-kHz speech data is used for recognition with 16-kHz HMMs, the recognition accuracy will be good. This pre-condition is maintained when using the wideband speech codecs where the encoded-decoded data from the network is also of 16-kHz rate. But when narrowband codecs are used in the transmission chains, the decoded data is of 8-kHz when using any of the narrowband speech codecs. For speech recognition with 16-kHz HMMs, the 8-kHz decoded data, after encoding-decoding process, may have to be up-converted back to 16-kHz before speech recognition process. This phenomenon may badly affect the speech recognition accuracy as the high frequency data is being removed because of sampling rate conversion and narrowband speech coding. But when using the 8-kHz HMMs for recognition for narrowband speech data, the accuracy may be good as the 8-kHz decoded data is matching to that of the 8-kHz HMMs. Along with the sampling rate conversions, the bit rate variations also further cause the amplitude and shape variations in the speech sounds.

In this paper, the influence of the sampling rate and bit rate changes with different wideband and narrowband codecs on the speech sounds/phonemes is analyzed. The effects of these sound changes are analyzed further on the ASR performance also. The different sounds are categorized according to their variations into other sounds based on the sampling rate and bit rate conversions when using different codecs.

The next sections in this paper, are organized as follows: Section 2 mentions about the standard speech codecs considered for this experiment with their bit-rates. Section 3 explains the experimental environment, the speech recognition setup, and speech sounds analysis steps. Finally, section 4 explains the ASR performance results with different speech coding standards both in narrowband and wideband modes and sound changes categorization based on the speech codecs and HMMs used for recognition.

2   Standard Speech Codecs Considered

The following popularly used speech codecs in VoIP and GSM wireless networks, standardized by ITU-T [4] and ETSI/3GPP [5] are considered for the analysis.

- ITU-T wireline codecs:
  - o   Narrowband: G.729AB
  - o   Wideband: G.722

- ETSI/3GPP wireless codecs:
  - o   Narrowband: AMR-NB
  - o   Wideband: AMR-WB

Summary of the different sampling and bit rates considered for the above codecs is given in Table 1.

Table 1. Speech and Audio Codecs with Different Bit Rates

Speech Codec	Sampling Frequency (kHz)	Bit Rate (kbps)
G.729A	8	8
AMR-NB	8	4.75 to 12.2
G.722	16	64
AMR-WB (G.722.2)	16	6.6 to 23.85

3   Experimental Environment

All the speech codecs referred in the table 1, from ITU-T, and ETSI/3GPP are integrated into the Sphinx ASR toolkit [6] under Linux environment. The c-source code for these speech codecs is downloaded from the ITU-T, and ETSI/3GPP websites, and the code is compiled to create the executables for encoders and decoders separately.

3.1   SPHINX ASR Toolkit

All the above speech codecs are evaluated with the SPHINX3 ASR tool kit with separate Context Dependent (CD) ASR HMMs generated for both 8-kHz and 16-kHz speech data. Tri-phone HMMs are created (76 Base-Phones, and 106209 Tri-Phones) with 5-states per HMM including 2 null states, with each state is modeled by 8 Gaussians. Language Model is used with Tri-gram Models (2385 one-grams, 5430 bi-grams, and 5556 tri-grams). 39 MFCC features (1Energy and 12 MFCC, and their DELTA and double DELTA values), are generated (for training and testing) per frame with 40 Mel Filter bands with 130Hz-6800Hz for wideband and 130Hz-3400Hz for narrowband frequencies.

3.2   TIMIT Speech Database

TIMIT Acoustic-Phonetic Continuous Speech Corpus is the most popular speech corpus available with Linguistic data Consortium (LDC) [7]. It is corpus of read speech, designed to provide speech data for acoustic-phonetic studies and for the development and evaluation of automatic speech recognition systems. Corpus design was a joint effort among the Massachusetts Institute of Technology (MIT), SRI International (SRI) and Texas Instruments, Inc. (TI). The TIMIT corpus includes time-aligned orthographic, phonetic and word transcriptions as well as a 16-bit, 16 kHz speech waveform file for each utterance. Training data contains a total of 6300 sentences or utterances, in which 10 sentences spoken by each of 630 speakers (female 192 and male 438) from 8 major dialect regions of the United States. The database contains a total of 6229 different words with 76 phonemes and 5 filler phones. Testing data (which is different from training data) contains a total of 1344 utterances spoken by a total of 168 speakers (56 females and 112 males).

3.3   Speech Recognition Setup

The original speech files in the TIMIT database are sampled at 16-kHz. Using this speech database, new speech database for 8-kHz sampling rate is also created by low pass filtering and down sampling. During ASR training phase, separate HMMs are created for both the 16-kHz and 8-kHz databases with corresponding ASR configuration parameters for testing purpose.

3.4   ASR with Wideband Codecs

For wideband codec analysis 16-kHz HMMs, are used. The encoded-decoded data from the wideband codecs is directly given to the ASR system with 16 kHz HMMs for recognition as shown in Figure 1.

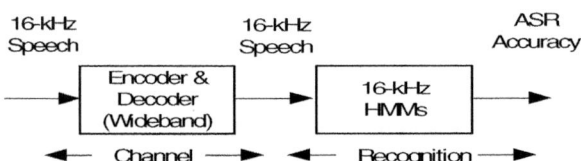

Fig. 1. Recognition with 16-kHz trained models (HMM) for wideband codecs

3.5   ASR with Narrowband Codecs

All the narrowband codecs work with 8-kHz sampling rates only. Figure 2 shows the procedure for testing narrowband codecs with 16-kHz trained models (16-kHz HMMs). The original 16-kHz speech data is down sampled to 8-kHz first. Then, this data is encoded-decoded with the respective narrowband codec. The decoded data is up-sampled back to 16-kHz before the recognition analysis.

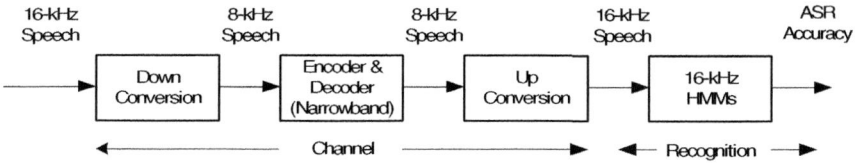

Fig. 2. Recognition with 16-kHz trained models (HMM) for narrowband codecs

As shown in Figure 3, when the 8-kHz trained models (8-kHz HMMs) are used, the decoded data from the narrowband codecs is directly given to the ASR system without any up-conversion, for the recognition analysis.

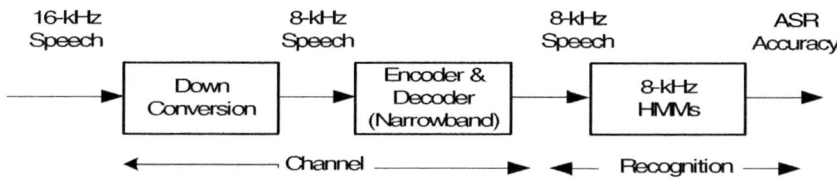

Fig. 3. Recognition with 8-kHz trained models (HMM) for narrowband codecs

3.6   Speech Sounds/Phonemes Analysis Steps

Once the recognition accuracies are found using the above setups, with the few randomly selected (36) speech files from the TIMIT test speech database, the actual phoneme changes are analyzed for different speech codecs with different sampling and bit rates.

The sequence of phoneme units is obtained for all the selected speech files without considering the language model (using "sphinx3_allphone" utility in the Sphinx ASR toolkit) i.e. by using only acoustic modeling. The following variants of speech coding and HMMs are considered in recognition for analysis purposes.

- Un-coded speech data when using 16-kHz HMMs for recognition.
- WB coded speech data when using 16-kHz HMMs for recognition.
- NB coded speech data when using 16-kHz HMMs for recognition.
- NB coded speech data when using 8-kHz HMMs for recognition.

Once the phones are recognized using the above steps, it is also attempted to increase the amplitudes of some of the sounds, in the encoded-decoded speech files, to investigate the phone recovery mechanism.

4   Results and Analysis

ASR Word Recognition Accuracy (A) [6] is measured by the following approach:

$$A = [H - (I+S+D) / H] * 100 \%, \text{ where}$$

H is the total number of words, I is the total number of Insertions, S is the total number of Substitutions, D is the total number of Deletions.

ASR Word Error Rate (WER) is defined as $WER = (100 - A) \%$

4.1   ASR Performance for Narrowband Codecs

Table 2 shows the ASR word recognition accuracies for the different narrowband codecs with different bit rates for both 16-kHz and 8-kHz HMMs.

Table 2. ASR Recognition Accuracies for Narrowband Codecs with Different Bit Rates

Codec @ kbps	ASR Accuracy (%) (16-kHz HMMs)	ASR Accuracy (%) (8-kHz HMMs)
Un-coded (Reference)	91	87
G.729A	54	81
AMR@ 4.75	41	75
AMR@ 12.2	52	86

4.2   ASR Performance for Wideband Codecs

Table 3 shows the ASR recognition accuracies for the different wideband codecs with different bit rates.

Table 3. ASR Recognition Accuracies for the Wideband Codecs with Different Bit Rates

Codec @ kbps	ASR Accuracy (%) (16 kHz HMMs)
Un-coded (Reference)	91
G.722	90
WBAMR @ 6.6	88
WBAMR @ 23.85	90

4.3   Sounds / Phonemes Changes w.r.t. Speech Coding

Once the sequence of phoneme units are obtained in section 3.6, the following tables 4 and 5 are prepared based on the phoneme changes for each sound i.e. vowels and consonants, w.r.t to the codecs and the HMMs used in the recognition. The sounds are categorized into respective classes with their changes with different narrowband and wideband codecs for different bit rates as below.

Table 4. Vowel/Diphthong Changes due to Speech Coding

Codec	Vowels / Diphthongs (WB_16kHz HMM)												
Un-coded	iy	iy1	iy2	e1	ae1	ae2	aa1	aa1/k	er1	uh	uh1/r	ow	ow1
G.722			ey1							ey1			ow2
WBAMR_6.6			ey1	ow1/l		ae1				ey1	axr		ow2/1
													er1
WBAMR_23.85				ow1/l									ow2/l
NB_16kHz HMM													
G.729	iy1	ix	iy1	ao1/l		ae1	ay1						eh2
	y												
AMR_4.75	iy1	ey1	iy	oy1/l	aa1	ae1	eh1						eh2
					ay1								axr
AMR_12.2	y	ix	iy1		aw1	ae1	ay1						eh2
NB_8kHz HMM													
G.729		iy			eh1			aw1	axr			l	ax
					aa1				axr				eh2
					aw1								
AMR_4.75		iy			eh1				r				ao1
		ih											eh2
AMR_12.2		iy			eh1			ow1	er				
		ih			ih1		axr						

Codec	Vowels / Diphthongs (WB_16kHz HMM)												
Un-coded	ao1	ah2	ay1	axr	ah1	ax	aw1	ey1	eh1	ix	ih	ih1	ih2
G.722	ay1	aa1							ae1	ax			
WBAMR_6.6	aa1						aa1						
WBAMR_23.85							aa1						
NB_16kHz HMM													
G.729		ao1		l/axr			ay1	oy1	ae1		ey1	dh	ih1
				er1			aa1	ow2			ix	ey1	
AMR_4.75		ae1	ao1	er1			ow1	uh1	ae1		ih1	dh	
							aa1	ax				ae2	
AMR_12.2			aa1	er1			ay2	l/ey1	ae1		ih1		
NB_8kHz HMM													
G.729						aw1	ih1		eh1			ey1	ax
									ih				
									ih1				
AMR_4.75	aa1					ae1	ih1		ih1	ae1				ax
									ih				
AMR_12.2						aw1	aw1	ih					ey1	ax
								ih1					

4.4   Sounds / Phonemes Changes Analysis

Vowel/Diphthong Changes: The following observations are made for vowel changes when using different codecs and HMMs for recognition based on the results from the above tables.

- The phoneme variations are minimal for wideband codecs, as the wideband spectrum during testing is matching with the 16-kHz HMMs
- The phoneme variations are high for narrowband codecs, as the narrowband coded spectrum during testing is mostly matching with the 8-kHz HMMs
- The phoneme variations are highest for narrowband codecs, as the narrowband coded spectrum during testing is highly mismatching with the 16-kHz HMMs.

- The high frequency components are removed during coding, but it is available in the 16-kHz HMMs, so the variation seen is high.
- All the Vowels are mostly changing into other near-by vowels only!

Table 5. Consonant Changes due to Speech Coding

Codec	Semi-vowels					Nasals		Voiced Stops			Unvoiced Stops		
	w	l	r	r/b	y	m	n	b	d	g	p	t	k
Un-coded	w	l	r	r/b	y	m	n	b	d	g	p	t	k
G.722							d	p	t	d		m	
												v	
												p	
WBAMR_6.6						n	d	p	th	d	t	m	g
							p	t	dh		th	hh	
												d	
												s	
WBAMR_23.85									t		sil		g
NB–16kHz HMM													
G.729	v/w						m	b	d	k	n		l/k
							ng		dh		v		
											v/y		
AMR_4.75	v		l					v	v/w	k	v		p
											n		d
											m		l/g
											v/y		
AMR_12.2	v		l				m		dh	d	k		t
									v				g
NB_8kHz HMM													
G.729	b/l			r/b	g	n	t/ih/n	g		d	t	d/dh	ch
								k					
AMR_4.75	d/w			d/m/v	v		t/ix/n	v	g	d	m	v	jh
								p				d	
												t/dh	
AMR_12.2	b/l			d/v	v		t	v	dh	d	m		jh
							d/n						

Codec	Voiced Fricatives			Unvoiced Fricatives				Whisper
	v	z	jh	f	dh	s	sh	hh
Un-coded	v	z	jh	f	dh	s	sh	hh
G.722						z	f	
						f		
WBAMR_6.6	f					z	v	
						f		
WBAMR_23.85	m					f		
NB–16kHz HMM								
G.729				jh	v	f	th	dh
							ch/hh	
							hh	
AMR_4.75				jh	v	f	th	
				dh			ch	
							jh/hh	
AMR_12.2				jh	v	f	sh/jh	th
				v			v	
							hh	
NB_8kHz HMM								
G.729	sh	s	sh	p				z
				t				
AMR_4.75			d	sh	th	z	z	
						f		
AMR_12.2			d	sh	p	z	z	
					b			

Consonant Changes: The following observations are made for all different consonants when using different codecs and HMMs for recognition.

Semi-Vowels: Unchanged for wideband codecs. Changed into other semi-vowels and voiced fricatives in case of NB Codecs with 16-kHz HMMs. Changed into other semi-vowels and voiced fricatives or voiced stops in case of NB Codecs with 8-kHz HMMs.

Nasals: Changing into other nasals and voiced/unvoiced stops.

Voiced Stops: Mostly changing into other voiced/unvoiced stops.

Unvoiced Stops: Changing into voiced/unvoiced stops, and changing into voiced/unvoiced Fricatives.

Voiced Fricatives: Changing into unvoiced fricatives, and changing into voiced stops.

Unvoiced Fricatives Changing mostly into other voiced/unvoiced Fricatives. As a special case, changing into voiced/unvoiced Stops for NB, 8-kHz HMMs case (especially for sound 'f').

4.5   Graphical Evidences for Phoneme Changes with Codecs

The phoneme changes due to speech coding with lower bit rates can be better explained using a selected speech file, "he spoke soothingly". From the spectrum analysis, by considering about 5 to 10 frames of speech data for different phonemes, as shown in boxes in figures 4 and 5 as an example, it is observed that speech codecs are either eliminating or reducing the amplitudes of higher frequencies as the bit rate is coming down.

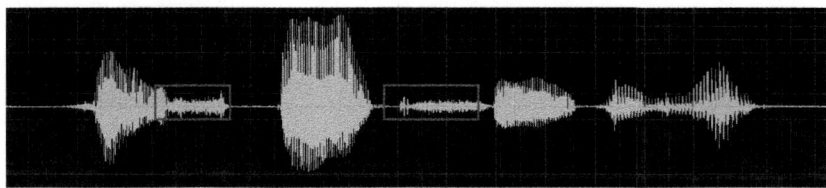

Fig. 4. Un-coded 16-kHz Raw Speech File

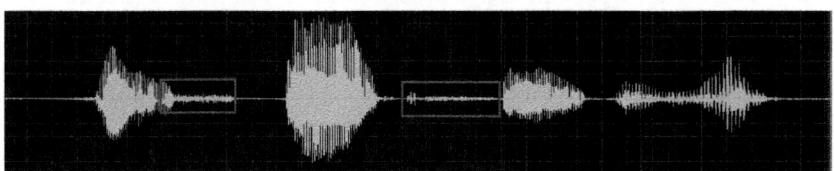

Fig. 5. WBAMR6.6 encoded-decoded Speech File

Most of the times, the higher frequency amplitudes are reduced in case of lower bit rates in wideband coding as shown in figures 6 and 8 for sounds "S" and "EY" respectively. But when narrowband codecs are used, most of the higher frequency components are eliminated and reduced in amplitudes as shown in figures 7 and 9 for the same sounds "S" and "EY" respectively.

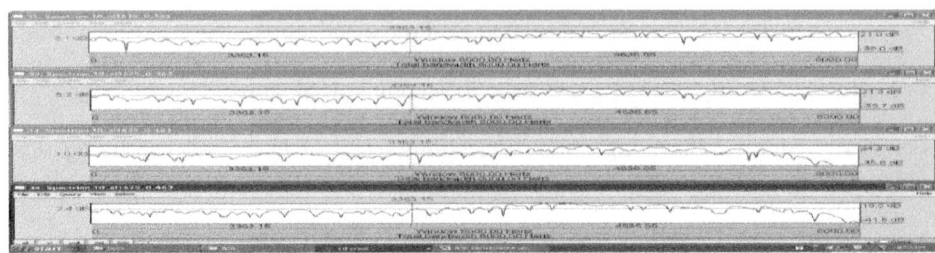

Fig. 6. Spectral variations of sound "S" for raw_16k, G.722, WBAMR23.85 and WBAMR6.6 rates

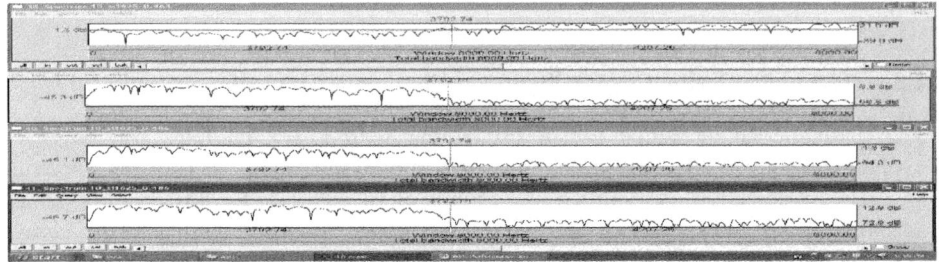

Fig. 7. Spectral variations of sound "S" for raw_16k, G.729, AMR12.2 and AMR4.75 rates

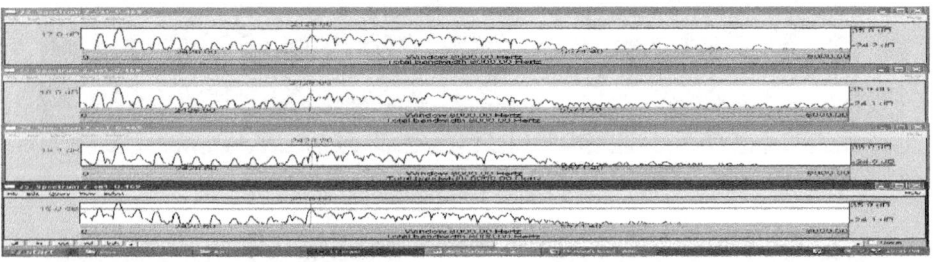

Fig. 8. Spectral variations of sound "EY" for raw_16k, G.722, WBAMR23.85 and WBAMR6.6 rates

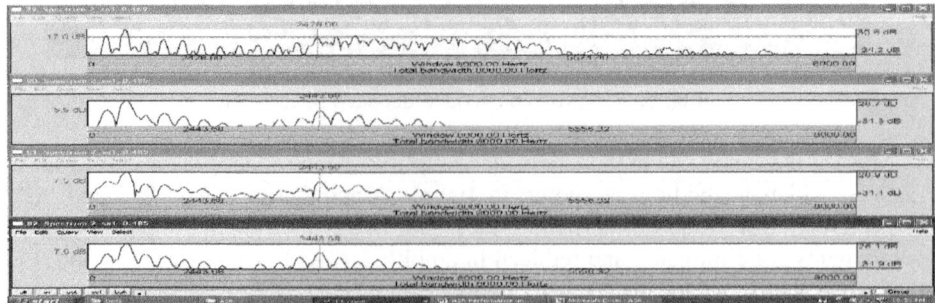

Fig. 9. Spectral variations of sound "EY" for raw_16k, G.729, AMR12.2 and AMR4.75 rates

5   Conclusions

The conclusions made from the above experiment are as follows:

WB Codecs are not much affecting the spectrum in changing the vowel sounds. The mismatched testing conditions (NB codecs with 16-kHz HMMs) are affecting the spectrum more and changing the vowel sounds greatly. Most of the consonant sounds are changing into voiced/ unvoiced stops and voiced/ unvoiced fricatives. The consonant changes are more when the codec bit rates are less. Most of the times, the higher frequency amplitudes are removed because of the speech coding (and lower bit rates), which is causing spectral changes. These sound changes with different codecs and bit rates are leading for wrong detection of phonemes and in-turn the wrong words, causing for the lower WAR!

6   Future Scope

The experiment can be extended for further analysis by using more speech database for vowels and consonants changes. We can identify the weakest sounds which are more prone to changes due to speech coding. By increasing the amplitudes (and/or duration) of the affected weak phonemes / sounds (in the affected speech files), we can see if there will be any improvement in the correct phoneme detection. It can also be focused to use the bandwidth extension / spectral band replication techniques to recover the upper band spectrum, which is lost because of the narrowband coding, from the available lower band spectrum for improving the WAR with narrowband codecs in ASR applications!

Acknowledgements. We would like to thank M/S Analog Devices - India, for partially supporting this work by sponsoring the multimedia and ADSPs laboratory at Department of ECE, Osmania University - Hyderabad.

References

1. Zaykovskiy, D.: Survey of the Speech Recognition Techniques for Mobile Devices. Department of Information Technology, University of Ulm, Germany (2006)
2. Tan, Z.-H., Lindberg, B.: Automatic Speech Recognition on Mobile Devices and Over Communication Networks. Springer, Heidelberg (2008)
3. Turunen, J., Vlaj, D.: A study of Speech Coding Parameters in Speech Recognition. In: Proceedings Eurospeech 2001, Scandinavia, Aalborg, Denmark, pp. 2363–2366 (2001)
4. ITU-T Recommendations, http://www.itu.int
5. ETSI Standards, http://www.etsi.org
6. Chan, A., Gouvêa, E., Singh, R., Ravishankar, M., Rosenfeld, R., Sun, Y., Huggins-Daines, D., Seltzer, M.: (Third Draft) The Hieroglyphs: Building Speech Applications Using CMU Sphinx and Related Resources (March 2007)
7. TIMIT speech database, http://www.ldc.upenn.edu/

Author Index